A Guide to Orchestral Music

A Guide to Orchestral Music

THE HANDBOOK FOR NON-MUSICIANS

ETHAN MORDDEN

OXFORD UNIVERSITY PRESS
New York

First published in 1980 by Oxford University Press, Inc., 200 Madison Avenue, New York, New York 10016

First issued as an Oxford University Press paperback, 1986

Oxford is a registered trademark of Oxford University Press

Library of Congress Cataloging in Publication Data
Mordden, Ethan
A guide to orchestral music.
Includes index.
1. Orchestral music—Analysis, appreciation. I. Title.
MT125.M72 785 79-19742 ISBN 0-19-502686-1
ISBN 0-19-504041-4 (pbk.)

Printing (last digit): 9 8

Printed in the United States of America

To Miss Pike,
the Toscanini of Friends Academy

The author wishes to acknowledge the guidance
of Sheldon Meyer and Vicky Bijur,
who both contributed strategically
to the experimental format used herein.

CONTENTS

Part I

Part II

Part I

HOW TO USE THIS BOOK

This is a guide through the world of Western orchestral music, designed for the use of non-musicians. It presupposes no experience of any kind, and is meant to be complete in itself. It is basic in its approach but intends to give the reader a thorough if informal "course" in the workings and overall effect—the meaning—of the symphony, concerto, overture, tone poem, and the like.

Music, like any art, does have meaning, though it is useless to attempt to get a musical idea by attaching extramusical pictures to it, as old-fashioned courses in "music appreciation" used to do. In certain cases—in what is called program music—a composer intends to suggest a specific image through music. But more often he intends his music to be nothing but—what is called "absolute"—music. One comes close to music on music's terms. That one does best, I think, by digesting the mechanics of form as one goes along, listening and learning, work by work. One starts to pick up terms. One distinguishes styles of composition. One develops likes and dislikes.

This book has been laid out with that sort of pilgrim's progress in mind. I assume the reader is a concertgoer, a radio or television listener, a record collector, or a combination of these on some regular if infrequent basis. Everyone has his own schedule and his own scene; some people who wouldn't miss a television concert have never attended a concert in person. Some make their way through the repertory via the radio, discovering new works by surprise. Some plot their trek through the oeuvre of one composer in particular, "doing" his sound till they get it down in depth. Some wander through symphony aimlessly without reference to who composed or when. However one does it, I presume he or she might profit by some informed company for a guide through the maze of historical evolutions, personal digressions, revolutions, counter-revolutions, and revolutions within revolution that comprise Western music.

This is meant to be a comprehensive volume, concise but far-ranging so as never to be outgrown: by the time one is graduated from this academy, one won't need a guide, I hope. For my intention is to educate the novice to the utmost, to make him or her an insider who comprehends symphony as well as anyone short of a trained musician. It isn't that hard, actually; as with so many other things, it's more a matter of informed exposure than of mystical concentration. The more you hear the more you know, until one day all the bits you've picked up have settled into a perspective. That perspective is expertise.

Start at the general introduction to symphony, immediately following. There's a lot to get down at first, and you may want to refer back every so often. (Those too impatient to plod can jump ahead to the dilletante's digest guide, which tenders essential briefing in short form.) And then? The music. Start anywhere, with a particular work. Read its little analysis and then hear it. Or hear it and then read. Or read while hearing—whatever way works best for you. (Try the lists of introductory works if you don't have anything specific in mind, or tune the radio in to the appropriate station and take potluck.)

Then, just keep on from there, trying new works at your pleasure. As you go along, you will pick up points of general or specific information incrementally, using the text at your own speed. Keep at it; perspective will gather. Use the front-of-the-book essays to fill out your education, the glossary at the back of the book for terminology, and the introductory articles on various composers when you want to consolidate your understanding of their position in the epic. When lost, reach for the index.

The composers have been arranged in chronological rather than alphabetical order so as to give a sense of historical space. Within each composer's chapter are, first, an introduction and, following, the works you would be most likely to run across. These are listed, *very* generally, in order of size from largest to smallest: symphonies first (in numerical order), then concertos and smaller *concertante* works, then large one-movement works and suites, and so on down to overtures and such.

The various forms are all filed together—all symphonies first, all concertos together after the symphonies, and so on by genre, regardless of how much they may vary individually in length. Because one comes to break repertory down in one's mind by forms, you will find this arrangement more efficient than an alphabetical listing, which gets complicated anyway in the sorting out of foreign-language titles (for example, *Ein Sommernachtstraum*) from their translations (*A Midsummer Night's Dream*).

A word on this: all works are listed in the text under the names or titles by which they are most commonly known in America. This book is designed to familiarize the reader with the vernacular of the American concert scene, not to parade academic precisions. We refer to the *1812 Overture,* not to the *Solemn Overture on the Year 1812,* which is its real name. Likewise, no one in America speaks of *Ein Sommernachtstraum.* We call it by the English translation, and so you will find it listed here. However, all reasonable possibilities are anticipated in the index.

Again, musical training is not a requirement. But neither is it a hindrance, and I've used a few musical examples on the supposition that a great many people undergo some sort of instrumental training in their youth. I hope no one will be irritated by some repetition in the way of definitions or historical commentary; better read it twice than miss it once. I assume as well that the reader won't be going straight through the book, so that it is necessary to repeat information where appropriate.

Now, a few smaller matters. The spelling of Russian names and words is an exact phonography of the originals rather than the inexact renderings one encounters in English. This is inconsistent, I admit, with my emphasis on common American usage, but the difference in spelling is too small to bewilder anybody, and I see no reason not to be correct here. Why write Chaikovsky when the man's name is pronounced Chaikofsky? These are transliterations from the Cyrillic alphabet; why transfer the irregularities of that alphabet into English when what one is really carrying over is the *sound* of Russian? Besides, if the lofty *New York Times* can revise the comparably traditional but inexact English spelling of Chinese names, who are we to hold the line on Russian?

Now to correct another misapprehension: "classical music." This term as generally used is a misnomer. "Classical" really refers to a certain period in music, that of Haydn and Mozart. To avoid confusions, I have used the word "symphony" in this book to mean all orchestral music. Thus, symphony comprises *the* symphony, the concerto, the tone poem, and so on. (As it happens, "orchestral music" is what the word originally meant, way back when the large-scale instrumental ensemble was being organized as the *sinfonia.*)

Lastly, on which composers and works to include here, I have tried to sustain a wide reach—but one must cut off somewhere. Everything popular is here, plus a great deal more that I feel is of interest, popular or otherwise. I admit to a definite American bias. This book is for Americans, and stretches a little to include American works that aren't often performed in hopes that American readers will be intrigued to learn how their artists have abstracted a national symphonic style.

GENERAL INTRODUCTION

All art is up to something. Art cannot just be; it always *does*—and what it does is hostile to stability. Of all the forces that influence our lives, whether the abstract or utilitarian, popular or arcane, positive or cynical, art is the most revolutionary, always in motion, always dissatisfied with what has been proved to satisfaction. Because it is concerned with humanistic ideals, it is universal. But because it is made by human individuals, it is elite, chaotic, and eternally in renewal, disproving what has been proved: subversive. Art teaches, art denies, art builds and destroys, justifying men's ways to God. It is a doing thing, forged for strife and change.

The artist who deals his hand in words or pictures has one advantage over the artist of sounds. All of them are sensually expressive, but words and pictures can make a more specific statement than music can. Yet music does make its own kind of statement. Melody, rhythm, and harmony are its content, but form is its statement—how these three elements are generated, developed, rounded off or left, disoriented, at the close. "Man's word," quoth Tennyson, "is God in man." But music is most Godly of all: pure expression, nothing but itself, perceived intuitively . . . until one understands its form. Then one sees within the sound and converses, in its code, with the ideal.

Thus, we want to catch the form in music, comprehend what the composer is saying through his shapes. We want to learn why a given piece of music starts this way, ends that way, does such or so in its middle. Perhaps this sounds complicated; it isn't. The only head start that a musician has over the layman in "knowing" music is the musician's grasp of form. I am taking it for granted that the reader cannot read a score to any appreciable degree, if at all. But the reader does have a mind and a working pair of ears—this is all he needs. We will do form, and when we have done, the reader should be able to route his way through the heritage—and future—of Western orchestral music unaided, his map, as it were, in his head.

Before we examine form as structure, let's run through the major categories of orchestral music, form as genre. First, naturally, is the symphony—first for its size, its terraces of communication, and its importance to the composers themselves, most of whom saved their most profound utterances for this form as opposed to all others. What is a symphony? There is no simple answer, but let's try one: a symphony is four movements of musical drama played by an orchestra. This is not "drama" in the sense of a story with a beginning, middle, and end. But there is a beginning, middle, and end in a symphony, and over the course of them, a kind of drama is expressed. It is abstract, but suggestive, a tracking of some expressive voyage. One doesn't need to know that Beethoven referred to the famous buh-buh-buh-*bum* of his Fifth Symphony as "fate knocking on the door" to understand that the work embodies a struggle of some kind and concludes triumphantly. One needs no particulars; there is no who, what, or where involved. Challenge and victory are implicit in the unfolding of the sound.

By the unfolding, I mean the progression of the Fifth Symphony's four movements. The first movement sets up the conflict. The second, a slow movement, heightens the experience with a lyrical, a poetic, a transcendent interpretation of the situation. The third movement stiffens the conflict for us by emphasizing its aggressive component in rhythm. And the last movement, the finale, resolves the conflict, triumphantly.

Of course, Beethoven's Fifth offers only one example of symphonic drama. The possibilities are limitless. Beethoven might have ended this work tragically—by making the music sound tragic—or might have expressed a different pattern of drama altogether. Symphonies are like snowflakes and unhappy families: no two are alike.

There are exceptions, too, to any definition, no matter how broad. There are three-movement symphonies, five-movement symphonies, symphonies in one movement that combine the functions of the separate movements in one organic structure. There are symphonies that include voices in the orchestra, a chorus or soloists or both. There are symphonies written for specifically limited orchestras, such as for strings only. There are what we call *program* symphonies, those which—either very loosely or in some detail—wrap themselves around an idea, or invoke images, or even narrate a story.

What's the difference between Beethoven's Fifth, with its unmistakable drama of conflict and triumph, and a program symphony? In one sense, none: all symphonies are made of music. But a program symphony goes out of its way to outline its subject matter in extramusical ways. The movements and the symphony as a whole may bear titles. Beethoven might have named his Fifth the "Fate" Symphony, and might have named the movements something like "Fate Knocks at the Door," then "Song of the Hero," then "The Hero in Battle," then "The Triumph." He didn't, of course. But that doesn't affect the allusive sensibility of the music itself.

There are many different ways for a composer to assert a program in a symphony. Beethoven did, for example, put titles on his Sixth, which he intended to suggest the human experience of the natural world. He named it the "Pastoral" Symphony, and titled its five movements to detail life in the country. Yet this is not a travelogue; the composer warns us that the work is "more an expression of a feeling than a painting." Music is drama, but it is dramatized in the abstract. Similarly, other symphonies with titles are not plays in music, not operas with the voices left out, but translations into music of an idea that is conveniently identified by words. Thus, Dvořák's Ninth Symphony, titled "From the New World," gathers up Dvořák's impressions of the folk-American sound. He doesn't attempt to "do" the Grand Canyon or Natural Bridge. He simply writes a symphony using melodies that, to him, represent the spirit of America. It would sound no different to the listener if he didn't know that the music was called the "New World"Symphony. He might say, after hearing it, that the second movement reminded him of the black spiritual. He might hear traces of the cakewalk, or of "Indian music." But his experience would be no more fulfilling if he knew what the music "meant"—because music doesn't mean in that way in the first place. It has character and expresses emotion. It suggests. It can be made to tell a story, yes. But its effect does not depend on anyone's knowing that story specifically.

Actually, neither Beethoven's "Pastoral" nor Dvořák's "New World" are what one might call hardcore program symphonies, because while they suggest, they do not narrate: they have no interior action. Even given that music is abstract art, some program symphonies really do attempt to exploit an almost textual meaning through music. Perhaps the most notorious example of this is Berlioz' *Symphonie Fantastique,* the "Fantastic Symphony." Here, there is a fully developed extramusical "situation" behind the sounds: an artist's exorcism of his obsession for a woman. Adoring her, despising her, needing her, rejecting her, the artist—Berlioz himself, confronting what was for him a real-life situation—uses the symphony as therapy. Tripping on opium, he scores the resulting "visions" for orchestra; each vision is a symphonic movement. The first movement offers a portrait of his obsession, the second a ball, the third a rural idyll, the fourth his own execution for having murdered the woman, the fifth a witches' revel. Throughout, one melody central to the dramatic *and* musical organization of the work represents the woman, and Berlioz uses this to exterminate his passion at last by sounding it in a grotesque transformation in the witches' sabbath movement—thus "transforming" the real-life woman into a hag.

Obviously, the listener is expected to understand a certain amount of prefatory material before hearing the *Symphonie Fantastique,* whereas the "Pastoral" and "New World" symphonies may be heard simply in the context of their subtitles. The "Pastoral" is a sense of the coutryside, the "New World" a salute to the United States. But the *Symphonie Fantastique* is an adventure, a sequence of scenes: a musical cinema. It is the very essence of the program symphony.

The next largest form of orchestral music is the concerto. It is generally smaller than the symphony, but it is older, and its primary characteristic is that it is based on the collaboration of a solo instrument (or several solo instruments) and an orchestra: a piano concerto; a violin concerto; a concerto for violin, 'cello, and orchestra; or even a concerto for orchestra, in which all the instruments take turns at playing the solos. The concerto usually has three movements, one less than the symphony, and its drama is personalized by the use of the solo, which plays both with the orchestra and against it. Where the symphony's layout tends to include a strong first movement, a lyrical slow movement, a rhythmic dance movement, and a strong finale, the concerto prefers a strong first movement, a slow movement, and a dancelike finale. Or, in other words, the first movement for drama, the slow movement for feeling, and the finale for fun. Throughout, the soloist is called on to display his technique at various intervals, but the slow movement emphasizes his sensitivity and the finale brings out the exhibitionist in him; after all, the concerto is a virtuoso's star turn by its very nature. At rare intervals, the soloist is invited to indulge in a cadenza, which is his show-off spot: the orchestra is silent, and he cuts loose, usually basing his pyrotechnics on themes from the movement at hand. In early days, the player actually improvised his cadenzas on the spot, but by about 1810 it was customary for composers to write out the cadenzas and for soloists to play them as written.

We should deal with the question of the soloist's playing "with the orchestra and against it." Exactly how does this work? To understand the concerto principle, it is necessary to go back in time to the Baroque era, the seventeeth and eighteenth centuries. This era predates the organization of the orchestra as we know it, even the orchestras we would think of as small. Ensemble groups consisted of only a few players, so each part counted heavily. There was nothing like the massed sonority of woodwinds, brasses, strings, and percussion we take for granted in Brahms or Prokofyef, say; they weren't even writing four-movement symphonies then. (When musicians of the Baroque used the word "symphony" they meant, simply, whatever orchestral group was on hand at the time. The *sinfonia* was the playing entity *and* whatever they happened to be playing, not an established form of composition.)

The major outlet of orchestral writing in the Baroque was the *concerto grosso,* or "grand concerto." What exactly does this word "concerto" mean? It is an ambivalent term, referring both to agreement and opposition (from the Latin *concertare,* meaning both "to unify" and "to dispute"). This ambivalence aptly defines the concerto principle. There is a general agreement in that all the instruments combine in a harmonious texture. But there is opposition in that certain instruments are brought forward to play in opposition to—yet in balance with—the others.

Before "our" modern concerto, with its star soloist, was derived, concertos utilized a group of soloists. These comprised the *concertino*—the disputants, as it were. The rest of the orchestra, generally strings and a harpsichord, comprised the *ripieno*—the "fuller group." Between them, they fostered a spirit of cooperative soloism, an equilibrium of back-and-forth gradations of volume and thematic interchange, between soloists and orchestra. This eqillibrium gives the *concerto grosso* its special aura of "classical" poise, and explains why many listeners who disdain Romantic "blood and thunder" relish the more serene intricacies of Vivaldi, Handel, Telemann, and the *summum bonum* of the Baroque concerto, Bach's six Brandenburg Concertos.

The balance implicit in the *concerto grosso* was completely overthrown in the 1800s. This was the Romantic era, a time when the individualism of self-expressive quest was the rage of time and place. Art always seeks to "follow nature"—but each generation has a different reading for where nature leads. If the Baroque saw the world as an essentially harmonious place, the Romantics envisioned a cosmic engulfment that could be broken only by heroistic strivings—by egomania, if necessary. In the seventeeth and eighteenth centuries, artists assumed that they fit into a world system and perhaps hoped to better it; in the nineteenth century, artists wanted to be Faust. He, too, bettered the world—but he could never fit in, though his most prominent biographer, Johann Wolfgang von Goethe, was a very model of the well-placed, well-thinking civilian artist-politician. This is a telling "hypocrisy" of the Romantic age: nonconformism was idealized in art while nonconformity in life was thought irritating and dangerous. Similarly, the Romantic concerto—the very model of the concerto as we generally think of it—tried to sit both sides of the fence, reveling in nonconformity (the disputation of concerto) while attempting to retain its balance (the agreement of concerto).

It could not be done. Nonconformity called up a new kind of concerto soloist, the intimidatingly brilliant virtuoso, accomplished to the point of blasphemy: Paganini on the violin, Liszt and Thalberg on the piano. To set the style, these men wrote their own concertos; later, composers wrote for talents like theirs as a matter of course, and the old equilibirum of the *concerto grosso* faded away in a blaze of charismatic exhibitionism. The *concerto grosso* died out (to be revived in the neo-Classical revival of the twentieth century). The solo concerto has predominated ever since.

The symphony is the grandest of orchestral forms, the concerto secondary in size and intention. Together, the two forms comprise the major part of the concert repertory and are the main outlets (or were until the second quarter of the twentieth century) for a composer's most intense strivings with himself: the bulk of his art. One always wants to know about a given composer, what does he do with the symphony? How does he bring off the concerto?

We especially want to know how he views the symphony as form, for it has evolved amazingly throughout its two-hundred-year history. The concerto today is a reasonable facsimile of the concerto of Haydn and Mozart's day, the only major difference being that the solo instrument is much more crucial now. But the symphony has grown remarkably in scope. When Haydn was crystallizing the form, it was frequently light in tone and at most half an hour long. Beethoven strengthened it, broadened it, made it an engine of profound and impetuous drama. Others followed his lead, and by the end of the nineteenth century many symphonies lasted over an hour, demanded gigantic orchestras unknown to Haydn and Mozart and used singers to make their "meaning" clear. The composition of a symphony was a quasi-apocalyptic event, then, no longer something finished a few days after it was started. Haydn wrote 104 symphonies, Mozart 41. But Beethoven only wrote nine, and very few composers after him broke that figure—they simply had to put too much of themselves into each one. Since then, composers have gone their separate ways in dealing with the symphony: some fear its size, and shrink it, while others fiddle with its shape, revising the progression of its movements.

Now we come to the smaller orchestral forms—smaller if only in terms of length. The most common of these is the tone poem, and here we are very much in the field of program music. The urge for abstract expression that called for the symphony and concerto was an urge for what we call *absolute* music, music for music's sake: "Oh, do not ask, 'what is it'? Let us go and make our visit." The tone poem was invented for exactly the opposite reasons, to write music that conjures up a story, images, ideas, the melodies specifically depicting characters or events. We speak of Symphony no. 3 or Violin Concerto in D Major, with an occasional title—Symphony no. 6 in F Major, "The Pastoral." But tone poems have names: *Night on Bald Mountain, Richard III, Thus Spake Zarathustra, The Golden Spinning Wheel.* Here one asks 'What is it'? What is it *about?*

It was the Romantic era, the 1800s, that invented the tone poem, for just as the Romantics needed bold and dashing celebrity virtuosos in the concerto and expansively emotionalized symphonies, they also put much emphasis on program, especially in the form of a poetic text that would inspire a translation of the poet's ideas into music. Accordingly, they devised the "symphonic poem," which is what the tone poem was first called: a poem in music.

Consider. Absolute music, without the help of a poetic key, tenders a kind of statement as it is. But this is a statement without specific characters or events—the overcoming of a threatening power that we seem to hear in Beethoven's Fifth, for example, or the raging melancholy perceived from movement to movement of Mozart's Fortieth. Program music, however, projects time, place, and action. Thus, Musorksky's *Night on Bald Mountain* gives us a picture of a witches' sabbath, Smetana's *Richard III* envisions the rise and fall of Shakespeare's devious king, Strauss' *Thus Spake Zarathustra* states in musical terms Nietszche's juxtaposition of human wisdom and the natural order of things, and Dvořák's *The Golden Spinning Wheel* recounts, episode by episode, a gruesome Slavic fairy tale.

The tone poem is usually one movement and therefore much shorter than the average Romantic symphony. But a few tone poems—especially those of Richard Strauss—are quite long, played in one continuous movement but containing interior sections not unlike the movements of a symphony. Since the tone poem is following a kind of narrative, it is more flexible than a movement in a symphony; it can change its rhythm, tone, and direction because unlike a symphonic movement it does not relate to a larger whole. The tone poem, long or short, is complete in itself—it doesn't depend on the lyrical release of a slow movement, or the aggressive dimension of a dance movement. The symphony and concerto erect a span over the course of several different kinds of movements, while the tone poem has just its one movement in which to tell its story.

One thing to keep in mind as one differentiates these major forms: there are no rules. These are general guidelines, not a code for behavior. For example, I have suggested that the symphony and concerto tend to be absolute music: music, period. Conversely, I have offered the tone poem as exemplary program music: music with a purpose. But there are tone poems whose "program" consists of nothing more than a title—Liszt's *Hungaria,* for instance, a simple celebration of the Hungarian folk sound, or Elgar's *Cockaigne,* a salute to the atmosphere of Cockney London. And there are program symphonies with as much program as the most depictive tone poem, such as Berlioz' *Symphonie Fantastique.*

Actually, examples of program music in one form or another may be traced back to the seventeenth century, and even the fully programmatic tone poem was not entirely an innovation of the Romantic era. It developed out of the overture, the traditional invocational preface of the theatre. Evenings of opera, ballet, and theatre customarily began with an overture, and by the late eighteenth century the opera and play overture especially aimed to prepare audiences for the action of the specific works to come. (Plays not only had overtures, but dance and choral numbers, preludes to each act, and assorted atmospheric filigree. A popular example is Grieg's *Peer Gynt* music, composed for a production of Ibsen's play.)

Obviously, the overture, which captures the spirit of a certain drama in one musical movement, is very like the tone poem, which also delineates a certain drama in one movement. The major difference between the two is that an overture is structured exactly like the first movement of a symphony, in a format called *sonata-allegro* which we'll get to shortly. The tone poem, however, is not necessarily structured like anything: it chooses its own format each time out.

Let's take an example of an overture—Mendelssohn's Overture to *A Midsummer Night's Dream.* Mendelssohn wrote incidental music for a staging of Shakespeare's comedy in 1843; accompaniments for scenes, choruses and solos, dances, all beautifully turned to portray Shakespeare's magic in music. And of course there is the famous overture. But as it happens, Mendelssohn had composed that overture seventeen years earlier (originally as a piano duet for his sister and himself), after a reading of the text. In other words, this is an overture just for the esprit of it—but an overture all the same, distilling the salient elements of the play in wordless but eloquent sounds. The overture *introduces* the play; one hears the fairies, the noble lovers, and the thespian bunglers who put on *Pyramus and Thisbe.* In fact, Mendelssohn provided a *locus classicus* for program music in this overture, in its opening: four hushed woodwind chords that seem to open up a Shakespearean forest of romantic imaginings. The overture also alludes to Bottom's "translation" into a donkey with a musical translation of braying. (Richard Wagner, whose forests of imaginings ran to the hefty side, dismissed Mendelssohn's delicate fairyland string figures: "Those are gnats," he said, "not elves." Still, the point is made. In program music, everybody hears something.) Though its structure clearly marks it as an overture, this piece of Mendelssohn's "after" *A Midsummer Night's Dream* might be thought of as an early tone poem called *A Midsummer Night's Dream.*

Let's go back to an issue raised briefly here earlier. If everybody hears something but not necessarily the same thing, how does one know if one is hearing the right thing? One doesn't. If Wagner insisted on hearing the Overture to *A Midsummer Night's Dream* as *The Flight of the Gnats,* that's his privilege. But this is why we can say that program music is like absolute music in that ultimately it is what you hear rather than what you have decoded through the advice of the composer's written-out program or a critic's gloss. Music will always excite some response in us of a quasi-particular sort, not always a response that can be verbalized. Sitting in the concert hall during a playing of Strauss' *Alpine Symphony*, one does truly seem to hear the climb, the thrill of the view from the summit, the afternoon storm, and the descent marked by the composer in the score and reprinted in the program notes. If nothing else, the title alone tips one off: *Alpine* Symphony. But another listener, switching on to a radio broadcast of the work too late to catch the title, might receive an entirely different set of images, images related to the immensity of Strauss' sound but far removed from his "pictures." I don't mean that the radio listener thinks, "Ah, a "Shipwreck" Symphony." Or, "Say, I believe I hear fate knocking on the door." Music is not a dumb language in need of translation. It speaks emotionally, dramatically, imagistically—not in translatable hieroglyphs.

Unless, of course, it wants to. Sometimes there is a "right thing" to hear. I said before the Mendelssohn's *A Midsummer Night's Dream* Overture depicts the fairies, the noble lovers, and the amateur actors in the play. But this is only my inference. Now, the fairies are unmissable because those gossamer violin lines sound like fairies. Okay. The donkey brays similarly must refer to Bottom and, by extension, his fellow thespians. But how do I get "noble lovers" out of the rest of the music? Well, they're the only other major characters in the play, and there's a theme that suggests them to me. But who knows? Maybe Mendelssohn had something else—or nothing else, just music—in mind.

However, often a composer makes it clear that a certain theme is meant to stand for something. Beethoven, for example, did apparently single out the all-important theme in the Fifth as a kind of Fate Theme. But there are more eliciting uses of allusive themes that we have to know about. How, for instance, does Berlioz' *Symphonie Fantastique* "tell" us about his obsessive passion for this woman? Simple: he uses a *motto theme*. This is a tune that appears in all five movements, always symbolizing the woman. How do we know that this is the woman? Does the motto theme sound feminine? No; nor masculine, nor does it have any identifying quality. It is simply a symphonic theme. But Berlioz tells us—in words—that this theme is "the Beloved," as he calls her, and once we've got it down, we can place it in a dramatic context each time it appears. One movement is called "A Ball," and it sounds like one, with the aid of a sumptuous waltz. At a certain point, we hear the motto theme—aha! The Beloved has turned up at the ball. "So," we think, "he cannot shake the spell; she still haunts him." Later, in a movement entitled "Dream of a Witches' Sabbath," sounding suitably grotesque, we hear the motto theme—but this time it has been transformed. It seems to hobble and croak at us. Why? Obviously, Berlioz has decided to rid himself of his passion by "turning" the Beloved into a hag; thus he can repudiate her, he hopes.

In short, hearing the "right" thing is a matter of picking up on the composer's characterization of his themes and following them as they develop. Music maintains a constant science of development. Seldom does a theme sound exactly the same way every time it appears. Even if it did, it would still be dealing out numerous variants of itself at other moments. One must be prepared to follow themes through their progress, for they often will change considerably.

We'll get back to the question of development later. Right now, let's complete this survey of categories. So far we have dealt with the major forms of orchestral music—or, as we're calling it in this book, symphony. These forms are: the symphony, the concerto, the overture, and the tone poem. Among the various other forms one encounters, the most common include, first of all, the theme-and-variations. This is exactly what it implies: a stated theme and a certain number of "other versions" of that theme. These versions, the variations, are worked out through a myriad of procedures. The composer might simply speed the theme up, or slow it down. He might alter a few but not all of its notes. He might come up with an entirely new theme altogether that is based on the rhythm, melodic outline, or harmony of the original theme. The possibilities are endless, and what makes the variation form so interesting is that as he goes along, the composer will often make new variations out of the variations, leaving the original theme way, way behind in the ear's memory. Often, he will finish off his set by sounding the basic theme in its original form.

Another common form is the suite, which is a work made up of shortish, separate numbers. For example, Holst's *The Planets,* in which each number represents a different planet of our solar system. Sometimes a suite is not an original composition, but a collection of excerpts from a composition. This is a standard practice for the concert performance of ballet scores and incidental music written for drama. Rather than play the entire ballet score (which could take up an entire evening) or all the pieces written for a production of a play, a few of the presumably more interesting pieces are collected and performed by themselves without reference to their theatrical context. For example, excerpts from Chaikofsky's ballet *The Nutcracker* are performed as the *Nutcracker Suite.* Similarly, the work generally called "Mendelssohn's Midsummer Night's Dream Music" is in fact a suite drawn from music used in a staging of the play. (The Overture referred to earlier is the first number in the suite.)

The serenade and divertimento will turn up every so often, especially in concerts of music from the Classical era (the age of Haydn, Mozart, et al.) or the neo-Classical revival of the 1920s and 1930s. These are forms of absolute music all the way, and basically they represent a lighter, less dramatic form of symphony, scored for a smallish, or chamber-sized, orchestra.

There are other forms, but these comprise the bulk of the repertory. One warning: when dealing with contemporary music, one will find that the older forms are less frequently used. Instead, a variety of new terms avoid any association with tradition. Ode, essay, dithyramb, expression, and so on proliferate after 1930 (which is about when the symphony fell out of fashion). Sometimes a composer will simply write "pieces," as in Alban Berg's *Three Pieces for Orchestra.*

This is very sparse, I know, but I am more concerned with the reader's getting down essentials without too much struggle than with comprehensiveness. There is, of course, an amazing vitality of detail in the way these forms have evolved over the years; furthermore, the many exceptions to even the general definitions laid down above run on for many pages. But I have arranged this book so that the reader may take his history and technical matter in stride as he proceeds through the main body of the text. Right now, let's concentrate on the basics so we can push on to the music.

We come to structure. The fundamental structural form of symphony is the movement, obviously. This word is used generally to mean a portion of music that is distinct but not necessarily independent, a section of an extended work such as a symphony, concerto, or serenade. We usually think of a movement as existing by itself, to be followed by another movement after a brief silence. But sometimes separate movements might be joined together. For example, the symphony is normally a four-movement work, with little pauses between each movement. Normally. But Schumann's Fourth Symphony was composed in one "movement" containing four sections corresponding in tone and function to the four symphonic movements.

So this term"movement" is a loose one. It might be better to think of it as a "type" of music rather than a length, for in fact it is in the interaction and contrast of succeeding movements that a composer builds a work. A symphony's four movements are not *any* four movements. If the symphony is to make anything of itself, there must be differentiation of instrumental texture, touches of color, sometimes even common melodic references from movement to movement. Four slow movements in a row, however beautiful in sound, would make a rather laborious entity. Four trivial movements would feel shallow. Four portentous movements would tease us; four self-affirmative movements offend. But one portentous movement followed by a beautiful slow movement followed by an apparently trivial movement followed by a self-affirming movement makes for a dandy symphony. It has a dramatic context. It has variety and—if done right—unity. It has a beginning, a middle, and an end. (The same goes for the three movements of a concerto, and the movements of any multi-movement work.)

Now, there are several different kinds of movements, several different shapes a movement can take. And each of these has about a hundred alternate forms. So I'd like to make the whole thing very elemental and assert one maxim that explains the structure of virtually any given symphonic movement—or of virtually any other musical subdivision as well:

All music is statement, variation, and restatement.

This assertion is contemptibly simplistic, but universally applicable. Most forms of music that one is likely to run into, from the most complex symphonic movement to a popular song, express themselves in this shape. Obviously, it is very versatile, especially because "variation" here means any kind of contrast or development. For example, take the song "Ol' Man River," from the Kern-Hammerstein musical *Show Boat.* The main part of this song—the refrain, or chorus—uses this shape in its simplest incarnation. The *statement* here is the main strain of the song, the part beginning "Ol' man River, dat ol' man River." That tune is repeated, not quite note for note, at the words, "He don't plant 'taters, he don't plant cotton." Then we get a contrasting tune, a kind of "middle section" at the words "You an' me, we sweat an' strain." That is the *variation,* so to speak. Then comes the *restatement,* with the repeat of the main strain at the words, "Ah gets weary an' sick of tryin'."

Symphonic movements work in just this way. The major difference is that the tunes as such are more extended then those in a song, and more plentiful. Statement, in a symphonic movement, might comprise some four or five different tunes. Variation is either a contrasting section, or the same tunes transformed in some way—varied, literally. And of course the restatement is just that, the original four or five tunes sounding more or less as they did when they first appeared.

Let's take the basic kinds of movements now, and put them together as composers put them together to make symphonies, concertos, and so on. The most important statement-variation-restatement movement is called *sonata-allegro* form, or, for short, *sonata* form. Its statement is called the *exposition.* This consists mainly of two very prominent themes, though there may be many subsidiary themes besides. The two themes are called the first and second themes (or first and second subjects), and they exemplify the symphony's need for constant conflict in melodic, rhythmic, and harmonic features: for contrast. If the first theme is assertive, the second might be poignant. If the first is lyrically pliant, the second is tautly dynamic. Thus, early in the first movement, a sense of conflict is set up in the confrontation of these two themes.

A standard sonata-allegro exposition might begin with a slow introduction, a short "preparation" for the work which may or may not anticipate specific themes in it. (The general rule is: before 1790, the slow introduction is likely not to anticipate; after 1800, it almost certainly will.) Then the tempo picks up, for the first movement tends to be a lively one; the movement proper has begun, and the first thing we hear is the first theme. (In a big symphony, this might be more of a first theme group, made up of several melodies acting as one.) After the first theme, a sense of transition may set in as the ear is moved into the different sound-space occupied by the second theme (or theme group). However it turns out, there is a true feeling of "contradiction" here, of dramatic opposition.

That much is all exposition, the statement. In Haydn and Mozart's day, when the symphony was young, this exposition was invariably repeated note for note so the audience could get the new material fixed in its mind. But since then the practice has fallen out of style. Nowadays, of course, we're much too familiar with the symphonies of Haydn, Beethoven, and Brahms to require exposition repeats. However, many listeners feel that observing the repeat adds to the experience and—since the composer did request it—is simple good manners.

In any case, now comes the variation part of a sonata-allegro movement, called the *development*. Here, between his statement and restatement, the composer varies, plays around with, and even completely transforms the material of the exposition. Frequently, he will deal with the first and second theme, but there is nothing to stop him from ignoring these in favor of some minor theme, or from introducing wholly new material. The main thing is the further sense of contrast. Just as the second theme contrasted with the first, so does the development contrast with the exposition. After all, the exposition is basically an orderly presentation of themes; the development is designed to shake order up, to throw things around a little and to emphasize certain elements at the expense of others. The Germans call the development the *Durchführung*, the "leading through"—and this is very exact. The development leads the exposition through a kind of sequence of variations, a game of repetitions and a climax to its drama. By the time the development ends, the ear has become disoriented; it longs for the return of the material with which the exposition launched the movement. It seeks order: resolution.

This brings us to the restatement section of sonata-allegro, the *recapitulation*. Here, the composer simply brings back the exposition in something like its original form. Actually, there are a few differences between the exposition and the recapitulation, but basically one has no trouble recognizing the first and second themes and the subsidiary themes and transitional material back in their old running order. Dramatically, it may sound redundant to have to hear "old" material all over again—but after the insecurity of the development, it has a very tonic effect. To complete the resolution of the movement, there is some kind of finishing piece tacked on after the recapitulation: the *coda* (Italian for "tail"). Statement, variation, restatement: exposition, development, recapitulation—that is sonata-allegro form.

The sonata movement is the most important movement in symphony, as it is used almost invariably for the all-important first movement of both the symphony and the concerto. The first movement is not just the start of a work: it is the basis for all that ensues. When the Classical symphony grew bold and expansive under Beethoven, the last movement was enlarged to balance the first movement, and it, too, became necessarily a sonata movement.

Before we go on to deal with the two middle movements in the symphony, let's deal with a tricky structural question. Since the first movement of a concerto is in sonata form, who sounds the first and second themes—the soloist or the orchestra?

Back in the days of the *concerto grosso* and its group of soloists, there was no problem. The main orchestral body opened the movement with one main theme, the solo group played off that theme with variations and contrasts, and structure was upheld by the orchestra's repetitions of the main theme. There was no second theme, no development or recapitulation as such. First movements were built entirely out of their opening theme, called *ritornello* ("refrain"). Thus, the balance of orchestra and solo group was assured: the one would sound the refrain and the other would "develop" that refrain between its appearances.

But the invention of sonata form changed all that. It made concerto first movements more complex, called for some effort in organization. This renovated concerto, devoted to the virtuoso soloist, was developed about the same time as the symphony (roughly the time of Haydn), and it is interesting to follow its development from Mozart through Beethoven to Mendelssohn and Liszt. The progression is one of streamlining, of cohesion and abridgement. In Mozart, the old orchestral *ritornello* survives. We call it the *tutti,* meaning "full orchestra" because in it the orchestra opens the first movement by stating the two principal themes before the soloist has played a note. Thus, a Mozartean concerto first movement has *two* expositions: one for the orchestra and one for the soloist and orchestra.

This makes for a problem of overstatement. When the soloist finally enters, is he to play the same themes all over again? Obviously, this would make for a rather limp movement. In his piano concertos especially, Mozart constantly experimented with the shape of the concerto exposition and the roles of the orchestra and soloist. Beethoven took the project over from Mozart, and then the process of abridgement began. Obviously, the solution was to dispense with the first of the two expositions, the one for orchestra, and to bring the soloist in right at the start of the movement. But this was not so obvious at the time, for at least the *tutti* gave the movement a structural foundation; this was preferable to launching a movement in chaos, with orchestra and soloist fighting each other to see who could sound a theme first.

As it happened, the concerto after Beethoven became something of a wrestling match anyway, and letting the orchestra share the exposition with the soloist—or even reducing the orchestra's role to that of mere accompanist—suddenly didn't feel like a bad idea. As it was, they were already sharing the development. By the late nineteenth century, a composer who respected the orchestral exposition before bringing his soloist in—like Brahms in his violin concerto—was looked on as somewhat old-fashioned.

So much for sonata-allegro movements. What about the rest of the symphony? The two movements in between the sonata end movements (the first and fourth, generally) are less complex in layout, though they, too, show the three-part situation of statement, variation, and restatement. The slow movement, usually the second movement in a symphony or a concerto, consists basically of a main section, a contrasting middle section (especially contrasted in mood), and a repeat of the main section, possibly in a somewhat altered form. (Theme-and-variation sets are also used in slow movements.) Using letters to stand for each section, then, the slow movement might be written as ABA.

The third movement in a symphony was used primarily for rhythmic purposes; when Haydn was consolidating the symphony as form, this was a *minuet*, also in ABA form. The A was the minuet proper, the B (called the *trio*) the contrast (contrasted not only in mood but in tempo as well), and the second A marked a note-for-note repeat of the minuet.

Early in the symphony's history, the minuet became the *scherzo* (Italian for "joke"). It still served a rhythmic purpose, but Beethoven, who invented it, found it more useful than the minuet for its fleet, tensile strength. The minuet was too tame for a Beethovenian symphony, and the scherzo replaced it almost universally within two decades of Beethoven's use of it. The scherzo has the same form as the minuet: ABA, with main section, trio, and repeat of the main section.

And this is a symphony:

sonata form	slow mvt	scherzo	sonata form
1st mvt	2nd mvt	3rd mvt	4th mvt

Compare that to the concerto:

sonata form	slow mvt	rondo
1st mvt	2nd mvt	3rd mvt

What's a *rondo?* It's a lighter form of finale than the symphony's sonata-allegro, and a more fluid and rounded form as well. It consists of a main theme, a subsidiary theme, and several episodes played in between repeats of the main theme and its subsidiary: ABACABA, for example, in which A is the main theme (the rondo's refrain), B the subsidiary, and C an episode. Haydn was fond of using the rondo, or a combination of rondo and sonata-allegro (called sonata-rondo) for the finales of his symphonies.

(There is one important feature about symphonic construction that does not really affect the listener on an awareness level, and since I don't think he need concern himself with it to any extent, I'm making it parenthetical to the text. This feature is harmonic, and it is, to the musician, as significant as melody and rhythm in the construction of a symphony. It is too technical for the non-musician to be able to use it actively in his understanding of symphony, but he will notice that symphonies, until recently, are always identified as being in a certain key. Beethoven's Seventh, for example, is actually Symphony no. 7 in A Major. Does the "A Major" part matter? Very much so, and in this sense: that in organizing the symphony, Beethoven arranges for the ear to distinguish a conflict between the home tonality—A Major—and opposing tonalities, so that certain movements, and the work as a whole, conclude with an almost subliminal sense of resolution by affirming the home tonality. One is probably not aware of any conflict on an intellectual level, and our modern ears have been so saturated with garbage and the ambiguous tonalities of modern popular music that we cannot exercise the hearing that Beethoven's contemporaries could. This is one good reason why symphonies and concertos are no longer composed in a home key: tonality, today, is gone haywire. But our ears do pick out certain basic sound patterns without our thinking much about it, and I can give you a very simple example of how the conflict of tonalities works as structure. Let's take that song "Ol' Man River" again. Remember, this is a typical sample of the statement-variation-restatement piece, in AABA form. But if you sing the song to yourself, or hear it sung, you must notice that the B section—beginning, "You an' me, we sweat an' strain"—seems to provide a certain "lift" to the music, a change of sound quality *besides* the change in the verbal information and the change in the melody. This is because the composer has moved from his home key, which in the case of "Ol' Man River" is usually C Major, into e minor. That is the conflict—one key temporarily replacing another. To understand how the conflict works structurally in symphony, imagine how "Ol' Man River" would sound if the music ended at the end of the B, the e minor section, without returning to C Major. The music would stop at the words, "Git a little drunk an' you'll land in jail." Try it—the sound is peculiar, uncomfortable. We *need* the resolution into C Major; our ears sense the disorder and anticipate a return to order. This is how a composer uses tonality to structure a symphony, and why we expect a movement to end in the key it began in, or change from the minor into the major or vice versa.)

Now let's take a sample symphony and see how the various structural and dramatic elements work collaboratively. Mozart's Symphony no. 39 in E Flat Major will serve nicely here: a traditional work, accessibly small-scaled, it will prove more rules than it will exceptions.

It begins with a slow introduction subtly connected to the rest of the work. At the change in tempo, to *Allegro* (lively), the first movement proper gets underway with the first subject, in the 1st violins (in the home key of E Flat):

This is an unusually delicate melody for a first subject, but the orchestra quickly steps in to build up some excitement, including the introduction, in the flutes and clarinets, of this subsidiary theme:

Easily recognized by its assertive repeated notes, this theme is slightly modified and combined with a new theme, a frolicsome little "tag" in the strings:

But meanwhile, we have arrived at the second subject, made of a flowing theme in the violins "answered" by those same repeated notes, further modified, in the woodwinds:

Two points should be raised here. One, to continue the parenthetical comment regarding tonality that I made earlier, is that along with melodic conflict—that is, first theme "versus" second theme—there is a harmonic conflict—home key versus other keys. In this case, we have moved from the E Flat Major that Mozart laid down both at the start of his introduction and at the start of the first movement proper, in the first subject, to B Flat Major, in the second subject. (B Flat is the "dominant" of E Flat, and functions as something like its oppositional alter ego.) Only those with what is called "absolute perfect pitch" will identify the shift in sound value as "E Flat to B Flat"—but, nonetheless, the ear does pick up on the change, if unconsciously. Ordinarily, the first and second subjects offer a greater contrast in mood than they do here, but the sense of conflict is still present because of the harmonic contrast.

The other point concerns Mozart's use of the repeated-note theme, changing it at each appearance according to his whim. Symphonic themes are plastic. They often undergo modifications of this kind—this is part of what gives symphony its dramatic motion. Naturally, we expect to hear such thematic transformations in the development section. But in fact the transformation process is going on all the time. Nothing, in music, is stationary.

With his first and second subjects (and subsidiary themes) set down, Mozart closes the exposition with the tag, the string line from example 3. As usual in Mozart, the exposition is repeated (that is, if the conductor wants to repeat it; the option is his).

Now comes the development. Mozart begins it with the tag—but with a switch: here it shows up in g minor:

The development is not long, lasting less than a minute, but it is crammed with action. Its special feature is an interplay of themes from the exposition. This is called counterpoint, an extremely important credential in a composer's portfolio. The trick of counterpoint is to bring two or more themes into play at the same time while creating a harmonious totality. You want to hear the separate elements functioning in an integral texture. Here is an example of what Mozart does with counterpoint—three different themes playing at the same time (actually, this passage from the development has already been heard in the exposition):

The climax of the development brings back the counterpoint of example 3, this time doubling it. Instead of two different themes playing against each other, Mozart now has four different parts working at once, as if to concentrate all the action of the exposition while expanding it.

That is as far as the development needs to go, and Mozart gentles it down, slipping back into the first subject as it first appeared: recapitulation. Now the entire exposition is heard again as it was first heard. The only difference is that instead of restating the harmonic tension originally used to oppose the second subject to the first, both subjects are now heard in the home key. This reassures the ear while resolving the work dramatically. An important question: how exact is the recapitulation in post-Mozartean symphonies? Much less exact as time goes on, for the Romantics sought a cohesion in the symphony that could not tolerate the full repetition of material already heard. Therefore, it is wise to think of the recapitulation not so much as a mirror of the exposition but as an artistic copy, with some rights of divergence. The themes may run in a different order in the recapitulation, or may be differently scored. But, as we see, in Mozart's time the recapitulation is an almost exact replica of the exposition (except for the harmonic change).

The slow [second] movement is much less complex than the first movement. Its "job," as such, is to widen the symphony's emotional parameters with music of a more interior communication than that of the first movement, and this it does not by reducing any sense of drama but by moving the ear from the "public" vitality of the first movement into a more private world. Here, there is less thematic interplay, more stress laid on the expressiveness of the themes themselves.

Harmonically, the slow movement is in A Flat Major (the subdominant of E Flat), a key of important subsidiary relation to our home key, E Flat. (As will be seen, the harmonic architecture of a symphony not only lies in movement-length conflicts, but builds the entire work.) The first theme, in the first violins, is simplicity itself:

By contrast, the minor-key second theme (also in the first violins) unleashes a searching rage:

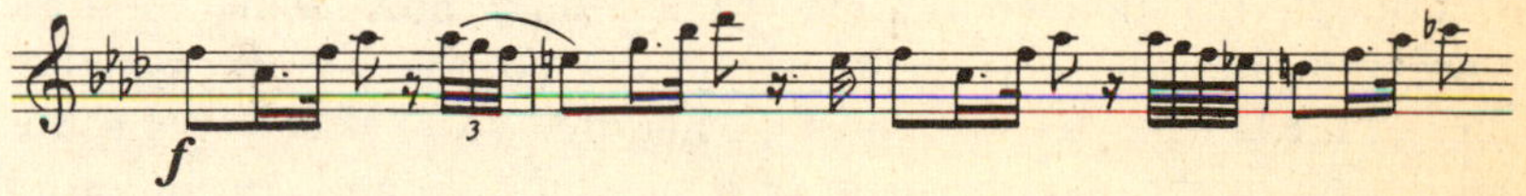

There is a third theme as well, but essentially the movement is run on the steam generated by the conflict between the first two themes. The more balanced first theme wins out, but the overall effect is one of great internal contest.

The third movement is the "plainest" of the four, a dance movement whose function is to break into the dramatic plan with rhythmic lift. As of Beethoven, this is the scherzo movement; before him, it was a minuet, as here. Where our statement, variation, restatement plan led us in the first two movements to a middle section in which familiar material was developed, in the minuet the middle section simply sounds a new theme. This is the trio section, called so because in earlier days it was played by three solo instruments. Thus, the entire movement (in E Flat, the home key) consists of a main theme and its subsidiaries:

followed by the trio section, launched by a clarinet solo:

which in turn is followed by the main part of the minuet all over again exactly as at first. (In fact, the repetition is so precise that composers do not even write out the repeat, but simply say, *da capo,* from the top.)

By this time, we have not just heard three periods of music, but have been led through a series of progressions within progressions—emotional, rhythmic, harmonic—that should now come to some resolution in the finale [fourth mvt]. In some of the complex symphonies of the late nineteenth century, a hundred years after Mozart, this resolution might take the form of a summing up and conclusion of all that has passed in the first three movements. Or it might refer most specifically back to the first movement, bringing it, as it were, "up to date" and finishing it off. Mozart's symphonies are less epic than that; here, he simply rounds off the work in a zesty close. The first movement balanced the lyrical and the dramatic, the slow movement opposed light and darkness, the minuet smiled and soothed. The finale sports.

It opens with a theme given to the violins, quickly joined by the full orchestra:

We are, of course, securely in the home key, E Flat, and we will end there, too. But first, this typical sonata movement draws us into the dominant (as occurred in the first movement) for the second theme. Note, however, that rather than come up with a *real* second (i.e., contrasting) theme, Mozart merely revamps the first theme, this time using woodwinds to "answer" the violins:

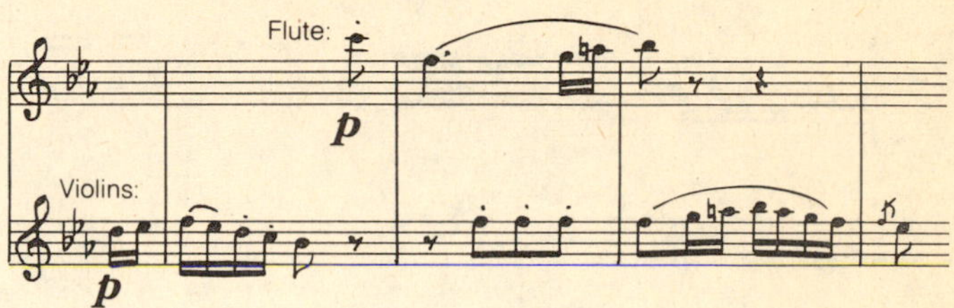

Thus, the finale is not as concerned with conflict as the first two movements were. Here, statement, variation, and restatement present a cohesive mood of almost non-stop vivacity. The exposition comes to a full close (with the "optional" repeat), then leaps into the development with the first theme very much to the fore. Often in movements of this kind, the development—or perhaps the coda of the recapitulation—would give us a fugal treatment of the theme. This means that the composer has different instrumental groups entering with the theme (or variants of it), one after another, until some four or five *separate* versions of the same theme are all playing at once. Mozart does this here, briefly, at the height of the development. At the same time, he pits the woodwinds against the fugal strings with a totally different theme. So what we end up with is a brilliant boil of string lines based on the first theme, topped by another melody that helps focus the ear:

The example above charts a condensation of what happens, for clarinet and bassoon are playing along with the flute's theme, while the second violins are doubling the first violins an octave below their line and the 'cellos and basses are doubling the violas' line in a similar fashion.

Having brought his development to a climax—having led his theme through its paces—Mozart slips quietly into the recapitulation and tops the whole thing with a firm, incisive coda. The very last thing one hears is "the" theme (for the whole movement has really consisted of one tune stretched to comprise both the first and second subjects) sounded twice and finally by the strings.

All this may seem like a lot to get down at once. But I think the reader will find that talking about form is never as clear as hearing it. After all, symphony doesn't follow these rules: it makes them. In other words, this statement-variation-restatement syndrome is the plan that was evolved, more or less fortuitously, as the overture, then the concerto, then the symphony, then the tone poem (in that chronological order) evolved. It seemed "logical," natural, spontaneous. No symphonist ever looked up this code for form in some book; it just happened to be what was going on in symphony. And, again, no composer ever held himself to these forms if he thought of something else to do.

Let's look at a few sample works in outline form, to see how different examples of different genres structure themselves by movement. Let's take Mozart's Thirty-Sixth, the "Linz" Symphony, as an example of the Classical symphony of the late eighteenth century, when the form had just recently evovled its shape:

sonata form	slow mvt:sonata form	minuet	sonata form
1st mvt	2nd mvt	3rd mvt	4th mvt

By the early 1800s, Beethoven enlarged the form, made it more powerful as drama. In particular, he strengthened the last movement, made it bigger to balance the big first movement. Also, he did away with the minuet of Mozart's time, substituting the more vigorous scherzo. This is the plan of Beethoven's Seventh:

sonata form	slow mvt: rondo form	scherzo	sonata form
1st mvt	2nd mvt	3rd mvt	4th mvt

Beethoven's type of symphony remained the model for the entire nineteenth century. Here is a prime example of the Romantic symphony of the 1800s, Dvořák's Seventh:

sonata form	slow mvt: ABA form	scherzo	sonata form
1st mvt	2nd mvt	3rd mvt	4th mvt

In the 1900s, some composers held to the Romantic format, or modified it slightly, while others joined the neo-Classical movement, reviving the fleeter forms of pre-Beethoven symphony. Here is a representative sample of the big (Romantic) symphony, *circa* 1945, from Prokofyef. Note that he has dropped the scherzo movement, slipping its rhythmic component into the slow movement and imposing its prankish tone upon the finale:

sonata form	slow mvt: ABA form	sonata form (without recapitulation)
1st mvt	2nd mvt	3rd mvt

The concerto has undergone less of a formal evolution than the symphony. Perhaps the only major structural difference between Beethoven's Third Piano Concerto:

sonata form	slow mvt: ABA form	rondo
1st mvt	2nd mvt	3rd mvt

and Chaikofsky's First Piano Concerto:

sonata form	slow mvt: ABA form	rondo
1st mvt	2nd mvt	3rd mvt

is that Chaikofsky, writing seventy-five years after Beethoven, brings his soloist in at the very start of the first movement instead of waiting for the Classical *tutti* (the orchestra's statement of themes) before bringing in the soloist.

Of course, in the 1900s, composers did not necessarily write concertos in three-movement form. Thus, Stravinsky's Violin Concerto (note that the composer has labeled his four movements by musical genre):

sonata form	slow mvt: ABA form	slow mvt: ABA form	rondo
Toccata	Aria I	Aria II	Capriccio

Now for one-movement forms. Here's a sample of the Classical overture, Beethoven's *Egmont* Overture:

sonata form (with extended coda)

Once the Romantic era got going, composers retired the overture in favor of the tone poem. Both, in essence, abstract an idea—*Egmont* tells of a hero fighting tyranny. But where the overture took the structure of a first movement in a symphony (sonata-allegro form), the tone poem has any number of forms it may take. For example, compare Strauss' *Till Eulenspiegel's Merry Pranks:*

rondo

with Chaikofsky's *Romeo and Juliet:*

sonata form

Debussy's *Prelude to The Afternoon of a Faun* is in simple ABA form, as if it were the slow movement of a symphony:

ABA form

Respighi's strictly episodic *Pines of Rome* takes another shape altogether:

A B C D

The next thing for you to do is start listening, using the entries on each specific work to guide you. Whenever you feel you need a brush-up, you might glance at the Digest Guide for Dilletantes, immediately following, which offers a shorthand version of this article. Two things to remember, above all: (1), all music is statement, variation, and restatement, and (2), there are no rules, including that one.

THE DIGEST GUIDE FOR DILLETANTES

This capsule guide is simplistic and approximate; its rules have many exceptions. However, it should serve as a fleet introduction for those who want the slightest coaching on form. It may also be used by graduates as a brush-up cram.

The major forms of orchestral music are:

1. The symphony, consisting of four movements:
   a strong first movement, a lyrical slow movement, a lively scherzo, and a strong finale
2. The concerto (which features one or more instrumental soloists), consisting of three movements:
   a strong first movement, a lyrical slow movement, and a lively finale
3. The overture, which is like the first movement of a symphony
4. The tone poem, which has no set form

The essential dynamic of symphonic music is:

statement, variation, and restatement

Accordingly, the basic symphonic movements follow that dynamic, in several different forms: sonata-allegro form, ABA form, and rondo form.

Virtually all first movements and many last movements are in *sonata-allegro* (or just sonata) form, consisting of:

1st and contrasting 2nd themes	the two themes (or other themes) varied	the two themes in original form
exposition (the statement)	development (the variation)	recapitulation (the restatement)

Most slow movements and scherzos are in ABA form, which is a simplified sonata-allegro:

main theme	contrasting middle section	main theme repeated
(the statement)	(the variation)	(the restatement)

In the scherzo, the middle section is called the *trio*.
Rondo form is usually used for lighthearted final movements. It consists of a main theme alternated with subsidiary themes:

main theme	subsidiary theme	main theme	"episode"	main theme	subsidiary theme	main theme

One other form is important, the *theme-and-variations*. It consists of one basic theme which undergoes a series of transformations. Often, after the last variation, the theme is restated in its original form.
Two basic terms to know: *absolute* music and *program* music.
Absolute music is music for music's sake.
Program music characterizes a person, place, or idea, or even tells a "story" in music.

THE ORCHESTRA

This is easier than you'd think. The whole business breaks down into four basic groups:

1. The Woodwinds
   These are the lighter-sounding wind instruments (those one blows into), which generally control tone production by the use of reeds, mainly: flute, oboe, clarinet, and bassoon.
2. The Brasses
   These are the heavier winds, controlling tone production by the use of mouthpieces instead of the woodwinds' reeds, mainly: French horn (usually called, simply, horn), trumpet, trombone, and tuba.
3. The Percussion
   These are the weirder instruments, those one hits, smashes, or otherwise assaults, mainly: the timpani (kettledrums) and other drums, cymbals, triangle, harp, and—in twentieth-century orchestration—the piano, celesta, and xylophone.
4. The Strings
   Two groups ("first" and "second") of violins, violas, 'cellos, and double-basses.

The size of the orchestra is not fixed. It has evolved from quite small ensembles consisting mainly of strings to the huge and extremely varied groups of Mahler's time, and since then has been big, medium-sized, or small at the composer's whim. Also, keep in mind that size is not only a matter of adding more players, but of adding different instruments to the basic ones.

Let's try some examples. A typical Classical orchestra takes us back to the time when the modern symphony orchestra was pretty much established and still on the small side. This is the time of late Haydn and Mozart and early Beethoven. Their scoring might call for:

woodwinds: 1 flute, 2 oboes, 2 bassoons
brasses: two horns, two trumpets
percussion: timpani
and all the strings

This would be roughly 1800. After that, the Romantic era saw the expansion of the orchestra. At the end of the nineteenth century, in the days of Mahler, a typical scoring would call for more players and other instruments:

woodwinds: two piccolos, four flutes, four oboes, English horn, four B-Flat clarinets, two E-Flat clarinets, bass clarinet, four bassoons, contra-bassoon
brasses: eight horns, four trumpets, four trombones, tuba
percussion: timpani, bass drum, snare drum, tambourine, triangle, bells, cymbals, two harps

and a great many more strings than Haydn or Mozart called for, to balance out the overall sound with the other instruments.
When you're sitting in a concert hall facing the players dead-on, the layout runs approximately so:

Percussion

← Brasses →

Percussion — Percussion

← Woodwinds →

2nd Violins — Violas

1st Violins — 'Cellos — Double Basses

Conductor

An ideal way to get all this down and enjoy some fine music as well is to invest in a recording of Benjamin Britten's *The Young Person's Guide to the Orchestra.* In essence a set of variations on a theme of Henry Purcell, the work demonstrates the contrasting colors of the various instruments with the help of a narrator. It's suitable for all ages, by the way; don't be put off by the title. (When you buy the record, make sure that it has a narrator—some versions offer just the music.)

SUREFIRE INITIATIONS FOR BEGINNERS

For those who don't know where to start, here are lists—in no particular order; choose by chance—of some of the more accessible works. All the pieces listed are dealt with in the book. There are two lists, the first comprising those works generally conceded to be ideal introductions to the world of symphony, and the second a less orthodox aggregation for the adventurous. In other words, list no. 1 indicates the beaten paths; list no. 2 recommends roads not always taken. (The first seven items in list no. 1 are also good starting pieces for children.)

Everybody's List of Introductory Pieces

1. Britten: *The Young Person's Guide to the Orchestra*
2. Mendelssohn: Incidental Music to *A Midsummer Night's Dream*
3. Beethoven: Symphony no. 6 (the "Pastoral")
4. Dvořák: Slavonic Dances
5. Chaikofsky: the *Nutcracker Suite*
6. Prokofyef: *Peter and the Wolf*
7. Saint-Saëns: *The Carnival of the Animals*

Baroque Era

8. Handel: The Water Music
9. Handel: The Royal Fireworks Music

Classical Era

10. Haydn: Symphony no. 92 ("Oxford")
11. Haydn: Symphony no. 94 (the "Surprise")
12. Haydn: Symphony no. 104
13. Mozart: Symphony no. 36 (the "Linz")
14. Mozart: Symphony no. 38 (the "Prague")
15. Mozart: Symphony no. 40
16. Mozart: Overture to *Don Giovanni*
17. Mozart: Overture to *The Magic Flute*

Transitionally Classic-Romantic

18. Beethoven: Symphony no. 5
19. Beethoven: Symphony no. 7
20. Beethoven: Piano Concerto no. 5 (the "Emperor")
21. Beethoven: Violin Concerto
22. Schubert: Symphony no. 8 (the "Unfinished")
23. Schubert: Symphony no. 9 (the "Great C Major")

Romantic Era

23. Berlioz: *Symphonie Fantastique*
24. Berlioz: any collection of overtures
25. Liszt: *Les Préludes*
26. Wagner: any collection of overtures and preludes
27. Franck: Symphony in d minor
28. Smetana: *The Moldau*
29. Brahms: Symphony no. 2
30. Brahms: Piano Concerto no. 2
31. Brahms: The "Haydn" Variations
32. Brahms: The Academic Festival Overture
33. Saint-Saëns: Symphony no. 3 (the "Organ")
34. Saint-Saëns: Piano Concerto no. 2
35. Musorksky: *A Night on Bald Mountain*
36. Dvořák: Symphony no. 9 ("From the New World")
37. Rimsky-Korsakof: *Scheherazade*
38. Rimsky-Korsakof: *Capriccio Espagnol*
39. Elgar: the "Enigma" Variations
40. Mahler: Symphony no. 1(the "Titan")
41. Mahler: Symphony no. 4
42. Strauss: *Don Juan*
43. Strauss: *Till Eulenspiegel's Merry Pranks*

44. Strauss: *Also Sprach Zarathustra*
45. Dukas: *The Sorcerer's Apprentice*
46. Vaughan Williams: Fantasia on "Greensleeves"
47. Rachmaninof: Piano Concerto no. 2
48. Holst: *The Planets*

Twentieth Century

49. Bartók: Concerto for Orchestra
50. Stravinsky: *The Rite of Spring*
51. Stravinsky: *Petrushka*
52. Prokofyef: Symphony no. 5
53. Weill: *Kleine Dreigroschenmusik*
54. Copland: *El Sálon México*
55. Copland: *Appalachian Spring Suite*

Introductory Pieces for Those With a Yen for the Offbeat

Romantic Era

1. Dvořák: Symphony no. 7
2. Janáček: *Lachian Dances*
3. Elgar: *Falstaff*
4. Mahler: Symphony no. 6

Twentieth Century

5. Nielsen: Symphony no. 5
6. Schönberg: *Pelleas und Melisande*
7. Ives: Symphony no. 2
8. Ruggles: *Sun-Treader*
9. Bloch: *Israel Symphony*
10. Villa-Lobos: Bachianas Brasileiras no. 2
11. Bartók: *The Miraculous Mandarin Suite*
12. Berg: Violin Concerto
13. Prokofyef: *Scythian Suite*
14. Milhaud: *La Création du Monde*
15. Piston: Symphony no. 2
16. Hindemith: *Symphonic Metamorphosis of Themes by Carl Maria von Weber*
17. Harris: Symphony no. 3
18. Poulenc: Concerto for Two Pianos and Orchestra
19. Copland: *Quiet City*

20. Shostakovitch: Symphony no. 5
21. Shostakovitch: Symphony no. 9
22. Hovhaness: *Mysterious Mountain*
23. Britten: *Four Sea Interludes*
24. Bernstein: *On the Town Suite*
25. Henze: Symphony no. 3

CLASSIC, ROMANTIC, AND NEO: A GUIDE TO STYLE

The adjectives "Classical" and "Romantic" are used a lot in this book—as, indeed, they are used in any analysis of Western art. These terms are not insider's lingo; they provide very handy, even necessary heuristics in the matter of establishing the "attitude" of a given work, a key to the creator's worldview.

In other words, it really does matter whether a symphony dates from the Classical era, or the Romantic era, or the neo-Classical revival and so on, because that label tells us a lot about the composer's approach on such matters as structure, emotional "meaning" (if any) of the music, size of the orchestra, length, and much more. There were, of course, other periods and quasi-periods before and during the ones defined below, but for simplicity's sake and because the massed ensemble of instrumentalists—the orchestra—did not come into being till late in music's history, you really need concern yourself only with those eras herein cited.

The Classical era, to reduce to picked bones what has filled volumes, emphasized the purity of music as absolute expression, music for music's sake. This was, generally, the late eighteenth century, the time of Haydn and Mozart, a time of symphonies, concertos, serenades, and divertimentos: absolute music. If a composer craved drama, he could compose an opera. There were no tone poems, no fantastic symphonies with extramusical synopses. Concerto soloists subsumed their personalities in the personality of the work. Formal integrity was secured by a clarity of structure—one always knew where one section of a work ended and the next began. There were always breaks between movements. Themes were not carried over from one movement to another: separateness of parts, clarity, precision. The world was in order, and music was meant to mirror that order.

The Romantic era, which lasted throughout the nineteenth century, corrupted Classical purity by taking music to be a dramatic expression, often inspired by a place, an event, a character, or even a text. This was music for some other sake: program music. Now composers who craved drama could bring it into the concert hall with the tone poem or with program symphonies. Music became less ceremonial, more personal. The Classical symphony was, in a sense, a public testament, a reflection of the age. The Romantic symphony grew more individually dramatic, a kind of self-portrait.

After a transition launched by Beethoven and seconded by Schubert and Mendelssohn, Romanticism officially took over with Berlioz and Schumann, and involved virtually every composer of the century except Brahms and Bruckner. It was an age of fantastic symphonies, of a disillusioned, chaotic, and self-obsessed worldview whose lack of clarity was mirrored in a tendency to blend sections of a work into each other. There were not always breaks between movements. Themes might be carried over from one movement to another. In particular, a kind of protagonistic musicality was encouraged in this personally protagonistic epoch with the use of motto themes, themes repeated over the course of a work like a composer's *cri de coeur,* or else transformed into other themes. Classicism was stability; Romanticism was transformation.

It was a time of quests and metamorphoses, a distrust of "order." It was a Faustian, a mystical and apocalyptic time, erecting huge structures in symphony as if to storm the heavens or wake the dead. New instruments were added to the orchestra, which grew to vast proportions. More woodwinds! More brasses! More strings to balance them out! Size . . . and personality. Concerto soloists were expected to be larger than the works they played; new concertos were written in which a charismatic virtuoso would conquer the orchestra as much as collaborate with it. Most important of all, it was a time when music emerged as a public commodity, gave up its privacy and sold tickets to a broad public.

And what happened after Romanticism? "Modernism" is a clumsy word with neither resonance nor, even, meaning. But we use it as a catch-all because the times get complex as of 1900, and no one word covers all that happened. On one hand, Romanticism seemed exhausted, flabby. Composers sought new disciplines for the act of composition. One approach was a return to the strict pre-Romantic world of absolute music and moderately sized symphonies: neo-Classicism. But even while reviving the sound styles and forms of Bach, Haydn, and Mozart, neo-classicism somehow got itself entangled in satire, jazz, and other commentative forms. It was as if they could not support a "Back to Bach" movement with a straight face.

While the neo-Classicists reduced the orchestra and worked in transparently small-scaled forms (such as twenty-minute symphonies), other innovators retained their Romantic roots, dallied with expressionism and other grotesquerie, and found their way at last into atonalism (music with rhythm and melody but no conventional harmony). This is where "contemporary" music begins to carry an unsavory air for many people—even now, there are many symphony buffs who refuse to hear Arnold Schönberg, Alban Berg, or Anton Webern. And they were contemporary before World War II.

What is modernism, then, if anything? There is no simple answer. Since about 1910, when Romanticism threatened to expire but never quite got around to it, we have seen neo-Classicism, neo-Romanticism, atonalism, twelve-tone music (Schönberg's precisely complex atonal method), electronic music, dada, and a host of minor flurries. Some people use "modern" to mean "anything avant-garde," some to mean "dissonant," some simply to cover the present time. It's best to use—and read—the word loosely as, I repeat, a catch-all: from Debussy on.

These are thumbnail breakdowns. For a more solid grounding, try reading the introductory articles to the composers listed below (chronologically by era), as these contain more detailed discussions of symphonic aesthetics as they have evolved from era to era. Because the modern orchestra and its compositional forms were organized mainly during the Classical period, I have not indexed the Baroque era below. However, some introductory comments may be found in the article on Vivaldi.

Classicism: Haydn
Transition from Classicism to Romanticism: Beethoven

Early Romanticism: Berlioz, Weber, Mendelssohn, Schumann
Middle Romanticism: Liszt, Wagner, Franck, Balakiryef, Musorksky
Classical Reaction to Romanticism: Bruckner, Brahms
Late Romanticism: Strauss, Mahler
Transition from Romanticism into the Twentieth Century: Busoni, Debussy, Ives
Twentieth-Century Romanticism: Janáček, Skryabin, Sibelius, Rachmaninof, Ruggles, Barber
Atonalism: Schönberg
Jazz: Gershwin, Weill, Copland
Neo-Classicism: Honegger, Milhaud, Poulenc, Ravel
Sui Generis: Stravinsky

A NOTE ON PERFORMING STYLES

One of the richer adventures of listening to orchestral music is discovering how different artists approach a given work. One might assume that because a composition is set down in black and white from first note to last it will sound more or less the same no matter who plays or conducts it. But it doesn't. If music were that exact, computers might run our concerts for us.

The personality of a musician bears heavily on the music he or she plays. True, we hope that performing musicians will reveal the original work, not manipulate it. But there is no such thing as "playing as written" if by "as written" one means without imposing any commentary on the work. Musicians who manage that do so not by suppressing their personality but by not having much personality in the first place. And these, of course, are not the musicians that anyone wants to hear.

On the other hand, the parameters of personal interpretation—of realizing the "truth" of a work—are very wide. Some musicians are famous for their attempts to follow a composer's directions (as to tempo, volume, and so on), to blend their spirit with what they believe to be the spirit of the work. Other musicians are famous for imposing their own will upon a score, ignoring or overdoing its directions at their whim. Which approach is preferred? The debate is hot and endless, and basically redounds to listener's taste—for who can say how deeply verbal directions speak to the soul of a work, or how far done is overdone? With the composer himself dead and out of the picture, what authority can define absolutely the spirit of a piece?

People have their opinions nonetheless. For example, some find the performances of Arturo Toscanini to be the classic instance of total fidelity to the score, expressed within a style that emphasizes precision, extraordinarily ecstatic lyricism, and dramatic excitement. Others will admit Toscanini's exactness in following directions but otherwise find him overly fast and rigid. So even if there is no denying that Toscanini did respect the "letter" of the manuscript as much as possible, it is also true that his personal slant affects the music. There is no one tempo, no fixed volume, no way to play music without *playing* it. The difference between Toscanini and some idealized impersonal perfection is the difference between art and a shrill-color snapshot of a robot eating a xerox machine.

The controversy over personal interpretation is not as old as one might imagine. It dates from the rise of the charismatic celebrity performer in the second quarter of the nineteenth century. Before then, music was largely made by those who wrote it, or performed by musicians under the composer's direction. In the seventeenth century, orchestral scores were frequently not even written out part for part, as the composer himself customarily settled on the instrumental parts in rehearsal for what he assumed would be the only performance a work would ever have. Our Baroque ancestors preferred novelty to revival.

Nor were there conductors then, in the modern sense of an all-powerful leader who keeps the orchestra together, cues in the various instruments, has a "view" of a piece, and is praised or blamed for its performance. Not till the late eighteenth century were instrumental ensembles large enough to need someone to keep them together; more often than not the concertmaster (the chief of the first violin section) would give the downbeat to launch a movement. Furthermore, there was less attention to the archeological aspect of musicology. Once a composer and his imitators had died out, that style was dead. No one cared to bring it back, to worry over its instrumentation, its special sensibilities. Nowadays, numerous specialists delve into forgotten repertory to exhume artifacts of the past—old church music, Baroque opera, or solos written for obsolete instruments. Not perhaps till Mendelssohn and Schumann reintroduced the virtually forgotten works of Johann Sebastian Bach to the public some hundred years after Bach's death was any attempt made to enrich the living repertory with the heritage of the past.

By Mendelssohn's time, orchestras had grown to such size and orchestra parts so dependent on synchronous diversities that conductors were needed. Mendelssohn was one of the first musicians to profess himself a conductor as well as a composer: he regularly performed other men's works. This was something new in music, and not till the end of the nineteenth century were there many people who went into music primarily to minister to the creations of others, whether as conductors or instrumental soloists. But the old usage of the all-around musicianship that knew no boundaries between composer and performer—everyone had been both—finally broke down. Already, in the nineteenth century, there were piano and violin virtuosos who composed only when they had to, and whose compositions were useful only to set off their virtuosity. They were performers, not—really—composers. And so we moderns have inherited a huge profession of conductors and instrumentalists known only for their gifts as interpreters.

However, the ancient caste of the composer-performer survives. Many conductors of the recent past and the present have, it is true, found little encouragment for their compositions. Otto Klemperer, Wilhelm Furtwängler, Victor de Sabata, and Jean Martinon, to name only a few, found their conducting careers overshadowing their careers as composers. But others such as Leonard Bernstein, Hans Werner Henze, and Benjamin Britten have played as well as made music. All are known for their interpretations of their own works, yes—but they also have exercised certain specialties in the classic repertory. Bernstein, for instance, led the Mahler revival in the 1960s after the death of Mahler expert Bruno Walter, and it is possible that many more listeners would be glad to hear Bernstein conduct Mahler than conduct Bernstein.

There is a cute sideline worth considering: are composers necessarily the best interpreters of their own music? Again, the debate rages. It seems presumptuous to discount the obvious advantage of personal authenticity that a creator can bring to his own work, but on the other hand there is no getting around the other advantages of technique and dramatic projection which a creator does not necessarily possess. The creator must know better than anyone how his work should sound, but he may not be as well equipped as others to effect that sound. It is for this reason that some listeners have found greater pleasure in, say, Bernstein's recording of *The Rite of Spring* than in Stravinsky's. A good illustration of the gap between ownership and expertise is found in two recorded performances of "The Carousel Waltz," the medley of waltz tunes that opens the Rodgers and Hammerstein musical *Carousel.* Rodgers himself put a performance on disc, leading the New York Philharmonic, and while Rodgers is no conductor, it's a fine performance, bright and lively. But a long-forgotten 78 r.p.m. single of the piece conducted by Fritz Reiner and played by the Pittsburgh Symphony yields a far more exciting performance, rhapsodic in the lyrical sections and tense in the dramatic ones, so precisely articulated that one feels Reiner and the Pittsburghers could have passed through the eye of a needle on that number. It's Rodgers' music, all right—but Reiner's is unquestionably the more interesting interpretation. In fact, next to Reiner, Rodgers isn't interpreting at all, just beating time.

This returns us to our main question about performers' interpretations: how much are they supposed to interpret? No one can say. The listener himself must decide which approach he prefers—which conductors he likes in which style of music, which pianists, violinists, and so on. There are whole schools of conducting, for example. One is the middle-European approach, especially associated with German symphony from Beethoven to Mahler: the Romantic era. This approach is called "subjective" by its detractors; actually, all conducting is subjective. But the more notable adherents of the German Romantic style are admittedly extreme, adding in all sorts of touches that the composer hasn't necessarily asked for in tempo and volume, applying an almost mystical ambiguity to instrumental ensemble and a strong architecture of rise and fall—all as if they were sculpting the music as they play it. Those who don't care one way or another about any presumed subjectivity might still find this approach too ponderous, too soupy, too slow. But those who respond to it find it profound, and tend to prefer their Beethoven, Brahms, and Strauss as played by the great Romantic conductors: Willem Furtwängler, Otto Klemperer, Hans Knappertsbusch, Clemens Krauss, Karl Böhm, Erich Kleiber, and Wilhelm Mengelberg. (However, outside the field of German Romantic symphony, these men could hit wide of the mark—Klemperer's recording of Berlioz' *Symphonie Fantastique* shows how the brilliant crispness of French music could elude the middle European.)

Of course, even within this stated arena, listeners have their preferences. Many who swear by Furtwängler's sacramental communion with the great German masters find Klemperer impossibly dense; some Klemperer buffs find Mengelberg's radical individualism unacceptable while seeing nothing extreme in the others. Too, there are the complications of history. For one thing, virtually all of these men are now dead, and survive only in the memory of their concerts or on recordings, often in antiquated sound. For another thing, the political upheavals of the 1930s and 1940s are the kind that weaken or even kill a musical tradition. The career of Klemperer, a non-Aryan, was disrupted by the rise of Nazism. The career of Furtwängler was disrupted by the fall of Nazism, for, though he hated the Nazis and actually used his powerful reputation as a shield in protecting their victims, he was smeared after the war and either barred from work or grudgingly tolerated by some opinion molders. The career of Mengelberg was not disrupted but finished in comparable circumstances: it happens that he was a Nazi sympathizer, and had the bad fortune to live in a nation—the Netherlands—where traitors are punished.

So perhaps it is no accident that the German Romantic approach is much less prominent today than it once was. In the post–World War II years, a fleeter, leaner style became popular, and this might be called the Italian approach, for its prime exponents include Arturo Toscanini, Guido Cantelli, Alceo Galliera, Carlo Maria Giulini, Claudio Abbado, and Riccardo Muti. If the German Romantics use the orchestra for a gestalt of sonority, a "whole idea" of massed sound, the Italian school seeks clarity of texture, precision more than immensity. The German Romantics play their orchestras as if they were huge organs; the Italians play theirs like harpsichords. Again, however, there is much divergence from any assumed model. Just as the Romantic school takes in a variety of views on tempo, volume, phrasing, and so on, the Italians are a diverse lot. One of the most popular and apparently secure generalizations about them—that they're generally fast and that Toscanini was the fastest—fell apart when someone troubled to time complete performances of Wagner's opera *Parsifal.* Pierre Boulez was the fastest, the German Romantics generally the slowest . . . but Toscanini was the slowest of all.

Speaking of exceptions to rules, an interesting case can be made for Herbert von Karajan, perhaps the most influential conductor today in terms of personality clout. Von Karajan grew out of the Romantic school, yet always seemed to be driving at a rapprochement of German and Italian techniques, combining the apocalyptic grandiosity of the one with the luminous precision of the other. This compromise became something of an extreme when von Karajan introduced his "chamber-sized" Wagner in the 1960s, an attempt to play Wagner's huge opera scores with unprecedented subtlety. The novelty felt all the more bizarre in comparison with Georg Solti's Wagner, huge and surging in the more traditional approach.

Lately, the German Romantic style has come slightly into fashion again as "neo-Romanticism." Such contemporary conductors as Daniel Barenboim and Zubin Mehta appear more in sympathy with Furtwängler than with Toscanini. As it happened, a connection between the middle-European masters and these younger men had been maintained by Leonard Bernstein, whose personal projection of Beethoven and Mahler—even of the Classical Haydn—was often cited as a "vestige" of Romantic conducting.

Bernstein's Mahler brings up a prime subdivision in music, the question of artistic "ownership." Some musicians become so identified with certain composers that the public grants them an informal copyright on performance, speaking of their interpretations as definitive. Much of this, in the past, derived from the concentrated consumerism of the 78 r.p.m. recording; with econimics limiting large or unusual projects to one performance at most, that performance *had* to be definitive, as there wasn't any room in which to give it competition.

Thus, a certain performer who recorded certain works just when they were ready to become popular become permanently linked with those works as the authority. Sir Thomas Beecham staked his claim on Sibelius and Delius by championing those composers when most conductors weren't playing them. Similarly, Artur Schnabel achieved great eminence as a Beethoven specialist when he made the first complete recordings of the piano sonatas and concertos. Of course, these were not stunts—the performers were genuine specialists, their personal commitment to the music very telling. (Old timers love to cite Schnabel's occasional failures of technique in the sonatas even as they extol his recordings as the only acceptable versions.) Despite the fact that they used modern instruments in place of the authentic Baroque ones, Adolf Busch, Rudolf Serkin, and a handpicked cohort virtually put out a patent on Bach's Brandenburg Concertos in their famous 78 set, the first complete recording of the Brandenburgs and the one that brought Bach home to two generations of listeners. (As witness to their status as classics, the Beecham Delius, Schnabel Beethoven cycle, and Busch-Serkin Brandenburgs continue to sell, ancient sound and all, on LP reissues.)

Obviously, records did much to bring underrated composers forward, since they made possible the repetition (in home listening) that acclimatizes the ear to unfamiliar idioms. In our own time, both Bruckner and Mahler moved up from tertiary status to the inner circle: records, mainly, did it. Veteran collectors can testify that the Mahler scene in the early 1950s consisted of Bruno Walter's recordings of the First, Second, Fourth, and Fifth Symphonies and *Das Lied von der Erde* plus a few odd items conducted by an unfamiliar name on a weird label of limited distribution. Then Leonard Bernstein took up the cause. Because his personality meshed so finely with Mahler's, the chemistry of Bernstein's performances made lightning in the concert hall and impressive profits on disc. (Stereo clarity helped, too, in domesticating that massive sound.) Bernstein was the first to assemble a Mahler cycle (i.e., all the symphonies). Then, such an undertaking felt like the discovery of a new world; now, encountering a new Mahler cycle is like walking into one's backyard.

Records make it easy for one to sort out not only which kinds of music he prefers but whose style he prefers in its performance. Cheaper and easier than steady concertgoing, records give one a chance to compare one musician's viewpoint on a given work with another's. Anyone who can afford decent stereo equipment is a critic, and comparisons are not odious but stimulating. The arguments over Horowitz versus Rubinstein on piano, Heifetz versus Menuhin on violin, Stokowski versus Koussevitsky on the podium are old ones, still hotly debated now that their successors have complicated the picture. This isn't contention for its own sake, but a *learning* clash of listening tastes.

That one will develop this taste is inevitable. But it does help to recognize that such considerations as tempo relationships, which instrumental line to bring out in a *tutti,* the very size and shape of sound vary from performance to performance. Hearing, for example, Furtwängler's, Mengelberg's, Toscanini's, Charles Munch's, George Szell's, von Karajan's latest, and—perhaps the best of them all—Carlos Kleiber's recordings of Beethoven's Fifth more or less at the same period in one's life is to undergo certain epiphanies as it were from within the work, to experience at first hand its ecumenism. All these men are playing what Beethoven wrote. Yet, in the end, all of them are playing different versions of the same thing.

Broadening one's experience in symphony, one may want to assemble a small collection of classic performances. This is a relatively inexpensive proposition, as the surviving recordings that predate the stereo era (*circa* 1957 on) have been "retired"on so-called budget labels such as Angel's Seraphim, Columbia's Odyssey, and RCA Victor's Victrola. The records are as well made as the more expensive American discs (which is to say, not very well made at all) and offer a fine opportunity to sample Beecham's idiomatic Delius, Sibelius, Mozart, and Berlioz; Toscanini's white-hot Beethoven and Berlioz and Classical Brahms; Walter's loving Schubert and Beethoven and authoritative Mahler; Furtwängler's cosmic Bruckner. (One warning—make sure that the original monaural sound has not been hoked up by "electronic rechanneling for stereo"—a contemptible hoax that should be firmly boycotted.)

Besides retaining great performances of the past, records document music's evolving styles of performance. A unique experiment in the phonograph's formalized intimacy between performer and public is the existence of three different Beethoven symphony cycles conducted by Herbert von Karajan. Each set was issued in a different decade: the first for Angel, with the Philharmonia Orchestra in monaural sound in the 1950s, the second for Deutsche Grammophon with the Berlin Philharmonic in stereo in the 1960s, and the third again for DG with the Berliners in the late 1970s. Unlike such men as Toscanini and Furtwängler, von Karajan is not fun to analyze—he's too ambiguous. He has no category, not even one compromised with corollaries and exceptions. Even these three Beethoven sets don't parse neatly for across-the-board differences—except in technical engineering—because von Karajan seems to have refined his relationship with each symphony on a separate basis, moving in so many different directions that any one of the three sets may be called the "best."

Those who would enjoy keeping up with the concert world have a problem in that music criticism in general is outrageously poor. There are few sources for competent reporting. However, there is a fine magazine devoted to the recording scene, *Fanfare,* featuring for the most part respectably opinionated and nicely detailed reviews of all major "classical" recordings issued in the United States. (The magazine's articles and reviews center on symphony, chamber music, instrumental work, and opera, with little of the hi-fi apparatus analysis that other record magazines emphasize.) Even more respectable, and relatively easy to find, is the British record magazine *The Gramophone*.

Also British is *The New Penguin Stereo Record and Cassette Guide* (paperback, 1982), which lists and assesses available recordings. Once one gets used to its slightly weird system of grouping recordings of major works by what's on the flip side, it should prove a valuable *vade mecum* for the aspiring connoisseur. And for historical perspective, the chronicle of choice is Paul Henry Lang's *Music in Western Civilization* (New York: W. W. Norton and Company, 1941), an exhaustive reading-and-reference work whose perceptions, comprehensiveness, and love of English are nothing less than dazzling.

Part II

ANTONIO VIVALDI (1675–1741)

In a book devoted to orchestral music, the Baroque era (roughly 1600–1750) offers peculiar problems. A few of the best-known works in the repertory were written in this time—Bach's Brandenburg Concertos and Handel's *Water Music,* for example, not to mention the present composer's *The Four Seasons,* cited below. On the other hand, by "orchestral music" we tend to mean large or middle-sized instrumental groups divided into woodwinds, brasses, percussion, and strings playing symphonies, concertos, and tone poems under the direction of a conductor who bends the original score through his personal prism.

Almost none of this applies to Baroque orchestral music. The Baroque orchestra eventually came to consist largely of strings and a harpsichord *continuo* (that is, a back-up providing "continuity" in harmony and rhythm). Alternatively, festive occasions might call forth orchestras of woodwinds and brasses. But there was no "orchestra" in the modern sense of a layered merging of woodwind, brass, and string timbres. Nor were there symphonies or tone poems. Nor were there conductors—who needed a conductor, with such small-scaled ensembles, perfectly capable of conducting themselves? Anyway, in those days no musician specialized in performing other people's music, as musicians do today: everybody wrote and performed his own. There were concertos then, at least—but even these were rather different from what most people think of as usual in the form.

The use of the term "Baroque" stems not from music but from architecture. A word that at root means "abnormal" and "grotesque" has been applied to the lavish building styles of the seventeenth and eighteenth centuries and, by extension, to the music of that time. Now it no longer means abnormal but "finely structured," for the taste-makers of the Baroque spent no little time in codifying genres and techniques. Cultural centers such as Venice, Naples, Florence, Paris, and Dresden informally established foundations in style; to speak of, say, "Venetian music" in the mid-1600s was to make oneself reasonably clear on a host of variables (the respective thrusts of church and secular music, the use of the voice, the attitude on opera and concerto, whether to emphasize one central melody in a composition—monophony—or to divide the ear's attention among several simultaneously competitive melodies—polyphony—and so on).

The structuring of Baroque music comprised not only the study of form (such as establishing a certain procedure for each movement of a concerto). Another important feature of Baroque thinking was an attempt to organize compositional policy—to figure out what different methods gave different results. There were, for instance, the "two practices," known variously as *prima prattica* and *seconda prattica* (first practice and second practice), as *stile antico* and *stile moderno* (old style and new style), as *stylus gravis* and *stylus luxurians* (serious style and decorated style). The first of the two practices referred to traditional usages in which musical form dominated compositional thinking, while the second referred to the modern novelty of letting feeling or textual meaning prevail over strictly musical considerations. (Feeling was defined in the doctrine of "affections": a systematic musical language to be used by all to depict universal emotional states such as anger, fear, boldness, and such.) There was even a compromise practice, the *stile misto* (mixed style), halfway from the *antico* to the *moderno*. For it turned out that the *seconda prattica* was a lot for anyone to handle, a kind of dry run for the aesthetics of nineteenth-century Romanticism in the importance it gave to the emotional instincts of art.

This is just a sample of the Baroque's love of structure; there were many others. Perhaps the most important for our purposes—certainly the one that bears most heavily on Vivaldi's work—is the era's experiments with individualized instrumental technique. The insistence on finding the right "color" of sound is a Baroque innovation. Musicians evolved schools of thought on how to exploit the idiom of a particular instrument; the art of singing and of violin playing flowered in this age. Certain instruments became obsolete and others grew in importance, so that by the time of the High Baroque in the early eighteenth century, the modern string family had edged out less efficient strings and furnished the basis for the Western orchestra, needing only the addition of a few woodwinds, the horn and trumpet, and the timpani (kettledrums) in the late eighteenth century to provide the setting for Classical orchestral composition.

Diversity of musical expression within a code of procedure: this was the Baroque. There were standards, but originality set them. This paradox made Baroque music as various as it was formalized. One example: it was typical of Baroque planning that the first operas were composed at this time (starting in 1597) according to fixed theories; it was also typical that scarcely a decade had gone by before the more talented composers were subverting those theories. Still, a firm mode was sought, and in the early eighteenth century there arose a centralized thinking about opera, on a new plan termed *opera seria* (serious opera, because it outlawed comic characters). This genre was designed to abstract a nobility of soul but—again, typical chaos—it was ruled by star singers who found nobility less telling than vocal gymnastics and ovations.

In general, the Baroque is a rich era for music. But for fully symphonic orchestral music it has its limits. The present volume concentrates on material composed for the totally integrated modern orchestra, and thus the great Vivaldi—along with Bach and Handel, the two presiding geniuses of the High Baroque—occupies a mere honorary position here. He is significant to us more for his influence on those who followed his lead than for his own work, as the forms open to Vivaldi are not analyzed here. The concerto was the only modern orchestral situation in use in his day, and this was not the soloistic concert we are used to; it preferred a *balance* of multiple forces to the *contrast* of a solo part and an orchestra. Not till after Vivaldi had put the solo violin into a position of quasi-leadership in the concerto did the "violin concerto" resemble what we mean by the term. Vivaldi's structure became known as the Italian concerto, whose three movements—fast, then slow, then fast again—remained the format for concerto ever after. But even so, Vivaldi's concertos lacked a basic structural principle of the modern concerto, harmonic conflict (in which the home key of a work, the tonic, is opposed to antithetical keys, thereby setting up an aural dissension that is resolved in the closing section of a movement).

An ordained cleric, Vivaldi was known as the "red priest" in his native Venice, perhaps the *Hauptkulturstadt* (cultural capital) of Baroque music. He traveled widely and left a prolific œuvre which has yet to be fully appreciated. Johann Sebastian Bach, however, made its acquaintance. Vivaldi's work in the concerto was carried on by Bach, and provided the experimental wherewithal from which Bach extrapolated a new idea in music, the harpsichord concerto. Those who respond enthusiastically to the four violin concertos described here may want to investigate the complete set from which they are drawn (see below). And then—there are a whole range of Vivaldi concerts to hear.

Le Quattro Stagioni (The Four Seasons), op.8, nos. 1–4 c. 1725

This "piece" is really four pieces, the first four of a set of twelve violin concertos that Vivaldi published under the title *Il Cimento dell'Armonia e dell'Invenzione* (The Test of Harmony and Inventiveness). Vivaldi wrote many such concertos, but this quartet has achieved a particular prominence for its engaging programmatic touches. One really does hear a musical depiction of the four seasons here, the solo violin, string orchestra, and harpsichord *continuo* stretching to evoke bird calls in spring, a summer storm, a peasant carousal and a hunt in fall, and shivery winter winds. All this precise imagism in an epoch that generally disliked extramusical allusions in music is refreshing to Baroque buffs and browsers alike.

In fact, one might go as far as to suggest a crypto-Romantic intention on Vivaldi's part, for each of the four concertos accompanies an anonymous poem (presumably by the composer) that states the textual basis for the music. This symbiosis of poetry and music was a favorite device of Romantic composers, which is why so many tone poems of the nineteenth century were inspired by poems—Dukas' *The Sorceror's Apprentice,* for instance, after Goethe; or Strauss' *Don Juan,* after Lenau. Still, one might easily receive the work as a quartet of violin concertos: as absolute music. Each concerto observes the standard format of the so-called Italian concerto—fast first movement, slow second, fast finale.

Spring, Concerto in E Major

"Spring has returned again, and festively
The birds salute him with their joyous song . . . "

And so it is in the orchestral *ritornello* (refrain); between the *ritornello's* appearances, the soloist supplies imitations of the birds' chirrups, of trickly streams, passing storm, and the birdsong again. The soloist leads off the wonderfully peaceful slow [second] movement, suggestive of the slumber of a goatherd and his "faithful dog." Whereas the outer movements of the Italian concerto tend to contrast the orchestral *ritornello* with the soloist's themes, the middle slow movement prefers to expand on one idea exclusively, drawing out of it a kind of continual motion in stillness. For its finale [third mvt], spring presents a dance of nymphs and shepherds in flowing $^{12}/_{8}$ metre. The orchestral *ritornello* (heard, as invariably, at the very start of the movement) suggests the bagpipes, its characteristic drone in the lower strings under the lilting violins.

Summer, Concerto in g minor

The first movement captures the intense drooping of the dog days. The orchestra leads off slowly, but the soloist's first entrance adds some brief vitality; the movement in general is insecure as to tempo, suggesting a nexus of events, true program music. Near the end of the movement, the strings tell of an ill wind rushing by, and the solo violin—supported by the harpsichord—imitates the lamentations of a shepherd apprehensive of a gathering storm. The brief slow [second] movement, too, is pressed by its subject matter, and the soloist's gentle song is menaced by the shuddering orchestra, showing that the shepherd and his fears are still with us. Sure enough, the third movement explodes in tempest. Vivaldi outdoes himself here concocting ingenious "storm effects" in solo and orchestra parts.

Autumn, Concerto in F Major

"With songs and dances country folk cheer
The satisfaction of a fruitful harvest . . . "

And, to top it off, a festive cup. The soloist suggests the inebriate spirits rising in scales and runs, and even attempts a few hiccups. The non-drinkers continue their more upright partying in the orchestra's repeated main theme (the *ritornello),* but the soloist, dealing with the wets in the crowd, closes his part in slower tempo, singing of the blissful sleep of the sated. Sleep is also the subject of the heavenly slow [second] movement, with a delicate but noticeable part for harpsichord. The third movement, subtitled "The Hunt," calls upon the soloist to depict the flight of a stag from hunt and hound, his wounding, and death.

Winter, Concerto in f minor

The first movement's *ritornello* introduces an odd effect in a hollow set of discordant repeated notes launched by the 'cellos and joined respectively by violas, then second violins, then first violins; together, they make a cold quartet, empty of feeling. The soloist enlivens the scene, "Shuffling a-tremble down the snowy street, Cut to the bone by the bite of the wind." The slow [second] movement repairs indoors to the blazing hearth. Note the violin *pizzicatos* (plucked notes) to suggest the rain plopping outside. Here the soloist is at his most expressive. The lively third movement, launched by the soloist, cites the perils of the season, mainly the slickness of ice.

JOHANN SEBASTIAN BACH 1685–1750

To those initiate in the mystery, Bach's music is absolute, beyond praise, dwarfing all that precedes and follows with the beauty of perfection, of order, of balance between extrovert action and introvert expression. It is an effortless rationalism, accessible even when most sophisticated. A fugue, a passacaglia, or any other tricky form appeals, in Bach, to the lay listener as well as to the musician. It is science and poetry at once, a universal epiphany that affects the first-time hearer as surely as the expert.

No other composer has excited such devotion on the part of his colleagues. Among symphony buffs, there is a Mahler cult, a Bruckner cult, a Mozart, Berlioz, and Ives cult. But among composers, there is only one cult, that of Bach. Said Schumann: "We are all bunglers next to him," and Beethoven suggested that he should be called not Bach ("brook," in German), but "Ocean." The passage of centuries has not in the least diminished the legacy of Bach's researches in sound, for either the avant-garde or the reactionary.

As it happens, Bach's reputation as a world-shaker dates not from his own time, but from a revival of interest in his music that was sparked by Mendelssohn and Schumann in the early nineteenth century. Until Mendelssohn's famous performance of Bach's St. Matthew Passion in 1829—the first of several resuscitations that returned Bach to the living repertory—Bach was known only to a few musicians as a kind of study. To the public, he was a closed book. Even his son, C.P.E. Bach, could sum up the father as "musical cantor to several courts and in the end cantor at Leipzig." Such a casual blurb. To his own family, Bach was . . . just another Bach. (The line of musicians died out in the 1870s.) But to other musicians he is a *summum bonum* of musical treatise, and to listeners—who can only sense his science as they receive his poetry—he is genius made manifold in spiritual expression.

Actually, for our purposes here, Bach must take a lower seat among the mighty in terms of output, for his many choral and solo instrumental pieces obviously don't fit into the scope of this book, and there is not too much real *symphony* by Bach. The symphony itself and the tone poem were not even in existence, really, in Bach's day. And while the concerto is very much of Bach's era, it is not exactly the concerto we moderns are used to. The outward formation is the same in its three movements—two fast ones flanking a slow one. But the solo concerto is less popular than the *concerto grosso.* This features not one but several soloists (called the *concertino*) more *in balance with* than *opposed to* the rest of the orchestra (called the *ripieno*). When the solo concerto does appear, it is still not the protagonistic concerto we get from, say, Liszt or Rachmaninof. Even the plan of the movements is different: instead of the extended sonata-allegro we expect to hear in the all-important first movement, Bach tends to build his first movement—indeed, virtually all his movements—out of one theme (rather than sonata-allegro's two or more) eternally developed and restated. Bach's architecture is smaller than what we're used to from composers who followed him.

Hailed as the inventor of nothing but the perfector of everything, Bach in fact may have invented the piano (it was harpsichord then) concerto in his Fifth Brandenburg Concerto. But this is a small point. What he did was demonstrate the innate universality of music as it had come down to him in the high Baroque era, building the science with his poetry. And it is universal: for the non-musician absorbs the sound no less enthusiastically than the expert.

The Four Suites for Orchestra c. 1720

Bach called them "overtures," but they are in fact suites, each one opened by a long overture and continued in a series of dance movements. The suites are French in style: the overtures follow the French format of a pompous slow introduction, a lively main section, and a short pompous coda; and the dances are French dances—the gavotte, bourrée, gigue (jig), courante. (These are sometimes in an extended ABA form, so that one movement will actually take in two different examples of the same species of dance. For example, a minuet movement might actually be two minuets—a first minuet (A), a second (B), and an exact repeat of the first (A).

Unlike the concerto, so prevalent in orchestral music of this time, the suites are mainly scored for balanced instrumental textures, with no special emphasis on solo work. However, each suite is scored for a different ensemble (except nos. 3 and 4 are almost identical), thus differentiating the overall sound from suite to suite.

Suite no. 1 in C Major

The orchestration calls for oboes besides the strings and the inevitable *continuo* (the textural "back-up" sound that plays along with the strings *ad lib*—usually harpsichord and sometimes also 'cello or bassoon). After a typical overture—slow, stately opening, lively main section, and slow close—the suite hits its streak of dances with a Courante, a Gavotte, a Forlane, a Minuet, a Bourrée, and a Passepied.

Suite no. 2 in b minor

This suite offers the one instance of a concerto-like texture in the set. The solo is a flute, whose bright ring stands out from the strings even when playing along with them. After the overture come the dances: Rondeau, Sarabande, Bourrée, Polonaise, Minuet, and Badinerie. The prize of the lot is the Polonaise: after sounding the theme, Bach provides a "double" (variation), in which the theme is repeated while the flute dances a jig above it.

Suite no. 3 in D Major

Opening up his scoring, Bach adds two oboes, three trumpets, and timpani (kettledrums) to the strings. The high color of the three brasses and the weight of the timpani make the French pomp of the opening even more pompous than usual. The second movement, however, is intimate, for strings only. This is not a dance, but an Air (song), made world famous as the "Air on the G String." The remaining dances—Gavotte, Bourrée, and Gigue (jig)—recall the oboes, trumpets, and timpani to business.

Suite no. 4 in D Major

Oboes, trumpets, and drums heighten the effect of no. 4 as they did no. 3. The plan is Overture, Bourrées I and II, Gavotte, Minuet, and a festive Réjouissance (celebration).

The Six Brandenburg Concertos c. 1720

They are named after the Margrave of Brandenburg, who had commissioned Bach to compose something for him. Too busy to create from scratch, Bach assembled some of his more-or-less recent work and sent it off with the appropriate humble dedication. It was standard, then, to produce works in quantities of six, so Bach gathered together six concertos for the Margrave—these six. Musical gossip loves tales of genius unappreciated, and it has often been told that the Margrave didn't think much of the package and never bothered to have any of it performed. He filed it away, they say, to be sold off for pennies after his death. Actually, it seems likely that the six concertos were too difficult for the Margrave's orchestra to play, and in fact they remained in the family after the Margrave's death and eventually were handed over to the Berlin State Library.

They are extraordinary: six concertos in the Italian style (three movements: fast, slow, fast), each totally different from the others in scoring and mood. Weird instruments fallen out of use since Bach's day give the set, when they are played in their original scoring, the peculiar shrill delicacy of the true Baroque—though the enthusiastic twentieth-century rediscovery of these six pieces poised on the verge between ancient chamber music and modern orchestral music was based entirely on performances that substituted modern instruments for the authentic Baroque ones. We heard flutes in place of Bach's recorders, modern trumpet in place of the old *clarino,* or clarin trumpet, and piano in place of harpsichord.

Some people still prefer the inauthentic but suaver modern instruments, even in these days when performers strive for accuracy in reproducing the sounds of bygone times. But one thing is generally agreed on—the Brandenburg Concertos constitute one of the unique documents in Western music. Not surprisingly, one of the musical selections chosen to represent the cultural self-image of the planet earth on the Voyager rockets in 1977 was an excerpt of one of the Brandenburgs (the first movement of the second concerto), on a 16⅔ r.p.m. long-playing stereo record.

To enjoy these concertos, one should first be aware of a significant difference between what we mean and what Bach's contemporaries meant by the word "concerto." We think of a star virtuoso dominating a work, challenging and conquering the orchestra with technique and charisma: a tug of war. But in Bach's day the concerto was more concerned with balance than with charisma, and sought a polished collaboration of solo and orchestra: a tug of peace. There were solo concertos then, but the preferred form was the *concerto grosso,* with not one but several soloists. The group singled out for solo work was the *concertino;* the main body of the orchestra (mainly strings and a harpsichord), the *ripieno.* Thus, you will seldom hear one instrument predominating, but will notice various instruments, singly or in groups, flitting in and out of the general texture.

Brandenburg Concerto no. 1 in F Major

If you're hearing a performance in authentic Baroque instruments, note the *violino piccolo,* the "small violin" pitched higher than the standard fiddle. The first movement is efficiently merry, completely overshadowed by the ornate melancholy of the slow [second] movement. However, the bouncy third movement brings back the high spirits. This third movement "should" have been the finale, but Bach tacks on an extra [fourth] movement, a suite of dances.

Brandenburg Concerto no. 2 in F Major

This concerto features the trumpet. If you can, hear the work performed on antique Baroque instruments so as to hear the trumpet of Bach's day, the piercingly bright *clarino*. Its perky metal sets off the lively first and third movements. In the middle slow movement, the composer opts for a delicate chamber scoring, giving the trumpet and the accompanying strings a rest and centering attention on violin, oboe, and recorder solos. With the trumpet back in play in the finale [third mvt], Bach shows us compositional detail in a fugue. Note the solo entries in turn—trumpet first, then oboe, then violin, then recorder.

Brandenburg Concerto no. 3 in G Major

No one soloist stands out in this concerto for strings only (plus harpsichord *continuo,* the back-up in the Baroque orchestra); it is the only one of the six Brandenburgs to emphasize massed sound or groupings of several players of one instrument (now violins, now violas, and so on). It is also the only one of the six to be missing a slow movement: the manuscript reveals only two chords where the slow [middle] movement would have been. Presumably a short slow movement or at least a cadenza was improvised here on these chords, as improvisation was very, very common in those days. In performances, players should improvise a cadenza here (exactly as a jazz group does). The modern habit of playing nothing here or playing the two chords "as written" is ridiculous.

The first movement is the usual lively concerto opening, as good an instance as any of Bach's ability to spin out a whole movement on the basis of its first few notes, endlessly developing. Then come the two enigmatic chords, squatting in nowhere unless modern players can recapture the Baroque gift for spontaneous ensemble. Then the finale, a Gigue (jig), rather frantic, highly Baroque.

Brandenburg Concerto no. 4 in G Major

From the first, you know that this will be a light piece, the sparkly gem in the collection. Two recorders and a violin are the soloists, very much to the fore on the quite lengthy first movement. The recorders dominate the slow [second] movement, alternating phrases with the orchestra. This is a very special slow movement in its meditations on airy contentment; it seems to move almost briskly. The finale [third mvt] bustles athletically.

Brandenburg Concerto no. 5 in D Major

This work stands out in the Brandenburg series for its harpsichord solo, which is surprisingly prominent in an era that did not recognize the harpsichord as suitable for solo work in the orchestra. (As the *continuo,* it habitually played along with the strings as an orchestral backup.) In fact, this work has been cited as possibly the first harpsichord (i.e., piano) concerto in history, though—in keeping with the group effect of the Brandenburgs—a flute and violin share the solo work.

The first movement is lively, on the gracious side, with a neat game of interplay between the three soloists. Eventually, the harpsichord emerges from the whole with a very lengthy cadenza, after which the opening music returns to round off the movement. The second [slow] movement, marked *Affetuoso* (sentimentally), reverts to the three soloists. The third movement, a chummy dance, brings the string band back in for a light finale.

Brandenburg Concerto no. 6 in B Flat Major

This one calls for an odd assortment of strings only–two violas, two violas da gamba (a special sort of viola, taller than the regular handheld model but uttering a more delicate tone), 'cello, and double bass (plus the harpsichord *continuo*). The two regular violas take the lead here, opening the first movement with a duet-like theme of "old-fashioned" gravity, a very technical theme, very artful. This theme serves as a *ritornello* (refrain), recurring throughout the movement. The two violas then more or less usurp the slow [second] movement as their duet, a closely entwined song of transcendant repose. Perhaps fittingly for this work, more serious than the other Brandenburgs, the finale [third mvt] tends to the serious, though like all the Brandenburg finales it is in form an agile dance. It's friendly, but vigorous, with a heavy-handed charm.

Harpsichord Concerto no. 1 in d minor c. 1730

Bach is sometimes credited with having invented the piano concerto in the Fifth Brandenburg Concerto, for the piano of his day, the harpsichord, was not considered suitable for solo roles in orchestral music. Brandenburg no. 5 did not start a revolution, however, and all seven of Bach's concertos for solo harpsichord apparently were arrangements of violin concertos, with the solo part rewritten for the keyboard. The violin originals may not all have been original with Bach, either—this one in d minor is said to have derived from a lost violin concerto of Antonio Vivaldi.

In its present form it's quite a work, regardless of its derivation. Many of the concertos that precede Mozart's (*circa* 1775–1790) are structurally rather flimsy, with little dramatic tension. Not so here. The solo part is nicely pianistic, from the heavily spry first movement through the reverent slow [second] movement to the vital finale [third mvt]. The slow movement, built on a bass line repeated six times under different melodies, has been known to hush a concert hall's most determined coughers.

Harpsichord Concerto no. 5 in f minor c. 1735

Like Bach's other solo harpsichord concertos, this one was apparently transcribed from a violin concerto. It shows a family resemblence, being less pianistic than it might have been. The format is standard for the so-called Italian concerto—three movements, fast, slow, fast. The two end movements feature famous "echo" effects between the soloist and the orchestra, but interest centers on the middle slow movement, which winds its florid way around one luxurious idea over light, almost disinterested time-beating in the strings.

Concerto for Two Harpischords in C Major c. 1735

Three movements, fast-slow-fast, in the Italian style. The first movement is really jolly, largely built on constant tiny back-and-forths between the orchestra (all strings) and the two keyboards. The very slow [second] movement brings the two soloists forward—the orchestra doesn't play at all. The movement is based on one theme alone, a sinuous tune that seems capable of coiling and uncoiling indefinitely. For a finale [third mvt], Bach brings the orchestra back in for a lively fugue. But this is begun by the soloists; not till they are securely on their way do the strings join them.

Violin Concerto in a minor c. 1720

It is difficult to get one's bearings on a Baroque concerto, for there is no first subject-second subject conflict to grasp, no overriding push towards resolution. The concerto of Bach's time has the general form we moderns are used to in its first movement, slow movement, and dancey finale, but they are unexpectedly succinct and based on one theme constantly developed. The main structural unit here is the *ritornello,* the orchestral passage that recurs in between the soloist's passages. This is used primarily in the brisk first movement and bouncy third. The middle slow movement presents the soloist winding long lines of embellishment over an orchestral "fixed bass" that repeats throughout.

Violin Concerto in E Major c. 1720

Only two of Bach's several solo violin concertos have survived, this and the one in a minor, above. Typical of the Baroque era, they have not yet discovered the confrontational politics of the later soloistic concerto, first developed by Mozart and Beethoven and brought to an apex in the personalized, charismatic 1800s. Baroque concertos used the soloist (or soloists, in the *concerto grosso*) to contrast a certain elegance with the less brilliant orchestral group—not to contrast themes and variations of themes in the dramatic style we expect. These concertos are more integrated, less confrontational—less dramatic. Generally, the movements are each based on one theme in endless development. The first movement is bright and lively, the slow movement meditative, the third movement an almost waltzlike rondo.

Concerto for Two Violins in d minor c. 1720

The distinctive timbre (sound color) of the two soloists makes this one of the most "antique" of all Bach's works, for the violin duet, a basic component of the Baroque sound system, is almost rare nowadays. We have expanded the orchestra since Bach's day, and depend on a large ensemble and exotic possibilities; Bach's age knew fewer instruments, fewer possibilities—plus, every composer was dependent, when he composed, on what instrumentalists were available for performance.

The Baroque concerto is built on balance rather than challenge, and you will note two species of balance working here: the two violinists playing with and off the rest of the orchestra, and the two violinists playing with and off each other. The orchestra is all strings, and the form is that of the Italian concerto: a lively, assertive first movement; very, very affecting slow movement; and a brisk rondo to close.

The two soloists help the orchestra open the first movement, announcing the main theme as if there were no soloists in the piece at all—soloist I playing with the first violins and soloist II playing with the second violins. This is the typical Baroque *ritornello*—the orchestral refrain. The two soloists finally get their own theme when the instrumental texture lightens, sounded by soloist I and echoed by his partner. The rest of the first movement is devoted to spinning out a web of running lines, now in mutuality, now in exclusivity, based on an opposition-collaboration of the *ritornello* to and with the soloists' theme.

The slow [second] movement is a remarkable duet of intertwined strings, the soloists endlessly echoing each other or initiating new ideas while the rest of the orchestra provides a respectfully sparse accompaniment. After so much "specialty" work from the two main players, it is—almost—unnerving to hear them and the other strings join in the last few notes for the simplest finish imaginable.

This d minor concerto has moved into F Major for the slow movement; now, properly, it returns to the home key of d minor for the finale [third mvt]. Here, the first movement's motion and the second movement's emphasis on the soloists are combined into a gala race led by the two leads and supported mainly by the little three-note "turn" heard throughout in the orchestra's parts. The turn is also heard, less crisply, in the soloists' parts—it is what one might call the melodic essence of the movement.

GEORGE FRIDERIC HANDEL 1685–1759

His fellow Germans still call him Georg Friedrich Händel, which is fair, though by the end of his life he had become so Anglicized that he himself had to admit that Georg (pronounced *Gay*-ork) was George forever. Like his exact contemporary Johann Sebastian Bach, he comes down to us from the remote past, in styles and structures so antecedent to what we're used to that they are not merely early versions but different forms altogether.

Bach and Handel lived in the Baroque era. There was no symphony then, not as we know it. The concerto was not "our" concerto but the *concerto grosso,* using a group of soloists rather than a central virtuoso. There were no tone poems at all. Orchestral ensembles were small, given to much improvisation. Church music was prominent; when was the last time you heard a Requiem Mass? Opera was popular, but a distillation of pastoral and historical gallantry that we today find hopelessly exotic. Symphonic Handel, except to buffs of the Baroque context, is a stranger.

Furthermore, those who know Bach will not stand that much closer to Handel, for the two contemporaries have very little in common. Handel was an international celebrity, prolific and highly original but drawn to glitter. Bach was unknown, prolific, and flawless, obsequious to public ceremony only in his church music, preferring the contemplative to the exhibitionistic. In technique, Handel was up to date, eighteenth-century current. Bach was both traditional and innovative, reviewing the seventeenth century even as he pushed forward into the future.

The Water Music c. 1717

Commentary on this attractive suite of dances in the French style can be very involved, as it must pin down a number of exactnesses left ambiguous in the passage of time. How many pieces were there when the *Water Music* was first played? When was it written? Exactly what was Handel's orchestration? And, most important for us of today, which of the several versions played in the twentieth century do we want to hear?

The original manuscript is lost, and the many contemporary publications of the *Water Music*—complete or in part—do not agree sufficiently for an absolutely authoritative reconstruction. Worse yet, the picturesque tale describing the premiere, first put forth by Handel's biographer John Mainwaring, is now discredited. So, not only the choice of pieces and their orchestration but even the event of their derivation is locked in mystery. The task of drinking in all the sources and thinking up a reasonable facsimile of the original yields a hangover only a scholar could love.

Still, the reports of those who were there or at least in the vicinity when the *Water Music* was first heard gives us an inkling of the situation. Some or all of what we now call the *Water Music* was played during a royal boat trip down the Thames at night in 1717, with the orchestra afloat beside the royal barge. (George I was the king in question, having recently succeeded Queen Anne; Mainwaring's discredited anecdote has it that Handel's concert reconciled king and musician, separated by the latter's French leave in England while the former was still Elector of Hanover and Handel's technical sovereign.)

However, as no one is certain which pieces that have come down to us are specifically *Water Music* and which not, and as they turned up in several different instrumentations, a number of different *Water Music* editions exist. Some one had to choose the pieces and settle on their scoring, but more than one person has done this. Also, until recently it was popular to play only a selection from the *Water Music,* referred to as "the Water Music Suite"—which only confuses the issue, since the original is a suite to begin with.

Today, the trend is toward authenticity wherever possible, and the suite of the suite is passing out of style. We want the full *Water Music* as it has been identified by trustworthy authorities; these have presented us with a grand document of the High Baroque style, with its squealing woodwinds, its arrogant brasses, its aggressive polish and touch-me-not grace. Depending on the authority, there are some twenty or so numbers, and not a single one is a dud. As mentioned, the genre is the French dance suite: a full overture in two parts (first grand, then brisk), succeeded by a chain of dances limp and lively. The order of the pieces as listed here follows that generally agreed on today, but different editions vary as to the numbering and titling. Note that the *Water Music* may be broken up into three suites, following tonality and instrumentation, without changing the order. I have taken the numbers and titles from Roger Fiske's edition, published by Eulenburg.

Suite no. 1 in F Major (with horns)

No. 1: The Overture, with oboes and violins trilling for attention in the slow opening and, in the fast section, a solo group of violins, in the style of the *concerto grosso.*

No. 2: *Adagio e staccato:* slow and clipped, with a fine oboe solo.

No. 3: *Allegro-Andante-Allegro:* what is called a *da capo* (from the top), with a lively first section, a slow middle section, and the first section repeated (i.e., *da capo*). The *Allegro* features more trills and a solo line for two horns in duet, the *Andante* two orchestras in opposition, woodwinds against strings.

No. 4: *Presto:* another *da capo,* moving from F Major into d minor and back again.

No. 5: Air: a wonderful effect here when Handel has the two horns playing softly in their higher range.

No. 6: Minuet for the French Horn: the horns launch the number, then are joined by the orchestra. Another *da capo,* this minuet digs deep into the minor tonality in its middle section, letting the dark bassoon define the tone.

No. 7: Bourrée: with the direction "3 times, 1st all the Violins [i.e., strings], 2nd all the Hautboys [oboes and bassoons], 3rd all together."

No. 8: Hornpipe: with the direction "3 times in the same manner [as the Bourrée]"

No. 9: (Untitled) another concerto movement for two orchestras, woodwinds versus strings.

Suite no. 2 in D Major (with trumpets)

No. 10: *Allegro:* the trumpets make their entrance in a sprightly business topped off with a drooping moment of minor-key coda.

No. 11: (Untitled) Perhaps the best-known number in the score, a hornpipe of such class that American public television uses it as a theme song.

No. 12: Trumpet Minuet: "3 times, 1st Trumpets and Violins, 2nd Horns & Hautboys, 3rd all together."

No. 13: *Lentement:* slowly, and with a rocking motion that suggests more $^6/_8$ metre than the $^3/_4$ that is marked.

No 14: "This Aire is to be play'd thrice"

Suite no. 3 in G Major (with flutes)

No. 15: (Untitled) This piquant item shifts the instrumental coloration of the suite to the metal brightness of the flute, which plays along with the first violins throughout.

No. 16: *Presto:* a quick dance, with a characteristic "turn" in the melody used effectively in the minor-key middle section.

No. 17: Menuet: the French spelling this time, perhaps because of the Gallic-pastoral charm of the minor key.

No. 18: (Untitled): Enter the recorders, now thought quaintly antique but in Handel's time a relatively vital member of the flute family. They, too, play along with the first violins.

No. 19: Country Dance: the step is rustic and hearty; the recorders make it even more rustic but less hearty.

The Royal Fireworks Music 1749

Like the *Water Music* a suite of dances designed for open-air performance, the *Royal Fireworks Music* was composed to accompany a pyrotechnical display in celebration of the peace of Aix-la-Chapelle that ended the War of the Austrian Succession. Handel pushed the limit in his scoring—over a hundred players, all on wind instruments (oboes, bassoons, contrabassoon, horns, trumpets) or timpani. (The effect, when performed in this original arrangement, is dazzling.) Later, Handel added string parts, but this refines the shrill Baroqueness of the original wind version, which may be heard on recordings.

The fireworks themselves seem rather to have fizzled; some of the most special devices did not come off, and at length the scaffolding from which the flares were launched caught fire. But the music itself is superb—self-possessed, imperial, and impervious to the manic quality of the evening for which it was drafted. The subject of Handel's discourse is royal successions, not fireworks.

The suite is shorter than the complete *Water Music:* six numbers, led off by a huge overture. This begins with all due ceremony, leading up to a grand chord, a mighty trill . . . and a fast movement is upon us, sweeping into the dance with gestures and throbbing dignity. (Many Handel buffs prefer this overture to anything in the *Water Music.*) A slowish intrusion late in the Overture holds us in check briefly, succeeded by a repeat of the fast section. The second number is a Bourrée, lithe and brisk, lightly scored, all too brief. Next comes "La Paix" (The Peace, an allusion to the treaty), a flowing pastorale, followed by "La Réjouissance" (The Celebration), invigorating for its drive of innocent energy and merrymaking trumpets. For a change of pace, a minor-key Minuet precedes the finale, which is itself a minuet, but a bright one, as befits its station.

FRANZ JOSEF HAYDN 1732–1809

A country boy from Lower Austria who rose to propounder of symphonic form and honorable Doctor of Music of Oxford University in his late heyday in London when he was the most widely hailed composer of his time, Haydn is too easily called "Papa," too lightly praised for the music that grins, too neatly dwarfed by his pupil, the shattering Beethoven. Yet there are those who will praise him too well. The symphony belongs to him, they say—and the string quartet: the grand and the small alike, the great cruiser and the lily. Haydn did help perfect the symphony, and he did it 104 times (plus two symphonies without numbers and one that is presumed lost). With Mozart comes the pure singing line, and with Beethoven the theatre of symphony. But Haydn, first of all, defined the evolving symphony, gave it a foundation on which to grow. Thanks to him, the symphony found an architecture in terms of melody, rhythm, and harmony.

The Classical symphony of Haydn's time had grown out of the old Italian overture. This was a three-part piece, first fast, then slow, then fast again. The three sections became three movements, sometimes four with the addition of the minuet, a graceful dance, just before the final movement. It was the German-Austrian school of symphony, primarily, that observed the four-movement structure. And it was Haydn who—more than anyone else—made it work. All aspects of symphonic organization intrigued him, and he ceaselessly fiddled with form until, by about 1790, he had certified the genre of symphony. Other fiddlers came after Haydn. But all, basically, worked from his model.

On the other hand, this is not to suggest that there would have been no symphony without Haydn. Some years before Haydn began composing, there was a thriving school of symphony in the German town of Mannheim, where a highly cultivated court supported what was at the time the world capital of orchestral music. Everything was in season in Mannheim, from opera to chamber works—but the pride of the place belonged to its orchestra, celebrated for their ensemble precision. The Mannheim players could start or stop on a dime, and were especially adept at getting louder or softer in an even texture, quite a novelty in those days. With better players to write for, Mannheim's composers wrote boldly; with bold music to hear, Mannheim's audiences demanded emotional and architectural expansion. This expansion was the Mannheim style, and that style *was* the symphony. By the time Haydn composed his mature symphonies, the Mannheimers were already into their third generation of symphonists. There had been the pioneers, Johann Stamitz, Franz Xaver Richter, and their colleagues. There were the younger masters, Ignaz Fränkl and his coevals. And lastly there were Haydn's contemporaries, a newer crop to finish off the Mannheim era even as leadership passed from it to the Vienna of Mozart and Beethoven. But before those two, there was Haydn.

On his way to defining the Classical symphony (Haydn as synthesizer), Haydn arrived in Vienna to do what any hopeful composer did in those days—sing, teach, perform, and arrange as well as compose (Haydn as musician). There were few if any "composers" in the mid-1700s: eighteenth-century musicians were compleat musicians, had to be. The living was precarious, horribly dependent on the monied classes and what they liked in the way of entertainment. A person who made his living in music might be teaching one minute, playing in a quartet for Someone's dinner the next minute, and spending the following weekend dashing off a serenade on commission for a wedding party, not to mention supervising the performance. Haydn worked in virtually every genre known to music, from opera to piano sonata; they all did. The practical experience equipped him to respond when fortune beckoned: twenty-nine years as musician-in-residence of the Esterházy family. Composing the works, rehearsing the players, maintaining the library of manuscripts and parts, acting as shop steward to the two Prince Esterházys on behalf of the orchestra, and provisioning the second Prince with some two hundred not-too-tricky pieces for the royal instrument, the now obsolete *viola di bordone,* Haydn passed three decades in isolation from the great capitals of music-making. It should have been disastrous—art needs stimulation. But, with nothing better to do than compose and perform, Haydn became the craftsman of the age. "As conductor of an orchestra," he was to write, "I could make experiments, observe what produced an effect and what weakened it, and was thus in a position to . . . be as bold as I pleased. I was cut off from the world; there was no one to confuse or torment me, and I was forced to become *original.*"

Symphony no. 31 in D Major, "Horn Signal" 1765

Haydn gave the work its subtitle, "Mit dem Hornsignal" (with the horn call) because it begins and ends with the same fanfare in the horns. There is another point of interest here. After a sturdy first movement the second [slow] movement turns concerto, with prominent solo parts for violin, 'cello, and four horns. The six soloists form a *concertino* to play against the orchestral *ripieno* just as in a *concerto grosso*. The third [minuet] movement is not unusual (even with its charming use of flute, oboe, and horns in the trio) but the finale [fourth mvt] is—a theme and seven variations, an unlikely finish for a symphony.

Symphony no. 45 in f sharp minor, "Farewell" 1772

Prince Nicolaus Esterházy, Haydn's boss, enjoys life at his rural estate so much that he spends interminable seasons there. But this keeps his musicians away from their families and "real" lives in the towns and cities. The musicians complain to Haydn. Shortly thereafter, the last movement of Haydn's latest symphony is not so much played as allowed to peter out: one by one the instrumentalists snuff their candles and depart, eventually leaving only Haydn and his concertmaster (the chief of the first violins), the impeccable Tomasini. Enough said? The next day, the estate is evacuated.

Haydn had made his programmatic point. But surely Prince Esterházy was more impressed by the telling rhetoric of the piece than by the stunt pulled in the finale. For this is a surprisingly dramatic work for its time. The first movement bears the kind of tension that focuses a statement, and the second [slow] movement carries the urgency through, though gently. The minuet [third mvt], too. Then the finale: the first half, a *Presto* (very fast), reaffirms the vehemence of the first movement. Then comes the farewell, an *Adagio* (very slow), diminished player by player. Modern performances invariably stage a farewell, sometimes in eighteenth-century dress. The Boston Symphony did it in the 1930s, wigs and all, with conductor Serge Koussevitsky as a Slavic Joseph Haydn.

Symphony no. 49 in f minor, "The Passion" 1768

It was not Haydn who called it "La Passione," and it is less passionate than foreboding, minor-key in all four movements. No. 49 emphasizes solemnity by starting with a slow movement, a usage that was soon to become virtually dead in the symphony. Enticingly sorrowful, the first movement gives way to "the same only more so": a fast, taut, and dour second movement. The two together are like a two-part study in tragedy, the first showing the somber interior and the second the face of fury.

The minuet [third mvt] at least offers some relaxation of the tension with a major-key trio (middle section). The Haydn expert H. C. Robbins Landon speaks of the trio's horns shining "only as gunmetal shines—glinting on a grey background." And just as the second movement was faster than the first but no less intense, so the finale [fourth mvt] is faster than the minuet, yet even more biting in its fury.

The "Paris" symphonies (nos. 82–87)

Symphony no. 82 in C Major, "The Bear" 1786

Called "The Bear" by the French, who heard a bearlike galumphing in the fourth movement, no. 82 is the first (in number, not in order of composition) of the "Paris" symphonies. Haydn had left his niche as court musician for the Esterházys and was taking all Europe. Elegance and vivacity are the mode of the entire "Paris" group. The first movement here sounds like a spicy fanfare. The slow [second] movement is a theme-and-variations, interesting because the first half of the theme is in the major and the second half in the minor. The third movement brings a ceremonial minuet colored by woodwind solos. Then the finale [fourth mvt], which belongs to "the bear" right from the start—or so the French thought. They heard growling in the first subject; actually, the effect is more reminiscent of bagpipes.

Symphony no. 83 in g minor, "The Hen" 1785

A rather dire first theme opens the work, but most of it is charming (no. 83 was written for Paris, and the French like their symphonies on the friendly side). The "hen" of the title derives from the first movement's second theme: the Parisians heard, in the oboe, the clucking of a hen. (Note that the "clucking" carries over delightfully into the development.) The slow [second] movement is touchingly lyrical, the minuet [third mvt] a minuet, and the finale a jaunty invitation to the dance. Note the odd pauses at the end, as if the music were coming apart—a typical Haydn joke.

Symphony no. 85 in B Flat Major, "The Queen of France" 1785

The subtitle refers to Marie Antoinette, who was said to adore this swank piece, written for Paris. A brief slow introduction heralds the first movement, a somewhat tense affair which utilizes the same accompaniment (a descending line of plucked strings) for both first and second (on solo oboe) subjects. The overall mood is calmed by the slow [second] movement, a set of variations on a French tune, "La Gentille et Jeune Lisette" (Dear Little Lisette). The minuet [third mvt] sounds like the Austrian Ländler (a forerunner of the waltz); a subtle touch of scoring highlights the trio (middle section), when one by one two oboes, a flute, and a bassoon each echo a melodic fragment just before the main theme of the minuet returns. The dapper finale [fourth mvt] is famous with historians because in it Haydn made his first experiment in combining sonata-allegro form with the rondo.

The sonata-rondo, as this hybrid is called, became one of the great features of the late Haydn symphony.

Symphony no. 88 in G Major 1786

One of the most popular of Haydn's symphonies, no. 88 conquers through sheer force of exuberance. This is a ground-zero of the "Papa Haydn" of light verve and little drama. It's a generally misleading image, but it does suit this vivacious work. After the slow introduction that was getting to be a habit with Haydn, the first movement takes off on the proposition that all themes are to be launched anapestically (bum-bum-*bum*!), a neat touch of unity in rhythm. This is frisky art, but not trivial art; it's too carefully organized, too alert, exact in its fundamentals and its expansion of them. But it is comical: at the very end of the movement, the woodwinds try the rhythm out one last time—like this?—the strings answer them—like this!—and all go bum-bum-*bum*! in accord.

The slow [second] movement, launched by two oboes and a solo 'cello, is richly scored, emphasizing solo work whenever the main theme is heard, and the minuet [third mvt] has its little joke in the jolting turn that launches each phrase. A typical Haydnesque rustic dance for strings and oboe with bagpipelike "drone" bass comprises the trio (middle section). A dazzling perpetual-motion finale [fourth mvt] closes the work to balance the vivacity of the first movement. Light is not necessarily unimportant.

Symphony no. 92 in G Major, "Oxford" 1789

The "Oxford" symphony just precedes Haydn's last set, nos. 93 to 104, written for England and known as the "London" or "Salomon" symphonies (Salomon being Haydn's English impresario). Still, the "Oxford" is associated with the series, as it was played on the occasion of Haydn's receiving an honorary doctorate from Oxford University in 1791. Those who would hear some "clue" to the spirit of Oxford life should be warned that (1) Haydn didn't write program symphonies, and (2) he composed this work in Paris two years before first setting foot on English soil.

That is simple Haydnesque sonata-allegro in the first movement, not the bustle of a university town; that is pure radiant slow movement, not some scholar loring over his books; the minuet shows its own good humor, not that of pranking dons; and the mercurial finale sings not for Oxford but for Haydn. So, let us take the work as the absolute music that it is. After the usual slow introduction, the first movement gets underway at a lively tempo with the first subject in the first violins. A raging *tutti* leads in the dainty second subject, also in the violins, with decoration by solo flute. Then the development, which uses all the themes just heard in what must be called a deft hodgepodge, climaxes and falls sweetly into the first theme again for the recapitulation. This time around, the second subject is introduced by a solo oboe.

Moving into D Major for the slow [second] movement, Haydn starts with a placid violin theme, interposes a heavy middle section in d minor, and assigns the recapitulation of the main theme to solo oboe. The minuet [third mvt] returns to G Major, bringing further flute and oboe solos. Haydn accents the trio (middle section) with bite, using contrasts of *legato* (smooth phrasing) and *staccato* (choppy phrasing) and launching the bassoon-and-horn theme on off-beats "corrected" by the strings.

The finale [fourth mvt] reaffirms the home key of G Major. It is one of Haydn's most delightful last movements, highly satiric in the clop-clop bass line given to the 'cellos and basses. Once again, flute and oboe solos set off the tone of the movement, which never loses its urge to joy—not even when Haydn passes the main theme through a few minor-key settings just to see how it might sound. He prefers it in the major.

The "Salomon" or "London" Symphonies (nos. 93–104)

Symphony no. 93 in D Major 1791

Proud, bold, and energetic, this was written to impress the English on Haydn's first visit to Britain; the fanfarelike slow introduction suggests a celebrity flourishing his passport of international fame. The first movement proper, *Allegro assai* (rather lively), is dignified, carrying a sense of occasion. The second [slow] movement, too, sounds serious, a set of variations on the theme that opens the movement in the first violins. The music builds importantly. But Haydn can take dignity just so far, and just as the movement is about to taper off gracefully, he blows a loud blatt! in the bassoons.

The minuet [third mvt] is vigorous enough to remind one that the Beethovenian symphony was just around the corner at the time; its trio presents a double-orchestra effect of hammering woodwinds and brasses against peaceful strings, which eventually surrender the battle and, not being able to beat the others, join them. The finale [fourth mvt] keeps to the general rule of formality, and is therefore less wittily dashing than Haydn usually likes to be in his finales. Altogether, this is a reasonably ambitious work in tone—except for that one moment in the slow movement. Ironically, that is the moment that everyone thinks of when the piece is mentioned.

Symphony no. 94 in G Major, "Surprise" 1791

The famous "surprise" is one loud chord that shatters the spell of the slow [second] movement, supposedly to startle the somnolent. (Actually, the chord had the reverse effect on a few of the audience, as some ladies were said to have fainted in the excitement.) For many years after Haydn's death, the piquancy of the chord's little legend made no. 94 the most frequently played of all Haydn's symphonies. But there is much more to the work than this one chord—especially in that same second movement, a set of variations on the "surprise" theme that retains the innocence of the original while putting it through some rather sophisticated paces.

First of all, the first movement, with the characteristic Haydnesque slow introduction, is in 6/8 time, which gives its lilting themes a curvy scan. Then comes the "surprise" slow movement. The strings state the theme, assisted by flute, oboe, and horn after the big loud chord. Then the variations: the first for second violins and violas with first-violin embellishment, the second in the minor key, the third—back in the major—led by the oboe, the fourth for full orchestra. Haydn starts a fifth variation, also for the whole band, but changes his mind and simply restates the first notes of the theme in the oboe and bassoon. The minuet [third mvt] is unusually hectic, the finale [fourth mvt] industriously fleet.

Symphony no. 95 in c minor 1791

No slow introduction opens no. 95, the only one of Haydn's late symphonies to leap right into its first subject. But this theme is a powerful one—the bare outline of itself, with no accompaniment—and it needs no prelude. It's a powerful work, but not specifically passionate. As early as the second subject of the first movement, a feeling of serenity steals in, though this is a minor-key symphony. The second [slow] movement finds the work mellowing out further with a taste of solo 'cello work, continued in the trio (middle section) of the scherzo [third mvt]. By the finale [fourth mvt], a *Vivace* in antidotal C Major, the symphony is all for joy. Haydn's earlier c minor symphony, no. 78, troubled to carry the minor-major conflict throughout the symphony into the finale. But by the close of no. 95, all sense of c minor is forgotten, as well it might be in a career bursting into final flower in a dazzling C Major of life.

Symphony no. 96 in D major, "Miracle" 1791

In Paris and London, Haydn had the luxury of writing for first-class orchestras, and could develop his gift for instrumentation as he could not have in his early years working as court musician for the Esterházy family. At Esterháza, there was a shortage of virtuosos, so Haydn concentrated not on scoring effects but on using the whole structure of the symphony for musical drama. Now, in London, he could try out *concertante* (instrumental solo) devices. The first movement offers the common-or-garden mature Haydn, with slow introduction and then a lively movement proper, emphasizing the cut of the first subject throughout as if the whole movement were spun of one idea. The second [slow] movement, however, pays homage to the ancient *concerto grosso* in its final pages, when all motion halts and a solo group of two violins, a flute, two oboes, and a bassoon play a kind of cadenza on the movement's main theme. The minuet, too, shows off its oboe in the waltzy trio, in folk-Austrian style. A compact, even tense finale [fourth mvt] winds up the show.

Oh, yes: the subtitle. The "miracle," be it noted and forgotten, obtained when a chandelier gave way and fell at the first performance. It happened to drop just when the audience had pushed forward to get a better view of the composer, so the accident occurred in empty space and no one was hurt—a miracle! Or so the story goes. Contemporary accounts actually report the mishap as having occurred at the premiere of another symphony, no. 102, four years later. Perhaps because the discrepancy discredits the subtitle, which is totally irrelevant to the music in the first place, the nickname is falling out of use.

Symphony no. 97 in C Major 1792

There is something in C Major that suggests to musicians the beginning and end of all coherent music—of all music that may be said to begin and end. C Major is fundamental, triumphant, a real blast. As so many composers after him, Haydn promotes the home key of this work with right-on, square-cut themes like battle cries, trumpets and drums to the fore, giving the work, especially the confident first movement, a martial character. The slow [second] movement is another of those theme-and-variations movements, but Haydn is still fooling around with effects and devices, and he directs the violins to play the final (third) variation *sul ponticello* (on the bridge of the instrument), yielding an overbright, tinny sound as if from some obsolete medieval instrument. Another quirk heightens interest in the minuet [third mvt]: a friendly violin solo in its trio (middle section) was designed especially for Haydn's British manager, Johann Peter Salomon, an accomplished violinist. ("*Salomon solo,*" Haydn allows in the score—"*ma piano*" [but quietly].) The fourth movement, as so often in Haydn, balances the self-assertive first movement to round off the whole, meanwhile offering a perky lift of its own as well.

Symphony no. 98 in B Flat Major 1792

One might almost date the rise of the dramatic symphony from this work—except that Haydn's coeval Mozart had already written his astonishing last two symphonies, nos. 40 and 41. Still, this is an important work in the evolution of the symphony as structure, for here Haydn developed most convincingly the sturdy balance of the two outer movements that gives the form its strength, its extension. This is not to downgrade the importance of the two inner movements—the slow movement and the minuet (which, as of Beethoven, would become the scherzo). But we want to see some dramatic foundation laid down in the first movement and some resolution in the fourth, to firm up, so to speak, the straight line of communication, from first to second to third to fourth movements.

What does Haydn do? For one thing, his characteristic slow introduction is clearly related to the first movement proper—they share the same main theme (in the minor in the introduction and the major once the *Allegro* [lively] is established). Furthermore, the first movement goes out of its way to extract all "meaning" possible from that first theme in the development section. The slow [second] movement, too, widens Haydn's emotional parameters in its gloss on "God Save the King." Earlier, he might have been content with a simple theme and variations, blithely saluting the English with an English tune and a touch of Haydnesque embellishment. But here he really digs into the theme, forcing it to the verge of something like terror in the middle of the movement only to withdraw poignantly after. (It has been suggested that this slow movement was intended as an elegy for Mozart, who had died the year before.) Likewise, the minuet [third mvt] carries through with a vigor unusual even for the vigorous Haydn, and the finale [fourth mvt] is not his standard devilish good rondo but a long, strong sonata movement. It is comparable to the first for breadth and weight, and *this* is resolution. True, it is vivacious—the work has definitely come to a happy ending. But the movement is not lightweight, for all its charm, and it sounds a little of the work's former sobriety in order to conquer it. Note the several violin solos in the finale; these were written for Johann Peter Salomon, Haydn's London manager and a sometime violinist. Haydn also wrote a solo for himself, just before the end, on the harpsichord. For, although orchestras seldom use it anymore, the orchestras of Haydn's day regularly employed the keyboard *continuo,* a kind of back-up that played along with the orchestra on an *ad lib* basis. Since the part was improvised, no composer wasted ink on it—but here Haydn actually wrote down a brief passage for himself, which of course must be honored by modern orchestras even if they have totally repudiated the *continuo* as a functioning member of the band.

Symphony no. 99 in E Flat Major 1793

A moody slow introduction leads on to Haydn's favorite opening gambit when the first movement proper takes off: a quiet statement of the first theme (for strings only) immediately followed by a restatement for full orchestra. The lyrical second theme brings out the clarinet in Haydn; this is his first use of it in a symphony, and he shows it off in duet with the first violins. This second theme dominates the development in its quiet way, passing from instrument to instrument till the recapitulation brings back the sturdy first theme. The slow [second] movement also offers a nice instrumental touch in its quartet for flute, two oboes, and bassoon early on, but their innocent charm is overridden by the rest of the movement, a sheerly powerful one. Consider the ongoing wholeness of the work, settling into a strong but pleasant minuet[third mvt] and then dispersing the tension established in the slow movement in a dashing finale [fourth mvt], one of Haydn's typical sonata-rondos. Another characteristic Haydnism: a sudden break in the tempo near the end, a full stop . . . and the orchestra starts all over again, as it were, building up steam for a vivacious close.

Symphony no. 100 in G, "Military" 1794

"Encore! encore! encore! resounded from every seat: the Ladies themselves could not forbear," reported the *London Morning Chronicle* of the ovation that greeted the exhilaratingly pugnacious second movement on the work's second performance. (In those days, one clapped after each movement, not once after the entire piece is played, as today.) This second movement is not the reflective slow movement we expect of Haydn, but a war piece, complete with expanded percussion section: cymbals, triangle, and bass drum as well as the usual timpani provide what was then known as a "Turkish" sound. It's military, all right. Its coda (tail-end), heralded by a trumpet call, was dubbed "the shortest war in history."

On the other hand, the rest of the symphony is hardly the work of war, though there is a glint of something hostile in the slow introduction to the first movement, which is generally non-belligerent. Then comes the military second movement; listening to it, we should keep in mind that though it sounds cute to us, noisy rather than vicious, its first audiences took it as a quasi-naturalistic description of the horrors of war. The *Morning Chronicle* cited "the sounding of the charge, the thundering of the onset, the clash of arms," but also "the groaning of the wounded." The minuet [third mvt] is fairly peaceable. If the finale [fourth mvt] is no conscientious objection, its military nature is nothing after the helter-skelter of the second movement, not even when Haydn brings in the "Turkish" battery for a last charge at the very end.

Symphony no. 101 in D Major, "Clock" 1794

The "Clock" symphony—nicknamed for the tick-tocky second movement—opens with the slow introduction usual in late Haydn. Soon it jumps into a sprightly *Presto* (quite fast) with some real snap in its development section, as if Haydn were not just playing with but fortifying his themes. Then comes the second [slow] movement, with its clockworklike string accompaniment. The main theme goes through some interesting changes in the course of the movement—a somewhat ferocious minor-key variation, a delicate transfer of the tick-tock to flute and bassoon, and a grand restatement, grandfather-clock style. A forceful minuet[third mvt] follows, featuring for its trio a perky tune for flute over a droning, bagpipelike background in the strings. In keeping with the partly aggressive nature of the work, the finale [fourth mvt] presents a constant contrast between the graceful and the assertive, including a stormy minor-key section followed by a dead stop, followed by a double fugue that has amazed and thrilled musicians for nearly two hundred years.

Symphony no. 102 in B Flat Major 1795

The slow introduction to the first movement is a regular feature of these late Haydn symphonies; some of them relate thematically to the rest of the work. Take heed of the opening note (all the instruments play the same one)—you will hear this again once the first movement picks up tempo and gets going. It appears twice before the appearance of the second subject, once at the start of the developement, and again in the recapitulation. Each time it appears this rather Beethovenish "No!" brings all action to a full stop. If the second [slow] movement is all forethought and simplicity until its surprisingly forceful ending, the bumptious minuet [third mvt] points the way to Beethoven, Haydn's (and Mozart's) successor and the reinventor of the symphonic minuet as the more energetic scherzo. Also prophetic of Beethoven is the loud-soft statement-counterstatement heard throughout the finale [fourth mvt].

Symphony no. 103 in E Flat Major, "Drum Roll" 1795

A startling opening, in its day: one great call to attention on the timpani (kettledrums). Then follows the usual Haydnesque slow introduction—but with a twist. For this time the introduction is not preparatory invocation, but a component, dramatically and thematically, of the first movement. Note the theme, a ponderous line in the low instruments, right after the drum roll. It turns up again several times in the course of the first movement, most provocatively near the very end when, after a noticeable deterioration of the general merriment into tragic warnings, the first few measures of the introduction—drum roll and all—are reprised with sharp dramatic effect. (A merry coda follows this, but still.)

The second [slow] movement emphasizes this contrast in tone in a series of variations on a plaintive theme, worked out so as to veer back and forth from c minor to the brighter C Major throughout the movement. The first variation favors the major, the second the minor, with some wailing commentary from the flutes and oboes. Then two solo violins take a major-key variation, brightening the atmosphere as well as recalling a day when orchestras were so small and the concerto so ubiquitous that solo parts rather than a massed ensemble sound were the rule. Back then to the minor and the full orchestra (with the timpani proving they can do more than roll). But Haydn closes in the major, handing the last variation to prankish woodwinds.

The minuet [third mvt] offers no surprises, but the finale [fourth mvt] yields one of the great experiments in symphonic construction: the whole thing, from exposition through development to recapitulation, is built not on first theme versus second theme but on one theme alone—on its energy, its outline, its possibilities. Toward the end we sense, briefly, the fraught drama of the end of the first movement, but this is quickly overrun with festivity.

Symphony no. 104 in D Major, "London" *1795*

Last of the line! We expect much from Haydn's final essay in the form that he more than anyone helped establish, and it is a triumphant work. It is a valedictory tally rather than a thrust into the future, a recapitulation, for once, not of one movement but of a whole method. Much that one has grown used to and fond of in Haydn is here—the forceful slow introduction; the devious first movement development, fastening on the hindquarters of the first subject (marked a):

to bring it back in at the heart of the recapitulation as a climax to the movement and a new theme in its own right:

Notice also the fierce minor-key outburst in the slow [second] movement; the grand cut of the minuet [third mvt], a temptation to conductors with overdeveloped senses of grandeur; and the folkish prance of the fourth movement's first subject, unveiled over a drone bass and identified as a folk tune by both English and Croatian folklorists. No, Haydn did not take the occasion to pass over into the future—but hadn't he done enough already to pull his own era into its present?

Piano Concerto in D Major c. 1782

This is the most popular of Haydn's few surviving ventures into the keyboard concerto (out of some twenty, by Wanda Landowska's count). Moderns enjoy a controversy over whether to play keyboard concertos of the late eighteenth century on "their" harpsichord or "our" modern piano; Haydn left the question open, for an edition of 1784 claims it "per il clavicembalo o fortepiano" (for harpsichord or piano). Furthermore, Haydn played both himself, so there one is. Of the work itself, there is little to analyze in the way of questing novelty, but much to enjoy of Haydn's unquestioned sociability in a snappy, squared-off first movement, a short and graceful second [slow] movement, and a finale [third mvt] in Hungarian style, featuring a minor-key section that sounds like "Three Blind Mice."

'Cello Concerto in D Major 1783

Haydn wrote the piece to set off the gifts of Anton Kraft, his prize first cellist at the country estate of Haydn's employer Prince Esterházy. But Kraft became more closely associated with the work than Haydn would have liked. Besides putting in a customary two cents on the working out of the solo passages, Kraft came to be thought of as the concerto's composer. A century or so of doubt ended in the middle of this century, when the manuscript turned up in Haydn's hand with his characteristic "Laus Deo" (Praise God) on the last page.

A most engaging piece. This is the only one of Haydn's six extant 'cello concertos to hold a place in the repertory. Opera buffs will catch the likeness between the first movement's opening theme and the middle section of the "catalogue" aria from Mozart's *Don Giovanni;* others will note the smallish orchestra (two oboes and two horns besides the strings) and wonder how much of this is due to the resources of Esterháza, the Prince's family manse, and how much to Haydn's care not to overshadow the 'cello. (For years, some meddler's expanded orchestration dating from the late nineteenth century was used in performances; nowadays, we prefer to play ancient music as authentically as possible. However, this means that a harpsichord—sometimes assisted by a bassoon—should play along with the strings.) The 'cello is favored in the amiable first movement, the songful second [slow] movement, and the spry finale alike.

Trumpet Concerto in E Flat Major 1796

This is a kind of stopgap work, composed after the days of the virtuoso Baroque trumpet had faded and before the flexible modern trumpet had been invented. The instrument had slipped in status to a makeweight in orchestral *tuttis* where it had once gloried in solos, and Haydn wrote this concerto to order for a newfangled "keyed" trumpet designed by one Anton Weidinger. No doubt the solo part sounds better today than it did on Weidinger's lips, for his invention apparently achieved its suppleness at the cost of tone. Not till the modern valve trumpet came along in the 1800s did Haydn's concerto show off the metallic trumpet sheen as a trumpet concerto should.

It's a late work, written after the last symphony. But Haydn seldom experimented with the concerto form as he did with the symphony, and what we have is a likable and harmless piece. The main feature, of course, is the solo line and its *squillante* (ringing) eloquence. A lively sonata-allegro first movement, a short but expressive slow movement like a barcarolle (boat music, suggestive of the roll of the ocean), and a vivacious finale filled with devilry.

Sinfonia Concertante for Oboe, Bassoon, Violin, and 'Cello in B Flat Major 1792

A great hit of Haydn's first English visit, this "concertoish symphony" harkens back to the era of Bach and Handel, the heyday of the *concerto grosso,* when concertos for groups of soloists (rather than one main soloist) were in vogue. The massed sound of the orchestra was forever being broken into by multiple solo lines flitting in and out of the texture. This was a time when balance and a kind of collaborative individualism were the rule, obviously, and composers tended to write these works to spotlight the best players on hand. Here, the two woodwind and two string soloists offer a quaintly witty complement to the rest of the orchestra; they enter the first movement early on and pretty much take it over, sharing a cadenza at the end. The solo violin leads off in the slow [second] movement, which is more a quartet than a solo movement. In the finale [third mvt], the violin again supervises the first pages, getting into a minor argument with the orchestra over what theme to use. At length everyone agrees, and the movement wends its lively way home.

The Toy Symphony ?1786

This isn't by Haydn, but everyone used to think it was, and we have to put it somewhere. Recent evidence declares the music to be the work of Leopold Mozart (Wolfgang's father), arranged as heard here by a Haydn, not Joseph but his brother Michael. The "toy" or "children's" symphonies were a popular subgenre dating back to when music-making was a regular activity in the home. Scored for instruments most people played, such as piano, violin, and 'cello, these compositions also called for a variety of simple instruments that could be entrusted to children—drums, ratchet (a sort of rattle), tambourine, triangle, bells, bird whistles, and sometimes even kitchen equipment. The present work, in three simple movements—*Allegro* (lively), minuet, and finale—calls for three varieties of bird call, a toy (i.e., one-note) trumpet, drum, rattle, triangle, and a few strings, mainly violins. It's a weird business, but not nearly so weird as Étienne-Nicolas Méhul's *Ouverture Burlesque* for piano, violin, and children's ensemble including three kazoos.

WOLFGANG AMADEUS MOZART 1756–1791

Hearing the oft-repeated statement that Mozart overflows with song—that his symphonies, especially, are rich in melody—the listener is apt to challenge that remark with a little common sense. Aren't all symphonies rich in melody? Music *is* melody, and a symphony is music, right? But not all melody is *song,* and there's the point. Beethoven's Fifth, for instance, begins with the well-known buh-buh-buh-*bum* that has no rival for dramatic clarity in symphony. A smashing first subject for a first movement. But it is not songlike—doesn't mean to be.

Mozart does mean to be: and is. Whether launching a dramatic movement, following with a development section, or ripping through a festive finale, Mozart transmits his symphonic "information" entirely through music that acts as "songs without words." This is not only a quality but a quantity as well—Mozart *overflows* with song. Where his contemporary Haydn might make one principal theme do for an entire movement; and where their successor Beethoven might build a movement out of the contest of two contrasting themes, Mozart might call up some four or five themes just to start with—and then introduce entirely new themes in the development!

His melodic gift was insanely rich, the more so when one considers how prolific he was in his short life, the child prodigy who made his first piano concert tour at age six, wrote a symphony at age nine, and was turning out operas at age eleven. His symphonies and piano concertos are not, however, accidents saved by song, but planned experiments in what were at the time relatively youthful forms. The symphony did not really get its bearings until Haydn finished with it, and Mozart was there, too, seconding Haydn's structural genius with his own melodic-dramatic one. And, for its part, the concerto was old, but the piano (as opposed to harpsichord) was new; it was Mozart more than anyone who laid out a kind of Old Testament for the piano as soloist in an orchestral sound-space.

Mozart wrote as Classicism was just getting ready to fade into Romanticism, and there is a streak of the style of the future in Mozart's autograph that we don't hear in Haydn. Both men, of course, were Classicists in their clarity of structure and pleasure in the forms of absolute music—symphony for symphony's sake. But Mozart shows some sense of Romantic self-dramatization. He wrote no Fantastic Symphony, as the arch-Romantic Berlioz would, a few decades later. Still, Mozart's mature symphonies (nos. 25, 29,

31–36, 38–41) occasionally utilize an emotional breadth that is almost fantastic in the context of formal, conservative, public Classicism. Mozart certainly was a public composer; he made that separation of self from work that musicians made in those days, saving their autobiographical affirmations for diary entries and letters. There was no Liszt, no Wagner, no Rachmaninof, no Bernstein in those days; nor was there Communications to centralize the production of personal celebrity. Beethoven, the first Romantic or the first of the last Classicists—depending on how one reads him—was the first compsoer to be personally felt through his music by those who did not know him as a person. As performers and composers, Classical musicians wrote to the order of the establishment, on commission, occasionally seeking wider audience in concerts and opera performances. Like his colleagues, Mozart wrote for occasions: serenades for celebrations, sonatas for pupils, "Paris" symphonies (in French style) for Parisians, piano concertos for his public appearances. Not that composers were aloof or "automatic"; simply that a symphony, in those days, was a symphony. Later, after Beethoven, a symphony was a personal affidavit—and, to a degree, Mozart anticipated this Romantic self-promotion in, for example, his two g minor symphonies, nos. 25 and 40.

However one parses Mozart's works, they are certainly universal, of immediate appeal to all ears: adored by laymen and admired by professionals. Perhaps there is no one who resists Mozart. David D. Boyden tells of an explorer among Indians in South America, who "found that a Mozart Symphony played on a portable phonograph was an *open sesame* to them. The Indians were indifferent to Sousa's *Stars and Stripes Forever* and to Louis Armstrong, but they were mad about Mozart."

Symphony no. 25 in g minor, K. 183 1773

This, the earlier of Mozart's two symphonies in g minor, is a small, intense work, passionate rather than tragic; the "color" of g minor invariably inspired expressions of torment and despair in the composer. The great popularity of the later g minor symphony, no. 40, has somewhat obscured no. 25, but the air of upreaching suffering is no less appealing here. The first movement is tempestuous and sudden, starting out with a few seconds of syncopated (off-the-beat) repeated notes in the strings before stating the swirling main theme. The second subject is also harsh, making for a very single-minded movement. The touching slow [second] movement offers relief in E Flat Major, but this is shortlived. The minuet [third mvt] is stark, back in g minor; its trio, in G Major, is scored for oboes, bassoons, and horns alone—a breath of country air—but the minuet theme of course returns, and the impetuous finale [fourth mvt] is very g minor. Note the reference, restated several times, to the syncopated repeated string notes of the first movement.

Symphony no. 29 in A Major, K. 201 1774

An exquisitely proportioned item, scaled down to the minimum in orchestration (two oboes, two horns, and strings) and transparently structured. It is a model of the "little" Classical symphony—little in size, not assertion. The first movement leans to the stately side, opening, without preliminary, with its famous "stepwise" first subject, more a pattern than a tune. The second subject, however, is certainly a tune—several tunes in a row, the last of them being a charmingly quainty item marked by trills in the strings. The tiny development pulls a typical Mozartean trick, presenting new material instead of developing what is already there.

Like the first movement, the slow [second] movement seems to be holding back, denying some secret passion. But the minuet [third mvt] is aggressive, interestingly nuanced and centered around a trio of spacious intimacy: strings dancing under sustained winds. The finale [fourth mvt] leaps into a vivacious 6/8 meter, putting some urgency forward; moreover, it takes its first theme (the first notes heard, in the first violins) through a strenous development. Late, but not too late, the work has thrust itself into palpable action, closing its space at last with an upward rush in the violins and two closing chords.

Symphony no. 31 in D Major, "Paris," K. 297 1778

In three rather than four movements, to accord with contemporary French taste (no minuet—that was a German innovation), K. 297 was composed for the famous Concerts Spirituels, a symphony society that prided itself on its opening *coup d' archet* (bow stroke), in which all the strings came in at exactly the same instant. Actually, Mozart found the level of playing below what he was used to in Salzburg and Vienna. But on the other hand the conductor of the Concerts was unhappy with Mozart's slow movement, an *Andantino* (rather slow), and had him write another, this one an *Andante* (slow). Both movements survive, and while Mozart expressed a preference for the second, the first is usually played today.

The modern listener may imagine for himself the peculiar tang of Parisian concertgoing by taking in the work not as that of an established genius, but of a new talent who, for all his success elsewhere, must now prove himself in Paris. The listener will expect homage to his culture, a work in French style: the three movements, yes—but also the proud, almost pompous tone cultivated by French musicians. This Mozart does attempt. Elsewhere, he is tender, or jokey, or tragic; here, he is a boulevardier in full strut. The listener will note with satisfaction the *coup d' archet* at the very top of the work, the frivolous nature of the lively first movement, the poised slow movement, and the racy finale. To ensure success, Mozart pulled a trick at the start of the finale, wherein the violins play a hushed rushing figure for a few seconds and are suddenly joined by all the instruments in a loud fanfare. Sensation!

Symphony no. 32 in G Major, K. 318 1779

Like several other less well-known Mozart "symphonies," this is in fact an overture. The difference between the two forms was not all that great in the 1700s, for the four-movement symphony in fact developed out of the three-section overture. (The sections were expanded and separated and a fourth section, a dance, was added in as the minuet movement by German-Austrian composers.)

The overture that gave birth to the symphony was the so-called Italian overture—what the present work is—with a fast opening, a slow middle, and a fast finale. The outer sections here really function as one sonata movement broken apart, as the slow middle section interrupts the opening just before its recapitulation, and the closing then presents that recapitulation. So it's like the first movement of a symphony with a slow movement dropped in two-thirds of the way through. It's fine music, trumpets and drums to the fore for the first subject and a frisky second subject (in the first violins) of great charm. Incidentally, the Mozart expert Alfred Einstein placed this piece as the missing overture to Mozart's comic opera, *Zaide;* recently, the Mozart expert William Mann exploded this theory. Scholarship marches on.

Symphony no. 33 in B Flat Major, K. 319 1780

This was originally written in three movements (first movement, slow movement, finale), but a minuet [third mvt] was composed for a performance in 1783. The first movement is pleasant but tricky—Mozart doesn't develop his main themes in the development, but rather introduces a new one. (Thus, the development offers not a variation of the exposition but a contrast to it.) The second [slow] movement is ravishingly Mozartean, the minuet [third mvt] intimate, the finale [fourth mvt] a swirly dance movement.

Symphony no. 34 in C Major, K. 338 1780

Three, not four, movements: Mozart started a minuet but then changed his mind. (He changed it again two years later, finally writing a minuet for the work—so we believe was the purpose of the minuet known as K. 409, sometimes played as the second movement of no. 34 and sometimes not.)

Intermittent passages in the minor key in the first movements of this C Major symphony suggest a threatening melancholy. But we expect joy, not anguish, from C Major, the key of marches and fanfares. Sure enough, Mozart opens the work with a fanfare of horns, trumpets, and drums, and the first movement is generally festive until the development section, opened by a glowering theme in the strings under sustained woodwinds and continually beset by a conflict of light and shade. Typically, Mozart does not "develop" the exposition in the development, but rather exposes entirely new themes. The minuet [second mvt, when played] is quite a find, richly sensuous; the slow movement is mainly silver, tenderly songful in its dovetailed string lines and understated bassoon assistance. But the finale, a skyrocket of perpetual motion in bouncy 6/8 metre, lifts the heart and mind.

Symphony no. 35 in D Major, "Haffner," K. 385 1783

This symphony is actually a serenade, slightly revised, originally composed in 1782 to celebrate burgomaster Sigmund Haffner's elevation to the nobility. That former serenade is not to be confused with the "Haffner" Serenade (discussed below), written for another occasion. But there is some confusion in the mind as to whether the essentially trivial serenade form can turn into a symphony by the simple elimination of two of its six movements and the addition of flutes and clarinets. A serenade is a serenade, one might say, and a symphony is a symphony. But Mozart was Mozart, and he often endowed the first movements of his serenades with the sturdy foundation on which a symphony depends.

What this is is a light symphony, though it begins with a portentous violin fanfare appropriate to Haffner's social ontogeny. One clearly hears delicate serenade-type melody in the second [slow] movement, buffoonery in the minuet [third mvt], and whiplash frolic in the finale [fourth mvt]. How much of Symphony no. 35 is true symphony and how much "spendthrift" serenade? And does it matter?

Symphony no. 36 in C Major, "Linz," K. 425 1783

Here Mozart opens with the slow introduction so often used by Haydn, but when the tempo jumps up to *Allegro spiritoso* (lively and spirited) and the first movement proper takes off, the sound is that certain graceful forthrightness that says "Mozart." The first violins lead off with the first subject, keeping it lean. But as motion pushes at the melodic line it expands, and oboes, bassoons, and horns as well as violins state the more complex second subject, a theme group more than a theme, and harmonically opposed to the C Major of the first subject in not one but two keys, first G Major, then e minor. Moving into the development on a little ascending-decending phrase in the first violins, Mozart decides to show it off in the strings as a new structural device until the home key is firmly reestablished and the recapitulation brings us home.

Structurally, the work is very fully conceived—every movement except the minuet is in sonata form, the most "symphonic" format there is. Accordingly, the slow [second] movement, in F Major, extends itself outward from its touching main theme in luxurious part-writing for the strings. The minuet [third mvt] refreshes the ear with some more C Major; the movement seems to want to be pompous but can't quite get up the necessary remoteness, especially when a rustic oboe and bassoon play along with the first violins in the trio. The wild finale [fourth mvt] naturally begins in C Major, speeds into

G Major for the second subject with every instrument going full blast, then pulls back for a tight development, with each instrument or group spotlighted in turn. They tear the movement apart thematically, then—slyly sidling into the recapitulation with no warning—put it back together.

Symphony no. 38 in D Major, "Prague," K. 504 1786

The "Prague" is the last symphony that Mozart wrote in three movements (French style), perhaps because the slow [second] movement is unusually persuasive. Actually, when the form we call symphony was new—an offshoot of the old Italian overture—it was in just these three movements; it is interesting to hear such a work as the "Prague" considering that this might easily have been *the* form that the symphony would have taken but for the addition (by German and Austrian composers) of the minuet movement, which later became the scherzo.

So here is one of the final examples of the symphony as it *almost* was, a circular trio of movements—solid *Allegro* (lively), tender *Andante* (slow), light *Presto* (quite fast). The slow introduction to the first movement sounds almost demonic in its forceful intimations. Of what? The first movement provides no clear-cut answer; this is a symphony that grows across the spaces between movements in a three-sectioned arc. At first, all is pleasant but somehow fierce. Not till the second [slow] movement does the consolation of Mozartean melody seem to conquer, or at least stay, the anger foretold in the introduction. At last, the bubbly finale [third mvt] ratifies the pleasant at the expense of the fierce. Even so, one is left feeling that the tense exhortation of the introduction really provides the key to this extraordinary work. The citizens of Prague, all Mozart buffs since the premiere of his *The Marriage of Figaro* a few months earlier, thought they heard more of its jaunty wit in the "Prague" Symphony. (True: the main theme of the *Presto* is borrowed from *Figaro*.) But even that comedy has its tense moments. This symphony is a work to be heard a few times before it may be fully grasped—and notice, each time, how much more important that introduction seems. Seeing how fluid this three-movement format is, you may understand why twentieth-century composers have gone back to it almost as often as they have retained the four-movement plan that replaced it.

Symphony no. 39 in E Flat Major, K. 543 1788*

This glowing work is a peaceable little kingdom of melody composed from the depths of penury and humiliation. Mozart was suffering one of the slowest times in his career when he wrote it, but you'd never know it from this music. Some listeners may make more of the occasional fierce outbursts than others, but a symphony finds its meaning in its completion, not in moments. No. 39 gets its sum in joy for joy's sake: art is not life.

What is this symphony? Delicacy infused with dash. For example, after the unusually powerful introduction to the first movement, we hear a dainty waltz for the first subject, then a taut transition theme to the likewise dainty second subject. The light touch vies with the vigorous—restrained slow [second] movement, hefty minuet [third mvt] with light clarinetty trio—until the finale [fourth mvt] secures the case for light vigor.

Symphony no. 40 in g minor, K. 550 1788

An intriguing conflict between gentility and fury permeates all four movements of this work, Mozart's most popular symphony and one of the cornerstones of the repertory. No doubt much of its popularity comprises simple pleasure in its melodies, so simply lovely that one wonders why they hadn't all been thought of long before. But perhaps listeners have also responded to the work's bimodal tone, one half shaking the fist and other half soaring in transcendance. Use of the minor key as the home tonality adds not melancholy, as it might, but a roughness unusual in symphonies of this era.

It begins starkly. There is no introduction: over the feverish thrumming of the violas, the violins enter immediately with the first subject, grieving and raging until the gentler, major-key second subject calms matters down somewhat—not for long. The development section emphasizes the feisty poignance of both main themes, and in the recapitulation the second subject is heard in the minor, underlining the tragic nature of the work.

The slow [second] movement provides some surcease in E Flat major, though the melodic line is often broken into with little chirp-

*A detailed analysis of this work may be found in the General Introduction, on pages 25 to 32.

ings. Then note the harshness of the g minor minuet [third mvt], as dignified as a minuet should be but unusually steely. The G Major trio (middle section) is suave, but when the minuet's main theme returns, all suaveness is erased, and the furious finale [fourth mvt] redoubles the tonal "pulse" of the first movement. Remember, tonality (the use of keys) is one of the foundations of the symphony; even the most untrained ear will respond, if unconsciously, to the sense of release provided by a return to a work's home key after pages of extrapolation in other keys. In a heroic symphony, the return of the home key, usually in partnership with the return of the first subject in the recapitulation, can be exhilarating. But in a tragic symphony—which no. 40 *almost* is—the same return is less exhilarating than nobly pathetic. So it goes here, then, as the final movment reaffirms the dark g minor at the close.

Symphony no. 41 in C Major, "Jupiter," K. 551 1788

The last, longest, and (some say) greatest of Mozart's symphonies bears its subtitle for a reason forgotten today, if there ever was one. But it is surely an Olympian work, expansive both emotionally and structurally. Mature is the word for it. For one thing, there is a pronounced relationship of themes from movement to movement. They seem to have been derived from or lead up to each other, and give a nice feeling of cohesion to the whole. Of course, this is not the only work in which Mozart did this—but here, even a non-musician can sense this relationship the first time he hears the music. For another thing, the finale [fourth mvt] is very full here, a finely detailed sonata-allegro movment that sounds like a fugue and uses its themes over and over again in dashing fluency as if in some miraculous improvisation.

The first movement is grand, but it has its quaint charm as well. Note the rumbling theme-fragment that opens the movement—this is used constantly as a structural building piece. The second [slow] movement is a rich one, interestingly embellished by the strings almost throughout. The minuet [third mvt] is shy, built on a falling melodic line subtly transformed into the oboe-violin tune of the trio section. But the minuet, too, is large for its genre, adding to the overall sense of size, and the finale [fourth mvt] retrieves the gala breadth of the first movement to close the work with admirable balance. This is the true "Jupiter" movement, this finale. It is a highly contrapuntal piece—counterpoint being the blending of several independent lines of melody into a harmonious whole. At the very end, Mozart pulls a brilliant stunt: he sounds all five of the movement's themes at the same time.

Piano Concerto no. 9 in E Flat Major, K. 271 1777

A special feature of this concerto finds the piano (or harpsichord, for authenticity) making its entrance right at the start of the first movement. This is contrary to established practice, which decreed that the orchestra first sound the first movement's themes alone and that the piano then enter. Mozart's is a very mild revolution, however: the piano finishes off the orchestra's first phrase twice, then drops out for a while to make a second entrance in his usual place. After the bright, lively first movement, the second [slow] movement shifts the work's tone with throbbing minor-key plangency. The finale [third mvt], however, is joyous, returning us to the major key, and—as an extra surprise—containing a dignified little minuet spang in the middle of the movement.

Piano Concerto no. 14 in E Flat Major, K. 449 1784

In this one, Mozart restrains the solo part to an unusual degree. True, there is the usual cadenza for virtuoso display at the end of the lively first movement—but the music up to that point has shown the delicate intimacy of a chamber grouping, almost as if this were a sextet rather than a concerto for piano and orchestra. This air of closeness hovers over the slow [second] movement, and Mozart pulls a real switch in the finale [third mvt]. We expect a vivacious fare-thee-well, but instead get a quite serious conclusion—lively, yes, but "not too," Mozart directs—*Allegro non troppo*. At the end, all seriousness disperses in a frivolous coda

Piano Concerto no. 15 in B Flat Major, K. 450 1784

K. 450 is generally thought to have the most difficult solo part of all Mozart's piano concertos (though concerto solos in this era were invariably much less difficult than what was to come in the nineteenth century of Liszt and Paganini). Mozart warned his father that this work would "make one sweat" to play it, with much bravura (heroic playing) called for in the not unprankish first movement. The second [slow] movement falls to more serious business with a gentle two-part theme and two double variations (variations in which each half of the theme is varied twice). But the rondo finale [third mvt] winds things up with the usual devilry.

Piano Concerto no. 17 in G Major, K. 453 1784

No fewer than six melodies grace (*just* the word) the orchestral statement of themes that precedes the soloist's entry; the third of these, a wry comment by the bassoon and flute leading from the first subject to the second, becomes a kind of motto for the movement. So far, the harmonic architecture has rooted itself in the home key of G Major; when the soloist enters the picture, an arch of tonality is raised, and we pass through a spectrum of harmonic "colors" until the recapitulation sets things to rights in G Major. The slow [second] movement is famous with analysts for its ambitious structure, a sonata form that might also be called a rondo or a theme-and-variations. Note that the main theme, which opens the movement in the first violins, is a slower statement of the theme that provided the second subject of the first movement. The finale [third mvt] is a clear-cut set of variations on a chirping tune (in flutes and first violins) that Mozart adapted from the repertory of his pet starling. The violins introduce a last new theme, *Presto* (very fast) to top the work off with a lengthy coda.

Piano Concerto no. 20 in d minor, K. 466 1785

The tense, jagged opening presages something new in Mozart's concerto line, a serious work. Using trumpets and drums for the first time in the genre, Mozart composed a work far from tragic but nonetheless weighty and intense, especially so because where one expects a Classical concerto of taut dramatic fibre to relax its tension as it proceeds, this one actually retains its tension right up to the last page, where it suddenly turns jolly. Perhaps because it seemed to exhibit a fierce Romantic melancholy, the work was a particular favorite in the Romantic nineteenth century, overshadowing others of Mozart's piano concertos that have since become much more popular.

The first movement sustains a struggle of great fury, anticipating the Romantic concerto of soloist-versus-orchestra. Rather than resolve the contest, it simply ends it, moving on to the slow [second] movement, a lyrical vacation in B Flat Major with, however, a stormy middle section. The finale [third mvt] is very much in the minor; if the storm has passed, this is a questionable peace at best. But at length, a change into D Major banishes all worry with a bright buh-buh-buh-buh-*bum-bum* on horns and trumpets.

Piano Concerto no. 21 in C Major, "Elvira Madigan," K. 467 1785

The nickname cited above is one of the rare instances of a work's getting a subtitle ages after it was first performed, said subtitle stemming from a weepily romantic Swedish movie of the late 1960s that incorporated K. 467's slow movement into its soundtrack. Calling this piece "the *Elvira Madigan'* concerto" annoys some people, but in fact it's much easier to distinguish one of Mozart's twenty-three piano concertos by a name than by number or Köchel listing (the "K." number). Furthermore, the nickname is in use, on record jackets and by listeners, whether one likes it or not. This concerto had a lot to offer *Elvira Madigan,* for this slow movement is one of Mozart's most beautiful compositions, almost ecstatically transcendent. But, as it happens, *Elvira Madigan* had something to offer this concerto—a wild popularity among people who don't ordinarily hear much Mozart.

The first movement asserts an identity in a marchlike first subject that dominates the movement. We hear it at the very top in the strings, very quietly. The woodwinds reply, the strings reply to the reply, and then the full orchestra hammers it home. Now, according to the rules, should come the second subject. But each of Mozart's concertos offers its little experiments, and first the piano soloist enters, playing around with a "false" second subject in a minor key, after which it settles down to work and provides a real second subject accompanied by the strings. Then comes development (the march theme much in evidence) and recapitulation. This brings us to the slow [second] movement, a nocturne of misty shadings. The finale [third mvt] is a crisp dance festival in miniature.

Piano Concerto no. 22 in E Flat Major, K. 482 1785

This has been cited as the queen of Mozart's piano concertos, probably because its sovereign grace appeals with a heavy underlay of great warmth. It may be noble, but it's friendly, too. As usual, Mozart stuffs the opening exposition of his first movement with a barrage of themes, letting the soloist enter with yet another one—the life was short but the art was replete. An important use of woodwinds here colors the movement quaintly, but dignity is the key to mood. Somewhat grandly, Mozart moves into the minor for the slow [second] movement, four variations on a tune (broken into by two episodes, both in the major) introduced by the violins. Again, the scoring is notable for the care with which the composer uses the woodwinds. The rondo finale [third mvt] is decorous rather than prankish, and emphasizes its poise in an unexpected slow interlude, stately but expressive.

Piano Concerto no. 23 in A Major, K. 488 1786

Mozart's piano concertos may at first seem pretty much alike, with their lively first movements, lyrical second movements, and dancey finales. In fact, each is different, featuring experiments in structure and dramatic progression that must amount to *the* major field work in the concerto. This one, for example, is generally singled out as the most songful of the series. (Since Mozart is never not songful, this is saying a great deal for the work's lyricism.) The first movement is less lively than serene, the slow movement unbearably lovely—a lullaby elegy—the finale less rousing than pert. Obviously, a songful concerto will show its great heart in its slow movement, the core of symphonic song, and there is much heart to show in this middle movement. The piano enters alone. Then the clarinets and violins make a counterstatement, imitated by the bassoon, that expands the soloist's grieving theme with a compassionate line of transcendent poise. At such a moment, the vigor of the first and the coming third movement are swept aside by the awesome, stationary eloquence of beauty. Some concertos are balanced on homogeneity, on their "all-aroundness." This one is balanced by the purity that sings in its core.

4 in c minor, K. 491 1786

rk, very exploitive of the minor key in the two om the first, a dark theme on strings and bas- ses to the full orchestra, the music is stark, full, and defiant. In this context, the piano sounds a poetic contrast, sometimes aided by oboe or clarinet. The second [slow] movement offers some release of the tension, but the finale [third mvt] returns us to the morbid minor key in a theme-and-variations set. The theme itself (the first thing heard, in the first violins) is consolatory, though sad, and there is a sense of release at the soloist's cadenza (his unaccompanied showpiece). But even then Mozart finishes off with a last, pathetic variation very much in the minor.

Piano Concerto no. 25 in C major, K. 503 1786

The main themes of the first movement bear an affinity to the "fate" theme of Beethoven's Fifth, though Beethoven's buh-buh-buh-*bum* is in c minor and Mozart's in the brighter C Major. Nonetheless, the rhythmic coincidence is hard to miss, especially since Mozart's version dominates the first movement of this work in a variety of thematic transformations. It first appears shortly after the fanfarelike opening, in a rising theme in the violins, and thereafter turns up in several different themes as a motto for the movement. Mozart, of course, uses the motto for C Major majesty rather than c minor defiance. The second [slow] movement is graceful, much embellished by the soloist, and the rondo finale [third mvt] manages to sound both lilting and important.

Piano Concerto no. 26 in D Major, "Coronation," K. 537 1788

This is one of the less popular of Mozart's mature piano concertos, mainly because it lacks the emotional power of its fellows. The first movement never quite seems to get somewhere, though the middle slow movement reminds us of the Mozart of importunate, songful vitality, and the pleasant rondo finale rounds things off with graceful purpose. The subtitle stems from the work's origin as part of the festivities attending the inauguration of Leopold II as Holy Roman Emperor.

Piano Concerto no. 27 in B Flat Major, K. 595 1791

Mozart's last piano concerto, written in his last year on earth, mixes a somewhat desolated quality with the spryer Mozart that we're used to. True, the first movement begins with the lively procession of tunes that one expects of the composer in his concerto first movements—but note how the first of them shows up in the minor key in the development section. Furthermore, neither the second [slow] movement nor the rondo finale [third mvt] yields quite the expansive consolation and dovetailing episodes of merriment, respectively, that these movements usually supply. It may not be a concerto of foreboding, exactly; let's not romanticize the case. But one does seem to hear snatches of an odd self-awareness that keeps cutting in on the spontaneity.

Concerto for Two Pianos in E Flat Major, K. 365 1780

The charm of a "double" concerto (one using two soloists, as here) is that the two star players get to add an extra layer of textural conflict to the conflict already inherent in the concerto form: besides playing off the orchestra, they can play off each other. Of course, Mozart's era was still close to the *concerto grosso* of the Baroque age, when balance rather than conflict was the aim of the solo group; Mozart wrote the piece to be played by himself and his sister Nannerl, so collaboration (and elaboration) is the urge here, not rivalry.

A delightful but unremarkable work. One hears the standard Classical concerto: strong first movement (with cadenza, of course, wherein the two soloists do not show off but dovetail their variations of the movement's themes); lyrical second [slow] movement; bright rondo finale [third mvt] with another cadenza.

Violin Concerto no. 3 in G Major, K. 216 1775

"German in melody, Italian in the violin technique," said Pitts Sanborn of this work—and a French influence in the *style galant* ("noble style"=simple tunes highly ornamented) is also evident. But, mainly, the piece is Mozartean in its rich outpouring of melody; this is youthful work, ingenuous, impatient to tell. The delightful first movement offers little development in the development section: instead, Mozart simply introduces new material. The slow [second] movement is very slow, and the finale [third mvt], folkish in tone, achieves breadth with the intrusion of a minor-key, gavottelike interlude amidst the major-key drollery.

Violin Concerto no. 4 in D Major, K. 218 1775

The martial opening, like so many of Mozart's military invocations, heralds a work neither contentious nor scrappy—as the soloist makes clear when he enters with the same opening music, playing it high in the violin's range to emphasize its lyrical bent. No, this is a playful work, though the slow [second] movement has its serious side. The rondo finale [third mvt] plays a lively "finale" tempo against a more sedate tempo, alternating the two as if gaming with the very idea of a frisky concerto finale. Note the pert duet of soloist and first violins over a solo oboe's sustained note near the end of the movement for further piquant amusement.

Violin Concerto no. 5 in A Major, K. 219 1775

Don't miss a wonderful little stunt that Mozart pulls off at the start of the first movement: he opens not with the expected first subject, but with the *accompaniment* to the first subject. This is sounded by the orchestra, and after a bit the soloist enters, to a strange halting lull in the proceedings. After appearing to warm up, the soloist rouses himself and plays his first theme—with the opening tune now playing along very nicely under him. The movement continues on its merry way after that, testing out a few minor-key outbursts in the development section but recovering its poise in the recapitulation. The slow [second] movement is purest song; interestingly, it, too, pulls a few minor-key switches in its middle section. By the time the minuetlike finale [third mvt] rolls around, we are prepared for a third minor-key middle section, and we are not disappointed: Mozart changes both the rhythm and mood of this finale in a bizarre "Turkish" episode—so such percussive sounds were called in Mozart's time and place. At length, the opening minuet theme returns to close the work.

Clarinet Concerto in A Major, K. 622 1791

One of the composer's very last works, written for Anton Stadler, who played a special clarinet commanding a greater range than those used today. This posed no problems to later clarinettists, however, as the manuscript had been lost and all surviving editions rearranged to suit the standard clarinet. But we don't want "arrangements" of Mozart, or of anyone. Luckily, musicologists have been able to reconstruct the original solo part, and technology has reinvented Stadler's clarinet.

The strings open the work with a pleasant first subject, eventually taken up by the soloist who of course decorates and develops it. Mozart makes much of the contrasting qualities of high and low in the clarinet's range, often in sudden juxtapositions—though in general the effect of the work is one of sunny relaxation. The slow [second] movement consists of embellishments on the theme introduced by the soloist at the start; many people consider it an outstanding example of Mozartean lyricism. For a finale [third mvt], the soloist leads the orchestra through a typical rondo, agile, harmonically adventurous, and finely balanced from episode to episode. Haydn's rondos are more vivacious, Beethoven's more dramatic. Mozart's—this one, for example—are sweet, more concerned with melody than with motion.

The Four Horn Concertos

These four works, presumed to be the surviving two thirds of a sextet of horn concertos, occupy a peculiar place in the repertory. They cannot be called popular in the sense of a Beethoven's Fifth kind of universality, yet a significant minority of the listening community has made them cult classics. (For years, a mono recording of these four concertos, conducted by Herbert von Karajan with Dennis Brain as soloist, stood as the best-selling item in the entire catalogue of Angel records right through the stereo era, until a disc of Scott Joplin ragtimes, wisely orchestrated by Gunther Schuller, edged it out of the way.)

Mozart's format here accords with the "Italian concerto" of strong first movement, slow movement, and virtuoso's rondo.

Concerto no. 1 in D Major, K. 412 ?1782

This work exists only as a first and last movement; either the middle slow movement has vanished, or—more likely—these are two unrelated movements of unplaced origin. Otherwise, why does the "first movement" call for bassoons and the "finale" not? But certainly no one needs any excuse to hear this music, of great jovial innocence.

Concerto no. 2 in E Flat Major, K. 417 1783

Two oboes, two horns, and strings support the solo horn, first in an *Allegro maestoso* (lively and majestic) that glows with peace even at the fast tempo and despite a minor-key session in the development. The slow [second] movement is thoughtful, the finale [third mvt] a succession of hunting-horn sallies and virtuoso stunts.

Concerto no. 3 in E Flat Major, K. 447 1783

Clarinets and bassoons yield a rich accompanimental texture here, and in general this is perhaps the most athletic of the four horn concertos. The first movement digs into its themes for some real dramatic grip (especially in contrasts of major and minor keys), the second [slow] movement emphasizes motion in its lyrical relaxation as if it were actively trying to connect the two faster movements, and the finale [third mvt] really dances.

Concerto no. 4 in E Flat Major, K. 495 1786

The first movement is outstandingly jovial, though it allows for some powerful statements from the soloist in the development. From the first note, the slow [second] movement belongs to the soloist, and a gifted performer can make this music the high point of a given concert. After such interior beauty, an extrovert finale [third mvt] such as the present one is just what one needs to come down to earth in style.

Concerto for Flute and Harp in C Major, K. 299 1778

Composed for the Duke of Guînes (flute) and his daughter (harp)—Mozart loathed both instruments, though he eventually came to admire the flute—the work is more of a curiosity than a treat. It's a light work, very basic, very C Major. Furthermore, one has to admit that the sound of the two solo instruments is peculiar, especially when they play together more or less unaccompanied. The flute is icily radiant, the harp giddy; as a duo, they sound like a nymph going bonkers in a plashing spring.

Perhaps apprehensively, Mozart keeps things moving right along. The first movement is busy, culminating in a detailed cadenza for the two soloists; the slow movement does what slow movements do: sing; and the rondo finale is justly famed for its variety of themes. Mozart discloses the secrets of his instrumental texture at the start of the finale by bringing in the players group by group—strings first, then oboes and horns, then (after some possibly resentful delay) the harp followed by the flute.

Sinfonia Concertante for Violin and Viola in E Flat Major, K. 364 1779

An early masterpiece of the "double concerto," K. 364 is one of those rare works that seems to exploit everything a composer has assimilated in the preceding period—a showpiece for the play as much as the players. The young composer (twenty-three at the time) had got down structure, orchestration, balance; this is a kind of celebration of technique. For example, in the first movement there is a solo for two horns, echoed by two oboes—this is matched by a similar moment for horns and oboes in the third movment.

Though the violin and viola are the nominal soloists, there is some elaborate spotlighting of other instruments as well; this, after all, is what a "concertoish symphony" is all about. Note also Mozart's adoption, at several points in the first movement, of the famous "Mannheim crescendo." Mozart had recently been to Mannheim to hear its celebrated orchestra, celebrated especially for the players' ensemble discipline. It seems they were so deft in their sense of balance that they could work up gradations of volume previously unheard of in the semi-amateur European orchestra, and gloried in their *diminuendo* (growing softer) and *crescendo* (growing louder).

For much of the work, Mozart has his violin and viola soloists playing in leap-frog. The rich first movement, *Allegro maestoso* (lively and grand), acts as a collaborative gala for all concerned, with the two soloists presiding from their entrance to their duo-cadenza at the end. The slow [second] movement, however, is so elegiacally songful that one notices the line of melody more than any one instrument. The joyous rondo finale [third mvt] plays the ear out with tunes in lively procession.

Sinfonia Concertante for Oboe, Clarinet, Bassoon, and Horn in E Flat Major, K. 297b 1778

Admirers of the Baroque *concerto grosso* should love this updated entailment on the old form, for in his solo wind quartet Mozart revives the *concertino* (solo group) and the *ripieno* (the rest of the orchestra: two oboes, two horns, and strings). Needless to say, this is an unusually concertoish concerto, what with four soloists to exploit. Classical usage calls for the orchestra to state the first movement's themes first, but once the quartet makes its entrance it sets to work, trading off solos as well as acting as a unit. In the slow [second] movement, the quartet completely takes over after an orchestral invocation, blending solos and ensemble in sometimes startlingly beautiful colors. For a change of pace, the finale [third mvt] is not the usual perky rondo but a slow theme-and-variations. The solo oboe presents the theme; ten variations follow, featuring the solo quartet. The overall mood is gently frivolous until a sorrowful passage right in the middle of one variation prompts loud chords of warning from the orchestra. Hold it!—don't lose the mood! Sure enough, a bouncy final variation ends the piece in great good humor.

One great pleasure in hearing this item is seeing the first-desk men and women of the resident orchestra (the best players of each instrument) come forward for solo work, as opposed to stars imported from the celebrity catalogue.

Serenade no. 6 in D Major, "Serenata Notturna," K. 239 1776

This "nocturne-serenade" for two small orchestras was surely composed for some occasion, but no account of such has come down to us. The two orchestras were probably separated on two sides of a gallery, for stereo effect, so there is much play with balance and soloistic touches, with a string quartet acting as a sort of solo group against an orchestra of strings and timpani. Actually, it's an odd combination, though the droll use of solos to relieve the sameness of texture provides much charm. There are three movements: a march, a minuet, and a rondo finale.

Serenade no. 7 in D Major, "Haffner" K. 250 1782

Mozart honored the Haffner family. Besides writing the "Haffner" Symphony (no. 35) to celebrate the senior Haffner's elevation to the nobility, Mozart donated a march and this serenade to the wedding party for Haffner's daughter Elise. Serenades are, by nature, trivial works, but the "Haffner" Serenade is titanic, comprising almost two symphonies' worth of material. This is dinner music, not meant to be studied; its mellow is much too extensive for the listener to follow any sort of dramatic progression. True, there are two sonata movements and a rondo with a part for solo violin, besides two slow movements and three minuets. But essentially it's a pleasing jumble, and should be heard as one.

Serenade no. 9 in D Major, "Posthorn," K. 320 1779

A brief slow introduction leads us into a spirited first movement with a picturesque theme in which the strings brusquely push in and the first violins timorously repel them. Next comes a minuet [second mvt] with a delightful trio (middle section) for flute and bassoon solos and strings. The third [slow] movement, called "Concertante," is a little *concerto grosso* spotlighting a pair each of flutes, oboes, and bassoons. Delight tops delight when Mozart arranges a cadenza for the group in which each soloist attempts a takeover, pretty much simultaneously. The lively fourth movement offers more soloistic effects, perfectly in keeping with the bantering nature of the serenade as form—but the fifth [slow] movement is an anomaly, a intense minor-key movement. This is heavyweight emotion for the lightheaded serenade, but then it seems likely that Mozart composed it not for some party but as a graduation exercise. The sixth movement, a minuet, contains a prominent posthorn solo (thus the serenade's nickname), and the finale [seventh mvt] wraps it all up in the manner of a symphonic finale. Altogether, this is a surprisingly adult example of the normally rather callow serenade.

Eine Kleine Nachtmusik
(A Little Night Music), K. 525 1787

This serenade for string orchestra is perhaps Mozart's most popular single composition. It was written simultaneously with the opera *Don Giovanni* hard on the heels of the smash success of another opera, *The Marriage of Figaro*—hit tunes must have been roaring out of the composer's brain. They are certainly in full supply here. "Night music," by the way, meant "serenade" in Mozart's day. This was not the nocturne of Chopin's time, with its haunted melancholy; a serenade was night music because it was ideal outdoor-party music.

There are four movements, though apparently there were five or six originally, the extra movements having been lost. The first movement is graciously precise, opened by one of the most familiar melodies in music, a call to arms in miniature. It chuckles, perhaps despite itself. The slow [second] movement isn't all that slow, though it fulfills the lyrical function of a slow movement with rich singing warmth. In a middle section, it gets just the slightest bit intense, but soon relaxes. The third movement is a minuet, short, firm, and sweet. For finale [fourth mvt], we get a bubbly rondo which never loses its poise despite a fast tempo and some surprising shifts in melodic direction.

Overture to Le Nozze di Figaro
(The Marriage of Figaro) 1786

Based on Beaumarchais' comedy about servants getting the better of their masters, *The Marriage of Figaro* takes in "one mad day" of intrigue, of foiling and being foiled. Naturally, the overture foreshadows all this. It starts quietly but with tensile exuberance that quickly explodes, subsides, and explodes again. And so on, with suggestions of whispers, signals, and dashes down the hall in a sonata movement too dizzy to contain a development: Mozart gives only an exposition and a recapitulation.

Overture to Don Giovanni 1787

The opening is tremendous. It means retribution for the rakehell; it is heaven screaming and hell opening; it is as if the night moved on you, gathered close and took hold. For: having killed the father of one of his prey, Don Giovanni (Don Juan) encounters a memorial statue of the old man and jokingly invites it to dinner. It comes. The music that accompanies the statue's appearance in Don Giovanni's house is the music that begins the overture—so we may know, right off, that judgment awaits the libertine. The opera unfolds within that Classical frame of world-order maintained.

But *Don Giovanni* is a comic opera melded on *opera seria* (heroic, non-comic opera), so these sounds of divine justice overtaking the anti-hero turn out to be just the introduction to the main movement of the overture, a lively business. Commentators of old liked to hear in this music the amoral Giovanni pulling his stunts and the "voice" of morality warning him to repent, but that's a little much. Treat the overture (composed only two days before the premiere) as a general preface to the tone of the show to come—that's what an overture properly is. *Don Giovanni's* tone is nobility, mock-nobility, and buffoonery intermingled. You'll hear all three. And notice the quiet ending—actually, the overture does not end. In the theatre, it runs right into the first scene: thus the unexpectedly subdued close.

Overture to Così Fan Tutte (All Women Are) 1790

All women are fickle—so say Mozart and his librettist Lorenzo da Ponte. Their comic opera *Così Fan Tutte* (literally All Women Do So) tells how two young soldiers bet an old boulevardier that he cannot prove their fiancées unfaithful. He wins, but all ends happily. The piece is almost all farce in its action, but Mozart lavished music of such great humanity on it that some people cannot approach it as a comedy. It's a kind of caviar for opera buffs, some of whom prize it above Mozart's more popular operas, *Don Giovanni, The Marriage of Figaro,* and *The Magic Flute.* Preparing the listener for the coming action, Mozart emphasizes the conspiratorial nature of the plot premise. But first, in a short slow introduction, he alludes to music heard late in the work when the old boulevardier tells his two friends that . . . well, *così fan tutte.* At the end of the overture, just before the coda, Mozart reprises the message one last time.

Overture to Die Zauberflöte (The Magic Flute) 1791

The Magic Flute, one of Mozart's last works, is an odd item. A fantasy involving the young hero's rescue of the young heroine (with the aid of a magic flute), it blends romance and farce with a profound humanism modeled on the order of Freemasons. (Both Mozart and his librettist Emanuel Schikaneder were Masons.) A complete analysis of the sociopolitical allegory in *The Magic Flute* needs a book of its own; the question here is, how does one write an overture—an emotional preparation—for so rich a work as this? Evidently, Mozart decided not to foreshadow the dramatic texture of *The Magic Flute* but to contain it, so to speak, in a study in vitality and stability. A slow introduction calls us to attention with fanfares associated in the opera with a Mason-like brotherhood, then moves into a lively tempo and the most ordered form in music, the fugue. Halfway through, Mozart emphasizes his seriousness of intention by repeating the fanfares; then the "busy music" takes off again. Strange—the piece is very solidly built, yet has the delicate air of faerie.

LUDWIG VAN BEETHOVEN 1770–1827

"I don't want to know anything about your whole system of ethics," he once wrote. "*Power* is the morality of men who stand out from the rest, and it is also mine."

Power was Beethoven's ethic, power of such presumption that the musical forms of his day were not large enough to contain that ethic. Beethoven made them titanic. Power: this was the morality of his symphonic outlook, power to extend the limits of the symphony, to free it for more imposing articulations of human will than his predecessors Haydn and Mozart could conceive of. Inheriting a model art from them, one of precision, balance, and tensile beauty, Beethoven evolved it over the course of a quarter-century into a grander form, no less precise but capable of greater drama, building a music of ideas as well as of melodies. With his Third Symphony, he fulfilled the symphony's potential for tragic poetry. With his Fifth, he devised a unity of heroic transformation through the use of one basic theme that grows more triumphant from movement to movement. With his Seventh, he proposed a quasi-Dionysian emancipation of spirit. With his Ninth, he idealized ecumenical communion, an elitist's populism, using text and singers to celebrate the fraternity of mankind.

Classicism was, on one level, a preference for equilibrium. Romanticism was a rage for power. Beethoven spanned the two eras, and by the time of his death he had so fully remotivated the symphony as a musicoemotional form that one may safely call his the single most significant achievement in the development of the Romantic Symphony, with its dramatic and heroic focus. No less famous for his expansion of the piano sonata and the string quartet, Beethoven remains the quintessential composer for many listeners, whether musicians or lay buffs. Bach and Brahms are worshipped for their domination of already established forms, not for their inventions; and such modern giants as Schönberg and Stravinsky are as much feared as admired for their experiments in the tone that music can take. But Beethoven stands foremost for the utopian energy of his innovations, colossal, sublime, elemental.

Biographers have emphasized Beethoven the wretched man—uncouth, bad-tempered, sometimes malign in his business and personal relationships, and possibly syphilitic (this to explain his loss of hearing, aggravated from a worrisome nuisance in his twenties to total deafness in his fifties). The catalogue of Beethoven's squabbles with publishers, musicians, patrons, family, and friends is inexhaustible, it seems. But all this is of little assistance in placing Beethoven the creator: a man's achievements far outweigh a man.

Moreover, we can only admire the man who dramatizes himself in such noble music as this. His work was a statement on man, on life: on power. Thus, his Third Symphony, the "Eroica," marked a major break with the "moderation" of Classicism—power is immoderate. Beethoven needed to find a grander engine of communication for this work, inspired by the messianic *fraternité* that the composer saw in the phenomenon of Napoleon (and which he was to consummate on an even grander scale in the Ninth Symphony). Similarly, Beethoven's sole opera, *Fidelio,* revitalized the genre known as "rescue opera" with a saga of tyranny overthrown by faith and endurance, capped by a scene of the liberation of political prisoners that has never been equalled for humanistic exhilaration. Power made him reinvent the very usage of music, its forms and content.

It was Vincent D'Indy, a composer of a later era, who divided Beethoven's oeuvre into three periods: Imitation, Externalization, and Reflection. This is astutely observed. Beethoven's Imitation is the apprenticeship of a traveler learning the routes. His Externalization (the period covering Symphonies 3 through 8, the last two piano concertos, and the violin concerto) is that of the pioneer who strikes out on his own. The Reflection is that of the discoverer laureate, retraversing his old trails to seek their profoundest mysteries. This third period, that of the last five piano sonatas, the last five string quartets, the Missa Solemnis (Solemn Mass), and the Ninth Symphony, is one of sublimation, of perfecting the innovations. Rather than break further with tradition, Beethoven draws closer to it, fulfilling his personal language to the utmost while working toward an abstraction of the forms that he had overthrown—the Ninth as the ultimate symphony, the Missa Solemnis as the ultimate Mass, the "Hammerklavier" as the ultimate piano sonata. It is horrible to reflect that for most of this time Beethoven had no hearing whatsoever.

Musicians argue over whether Beethoven might be thought of as a Classicist or a Romantic; but what is important is that he supervised, in music, the transition from one to the other. The key, of course, is in the word "power." Beethoven's was a time of great upheaval, a revolutionary time in many ways. A new urgency inflamed life, thought, and art—a need to force wide the structures set up in the past. Romantics were the agents provocateurs as poets and politicians; Romantic art had to develop more complex forms than were known to—or needed by—Classicism. "In the beginning," says Goethe's Faust, "was the Deed." This is what Beethoven means by power.

Symphony no. 1 in C Major, op. 21 1799

We cannot hear this work with the Viennese ears of 1800 that heard it when it was new, some in mild horror and some in admiration. But with our hindsight, we can place it historically as a Haydnesque symphony as Beethoven might have written it—and this, of course, is exactly what it is. The format is Haydn's, but the agressive oomph is Beethoven's. The very beginning, for example: we start with Haydn's slow introduction . . . but Beethoven launches it with an unorthodox harmonic procedure, a sequence of chords leading into—rather than starting with—C Major, the home key. (This, for 1799, was unheard of.) The first movement is Haydn-lively but Beethoven-pushy, and if the second [slow] movement is the most conventional of the four movements, the so-called minuet [third mvt] is no minuet at all but the first-ever example of the more vigorous and less refined scherzo, with which Beethoven replaced the minuet as a symphonic organ. The rondo finale [fourth mvt] is cute; Haydn, too, showed a sense of humor. But even his brilliant final movments lack the deft melding of brawn and brevity we hear here, with surprises of sudden loud and sudden soft and a rhythmic kick that points to the Beethoven who would shortly revolutionize the symphony for ever.

Symphony no. 2 in D Major, op. 36 1802

Composed in the shadow of an emotional depression, this sunny piece doesn't bear the slightest hint of Beethoven's state of mind. It is a formal exercise, a "pure" symphony, without meaning. Like the First Symphony, it places the Beethoven of the supervening will in the context of the Haydn-Mozart symphonic structure—their form, but his expression. Its finale [fourth mvt] is so bold, it threw a generation of critics into confusion. Hector Berlioz, who did no little confusing on his own, thought this finale "playful" and "delicate." But to one writer of the day it seemed "a repulsive monster, a wounded, tail-lashing serpent, dealing wild and furious blows as it stiffens into its death agony in the end."

On the way to this finale, we pass through a forceful first movement preceded by the longest and grandest slow introduction composed to that time. (At one point, sharp ears will pick up a brief foreglimpse of the Ninth Symphony.) There follows a sturdily lyrical slow [second] movement and a scherzo [third mvt] of fierce loud-soft confrontations, momentarily calmed by its trio, led off by oboes and bassoons. Their little tune is another anticipation of the Ninth, this time of the exactly comparable spot, the trio of the scherzo. More important is it to note that this third movement marks the first time that Beethoven officially called his scherzo ("joke"), which he devised to replace the old minuet, a scherzo.

The forceful, the lyrical, the fierce—and we have arrived at the infamous finale, with its first theme that sounds like a back flip. What is it about this movement that so alarmed conservatives of 1803, when it was premiered? It's too fast, too changeable, too happy to be radical. Beethoven resolves the tension of the first three movements by knitting their different energies together. It's a brilliant stunt, a gleeful fury. Note how early the second theme (in the 'cellos) glides in, pretending to be serious, how Beethoven thinks nothing of being most lyrical *while* he is being most fierce, how long he takes in winding things up. He can be raucous, comical, and beautiful in the same movement—at the very same second! This richness of mood was too much for some people. We all know the kind.

Symphony no. 3 in E Flat Major, "Eroica" (Heroic), op. 55 1804

No spacious introduction here. Two abrupt chords launch the work, one of the most unpretentious openings ever. Yet this is perhaps the great moment in the history of the symphony, the great leap forward of contagious genius. Here, for the first time, Beethoven leaves eighteenth-century tradition behind.

"Composed to celebrate the memory of a great man," according to the score, it was actually written to honor Napoleon. Beethoven rededicated it in fury when Bonaparte crowned himself emperor of France; this was to be an epic lay for a leader of men, not a tyrant. The moral imperative of what Beethoven expected of his hero is written into every page. In its imagination and thrust, its impartive virility and breadth of communication, the "Eroica" amplified the symphony of Haydn and Mozart to immense proportions, and quite simply inaugurated the future of the form.

The first movement presents "the great man" of the dedication at his apex of glory. Then comes the "memory"—for the slow [second] movement is a funeral march in ABA form. The A, in the minor, represents the cortege; the B is an interval of inspiring major-key faith. Beethoven contrives to maintain the hopeful tone when the mourning A section returns, but the catastrophe is too great, and the movement seems to dissolve in living bits at its close. The scherzo [third mvt] brings release in its lighter look at heroism, with a lively trio (middle section) based on horn calls, calls to action as if in defiance of death. From the second movement's stuttering tragedy, Beethoven conquers despair with a triumphant finale [fourth mvt]. He builds the movement on two themes borrowed from his ballet *The Creatures of Prometheus,* drawing the listener into his personal view with great gallant urgency. The funeral march is now seen in the context of deliverance rather than futility: this celebration of the memory of a great man is the resurrection and the life.

Follow the finale (a combination of sonata form, rondo, and variation) as calibrations of triumphant catharsis: a brief introductory tumult, a pause, then the first *Prometheus* theme, a skeleton of melody. Two variations. Then the second *Prometheus* theme, this one lyrical, on the oboe. As it appears, the skeleton is heard below it—the two are really two halves of one theme: a lyrical tune and its skeleton bass. Variational episodes and new themes intensify the trip, leading up to a grand slow passage. This becomes broader, quieter, and at last explodes into a thrilling coda. Heroic is right.

Symphony no. 4 in B Flat Major, op. 60 1806

Flanked by two such terrific propositions as the Third and Fifth Symphonies, the sunny Fourth suffers a qualified eclipse: Schumann dubbed it "a slender Greek maiden between two Norse giants." It is an irresistible work, fleet and convivial. Though it is certainly not comparable to its heroic neighbors, it is no lightweight. Beginning with a slow introduction of ominous mood, Beethoven suddenly leaps into a bright and engaging first movement. The slow [second] movement has had champions among commentators, who protest much as if making up for its failure to assault the heavens. But Beethoven shook his fist at fate enough elsewhere; here he exhibits his too easily overlooked good nature—and note the odd accompanimental figure that characterizes the movement (the first music heard, in the second violins). Is it pleasant or menacing? Even at the movement's end, when it steals in for one last rhythmic comment, we still don't quite parse it. The scherzo [third mvt], however, is clear-cut fun. Its trio (middle section) is so delightful that the composer can't help giving it an encore. Instead of the usual ABA, this scherzo ends up as ABAB and coda—not a note too many, either. The finale is quicksilver fun, closing in a very Haydnesque joke: the main theme is played in slow motion . . . and the whole thing springs back into tempo and promptly ends.

Symphony no. 5 in c minor, op. 67 1807

The Fifth!—most awesome of all symphonies, most humbling even though it would incite us to defy and conquer. That is "fate knocking on the door" that we hear in work's famous opening bars (so the composer himself tells us):

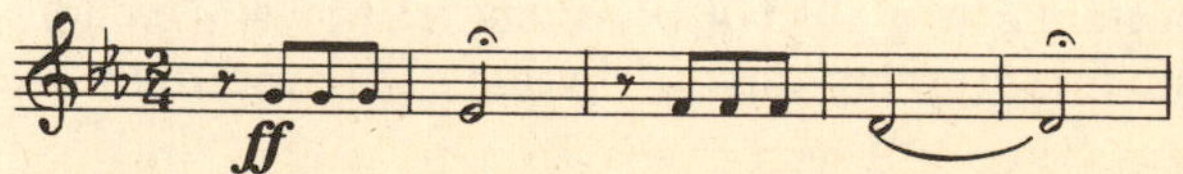

and the question posed by the symphony is, "Shall we or shall we not overcome fate?" The answer is, "We shall!," with a shattering victory over the forces of destiny. But how does Beethoven portray the victory? The *sense* of the music makes the conclusion clear, especially in the transition from the third movement to the fourth movement (the two are connected), when mounting pressure bends all sound into a cheer that at last explodes as the thrilling first theme of the finale. The sense of the music, its emotional drift, pushes on to triumph.

Beethoven presents the victory in another way: he uses the "fate" theme that opens the work as a kind of protagonist, changing it as the symphony progresses into a motto of heroic vitality. In its original form, this motto theme so dominates the first movement that, after serving as the first subject, it hangs on to menace the second subject on the timpani:

It is still in control at the end of the first movement, almost the last thing one hears. But that is not the end of it. After the serene beauty of the slow [second] movement, just after the scherzo [third mvt] has begun, what should we hear but this same four-note theme, in the horns, transformed now from the threat of dispassionate fate to something more human and noble:

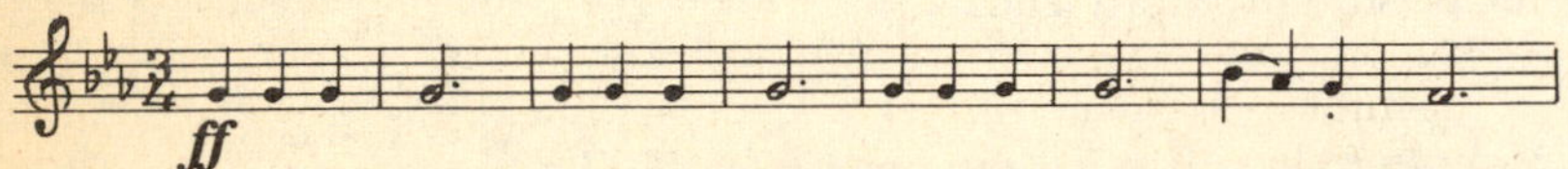

It is as if the theme had two sides, two meanings: one as obstacle and one as the runner of the course. Both adversaries, man and fate, are joined in a musical pathology devoted neither to one nor the other, but to the conflict itself. At the transition that connects the scherzo to the finale, the strings sustain a long hush of expectant trauma while underneath them the timpani softly rap out the rhythm of this motto theme:

It appears again in its noble version in the last movement, but only briefly, for by then the victory has been announced in a change of key from the dark c minor of the first movement to the joyous C Major of the last. The battle over, the theme is not heard from again.

To be fair, not all analysts accept this theory of the heroistic motto theme. Some say there is no intended connection between the themes quoted above; others have sleuthed out incarnations of the motto in all four movements. Both sides have gone to ridiculous lengths to prove their claims and debunk each other, but one thing is sure—the symphony prosecutes the *dramatic* implications of those first four notes in every page that follows. Even such spare material as that provides Beethoven with foundation enough for an entire work.

Symphony no. 6 in F Major,
"Pastoral," op. 68 1808

This is no Wordsworthian nature poem: Beethoven's natural world teaches less of man and morality than of its own immortal truth, of the chastity of Creation and the cyclic beauty of the green world. Accordingly, the "Pastoral" Symphony is less wracked than Beethoven's other symphonies. They are concerned with defiance and overturn—this one is concerned with the epic of a timeless, never-changing scene. It is natural rather than dramatic, suggesting a brook, tiny animals, a farm festival, a storm, and the sun. It is a strangely "pure" work, perhaps the most spontaneous-sounding of all symphonies, as if Beethoven were simply taking down dictation from nature. The reason for this is that the harmony is kept elementary—basic. Using the natural tension of fundamental Western harmonics, Beethoven reduces the world, as it were, to *its* fundamentals. The whole thing is like a cycle of folk tunes, unpretentious, apparently artless.

Beethoven himself gave the work its name, and there is a slight program. The first movement is entitled "The Awakening of Joyful Impressions on Arriving in the Country," and its simplicity is emphasized from the first moment. A feature of this movement is the use of a crescendo (gradual intensifying of volume) while a phrase is repeated over and over—and this, too, is introduced early on. (Beethoven uses it most startingly in the development section.) But in essence this movement amounts to variations on the "theme" stated in the subtitle: the exhilaration of discovering the special solitude of a day in the country. For his slow [second] movement, the composer presents a brook in its trickles and flows. At the very end, we get imitations of a nightingale (on the flute), a quail (oboe), and the cuckoo (clarinet). There are impressionistic touches, too, in the scherzo [third mvt], a peasant hoedown with a lot of woodwindy frolic, and the little fourth movement—a kind of introduction to the finale—features a storm. Then the finale [fifth mvt] returns us to the glad calm of the first movement in a "Shepherd's Song," with the landscape once more in radiant peace.

Symphony no. 7 in A Major, op. 92 1812

"The apotheosis of the dance," Richard Wagner called it, suggesting that, upon hearing it, "tables and benches, cans and cups, the grandmother, the blind and the lame—even the children in the cradle—fall to dancing." Others, too, have seen a message in the Seventh; it has been reported as, variously, a peasant wedding, a Bacchic orgy, a democratic revolution, a chivalric ballad, a celebration of the dissolution of Napoleon's empire (note the year of composition—the tide was running against Bonaparte by then). The slow movement in particular seems to have suggested pictures to commentators—a visit to Roman catacombs, a houri's reverie, a hero's cortege (though Beethoven had already written one as the slow movement of his Third Symphony, the "Eroica").

Of all interpretations, Wagner's holds up best, for this is a very rhythmic work. It sounds simplistic to say so, but it is in how much or little a rhythmic impulse dominates a piece that the word "rhythmic" applies. In the Seventh, we feel that impulse importantly throughout. It is a profound but very exuberant work, of an almost Dionysian sensuality. Still, there is much Apollonian equilibrium as well. For example, the first movement is without question a dance movement, but note the courtly poise of its long slow introduction. An interior calm keeps the dizzier movements in perspective; it is like a battle between balance and frenzy. Thus, from the slow introduction and the lively first movement, we move into the incomparable slow [second] movement in a minor, with its steady rhythm outlined at the start in the lower strings. Themes are sounded over this rhythm, or counterstate it, but it is inexorable, and it finally ends the movement in a weird sort of question.

The tug of war is continued in the F Major scherzo [third mvt], where Dionysian frenzy maintains the main section and Apollonian resistance controls the D Major trio (middle section). This may be the most dancelike of all movements, though the sudden grandeur of the trio, with its singing clarinets and horns and high, sustained violins, calls for more of a sumptuous slow-motion mime than any true "steps." Beethoven likes the effect of the trio's cutting in on the scherzo's energy so much that he repeats it, making this movement not the usual ABA but ABABA. Then, note the interesting coda—a last tiny hint of the trio, the same hint suddenly shifted into the minor key, and a fast exit.

So far, Dionysus and Apollo have shared the work; Dionysus wins out in the finale, reinstating the home key of A Major, wherein an almost non-stop rolling boil concludes the work in pagan delirium.

Symphony no. 8 in F Major, op. 93 1812

The Eighth is Beethoven's salute to tradition, a delightful symphony patterned on the old style: short, playful, and Haydnesque. Indeed, it is almost a self-spoof, "exposing" the tumult of Beethoven in the "contained" context of Haydn. An ebullient first movement, an almost silly second [slow] movement. There's even a minuet [third mvt] instead of the more dynamic scherzo that Beethoven habitually used. Every page of the work bears the autograph of the revolutionary Beethoven, but its overall shape is that of the more . . . well, "orderly" nineteenth century. Only in the finale [fourth mvt], *Allegro vivace* (Vivaciously lively), does the uproarious nature of the younger master totally overcome the orders of the past.

Symphony no. 9 in d minor, "Choral," op. 125 1824

The use of singers in the last movement of the Ninth precipitated a controversy that has never been settled, for the intrusion of the human voice (and a text of extra-musical poetry) was unheard of in symphony till Beethoven tried it. Since then, others have used text and singers and symphony. But the question remains: does it work? Is music absolute unto itself, or can it successfully subsume elements of other media? On the other hand, if it "works" for the composer, who is the listener to say it doesn't? Isn't it ridiculous to hear people announce the "failure" of the Ninth Symphony, one of the most stupendous and exhilarating instances of Western art? The Bostonian critic Philip Hale, some fifty years ago, likened the vocal finale to "an irritated kennel," and thought it "better to leave the hall with the memory of the Adagio [the slow movement] than to depart with the vocal hurry-scurry and shouting of the final measures assailing ears and nerves."

I'll tell you about this vital question on aesthetics: only the composer is in a position to answer it. Beethoven added the text into the till-then text-less symphony because he had evolved the symphony, as form, as an engine of dramatic communication, a conceptual symphony. But concept, in music, can only go so far; Beethoven wanted to go farther. This is a symphony "about" something: the solemn joy of universal brotherhood. There was no way to bring this forward, in music, without words. So Beethoven borrowed words from Friedrich Schiller (his ode *An die Freude,* "To Joy"), called for soloists and chorus to sing them, put them in a symphony, and so produced extraordinary music.

What happens that necessitates this vocal finale? The first three movements of the Classical four-movement plan are each bigger than such movements usually have been. The first movement immediately suggests the Ninth's overall innovative immensity in its slow introduction, a bizarre soundspace made up of *harmonic* rather than *melodic* fragments. It is an almost cinematic device, for till this work came along, the symphony depended on more-or-less equal parts of melody, harmony, and rhythm. Here, Beethoven underplays the rhythmic element and virtually negates the melodic: an indistinct imagism as opposed to a coherant picture. But finally a theme does flash out of the "space," a powerful *tutti* (full orchestra) line. Then Beethoven repeats the introduction (in a different key than previously) and launches the movement all over again. A host of ideas turn up in the exposition, corollaries to the central concept of power—knowing and using it. To define his aggrandized structure, Beethoven uses the introduction to signal the start of the development and the recapitulation, and through rehearing it takes on a melodic identity. It becomes a theme, at least, if not a tune.

The sense of writing a symphony in the approved form that is nonetheless a total novelty also informs the scherzo [second mvt], a dance cut from solid rock. Besides being in the "wrong" order—the scherzo invariably followed the slow movement rather than preceded it—this scherzo expresses a thundering cheerfulness, with its timpani blows and rollicking, intertwining string lines. Remember, until Beethoven this movement was given over to the gentle minuet; its space was meant for a rhythmic release rather than dramatic statement. But here it is used to develop the feeling aroused in the first movement. That was power. This is joy. And notice that though it is frighteningly huge, its little woodwindy trio runs mainly to the tiny without subverting the overall assertiveness.

From power and joy, we move to beauty in the slow [third] movement. Very slow and very songful, it is the least unusual of the movements, but like the others it is also of great breadth. The question is, what can cap all this hugeness of utterance, what resolution is called for? As if even the composer himself doesn't know, the finale [fourth mvt] opens in cacophony. Then the lower strings enter in smooth recitative, a kind of speaking song; the effect is that of the strings trying to pacify the other instruments. The storm breaks out again, the strings again attempt to assuage the turbulence, and then, *most* unexpectedly, the orchestra reprises the opening of the first movement; this the recitative brushes aside. We hear recollections of the scherzo and slow movement, and these, too, are rejected. On the fourth try, the movement finds its theme—its music and statement—in a hymn tune of great purity and strength.

Thus the forces of power and joy and beauty, heard in the first three movements, are resolved in a new force, this one of freewilling human brotherhood. But how to make this clear? Power, joy, and beauty can all be expressed in music alone, but "brotherhood" cannot. The symphony, as Beethoven has inherited and evolved it, is still not eloquent enough. The cacophony again bursts in, as if cursing its limitations of communication; but this time it is not the lower strings but a human voice that takes over—"O friends, not these sounds! Rather let us raise up a more agreeable and joyful song!"

And now the fourth movement proper begins, *Allegro assai* (rather lively), shaping in music and words an end for the means of defiance and hope outlined in the first three movements. Voices in a symphonic movement? Not only a chorus, but a soprano, mezzo-soprano, tenor, and bass right out of some cantata? There are no rules; form bends to content. This is a manifesto, a cosmic evangelism: "Brothers, surely over our starry canopy, a loving father dwells."

Piano Concerto no. 1 in C Major, op. 15 1797

Although numbered first of the five piano concertos, this is really "no. 2," the official no. 2 being two years younger than this one. (It was revised for a performance in 1798 and thus got a later opus number.) You can hear the difference for yourself: no. 2, in B Flat Major, tends to look backward to Haydn and Mozart in style; it's even a little limp. But this one, like most of Beethoven, charges forward vitally.

Still, it is a product of its age. A Mozartean layout—strong first movement, lyrical second, bubbly third. Further: a keenly Mozartean flavor in the first movement, Mozart's ability to draw out a theme without "tampering" with it, Mozart's grace. (The later Beethoven will do much tampering.) Note the pretense at politeness at the very opening: the violins are marked *pianissimo* (very quiet), but the theme they play is very pushy.

The slow [second] movement, however, shows a more self-willed composer; it is more aggressive, more Beethovenian, albeit pliant and—in its use of solo clarinet—darkly tender. The piano is almost the whole show here, taking the lead at transitional points and decorating the orchestral line when not sounding the tunes itself.

In the rondo finale [third mvt], Beethoven asserts himself—that forceful main theme might have occurred to Mozart, but he would not have scored it so lustily as Beethoven does. Also, the themes heard between recurrences of the main theme—the "episodes" of the rondo—foreshadow the rough vigor of the later Beethoven. And note the sudden ending, based on a surprise alternation of soft and loud—*very* characteristic.

Piano Concerto no. 2 in B Flat Major, op. 19 1795

Published second but written first of Beethoven's five piano concertos, no. 2 is the least admired, though it has its champions. Scott Goddard has pointed out the the opening of the first movement presents "an immediate contrast . . . between a feeling of vivacity and a mood of contemplation" in two melodies heard back to back in the span of about five seconds. This bimodal escort of "outward semblance, the instantaneous gesture" on one hand and "inward image, a sign of the questing mind" on the other carry the work through all three movements. An interesting novelty finds the "inward image" taking over just when one would expect the soloist's cadenza at the end of the lyrically intense second [slow] movement: instead of the usual virtuoso display, the pianist is given a delicate little line to play, the very antithesis of display. However, we expect a concerto finale [third mvt] to emphasize vivacity over contemplation, and this one does—though an important, restrained second theme keeps the vivacity from taking over.

Piano Concerto no. 3 in c minor, op. 37 1800

A conservative work: grand first movement, lyrical second, light and lively third. Notice, for instance, the full "double exposition" that opens the first movement, wherein the orchestra first sounds the themes and the pianist enters second to sound them again. But the minor key imposes a certain turbulence on the mood of the piece. This is most felt in the end movements (the first and third); the middle slow movement is an almost Chopinesque nocturne with an odd middle section in which flute and bassoon exchange fragments of themes while the piano rumbles with embellishments. It's a harmonic rather than a melodic period: it has an atmosphere but no real sense of a tune going on. The closing rondo [third mvt] is hard-edged, but finishes in a jolly coda in the major.

Piano Concerto no. 4 in G Major, op. 58 1805

The hushed opening, announcing the first subject without any preliminary ado and played by the pianist alone, signals a defter Beethoven than the one who composed the first three piano concertos. It had been the rule for the orchestra to sound the principal themes of the first movement in a solo concerto *before* the soloist played a note. But here Beethoven emphasizes the generally lyrical context of the work by bringing the soloist in—so gently—before the orchestra. But then the piano drops out to await a more traditional (re-)entrance after the orchestral *tutti* (the statement of themes). That first theme, though, dominates the movement; the piano is already delivering variants of it when it returns. Beethoven, honcho of the forceful symphony, shows his tender side, especially in the unusually compressed slow [second] movement, a dialogue between proud strings and palliative piano. Franz Liszt likened it to Orpheus soothing the savage breast. This startling lull does not quite end—the vivacious finale [third mvt] leaps in with a muted statement of its soon-to-be-boisterous main theme (in the strings). Then we're home free, with the lyricism of the first two movements elbowed out of the way by the aggressive finale.

Piano Concerto no. 5 in E Flat Major, "Emperor," op. 73 1809

It opens majestically, with solid chords from the orchestra and a cadenza from the soloist by way of introduction. Then the orchestra starts off the movement proper with the exposition: solemn first subject, the oddly dainty second subject, and a transition theme, bringing the soloist in for the second exposition (the first is traditionally for orchestra alone, the second for piano and orchestra). This includes a dazzling piano-only version of the second subject, now even more delicate. But this is immediately echoed by the orchestra in a transformation that brings out the theme's jaunty solidity—it has turned into a march. As the movement proceeds through development, the assertive character of the themes overshadows their warmth, and the piano exordium that began the movement recurs to begin the recapitulation. We expect a cadenza, of course—what concerto first movement of this era doesn't have one? This one doesn't. Not only that; it goes right up to the customary noises that prepare the cadenza—and the piano seems to start a cadenza—but instead it reworks the principal themes with the orchestra in a kind of second recapitulation, making for a very expansive first movement.

Actually, the whole work is grand, which perhaps explains its nickname (no one knows for sure how it got there). The second [slow] movement opens with its main theme, a melody of moving distinction, and maintains this transcendant tone right up to the surprise eruption of the finale [third mvt]. There is no break between the two movements: over a low, held note in the bassoons and horns, the piano anticipates a new theme, then uses it to launch the last movement, a joyous rondo in sonata form. Connecting two separate movements was unheard of at this time, but Beethoven had already done it two years before in his Fifth Symphony; many others were to do it after him. Meanwhile, notice the odd journey in tone we have made through the work: from a confrontation of the sublime and the impetuous in the first movement, utter spirituality in the second, to, now, dancing exhilaration. And at the very end, another reminder of the Fifth Symphony's linkage of the last two movements in a brief duet of piano and timpani (recalling the important use of timpani in the Fifth). In a composer's evolution, no work is an island.

Violin Concerto in D Major, op. 61 1806

Notice the five quiet taps on the timpani at the very top of the first movement—they are not there for mere attention-getting, but rather form a structural component of the movement. One hears the rhythm of those five notes in alternate versions throughout the work. Indeed, they have already passed into the strings scarcely a moment later, using different notes but the same rhythm. Meanwhile, attention turns to the soloist, who has waited out the traditional orchestral statement of themes (the *tutti*) and then, in a hush, enters with a brief cadenza. As one expects, the soloist deals with the main themes in his fashion, Beethoven retailoring them to suit the violin. Perhaps not the first time, but eventually as you hear this movement, you will notice how the five repeated notes subtly dominate the movement; generally, first-time hearers are too absorbed in the noble beauty of the music to pick out the details of Beethoven's construction. But you will surely note the careful separation of soloist and orchestra, so Classical, that Romanticism would blur, making the soloist not the collaborator with the instrumental body, but the very essence of the concerto.

The second [slow] movement is understated, almost self-effacing—but it contains a surprise. Instead of ending, it lets the soloist's cadenza lead us directly into the dazzling rondo finale [third mvt]. The refrain of the rondo (first tune heard, on the solo violin) is robustly humorous, the subsidiary theme (soloist over the horns) more lyrical though still bouncy. An intermediate episode takes us into a minor key for the singing "heart" of the movement. But in a rondo the refrain tune always triumphs, and the work ends on an up note with the soloist's cadenza and a coda that takes the refrain from dainty to sturdy.

Concerto for Violin, 'Cello, and Piano in C Major, op. 56 1805

A triple concerto poses a problem: how to spread the material fully among the central trio without creating too diffuse a work? Beethoven unquestionably worked it out, but the result is a little on the dry side, at least in the first movement. Somehow it never seems to spark the level of drama or rhapsody that one expects of the all-important first movement of a concerto. On the other hand, the composer writes for his star trio so aptly that the work develops a nice chamberlike intimacy. Notice that with the bright violin and percussive piano threatening to overshadow the 'cello, Beethoven handicaps the first two by leading off solo sections with the 'cello throughout the concerto. It slips quietly into the start of the second [slow] movement, taking over the main theme from the strings, and is in turn assisted by the piano and violin. Gradually, the solo trio take us from the songful to the stirring, and as the slow movement dies down, again it is the 'cello that conducts us (without a break) into the finale [third mvt], a rondo *alla Polacca* (in the style of a Polish dance). This is the highlight of the work, glittering with really characterful themes played for lightness rather than pushy display or simple freewheeling energy. Note, at the coda, the change in rhythm that transforms the rondo's refrain into something more outspoken, more square-cut. At the last minute, it returns in its original form.

Wellington's Victory at Vitoria, op. 91 1813

War was a commonplace of Beethoven's time and "battle symphonies" popular. This one, incredibly, was in Beethoven's lifetime considered one of his best works; today it is seldom played. It was commissioned for an unusual medium, a mechanical band called the panharmonicum (devised by Johann Nepomuk Maelzel, the inventor of the metronome). Ultimately the piece surfaced in a scoring for orchestra, celebrating Napoleon's defeat by British forces under Wellington at Vitoria in Spain in 1813.

The work is in two movements. First is "The Battle" (with an introduction presenting the English and French armies respectively with "Rule Brittania" and something called "Malbrook s'en Va-t-en

Guerre" [Marlborough Goes to War], which bears a disconcerting resemblance to "The Bear Went Over the Mountain"). Second is a "Symphony of Victory." This utilizes "God Save the King," appropriate for the situation but rather queerly arranged.

Overture to The Creatures of Prometheus, op. 43 1800

Die Geschöpfe des Prometheus, a ballet, salutes Prometheus not as the trickster titan and fire-bringer, but as teacher of art and science. Today, only the overture is heard. It is a piece of Mozartean lightness, early Beethoven. A slow introduction (featuring the oboe) ushers us in, as solemn as the main part of the movement is prancy. Note one structural quirk—no development section. Beethoven goes right from the exposition to the recapitulation. He does extend himself, however, in a fine coda.

Overture to Coriolanus, op. 62 1807

Give Beethoven a hero to hymn; that's his metier! Haydn was as humorous, Mozart as lyrical. But no composer of the Classical era can rival Beethoven for musical depictions of the heroic will. Coriolanus, familiar to readers of Plutarch and Shakespeare, is the Roman general too stupendous to be tolerated in stupendous Rome; exiled, he hires out to the enemy Volscians, lays siege to Rome, is talked into a cease-fire by his wife and mother, and, his will shattered, is destroyed. In Shakespeare, Coriolanus is assassinated by Volscians, but Beethoven wrote his overture for a production of Heinrich Joseph von Collin's *Coriolanus*, in which the general ends in suicide.

A tone poem before tone poems had been invented, Beethoven's *Coriolanus* music prepares the spectator for the central struggle of the play, the hero's personal will against his public, Roman will. Step by step, this sonata-allegro movement limns the event: first an introduction offers taut, declamatory chords of great resolve. The first subject presents the defiant general; the lyrical second subject, the pleas of his wife and mother. Then the development gives us the conflict in Coriolanus' mind, and the first subject loses its authority, almost stutters. Toward the end, the chords of the introduction return, diminished in stature, and at last the first subject—so unconquerable at first hearing—virtually ebbs away into nothingness.

Overture to Egmont, op. 84 1810

Like Beethoven's one opera, *Fidelio,* Johann Wolfgang von Goethe's drama *Egmont* deals with man's battle against tyranny; unlike Florestan in *Fidelio,* however, Egmont is cut down for his defiance, though hope for mankind's free future is granted him in a vision on the eve of his execution. Thus, this quite tragic overture, which at one point seems about to close on a mournful note, suddenly blazes into a glorious coda. Goethe's message, and Beethoven's: live free or die.

Overture to The Consecration of the House, op.124 1822

This late work, like Beethoven's Eighth Symphony, deliberately imitates an older style. The composer had been wanting to try out an essay in the Handelian manner, and this was his chance. The work did, in fact, solemnize the inauguration (actually the refurbishing) of a theatre, but its title stems not from the occasion, but from the play for which it was written. (This play, *The Consecration of the House,* was another refurbishing: a revision of *The Ruins of Athens,* for which Beethoven had written incidental music some years earlier.)

A solemn introduction leads in with a finely judged self-importance that never turns pompous. It is a long introduction; eventually, it is the strings that start the main part of the movement with a typically Handelian fugue. This is the meat of the movement, fit for a festival.

The Four Fidelio Overtures:

Leonore no. 1, op. 138 1805
Leonore no. 2, op. 72a 1805
Leonore no. 3, op. 72b 1806
Fidelio, op. 72c 1814

Beethoven suffered terrible pains in launching his sole opera, *Fidelio.* Dealing with the rescue of a political prisoner, Florestan, by his wife Leonore (who dons man's clothes, dubs herself "Fidelio," and takes a job in a prison to protect her husband), the opera was not at first successful. Beethoven revised it twice before a third version succeeded in 1814. While deleting some numbers and reworking the rest, Beethoven also wrote a new overture to replace the original overture . . . three times. (Actually, he had already written his second of the four overtures while the first version of the opera was still in rehearsal.) The four are listed above in a presumed chronological order. Note the change in name: the 1805 and 1806 versions of the opera were called *Leonore,* but the final version was retitled *Fidelio.*

Here we have four different approaches to one challenge: how to prepare an audience for a dramatic work of some ideological consequence? *Fidelio* is about constancy, the husband's faith in freedom, unbroken even after two years of solitary confinement, and the wife's resolution in saving her husband. Leonores 2 and 3 actually dramatize in little the action of the opera; *Leonore* no. 1 and *Fidelio* only suggest the action. But all four draw on the same spirit of joyful overcoming that attracted Beethoven to the subject in the first place—the valiant woman, the unbreakable man.

Leonore no. 1 is the simplest of the four, and opinion holds it too inconsequential a piece to suit *Fidelio. Leonores* 2 and 3, the big ones, are much like each other. Calling no. 3 bigger than 2 is like calling Goethe bigger than Schiller: both are pretty grand to start with. (Note, by way of programmatic allusion, the trumpet call that bursts into the proceedings in both no. 2 and no. 3. In the opera, this heralds the arrival of a state minister at the prison and the end of the husband's captivity.) However, no. 3 ends much more grandly than no. 2. Both are sonata movements, but no. 2 leaves out the recapitulation—since the trumpet call is the climax of the drama, the overture logically should speed to a conclusion lest it supersede the opera itself. But in no. 3, Beethoven lets music, not theatre, set the form; the trumpet call is followed by a sweeping review of the material capped by a whirlwind coda of astounding emotional catharsis. (Because it's too marvelous for conductors to resist, Leonore no. 3 is sometimes played in productions of *Fidelio* just before the triumphant last scene. Its dramatic power makes whatever succeeds it rather anti-climactic.)

The *Fidelio* overture strikes a mean between the overpowering *Leonore* nos. 2 and 3 and the relatively flimsy *Leonore* no. 1. Since it prepares the action without giving it away (as the two big ones do—no. 3, especially), it is the overture now used to introduce performances of the opera.

NICCOLÒ PAGANINI 1782–1840

Rumor had it that Paganini had sold his soul to the devil in return for a violin technique beyond that of any of his colleagues—indeed, beyond what was thought to be mortal possibility. Paganini laughed such nonsense away, but his public sniffed for sulphur. And Paganini rather encouraged the imaginative awe of his following by shrouding much of his offstage preparation in secrecy. He refused to publish most of his own compositions—of course: the devil penned those notes in blood! (Actually, Paganini merely wanted to maintain an exclusive repertory.) He claimed not to need the virtuoso's daily workout—yes: the devil plays those fingers! And before a concert, he always tuned his instrument in secret—ah so: the devil chooses that pitch! (No, another example of the canny showman: Paganini tuned up privately so no one would know that he tightened his strings to sound extra brilliant. When accompanied by an orchestra, he could thus outshine all the other violinists without doing anything that they weren't.)

The second quarter of the nineteenth century was the age of the charismatic solo recitalist—singers, pianists, violinists. Paganini helped make that age. In Mozart's day, and in Beethoven's as well, a musician was a musician, proficient in composition and performance. Paganini was among the first to specialize. He composed, but only to furnish himself with vehicles for his demonic musical trip: mainly, he was a performer, and quite a one. An English critic wrote of Paganini's playing of his first violin concerto (cited below): "he commenced with a soft, dreamy note of celestial quality and, with three or four whips of his bow, elicited points of sound that mounted to the third heaven. A scream of astonishment and delight burst from the audience at the novelty of the effect."

Daredevil that he was, the man expanded the technical capabilities of the violin. And after him, others confirmed the idea of the star performer-personality as vocation; it caught on, revolutionizing the profession of musician. Nowadays, more often than not, composers compose and performers perform.

Violin Concerto no. 1 in D Major, op. 6 c. 1810

Since Paganini hoarded most of his compositions, no one knows exactly when he wrote this concerto—or, for that matter, if this really was his first. It is the only one of a possible dozen Paganini violin concertos that still holds the podium with any frequency—and, as it happens, it was not composed in D Major but in E Flat Major. The reason for the discrepancy is that just before a concert, on the quiet, Paganini would tune the strings of his violin one half-tone higher than the norm. The orchestra would play in E Flat. Paganini would play in D Major on strings tuned to *sound* in E Flat. But the effect was that of a demon talent playing music that—given the violin's topography—could not possibly be played in E Flat. Magic! (Thus the demonic legends about where Paganini derived his talent.) Today, violinists play openly in D Major, the orchestra plays in D Major, and that's the end of *that* little dido.

Apparently Paganini was violinist enough to need no "magic," and in this concerto he contrived an extravaganza of effects and devices. Ironically, the taste today is for players to de-emphasize the exhibitionistic side of the work and concentrate on its musicality. But then violin technique has advanced well beyond the standard of Paganini's day, and his crazed tricks are the modern player's everyday exercises. In playing this music, some soloists will revive Paganini's trademark "springing bow" trick (in which the bow is virtually thrown onto the strings to create a kind of *ping!* of the notes), his scale passages dizzily veering from sweet phrasing to sharp phrasing, his one-finger slides, and guitar imitations.

The first movement is mainly pyrotechnical. Paganini chose his first theme with a keen sense of the star entrance, and the second theme presents the fiery warmth of the protagonist, now displaying not his prowess but his steely heart. However, the second [slow] movement is quite touching, a rendition of minor-key Romantic melancholy, though the rondo finale [third mvt] returns us to the mindset of the virtuoso showpiece—the springing bow, for example, is called for right at the top of the movement. Musically, Paganini's finale is no more imposing than the finales of any number of minor violin concertos of the era. It lacks the emotional foundation—the sense of completing an arc plotted in the first movement—of the finales in Mendelssohn's or Brahms' violin concertos. Perhaps because he didn't like to share his specialties, Paganini's own cadenzas for the work died with him. There are traditional substitutes, but a true virtuoso of the Paganini school should dazzle us with his own.

CARL MARIA VON WEBER 1786–1826

Pronounced interests in nationalism, folklore, fantasy, and Gothic horror made Weber a charter member of the Romantic era, but much of his reputation rests on his stage pieces rather than on his orchestral work, which emphasized concertos in Mozartean style. A vogue is slowly growing around his till recently ignored operas *Euryanthe* and *Oberon,* though both suffer from libretto trouble. Still, the music is gaining admirers to rival the cult following of his best-known opera, *Der Freischütz* (The Free-Shooter).

Weber was, perhaps, less a great composer than the right man at the right time. Its folklore and nationalism made *Der Freischütz* the sensation of the day in Germany, while fantasy sparked *Oberon* and Gothic horror enlivened *Euryanthe:* Weber was there with the information to help the new era find itself. He had a professional's craft as well as the individual's vision, yet today he is the least heard of the best known: everyone knows the name, but only the opera buff can really place him.

This may change in the near future. Since the rise of the long-playing record as a museum of the obscure, Weber's memory has come to life. The listening ear has picked him up, particular for his zesty *concertante* pieces for bassoon and clarinet. Then, too, the recent rediscovery of Gustav Mahler's realization of Weber's unfinished comic opera, *Die Drei Pintos* (The Three Pintos), has added the luster of a familiar name to a neglected one. Who knows? Mahler was thought offbeat in the early 1950s; today he is part of the standard repertory. If anyone deserves revival, it is Weber, a seminal figure who died before he could age into a prime.

Symphony no. 1 in C Major, op. 19 1807

A brisk fanfare, some murmurings in the strings, the fanfare again, and the symphony is on its way, highly reminiscent of Haydn and Mozart. But Weber shows himself in the second theme, a perky march touched up by woodwind solos. This theme opens the development; the fanfare closes it. Recapitulation of the two themes affirms Weber's foremost characteristics at this early stage of his career: sheer melting charm. The slow [second] movement places the composer as one of the important transitional figures in music—from the Classical to the Romantic—in its plaintive juxtaposition of light and shade, its murmurs and roars. Here, too, the woodwinds are prominent. (Weber was one of the composers most sympathetic to the personality of the woodwind family, an underrated group at the time.) Unlike many of his contemporaries, Weber was quick to seize on Beethoven's scherzo to replace the old minuet as the dance form of the German symphony's third movement—but this is a light scherzo, more suggestive of Mozart than the formidable Beethoven.

The finale [fourth mvt] is vivacious, all churning strings and frisky woodwind turns.

Piano Concerto no. 1 in C major 1810

One of the founding fathers of the Romantic movement in music, Weber offers numerous studies in the changeover from the Classical world of Haydn and Mozart into the Romantic world of Schumann and Liszt. Here is such a study: a concerto that is Classical in format but Romantic in its use of chromatic (what one might call "decadent") harmony and a piano part tricky enough to point to the coming era of the virtuoso performer. Still, the overall effect is Classical, with many Mozartean echoes. A proper Classical *tutti* presents the themes, after which the soloist steps in with a bit of showy pianism, including a very difficult upward run for *legato* (connected) thirds in both hands—something Mozart never asks of his soloists. Otherwise, however, the piano part is not all that challenging, favoring a lot of portent and filigree. The brief slow [second] movement seems to anticipate Liszt in its piano flash. Note the highly Romantic keyboard "shudder"—played against one hushed note on a solo viola—just before the end. For his rondo finale [third mvt], Weber resorts to one of his most ingratiating devices, a heftily flowing dance in three-quarter time that would feel right at home at a rustic wedding. Near the close, he asks for another difficult upward run from the pianist, this one in octaves. Thirds are harder.

Konzertstück (Concert Piece) in f minor for Piano and Orchestra, op. 79 1821

A piano concerto in an unusual format: one movement in four distinct sections—slow, fast, march, and finale. Weber didn't call it a concerto because in his era the word applied almost exclusively to works in three separate movements with no dramatic program—and Weber, always at his best with a story to tell, had thought one up to explain the music: a knight's lady awaits her crusading lord, experiences a dream of his death, and is at last reunited with him. Thus the title, "concert piece": it was a tone poem before there was a term to call it by.

Knowing the program, one may follow it in the music—first, the affecting evocation of the lady's love for her knight, then the turmoil of her nightmare vision. The march brings her hero home (note that the piano is silent throughout the march except for one jubilant glissando—a slide up the keys like a whoop of joy), and the finale throws the party in his honor.

Clarinet Concerto no. 1 in f minor, op. 73 1811

Weber wrote a number of clarinet *concertante* works for his friend Heinrich Bärmann, all designed to exploit the resources of the instrument, from its edgy top to the rich *chalumeau* register (as it is called) in its depths. The first movement is rather stormy, demonstrating the Romantic flair that would make Weber one of the most important opera composers of his time. Much of the solo part in this movement captures the wistful rusticity that the Romantics recognized as an emblem of their mindset; much of it also offers the player one of the great showpieces in his repertory. As it turns out, the stormy passages belong to the first theme and are given to the orchestra, leaving the clarinet to hold up the more lyrical end of things, a nice contrast. The slow [second] movement, naturally, soothes the mood of the work. Moreover, its C Major states a refreshing opposition to the f minor of the first movement. Note an especially Weberisch touch, two passages in which the clarinet plays against a horn chorale. Slipping into F Major for his finale [third mvt], Weber tenders one of the most engaging rondo finales in all concerto, a deft blend of rhythmic lift, clarinetty showmanship, and heartful song, a very festival of small-town exhibitionism. Anyone who doesn't stand up and cheer for the soloist's last shrill high note hasn't a soul to speak of.

Concertino for Clarinet and Orchestra, op. 26 1811

Famed for his woodwind concertos among buffs of that particular timbre, Weber seconded Mozart in bringing the clarinet and bassoon out from under the strings and into the limelight. Weber calls this a "concertino" (small concerto) because it is a mere one movement's worth of concerto. It opens with a portentous slow introduction dominated by the soloist. But this soon gives way to a theme-and-two-variations, the sunny theme sounded by the clarinet. After a dash of orchestral excitement, the clarinet leads the two lively variations, rounding them off with a slow, minor-key episode and a vivacious coda—in effect, a last variation—designed to exhibit technique.

Overture to Der Freischütz (The Free-Shooter) 1820

The shooter is free in that he makes a pact with an agent of the devil to obtain "free bullets," six of which will invariably hit the hunter's mark—but a seventh flies for the devil. Try to hear this music in the context of the Gothic frisson that Weber's contemporaries enjoyed, for this prototype of the folk-German *Singspiel* (musical play) set a tone for the blending of true romance, rustic comedy, and the occult that was to dominate the era through the 1860s. Typically, the overture prepares one for the action, from the opening horror sequence and battle of innocence and evil to the jubilant conclusion, innocence triumphant.

Overture to Euryanthe 1823

The libretto to this opera, which bears more than a passing resemblence to Wagner's *Lohengrin* of some years later, is so ridiculous as to resist any salvage in the way of revision or translation. But the music is outstanding. The time is the Middle Ages, the place chivalry, and the characters a good knight and his good lady and a bad knight and his bad lady. Thus the exposition presents nobility (first subject) and courtly love (second subject), ceding in the development to a slow section for muted strings—ghost music. (Don't ask why; answering necessitates reference to the impossible plot, and you'll only laugh.) Then the music picks up in tempo, turning tense as the bads plot against the goods. But the joyful recapitulation brings an affirmative restatement of the first and second subjects—note the new timpani blast in the latter.

Overture to Oberon 1826

Like Weber's *Euryanthe, Oberon* is an opera burdened with a preposterous libretto. But the overture, like *Euryanthe*'s, remains a familiar treat in the concert hall. The horn that opens the piece is a magic one, and note that the sprightly chortles of the elfin kingdom dance about the horn call in woodwinds and strings. (This is a fairy tale, but not *A Midsummer Night's Dream,* though Shakespeare's Oberon and Puck are involved in the story.) After this introduction, the movement gets underway with a stirring first theme. The horn call and elfin music slip in again, followed by a second theme in the clarinet taken from an aria sung by Oberon's hero, Huon. Then comes a sweeping tune in the violins associated with Huon's beloved, Reiza. Now we are ready for the development, warning of the clash of true love and villainy that opera specializes in, and at length giving way to a happy recapitulation emphasizing the reaching grandness of Reiza's tune.

FRANZ SCHUBERT 1797–1828

Schubert was a natural. His melodic well had no bottom. Where other composers might play with a first-rate melody—develop it—Schubert would just as soon top it with another: his supply was limitless. Not the founding father but certainly the first great master of the song as art form, he worked in all types of music, leaving in his horribly short life—shorter than Mozart's, even—a bequest of sheer melody unrivaled by any other.

A natural gift has its drawbacks. When the tunes come so easily, one might get lazy about developing and structuring them. One can't build a symphony out of mere tunes. Some critics would give Schubert all the credit in the world for "inventing" the *Lied* (art song, of high textual and dramatic quality) and praise his chamber music, yet patronize his symphonies. Charming, they tell us—but lightweight. They will except the two movements of the "Unfinished" Symphony (no. 8) and no. 9: because they have to—these are masterpieces. But they like to think of Schubert as a hasty primitive, making up in melody what he lacks in technical expertise.

In fact, Schubert *was* hasty. He was too full of song to organize through sketches and trial runs, too fearful, perhaps, of locking inspiration in the cage marked Careful Planning. But he was no primitive. Organization may belong as much to instinct as to forethought, and no slapdash tunesmith lucks into a Ninth Symphony as brilliantly conceived as Schubert's.

Indeed, Schubert wrote symphonies of melody more than of drama; they owe more to Haydn and Mozart than to Beethoven, though in his Ninth Schubert turned radical, using Beethoven's expansive format and his own melodic gift to create a dramatic-lyric hybrid form unique in the repertory. Stendahl said of him, "He lived, he suffered, he died." One could say as much of many another. But he was a natural, and that is rare. He couldn't be bothered to keep track of his output, so there are few opus numbers to guide us; instead we use the "D" number, named for Otto Deutsch, who catalogued Schubert's oeuvre.

Symphony no. 1 in D Major, D. 82 1813

An amazing work for a sixteen-year-old, but then, like Mozart and Mendelssohn, Schubert was a prodigy. Tradition looks over his shoulder in the zesty tutorial of Haydn and Mozart, but the youngster is no slavish imitator: note that the slow introduction to the first movement turns up later in the movement, just before the recapitulation, retaining its gravity even at the faster tempo. The slow [second] and minuet [third] movements are more conventional, but the finale [fourth mvt] has a bright vitality that is very Schubertian.

Symphony no. 2 in B Flat Major, D. 125 1814

One feels the influence of Mozart here, though the first movement extends sonata-allegro form to great reaches of development in the manner of Beethoven. The delicate second [slow] movement is especially Mozartean—a theme, five variations, and coda such as Mozart often used, and with the older composer's habit of sticking close to the outline of the theme as he varies it. The third movement, too, is more like Mozart's minuet than like Beethoven's raucous scherzo, and the finale [fourth mvt] is one of those deft sonata-rondos, in a light vein, that the Classical symphonists preferred and which Beethoven reinvented as an intense sonata-allegro finale.

Symphony no. 3 in D Major, D. 200 1815

As sunny as the sunniest Mozart, Schubert's Third might be good-natured to a fault, for it feels somehow less dramatic than it ought to be. For example, the first movement: we get the usual (in those days) weighty introduction, then the movement proper begins with a slightly Tyrolian-sounding first subject. Notice the very Schubertian transition to the second subject, a forceful orchestral statement culminating in a loud chord and a short silence—but notice how much the second theme (first heard on the oboe) sounds like the first.

Without the necessary contrast between the two themes, the all-important first movement loses some of its dramatic potential, as if it were a football game played by one team.

On the other hand, this understating ease may be just what Schubert is after. Small-scaled slow [second] and minuet [third] movements hearken to Haydn and Mozart's lighter symphonies, and not till the finale [fourth mvt] is there anything out of the ordinary—a tarantella, that tireless skipping Italian dance so useful for lively finales. The work dances itself out with scarcely a breath taken.

Symphony no. 4 in c minor, "Tragic," D. 417 1816

Why tragic? Schubert gave the work its subtitle himself, yet it's hard to find much tragedy here. Despite the minor key and some powerful moments in the two end movements—always the "heavy" components of the Classical symphony—the Fourth is no more tragic than any other of Schubert's early symphonies. The first movement opens with a slow introduction of importunate pathos, reaching a fierce climax with two whacks on the timpani—now, this does portend tragedy. And when the first movement proper gets going at a fast tempo, the tension is retained. But the slow [second] movement is the usual Schubertian slow movement, as lovely as any. No tragedy there. And the minuet [third mvt], though sporting a sharp outline in its odd accents, is the minuet one expects of Schubert in this period, still unprepared to take on the more animated scherzo developed by Beethoven to replace the minuet. And the minuet's trio (middle section) is as cute and waltzy as possible, right out of a Viennese dance hall. The finale [fourth mvt] returns us to the tragic tension, true. But notice how the c minor first subject that opened the movement comes back in affirmative C Major in the recapitulation. The resolution is not tragic, but triumphant.

Symphony no. 5 in B Flat Major, D. 485 1816

Once known as "the symphony without trumpets and drums" because of its small orchestration (clarinets are also omitted, an unusual touch for the day), Schubert's Fifth is a beautifully balanced work, not so much small as tightly structured. Still closer in spirit to Haydn and Mozart than to Beethoven, Schubert provides a momentary hush of introduction before launching his first movement—one of the most unportentous openings in all symphony. In fact, this is one of the great unportentous symphonies altogether, from movement to movement, even if the minuet [third mvt], in a minor key, starts out with a hint of the aggressive Beethovenian scherzo. But the crisp finale [fourth mvt] returns us to the Classical Schubert of the keen proportions, never too much or too little and all for song. Hearing his symphonies in order, one begins to notice that his sense of sectional interplay is flawless. He can stretch an exposition or development to unusual lengths without losing interior propulsion, amplifying but never straining a movement's overall shape.

Symphony no. 6 in C Major, "Little C Major," D. 589 1818

An introduction somewhat Beethovenian in character (manic assertions of loud and soft surround a central idea) ushers in a first movement totally Schubertian in its velvety musical energy and lightness of touch. The second [slow] movement is likewise tenderly Schubertian, but the third retires the old minuet to adopt Beethoven's headstrong scherzo. Even the trio (the scherzo's middle section) shows a Beethovenian tension amidst the Schubertian spontaneity. Commentators argue the merits of the odd structure of the finale [fourth mvt], which amounts to a sort of idle rondo, but all do agree that in it Schubert was trying out a technique that he would perfect in the finale of his momentous Ninth Symphony, wherein the musical information is not melodic but rhythmic. Certainly this "little" finale feels right for this "little" symphony—called little so as to differentiate it from the Ninth, also in C Major but of far greater dimension.

Symphony no. 8 in b minor, "Unfinished," D. 759 1822

Why didn't Schubert finish the work? No one knows. Two movements and a third in shorthand tell us it would have been quite something, for the "Unfinished" explodes the fancy that "popular symphonies are simple symphonies." There is a certain simplicity in Schubert, but a deceptive one: that graceful, unstoppable melodic flow that sounds so spontaneous actually falls in with—obeys—an artist's scheme, an organizational imperative. What sounds more "natural" than the famous second subject of the first movement of the "Unfinished," the theme everybody thinks of when the "Unfinished" is mentioned? And it is "natural." Yet it is brilliantly developed to artistic (unnatural) ends as the movement proceeds.

A sad symphony, a minor-key symphony, the *Unfinished* opens in an atmosphere of Romantic self-dramatization, unlike the more "public" (i.e., Classical) introductions to Schubert's earlier symphonies, modeled on those of Haydn. A deep phrase in the lower strings draws us into personal realms, then nervous violin figures accompany the first theme, a keening of oboe and clarinet. The harmonic foundation brightens a bit from b minor to G Major, and we hear the second subject on the 'cellos, one of the best-known melodies in the Western world. All else in this movement stems from this first dualistic impression: sorrow balanced by beauty. The sorrow builds impressively in the development section (heralded by a long-held chord on the woodwinds over a portentous descending line of plucked strings, a dramatic transition as clearly marked as any king's entrance in a chronicle play). Impressively—what an incompetent image! There is no music in all symphony that finds the nobility in *feeling* as aptly as this. Notice how the recapitulation, though using themes in their original form even after the development has brought us more deeply into them, does not feel tautologous, so pure is their essence. The coda rounds it off perfectly by returning us to the opening music, dying away until three firm chords cut it short.

It is no different in the slow [second] movement; the melodies file by, each subtly related to the others, then return. Gradually the movement ebbs away. And what was to follow? Schubert sketched out a third movement but never scored it, so the music ends here, after two movements–two so finely developed images of tragic nobility that some musicologists have suggested that Schubert left the piece unfinished because it was finished as it was. Ridiculous. This would have been unthinkable in Schubert's day—symphonies just didn't consummate themselves in two movements. What about the scherzo and finale, to complete the statement launched in the first movement and extrapolated in the second? The work is, for all its sorrowful power and eloquence, unfinished.

Symphony no. 9 in C Major, "Great C Major," D. 944 1828

Called "the Great" to distinguish it from Schubert's other (and littler) C Major symphony, no. 6, this is one of the few really large symphonies of the early nineteenth century not by Beethoven. This was a time of transition, from the more contained statements of the Haydn-Mozart era into the grander exordium of Romanticism. Everything is bigger and more intense than before: the structure, the expression. Yet if Schubert did succumb to a Beethovenian heroic influence, note that unlike Beethoven he does not seem to be portraying anything in his music. It is heroic—but not about a hero.

From the first notes, we can tell that this is to be an extraordinary experience: two horns call us to attention, heralding a lengthy slow introduction in which their call is built on, built on, and built on. That is the essence of the work's architecture in every movement, and why it takes so long to play: Schubert uses the structure of symphony to its utmost through constant development of his melodic kernels. For once, the spendthrift melodist makes a few stingy themes accommodate an entire work, redefining them to make them last, tell, interconnect, and thus define. And he built one of the biggest symphonies of his century.

When the introduction gives way to the first movement proper, the tempo turns lively, but the time scheme broadens. A new listener will be hard put to tell when the exposition has ended and the development begun, so determined is the development of the themes even when they first appear. As if clearing the way for the huge symphonic tapestries of Bruckner and Mahler, Schubert extends his line as far—yet as tautly—as possible. Unperturbed by length, he provides a full recapitulation—and a reprise of the introduction—before moving on to the slow [second] movement.

The slow movement manages to convey the needed lyricism without losing the impetuosity of the first movement. Notice how the lower strings start the first theme, suddenly yielding to the oboe after a few seconds. From a minor key we move to the major in the middle section, then the minor returns. But the aggressive nature of the work is always felt—as in the stolid repetition of notes, a special feature of the piece.

In the third movements of his earlier symphonies, Schubert often held to the old minuet, but this third movement is a Beethovenian scherzo. The work is big, so the scherzo is burly, veering from the light touch to the smash. The trio (middle section) offers one of Schubert's longest-breathed tunes ever. The woodwinds take the melody, the brass and strings quietly pound out a rhythm—yes, a quiet pounding—and then we take the scherzo's main section from the top.

After all this, the composer is going to have to come up with something rather awesome to finish off this dynamic hulk of joy and belligerance. He does. C Major, our "home" key for the work, is pronounced straightaway and off we go—this is a whirlwind finale to make good all that was promised in the work's construction thus far. Here the sense of building sounds out of action rather than melody is most clearly felt. For long stretches, the rhythmic pattern set up in the first notes of the movement edges out any attempt at thematic development. (For their part in the second subject—announced by four repeated notes on the horn and clarinet—the strings must play a tiring figure endlessly under a tune in the woodwinds and brass; at a rehearsal for an early performance in London under Mendelssohn, the violinists burst into giggles and fury at that point. What nonsense, they thought—they should have heard what it sounds like from out in the audience, with the two parts together.) Grander even than the first movement, the finale at last comes home in a blaze of C Major, having exhausted the players, the imagination, and the memory of symphony as practiced by Schubert's inferiors. The fulfilling vastnesses of Romanticism have arrived.

Incidental Music from Rosamunde, D. 797 1823

Wilhelmine von Chézy's play *Rosamunde, Princess of Cyprus* seems by all accounts to have been as awful a concoction as Schubert's score of entr'actes and ballet music is wonderful. Von Chézy's plot is loaded with such devices as a royal heroine living among the people and a poisoned letter, but the overture doesn't attempt to suggest any of this because Schubert was trapped by his deadline and borrowed an overture left over from an earlier work. (As it happens, the borrowed overture came from his opera *Alfonso and Estrella,* but through an accident the so-called "Overture to *Rosamunde*"—the one we hear by that title today—belongs to another Schubert work, *The Magic Harp.)*

With Von Chézy's script forgotten, we can enjoy these ten *Rosamunde* pieces plus the *Magic Harp* overture as music for music's sake. The overture, like all overtures of its day in sonata-allegro ("first movement") form, starts with a slow introduction and soon turns lively for first and second themes. Try to notice a spot midway along in which the wind and string instruments play against each other with a hair-raisingly brusque lightness; it is one of the great novelties of orchestration of its time.

There is no routine set down as to which of the pieces gets played in concert—this is up to the conductor. Some play them all, some select. The overture, at least, is always heard, and one can also count on hearing the Ballet no. 2 in G Major, a heavenly parade of melodies delicately served. The ear feasts.

HECTOR BERLIOZ 1803–1869

With Berlioz more than with any other composer, symphony leaps the Classical precipice for the questing flight of Romanticism. Beethoven may be said to have prepared the takeoff with his experimental translation of purely musical ideas into programmatic images—a "heroic" symphony (no. 3—the "Eroica"—and no. 5), a "Pastoral" symphony (no. 6), and at last a symphony so in need of visual clarification that human voices and a text are required to "explain" it (no. 9). But all this was only by way of suggesting the Romantic symphony to come.

It came with Berlioz. He regarded himself as Beethoven's heir, yet had his eye less on Beethoven's sense of structure and more on Beethoven's programs. Suddenly, with Berlioz, we begin to lose the platonic ideal of music as sound. Now, music is meaning. No more symphonies, concertos, overtures per se: in Berlioz, everything has a title, sometimes even a story. His personal entailment on the viola concerto turns up as *Harold in Italy,* a rendering of Lord Byron's *Childe Harold.* His overtures, too, all bear titles even when written strictly for concert performance, and sometimes use music to suggest dramatic action, as when a drum roll in the *King Lear* Overture is meant to portray Lear's entrance into his council chamber. When Berlioz composes a symphony, it is not your common or garden Symphony no. 1 but a *Fantastic Symphony,* "an episode in the life of an artist," as the subtitle tells us, full of melancholy and terror, the favorite styles of the age. As the composer Paul Dukas put it, "With Berlioz, *everything*—symphony, oratorio, sacred music—becomes drama."

Romanticism, fully understood, needs a book of its own. But we can capture the essence of the movement in a survey of Berlioz' works. The contemporary of Hugo, Dumas père, Saint-Beuve, de Nerval, and de Vigny, Berlioz spoke for his generation in conceiving symphony as "instrumental drama." He was always willing to transform a literary property into music, especially a certified Romantic source from such as Goethe *(Faust),* Sir Walter Scott *(Waverley, Rob Roy),* James Fenimore Cooper *(The Red Rover),* or Shakespeare, the composer's favorite *(Romeo and Juliet, King Lear, Much Ado About Nothing, The Tempest).* Like his colleagues elsewhere in the 1800s—Mendelssohn, say, or Schumann or Dvořák—he sought an inner unity for the largest forms by carrying themes over from one movement to the next, or by varying a central theme into several subsidiary themes. But unlike them, he just didn't care to write a concerto and call it a day. No: his concertos have plot lines and, therefore, titles. Music is meaning.

Plus romantique que le romantisme, too romantic even for a romantic period in high gear, Berlioz suffered terrific ups and downs throughout his life; not till the 1960s was he granted full international recognition as one of music's great revolutionaries. Most frustrating to him was his failure to raise popular taste to his own enthralled level. A composer who loves a good story is naturally attracted to opera, and Berlioz saw his really quite brilliant operas continually rejected either by impresarios or, when performed, by audiences. The only reason that anything by Berlioz ever got done at all was his fanatic militancy and endless pushy insistence. Wildly innovative, this was "difficult" music; the man, too, was hard to like. In her superb biography of Franz Liszt, Eleanor Perényi lays her pen on the Berlioz problem:

> With his eagle's countenance and his hedge of hair he looked like a French-speaking bird of prey and was every bit as daunting as he looked. It took nerve to make friends with him, and more still to hang on. He combined intellect with bad judgment, wit with irrationality to a staggering degree and was unusually disaster-prone. Let everything hang on the fate of a certain concert and the heavens opened. . . . His love-life is summed up in the grimly comic heading to the forty-fifth chapter of his autobiography: I AM INTRODUCED TO MISS SMITHSON—SHE IS RUINED—BREAKS HER LEG—I MARRY HER.

Miss Smithson, the inspiration for the unnamed love object of the *Fantastic Symphony,* brings us to another Berlioz' past-times—passion—past-time as well of the era, along with melancholy and terror. It was like Berlioz to develop a fetish for Smithson, an Irish actress he saw as Ophelia in the famous Charles Kemble production of *Hamlet,* which revealed Shakespeare in a "new" guise as the precursor of Romantic melancholy, terror, and passion. Not having met Smithson except across the footlights, Berlioz went on a personal rampage of idolatry, finally trying to exorcise the delicious demon by writing her into his *Fantastic Symphony* as an *idée fixe,* a motto theme that occurs in all five movements, grotesquely transformed in the last into a hag at a witches' ball. But even this was not enough; in the end, he married her.

Lest we take the amusing extremism of Berlioz too far, remember that he is one of the geniuses of music, an extraordinary transitional figure whose work, once the transition is made, does not vanish forever, his role over, but retains and even grows in vigor. His abilities as orchestrator still amaze. Unlike the piano- or violin-virtuoso composer of his era (like Liszt or Paganini), he played no instrument but mastered them all to learn what effects lay undetected in them—what stories they might tell. The full orchestra alone intrigued him—he left no chamber music, no piano studies, no violin sonatas. As scorer, he reminds one of Rimsky-Korsakof, for both wrote classic treatises on orchestration. But Rimsky is bright, neat, glittering; Berlioz is audacious, bizarre.

This, too, may be taken too far. When art demanded it, Berlioz was reasonable. His operatic masterpiece, *The Trojans,* a huge gleaning from Virgil (plus one excerpt snatched from the mesmerizing Shakespeare), manages even amidst some melancholy, terror, and passion to meet Classical art on its own terrain and terms. Disdained by the trivial society of the Second Empire, *The Trojans* finally got itself discovered in recent years and is now regarded as one of the most awesome experiences at the disposal of the lyric stage.

It would be shattering to think of the neglect that Berlioz suffered were it not that his character seemed to invite and perhaps even thrive on it. Far more shattering is the realization that even today not everyone can appreciate him. You will still read some idiot's much-quoted assertion that Berlioz had "genius but no talent"—i.e., long vision but faulty craftsmanship. Rubbish! He does have an odd sound to him—angular, shrill, nervous—but this is largely the idiosyncrasy of personal expression, not a failure to subdue idiosyncrasy. As a romantic, Berlioz would be autobiographical in art—that's he in Italy, not Harold; he the artist whose "episode" provides the gist of the *Fantastic Symphony;* he damned as Faust, praised as Benvenuto Cellini, crushed as Lear: episodes in the life of an artist.

Symphonie Fantastique (Fantastic Symphony), op. 14 1830

Fantastic is right! Subtitled "An episode in the life of an artist," the work takes in an elaborate program, involving the lovesick drug trip of a "young musician of morbidly sensitive character." Hoping to O.D. on opium, he instead merely dreams—five dreams, five symphonic movements—and in each, he at some point recalls or encounters the woman who drove him to attempt suicide.

First of all, don't try to fit Berlioz' logistical plan into the standard four-movement layout of the Classical symphony, still the preferred form when the *Symphonie Fantastique* was written. Here is Berlioz' plan:

1st mvt: introduction and standard sonata-allegro form
2nd mvt: a waltz
3rd mvt: slow movement
4th mvt: scherzo
5th mvt: rondo finale used as a second scherzo

So far, it's not all that unusual. However, Berlioz' detailed narration amounts to making this the first completely programmatic symphony. Never before did a composer so fully put his musical art at the service of an extra-musical narrative. Here is the story, with Berlioz' titles:

1st mvt:
Reveries. Passions. In his narcotic coma, the hero writhes and moans, envisions his Beloved, and dreams of his obsessive *amour.*

2nd mvt:
A Ball. At a brilliant soirée, he sees his Beloved.

3rd mvt:
Scene in the Country. Two shepherds pipe away (English horn and oboe). He longs. She appears. Is she false or true to him? One of the shepherds reprises the pastoral call (English horn again); the other does not answer. Sunset. Loneliness.

4th mvt:
March to the Gallows. The dream turns nightmarish. He has murdered her and is being led to the scaffold. He thinks of her—and the axe falls.

5th mvt:
Dream of a Witches' Sabbath. At a goblins' revel, the Beloved appears in the form of a hag and joins the orgy. A bell tolls for the dead, heralding a Dies Irae. The witches dance. The Dies Irae and the dance compete.

Now that, for 1830, was revolutionary.

To follow the central action of the Beloved's manifestations, one should take note of the symphony's motto theme, the *idée fixe* (as it is known), for by this tune Berlioz characterizes his Beloved. Generally associated with the woodwinds and strings, it first appears after the long slow introduction to the first movement, just as the main *Allegro* (lively) gets going:

The *idée fixe* changes slightly at each appearance, especially in the last movement, when the Beloved, so graceful and inspiring earlier, shows up as a crone at the witches' sabbath. Now she prances grotesquely on the clarinet:

Another cute effect is heard in the last movement: Berlioz cuts off the grotesquerie of the goblin party with the tolling of bells, then introduces on bassoon and tuba the menacing Dies Irae (a medieval plainsong melody foretelling the Day of Judgment, often used by composers). He follows this with a frenzied dance of witches, then—tremendously exciting!—he plays both at once, a typical Berliozian touch. It's quite a finale.

Not only is this the first program symphony; it is also one of the few symphonies to claim a sequel, *Lélio; or, The Return to Life* (those interested may find it directly following). The Beloved, by the way, was Harriet Smithson, a gorgeous but not much gifted actress whom Berlioz saw as Ophelia, adored from afar, and attempted to dislodge from his consciousness in this extravagant shriving. It didn't work; so he married her.

Lélio; or, The Return to Life, op. 14b 1832

With its windy narrator, three vocal soloists, and chorus, *Lélio* has no place in a book limited to orchestral music. But as the sequel to the *Fantastic Symphony* it deserves a mention, if only to whet the curiosity of new Berlioz buffs.

Lélio covers the spiritual cold turkey of the "young musician of morbidly sensitive character" who dreamed the adventures outlined in the preceding work. Awake now and still trying to free himself of the Beloved's power over him, he soliloquizes in between musical "acts"—a nostalgic song, a daydream of the bandit's life, a rehearsal of his Fantasy on Shakespeare's *The Tempest.* Ultimately, however, he remains haunted by memory of the Beloved.

Berlioz planned *Lélio* to follow the *Symphonie Fantastique* in performance, thus making up a full evening's entertainment (it almost never happens: *Lélio* is too difficult—and unpopular—to mount). He had another purpose in mind: the six musical numbers in *Lélio* had been written earlier and ignored—now, a remaindered miscellany, they might succeed the second time around. Are they worth hearing? Yes, especially the *Tempest* fantasy, an imaginative piece for chorus and orchestra (sung in Italian, and thus emphasizing *Lélio*'s heterogeneous derivation). Those who love the *Symphonie Fantastique* will recognize the *idée fixe* (the motto theme portraying the Beloved), played near the start and at the very end of *Lélio* on the first violins.

Harold in Italy, op. 16 1834

The violin virtuoso Niccolò Paganini asked Berlioz to write him something to show off a Stradivarius viola that he had laid hold of; obviously, he had a dazzling concerto in mind. Berlioz, however, wrote not a concerto but a symphony with an understated solo line for viola. Finding his part "too full of rests," Paganini begged off. Later, he was to hear the piece and be *very* impressed—but, V.I.P. to the core, he never played it.

Not only Paganini but Lord Byron, too, inspired this work, the Englishman through the fascination of his picaresque romantic hero, Childe Harold. This is not a direct "adaptation" of Byron—the indispensable commentator Donald Francis Tovey spoke of Berlioz' "encyclopaedic inattention" to the original. Instead, Berlioz invokes the romantic's fascination with wild, natural Italy, melding it with recollections of his own visits there and a generalized portrayal of the Byronic avatar. As with the *Symphonie Fantastique,* there is an *idée fixe,* a motto theme appearing in all four movements, invariably the property of the viola solo and first heard in the slow introduction to the first movement, accompanied by the harp.

One can see why the flamboyant Paganini distrusted the viola part; its charisma—so subtle, dreamy, sensitive—lacks what he would have called star quality. But for Berlioz' purposes it works beautifully, relating the loose program in each movement to the central idea of Harold's reflections. The first movement presents Harold in the mountains, the second [slow] movement a pilgrims' march, the third [scherzo] a mountaineer's piping serenade of his mistress, the fourth an orgy of brigands. Harold's motto theme is heard in all four.

As Paganini's disdain tells us, this is no concerto despite the prominent (but not showy) viola part. As a symphony, it reminds us of Berlioz' stated intention of carrying on where Beethoven left off, for the last movement begins with a structural device introduced by Beethoven in his Ninth Symphony. Just as Beethoven launched his finale with quotations from each of the first three movements, Berlioz unifies his conception of Harold's tour by interspersing the brigands' orgy music with quotations of themes heard earlier—the introduction to the first movement, then the pilgrims' march, the serenade, the main theme of the first movement, and at last the first notes of Harold's motto. The orgy now takes over; Harold is silent, disapproving. (Paganini, too, disapproved. His viola would top an orgy any day, with scales, cadenza, and tricks. But that wouldn't have suited the narrative.) Not till the final pages of the work, at a last appearance of the pilgrims' march, does the mournful viola comment—and a closing orgiastic eruption silences it for good.

Excerpts from The Damnation of Faust 1829; revised 1846

Concerts tend to program (in varying order) three orchestral numbers from Berlioz' "dramatic legend" after Goethe, each of the three a witness to the composer's insane flair for orchestration. A conflation of the separate functions of opera, oratorio, and ballet, *La Damnation de Faust* in its complete form concentrates on the questing Faust, the woman he loves, and the devil with whom he bargains, but the three snippets cited here have little to do with plot or character. This is why they are so enjoyable out of context. The "Dance of the Sylphs" offers a waltz as airy as a ballerina's ghost. So light and wraithlike is it that Saint-Saëns borrowed it—rescored for double-bass and transformed by comic irony—to characterize the elephant in his *Carnival of Animals.*

The "Minuet of the Will-o'-the-Wisps" stars the woodwinds in another of Berlioz' ingenious colorations, this one less airy than saucy. His choice of the minuet for this dance comes off as a bit of antiquing, since the minuet was just about dying out as a vital form at the time.

The "Hungarian March" is a real corker, Berlioz' arrangement of a traditional Hungarian tune in the form of a nationalistic battle cry. Heard very early in *The Damnation of Faust,* it is played last in concert because, really, what could possibly follow this?

Excerpts from Romeo and Juliet 1839

Shakespeare was one of Berlioz' passions, the "dramatic symphony" another; here they fuse as a huge fresco of orchestral, solo vocal, and choral romance. The story is familiar, and taking in original order the three pieces pulled from the whole for concert performance (orchestra alone, no voices), we may follow The Meeting, The Balcony Scene, and Mercutio's salute to Queen Mab, "the fairies' midwife," who "gallops night by night through lovers' brains, and then they dream of love." All the music below, in short, is devoted to the adolescent love story at the heart of the play.

The Meeting is outlined in "Romeo Alone—His Sadness—Concert and Ball—A Great Fête at Capulet's House." Romeo's surging melancholy, Juliet's innocence, and the sounds of the party provide the three musical ideas, each identified by Berlioz' orchestral characterization—Romeo all yearning strings, Juliet a solo oboe, the party a rampaging *tutti* (full orchestra). At the height of it all, Berlioz achieves a magnificent effect by playing Juliet's theme against the party noises, as if picturing Romeo in his mask surrounded by a swirl of merrymaking but seeing only Juliet: The Meeting.

The famous Balcony Scene, entitled "Love Scene," acts as a kind of slow movement, and depends less on Shakespeare than do the other two excerpts. Don't listen for evocations of "A rose by any other name" or "Parting is such sweet sorrow." This is Berlioz' personal reading of the situation.

Mercutio's Queen Mab speech turns up twice in Berlioz' *Roméo et Juliette.* Early on, a tenor sings it; later, as the "Queen Mab Scherzo" (the present number), it becomes a full-fledged symphonic movement, comparable to Mendelssohn's *A Midsummer Night's Dream* music in suggesting the fleet cunning of the fairy kingdom. Berlioz' instrumental touches are too many to single out; listen as you might for a leprechaun, with an agile ear.

Royal Hunt and Storm from The Trojans 1859

This danced intermezzo from Berlioz's vast opera on the *Aeneid* opens with evocations of the green world, a "virgin forest" at dawn with strings humming and woodwinds rustling. Then the hunt: horn fanfares, the chase, and an interfering storm, the natural world in upheaval. Eventually, things quiet down and a certain purity returns. The horns are heard briefly, heading homewards. Peace.

The Corsair Overture, op. 21 1844; revised 1852

Oddly, the model for this piece is not Byron's poem *The Corsair* (as is often thought), but James Fenimore Cooper's novel, *The Red Rover.* It doesn't much matter either way, though, as this is absolute music, not a rendering. Berlioz was too much of a dramatist not to give his overture a title, but this is generalized Romantic crise—melancholy, terror, and passion (as cited in this chapter's introduction). The melancholy here leans to a peaceful idealism and the terror to fiery action; the passion, however, blazes away as ever. The ear will be caught first by a beautiful slow introduction, after which the pirate's life is treated to a nicely varied sonata-allegro movement, much friendlier than the title would suggest.

The Roman Carnival Overture, op. 9 1844

A tricky piece for the players. When composers such as Berlioz wrote, they set standards for orchestral togetherness and solo brilliance that many orchestras of the day could not meet. Nowadays, playing is on a much higher level (though *The Roman Carnival* still brings out a clinker here and there from the best groups). This glittering, chatterbox festival was composed to open the second act of Berlioz' opera, *Benvenuto Cellini.* It begins with a hint of the coming carnival, then lapses into an extended slow section (using music sung as a love duet in Act I of the opera, here assigned to the English horn). Only after this does the carnival prevail—but notice how the beckoning whoop-de-do first sneaks in under the slow love music. Who can resist the *ping!* of the triangle? Love can—the lovers' duet soars away unmindful of the insistent carnival noises playing right along with it—a delicious, very Berliozian moment. Soon, the lovers cede to the fun, and the overture expands itself in all directions to live up to its title.

Waverley Overture, op. 26 c. 1827

"Dreams of love and Lady's charms
Give place to honour and to arms"

is the epigraph found in the score; it decodes the composer's musical message with an economy all analysts should envy. The words belong to Walter Scott, author of the novel *Waverley.* So: an overture on the gallant life and its priorities. Dreams of love are heard first, probed by the 'cellos; these give place, as Scott directs, to honour and arms. Oddly, there is no hint of Scotch atmosphere (for which the novel was famous at the time). In fact, the unmistakable savor of Italy guides the tone, not least in the Rossini-like lightness of the scoring and the "Rossini crescendo" (the same tune played over and over in a steady rhythm, louder each time) that Berlioz adopts in the coda (tail-end).

King Lear Overture, op. 4 1831

There is a trap in pictorial music: one might get so rapt looking for the pictures that he will forget to hear any music. True, there are some precisely turned images to be found—there are such in this very piece—but one is not expected to hear everything that a composer puts into a work. One may not, after all, hear the work *his* way at all. Do I hear Cordelia on the oboe? Is that stirring Goneril and Regan at plot, or poor, blind Gloucester? Don't ask. Let the music happen.

In other words, regard the *King Lear* overture as a loosely scoped realization of tragedy. It suits the work: it sounds "Shakespearean." Opening with a bold recitation on the lower strings, *King Lear* asserts a portentous self-importance somewhat mitigated by a pliant theme on the oboe accompanied by plucked strings. This opens up beautifully on trombones and horns over soaring strings, but the lower strings intrude with their recitation and the tempo changes. The foregoing, it seems, has been just so much introduction, and now comes the meat of the movement, an *Allegro disperato ed agitato assai* (lively, but rather desperate and agitated) in sonata-allegro form. It takes some time to work up to real desperation; still, one senses, if not the vastness of tragic futility, the struggle of a human will. In the development section, the agitation rips at the main themes, and the recapitulation—when a Classicist might have put things to rights with full repetition—is interrupted by the recitation from the introduction, reflecting a Romantic's need to subvert form with dramatic urgency. An agitated coda winds things up—note the tiny menace of the recitation one last time just before the final chord.

Overture to Benvenuto Cellini, op. 23 1837

Berlioz identified a great deal with the "characters" in his music, and the innovative sculptor, musician, and goldsmith Benvenuto Cellini in the opera of that name suits the composer: the work is replete with bohemian elan. Now, the question is, how was Berlioz to anticipate a whole opera's worth of riotous artistic quest in an overture?—for that is what an overture does: express in one sonata-allegro movement the essential quality of the coming entertainment. How? In a tumult, for the most part. A whirling dervish opening limns Cellini's iconoclastic temperament, but only briefly. In a typical Berliozian trick, the movement halts just as it has begun, ceding to a slow introduction. Not till this has had its say does the opening theme return to carry on. As impetuous as Cellini in the opera, so is this music, one of Berlioz' most popular works. Toward the end, the "Cellini" theme—the first subject—is played against a theme from the introduction (another of Berlioz' habitual touches), *tutti fortissimo* (full orchestra, as loud as it can blow, bow, or pound).

Overture to Les Francs-Juges (The Secret Court), op. 3 c. 1827

Composed for an opera that was never completed, this overture opens with a slow introduction. (Haydn's influence on the basic sonata-allegro movement was considerable, but notice how much more dramatic—fiercely so—is this slow introduction than any by Haydn. Here the rhetoric owes more to Beethoven, Berlioz' personal favorite among his predecessors.) With much alternation of loud and soft and with bold recitations on the brass instruments, the introduction prepares for an atmosphere of conflict, fully borne out when the tempo speeds up and the movement proper gets going. Villainy menaces purity—this is pretty much what the opera would have dealt with. The former intrigues in the busy first theme; the latter resists with its cool, upright second theme, which caps the movement heroically after a fraught development section. It's a youthful work (note the opus number), but not immature—especially with such piquant details of instrumentation as abound within.

Overture to Béatrice et Bénédict 1862

Berlioz' opera, adapted from Shakespeare's *Much Ado About Nothing,* carries over much of the original's testy frolic; likewise the overture, a trim potpourri of tunes from the show, sets up the evening with caprice and dash, opposing a flirtatious first theme to a lyrical second theme. As all symphony is confrontation and repetition, so goes the overture, as surefire in the concert hall as in the theatre.

FELIX MENDELSSOHN 1809–1847

It is often said that there is in all the world of music no more astounding exhibit of precocious genius—not even in the prodigious infant Mozart—than in the seventeen-year-old Felix Mendelssohn's composition of the Overture to *A Midsummer Night's Dream,* not only for its mastery of form, but for its originality as well. Noted less often, however, is the boy Mendelssohn's deft synthesis of the disparate elements of Shakespeare's comedy—mortal lovers, fairies, and *hoi polloi* bedeviled by the "truth" of transformation in the enchanted wood. So remarkable is this early work that it equals anything else that the composer wrote the rest of his days.

And that, in itself, poses a problem for Mendelssohn's admirers, for this most fortunate and engaging life shows little of the upward mobility of the more imposing (and, perhaps significantly, less fortunate) composers. No Beethovenian struggle against the sports of the gods here, no chaotic emotional deluge such as continually threatened to drown Hector Berlioz, no Wagnerian obsession with the dark passages of human love. Whether because he had it easy, as they say, or because he lacked the grasping hunger of temperament, Mendelssohn somehow never rose above and past his early brilliance (though he seldom fell below it, either). Even his greatest works amount to a protraction of the youthful gift that at first seemed to announce the next titan.

Mendelssohn did, it is true, have the ostensible advantages. Born to a wealthy and cultivated family, grandson of the famed philosopher Moses Mendelssohn, young Felix came into all the luxury of art and science that early-nineteenth-century, upper-middle-class German breeding could offer. (Pity the senior Mendelssohn, a mere banker, plunked down between two creative generations: "I used to be the son of my father," he once observed, "and now I'm the father of my son.") With such a background, with travel to fire the imagination and position to open the Right Doors—with the freedom to *become*—Felix had the chance to mine his resources, and in truth he did, though he often felt that he was becoming too much a performer of others' music and not enough a writer of his own. In his day he carried a vigorous reputation in European music, as composer, conductor, pianist, pedagogue, and impresario in the revival of interest in the works of the until-then largely forgotten Johann Sebastian Bach.

Mendelssohn's career occurred in the transitional period between Classicism and Romanticism, when the architectural clarity and rationalism of the former was giving way to the egocentricity, complex forms, and "dissolute" harmonies of the latter. The Classicists had founded the symphony, a pure form, absolute music—but Romantic Berlioz could only write a "Fantastic Symphony" or symphonies that were part opera, and Liszt, too, put stories in his music.

Mendelssohn would have none of it. He regarded himself as heir to the past, heir especially to J. S. Bach and the discipline implicit in Bach's musical structures. Compared to Bach, the romantics were self-indulgent renegades. How did Mendelssohn put it? "One ought to wash one's hands after touching Berlioz' scores." This opposition to the avant garde of his day has made it easy for certain writers to promulgate the legend that Mendelssohn constituted a smug and sentimental deadweight to symphonic development. But, indeed, he had much to offer his coevals in the matter of experimentation. To pick one major instance, Mendelssohn in his concertos did away with the traditional double exposition of the first movement, in which first the orchestra and only secondly the soloist each introduced the same set of main themes, thus saying one thing, more or less, twice. Mendelssohn cut right to the soloist, thus virtually reinventing the all-important first movement of the concerto principle.

Classicist that he was, Mendelssohn still reveals a slight Romantic overlay in his style. In structure he is largely Classicist. But in subject matter, Mendelssohn shares with the Romantics a fascination for the wilder outback of the natural world (as in the "Hebrides" Overture, devoted to the savage geography of the Scotch frontier) and an attraction for program music, however slight the context. (There is, for example, an undebatable Scotch flavor to at least one movement of his "Scotch" Symphony, but no overall point of view.) Moreover, there is that Overture to *A Midsummer Night's Dream,* inspired by a reading of one of the most romantic plays in literature and written to jibe with the moods of the original. It is wrong to harp on this one piece, but unavoidably one returns to it. It stands as a hallmark of sound dramatic structure, balanced, complete—this much is Classicism. But its program is pure Romanticism. Berlioz, too, loved his Shakespeare and set him to music. Perhaps the Romantic and the Classicist had more in common than Mendelssohn knew.

Symphony no. 3 in a minor, "Scotch," op. 56 1842

A visit in 1829 to Holyrood Castle in Edinburgh "where Queen Mary lived and loved" gave Mendelssohn the idea for the wan first theme of the work, though he was not to write the rest of it until some years later. It was he who devised its unofficial subtitle, but, as with Beethoven's "Pastoral" Symphony [no. 6], the intent is a general impression of Scotland and there is no program as such.

Following in Beethoven's shadow, Mendelssohn put the scherzo in second position, ahead of the slow movement; this provides the one palpable moment of more-or-less-authentic *doch-an-dorrach,* in the vivacious bagpipe-like clarinet theme that opens the movement, though Mendelssohn did pass up the chance to set it over the droning bass of true Scotch pastiche. It is the savage finale that has kept people guessing—is it a gathering of the clans for a highland wapentake? A wild ride to battle? Writers have exerted themselves trying to coordinate this fourth movement with some coherent program—none convincingly, as Mendelssohn intended none, and the stirring but slightly underpowered coda (tail-end) is German symphony, not

Scotch, at its purest, bringing the work home from its sad little commencement in a minor to a stolid A Major.

This suddenly homiletic coda shows us Mendelssohn at his most Victorian—a little too glibly Tennysonian, the elated grandee of the "Prom" concerts—but all that precedes these final moments shows us the Mendelssohn who deserved utterly the respect that was his in his day for craftsmanship, invention, inspiration. Not the last bars of the symphony but the first capture us: Scotch or not, the opening theme sets the scene for a curiously martial work, curiously because only in the finale [fourth mvt] does main force as such really urge itself upon us. The first movement is moody, true—now sullen, now tender—but the bubbly scherzo [second mvt] and the partly gentle, partly dire slow [third] movement either dispell or compromise the dourer qualities of the opening. What *is* the work, then? It is neither lyrical nor martial, but both—its drama is the conflict of the two (as so many symphonic conflicts are), the dark side of romance. Perhaps we would feel more convinced had Mendelssohn not closed the whole with that Victorian coda. But then, here as everywhere, the composer is the only authority on how his music ought to go.

In a way, the coda to the "Scotch" is like Mendelssohn's final years, as nobly spent as anything that had preceded them yet disappointing for not being more noble, for not somehow consummating the nobility in a blaze of communication to tally the whole at a sweep as the spire tops the cathedral. On an up note, the last word on the exact location of the Scotch's last movement is supplied by Robert Schumann. *He* thought it sounded Italian.

Symphony no. 4 in A Major, "Italian," op. 90 1831

As a trip to Scotland evoked a "Scotch" symphony [no. 3] of the impressionable Mendelssohn, so did Italy inspire an "Italian," a more lithe and outgoing piece than its northern brother—and, for that matter, more readily accomplished, as the "Italian" was finished scant months after the trip, while the "Scotch" simmered in the composer's mind, after the initial idea for its opening theme was jotted down, for thirteen years.

Though the "Italian" precedes the "Scotch" chronologically, it is numbered after it for having been published later: Mendelssohn withheld it from the printer in his lifetime because of some dissatisfaction with the last movement. As it happens, it is this finale that promotes what little ethnic program the work has to offer. The "Scotch" symphony tendered a bagpipe tune; the "Italian" gives us a saltarello (a breathless Roman dance akin to the tarantella). What it was that so disappointed Mendelssohn about this movement has never been explained, for it is a fine piece of work, the jumpy themes developed in counterpoint—that is, with two or more independent orchestral voices played at the same time.

A generally sunny work, the "Italian" offers less dramatic contrast than most symphonies, poised as they are on the fulcrum between the forceful and the pliant. Leaping headlong into a first theme, the "Italian" 's first movement is all light and air—a dance—and while the second [slow] movement pauses for a processionallike dolefulness, the third movement recalls the minuet and trio of Haydn at his happiest—another dance—and the fourth movement wraps it all up with the dizzy saltarello, most dancy yet. An amusing coda seems aimed at fading out, but at the last moment a *tutti* (the whole orchestra) gives us a big bang, and so joyful is this . . . what, Roman carnival, perhaps? . . . that one has scarcely notices that the joy has been pitched in a minor key.

Symphony no. 5 in d minor, "Reformation," op. 107 1830

Actually Mendelssohn's second symphony in order of composition (but published and therefore numbered last), the "Reformation" like the "Scotch" [no. 3] and "Italian" [no. 4] aims only to suggest its subject, not to portray it. It is not a favored repertory item, possibly because it is laid out with the expected "big" outer movements but with two rather underpowered middle movements, and thus feels unbalanced: the drama in movements one and four overshadows the forbearance of movements two and three.

Certainly the "Reformation" has atmosphere. The first movement is as militant and ungiving as an army in a holy war, and further proves the overall program by quoting the so-called "Dresden" Amen. Similarly, the Finale [fourth mvt] is dominated by Martin Luther's "A Mighty Fortress Is Our God." (The Dresden Amen, which dates from the eighteenth century, has no connection with the Reformation, as does "A Mighty Fortress"—a kind of theme song for Protestant dissent—but it lends a nice ecclesiastical touch. Wagner used it prominently in his opera *Parsifal,* which couldn't have less to do with the Reformation if it tried.)

The middle movements make their points more gently, in a scherzoish *Allegro vivace* (vivaciously lively) [second mvt] and a tiny slow [third] movement, more like a song among the first violins than a real symphonic movement. Mendelssohn uses this *Andante* for dramatic emphasis by quoting, climactically, the second subject of the first movement, as if to subdue the holy war with a plea for peace.

Piano Concerto no. 1 in g minor, op. 25 1831

One perceives here some awareness of the changeover in era from Classicism to Romanticism in Mendelssohn's anticipation of the Romantic's cyclic unity: the three movements are joined at the edges rather than separated by pauses, and themes from the first movement are reprised in the last. Note the "sudden" opening of the now-fiery now-lyrical first movement, with the piano leaping in a scant moment later. The slow [second] movement clears the air with gentle melody of the kind that was so popular in the Victorian era and which tends to embarrass our hard-edged, heartless modern critics. But no one should resist the finale [third mvt], which starts out turbulent but soon turns merely vivacious.

Violin Concerto in e minor, op. 64 1844

Never before in a violin concerto had the soloist made his first entry before the orchestra had outlined the themes, but here the soloist soars right in with the first subject after a few seconds of hushed orchestral tension and goes on to dominate the concerto as a hero dominates his epic, albeit loving more than fighting.

First movement, passionate; second, tender; third, chipper: this is the mode of the piece, one of the best loved in the repertory—highly *violin,* as one might say, especially in the main theme of the last movement, one of those zippy, flexible melodies that dart up and down the scale in diction that simply wouldn't work on any other instrument. A counterstating second theme by the orchestra actually borrows a bit of the soloist's theme, emphasizing the collaborative atmosphere in which the concerto must function. Yet the soloist runs the show, and this is as it must be in this place and time, Mendelssohn in the high youth of the Romantic era.

One has only to consider the violin concertos of, say, Mozart in the light of this later one by Mendelssohn to realize how much more the form was streamlining its *tutti* (orchestra only) passages and featuring the soloist—how the principle of Classical balance and discrete structuring was turning into Romantic competition and cohesion. Note that the final chord of the first movement does not actually finish it—for the bassoon holds one note of the chord, the flute and strings join it, and suddenly the slow movement has begun without the first movement's ever quite having ended.

Incidental Music to A Midsummer Night's Dream, op. 21;61 1826;1843

"Those are gnats, not elves," cried Wagner of Mendelssohn's Shakespearean fairy music. "Look at [Carl Maria von] Weber's [opera] *Oberon;* there you will discover the fairies." Wrong. Mendelssohn was every bit as successful as his predecessor Weber in assessing the fleet, fey spell of the Other World, and the wonder of it is that his overture, written for its own sake when Mendelssohn was seventeen, is perfectly matched in style and tone with the songs, dances, and interludes that he wrote for a production in Berlin seventeen years later. But then, Mendelssohn's genius did not so much develop as materialize, fully fashioned, in youth.

This is sharply delineated music. With Grieg's *Peer Gynt* score, it stands as a rare example of background accompaniment for a spoken text that not only outlasts a few early productions but becomes associated with the play to the point of symbiosis. True, the inflationary economics of today's theatre militate against the use of a symphonic cohort in the pit; tape, a fluty quintet, or no music at all are the alternatives open to modern producers. Yet Mendelssohn hit on so apposite a context for Shakespeare's comedy that performances of the play are bound to be haunted by the music even when it isn't used. Was ever elsewhere in music as much made of less than in Mendelssohn's famous four woodwind chords which launch the Overture and cap the play's finale?: two flutes first, then the clarinets added, then the bassoons join them, and at last the oboe and horns, too, all singing the cool green shimmer of the forest. Gnats? Nonsense. "Lovers to bed, 'tis almost fairy time."

Mendelssohn wrote about fifteen numbers for the play, including two sumptuous songs, for "Ye spotted snakes" and "Through the house give glimmering light," but concerts invariably program five non-vocal selections. The Overture, in sonata-allegro form, introduces—all in its exposition—the fairy sodality (a tiny hubbub of strings) as its first subject, Theseus' court (hunting horns) as a transitional theme, the young lovers as a second subject, and the roughhewn amateur actors as a closing theme with the unmistakable braying of Bottom "translated" into a donkey. The chortling Scherzo brings Puck forward in the "person" of two flutes (note the agile flute solo towards the end), and the Intermezzo follows Act II and Hermia's dash after Lysander—"either death or you I'll find immediately." Then comes the famous Nocturne, devoted to the four sleeping lovers and Puck's "country proverb" on the course of true love: "Jack shall have Jill; naught shall go ill." Here the magic is worked out by use of a solo horn. The familiar Wedding March provides a regal finale for these concert extracts, but one should remember that Mendelssohn's score really ends in its full theatrical version, as Puck speaks the epilogue, with those same four woodwind chords that launched the adventure. Perfection.

The Hebrides Overture (Fingal's Cave), op. 26 1830

Like the Symphony no. 3 a bonus of Mendelssohn's tour of Scotland, "The Hebrides" attests to the composer's romantic leanings toward savage places and faery marvels. Fingal's Cave is a phenomenon of nature's sculpting hand, located on a tiny island just west of Mull (and not, in fact, in the Hebrides at all); its remote beauty struck off sparks in Mendelssohn. Consider it as a seascape, for salt spray and seagulls, wild life in peace and fury, are here as palpably as music can phrase it.

Calm Sea and Prosperous Voyage, op. 27 1832

Despite the foaming resistance of some who have come to misadventure in what sailors refer to as "heavy weather," a calm sea was not always a boon. Before the machine age, indeed, a blank and windless prospect along the whale-road was liquid death, and Mendelssohn—not to mention commentators of the steam-and-motor power days—would have one know that the "calm sea" music is meant to chill, the "prosperous voyage" to cheer.

Mendelssohn based this overture on two short poems by Goethe, *Meeresstille* and *Glückliche Fahrt.* The calm functions as a long introduction (not unlike one of Haydn's adagio introductions to a symphony's first movement, except much more developed), the voyage as the movement proper. Effectively suggesting the vast stupor of sea and sky in the introduction, Mendelssohn then provides a surge of salty locomotion for the trip itself, culminating just before the coda in a thrilling and rather Beethovenian tattoo on the timpani.

Overture to Ruy Blas, op. 95 1839

The Leipzig Theatrical Pension Fund, a worthy charity, begged this and a song of Mendelssohn for a benefit production of Victor Hugo's *Ruy Blas,* an excursion into the ecstatic new romantic drama (Ruy Blas is a Spanish nobleman's valet riding melodrama's carousel of brave and base natures, court intrigue, disguise, blackmail, and poison). Mendelssohn read the play, denounced it as rubbish, told the Pension Fund people that he had no time to write an overture, and handed over just the song—a chorus, actually. But then, thinking about it, Mendelssohn relented and literally dashed off the overture as well, filling it with the blood-and-thunder convulsion that melodrama craved. This is total Romanticism—at least in tone. Note the schizophrenic introduction, the harassed fury of the first theme, the stuttered stress of the second theme, the overall violence. But note as well a Classicist's touch in the change from the doleful c minor of the beginning to the more positive C Major of the end. At length, Mendelssohn declared himself amused by the entire business, though he preferred to think of the piece as the Overture "not to *Ruy Blas* but to the Theatrical Pension Fund."

The Beautiful Melusine Overture, op. 32 1834

Inspired by a tale of the archetypal water-sprite who destroys the mortal men who love her, this piece is famed for its highly suggestive water music (heard as the first theme at the very start), an early example of pre-Debussy impressionism. A fiery second theme (in the strings) and an ardent closing theme (first violins) complete the exposition's outline of moist beauty, mortal swain, and mutual love, but as the sonata-allegro movement continues, the water music appears to act as an agent of destiny, parting the pair. Few of Mendelssohn's colleagues failed to remark the pictorial undulations of the water theme—least of all Richard Wagner, who borrowed it to characterize the Rhine River in his opera epic, *Der Ring des Nibelungen.*

FRÉDÉRIC CHOPIN 1810–1849

Chopin poses a problem of categorization for this book, for while he was certainly one of the significant composers of the Romantic era—one of its founding fathers, perhaps—he was not much of a symphonist. Two engaging but virtually incompetent piano concertos constitute a weak case for the man, so it is well to remember that Chopin wrote them mainly because aspiring instrumental soloists of the early nineteenth century *had* to write themselves full-concert display pieces; tradition deemed it necessary and the public held them accountable to tradition. Mozart, an aspiring pianist, wrote his own concertos; Beethoven, likewise. What could descendent upstarts do but follow suit? It was an age of concertos. Everyone wrote them, played them, heard them, discussed them. But the main thing was you played your own.

Chopin dispatched his obligations early and, made famous, left sonata-allegro movements, orchestration, and so on to others. The two piano concertos and four other large-scale piano-and-orchestra works were all written by the time he was twenty-one, dues paid out for membership in the performing elite. Thereafter, he concentrated on what he did best, solo—mainly short—piano pieces that didn't require the extended structural development sections or long-term thematic penetration of symphony.

This is not to patronize his art, however. The sickly physique and underpowered playing style of the man in life (not to mention the loony suaveness of the man in Hollywood versions of his life) are misleading. As poet, Chopin was that best of all things in art, an original, and a strong one. The pianist John Field, so-called "inventor of the nocturne," termed Chopin's gift "a sickroom talent"—but finesse is not the utmost of Chopin. The aggressiveness of the polonaises, the vigor of the scherzos, the for-those-days shocking moodiness of the nocturnes and mazurkas, the grace of the waltzes, the technical pedagogy of the études, the curious beauty of the tiny préludes—these are no sickroom's bouquets and candyboxes. With our modern ears dulled by the anarchic onslaught of muzak and heavy-metal rock, we are in no position to appreciate Chopin's revolutionary use of harmony. Anyone can enjoy and value his work, the faulty concerts included. But it takes a trained musician to credit his historical achievement.

Piano Concerto no. 1 in e minor, op. 11 1830

Actually written after no. 2, no. 1 struck its composer as being "far too original"; actually, Chopin's originality still lay head of him in 1830. A strictly traditional concerto in format, op. 11 so respects the Classical *tutti* (wherein the orchestra announces the principal themes before the soloist enters) that conductors have taken to cutting it down to get the soloist in earlier on. When he does enter, he restates themes already heard, with the characteristic Chopinesque embellishment of little extra notes, trills, and other decoration. Sadly, the firm profile of the first movement's opening theme never quite captures the movement in general; it is merely one of several themes, not—as sometimes happens—a tone setter. The second [slow] movement is almost entirely built of piano decorations of themes; the third movement, a lively rondo, perks up interest if only because it's always got something going in a fast tempo. Still, for all its loose construction, the concerto pleases for the glittering pianism of the solo part. No one can deny that the concerto principle is little activated here: where is the collaboration/conflict of solo and orchestra? Except in the opening *tutti,* the orchestra is hardly there at all. But it works. The tunes are engaging, and Chopin knew how to write for piano for sure.

Piano Concerto no. 2 in f minor, op. 21 1829

Numbered second but composed first, the f minor is generally preferred to Chopin's other piano concerto, the e minor. Schumann and Liszt in particular appreciated the slow [second] movement as a ratification of the Romantic (i.e., their own) worldview—which, in its alternation of rhapsodic delicacy and "operatic" dramatics, it undoubtedly is. On the other hand, one may make an amusing experiment in the arena of Classic-versus-Romantic by listening to this slow movement of Chopin and then to a slow movement from one of Mozart's mature piano concertos (no. 14, let's say). Does one notice all that much difference in tone? No, not really. Either Mozart is not quite so Classical as he "should" be or the pure Romantic Chopin inadvertently proves how much the two sensibilities have in common.

The concerto shows the same lack of employment for the orchestra as Chopin's other concerto does. In fact, after the first movement's opening statement of themes, the orchestra more or less vanishes from the scene. As for layout, the work accords with tradition: a strong first movement, a slow movement, a bright and bouncy finale. The finale tenders us a look at the Chopin of the assertive Polish dances—the mazurka, the polonaise—for solo piano, and one theme calls special attention to itself by being accompanied by the strings *col legno* ("with the wood," playing with the bow reversed so the wood side hits the strings for a hollow effect).

ROBERT SCHUMANN 1810–1856

Schumann is one of the arch-Romantics, as necessary to the musical developments of the mid-nineteenth century as that other arch-Romantic, Hector Berlioz. But where Berlioz concerned himself exclusively with large forms, blending orchestra, vocal soloists, and chorus into operatic symphonies and never writing anything smaller than an overture, Schumann made a specialty of piano music and songs, the sort of things one might perform in a small room by oneself. As the entries below attest, Schumann did eventually turn to the symphony and concerto, though critics, luxuriating in their foul sensitivities, have warned us that Schumann was not a first-rate symphonist—that his sense of rhythm is dull, his orchestration puerile, his development sections stagnant.

Never believe a critic. Yes, there is a certain squareness to Schumann's symphonic movements, not enough rhythmic variety; and he was not one of the most imaginative orchestrators. But compared with his gifts, these faults don't matter much. As melodist and as musical dramatist, Schumann was a first-rater. As arch-Romantic, he followed Beethoven in experimenting with the form of symphony, in unifying and conceptualizing it. His Fourth Symphony is an early document in symphonic unity, merging the four movements into one. And his superb piano suite, *Carnaval* (subtitled "Cute Scenes on Four Notes"), offers twenty-one short pieces, almost every one based on one of three basic melodic fragments. Schumann craved concepts, too: the Carnival of the title is held by an imaginary fraternity of anti-Philistines, alter-egos of Schumann and his friends. Music was not just music anymore, but an engine of personal expression. This is one angle of Romanticism.

Schumann, like most of his contemporaries, was a performing musician, not just a composer. But he ruined a promising career as a pianist by the use of a homemade "machine" designed to strengthen the right hand, and his piano music was largely brought forward by his wife Clara, the only woman pianist of the day to rival the stupendous Liszt and Thalberg. Schumann had a third career—as critic. Perhaps it serves a kind of justice that critics have underrated Schumann's orchestral music, for as critic he was pretty awful. He knew what he liked, but he had no real standards, although he more or less launched his career by discovering Chopin. "Hats off, gentlemen," runs his famous squib, "a genius!"

Symphony no. 1 in B Flat Major, "Spring," op. 38 1841

Composed posthaste in celebration of Schumann's marrying Clara Wieck after years of opposition from her father, the "Spring" Symphony originally bore a slight program, read in the titles of the four movements: "Spring's Awakening," "Evening," "Jolly Playmates," and "Spring's Farewell." These Schumann discarded before publication; nonetheless, they sum up the tone of this sprightly work. First novels, they say, tend to the autobiographical; perhaps the Robert-Clara love affair, at last consummated, inspired Schumann to create his personal spring in this work.

It is Classical in form, with first and second themes in place. But it reaches for a Romantic's sense of self. The theme of the slow introduction turns into the first subject when the first movement gets going at *Allegro molto vivace* (lively and quite vivacious), but returns to its original form to lead off the recapitulation, an arresting ambiguity of transformation. The touching second [slow] movement sounds almost monothematic in its consistency of mood; it leads without a pause into the scherzo [third mvt]. "Jolly Playmates," Schumann had called it, though for a scherzo it lies on the serious side. Instead of the usual ABA form, Schumann supplies two trios (the B), turning the scherzo into a rondo: ABACA. The finale [fourth mvt] takes up the vital "rustle of spring" air of the first movement, yet with an autumnal nostalgia—this, remember, is "Spring's Farewell." Those who haven't yet got the hang of knowing when the development ends and the recapitulation begins get a hint from the composer, who separates the two sections with a surprising interlude of horn calls and a cadenza for solo flute.

Symphony no. 2 in C Major, op. 61 1846

Take note of the delicate fanfare in the brass instruments that opens the work: it serves as a motto theme for the whole, recurring several times (always in the brass) as a binding force, most effectively at the end of the last movement in a triumphant transformation of self-assertion. Schumann himself felt that he suffered from lack of self-assertion during the composition of the symphony, for he was not well; not till the end of the work does he bestir himself out of dark into light.

Not that this is in any way a perfunctory entry, though its critics find the first movement too scattered to be effective. The scherzo [second mvt], however, lifts the spirit with infusions of energy and two different trios (that is, two contrasting "middle" sections: ABACA). The slow [third] movement offers minor-key ruminations, and one can see why Schumann felt so relieved about the finale [fourth mvt], which leaves everything on an up note in heroic affirmation of the motto theme.

Symphony no. 3 in E Flat Major, "Rhenish," op. 97 1850

Named for the Rhineland and supposedly inspired by Schumann's first glimpse of Cologne Cathedral resplendent in sunlight, the "Rhenish" takes off on a thrilled flight at once. That first theme and its subsidiary raptures dominate the first movement, though the second subject naturally offers contrast in its pensive pleasure. Surely no one since Schumann has been so excited by a visit to Cologne—note how the first theme turns into a vibrant horn call in mid-movement, a swinging brass fanfare in its final measures. The scherzo [second mvt], originally designated as "Morning on the Rhine," tenders a rural folksiness, and the slow [third] movement grows yet more introspective, as slow movements tend to. But the fourth movement draws us to public precincts—a church ceremonial, from the sound of it. Schumann was wild about Bach; here he pays homage in solemn Bach-like counterpoint (two or more melodic lines running against each other). The pageant gives way to two fanfares for brass and wind, "answered" by the strings. Majestic chords close the picture. But this is not the finale: Schumann supplies a fifth movement to round off his sort-of paean to life in the Rhineland. Unlike the enthralled sweep of the first movement, the tone here is jolly, the light touch—but lo, sharp ears will catch, at the very end of the work, a last reference to the explosive first theme of the first movement.

Symphony no. 4 in d minor, op. 120 1841

Although numbered fourth, this is actually Schumann's second symphony. It is also one of the most important documents of evolution in the form, a halfway house for errant Romanticism on its journey from the confines of Classical separation-of-parts to the elasticity of organic unity. In other words: the symphony of Haydn and Mozart was constructed of discrete parts; the Romantics of the 1800s wanted to meld those parts into one organism.

How to achieve this unity? For starters, Schumann did away with the pauses between movements. The four major sections remain, but strung out in one musical entity. Furthermore, Schumann linked the third and fourth movements with a bridge passage, drawing these two sections even more closely together. Most importantly, Schumann carried over themes from one section to another, sometimes with little change and sometimes in a transformation.

Truly, a remarkable work, directly inspired by Beethoven's experiments in linking movements and using themes in more than one movement, but a strictly Schumannesque piece in sound style. No one should have any difficulty following the progression of first movement, slow movement, scherzo, and finale, even without the tell-tale pauses between movements, for the general atmosphere follows a dramatic progression: moody, lyrical, taut, impetuous. Those who would like to sample Schumann's Romantic unification process for themselves might look out for three reasonably easy-to-spot procedures. One is the use of a loud, sudden low note in the brasses to herald the development sections in both the first and fourth movements. Another is the transformation of the symphony's opening slow introduction into a pleasant middle section of the slow [second] movement, ornamented by a solo violin. (This introduction tune, the first thing heard in the work, acts as a motto theme, turning up yet again in the repeated trio of the scherzo [third mvt], and thus adding to the impression that all the movements are parts of one overall "movement.") Most striking of all Schumann's devices for unity is the bridge passage connecting the third and fourth movements, for here he uses the main theme of the first movement, dragged down to a slower tempo, gray and lowering. Hearing this passage grow and finally burst into the lively finale with a cathartic release of D Major, one should remember that such innovations were once considered scandalous self-indulgences.

Piano Concerto in a minor, op. 54 1845

Admirers of the piano concerto, rally 'round—this is one of the most popular. As in many a Romantic concerto, the soloist comes crashing in early on, skipping the orchestral presentation of themes observed by Classicists. Note the wonderful fluency of this movement, each new theme growing out of the last as if in a theme-and-variations. Indeed, the first subject (introduced on the oboe) does appear to control the proceedings, as it recurs (in the clarinets) in a bridge passage connecting the tender slow [second] movement to the vivacious finale [third mvt], meanwhile celebrating the occasion by turning into the first subject of the finale. By this time, the a minor of the first movement has been overthrown by the peaceful F Major of the slow movement, with its radiant middle section (a dialogue of 'cellos and piano), and the dynamic A Major of the finale. Schumann has his detractors, yet: "Fashion and musical party-politics have tried to play many games with Schumann's reputation," says the wise Donald Francis Tovey, "but works like these remain irresistible."

'Cello Concerto in a minor, op. 129 1850

A much-maligned piece from Schumann's maturity. One thing no one denies: he did manage the tricky balance between soloist and orchestra without drowning out the 'cello—not easy to do, as that instrument projects not unlike an old shoe. However, many find the work limp, repetitive, weak in its final movement. It's listener's choice, really—and one should take into account that 'cellists have always found the work extremely satisfying in terms of what it allows the instrument to express.

Typically Romantic, Schumann ushers in the soloist at once; untypically for the era, he does not allow the soloist much exhibition. The point here is the music and its organization, not the celebrity spotlight. Still, in its mellow way the 'cello dominates the work—one begins to notice that the orchestra is, perhaps, too laid back. From the first movement, Schumann cuts to the second [slow] movement without a break, slipping into it just where one might expect a cadenza from the soloist. The third movement, too, is joined to its predecessor, so that the three movements—soaring, then pensive, then limber—play as one grand sweep.

Overture to Manfred, op. 115 1848

Lord Byron's verse drama *Manfred* so efficiently captured the spirit of rebellious continental Romanticism that it proved more popular in France and Germany than in Byron's native England. "Wild, metaphysical, and inexplicable," Byron himself described it, not very helpfully. "Almost all of the persons are spirits of the earth and air, of the waters; the scene is in the Alps; the hero is a kind of magician, who is tormented by a species of remorse." The poem bewildered many, but everyone read it, if only to encounter the Zeitgeist. Chaikofsky used it as the basis for an expansive symphony; here we have all that modern audiences ever hear of Schumann's incidental score for a production of Byron's not very dramatic "dramatic poem." Musically, this is a sonata-allegro movement, with slow introduction and slow coda. Some analysts regard it as a tone poem for its detailed character study. The "species of remorse" seems to dictate the tone, bittersweet despair in the introduction (the oboe is useful here), then enthusiastic waves of breast-beating self-dramatization. At length, a coda refers us back to the material of the introduction.

Overture to Genoveva, op. 81 1848

Schumann's one opera, about a faithful wife wrongly accused of infidelity, enjoyed a temporary success, fading from the scene by the end of the nineteenth century. But its overture survives, a fine saga in little, slowly pulling out of c minor into C Major. After a plaintive slow introduction, the movement proper takes off in fast tempo with an agitated violin theme, threatened by the lower strings and buoyed up by woodwinds. A "hunting horn" second theme offers noncommittal surcease. Not till the development and recapitulation have been played out does a victorious coda smooth things over with unmistakable sounds of happy ending.

FRANZ LISZT 1811–1886

One of the most important composers in Western music, Franz Liszt served more as an influence on others than as a bastion of popular repertory. His orchestral music, other than the two piano concertos, is not heard that frequently. But as composer, pianist, conductor, advisor, and encourager, Liszt acted as a seminal figure for High Romanticism, a sentinel of the midpoint between Beethoven (Classicism moving into Romanticism) and Debussy (Romanticism moving into Modernism). The layman recalls Liszt mainly as a pianist—a stupendous one, crystallizing the ideal of the demonic genius who pounds passion into ideology and keyboards to rubble. But his fellow composers knew him better as a kind of teacher, an experimenter who funded their own research with his discoveries.

The structure of musical Europe had changed remarkably by the time that Liszt, the boy wonder, first toured out of Hungary as a recitalist. Formerly the semi-private exercise of house musicians or commissioned freelancers, rented by the elite, music now wore a public face: concerts were given, and anyone who bought a ticket might attend. Bach, in the early eighteenth century, wrote for the church or private patrons; Haydn, in the late eighteenth century, started as a court musician but ended with international glory in London, his music heard by one and all. Now, in Liszt's 1800s, composers reached a wide public in the cosmopolitan centers as a matter of course. (Why play at a party when you could sell out a recital hall?) Along with the inevitable interaction of audience and musicians came a new fellowship of the musicians themselves, who could assess and debate each others' work with ease—night after night, concerts, recitals, musical salons: a learning process.

The public knew—and preferred—Liszt the Herculean pianist, virtually the inventor of a flamboyantly extroverted style of playing. Later, they knew Liszt the composer and conductor. But Liszt's fellow musicians knew Liszt the coach, the darer, the synthesizer of new forms of composition and harmony. Synthesizer: Liszt drew on the recent past, on Beethoven, Schubert, Mendelssohn, Schumann, extending his retrospective to build anew on their foundation. They were some combination of Classicism—sharpness of form, absolutism of pure musical expression, separateness of parts—seeking Romanticism—renovation of form, pictorial or emotional imagery in music, unity of parts. But Liszt was entirely Romantic. He brought them up to date, and prompted further updatings by others.

For example, the concerto. Mendelssohn had already revised the Classical model in his violin concerto, making the first attempt to draw the three distinct movements together at their edges and dispensing entirely with the traditional orchestral statement of themes that precedes the soloist's entry in the first movement. Mendelssohn's approach, mildly shocking in its day, traded stateliness for intensity. Liszt, in his two piano concertos, took such renovation for granted, and sought further unity by using themes from one movement in other movements.

He also took for granted the premise that music was not necessarily "absolute" in itself—that it might deal in imagistic and even narrative suggestion. Program music was not a Romantic invention by any means, but before the 1800s it was an exception to natural rules of composition; in Liszt's time, it was proving its own rules—and this practice, too, Liszt helped promulgate. He wrote two works called symphonies, yet they are not Symphony no. 1 and no. 2 but *Faust* and *Dante,* derived from Goethe's play and the *Divine Comedy,* respectively, and using musical themes to reconstruct the intellectual or emotional apparatus of the two sources. Moreover, Liszt devised a plastic, one-movement form for musical illustration, the "symphonic poem." Again, this was not entirely new. Liszt developed it from the dramatic opera overture of Mozart and Beethoven. Also again, it proved a godsend to Liszt's successors, who made of it, as the tone poem, one of the glories of the late Romantic era.

In the matter of harmony, too, Liszt was an innovator, moving sometimes quite boldly into chromaticism—i.e., using all the notes in the Western scale instead of the fraction of them that form an "orderly" sound-space. In this, one of Liszt's most important bequests was the enriched harmonic palette of Richard Wagner, Liszt's son-in-law and one of the many musicians who profited from a friendship with Liszt even more creatively than personally. Remember, the popular pieces by which Liszt is known today—and was known in his own time—are only a small part of what the man accomplished. Hearing the *Hungarian Rhapsodies* for piano or the orchestral tone poems, one might give credit to Liszt's pioneer work in establishing a full-blown-virtuoso piano style for his age. One might note his obsession with sonorities, the textures of sound. But one will grin at the overstatements, the epochal *style énorme* with its self-love and sensationalism. This is unfortunate, for Liszt's subtler pieces would give a vastly different impression; too bad they are not heard more frequently.

It should be clear, then, that Liszt was far more than the hottentot pianist of unprecedented technique and crypto-sexual charisma. He was that most specialized of revolutionaries, the continuity-master. Liszt's halfway house rehabilitated the genius of the old and fired that of the new. Perhaps no one else in music was as open to contemporary novelty as he, and so unaffected by musical politics—it was lucky, then, that he was one of the age's most influential conductors. When Liszt played, they listened! A tireless student of method, constantly revising his work, he must have rethought his aesthetics a thousand times. He could change, evolve; he literally *grew* with his times. But he led, them, too. And that is awfully rare.

A Faust Symphony 1854; revised 1857, 1861

Outsize, weirdly shaped, Romantically topical, and even partly vocal (tenor solo and male chorus at the end), Liszt's major attempt to bend his individualistic vision to symphonic form both excepts and proves rules of mid-nineteenth-century symphony. Even its oddities were approved, sought-after Romantic oddities. It's a long work—seventy minutes—but symphonies were getting longer; longer meant more, and more is the motto of Romanticism. It's in three, not four, movements—but this suggested a circular shape not unpleasing to Romantic experimentation. As for the vocal finale, had not the supreme Beethoven started that off in his Ninth? Best of all was the topic (for symphonies now had topics almost more often than they didn't): Faust, the fascinating alchemical mystic, the groper—like Romantic art—toward some profound new revelation. Some Romantic heroes were melancholy and wandered, some fought battles and were consumed by power, some delved into magic. Goethe's Faust, the hero of an epic two-part verse play, did all of the above, the compleat Romantic hero. That Liszt, the compleat Romantic composer, performer, advisor and—somewhat incredibly—priest, should write a *Faust* symphony was righteous and opportune. That he should write it so well says as much for Liszt's influence on middle and late Romanticism as for Romanticism's influence on Liszt.

To begin with, Liszt organized the work in three movements, each devoted to a character in Goethe's play: first Faust, then his beloved Gretchen (short for Margarethe), then Mephistopheles. The music in each movement is conceived not only to describe the character, but to relate him or her to the others. Thus, music from one movement is used in others. There is, however, no "story," but rather three portraits—Faust ardent, Gretchen tender, Mephistopheles antagonistic—capped by a cathartic setting of Goethe's final lines (roughly, "The indescribable can be accomplished: Eternal Woman draws us on to heights"). In form, the music will not sound much unlike what one is used to in symphonic movements of the mid-nineteenth century. Both the first and second movements, "Faust" and "Gretchen," might have been the first (sonata-allegro) and slow movements of any number of Romantic symphonies, and the third movement runs rather like Liszt's symphonic poems (what we now call tone poems). The first movement, "Faust," opens with a manic-depressive introduction, then moves into an orderly statement of principal themes, by turns desperate, passionate, and heroic. This is Faust the eternal striver, no mere deputy of the Schiller-Berlioz-Stendahl-Byron axis but a human symbol of no one place or time who seeks answers to disturbing questions.

After "Faust," "Gretchen" [second mvt] comes as a wildly unexpected mellow. Some of Faust's themes are carried over to depict the love affair between these two but this is always delicate music, all for love. The main theme comes in early on oboe solo accompanied by a solo viola—a nice evocation of innocence—and this cedes to the symphony's one pictorial moment, a clarinet and two violins voicing the "he loves me, he loves me not" that Gretchen plays with a flower in a scene of Goethe's drama. Later, the tone turns more sensual as Faust and Gretchen consummate their romance, followed by the Gretchen theme again, now given to a violin quartet.

The third movement, "Mephistopheles," turns on an ingenious idea. Since the devil defines himself in Goethe's text as "the spirit that always denies," Liszt portrays him in parodies—denials—of Faust's themes. A buffoonishly vicious movement, as cynical as a post–World War II existentialist, Mephistopheles spoofs and shrills. Significantly, the only musical idea he cannot ridicule is that of Gretchen; her theme, undefiled, appears at length on horn and 'cello, introducing the vocal finale and a total change of mood.

Originally, Liszt ended the work at this point, and occasionally a conductor will elect to perform the first version. But the work concludes more satisfyingly in the final version with the tenor solo and male chorus singing Goethe's words about Eternal Woman *(Das Ewig-Weibliche),* because the image of the female anima encapsulates the goal of Faust's (man's) struggle to achieve belief in the self through positive action. Thus, when the tenor makes his entrance, he sings of Eternal Woman to the beautiful purity of the Gretchen theme, bringing both musical and topical schemes to a fine resolution.

Piano Concerto no. 1 in E Flat Major 1848

A reasonably daring idea for the day—a piano concerto in one continuous movement, containing subdivisions corresponding to not the concerto but the symphony: first movement, slow movement, scherzo, and finale. Liszt did not kid himself that his daring would go over easily. He is said to have sung "Das versteht Ihr alle nicht" (This none of you understands) to the seven notes that open the piece. Planning the work to play in one swell foop is no stunt—Liszt sought a unity for the concerto, and to this end he not only discards the silences that separate movements but also the climaxes that end them: so as to *flow* each section into the next. Moreover, he carries themes from one "movement" over into another. In all, though the tempo changes mark four distinct sections, this really does feel like one rich movement's worth of concerto.

After the famous seven notes of Liszt's contempt for his slow public, the piano leaps in with a mighty flourish and a lengthy cadenza, reminding us that Liszt was (1) perhaps the most physical pianist of his era and (2) no shrinking violet in the matter of egoism. A heroic but not climactic first section cedes to a poetic slow section topped off by a refreshing flute solo. Suddenly, we have arrived at the scherzo. Note the triangle—percussion instruments were considered ridiculous at the time, and this rather stellar use of the triangle prompted much hilarity at Liszt's expense. The influential and utterly unimaginative critic Eduard Hanslick dubbed the entire work "the triangle concerto." But just wait—a further percussion solo from a busy cymbal awaits us in the finale, by which time one will have noticed that themes associated with earlier sections have been reappearing frequently: unity. One grand movement, a classic.

Piano Concerto no. 2 in A Major 1848

Like Liszt's first piano concerto, no. 2 is in one long movement subdivided into sections. However, while no. 1's sections correspond to the four movements of the symphony, no. 2's layout is more individual, less easy to describe. One wants to call it more meditative, less showy—but it, too, has its passages of *bravura* (heroic) display. The American critic William Foster Apthorp suggested a subtitle for it—"The Life and Adventures of a Melody," for Liszt's primary activity here is the transformation of one theme (the opening wail of clarinet and oboe) into numerous subthemes, thus building a whole concerto out of one tune. (Don't attempt to listen for the transformations; it takes a musician and some hours of study to plot them out in the printed score.)

Rather than look for the equivalents of slow movement, finale, and such, listen to the progression of moods in the piece. Note how Liszt veers from the dreamy to the jerky to the tender to the decisive without ever letting the architectural tension lapse. Given the tradition of the three-movement concerto (fast-slow-fast) with pauses between movements, a tradition very much alive and jealous of variation in 1857, when the work was first performed, this was a rather extraordinary prospect. Those who like a highly *piano* sort-of-concerto will thrill to the coda (tail-end), involving a series of terrific *glissando*s (slides) up and down the length of the keyboard.

Hungarian Fantasia for Piano and Orchestra 1853

Perhaps because it is a reworking of a piano solo (the Fourteenth Hungarian Rhapsody), this *Fantasy on Hungarian Folk Themes for Piano and Orchestra* (as the title properly runs) sounds less like a concerto movement than a piano spectacular on which an orchestra is occasionally permitted to intrude. In true concerto, the soloist and orchestra collaborate integrally; here, they tend to alternate, and when they do play together, the piano still feels separate, as if it were thinking back to the smug independence of the original piano-only version.

Anyway, it's an enjoyable piece, filled with regional effects—the oddly placed accents of Hungarian folk song, the "gypsy" violin, and a cute pianistic imitation of the cimbalom, a Hungarian form of dulcimer. The melodies are, as the title implies, authentic native tunes, and while the opening *lassan* section sounds vigorously soulful, the faster *friska* brings the piece to an explosive conclusion.

Totentanz (Dance of Death) for Piano and Orchestra 1853

This is a series of variations on a medieval plainsong theme known as the "Dies Irae" (Day of Wrath) because of its use with words warning of the Day of Judgment. The theme is heard at the start of the piece—long, somber notes over rumblings on timpani and the piano, followed by brilliant keyboard flourishes and further statements of the theme. The first variation makes prominent use of the bassoon; throughout, however, the piano leads the band, emphasizing the diabolism that a dance of death requires. The piano hammers, shivers, moans—one can see how far the instrument had come since the time of Mozart and Beethoven some fifty years earlier.

In a longer piece, the variations might range far from the original theme, but here the Dies Irae outline remains within hearing distance, returning to its original form at the end after a dazzling final variation for which the strings play *col legno* (with the reverse, wooden, side of the bow, yielding a spooky effect) and the piano plays upward-rushing, double *glissando*s (slides across the keyboard, "double" meaning with both hands—two slides at once).

The Symphonic Poems

We call them tone poems nowadays, but Liszt had to invent his own term because this was a new, not to say daring item when he devised it. Essentially, it dates back to the opera overture of a previous age: program music. If a Classical-era composer wrote a symphonic movement, it was a symphonic movement, music *qua* music. But if he wrote a symphonic movement as overture for an opera or play, that was something different—an introductory abstraction of the dramatic event. Thus, Mozart's Overture to *Don Giovanni* warns us in its thunderous opening measures of the damnation awaiting the hero, then seems to characterize the heedless, debonair hero himself. In a way, Mozart's Overture to *Don Giovanni* might have been a tone poem called *Don Giovanni*.

Liszt's tone poems, however, are not overtures by another name. Not only do they have subjects; there is also a purely musical aesthetic involving the metamorphosis of one theme into several different forms. Mozart, again, would give us two principal contrasting themes. Liszt gives us one protagonistic theme that develops throughout the piece, thus tying the various sections together organically. Liszt's symphonic poem is not unlike a "theme and variations," except not so formal as that, not so clearly cut as to where one variation ends and another begins. This basic melody (or ur-theme) is a strategic bid for unity in a form that lacks the structural principles of a symphonic movement—the exposition, development, and recapitulation of sonata-allegro, the scherzo-and-trio, the alternating episodes of the rondo. No, tone poems make up their structural principle each time out—no two are alike, and the term for their structural individualism is "fantasy," meaning free in form.

Liszt wrote twelve symphonic poems, kicking off a vogue that eventually gave us such items as *The Sorceror's Apprentice* (Dukas), *Till Eulenspiegel's Merry Pranks* and *Don Juan* (Strauss), and *Finlandia* (Sibelius). As with Mozart's opera overtures, the tone poem relates to some specific program material—but the level of narration or characterization is up to the composer. Thus, the Dukas actually narrates a story, *Till* dances around the vague outline of a life story, *Don Juan* is a non-specific character sketch, and *Finlandia* little more than a misty image. Liszt's tone poems generally shy away from outright program, but as they all have titles—names, pictures, ideas—they are all, in some way, about something.

Symphonic Poem no. 2: Tasso: Lament and Triumph
1849; revised 1854

The sixteenth-century poet Torquato Tasso was just the sort of erratic genius beloved by the nineteenth century (a golden age of erratic geniuses); he makes a perfect subject for a Romantic tone poem. Liszt wrote it first as an overture to Goethe's play *Torquato Tasso* (Goethe and Liszt both were the least erratic of geniuses, but they appreciated the quality in others). Later, he redeveloped it, as he redeveloped the Classical overture in general, into this more fluid, less Classical, form. Like Liszt's other attempts in the field, the score is based on one theme which constantly changes its shape or reasserts its original guise, depending on the thrust of the music. The theme is heard immediately in a minor key on the strings; out of it, the entire work progresses. A melancholy nostalgia and stormy interlude—the Lament of the subtitle—eventually yield to a minuet, with the theme assigned to two 'cellos. This in turn grows passionate and waltzlike and yields to the storm again before the theme is revitalized in the major—the Triumph.

Symphonic Poem no. 3: Les Préludes 1850

A granddaddy of tone poems, one of the oldest and most popular. The title refers to a poem by Alphonse de Lamartine, from which Liszt drew an epigraph: "What is your life but a series of preludes to that unknown song of which death strikes the first solemn note?" The quotation goes on, but that's all one needs to know: here are life's various preludes to the universal climax. As in all Liszt's symphonic poems, the entire work flows out of one basic theme, here sounded at the start of the slow introduction (those who know César Franck will note a resemblance to the first theme of his Symphony in d minor) and again, already beginning to alter its shape, just after the introduction in a heaving *tutti* (full orchestra) in C Major. Then the "preludes" file by as scenes from a life—tenderness, fury, triumph, suburban stasis (literally—Lamartine alludes to the "serenity of rural life" and Liszt obliges with piping woodwinds and a sprightly folk dance in $^6/_8$ metre). The *tutti* passage from the work's opening is reprised at the end, back in its original C Major, presumably to emphasize life's triumph rather than death's.

Symphonic Poem no. 4: Orpheus 1854

As one who struck one of his era's more prominent lyres, Liszt understandably felt some kinship with the Greek musician of legend. In the event, he produced a tone poem notable for a dignity and nobility quite unlike the hyperactive Liszt of the better-known Hungarian Rhapsodies or *Les Préludes*. Here he plays the orchestra as if it were a gigantic lyre (the harp is, of course, ubiquitous) soothing the savage breast. One basic theme does duty throughout the work, developing tension not out of contrast with a second theme (there is none, really) but out of its own urgent continuity. Note the haunting little coda, a series of chords answered by the woodwind. Perfect understatement.

Symphonic Poem no. 5: Prometheus 1850

The Romantics preferred heroes with self-doubt, but they could take a titan in a pinch. "*Malheur et gloire!,*" Liszt wrote in preface to the score—Misfortune and glory!—viewing Prometheus in terms that the 1800s could understand. Misfortune and glory do indeed inform the music, "a devastation conquering through the perseverance of lofty energy." (Prometheus' misfortune was his punishment for stealing fire from the immortals and passing it on to humankind: daily, an eagle visited Prometheus at his rocky captivity and gorged on his liver. His glory as man's benefactor is the knowledge [fire] that is power.) Two distinct themes alternate here, one threatening misfortune, the other promising glory.

Symphonic Poem no. 6: Mazeppa 1851

The only one of Liszt's twelve tone poems that can really be called pictorial, *Mazeppa* traces the ghastly ride and rescue of its titular hero, who paid too nice an attention to a nobleman's wife and was tied naked to a wild horse. Liszt's source was a poem by Victor Hugo. As Hugo starts right in with the galloping horse, so does Liszt: rushing strings build to a thrilling statement of the principal theme in the brass and lower strings. The breakneck ride continues till a change of mood brings a sadder version of the theme (note the odd accompaniment in the strings, some of which are directed to play *col legno*—"with the wood," i.e., using the wood rather than the string side of their bows). The ride is heard again, but Mazeppa's theme is defiant. Ultimately, Hugo tells us, it is the horse which falters more than the hero and which at last falls "to the cries of a thousand birds of prey." Silence. Then moaning strings. A solo bassoon, a solo horn. Now a thrill sparks the lower strings, and a trumpet calls—Cossacks of the Ukraine find and liberate Mazeppa, make him their chieftain, follow him into battle: a rousing march. Mazeppa's theme has now evolved into a brash, gypsyish fanfare, a warrior's glory.

Symphonic Poem no. 9: Hungaria 1856

The vaguest of Liszt's tone poems in terms of program, *Hungaria* is an emotional hymn to his homeland; eventually the doleful, minor key of the opening strain gains a sturdy major-key uplift in the final section, based on a Hungarian folk tune that turns up in a number of Liszt's works. Note, for regional savor, the solo violin of the earlier pages, used in the cadenzas expected of a gypsy fiddle.

RICHARD WAGNER 1813–1883

Because his field was opera almost exclusively, Wagner takes his place in this book for concert "bits": overtures, preludes, or orchestral interludes. Unlike a given symphony or concerto, these pieces were not composed simply to be heard, but to illuminate a dramatic context. They set mood for the action to come, or sum up what has preceded. More importantly, because Wagner depended heavily on the leitmotif (leading theme), a tune associated with a character or idea that changes according to the subject's use in the story, these pieces are symbiotically dependent on their theatrical contexts to make their proper effect.

In Wagner, meaning is both musical and dramatic. Anyone may sit back and listen to, say, the *Flying Dutchman* Overture without having the faintest idea of its meaning. But listening without knowing the narrative "code" is not unlike reading in the dark. Wagner uses his themes as symbols for dramatic ideas—objects, people, drives, concepts. His development of the themes follows their dramatic function—the transformation of objects and people, the urgency of drives, the triumph or collapse of concepts. So, to get the most out of Wagner, the listener must know (1) what the leitmotifs in a given piece represent and (2) what the use of the leitmotifs is telling us dramatically.

Wagner did not invent the leitmotif, but he made it supreme in opera. When he began, he was sparing with it, composing operas that *contained* a few leitmotifs referring to the most important persons and ideas in his librettos. By the end of his career, however, he had evolved a type of operatic composition in which virtually every note of score is *comprised* of leitmotifs being stated, restated, and endlessly developed into new leitmotifs. For example, anyone can pick out the two principal letimotifs in the *Flying Dutchman* Overture, from relatively early in Wagner's career. The overture is a sonata movement, and the two leitmotifs appear as first and second subjects in the exposition—one for the ghostly hero and the other for the redemptive woman he seeks among mortals. These leitmotifs *sound* like what they are: the first is stormy and obsessed, the second tender and yearning. (There are other leitmotifs in the overture, as in the opera, but these two are all that one really needs to appreciate what Wagner is doing in the overture—especially as he closes with the redemptive theme restated triumphantly.)

In late Wagner, however, the leitmotifs not only are numerous, not only change their shape, but do not invariably sound like anything in particular. A leitmotif symbolizing a cursed phantom captain driving his phantom ship through the ghost world is reasonably easy to characterize in music. But ideas, inanimate objects, and psychology are less easy to describe. For example, *The Ring of the Nibelungs.* This is an epic opera of human conflict seen against the cycle of nature, and its fundamental leitmotifs, eternally reinvented, create a web of meaning that illuminates the action in commentary. Thus, the theme associated with the sempiternal flow of life-water:

is played in a dark, minor key to yield the theme associated with the Earth Mother, the placeless, timeless consciousness of natural wisdom:

This second theme, in turn, turns into yet another theme related to the downfall of the old order. Because this order has sinned against natural wisdom, the notes of the second theme are inverted to sound like a fall into darkness:

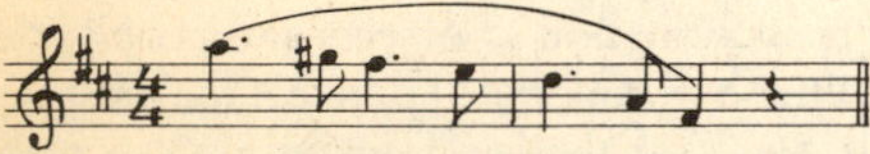

Theatre, then, was Wagner's field; all but the first two items below are excerpts from operas (and one of the first two is made up of themes from one of the operas). The listening experience will be almost entirely programmatic, rather like a succession of tone poems and completely unlike what one is used to from symphony except for a few of the overtures. Don't proceed with caution: leap in—it's terrific music. Just make sure you know what's going on dramatically in each case. (Sometimes this is absurdly simple, as with, say, "The Ride of the Valkyries." What should one know about it except that Valkyries are riding through the sky? On the other hand, the prelude to *Tristan und Isolde* deals in a psychological subtext that should be understood if the music is to matter.)

This is not the place to go into Wagner's overall importance as opera composer, opera librettist, revolutionary of theatre technique, and expander of the symphony orchestra: there is far too much to tell, though his extraordinary use of the colors of the orchestra—the doom-laden darkness of the brasses, especially—as narrative forces in his music drama should be mentioned here. Suffice it to say that the popular clichés about overloud orchestration, endless boredom, freaky mythopoeia, and bosomy damsels wearing overturned urns on their heads and holding pitchforks is all simplistic drivel. The man was a titan of art, and repays as much serious investigation as one puts out. Those who feel up to it should try one of the operas at first-hand—*Die Meistersinger von Nürnberg* (The Mastersingers of Nürnberg), a charming but huge comedy, is a good place to start. However, do not drop in on this work in the opera house unless it's being sung in English. Better prepare for a live performance by hearing it first on records *while following along with the printed libretto*. Remember, this is theatre—the music is only one component of the totality. You must understand the words as well as enjoy the melodies.

Siegfried Idyll 1870

A chamber work, free in form, and a cross between absolute and program music. It was composed as a birthday treat for Wagner's second wife Cosima (the illegitimate daughter of Franz Liszt and, until she met Wagner, the loving wife of the conductor Hans von Bülow) and first performed on the staircase of the Wagners' villa in Lucerne, Switzerland. Thus, it had to be scored for a small group of players (a fuller instrumentation is commonly played in concerts and on records). This *is* absolute music in fact, but as most of its themes were drawn from the love scene of Wagner's *Siegfried* (the third opera of his *Ring* tetralogy), as Cosima had presented Wagner with his first son, also named Siegfried, and as the entirely joyous music reflects the meeting of two lovers, the *Siegfried Idyll* may be taken as program music as well, the subtext being domestic tranquility. Opera buffs familiar with *Siegfried* will place most of the themes (two are drawn from other sources) and will note that a bird call on clarinet and flute is, amusingly, only similar to—not a replica of—the bird call that in the opera leads Siegfried from his dragon slaying to rescuing a virgin Valkyrie on her fire-girdled mountain crest.

A Faust Overture 1840

One of Wagner's few forays into the concert hall in music not first composed for the opera house. This is very early Wagner, and looks back to the era of Mendelssohn and Schumann (i.e., early Romanticism) with a clear-cut sonata form of first and second subjects, development, and recapitulation. The Romanticism is also clear-cut. Note the vaguely programmatic title, focusing one's attention on music as idea: an overture about Faust. Goethe's alchemist, soul-searcher, and hero cut quite a swath in those years; Wagner's contribution to the cult is shorter than Liszt's huge symphony and Berlioz's huger opera-ballet-symphony, but no less worthy of the *Sturm und Drang* (Storm and Stress = code words for continental Romantic consciousness-raising).

Rienzi (1840): Overture

Written before Wagner had matured his revolutionary theories of opera composition, *Rienzi* shows the outward format of commercial, establishment grand opera as developed in Paris by the composer Giacomo Meyerbeer and the librettist Eugène Scribe: five absolutely grandiose acts, historical setting, spectacular decor and effects, huge cast, much chorus, a big ballet number, the works. *Rienzi*'s plot was based on Edward Bulwer-Lytton's novel (based, in turn, on history), telling of the rise and fall of a popular hero in fourteenth-century Rome beset by arrogant, squabbling patricians. Wagner followed form so carefully that the generous and at present horribly underrated Meyerbeer thought *Rienzi* the best grand opera ever, while wags of the day enjoyed calling it "Meyerbeer's masterpiece." In truth, *Rienzi* shows a little too much of the fanfares, flourishes, and vast other rhetoric of the grand opera style, and since an overture prepares one for what is to unfold onstage, brace yourself for fanfares.

It's a rousing piece, a potpourri of themes from the opera worked into traditional sonata-allegro form with a long slow introduction. The muted martial opening, three notes on the trumpet, signals Rienzi's call to the people to fight for liberty; this shortly yields to a flowing theme heard in Act V as "Rienzi's Prayer." After a fiery restatement of the prayer with string figures roiling about the melody, the three-note trumpet call launches the main, fast section of the overture, including another statement of the prayer theme in swifter tempo and several heroic attitudes in the brasses. A brief development cedes to the three trumpet notes and a recapitulation. This features a zesty bit, culled from the Finale to Act II, when two separate fanfare themes are played simultaneously. Altogether, very bracing.

The Flying Dutchman (1842): Overture

Readers of the television generation (circa 1945—   ) will recognize the stormy opening theme as the sign-in music of Captain Video, a sound-stage space ranger who brightened young lives of an evening in the early 1950s. In Wagner's opera this music announces the Flying Dutchman, a ranger of the seas who defied the devil and suffers his curse to wander the world in a ghost ship till a faithful woman shall redeem his soul. Two focal images command our attention: the Captain Video theme and a second, lyrical theme representing the Dutchman's redemption. Around them roar the sounds of the seacoast, gales, thunder and lightning, and, in a lighter mood, a

Norwegian sailor's song. The climax is signaled by a breathless upward rush in the strings and a thrilling restatement of the redemption theme. In his first version of the overture, Wagner closed with the pounding fury of the Dutchman's theme, but today we almost invariably hear a more optimistic finish utilizing the redemption melody.

Tannhäuser (1842): Overture and Venusberg Music

Tannhäuser (pronounced *Tann*hoyzer), medieval poet and musician, is caught between the dark lady and the blonde lady: profane and sacred loves. The dark lady is Venus, the blonde lady Elizabeth, one of the redemptive womanly animas so strategic to German art. Thus, the overture encapsulates the opera's conflict between the fleshly and the spiritual. The latter is sounded first—the famous "Pilgrims' Chorus"—quietly, then gloriously. But as it calms down again, mysterious revels rise up in the orchestra. The music surges, boils, desires (this is amazingly sensual sound for its day), and then soars into Tannhäuser's hymn to Venus, which, to be fair, sounds like a Teutonic drinking song. The orgy reconvenes, dwindles to a lush clarinet tune, and reconvenes anew only to give way to a reprise of the Pilgrims' hymn. The spiritual triumphs.

At that point, the overture ends. But some conductors will skip the restatement of the Pilgrims' hymn and go right into the opening of Act I, a bacchanal inside the Venusberg (Venus' mountain), where Tannhäuser is already tiring of the hedonist scene. Because Paris was the center of the opera world, Wagner had hoped for a production of *Tannhäuser* at the Opéra; this, he felt, might make his reputation. He did get the production after all, but as a concession to Parisian taste he had to extend the bacchanal to include a lengthy ballet. (As it happened, the ballet did not concede enough—Parisians liked to come late and catch the dance midway through the action, not in the first scene.) Bacchanals in opera tend to the ridiculous, but the Paris version of the *Tannhäuser* score is a treat, for as sheer music this lengthy saturnalia offers an amusingly salacious earful.

Lohengrin 1850

A chivalric melodrama that plays spiritual purity against evil. Its three acts each begin with a prelude (music that runs into the action rather than comes to a full stop before the curtain goes up, as an overture does). The Prelude to Act I deals in holy spirit, that to Act II in evil, and Act III takes off with a whirlwind of wedding preparations. Only the first and third preludes are heard in concert.

Prelude to Act I

This study in nearly motionless music is meant to suggest a vision of the Holy Grail descending to earth, a gift of the heavenly host to a love-starved earth. (Lohengrin, it turns out, is one of the keepers of the Grail. He doesn't stick around long.) Wagner plays the vision at first in an immobile string sound—an atmosphere rather than melody. Eventually a very slow, celestial tune begins to unfold as the Grail descends to earth. Slowly, the other instruments enter the ether. The arrival of the Grail brings on a great crescendo, twice climaxed by a cymbal crash, and the host then reascends to the string sound of the opening.

Prelude to Act III

Lohengrin is marrying Elsa; the wild pyrotechnics heard here express the joy of the wedding party. In ABA structure, we hear both extroverted excitement (the A) and less uninhibited material (the B), no doubt referring to the bride's blushes. In the opera, after the A repeats the curtain rises on the well-known Bridal Chorus ("Here Comes the Bride!").

Tristan Und Isolde 1865: Prelude and Isolde's Liebestod (Love-Death)

Tristan marked the emergence of the mature Wagnerian style, difficult but enthralling. Pushing out the parameters of harmony past what many thought of as reasonable, even listenable, bounds, Wagner created for this tale of cosmic love a sound space of vivid sensuality. It was unusually metaphysical, difficult to sing, and revolutionary in other ways as well. But, mainly, it was shocking.

The Prelude opens and the "Love-Death" closes the opera. However, they often appear together as one piece in concert. The music consists of melodic fragments repeated and remade ad infinitum, and is a highly ecstatic business. Know that Tristan and Isolde are, technically, enemies. English Tristan is bringing Irish Isolde as war booty to wed his uncle, but a love potion throws them into each other's arms. The Prelude sets this up before the rise of the curtain, starting with two themes dovetailed as one—a yearning moan on the cellos and four rising notes in the oboes. Silence. Cellos, oboes again. Silence. Same thing again, the oboes echoed by the flutes. Silence. Now the strings echo the flutes, woodwinds echo the strings, and a burst of sound sets the piece in motion. Each tune echoes another in burning desire until a climax returns us to the hesitant opening music, and we go right into the "Love-Death," without its vocal line in which Isolde more or less rationalizes her organically inexplicable death beside Tristan's corpse. (This is not an arrangement of the aria for orchestra: it is the aria performed with the voice part missing.) The two have been seeing Love as Death all night; at last, they have both. More ecstasy here, line upon line in parabolic profusion until the oboe theme from the Prelude at last resolves—as it has not once in the entire opera—and two harp chords close the show.

Die Meistersinger von Nürnberg
(The Mastersingers of Nürnberg) 1867

This grand and delightful comedy bears a serious message about the necessity of re-evolving the tenets of art through the teaching of tradition: new blood is requisite, but only as a transfusion into existing culture, not as wholesale destruction. In the opera, set in the sixteenth century, tradition is upheld by the mastersingers, a guild of well-studied amateur musicians; regeneration is provided by an iconoclastic young knight, Walther von Stolzing. He is like unto Wagner, and the composer makes it clear how he expects to be treated by comparing von Stolzing to two other figures. One, Hans Sachs, is conservative but open-minded enough to appreciate the freshness of the avant garde. The other, Sixtus Beckmesser, is a hateful pedant. Wagner admires Sachs and excoriates Beckmesser; he clearly intends for us to do the same. And as for von Stolzing, he wins a song contest and gets the girl. So, the old school and the new wave make their peace.

Overture

(Technically this is a prelude, as it runs into Act I without a break. When played on its own in concert, the piece is finished off with a "concert ending," a few chords borrowed from the last page of the opera.)

Setting up the work's central conflict, Wagner opens the overture opposing music later associated with the mastersingers (tradition) to that associated with his young hero (artistic regeneration). The masters take the opening page, pompous, confidant of their doctrine; the hero enters in a pliant "love" theme, which quickly cedes to a violin run introducing a second masters' theme, the festive march of the masters. Note how Wagner expresses their orthodoxy in vigorous, squared-off rhythm and very fundamental harmony: back, they seem to cry, to basics! More love music follows, warm and urgent, followed by a "miniature" version of the opening masters' theme (this represents the villain of the piece, Beckmesser—the "little" sound suggests his pettiness). When this climaxes, Wagner comes up with a tour de force of dramatic abstraction: he plays both of the master's themes *and* the hero's love music simultaneously. For resolution, Wagner treats us to a gala restatement of the stolid march, topping it off with the first masters' theme.

Prelude to Act III

Hans Sachs, custodian of all that is bright, wise, and noble in Nürnberg's sixteenth-century middle-class culture, considers the state of his worlds, public and private. His musings Wagner captures for us before the curtain rises, in music meditative, proud, ponderous, aspiring.

Der Ring des Nibelungen
(The Ring of the Nibelungs) 1876

Four separate operas comprise this epic on love and the lust for power among gods, mortals, and goblins: *The Rhinegold, The Valkyrie, Siegfried,* and *Twilight of the Gods.*

The Ride of the Valkyries (from Die Walküre, Act III)

The Valkyries are Odin's daughters, who collect fallen warriors and take them to Valhalla, the mead-hall of the gods. This passage, which opens the third act of the second *Ring* opera, depicts their ride through the sky from battle to battle. Note how Wagner starts with a swirling motion suggest of airflight, spurs the valkyries' horses with a rhythmic attack, and only then brings in the tune, in the brasses.

Forest Murmurs (from Siegfried, Act II)

Early impressionism, this snippet of the third *Ring* opera abstracts the mysteries of the green world as experienced by the hero of *The Ring,* a stripling raised in the wild. It sounds like Jean-Jacques Rousseau's prescription for the ideal education, though the evil dwarf who brought the boy up and the oafish dragon he is about to slay would have raised hell with Rousseau's syllabus. The deep rustling in the strings gives way to a twittering on oboe, flute, and clarinet, each with his special figure. This represents a bird who directs Siegfried to the fiery mountain where the love of his life, Brünnhilde, awaits him in sleep. As the satirist Anna Russell puts it, "She's his aunt, by the way."

Siegfried's Rhine Journey (from Götterdämmerung, Act I)

Felling a dragon and rescuing a distressed damsel are not sufficient exploit for a Wagnerian hero: Siegfried is heard here setting out in search of further adventure in an intermezzo connecting the prologue of the fourth *Ring* opera to its first act. As with any chunk hacked out of the score of an opera other than a self-contained overture, some arranging has to be done to fit the music into the concert hall. The usual practice is to start with sounds descriptive of sunrise on the rock where Siegfried has met and won Brünnhilde, cut past their duet and go right into the intermezzo proper, the "Rhine Journey." This is program music, specifically descriptive. The horn call, for instance, is Siegfried's farewell salute to his lady; and a bit later on comes the unmistakable gurgle of the Rhine, which plays a cosmic role in the *Ring* as a primeval all-water of life. Purists end the intermezzo as written in the score, petering out into the next scene, but concert performances ususally tack on a rousing coda drawn from an earlier passage in the piece.

Siegfried's Funeral Music (from Götterdämmerung, Act III)

A climactic moment in the fortunes of gods and mortals: Siegfried, the once-and-future free man and the hope of the world, has been treacherously murdered. In this intermezzo bridging one scene with another, Wagner retraces the hero's career in music, characterizing on the personal level his nobility and on the public level the tragedy of the martyred redeemer. There is no space here to list the many leitmotifs and their associative meanings in the drama, but perhaps with such exhilarating heroistic tragedy it is better to listen with the heart than the mind anyway.

Parsifal 1879

Many Wagnerians find Wagner's last opera uncomfortably sanctimonious. Musicians admire it for its experiments in harmony that presage certain avant-garde trends of the twentieth century, but its mytho-Christian extemism sends some listeners running for the comics page for a naturalistic-heathen antidote.

Prelude

Themes denoted by the composer as representing Love and Faith comprise the prelude, with the assistance of a quotation of the "Dresden Amen," an eighteenth-century hymn tune associated in *Parsifal* with the Holy Grail. Strange music, the tunes largely unaccompanied, it sounds as if out of a vacuum, or from within a cathedral. Note the almost total lack of motion, to suggest the transcendental endurance of faith.

Good Friday Spell

This excerpt from Act III, often joined to the opera's prelude to form one piece, is Wagner's essay in sustaining a state of grace through orchestral means. If the prelude is (as some think) too holy and too slow, this Good Friday music at least yields a tender oboe tune to depict the splendor of a fine spring day in a misty meadow in an atmosphere of rebirth and transformation.

CÉSAR FRANCK 1822–1890

A deeply religious man whose sense of spiritual transcendance rooted itself as much in the ways of Johann Sebastian Bach as those of God, César Franck is known for a small body of work, for he spent his days more as a teacher of composition and deviser of organ improvisations than as professional creator. One symphony, one string quartet, one violin sonata, one (sort of) piano concerto sufficed to articulate Franck's interest in those fundamental musical structures. True, he did write two operas, five oratorios, four piano trios, and numerous short works for organ, but these are not the works we hear today. Even his several tone poems, all of note, are not often heard outside France.

Belgian by birth, Franck arrived in Paris when it was the cultural capital of the Western music world. It was the heyday of middle-period Romanticism, when Franz Liszt and Richard Wagner forced the issue of cyclic composition, a method of imposing unity on musical forms by either relating a number of themes to each other (so that ultimately all relate to one basic theme) or by the use of a "motto" theme, reprised at various points. Liszt worked in piano music and orchestral "symphonic poems" (tone poems), Wagner in opera. But their revolution changed the thinking of composers in all music's niches. Unity was the battle cry of high-strung nineteenth-century music.

Franck was impressed, and joined up. If the cyclicism in his popular Symphony in d minor strikes many as self-conscious—imposed on the work rather than evolved out of it—it remains a landmark of cyclic symphonism. But what detractors Franck had in his day! Charles Gounod, composer of the opera *Faust* and riding high in a Faustian era, called Franck's symphony "the affirmation of impotence pushed to dogma."

Symphony in d minor 1888

A three-movement symphony was an odd item in the late nineteenth century, but there are reasons why Franck had to write one. For one thing, the old French symphony of the late eighteenth century held to three movements (it lacked the minuet—later, scherzo—movement); thus this French, or, rather, Belgian, symphony is only reviving an ancient historical precedent. Moreover, Franck was working on the cyclic unity described in his introductory article, and the tripartite layout offers a somewhat circular structure as compared with the squared-off four-movement plan of the standard symphony. Anyway, Franck includes all four movement types in his three movements, for the second movement is a combination of slow movement and scherzo.

How does this cyclic unity affect the ear? Not all that much, except when the final movement quotes from the two preceding movements to connect all three organically. In fact, it shouldn't make much difference to the listener to learn that all the themes in this symphony are variants of each other, for the relationship is one that only a musician could reckon, and at that after much study of the score. Then why did Franck bother? Because artistic truth is not subject to one-time hearings. It's there if you want to find it; if not, enjoy what you do find.

There is much to enjoy. The work "begins" slowly, but grows more athletic as it proceeds, and culminates in an invigorating finale. Essentially, it runs on a dualistic energy—a struggle between forces of minor-key fatalism and major-key affirmation. All is gloomy at first in what sounds like a slow introduction. But Franck reuses this slow passage several times over in the movement, veering back and forth between a sad *Lento* (quite slow) and a fiery *Allegro non troppo* (lively but not too). The portentous utterance of the lower strings at the very start of the work in the first *Lento* becomes a clear-cut first subject when the tempo changes to the *Allegro*. Then the *Lento* passage returns again before a second *Allegro* brings us a second subject, plus a grand third, or closing, theme. This third theme is a bright standout in this restless movement, and our first evidence of the symphony's heroic character. The development continues in the *Allegro* vein, but the recapitulation brings back the *Lento-Allegro* trade-off, closing with a more positive-sounding coda. Affirmation is winning out.

The second movement, a slow movement *containing* a scherzo, redoubles the growing optimism. After the battle between the dark *Lento* and the vital *Allegro* in the first movement, won by the latter, Franck will not drop us back into the abyss. No tragic lyricism here. The "slow movement" sections of the second movement reassure even in their understated melancholy, and the nimble "scherzo" at the heart of the movement—rocking clarinets over suave 'cellos and nervous strings—casts even brighter light around. (Historical note: pedants of the day scoffed at Franck's use of the outlaw English horn. Hear it for yourself at the top of the movement, over harp and plucked strings.)

Then the finale [third mvt], an excited conclusion to the conflict of darkness and life. To emphasize the wholeness of the work, Franck quotes from the first two movements, very prominently. The controversial English horn of the second movement briefly reprises its theme at the close of the exposition, echoed near the end of the work by the whole orchestra, which further rounds off the shape of the piece by playing around with the big theme of the first movement. An affirmative finish vanquishes all darkness, celebrates life.

Symphonic Variations for Piano and Orchestra 1885

Leave it to the individualist Franck not to write a common-or-garden piano concerto. Ostensibly an introduction, theme and variations, and finale—all in one movement—the work in effect accords with the three-movement layout of the classical concerto (fast-slow-fast), and the piano is used as soloistically as in any concerto.

The slow introduction sounds as if the variation process is already underway, as the first themes that one hears begin at once to vary, slither in and out of shape. But not till the tempo picks up some minutes later do the variations proper occur. The theme to be varied is announced by the piano; six variations follow, the sixth given to the 'cellos while the piano gently serenades them by way of accompaniment. A double trill on the piano signals the finale, no mere coda but a little symphonic movement in its own right, with first and second themes, development, and recapitulation.

But why does Franck call it *all* symphonic variations if the variations occupy only the center third of the work? Because the themes in all three sections are all variations on the melody sounded by the piano at the very start of the piece—a motto theme. This is another example of the cyclicism basic to nineteenth-century symphony: unity, one theme growing into many others.

Rédemption 1872; revised 1874

Actually a morsel of a grandiose choral work bearing the same title, *Rédemption* pictures the triumph of spiritual affirmation over despair. Here, however, Franck gets more ecstatic than dramatic, emphasizing the opaque radiance of the string choir with the characteristic religiosity that analysts have analyzed with shudders of secular distaste. Those who associate *Rédemption* with the equally devout string sound of the prelude to the first act of Richard

Wagner's *Lohengrin* will have noted an odd point of cultural coincidence. But where Wagner's strings quietly declaim as if woven into a fairy tapestry, Franck's strings rumble with a fundamentalist glory in revealed religion. At the close, brass fanfares celebrate the remission of sin by the Word of Christ.

Les Éolides (The Daughters of Aeolus) 1876

They are the wind, sighs and teasing, the zephyrs of Father Aeolus. Soon, playing about each other, they gather strength, but gentle intervals intrude, and the threatened storm never quite happens. As so often, Franck makes one basic theme do a lot of work: notice that all the tunes sound related. And indeed they are—sisters, daughters of Aeolus, the wind.

Le Chasseur Maudit (The Damned Hunter) 1882

Hunting horns invoke a forest for us, interrupted by church bells: it is Sunday morning, and only the blasphemous would indulge in a hunt. Apparently, someone will indulge, for the horns and bells battle until the hunt wins out. This is the crux of this vital tone poem—the hunter defies piety for a lark, and is rewarded by the Flying Dutchman–like curse that he must ride forever, himself hunted by the dogs of hell. The horror of the hunter's peculiar Sunday is fully borne out by Franck's frenzied hunting music. A more subdued middle section portrays the creepy-crawly aspect of the curse, but the hunt returns for a rampageous finish. Those who golf on the Lord's day, be ye warned.

Les Djinns (The Demons) 1844

Here's a tiny piano concerto—no, more exactly a tone poem with the embellishments of a solo piano. (A proper concerto calls for a more pronounced structural basis than is possible in one short movement, as here.) *The Demons* takes its inspiration from a poem by Victor Hugo in which man is tormented by the spirit world. The piano voices human horror, the orchestra the haunting grotesquerie of the Beyond, until a quiet middle section seems to effect a peace. The piano becomes more prominent now developing themes heard earlier, and the "haunting" music gradually dies away. Notice how Franck uses the piano partly as a member of the orchestra and partly as a soloist, but never for celebrity display. This makes the piece a rare item, as stars find it too piffling for their status quo while the public lacks the curiosity to hear the piece unless a star is announced for it. Catch-22.

ÉDOUARD LALO 1823–1892

Lalo had flair. Of French nationality and Spanish origin, he dealt in exotica—a Norwegian Rhapsody, a "Russian" violin concerto, an opera called *The King of Ys* set in ancient Brittany and peopled by imaginary Bretons with real names: Margared, Rozenn, Karnac. Like many others, he faded from the scene when his era ended, but he still holds the list for one work of enduring delight (and yet more folkloric charisma), the Spanish Symphony.

Symphonie Espagnole for Violin and Orchestra, op. 21 1873

The middle nineteenth century was the heyday of the virtuoso violin concerto, and many of the best-known such were written with a specific virtuoso in mind. Mendelssohn composed for the great Ferdinand David, Brahms for Joseph Joachim—and the stars themselves wrote showpieces, though few of these are still played today. Similarly, Lalo conceived his "Spanish Symphony" as a bud to be opened—wistful, ardent petals—by Pablo Sarasate: despite the title this is a concerto, not a symphony. In five rather than the concerto's traditional three movements, the piece earns its great popularity for a wealth of melody lightly scored—for Sarasate led an avant-garde among violinists for the delicate *ping!* of his attack, so unlike the tempestuous heroism of the Paganini school.

Thus, though the soloist is not denied the chance to parade the intricacies of his art, we get no storming of the heavens or descents into the abyss. Actually, this is a suite scored as a concerto, the five "numbers" rotating views of the Spanish soul in authentic Spanish rhythms. This is why Lalo wrote the work with two more than the usual movements—besides the basic fast-slow-fast movements of the standard concerto, he included two scherzo movements to fill out his dossier on Spanish style. (Performers often omit the third movement, one of the two scherzos, figuring that one scherzo is enough. But if one were enough, Lalo would not have written two.)

After a hefty introduction anticipating the main theme, the first movement takes a regular sonata-allegro course of first theme, contrasting second theme, their development and recapitulation. The Spanish atmosphere, touched on there, floods the second movement, a moody scherzo based on a rhythm known as the seguidilla, and the third as well, a slower scherzo dominated by the soloist. (Note how the soloist's theme is first presented in the minor and then dressed up in the brighter major mode.) The fourth movement is the slow movement, a sombre situation colored by the low brass instruments in the beginning and the pulsing kettledrums toward the end. Lalo pulls a curious stunt at the start, giving the orchestra an accompanimental figure to play thirteen times, getting louder and softer until at last the soloist slips in with a tune. A rondo (in which one main theme predominates throughout the movement, usually without changing, while "episodes" trade off between its appearances) provides a typical concerto finale [fifth mvt].

BEDŘICH SMETANA 1824–1884

A true son of Bohemia (part of modern Czechoslovakia), Smetana inherited his nation's celebrated musical tradition at a time when a nationalistic trend in music spurred composers to root out and exploit the folk information in their native cultures. Smetana needed a little brush-up before he could join the movement: his education was more German than Bohemian, and he couldn't even speak his native language. But once he placed himself he did so well for the homeland that he became known as the Father of Czech music. Yet he was only carrying on an ancient line, ancient even by European standards. As early as the Renaissance, Bohemian musicians roamed all Europe as teachers, minstrels, and instrumentalists, and poor indeed was the Bohemian household that could not count a folk ensemble among its members.

What Smetana did father was a movement devoted to working folk music, folk color, and folk legend into symphonic form. His successor, Antonín Dvořák, could not turn his back on the international scene entirely, but Smetana willingly embraced the all-native muse. His operas delve into local history and saga, and his great orchestral achievement is a series of six tone poems collectively called *My Native Land.* One of the countless discouraging tales that blot the course of art like oil on velvet informs us that Smetana, like Beethoven, grew deaf in mid-career and composed most of *My Native Land* in silence, hearing it only with the musician's secret ear.

Má Vlast (My Native Land) 1879

This cycle of six tone poems on Bohemian saga and topography may be taken as exhibit A in the case of nationalistic art. For rhythmic vitality, melodic self-expression, and sheer narrative sweep all six prove irresistible. Detailed programs were run up for them (by someone else with Smetana's approval), and while any one of the six may be heard separately, they work best as a series because Smetana organized them to relate to each other thematically. (For example, the main theme of Vyšehrad, associated with the ruined glory of an old fortress overlooking the Vltava River, turns up again in Vltava, when the music pictures the same fortress.) As regards structure, the forms vary from piece to piece.

Vyšehrad

Picture in your mind a great lump of rock jutting out of the Vltava River near Prague. Here ancient kings raised up a castle, the Vyšehrad (pronounced *vi*-zhe-hrad), and the tone poem acts as might a bard, striking his harp and singing of the chivalric past. One hears the harp at the very start, by way of poet's prelude, and gradually a noble theme grows out of the orchestra's cautious warm-up: an epic takes a while to get going. At last it appears in full raiment, heralded by cymbal crashes. Note how, though the tempo changes at times, the theme remains in view, changing its tone to accommodate the retrospective of heroism and the passing of glory in the world.

Vltava (also known as The Moldau)

A remarkable idea: to follow the course of a river from its tiny sources down to the heaving causeway of a metropolis. The river is the Vltava, called the Moldau by Western Europeans, and it starts with flutes, then clarinets, representing different brooks whose waters collide to grow into the flowing Vltava. The theme allotted to the river is unmissable, a charming folkish tune in the minor key. Moving on its way, the river passes through woodland—horn and trumpet calls—and then through more settled territory, where a peasant wedding is in progress: bumptious dance music on clarinets and strings with an um-pah bass.

Then night falls in a strange quasi-silence that evolves into a dance of water nymphs on flutes and clarinets accompanied by a plashing harp. The next episode follows the water into rapids, where the Vltava theme sounds jagged and bitten. Shooting through the turbulence, the river passes the great Vyšehrad fortress, and we hear the Vyšehrad theme from the preceding entry in this cycle of tone poems. Now the Vltava has reached Prague, city of spires, and the theme rolls out gloriously in the major key.

Šárka

Radical feminists will enjoy this tale of a Bohemian Amazon and her man-slaughtering army, for though Ms. General Šárka (pronounced "*shar*-ka") tastes of love, war ultimately conquers all. After a fiery introduction, a light but testy strain sets up for the central episode of the piece—a meeting between Šárka and the knight Ctirad. (For reasons not worth going into, Ctirad finds Šárka tied to a tree. He . . . uh, liberates her.) Šárka is portrayed on the clarinet, Ctirad on the 'cello; love music follows. Suddenly, a martial, even jaunty section intrudes: Ctirad's knights are celebrating the coming marriage of hero and heroine. But clarinet and horn call Šárka's Amazons to arms; one cannot make both love and war. Ctirad and his fellows are wiped out.

Z Českých Luhôv a Hájův
(From Bohemia's Meadows and Forests)

A bizarre rustling of nature noises opens this pastoral tone poem, at length giving way to the principal theme in clarinets and horns. This is repeated over string trills, then by the full orchestra. Something basic and beautiful in it tells of man's love of his homeland, of earth, air, and sky—and of his fellow man: two sudden snatches of polka depict a village do, and finally the polka takes over altogether—a harvest festival, doubtless. Toward the end, the main theme returns, followed by the odd nature rustling of the opening.

Tábor

In form a fantasia (a free construction), *Tábor* blends, mosaiclike, military themes and an old Hussite chorale, "You Who Are the Warriors of God," for like the succeeding tone poem *Blaník* it deals with the Hussite Rebellion of the early fifteenth century. Jan Hus was burned in Constance by Calvin, but his movement for Bohemian independence and, incidentally, Protestant rationalism, triumphed. Smetana celebrates the terror of the Hussite army in this salute to their war camp, Tábor, some fifty miles south of Prague.

Blaník

As this is a sort of continuation of *Tábor,* the preceding piece in the cycle, please catch up on the Hussites and their rebellion in the paragraph directly above. Tábor was the Hussites' encampment; Blaník is the hill in which, so legend tells, their corporeal beings sleep until the day when Bohemia is again threatened by foreign invasion. Strangely, they seem to have slept right through invasions by both Nazis and Soviets in recent years.

Musically, *Blaník* is episodic. After a martial opening, Smetana portrays the timeless peace of the sleeping army via pastoral woodwinds. Not for long, though—not for Bohemia, one of Europe's most central battlegrounds, a favorite raiding place for imperialists of all kinds. The Hussite chorale that sparked much of *Tábor* is also heard here, and at the very end we hear for a few seconds the broad theme of *Vyšehrad* (the first tone poem in this cycle) to put the final stamp on this patriotic exercise.

Richard III 1858

Richard III marks Smetana's graduation as a Lisztian, seeking an aesthetic for program music in the ceaseless variation and development of one all-important theme. Smetana claimed to have characterized Shakespeare's king in the first moments of the work, carrying the theme through struggle, then victory, then crisis and collapse.

Wallenstein's Camp 1859

A tone poem inspired by Schiller's play. The first section covers the bustle of soldiers on active duty, the second an impromptu dance with fiddle and bagpipe. (Note the intrusion of the trombones, intoning—as does a Capuchin friar in Schiller's play—a sermon against the carousing of the impious.) A third section offers a dreamy nocturne—peace—and a final section, heralded by trumpet calls—reveille?—presents the troops on dress parade. Thus, Smetana has made a kind of one-movement symphony out of a tone poem: the first section is like a first-moment exposition, the second a scherzo, the third a slow movement, the fourth a shortened finale.

Overture to The Bartered Bride 1866

Smetana's comic opera *The Bartered Bride* remains a classic folk piece, nicely prepared for by this racy sonata-allegro movement. Note the gradual and separate entries of the different string instruments after the opening bit, building in volume until a very Czech-sounding dance tune comes roistering out in the full orchestra (not least on the timpani). A tender second theme follows, but the busy strings push right in with a brief development, and recapitulation is not far behind, the timpani outdoing themselves. This time, the gentle second theme hesitates, prompting a wild coda.

ANTON BRUCKNER 1824–1896

Pious, modest, naive, and easily bullied yet quietly tenacious in the face of consistent public and critical disdain, Bruckner has only recently come into his own as one of the great symphonists. Probably no other composer is so disliked by those who dislike him as Bruckner is. But that is the price that extremism sometimes must pay. A Bruckner symphony (there are eleven in all, numbers 1 to 9 and two early works, known as the "Student" symphony and, charmingly, no. 0) could not be mistaken for any one else's symphony. His large is a certain kind of large, clumsy and overbearing to some. His slow movements are "slower" than any others'—and dull, say some, with the mystical radiance of the idiot. His sense of form was set so early on that he wrote all his mature symphonies in the same style—his detractors say that Bruckner didn't write nine symphonies, just one symphony nine times.

Forewarned is forearmed to defend the amazing Bruckner. I cite the arguments of the anti-Brucknerite only because such attitudes are not rare. You will hear these diatribes often, from critics and lay buffs alike; don't let them discourage you from trying this huge art for yourself, for as sheer symphony it ranks not only high but unique. Bruckner *is* extreme: loud, deep, repetitive, and long. He is the last word in symphonic flamboyance, world creation and world's end. His format may sound weird at first, but in fact it is simply the Classical symphony of Beethoven pushed out to wide limits that Beethoven himself indicated as possible, even necessary. Beethoven's Ninth without singing in the last movement, if you can imagine it that way, is a precursor of the standard Bruckner symphony.

In fact, that quip about Bruckner writing the same symphony over and over is not whistling Dixie. Bruckner did work from the same plan each time out. But while the plan does not vary very much, its effect on the different combinations of melody, harmony, scoring, and so on varies greatly. Therefore, it pays to lay down the general structure of the most commonly heard of Bruckner's symphonies, nos. 3 through 9, for of strictly orchestral music Bruckner's output really consists of those seven works. No concertos. No tone poems. No serenades. Just symphonies, simple but big.

To begin with, the layout is orthodox: four movements, with two powerful sonata-allegro movements at the ends and a slow movement and scherzo in the middle (the slow movement precedes the scherzo in all but the last two). The first theme of the first movements is all-important in Bruckner, the initiative for the musical drama. This first theme sets up a dramatic conflict for the whole work that spins out in a straight line through the movements to resolution at the very end: it is the essence of the symphony, and is usually restated at the work's end. The slow movement is *very* slow and deeply spiritual. The scherzo is bluntly rhythmic, usually with an unbelievably naive-sounding trio (the middle section), and always closes with an exact repeat of the scherzo proper after the trio. The finale balances the first movement, concluding the drama either tragically or victoriously. Thus:

statement of conflict	reflection of conflict	dynamics of conflict	resolution of conflict
1st mvt	slow mvt	scherzo	finale

Much of the above is derived from Beethoven's Ninth. Bruckner, going back to an early foundation for the symphony at a time when many composers were deeply into experimentation, is at heart a Classicist working in a Romantic age. He is often mistaken for a Romantic, not least because of his devotion to and influence by the arch-Romantic Richard Wagner. But in his insistence on ancient structures, he shows himself a Classicist. Indeed, he goes as far as to de-Romanticize Beethoven's Ninth, writing his own versions of it without the heretical (i.e., Romantic) intrusion of the singers in the finale.

One of the things that most exasperates non-believers about the way Bruckner sounds is his extremely expansive architectural procedure. With other symphonists, one hears themes come and go, intrude on each other, cooperate, even combine. It all seems very fluid. But Bruckner builds his works out of huge blocks of sound: a theme comes, and stays, and grows immense, and only then goes, followed by the next theme, which stays, and so on. It's not fluid; it's episodic; it's also spectacular. It's like a cathedral making a pilgrimage: it may lack zip, but it sure has effect when it arrives.

Obviously, this is an extreme style, and as it takes some getting used to, Bruckner had the devil of a time getting himself established. Bruckner's Vienna was enjoying a musical heyday, with all the intrigue and dirty politics that any art community suffers from and luxuriates in, and poor Bruckner was made a pawn in a feud between pro- and anti-Wagner factions. A devoted disciple of the huge Wagnerian orchestra, Bruckner was in fact much less Wagnerian than he was thought to be, including by himself. Size is all they have in common, for Wagner was the very paragon of literary, sensual, pagan Romanticism while Bruckner was absolutely musical, ascetic, and Christian. Still, they seem to share a sound-space—and that was enough in itself to insure Bruckner a campaign of hostility on the part of the anti-Wagnerites, led by Vienna's most mean-spirited critic, Eduard Hanslick, who was unfortunately Vienna's most influential critic as well.

Eventually, Bruckner caught on, but until very recently he was more heard of than heard outside Germany and Austria. The strong hymnic derivation of his chorales, the folkish *Gemütlichkeit* of the trio tunes in his scherzos, and the reminiscences of Beethoven all appealed naturally to Germans while sounding alien to everyone else. The phonograph, however, made him universal; it gave the ear a chance to pick up on Bruckner in steady helpings, domesticated him in the living room.

One last item: Bruckner's scores are bedeviled with a problem of edition, for throughout his life his friends convinced him that his unpopular symphonies needed improvement of one kind or another. Too quick to doubt himself, Bruckner made his own revisions and sometimes let others maim his work for him. Now, it isn't clear exactly which of several versions of each work is the authentic one. In certain cases, the differences are not significant. In others, such as no. 5, they are vast, offering what amounts to totally unlike "soundings" of the same material.

Where to start? Nos. 4 and 7 seem most successful at enchanting the newcomer. Everest-climbers might want to scale the summit and tackle the greatest of the lot, no. 8—because it's there.

Symphony no. 3 in d minor, "Wagner"
1873; revised 1877; revised again 1889

Bruckner himself called his Third the "Wagner" Symphony because he was hoping for Wagner's support in some small way, such as being permitted to dedicate the score to him. (At first, Bruckner quoted themes from Wagner's operas in the score, though revisions deleted all but one of these.) Like many symphonic subtitles, this one is misleading. Bruckner was strongly influenced by Wagner, especially in the field of orchestration. But this work is no more Wagnerian than any other Bruckner symphony.

It is a big work. One can tell right from the start that one is in for a heavy trip because the music is highly (and deliberately) reminiscent of the opening of Beethoven's Ninth. Bruckner means to show his scale at once, produce his references. (The key of this symphony is the same as that of Beethoven's Ninth; among musicians such a correspondence is no coincidence.) After a movement that fully bears out its beginnings, the slow [second] movement continues the drama in less trumpeting terms. (It is here, at the very end of the movement, that Bruckner slips in the "Magic Slumber" theme from Wagner's *Die Walküre.)*

The scherzo [third mvt] brings things back up to an earthy level. The main theme is tumultuous, the trio a rustic waltz of great charm—note the bird calls. Then the finale [fourth mvt], which matches the first movement for grandeur, though an odd episode early on pits a frivolous dance tune (on the violins) against a solemn chorale in the brass. (Bruckner told his biographer that this passage was meant to capture life's humor simultaneously with life's sorrow.) Climax builds on climax, and at length the ultimate climax is reached, and the fourth movement closes rather as the first movement began.

Symphony no. 4 in E Flat Major, "Romantic"
1874; revised 1880

Bruckner gave this, his most popular symphony, its subtitle on the advice of friends who wanted to Romanticize him, get him into program music. Poor Bruckner was even talked into running up programmatic captions for the individual movements—all after the totally non-programmatic music was written!

It's the most "pleasant" of the other Bruckner symphonies. A solo horn call opens it, followed by the usual Brucknerian build-up and climax. The second theme lightens the tone—a quainty tripping passage for the strings. The usual brass chorales and climaxes lead to a triumphant close, and while the second [slow] movement suggests a funeral march, it really isn't all that gloomy. Note the principal theme, right at the start, on the 'cellos; it returns several times, stronger at each hearing until it explodes in the full orchestra over upward-rushing strings near the end. The scherzo [third mvt] Bruckner at one point called "The Hunting of the Hare," though this excited pride of hunting horns sounds as if it's after grander quarry—an elephant, perhaps. The slender, waltzlike trio (middle section) Bruckner termed "Dance-Melody During the Huntsmen's Meal." As always, the first section is repeated after the trio. The finale [fourth mvt]—which occasionally quotes the hunting horns from the scherzo—balances the power of the first movement. Like it, the triumph at the end is not one of despair but of triumph for its own sake. A happy symphony.

Symphony no. 5 in B Flat Major
1876; revised 1878

No. 5 is the only one of Bruckner's symphonies to begin with a slow introduction. It is a fragmented declaration of purpose: quasi-melodic noises over quietly plucked strings, then a fanfare, then a bit of brass chorale. (All of this will return later on.) The movement proper takes off in fast tempo, building in Brucknerian climaxes, and does not end for twenty minutes. This is one of the longest of symphonies, but familiarity will breed confidence in Bruckner's great time-spans—after all, Beethoven and Schubert were reaching for this grandness of statement in their respective Ninth symphonies. Bruckner is only carrying their work forward.

The slow [second] movement, too, is long—but simple. Two basic themes alternate and vary slightly; after a few hearings it will all feel—as indeed it is—tightly organized. The first theme opens the movement (solo oboe over string accompaniment); the second theme appears shortly thereafter, a broad flow in the strings.

Interestingly, the string accompaniment of that first theme, speeded up, defines the pulse for the scherzo [third mvt], like all Bruckner scherzos a strict ABA form. The string figure dominates the A, riding it through alternations of rustic gaiety and furious power. The B is like a miniature A, a pert rustic dance that builds to a ferocious climax.

The fourth [finale] movement opens with the solemn tread of the introduction to the first movement, and further unity is established by the quotation of the first subjects of both the first and second movements. Bruckner draws our attention to what has preceded to make the sense of conclusion more immediate. The finale comprises an immense series of archlike sections, rising and reaching to a last climax, a festival outburst punctuated by the brasses, blazing in primary colors. A heroic and much underrated work—one, incidentally, that the composer never heard performed.

Symphony no. 6 in A Major 1881

This is less tragic, less ferocious than most of Bruckner's symphonies. The first movement gets off to a quiet but flying start, braking slightly for the lyrical second theme group. The expected development leads, in a breathtaking crescendo, to the recapitulation in a great release of harmonic tension—even a non-musician can "hear" the reinstatement of the home key, A Major, after forays into other keys. Bruckner finishes off the movement in a coda so long it amounts to a novel fourth (exposition-development-recapitulation-coda) section of sonata form.

A consoling complement to the fiery first movement, the second [slow] movement traces the more songful side of things. The water-ripply scherzo [third mvt] brightens the overall tone. Bruckner marked the A section of the (ABA) scherzo *Not fast,* but a racy inner voice on the second violins and violas gives the impression of speed, an interesting effect. (Also interesting is Bruckner's suggestion of the Rhine music from Act III of Richard Wagner's *Götterdämmerung,* possibly in homage to Wagner or possibly just accidentally.)

The finale [fourth mvt] is tricky, an episodic march. The conductor must hold together a series of ideas, all of them straining toward a final great junction point at the close in which the entire work fulfills its statement (note the trombones blazing with the very first theme of the first movement to add to the sense of cyclic completion). When a first-rate Bruckner conductor takes the podium—Wilhelm

Furtwängler, Otto Klemperer, or Eugen Jochum, for example—the fulfillment is patent.

Symphony no. 7 in E Major 1883

Perhaps this is the most beautiful of Bruckner's symphonies, the least overbearing, the least incessantly climactic. Each movement, in its separate way, seems to emphasize the Brucknerian character in symphony: the first and fourth movements sound triumphant without forcing the issue, the second [slow] movement unwinds a beautifully long-lined elegy, the scherzo [third mvt] contrasts earthy rhythm with a touching lyrical introspection.

Horns and 'cellos open the work with a strong first subject, setting up for an affirmative movement. But the second [slow] movement is a dirge, apparently inspired by the death of Richard Wagner. The passing of a great man is not all despair—his great works must be celebrated—and the second group of themes has a rather Viennese lilt. As the movement grows in splendor, the theme that opened it glows over a running figure on the violins which swells like sunlight bursting through clouds. A controversial cymbal crash signals the climax—controversial because Bruckner apparently had second thoughts about it, leaving the choice of whether or not to use the cymbals up to the conductor.

The scherzo [third mvt] brings us back up to a more extrovert plane with its jaunty cock-crow on the trumpets, leaving the grand fourth movement to sum up the proceeding in a fine blend of fanfares and chorales. As usual with Bruckner, the final pages assert the cathartic closing in a rush of excited theme fragments that at length resolve in glory.

Symphony no. 8 in c minor 1887; revised 1890

This is the grandest of all Bruckner's symphonies. Only the Fifth is as long, and not even the Fifth offers so tremendous an experience in the transcription of power as a musical conception. A work this big makes one ask, What is a symphony for? Why this shape, this size? How does it use space, time, color?

In shape, the Eighth poses only one innovation in Bruckner's usual practice—the middle slow and scherzo movements are in reverse order. We have the two strongest movements on the outside, the most lively (scherzo) and most lyrical (slow movement) in between:

	scherzo	slow mvt	finale
1st mvt	2nd mvt	3rd mvt	4th mvt

Generally in Bruckner, the two outer movements are the biggest ones, framing the middle movements with granitic force. But here the slow movement is the longest of the four, and the one that for many makes the deepest impression.

How does the work *use* its space, what of its substance? We speak of power, liveliness, lyricism, yes—but to what end? The first movement, for example, agonizes in its several climaxes—but note how it finally dwindles away, its main theme breaking down into a fragment as the texture peters out. Immediately, the scherzo [second mvt] replenishes the vital heart of the work with typical Brucknerian gusto, pounding out its rhythm—but then the trio (middle section) complicates matters with mingled tenderness and brashness. Then the first section of the scherzo repeats, as always. How far have we come? From tragic density to a fleet mixture of joy and sorrow. But now the slow [third] movement deepens the tragedy even as it consoles—and this, too, peters out at its close. It is up to the finale [fourth mvt] to make some account of the whole, referring to both the tragedy and vitality that we have heard and building them into a new, fourth-movement energy for triumph. The sense of time in the work, the *interaction* of movements, has led us progressively into emotional recesses:

dynamic tragedy	Vitality–tenderness/ force–vitality	static tragedy
1st mvt	scherzo	slow mvt

But the finale carries us upward—on the motivation of music already heard—to a summit of release:

dynamic victory
finale

The colors in the work, the identities of the movements, are less separated than integrated: this is the Romantic in Bruckner, seeking unity in the hugest structures. Certain moments stand out—the crushing coda of the first movement, as the all-important first subject falls away to nothing; the rhythmic insistence of the scherzo; the ethereal string chords and harp accompaniment heard at the start of the slow movement; and the cymbal crashes at that movement's climax. But how, then to "receive" all this, to project its conclusion, in the finale? Bruckner does this by transforming the crestfallen first subject of the first movement into a confident first subject in the finale, a fanfare for growth and glory. Most momentously, he finishes off the movement—and the entire work—by playing the first subjects of all four movements simultaneously in a radiant epilogue, the c minor of the opening now blazing in C Major and the four themes like a quartet of fanfares.

Symphony no. 9 in d minor 1894

Unfinished. But it is so fulfilling an experience even lacking a final movement that it has been suggested that it is finished as it is—that even Bruckner could not have written a fourth movement great enough to follow the glorious third, a slow movement of infinite lonely transcendance. Tommyrot. Bruckner was too much the Classicist to consider a three-movement symphony a finished work. He was at the height of his powers then; he would have found the way, however difficult, to top the third with a fourth. It must be admitted, though, that the last movement was giving him trouble. Realizing that he was not going to survive his eleventh symphonic slow movement (there are two earlier, unnumbered symphonies before no. 1), he quoted from other works of his in its last pages in nostalgic requiescat.

If one had to describe this symphony in one sentence, one could say that its three movements are like all other Bruckner first movements, scherzos, and slow movements, only more so. The mysterious opening, blasted by a heroic first theme building up in climaxes and falling back in sorrow at the finish, we have heard before. Perhaps because we know it the last of its line, we hear more in it. But more *is* heard. Likewise, the scherzo [second mvt], while pounding out its rhythm in characteristic Brucknerian fury, seems more furious than any, with a wild string theme that plunges from on high and storms back upward, giving the impression of an immensely reverberant space. Its trio (middle section), instead of leveling off the tension, rather urges it on in quieter, but no less gripping, terms.

Then comes what we must reluctantly accept as the last—but not final—movement, the third. This is surely the most intense, remote, gigantic, solemn music ever to "close" a symphony. All of Bruckner's slow movements sound as if echoing from out of a cathedral. But here the walls and roof vanish—the knowledge that here is the end of Bruckner again lets us take more out of the movement than Bruckner put into it. Shattering, this last movement, but a cheat. We are told it is the end because of its great store of resignation. But it is no end. Knowing that he was dying with the fourth movement a mere set of sketches that no one could put into even provisional working order, Bruckner suggested that his Te Deum, a choral piece, be used as a finale (thus making his Ninth something like Beethoven's Ninth, the work that most inspired his sense of symphonic organization and thematic substance). But this is seldom done. We must hear the work as it stands, and imagine what conclusion Bruckner might have put to it.

CARL GOLDMARK 1830–1915

Rarely if at all mentioned today, Goldmark was once one of the most famous men in music through the wild popularity of an opera, *Die Königin von Saba* (The Queen of Sheba). It is seldom heard today, however, and even his *Rustic Wedding Symphony* has lost its old chestnut status. I cite it and Goldmark's violin concerto below as insurance against an unexpected (and, frankly, unlikely) Goldmark revival.

The Rustic Wedding Symphony, op. 26 1876

Despite its title, this is really more of a suite of five numbers than an organic unity of symphonic movements. The theme is, as the man says, a country wedding (Ländliche Hochzeit)—more a romanticized rural idyll than a populist manifestation. There is no detailed program, but each movement bears a title and strikes a generalized pictorial attitude. First comes a "Wedding March," a simple tune on the lower strings put through thirteen variations, each in a different mood; at length the march returns in its original form. The second movement is a "Bridal Song," not exactly blushing—on the flirty side, in fact. Then comes a "Serenade," with a bagpipe imitation (tune in the oboe and clarinet drone on bassoon and 'cello) by way of country bumpkinism. Taking the work as a true symphony (and it does at least show some signs of the thematic and harmonic organization suggestive of symphony), we might think of the Bridal Song as an interlude, the Serenade as a scherzo, and the following "In the Garden" as the slow movement. The garden scene opens the work up lyrically; this is an occasion for strings, with operatic "love music" welling in the violins. After a *tutti* climax, a wild downward run from the violins to violas to 'cellos and basses brings back the quiet music that opened the movement. The last number is called simply "Dance"—and it's a rouser, the only sonata-allegro movement in the symphony. As a treat, Goldmark interrupts the development section to reprise the main theme of the garden movement. The respite is brief, however, and the whirlwind dance takes over again till the finish.

Violin Concerto in a minor, op. 28 1878

One writer called Goldmark "the Casper Milquetoast of the composing fraternity"; he seems to have been unusually bashful. Sometimes his music is, too—here, perhaps. The Violin Concerto is a reasonably appealing example of the Romantic virtuoso concerto, with much soulful singing in the solo but too little dramatic challenge from the orchestra. There are the usual three movements, fast-slow-fast, and for balance, the two end movements both exhibit some *fugato* (fugue-like) writing for the orchestra. In brief, the piece works if the violinist really likes this kind of music, and can make its pallid sound elegiacal and its bombastic thrill us as boldness—Nathan Milstein, for instance, who has championed it eloquently in recent years when it might otherwise have disappeared altogether.

After a vaguely martial opening in the orchestra, the soloist completely changes the mood of the first movement to one of gentle lyricism. The orchestra humbly plays along with the soloist, eventually growing daring enough to restate its opening theme; the soloist is clearly not impressed with this tune—he'll play it, but he prefers his own more pliant melodies. The shortish second movement offers a very basic concerto slow movement: a solo line of non-stop song supported by the orchestra. The firm G Major tonality of the main theme sounds a refreshing release from the work's center in a minor. The return to the minor in the third movement is strengthened by

Goldmark's urging the soloist on to a display of technique. Typically for its day, this finale has a folk flavor in its dancier passages. Untypically, however, it is never energetic enough for a finale, though the soloist is put through some wild hairpin turns at the last moment.

ALYEKSANDR BORODIN 1833–1887

A doctor and professor of Chemistry at the Petersburg Academy who composed only in his spare time, Borodin engages us for his wild oriental-Slavic flair, his high coloring. He was one of the *Moguchaya Kutchka* ("mighty grouplet"—known hereabouts as "the Russian Five") that spearheaded the nationalist movement in Russian music. The Five lorded their natural gifts over academic training and symphonic tradition, but being self-taught gave Borodin the curse of self-doubt, and he was forever needing encouragement and counsel (especially in the matter of orchestration) from his fellows of the Five—Rimsky-Korsakof, Musorksky, Cui, and especially Balakiryef, the Nestor of the movement.

Borodin is mainly remembered in the West for his opera *Prince Igor,* based on the ancient epic, *The Song of Igor's Campaign.* Actually, the rest of his oeuvre shows the same attractive blend of Slavic ferocity and eastern sensuality. In America his music is well known to many who couldn't cite him offhand through the Broadway "musical Arabian night" *Kismet,* whose authors borrowed some of Borodin's best tunes for their score. (*Kismet* was revived in a poor revision in 1978 as *Timbuktu!*) Thus, "Stranger in Paradise" is—or, rather, was—a section of the Poloftsian Dances in *Prince Igor,* "The Olive Tree" derives from the big third act trio of that opera (and is heard in its overture), "And This Is My Beloved" from the nocturne movement of the Second String Quartet and so on, with bits of *Kismet* cropping up in Borodin's works like old friends suddenly introducing you to their parents after all these years.

Symphony no. 2 in b minor, "The Valiant" 1877

It was the critic V.V. Stassof who gave this work its subtitle, which has not quite caught on in the West. Borodin had been steeping himself in old Slavic lore in preparation for writing his opera *Prince Igor,* and he meant this symphony to recall the roughhewn feudal chivalry of medieval Russia, barbaric and triumphant. Another critic, one Ivanof, wrote, "Hearing this music, you are reminded of the ancient Russian knights in all their awkwardness and . . . greatness."

You are, to be sure. The two outer movements feature the awkwardness, the two inner ones seek romance. One should not attempt to take the stated program too far, though, for while we may go along with Borodin's suggestion that the coarse and brilliant first movement describes a gathering of Russian heroes, the third [slow] movement a recital of bardic lays, and the dancelike fourth a feast of heroes and cheering populace, what are we to do with the second [scherzo] movement, a dizzy business of plucked strings with a lilting trio led off by the oboe? How does it relate to valor? Even Rimsky-Korsakof, that arch-architect of program and advices, was stumped.

In the Steppes of Central Asia 1880

Fiercely Russian yet possessive of his partly Oriental blood, Borodin inlaid both fractions of himself in this tone poem, a depiction of a caravan convoyed by Russian troops through the gritty arabesques of the Asian desert. The music was written to accompany a *tableau vivant*—camels and all, one presumes—performed as part of Tsar Alyeksandr II's twenty-fifth anniversary celebrations, a year before he was assassinated. Borodin himself assures us of the intended program in the manuscript of the score, explaining that the songs of the Russian soldiers and Asiatic natives play off each other, commingle, and fade as the caravan nears and passes. Note the static opening, a long-held note in the violins suggesting the endless desert void, repeated briefly at the very end.

Overture and Poloftsian Dances from Prince Igor 1890

The opera *Prince Igor* occupied Borodin on and off for eighteen years, from 1869 until his death, when Rimsky-Korsakof and Alyeksandr Glazunof undertook to bring the unfinished work to the stage. Much of what Borodin wrote had not been orchestrated, and some (though not all, as is sometimes reported) of the third act hadn't been written at all. As it was, Glazunof had to set down the overture from memory, as Borodin had played it for friends but had not committed it to paper. Luckily, Glazunof exercised one of those fluke gifts for total recall in matters of intense musical interest; apparently, this overture as recorded by Glazunof is Borodin's to the note, a neat sonata-allegro movement with slow introduction, the whole drawn entirely from themes heard in the opera. Brutish vitality and yearning beauty are its urges, as the plot deals with Russian Igor's battle against nomadic Poloftsy invaders from the East, his defeat and capture, and his escape. (Interesting that Borodin, whose veins raged with both Slavic and Oriental blood, should concentrate most of his composing career on a conflict of Mother Russia and barbarian invasion.) After the slow introduction, martial fanfares race into a lyrical but restless first theme group, and the second theme group also blends assertiveness with pliancy. The development reminds us that much of the opera's action is war and intrigue, and after a regular recapitulation, the fanfares return to end the movement.

Vitality and beauty too inform the famous Poloftsian Dances. These occur in Act II, when the big-hearted Khan of the Poloftsy, Konchak, entertains the captive Igor and his son with a feast, chorus, and ballet. (The chorus is not always used in concert performance—i.e., out of the opera house.) The first section of the dances, after a short woodwindy introduction, is a lyrical tune used in the operetta *Kismet* as "Stranger in Paradise." Actually, much of this piece turned up in *Kismet:* the next section, a viciously exuberant movement, offers two melodies in counterpoint, both familiar from the *Kismet* score. Yet more primitive revelry follows, first a rude waltz, then a kind of war dance. "Stranger in Paradise" returns with an intriguing effect—a new melody played over it high in the flute. Earlier material now returns, leading up to a furious closing.

JOHANNES BRAHMS 1833–1897

So used are we to Brahms as the youngest of The Three B's that it might come as a surprise to learn that when the phrase was coined (by the conductor Hans von Bülow), eyebrows shot high all over the Western musical community. Nowadays it feels right to align Brahms' finely articulated musical absolutism with Beethoven's heroically clenched fist and Bach's extraordinary intellectual rebuses; in Brahms' own day it seemed controversial. (As far as that goes, however, Beethoven had a few ridiculous detractors even in his triumphant last years and Bach lay more or less forgotten for nearly a century after his death: in music, universal popularity is an applied, and often posthumous, science.) On the other hand, this "Three B's" business is strictly a shorthand of the midcult. Musicians never refer to it.

The music itself is the reality, anyway, not someone's judgment on it. Sample for yourself Brahms' symphonies, four concertos, two overtures, or the "Haydn" Variations: experience his way with compositional structure and consider him in the light of such other composers of the nineteenth century as Berlioz, Schumann, and Liszt—there's your perspective on Brahms. Those others sought new horizons in their art. They commingled symphony with opera, they worshipped the permutations of the leitmotif—melody that means something—and they began to see music as a means to an end, a vehicle of expression. To Brahms, music was the end; music expressed itself. His symphonies have no titles (as some of theirs did), likewise his sonatas, trios, quintets, and such. When Schumann wrote short piano pieces, he often put names on them: "Lonely Flowers," "Shelter," "Why?." Brahms' many piano pieces bear no titles, only generic descriptions: Capriccio, Ballade, Intermezzo. Brahms' *Academic Festival* and *Tragic* Overtures, vaguely titled, tell no story.

Strange that one should define Brahms' trajectory as much by what he wasn't as by what he was. But then what Brahms wasn't—a full-fledged Romantic—is important in that he inhabited a full-fledged Romantic age. But note that Brahms' symphonies and concertos, so sturdily looking back to Beethoven and ignoring everything in between, offer no less an emotional experience than do the more Romantically colored works of Berlioz, Schumann, or Liszt. Music, again and still, is music.

Symphony no. 1 in c minor, op. 68   1876

So seriously did Brahms take the idea encased in the word "symphony" that he waited till he was forty-three to complete his first, moving towards it with notes, studies, and false tries for over twenty years. In the Classical era of Haydn and Mozart, symphonies were trade; one wrote many, tossing them off sometimes in a matter of days. Yet Brahms, often thought of as the lone Classicist of the Romantic era, lacked the typical Classicist's spendthrift prolificacy. He saw himself as Beethoven's humble heir, heir to a more momentous symphonic worldview. After Beethoven's Nine, a Gospel for true believers, one could no longer toss off a symphony. One had to devastate.

Brahms does, and on very Beethovenian terms. The conductor Hans von Bülow referred to Brahms' First admiringly as "Beethoven's Tenth"; its detractors have taken up the phrase to suggest that

Brahms copied Beethoven's manner without rivaling his talent. They're wrong. This is a big work with a big stretch, from its tragic opening in the minor to triumphant conclusion in the major.

Brahms opens the first movement with a slow introduction of discordant foreboding over a pounding drum. At the tempo change to *Allegro* (lively) and the first movement proper, the rising introductory theme becomes the first theme of the movement, and even the gentler second theme (on the oboe) is based on the same rising figure. (Familiarity with Brahms will reveal many such economies, in which one theme is varied to create other themes.) On these essentially tragic materials the entire movement makes its case, one lightened by the second [slow] movement's plangent but hopeful woodwind coloring and by the third [scherzo] movement's rhythmic insouciance. What's going on? Should so tragic a first movement bc followed by two so impervious intermissions? Indeed, the scherzo is hardly a scherzo at all, more of a second slow movement with occasional scherzoish thrust. But Brahms is saving up for a *big* finale [fourth mvt]. This, like the first movement, has a slow (and ominous) introduction, gradually working up out of c minor into C Major at the revelation of a thrilling horn call. Then comes the great finale itself, led off by a hymnlike melody in the violins that reminds almost everyone of the last movement of Beethoven's Ninth."Any fool can see that," said Brahms when someone mentioned the resemblence. Good old Brahms.

Symphony no. 2 in D Major, op. 73 1878

Having composed the powerful Symphony in c minor a year earlier, Brahms now felt confident to toss off, as it were, a light number in the cooler precincts of D Major. Note the opening three notes, in the lower strings: much of the melodic material for the entire symphony derives from that kernel. Sometimes referred to as Brahms' "Pastoral," the piece glides happily through four movements' worth of warmth and contentment. It has its interior contrasts, of course, but its essence is found more in the first movement's reassuring second theme (in the lower strings, sounding rather like Brahms' famous lullaby) than in the occasional fierce outline of its other tunes. The second [slow] movement has proved difficult for first-time hearers to assimilate; it's complex, so give it a second or third hearing. The scherzo [third] movement is as easy to understand as the second is tricky: instead of an ABA main section-trio-main section repeated, Brahms provides two trios (ABACA), each trio being a variation of the main section. Thus, what one really gets is A A^1 A A^2 A—and anyone who finds the general tone reminiscent of Schubert gets a gold star. The finale [fourth mvt] rounds off the whole in a lively fashion, borrowing yet another old reference—Haydn—in its transparent vitality and technical expertise in relating each melody to the next (and all melodies, ultimately, back to the three-note kernel that launched the work).

Symphony no. 3 in F Major, op. 90 1883

What could have possessed the conductor Hans von Bülow to call this "Brahms' *Eroica*" (thus comparing it to Beethoven's Third, the "Eroica," a work of extraordinary dramatic power)? For Brahms' Third is no heroic symphony. True, it has a heroic opening and a heroic finale. But otherwise it shows a Brahmsian warmth and pliancy that recalls the idyll of, say, Schubert rather than the defiance of Beethoven.

The passionate commitment of the first movement's first measures cedes to a delicate theme on solo clarinet, and it is the latter that sets the tone for the work, at least until the last movement. Both middle movements emphasize the lyrical, the second an expansive slow movement (*very* Schubertian) and the third a scherzo so restrained and graceful as to feel like a second slow movement. Its principal melody strikes an odd balance between sad and not sad; it launches the movement on the 'cellos, *espressivo* (expressively) and returns, after the middle section, on the horn. A minor-key melody, it has every right to sound mournful, yet doesn't, for the accompaniment is scored so as to offer a light consolation.

The finale [fourth mvt], however, changes the tone of the work, taking the key center from F Major to f minor and basing its melodic identity on sharply angular phrases and a cutting rhythmic penetration. Starting *sotto voce* (in an undertone) but quickly flying into the eye of a storm, it sustains the agitation until a lengthy coda returns us to F Major and quiet calm. The sense of completeness is aided at the end by a reference to the first theme of the first movement in the shimmer of the first violins.

Symphony no. 4 in e minor, op. 98 1885

Perhaps the most exalted of the four Brahms symphonies, almost mystical in its stimulation. More than ever the Classicist holding the line of tradition at the height of the revolutionary Romantic era, Brahms demonstrates the ability of Classical technique to expand emotionally. He disproves the apprehension that Classical procedures yield dryness. (Is Mozart dry?) An analyst would have a field day parsing this work by structure, thematic congruency, and such—yet the analyst, too, must succumb to the magic in performance. It is as if Brahms had a mathematics for rhapsody.

What happens here? Tragedy? Heroism? Not specifically: the air of the first movement is one of a temporary truce of some kind, its melody more entrancing than devastated. As usual with Brahms, the entire symphony seems to grow out of its first few notes; again and again, subsidiary themes surface on a shared energy, resurface as new themes only to return to their original form. With aplomb and no prelude, the first theme sails in on the strings, challenged later by a fanfarelike second theme in the woodwinds. Beethoven, whom Brahms regarded as a predecessor of almost unassimilable hugeness, might have beaten these two themes into bloody bits in the development section; Brahms gentles them, and when the first theme leads off the recapitulation (on oboe, clarinet, and bassoon), it is more restrained than ever. But as the recapitulation progresses, the fanfare theme sets up a vigorous coda, ending the movement on a tougher note than that of its beginning.

The second [slow] movement picks up on this, deepening the feeling of profound melancholy, and the following scherzo [third mvt] emphasizes tautness in high Beethovenian style. In other words, rather than launch the whole symphony in pity and terror, Brahms lets its inner core evolve in the progression of movements. What can follow? The finale [fourth mvt] takes the cake for restless grandeur and minor-key passion in a parade of variations on the opening eight-note melody, one variation after another, each as short as the original theme. Hear it in its pure form: a stark pronouncement of woodwind and brass, the first eight notes of the movement. Now come the variations, thirty-one studies in how to play the same thing "only different." (This particular technique is called the passacaglia, because the lower instruments repeatedly sound the same shape while the actual variations play over them.) Unyielding at first, the variations relax at the twelfth variation for flute solo, then broaden out solemnly to complete the passage made by the three previous movements in a fierce e minor coda.

Piano Concerto no. 1 in d minor, op. 15 1858

Young Brahms' friend, patron, and least severe critic Robert Schumann threw himself into the Rhine and was fished out mad; shortly thereafter Brahms composed music that in part became the first movement of the present concerto, inspiring the conjecture that Brahms was attempting to portray Schumann's agonies in the agonized music. (The slow movement likewise was arrogated as a requiem for Schumann, and the striding third movement presumably fits into the scheme, too—Schumann's truth going marching on, perhaps.)

Such tales misrepresent Brahms, whose music portrays only itself, never anything else. But the piece is suggestively dramatic; it starts huge, develops huge, and ends huge. Even granted that the Romantics liked things big, Classicist Brahms presented the Romantic era with a piano concerto that was immediately attacked for its generous proportions (yet Brahms' Second Piano Concerto would be even bigger). The opening, first theme over a thunder of drums, seems to resound through some infinity of space, and while what immediately follows is on the lyrical side, the texture of the sound reaches broadly out beyond the simple dimensions of the concerto for the grandeur of the symphony.

When the piano at last makes its entrance (waiting out the *tutti,* or orchestral exposition) it is not as a fiery star but as a mournful second—but on a very elaborate scale. Brahms asks for the most from his soloist in terms of technique and endurance—he wants a Romantic hero as well as a keyboard athlete. Luckily for him, the soulful slow [second] movement affords some relaxation of the passion that stalked the first movement so unceasingly. But the rondo finale [third mvt] returns us to the dynamics of size and power. It's interesting to note that the rondo, so useful in finales of the showpiece concerto—when the music services the virtuoso's thirst for personal exhibition—does equally well here in a far more artistic context. Most rondos would sound too trivial for this concerto, too light and pranksome. But *this* rondo does the job, matching the first movement in weight and thrust. One episode along the way even signals a short adventure into fugue, which is as much a gesture as Brahms will make in the direction of divertissement, and he ends the work as it began: highly symphonically.

Piano Concerto no. 2 in B Flat Major, op. 83 1881

The biggest piano concerto ever written till then, op. 83 takes four movements, not the usual three. In its structural breadth it resembles a symphony more than a concerto, then—but the piano soloist keeps the concerto principle in operation. Indeed, the understated opening of the first movement is misleading: this is a mighty work, with one of the most difficult piano parts in all concerto.

At first, it looks as if Brahms has given in to the post-Classical habit of bringing the soloist in before the orchestral exposition is over. But, after its first intrusion, the piano lays out to let the orchestra state the main themes alone. Once the soloist jumps back in, he is seldom out of the picture for the rest of the work. Whether accompanying other instruments or sounding his own melodies, the soloist holds the center together—*is* the center, truly. After the sensitively heroic first movement comes Brahms' novel addition to concerto form, a scherzo [second mvt], and a dour one at that, adding symphonic gravity to the relatively light-headed three-movement plan of the concerto. In a symphony, the scherzo lends rhythmic vitality to the overall plan; so it does here in a virile *Allegro appassionato* (impassioned and lively). The slow [third] movement opens the work with a deep vein of lyricism from its touching 'cello solo to a lovely hushed interlude in slower time for the pianist and two clarinets; the 'cello returns with its tune at the end under the piano's filigree of trills and scales. The use of solos has lent a touch of intimacy to the work; now Brahms pulls back in an extroverted finale [fourth mvt] that upgrades the merry rondo of old into a *summum bonum* of sophisticated innocence. For without forgetting that the quasi-comic rondo makes for a pleasantly cathartic finale, Brahms manages to expand it to fit the scale of the rest of the work. Such delight made Mozart's concerto finales the touchstone of bright symphonic resolution. But here Brahms reinvents the idea to accord with a grander epoch.

Violin Concerto in D Major, op. 77 1878

Brahms' violin concerto is of a type very popular in the late nineteenth century, with a first movement exploiting the considerable sweetness of tone that the instrument commands, a slow movement of seductive intimacy, and a "Hungarian" rondo finale designed to show off the soloist's "gypsy fiddle." The vogue has passed, taking most of the "Hungarian" concertos with it, but Brahms' remains one of the most popular of violin concertos. It contrasts remarkably with his two piano concertos: they are heroic, this is lyrical—especially in the first movement, which blends the structural broadness of a symphony with the pliancy of the Romantic violin. Brahms even allowed for a soloist's cadenza—he didn't always—in its usual spot near the close of the first movement. The cadenza traditionally used is the work of Joseph Joachim, a champion violinist who gave Brahms much advice in the writing of the solo part.

After the mellifluous first movement, a slow [second] movement might appear too much of a good thing but for the former's rhythmic drive; only with the second movement does Brahms really lay peace on the landscape, in a simple oboe melody varied by the soloist and counterstated in a middle section until the oboe reprises the first theme. (The eminent violinist but not especially Brahmsian Pablo de Sarasate, asked if he would play the work, replied, "Do you think I were so tasteless as to stand on the platform holding my violin while the oboe plays the *only* melody in the whole work?")

The "Hungarian" finale [third mvt], delivered with the right oomph, sounds exceedingly Hungarian; its rondo structure is transparently easy to follow. Note the coda's amusing transformation of the main theme, the rondo refrain, into a sprightly, ridiculous march.

Concerto for Violin and 'Cello in a minor, op. 102 1887

A problematic work. For one thing, the 'cello doesn't carry as well as the violin and can too easily be overshadowed either by the violin's bright sound or the volume of the orchestra. For another, this "double concerto" was Brahms' final bout in the symphonic arena (chamber music, songs, and keyboard works are all that followed), and he emphasized the autumnal intimacy of the concerto rather than its flashy virtuoso exterior. Vastly less showy than most concertos, op. 102 disappoints some people for its lack of exhibition and its gravity.

However, the work represents a fascinating use of two solo instruments without the orchestra's being demoted to mere accompanist status. The opening of the first movement, for instance: the orchestra anticipates the first subject briefly as the 'cello snaps in as if accepting a dare, borrowing the orchestra's last few notes for a cadenzalike recitation. Then the woodwinds anticipate the second subject—and this, in turn, is appropriated by the violin. Soon the 'cello has joined it, and we have the two soloists engaging in accompanied dialogue, building tension until the orchestra again shoves in with a full statement of the movement's main themes, a full Classical *tutti.*

Thus the "whole idea" of the concerto has been announced: the violin and 'cello in partnership and something of a challenge to the orchestra. In this way, Brahms acclimatizes us to all that must follow, reflective and thematically pungent but not show-offy—another reason, perhaps, why the work is not heard that often. (Why would soloists play something reflective when the public would much rather hear them show off?) Meanwhile, note how the main theme of the slow [second] movement develops out of the horn and woodwind calls that launch it, and enjoy the tensile energy of the final rondo [third mvt]. If there's one thing one may count on in a concerto (at least, usually), it's a vivacious rondo finale.

Serenade no. 1 in D Major, op. 11 1859

Mozarteans, used to the particular charm of the serenade, will feel right at home here, though noting Brahms' more advanced harmony. Since the serenade is basically a frivolous symphony with no fixed number of movements, Brahms gives us two scherzos and two minuets, back-to-back. The general plan is: a lively, Haydnesque first movement; scherzo; slow movement; two minuets; scherzo; and rondo finale. Obviously, the emphasis is on the higher sorts of spirits. But the slow movement is the emotional heart of the work, rich in woodwind solos that recapture the sound of the Classical era, the serenade's heyday. (Two birds, one stone: (1) instrumental solos were more noticeable in the days when orchestras were smaller and the concerto more popular, and (2) the light quality of the serenade depended particularly on the flirty color of the woodwinds.)

Serenade no. 2 in A Major, op. 16 1859

Scored for a small group (no violins!), this serenade reaches for dark, brooding colors. There are five movements, like a symphony with an extra scherzo just before the finale. The general tone is light drawing into shadow dancing out again into light, the shadow's center occurring at the middle section of the slow [third] movement, when two horns sound a theme of resignation, odd in the context of the traditionally light-hearted serenade. The remaining two movements return us to happier realms, especially in the rondo finale [fifth mvt], led off by two tom-fool clarinets heading for the dance floor.

Variations on a Theme by Haydn, op. 56a 1873

One of the most invigorating works in the repertory, the "Haydn" Variations take as their theme a tune known as the St. Antoni Chorale; its authorship, once ascribed to Haydn, is at present in doubt. Whoever wrote it, it supplied Brahms with a dandy jumping-off place for rhythmic, harmonic, and melodic transformations so deftly turned that he never has to stray far from the original shape of the theme to float his parade.

The structure is simple: the theme itself, AABA (a tune repeated, a contasting middle section, and the first tune again), nine variations, and a final statement of the theme in its pure form. Now, let's take the variations as they come:

Var. I: bassoons and horns sound the theme's basic shape under flowing strings.

Var. II: the first four notes of the theme inspire a lively new version.

Var. III: a lissome melodic variation, with the outline of the theme still implicit. Note the sighing horn in the B section.

Var. IV: A slower tempo, pulling away from the original theme.

Var. V: The tempo picks up again, bustling like a Mendelssohnian scherzo.

Var. VI: The theme is more recognizable here, squarer and stiffer.

Var. VII: Now as supple as a court dance, the theme shows its harmony with a lilting new melody phrased as a barcarolle (boat music, suggestive of the rocking of the waves).

Var. VIII: slightly introverted, hushed so as to prepare for a grand finale.

Var. IX: the last and most intense variation. Here the theme is buried in the lowest notes of the orchestra, repeated over and over while other ideas pass over it. (This procedure is known as a passacaglia and is in itself a format for variations; thus the last variation is actually a tiny set of variations.) As the music grows more and more majestic, we hear the original theme push through the veil of melody, and at last it appears in full voice, flowing and grand.

Incidentally, the a in the opus number, 56a, is there to separate this orchestral version of the variations from an alternate version written for two-piano duet, op. 56b.

Academic Festival Overture, op. 80 1880

When the University of Breslau decided to award Brahms an honorary degree for being *artis musicae severioris in Germania nunc princeps* ("the first master of rigorous musical art in Germany today"), it naturally expected a sample of Brahms' rigorous art to solemnize the occasion, something—well, solemn. Instead, he wrote one of the most comically jubilant pieces ever, extra-heavy on the Festival. For Academic context, Brahms happily borrowed four tunes from collegiate folklore.

We open with a portentous invocation, a slow introduction to a sonata-allegro movement. It leads up to a lovely horn-and-trumpet call based on the first of the four student songs, "We Had Built a Stately House." This song also supplies the first subject when the movement proper gets going. For a second theme, we are treated to a rolling string setting of the "Hochfeierlicher Landesvater," "Hear, I Sing the Song of Songs." The racy closing theme of the exposition bubbles first on the bassoon, then more orchestrally; this is the "Fox Ride," "What's Coming from the Hills?," an initiation ditty celebrating the oafishness of a freshman from the boondocks. A short, stormy development and gala recapitulation build up to—what else?—"Gaudeamus Igitur" for a splendid coda, cymbals crashing, triangle cheeping, violins rushing up and down, and brass and woodwind in full cry. All told, the biggest orchestra that Brahms ever used.

Tragic Overture, op. 81 1880

No tragedy in particular, says Brahms—absolute music in a generally tragic tone. Two sharp chords lead off. The fast tempo of the bitter opening section holds sway until a lyrical second theme offers temporary consolation. Note that the two opening chords return to divide the exposition from the development, wherein the oboes transform a theme heard earlier into a wan little march somewhat reminiscent of Schubert. The strings take up the march, emphasizing pathos rather than tragedy, and the oboes return shortly to continue their woeful tread. But as the piece moves into the recapitulation, the tragedy hardens, deepens, rages (the two chords again).

CAMILLE SAINT-SAËNS 1835–1921

Saint-Saëns, whose career was one of the longest in Western music, was so industrious that he sometimes wrote when he had little of real moment to express. The act of composition was for him a work of minutes; perhaps it was this fluency that cursed so much of his issue with shallowness. He had much craft, the *savoir faire* of art. But he was glib. "That youngster knows everything," observed Berlioz of the young Saint-Saëns. "But he lacks inexperience."

On the other hand, he was no mere pedant. He loved tradition and innovation both. He brilliantly telescoped the ancient form of the concerto into a fluid, integrated whole. Like many French musicians of his day, he was heavily influenced by Liszt's cyclic transformation of themes, the system by which one basic theme would be varied and reshaped into several different melodies in the course of a composition. That would be Saint-Saëns, the modernist. As for tradition, he had more than a touch of the Bach devotion felt by all composers, and often made his orchestra sound like a gigantic Bachian organ.

This is the paradox of Saint-Saëns: an allegiance to the past and a belief in the future incorporated in a too-often superficial artwork, one that has little more to express than its own technical competence. At his best, though, he is formidable: the "Organ" Symphony, the Second Piano Concerto, the surprisingly whimsical *Carnival of the Animals,* and his best-known work, the opera *Samson et Dalila.*

Symphony no. 3 in c minor, "Organ," op. 78 1886

Some of us wonder, sometimes, why the symphony has so much repetition in it. Why recapitulate all the themes in sonata-allegro (usually first and fourth) movements? Why is the scherzo ABA—why not just AB? Well, Saint-Saëns seems to have wondered, too. In this best and last of his five symphonies (the first two, unpublished, had no numbers), he tried writing a symphony without those traditional repeats.

Superficially cast in two movements, the work clearly follows the usual four-movement format: first movement, slow movement, scherzo, finale. The catch is that the first two and last two movements are joined together:

	slow mvt		scherzo	
1st mvt	2nd mvt		3rd mvt	4th mvt

This join occurs just where the first and third movements would have "repeated"—after the first movement's development section and after the trio (the B) of the scherzo.

The subtitle: we call it the "Organ" Symphony simply because the scoring includes an organ (a piano, too) for a few special effects. Also, this is a symphony with a motto theme, a generative melody basic to the spirit of the piece and the source of its major themes. (Not surprisingly, Saint-Saëns dedicated the work "to the memory of Franz Liszt": Liszt was the prime mover behind the theory of "cyclic unity"—of one theme constantly changing its form as a work proceeds.)

As so often, the motto theme is the first subject of the first movement (after a slow introduction), a nervous figure in the strings. (This theme will reappear in each of the work's four sections in different guises—at different tempos and with altered notes—until it takes over in a thrilling transformation at the end.) Almost everybody's favorite moment in the work is the "slow movement"—the second half of the first movement, a *Poco adagio* (almost very slow) of silvery, impenetrable contentment in D Flat Major. (The moment is impossible to miss, for it is ushered in by the organ's first appearance.) Here the strings take over, with a heavy grandeur. Their theme is repeated, with help from the woodwinds, then developed, retaining its air of spiritual mystery—Saint Saëns is often called frivolous, but this is undebatably profound music. A touch of Bach informs a variation of the theme for violins, now reaching higher in their range as if circling into the dome of a cathedral. Then, a restless sequence for plucked strings continues under the theme, which loses none of its beauty in so much repetition.

The second movement begins with the scherzo section, a furious business in c minor launched by the strings. A faster, lighter trio section featuring woodwinds, piano, and triangle follows, cedes to a repeat of the scherzo, tries to assert itself again—but immediately a cacaphony intrudes. This in turn gives way to a peaceful violin theme by way of transition, and suddenly we are thrust into the closing half of the movement, the finale of the work (again, the organ marks the spot). In C Major, violins and rippling piano scales lay a masterful peace upon the work which grows into a conquering glory. Here, particularly, is felt the searching grasp of "cyclic unity," for the motto theme in its last and most brilliant transformation totally takes over the score, forcing it to an amazing breadth of development, one of the most structurally impetuous climaxes in symphony.

Piano Concerto no. 2 in g minor, op. 32 1868

Saint-Saëns greets us in a Classical mood, launching the work with an unaccompanied cadenza for the soloist that sounds like Bach improvising. The orchestra enters with a few calls to order, and then the first movement takes off with its first theme. This so overshadows the faint-heartened second theme that the latter does not return in the recapitulation, letting the movement close as it opened, with the Bachian cadenza. A traditional concerto would by all rights give us a slow movement next, but Saint-Saëns instead provides a scherzo (in rondo form, by the way, more fluid than the ABA of the strict scherzo-and-trio), with a quicksilver main theme and one of the most irresistible second themes in the repertory. We have completely passed out of the sombre air of the first movement, and the fast, furious finale [third mvt], a tarantella, seconds the motion.

Piano Concerto no. 4, op. 44 1875

Here is a concerto for those who weary of the three-movement (fast-slow-fast) formula. Saint-Saëns organized this work so unusually that musicologists aren't sure how many movements it has. The composer himself counts three. But the first movement seems to turn into a slow movement halfway through, and another, tiny slow movement slips into the last pages of the second movement. But the work does have a nice organic completeness, the clearcut relating of each movement to its fellows. Saint-Saëns manages this by a device familiar to composers of the Romantic nineteenth century: using the same themes in several different movements. For example, notice the first subject of the first movement (in the strings, answered by the piano, right at the start, and promptly used as the basis for a lengthy theme-and-variations episode). This same theme will turn up again in the second [scherzo] movement. For another example, notice the hymn-like theme played by the woodwinds in the "slow movement" second half of the first movement. This chorale will turn up as the triumphant main theme of the finale [third movement].

Violin Concerto no. 3 in b minor, op. 61 1880

Few composers of the late nineteenth century cared as much about the concerto as Saint-Saëns did. His colleagues might write one each for the violin and 'cello and perhaps two for piano, but Saint-Saëns wrote ten in all—three for violin, two for 'cello, and five for piano. Though he experimented with set form often in the concerto, here he turns conservative, constructing the work along strictly traditional lines. The composer has something of an off-day in terms of melody, but at least the writing for the soloist shows off much audacity, brilliance, and sensitivity (if he has such to show). A star violinist is the big cheese here, more or less standing alone, whether introducing the aggressive first subject at the top of the first movement, setting the Palm Court tone for the second-movement barcarolle (boat song, in a rocking rhythm suggestive of watery motion), or launching the finale [third mvt] with an unaccompanied cadenza.

'Cello Concerto no. 1 in a minor,
op. 33 1872

A brilliant tour de force of structure and beautiful writing for the soloist make this a historical study as well as a treat. Its three movements are connected into one large movement comprising an exposition and development in the first movement, a trim, antique minuet in the second movement functioning as a kind of interval, and a recapitulation (with new material) in the last movement. In other words, the whole work acts as one large and varied sonata-allegro movement: statement and development, then a musical intermission, then restatement. Notice how Saint-Saëns exploits the intimate nature of the 'cello sound in the middle movement, beautifully subdued yet all the more noticeable for its lack of exhibit. The composer uses song, not sensation, to draw one in.

Introduction and Rondo Capriccioso for Violin and Orchestra, op. 28 1870

One movement's worth of showpiece miscellany for the soloist, opened by a melancholy introduction with a slightly folkish flavor; the accompaniment of plucked strings suggests a guitar serenade. Saint-Saëns spins out an inconsequential but pleasant rondo here, topping it with a virtuoso's coda of the sort designed to set off the violin as the television talk show sets off the celebrity.

Le Rouet d'Omphale (Omphale's Spinning Wheel), op. 31 1871

Heracles was always getting into trouble. Scarcely had he completed his twelve labors to atone for one crime than he committed some new outrage and did penance by being sold into slavery. Omphale, queen of Lydia, bought him; it is their relationship that Saint-Saëns dramatizes in this tone poem. Robert Graves points out that classical writers tended to view the tale as that of a strongman sapped by a designing woman, and so Saint-Saëns sees it. But the spinning wheel is not found in the original. "The subject of this symphonic poem," the composer states, "is feminine seduction . . . The spinning wheel is only a [musical] pretext."

Well, it's Saint-Saëns' story—let him tell it. After a brief introduction, we hear Omphale in light, mocking music redolent of the festive emptiness of the ballet stage. Then we hear a lowering theme in the darker instruments (lower strings, bassoon, contrabassoon, and trombone): Heracles. This is meaty music, but the tone lightens as the wheel turns to Omphale's theme. Eventually the motion of the wheel gives out and the piece dies away. And what happened, then? Legend tells that Omphale and Heracles made a nice, if temporary, couple.

Danse Macabre (Dance of Death), op. 40 1874

A graveyard bash, from midnight to cockcrow—a waltz, pepped up with xylophone (for rattling bones, one presumes), an out-of-tune solo fiddle, and a whimsical quotation of the medieval *Dies Irae* plainsong. "Intense and coarse realism" was the verdict of a British critic when the tone poem came to London, but the passage of time has painted over Saint-Saëns' grisly chalk with the pastel of nostalgic charm.

The program is a light one: Death summons ghosts to their revels, the winter wind groans as they frolic, and all scatter gravewards as dawn breaks. In form a rondo in g minor, the piece gets going quickly. First the harp chimes twelve o'clock, then the violin soloist (as Death the fiddler) plays warm-up chords with one string tuned flat, and we're off with the main theme in the flutes. In proper rondo style this theme vies with a second (introduced by the soloist), taking turns until Saint-Saëns plays them simultaneously at the climax. But ho, as suddenly as it started, it ends: a cock crows (on the oboe), Death fiddles us a wan adieu, and flick! all is still.

The Carnival of the Animals 1886

This witty suite, scored for small orchestra (including two pianos), tours us through the animal kingdom in short bits; one absolutely must follow the music noting the titles of each number to enjoy the characterizations:

1. Introduction and Royal March of the Lion: Pianos and strings bow to the king of beasts, who roars in menacing keyboard runs.
2. Hens and Roosters: A lot of squealing here, especially from the clarinet.
3. Wild Asses: racing up and down the pianos.
4. Turtles: To express the cagey torpor of the turtle, Saint-Saëns borrows two racy themes from Offenbach's musical comedy, *Orpheus in the Underworld* (one of them the famous can-can), and simply slows them down to a . . . snail's pace.
5. The Elephant: Another borrowing, this one from Berlioz' *The Damnation of Faust.* What could be more apt for the lugubrious elephant than Berlioz' delicate "Dance of the Sylphs"—played

on the double-bass? (Sharp ears may detect a tiny quotation of the Scherzo from Mendelssohn's *A Midsummer Night's Dream.*)

6. Kangaroos: doing what they do.
7. Aquarium: Sea creatures glide and glimmer in lush ripples on piano, strings, flute, and harmonica. (This number was used to excellent effect in Terrence Malick's film *Days of Heaven.*)
8. Long-Eared Characters: A shrill interlude.
9. The Cuckoo Deep in the Forest: on the clarinet.
10. Flight: A flutey bird, hither and yon.
11. Pianists: the most beastly of all in the carnival, practising their elementary scales. Saint-Saëns directs the two pianists to "imitate the gaucheries of a novice." There are no wrong notes, but waggish performers will suggest the fumbling tyro by slowing down at the tricky parts and speeding up at the home-free.
12. Fossils: Five old tunes, including snippets of Saint-Saëns' own not-so-old *Dance Macabre,* Rossini's *The Barber of Seville,* and "Ah! Vous Dirai-je, Maman" ("Twinkle, Twinkle, Little Star").
13. The Swan: The most famous piece in the carnival, vulgarized as "The Dying Swan" by generations of ballerinas no better than they should be. Saint-Saëns set it for 'cello accompanied by the pianos, but the melody proved so popular that his publishers, after his death, arranged it for home use by every conceivable combination, including harp, harmonium, mandolin, and piano; two mandolins and piano; and even a vocal version.
14. Finale: at the gallop, with recollections of the Wild Asses and Roosters.

MILY BALAKIRYEF 1837–1910

Balakiryef is better known for what his colleagues composed than for what he wrote himself. A Russian guru, on the earthy side, but not lacking in the mysticism that endows the natural leader. Balakiryef's following, in fact, founded at his tutelage the first nationalist movement in Russian music, which had till then been largely (but not exclusively) dependent on Western forms and practices.

Balakiryef's movement was known as the *Moguchaya Kutchka* ("mighty grouplet"), generally called the "Russian Five." It was the Five's intention to launch a purely Russian art through Russian modes and structures. They regarded the symphony and concerto as items of ultra-Western derivation, fit for a cosmopolitan such as their coeval Chaikofsky. The Five preferred the song, the tone poem, and opera, where written text or a musical program would relate the listener to Russia's rich log of history and folklore. Reasoning that Russia was crude rather than graceful, they exulted in their lack of craftsman's polish—indeed, the "cruder" his protégés' music, the better Balakiryef liked it.

Eventually, Balakiryef's messianic amateurism, his disdain for all Western music and distaste for proper training annoyed the critics and alienated Nikolai Rimsky-Korsakof, the most accomplished of the group. But a Russian school had been founded. "We are self-sufficient," Balakiryef announced: Russian instinct, not academics, would provide for Russian music.

The Five's aesthetic may be experienced first-hand in the works of Balakiryef's four tutees, Borodin, Musorksky, Rimsky-Korsakof, and the runt of the litter, the almost nonexistant Cui. (Chaikofsky, too, belongs on the list as a part-time disciple.) Unfortunately, Balakiryef himself wrote little—and little that he wrote is heard outside Russia. It's perhaps typical of the situation that his most popular entry, an Oriental piano solo called *Islamyey,* is so difficult to play that it remains more popular with listeners than pianists.

Symphony no. 1 in C Major 1888

Although Balakiryef felt that the tradition of Russian music which he was trying to found must seek its own forms out of Russian instincts instead of Western influences, this symphony accords with general Western practice—strong first movement, buoyant scherzo, lyrical slow movement, and strong finale. The difference between Balakiryef and any Western composer lies in the distinctive flavor of Russian song, which Balakiryef liked to leaven with the languorous line of the Orient. Throughout, one hears tone of unmistakably Slavic-*cum*-Eastern derivation, and Balakiryef builds his last movement on a real Russian folk song just in case anyone hasn't yet gotten the point.

The two themes that dominate the slow introduction to the first movement—one low and brooding, the other flutey and brighter—dominate the entire movement as well, for Balakiryef will have none of your Western sonata-allegro. He gives you first and second subjects, but not exposition-development-recapitulation; no, the whole movement, really, is a development of the introduction, free-form (what musicians call fantasia, a fantasy). The scherzo [second mvt] bows to Western usage in its ABA setup, and the wonderfully lush slow [third] movement, with its sinuous clarinet melody and more energetic, rising string theme for contrast, will not bewilder the beginner. But the finale [fourth mvt] returns us to the private world of the Russian fantasist, working a few themes over and over again to see how many different ways they can be played. (The opening theme, a roughhewn tune presented in the lower strings, is the authentic folk song mentioned above.) It's shameful that this expansive, brilliant work isn't heard more often—what limited currency it has is courtesy of Thomas Beecham's insistent performances—for its charm is surefire, and it certainly does not lack for orchestral fireworks.

Overture on Russian Themes 1858

As committed nationalist, Balakiryef was bound to offer something of this nature, a somewhat freestyle slow introduction and lively movement made of three native melodies: art drawing on life, sort of. The three themes are excitedly sounded, varied, and dovetailed—Balakiryef did not especially revere the sonata-allegro formality of exposition development and recapitulation taken for granted in the West—until a sudden rather inexplicable hush descends and cuts the whole thing off. Incidentally, Balakiryef and his nationalist fellows in the Mighty Grouplet were not the only Russian composers to borrow folk themes for symphonic use, and two of the three folk tunes here employed turn up again in, respectively, the fourth movement of Chaikofsky's Fourth Symphony and in Stravinsky's ballet *Petrushka*.

GEORGES BIZET 1838–1875

Bizet is so well known that it's a shock to see so few works listed here. But then he is known mainly for an opera, *Carmen,* and seems to have enjoyed few prerogatives as a man of symphony. In fact, his major excursion in the form was not even heard, having been lost, till 1935. It is for operas that Bizet is recalled and in opera that his style was set. Not one of the pieces listed below, for all their charm, is even remotely competitive with *Carmen,* one of the greatest operas ever. Those nervous about opera, but intrigued by *Carmen,* should pass by the various recordings of the *Carmen* Suite (for reasons cited below) and invest in a one-disc "highlights" album. Or, maybe better, buy a recording of Oscar Hammerstein's Americanized version of *Carmen, Carmen Jones.*

Symphony in C Major 1855

This was a lost classic, mislaid in Bizet's papers and not discovered until eighty years after it was written. Though in *Carmen* Bizet would write one of the most original operas of the era, his symphony is standard-make; buffs of Haydn and Mozart will find their way about here with ease.

After a zesty first movement, a solo oboe graces a moving slow [second] movement, and the work's one novelty turns up in the scherzo [third mvt]: both the main theme and the trio (middle section) theme are the same tune. In the trio the tune is lightened and played over a bucolic "drone bass" suggestive of bagpipes. The finale [fourth mvt] balances the first movement in tone. Many have commented on the taste of Mendelssohn (among others) in this movement; keep in mind that Bizet was only seventeen when he composed the work, still a student, still feeling his way into history.

Roma 1868; revised 1871

This was originally intended as an "Italian" symphony, like Mendelssohn's Fourth and Richard Strauss' *Aus Italien*. Each movement was to abstract the atmosphere of a city—Rome in the first movement, Florence in the frivolous scherzo, Venice in the slow movement, and Naples in the busy finale. As it now stands, however, the work is a "concert suite" and all for Rome. The first movement has become a forest hunt, the third a slow procession of some kind, and the fourth a Roman carnival. (And the second? It has no program—when Bizet was making up his subtitles, he had temporarily withdrawn the scherzo because of its poor reception at the premiere.)

Jeux d'Enfants (Children's Games), op. 22 1873

A suite of five extracts pulled from an earlier and bigger piano suite, all devoted to the innocence that adults assume to be the mode of childhood. Someday a composer will tender us a look at youth with the wryness of *Peanuts* and the sting of Anne Sexton's Mother Goose retellings, *Transformations*. Meanwhile, we enjoy Bizet's tidy summary.

First comes a march, "Trumpets and Drums." Next, "The Doll," a woodwindy rockabye. "The Top" does what tops do; then comes "Little Husband, Little Wife," scaled down for size. The finale is a gallop, "The Ball," a racy piece that sounds more like kids running around aimlessly in that way they have than like any dance known to the ballroom.

L'Arlésienne (The Woman from Arles) Suites 1872

Bizet's incidental music for Alphonse Daudet's play *L'Arlésienne* was too good not to succeed on its own in the concert hall, though composed to dovetail with the character of Daudet's melodrama so neatly that we are missing the heart of the score by not hearing it in its intended dramatic context. Still, there is wonderful vitality here, especially in the dances designed to reflect the play's setting, the highly ethnic territory of Provence, in Mediterranean France. The hefty march that opens Suite no. 1 is an old Provençal tune, in fact, as is the folkish dance that closes Suite no. 2 (arranged not by Bizet but by Ernest Guiraud and including a minuet from Bizet's opera, *The Pretty Maid of Perth,* as a filler).

So, listen to these eight pieces as music pure and simple, keeping it in mind that their original function was to accompany a play—for suspense, relief, irony, characterization. Notice, here as elsewhere in Bizet, the aptness of instrumentation—the pipes-and-tabors shrilling in the last item in Suite no. 2, for instance, or the piquant call of the combined saxophone and clarinet in the middle section of the second item in Suite no. 1, a minuet.

Carmen Suites 1875

Suites from operas are a terrible idea. Not only do they shear hulks off a dramatic tapestry, rendering them senseless, but they sometimes rearrange vocal music for orchestra without voices, which is really rotten. In *Carmen*'s case, there is one suite that simply excerpts the four act preludes, which is acceptable—this is usually called *Carmen Suite no. 1*. But it's really up to the conductor which excerpts to play, and there is a spurious *Carmen Suite no. 2,* a cheap collection of what deserves to be called *Carmen's Greatest Hits*. Avoid this at all costs.

The usual order of Suite no. 1 is the reverse of how these four numbers appear in the opera: the introduction to Act IV first, then that to Act III, and so on. The fourth introduction is the most "operatic," for under all the hoopla of Spanish danceorama, one picks up the trace of something uncomfortable, disturbing. It is a device called the "dominant pedal," best explained as an anticipatory bass note. This pedal note, resting heavily under the frivolous oboe melody and busy woodwind figures, warns of the ugly scene to come between Carmen and her cast-off lover: her contempt, his rage, the knife.

The suite continues its course backwards through the drama. The Act III prelude offers a pastorale on flute and clarinet (accompanied by the harp), the Act II prelude a martial tune (a favorite of Friedrich Nietzsche, who thought *Carmen* the prize opera of the day), the Act I prelude a splashy evocation of torero glamor with a middle section drawn from the famous aria, "Toréador, en garde!" All of these refer to the action ironically: Carmen's lover, Don José, abandons his village sweetheart and army position for Carmen, only to be tossed aside for a new love, the torero Escamillo.

Patrie (Fatherland) Overture, op. 19 1873

A case of Gallic jingoism here. Nobody takes this at times pushy piece seriously, but it is fun. Bizet was too deft not to mitigate the aggressive first subject with subsidiary themes of a more congenial nature. One such in particular will catch the ear about two thirds of the way through, just before the recapitulation: a wistful melody, having nothing to do with topics of war and patriotism, that returns unexpectedly in the last few moments of the piece.

MAX BRUCH 1838–1920

Versatile and vigorous, Max Bruch offers a classic example of the artist who suits his era too well to survive it. As a musical conservative he never suffered the revolutionary's ostracism; as a gifted melodist he won favor. But posterity demands revolution as much as melody of its protégés, and Bruch lacked idiosyncrasy. Operas, symphonies, cantatas, concertos, chamber works—all of Bruch has vanished except for the two works listed below and the *Kil Nidre* variations for 'cello and orchestra, a not very popular piece kept alive by grateful 'cellists.

Violin Concerto no. 1 in g minor, op. 26 1866

Generally, the first of the three standard concerto movements is the Big One, sometimes as big as the other two put together. The first movement is the dramatic foundation of the concerto, the plotted tangent of its expressive arc—so much so that a weak first movement is a sudden death. This concerto has so small a first movement that Bruch wasn't sure, when he finished, that he ought to call the work a concerto. Still, that first movement is far from weak, serving as a preface to the two following movements rather than as much of an entity in itself. Opening and closing with a rhapsodic dialogue between orchestra and soloist, it acts as the first one-third of a sonata-allegro movement—exposition but no development or recapitulation. Just where the development *would* occur, the orchestra bursts in and leads back to the opening dialogue, then provides a keening transition to the second [slow] movement. This takes up the slack thrown out by the shortened first movement in long lines of rhapsodic violin tone, highly concerto. It's a great movement, very "natural" in effect, built mainly on the E Flat Major motive introduced by the soloist at the start of the movement. This theme is decorated, varied, restated, and built to a thrilling climax. As the sound dies down, brief drooping lines in solo flute and horn urge the violinist on to a last statement of the theme.

The third movement, a "gypsy" finale (in G Major) of the kind so common to violin concertos of the middle and late nineteenth century (Brahms', for example) is surefire: brilliant, tautly varied, extravagant yet somehow not losing the "natural" air that distinguished the second movement. The gypsy quality inheres in the Hungarian-sounding first theme, anticipated by the orchestra and finally sounded full out by the soloist.

Scottish Fantasy for Violin and Orchestra, op. 46 1880

". . . With the Free Use of Scottish Melodies," the title goes on. Composers of the nineteenth century often exploited a dainty populism, romanticizing the nationalistic sociopolitics of the day for non-ideological musical purposes. Mendelssohn's "Scotch" Symphony (no. 3) merely invoked Scotland in a general way; Bruch delves intently, borrowing real Scotch melodies for virtually all his main themes.

Four movements, opened by a somber introduction which leads into a slow first movement, spotlighting the soloist in the tender "Auld Robin Morris." Follows then a scherzo [second mvt], doing what scherzos do: energize, with much high-flying exhibition for the soloist and leading without a break into another slow [third] movement, this one on "I'm a-Doun for Lack o' Johnnie." Bruch makes common cause with Mendelssohn in his finale [fourth mvt], for both composers end their Scotch retrospectives with what sounds like a parade of warrior clans. The familiar "Scots Wha Hae Where Wallace Bled" sets the tone, elaborated by the soloist, all for fire and battle. Just before the end, the soloist reprises "Auld Robin Morris," and the orchestra winds it all up with a last skirmish. Scotland wins.

MODYEST PYETROVITCH MUSORKSKY 1839–1881

Except for his piano-accompanied songs, a treasury of folk-naturalistic Slavic melody, little of Musorksky's powerful, awkward musical legacy has been shared without some interference by uninvited executors. Citing his disorderly, unlearned technique, they have reorchestrated him, reshaped him, retuned him. They refined him; but he wanted no refinement. "Life, wherever it is shown; truth, however bitter; speaking out boldly, candidly, point-blank to men—that is my aim," said Musorksky—and he attained it, in works of barbaric vitality.

True, bold, and point-blank, Musorksky was, however, an unschooled musician; thus, it was easy for his editors, after his death, to assume that his bold was born of ignorance and his point-blank the over-eagerness of the amateur. In their cultivation, they missed the truth. The most unvarnished of the raw musical coterie known as the *Moguchaya Kutchka* ("mighty grouplet"), or the "Russian Five," Musorksky essentializes their quest for a national art of no allegiance to the forms and symbols of Western music. (For a discussion of the Five—who also included Nicolai Rimsky-Korsakof, Alyeksandr Borodin, Mily Balakiryef, and Cesar Cui—see the Balakiryef article.) Since Peter the Great, Russian technology had been Western (largely German) technology, and Russia's belated musical insurgence in the mid-nineteenth century might easily have bowed to the tradition of Western symphony and song (as it did, somewht, in the work of the cosmopolitan Chaikofsky). But this was a mighty if largely untutored Grouplet, and each of the Five held to his folk-national code, seeking ways to connect his sound to the substance of Russian life, letting form be whatever form would so that content be satisfied. Musorksky's scope was not the visionary beauty of the poet, but the vivid truth of the realist—though the realist, too, has his ideals. Musorksky's operas particularly reveal this fixation on art as revelation of life rather than poetic synthesis, where ignominious man, conniving at power, provides his material.

Even Musorksky's friends felt that he could use some emergency cramming in a harmony class, and his detractors might have added that he wouldn't have passed the course. But Musorksky's natural talent was talent enough, and though as a "weekend musician" (his professional identity belonged to the civil service) he did not leave a large body of work, what there is needs no patronizing. True, it does sometimes take a while for us to comprehend genius on its own terms. For almost a century, Musorksky's opera *Boris Godunof* was almost always performed in a version prepared by Nicolai Rimsky-Korsakof (the most resourceful of the Five), and many experts decreed the original vastly inferior, too uncouth and untheatrical. But the gyres have turned, Musorksky's unedited *Boris* is heard more and more, and lo, it turns out that Musorksky's original is a masterpiece of uncouth and highly theatrical splendor. (For his part, Rimsky-Korsakof had only intruded with his revision to keep the "difficult" work alive, and would doubtless be glad for his comrade that the original is taking its rightful place on the world stages.)

Do not look, then, for sonata-allegro and other finesses of Western derivation in Musorksky's work, but hear the "sound" of the Russian character, phrased at an instinctually primitive level, psychology taught by a folklorist. "I foresee a new kind of melody, which will be the melody of life," said Musorksky—but he could not wait for it and so worked it out for himself. Russian music had no tradition, no indigenous formality; the Mighty Grouplet had to start from scratch. Of the gang, only Musorksky and Rimsky-Korsakof proved giant, and each in his own way. If Rimsky's way yields more sensual allure, Musorksky's tenders the savagery of realism. Rimsky raises the icon . . . but Musorksky bears the axe.

Pictures at an Exhibition 1874; orch. 1923

A perennial of the concert platform, this work leads a double life, for it began (and maintains much of its present career) as a piano suite; the orchestral version is an afterthought—and not Musorksky's. It was Maurice Ravel who scored *Pictures* for orchestra, at the suggestion of Serge Koussevitsky (in Paris then, prior to his days with the

Boston Symphony), and Ravel's brilliant instrumentation has competed with the original piano version ever since.

Musorksky's premise is intriguing: a turn through an art exhibit, each musical number conveying the mood of a different picture. More intriguingly, the situation takes its cue from life as well as art in that the artist was Victor Hartmann, a friend of Musorksky's who had died a year before the show of his sketches and watercolors was mounted at the St. Petersburg Architectural Association. Hartmann's pictures inspired ten studies from Musorksky, each a little tone poem, somber, comic, grotesque, or imperial, and the whole is bound together by a motto theme, the so-called Promenade.

Consider: a spectator wanders through this exhibition, now here, now there; here he stares bemused for minutes, there he passes quickly by, here a guffaw at some freak of design, there a sad contemplation—like Musorksky's, in life—at the untimely death of a gifted artist. All this is suggested by the "Promenade," which launches the suite, turns up slightly disguised in two of the "pictures," and roams in and out of the proceedings as the spectator roams the gallery:

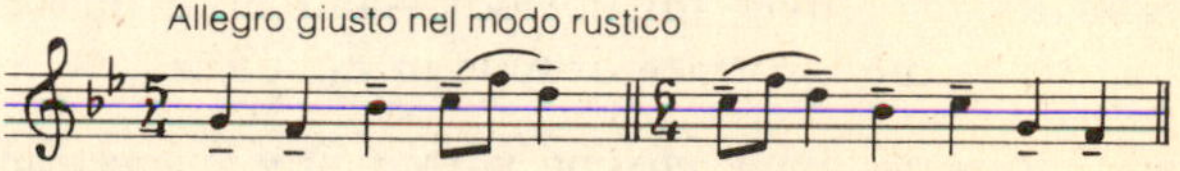

One may, of course, listen to *Pictures at an Exhibition* as a simple musical experience, but to appreciate Musorksky's memorial to his friend Hartmann one ought to be aware of the title of each of the pieces as they are played so as to receive Musorksky's own pictures. For there really are two exhibitions contained here—one is Hartmann's, in the pictorial apprehension of art; the other is Musorksky's, in the sometimes no less pictorial language of music. Note, for example, the bittersweet air of the second picture, "The Old Castle," conjured up in a medieval troubadour's hollow plaint; or the capricious shrillness of "Tuileries," the third picture, a watercolor of Paris' famous garden animated by the squabbles of schoolchildren; or the ferocious ninth picture, "The Hut on Fowl's Legs," which Hartmann depicted as an ornate clock but which, as the home of the witch Baba Yaga, Musorksky depicted as a wild ride through the air en route to what is almost certainly a sordid picnic.

Let us take the pictures one by one, in order:

The "Promenade" comes first, of course, followed by

"Gnomus" (The Gnome): a grotesque nutcracker, nervous and all a-crack. At one point, blurry, hushed motions in the strings playing *sulla tastiera* (on the fingerboard, thus producing a lifeless tone) testify to Ravel's ability to redouble Musorksky's effects even as he translates.

A pensive "Promenade" takes us to

"Il Vecchio Castello" (The Old Castle): set off by a sadly wistful alto saxophone portraying the song of a medieval balladeer.

Another "Promenade," on the vigorous side, precedes

"Tuileries": children playing and quarrelling, with a plangent middle section but the games reorganized by the end.

"Bydlo": This Polish word meaning "cattle" refers to an ox cart which we hear approach, pass, and fade away in the distance. At first a tuba solo appears to "play" the heavy, sagging wagon, but later other instruments take over the melody—and note that a horn, not the tuba, offers the last trace of tune in the piece.

Another "Promenade" jogs us along, closing with a tiny suggestion of the quaint

"Ballet of the Chicks in Their Shells": which sounds exactly as the title suggests, in standard scherzo form (ABA).

"Two Polish Jews, One Rich, The Other Poor" (sometimes called "Samuel Goldenberg and Schmuyle"): First we hear the haughty plutocrat, proud of purse, next, a stuttering trumpet solo for the beggar—"please, just a kopyeck!"—and at last the two simultaneously. It is left to the listener to decide whether poor Schmuyle's plea is successful.

"Limoges—The Marketplace": Gabbling like old hens, the women of Limoges review the local dish. Following Musorksky, Ravel directs the piece to run without a break into

"Catacombs": a properly deep and weighty situation, no life, no breath—chords rather than a melody. Since we have not heard the

Promenade of late, Musorksky obligingly quotes it in the next item.

"With the Dead in a Dead Language": a Latin "text" of great mystery, launched by the violins trembling on high as the oboes and English horn give us, as if through a veil, the Promenade theme. Moved, no doubt, by the Catacombs picture, the promenader is lost in sepulchral thought, but the spell is dispersed by

"The Hut on Fowl's Legs": another ABA scherzo, this one on the macabre doings of the man-eating witch Baba Yaga. Ravel pulls the stops out here for wicked effects, but a grand finale is yet to come (again with no warning break) in

"The Great Gate of Kief": based on Hartmann's design for a fantastical triumphal arch that was never built. The Promenade is heard once more, now sounding like a great tolling of bells, and the climax is far and away one of the biggest things in the orchestral repertory, fully justifying—as if Ravel has not already—the work's reputation as a showpiece for orchestral superskill.

One final note: the listener owes it to himself to check out Musorksky's original piano version, for while Ravel's scoring is dazzling, the quintessential Musorksky of the rough, unvarnished truths may be found only in work of his own hand.

A Night on Bald Mountain 1867

Here is the most barbaric witches' sabbath in all music, obscenities and unnatural acts from midnight till dawn, when a bell tolls six and the satanic crew disperses. Bald (or Bare—"barren" is the meaning intended) Mountain is Mt. Triglaf near Kief, where St. John's Eve, June 23, is annually celebrated by a revel of evil presided over by Chernobog (dark god) in the form of a black goat. This music more or less invents its own structure as it goes along—"everything firmly linked," as the composer himself very smartly assessed it, "but without any German [i.e., Western academic] transitions." How the woodwinds seem to caw at the topmost shrill of their range, banshees; how extra-heavy the heavier instruments (the brass and lower strings) sound, dybbuks. What a pride of demons! Perhaps what gives the piece its power is Musorksky's juxtaposition of folkish tunes with grotesque orchestration, thus asserting the primitive humanity of his goblins—but then for this realist of musicians, the line between the human and the ghoulish is often drawn thin.

This is thrilling work, truly. Nothing of its day approaches it for an articulation of the stark nakedness of evil, but—as always—even Musorksky's supporters fussed at his nakedly idiosyncratic sound, and the work is heard today as glossed over by Nicolai Rimsky-Korsakof.

Introduction and Dance of the Persian Slaves from Khovanshchina 1874

Virtually everything that Musorksky wrote was meant to vindicate the "Russianness" of Russian art, whether in subject matter, melody, or even shape. In his opera *Khovanshchina* (The Time of the Khovanskys), Musorksky undertook a complex and perhaps only partly fulfilled vindication (left unfinished at his death and completed by Nicolai Rimsky-Korsakof). Set in and around Moscow in 1682 (the first, madly chaotic year of the reign of Peter the Great, aged ten at the time), the opera deals with Slavic resistance to the Westernization of Russia in religion and politics—much as Musorksky resisted the Westernization of Russian music.

The introduction, subtitled "Dawn on the Moscow River," opens the opera just as it is played in the concert hall with a series of variations on a theme heard almost immediately in the violins and oboes, each variation so slight that the introduction comes off as a tune in several verses. These variations refer to a folk practice common to Russian peasant musicales: as they progress from verse to verse, the singers change the melody a little bit at each repetition. So, Musorksky treats his theme the same way—each replaying is a little different from the last. A quiet beginning (note the bird calls and cockcrow in the woodwind), an increasingly refulgent continuation, and a quiet ending; restful, this dawn, except for an ominous hint near the close of the bloody days that are to follow as the opera progresses.

The *Dance of the Persian Slaves* is a sumptuous Oriental exercise extracted from the opera's fourth act, when Persian girls entertain old Prince Khovansky with a sample of what ballerinas do best. The music is highly schizophrenic in mood, hectic one minute, luxuriating the next.

PYOTR ILYITCH CHAIKOFSKY 1840–1893

The Russian art world in which Chaikofsky lived was like a play on native life and love performed in French, superintended by a German technical staff, and decorated with sets depicting an English garden, an Italian piazza, and a Viennese ball. There was no strong feeling of Russia in Russian art—the character of its people, their language, their cultural imagery. Everything had been inherited from the West—literature, science, music, philosophy—when Peter the Great remade his native land along modernized Western lines.

Thus it was wholly understandable that, when Russian artists undertook to enjoy a nationalist era, they must overstate their case, reject totally the Western influence. In music, the nationalist school proved so radical that it rejected not only Western forms (the four-movement symphony, the three-movement concerto) but most technical training as well. Who needs to learn harmony, counterpoint, orchestration?, the line ran: we are self-sufficient. Such was the scheme of Balakiryef, the godfather of the nationalists and head of the anti-Western group known as the *Moguchaya Kutchka* (mighty grouplet), or the "Russian Five." Having undergone little formal training himself, Balakiryef figured no one needed it, and encouraged his four colleagues—Musorksky, Rimsky-Korsakof, Borodin, and Cui—to be Russian, innovative, clumsy if necessary: self-sufficient. But a sixth composer, while often encouraged and advised by Balakiryef, expressed his nationalism through Western forms—yet couldn't have felt, or sounded, more Russian. This, of course, was Chaikofsky.

He never doubted that the forms of European tradition could be bent to his personal will as a Russian artist, and he was right. While the Five struggled to found Russian music, Chaikofsky worked out a no less national plan without having to invent any new forms or styles. One thing he had that they didn't: polish. His use of folk melodies is judicious, almost suave, though Russian folk music is if anything roughhewn and dumpy. His ballet music (though thought undanceable by the companies for which it was written) remains a touchstone for charm and urbanity. His songs are subtly developed, his concertos show a knack for encouraging the virtuoso's sensitivity, making it shine. Whether athletic, sentimental, folkish, humorous, or tragic in tone, Chaikofsky wrote with a deft hand.

You might not think so if you listen to the clichés of music journalism, which characterize Chaikofsky as a tormented soul pouring out whole symphonies of trauma and self-pity. This is an outrageous libel. Chaikofsky's was not a happy life, it's true, and his three very popular symphonies—nos. 4, 5, and 6—do sound personally expressive. But, to pick one example, so do

Mahler's. Yet Mahler is not sneered at for his subjective approach. Whatever you may hear to the contrary, Chaikofsky was far more than a mere melodist, a symphonic tunesmith. His sense of structure has control to spare; without ever appearing to be a revolutionary, he helped develop the dramatic dimensions of the symphony. The Fourth and Sixth are highly original, in fact. We may find them immediately appealing, but the composer's contemporaries found them boldly avant garde and difficult to enjoy.

Symphony no. 1 in g minor, "Winter Dreams," op. 13 1867

Chaikofsky called it "a sin of my sweet youth" and "immature," but it has charm and an appealing folkish sound, though apparently only one or two themes at most are authentic folk tunes. It's old-fashioned: assertive first movement, slow movement, scherzo, and festive finale. (A curiosity: the first two movements have programmatic titles—"Dreams of a Winter Journey" and "Land of Desolation, Land of Mists"—but the third and fourth movements do not.)

The first movement begins with its first subject on flute and bassoon over trembling strings, eventually to cede to the expressive second subject on solo clarinet. One is impressed by the composer's sure sense of self in this "sin" of a first symphony, for the style is mature, exemplary Chaikofsky in every way—his plangent lyricism, his energy, sorrow, surprise. The work takes its dares, too, as in the odd transitional passage connecting the development to the recapitulation, in which the horns play against the lower strings in the barest semblance of what generally gets called "music."

By this time, the listener must be thinking that Chaikofsky's dismissal of the work as "immature" is undeserved. The second [slow] movement, opening and closing in a string chorale that encloses a wan little tune introduced on the oboe, is a winter gem. So far the minor key has kept things plaintive; the third [scherzo] movement holds to this tone, though its trio (middle section) offers a luscious major-key waltz. (Another dare taken: the prominent timpani part near the end of the movement.) The finale [fourth mvt] opens with a ponderous slow introduction that returns near the end of an otherwise gala movement as a reminder of the minor-key reveries that have already resolved into more affirmative major-key expectations—great ones, truly, given what was to come from this pen.

Symphony no. 2 in c minor, "Little Russian," op. 17 1872

"Little Russia" is the Ukraine, and the subtitle refers to two Ukrainian folk melodies used, one each, in the first and fourth movements. One of the pair opens the symphony in a plaintive horn solo leading to a longish slow introduction. This is ended, as begun, by the horn, yielding to the first movement proper at a swift pace, turbulent at the first theme, ardent at the second. The second [slow] movement is a march, keyed at beginning and end to the left-right-left-right of the timpani; the third [scherzo] movement lightly whizzes by, a study in rhythm. Whatever popularity the "Little Russian" has earned is largely the work of the last movement, as staunchly high-spirited a finale as ever was written. This, too, opens with a Ukrainian tune, a squared-off dance theme in the major key: happy ending. The folk tune at first serves as the focus of a ceremonial introduction slightly reminiscent of the Promenade Theme from Musorksky's *Pictures at an Exhibition,* but the ceremony is a brief one and the movement cracks off bright and bounding, stating and restating the folk tune in variations. At length, we get a softer second theme, a development contrasting the two, a joyous recapitulation, and a coda more joyous yet.

Symphony no. 3 in D Major, "Polish," op. 29 1875

Strongly devoted to the Classical model for the symphony, Chaikofsky was as strongly motivated to personalize it. His most brilliant, "Chaikofskyan" experiments would be made in the Fourth and Sixth Symphonies; here, he is content with adding in an extra, a fifth, movement, an "alla Tedesca" (in German style) after the first movement. The symphony's subtitle refers to the "in Polish style" fifth movement, a polonaise. The symphony, then, is no more Polish than it is German; and is neither, being Russian all the way. Chaikofsky's only symphony in a major key, it still shows the composer's characteristic conflict of worry and confidence. A short funeral march opens, as a slow introduction, the otherwise vigorous first movement, and a plangent air marks the "extra," German-style second movement. (Note the prominent use of the bassoon, unusual for the time.) The slow [third] movement evokes a pastoral innocence of the kind also useful to Dvořák and Mahler; the scherzo [fourth mvt] dances, lithe, pert, and woodwindy, as on air. Last comes the polonaise [fifth mvt], effectively balancing the first movement with like vitality. Its all-around esprit reminds one that Chaikofsky is still unsurpassed as a composer of ballet scores.

Symphony no. 4 in f minor, op. 36 1878

This remarkable work has proved itself both as popular success and analyst's touchstone—though, as usual with Chaikofsky, it was enthusiastically disliked when first performed. There is a slight program: the famous fanfare that dominates the first movement and returns so crushingly in the last is Fate. (Beethoven also opened a symphony with the challenge of Fate, but his Fifth works out that challenge far differently than does Chaikofsky's Fourth.) Shadowed by the inexorable force, we seek refuge in sweet dreams, but to no avail. The second movement deepens the melancholy; the livelier third complicates it with what the composer called "a succession of capricious arabesques." The fourth movement presents a public fair, where one goes to escape his sorrow by sharing others' joy. The Fate theme, however, reappears to remind one of his alienation.

The above sounds pat; the music is anything but. After uncountable hearings, the fanfare—Fate—still evokes a thrill of menace. The huge first movement, built mainly on repetitions of the swooning waltzlike first theme (heard right after the fanfare), is a textbook case of the historical expansion of the Romantic symphony: more to say, more irony and ambiguity, longer symphonies. To make it easy for his public, Chaikofsky marked the blueprint for his unusually grand first movement by sounding the "Fate" fanfare at the major junction points—after launching the movement, it leads off the development, recurs just before the recapitulation, and heralds the start of the long coda.

A solo oboe introduces the sad main theme of the slow [second] movement, which rises to a hopeful affirmation in its middle section and yields again to sadness as the violins inherit the theme. At the end of the movement, the composer passes the little melody from instrument to instrument without losing its wan coloration.

But cheer up—now comes the scherzo [third mvt], on an interesting technical premise: a principal section made up of rushing plucked strings surrounding a trio which sports a boozily energetic tune for woodwinds and a quiet march for brass. At the end, we get all three parts together, each group playing its own music.

The finale [fourth mvt], an attempt to evade Fate by mingling with simple people (a rather Thomas Mannish idea), is a whirlwind carnival complete with quoted folk tune, very Slavic on oboe and bassoon. Near the end, Fate breaks through a last time with its fanfare, but the carnival recovers and carries on.

Symphony no. 5 in e minor, op. 64 1888

One of the oddities of symphony is that the garbage does not rise to the top. In all the other arts—fiction, poetry, theatre, and so on—the most popular is most often the least penetrating. *Love Story,* Rod McKuen, and *Grease* remind us that popular taste is not necessarily good taste. But in symphony, the reverse is true. Who are the greatest symphonists? Haydn, Mozart, Beethoven, Brahms, Chaikofsky, Mahler, and so on. Who are the most popular? Haydn, Mozart, Beethoven, Brahms, Chaikofsky, Mahler, and so on.

Chaikofsky is especially relevant here, for he is the only first-rate symphonist vulnerable to critical condescension. But we listeners aren't going to be misled—not with such splendid dramatic vitality as this, not with Chaikofsky's masterful grasp of organization and development. The Fifth has been particularly the subject of derogation by critics, but our own ears tell us that critics have bananas in their ears and sludge in their hearts.

This is a symphony with a motto theme, a central melody used throughout the work to relate each movement to the emotional foundation of the whole. Naturally, Chaikofsky emphasizes it by opening the piece with it: a brooding tune in the low register of the clarinets. Having stated this motto, he begins the first movement proper with a march theme. (Watch the tempo here; conductors sometimes overplay the somber Chaikofskyan atmosphere by taking the movement under tempo. It is marked *Allegro con anima,* lively with spirit—not *Andante,* slow.) The second-theme group brightens the tune a little, but this is essentially a dejected movement.

We get a soothing, highly lyrical second [slow] movement, however, perhaps the most familiar slow movement in the entire symphonic repertory, beautifully built from its opening horn solo to a refulgent climax—and note, again, the furious intrusion of the motto theme midway through the movement. For his scherzo [third mvt] Chaikofsky tries something new, a graceful waltz rather than the more usual rhythmic piece; again, the motto breaks in, quietly this time, at the very end of the waltz.

That motto also leads off the finale [fourth mvt], but now we hear it in the major instead of the minor as before, suggesting a triumphal finish. Chaikofsky works over the theme in a portentous introduction, roars it, tames it, and then launches the finale proper, a racy *Allegro vivace* (lively and vivacious). Always seething, now loud now soft, the finale brings the work to a head as if in direct line through the appearances of the motto theme, and further cohesion is provided by a reprise of the first theme of the first movement at the very end of the piece.

Symphony no. 6 in b minor, "Pathétique," op. 74 1893

Those making their first acquaintance with this work are often surprised to hear symphony buffs discuss the "different" *Pathétiques* of different conductors: how can one symphony, the music all written out, sound different under different batons? Well, it can—slower, faster, denser, lighter, defeated, defiant. It is a matter of what components of the whole a given conductor emphasizes. I raise this point here because the *Pathétique* is one of the most "interpretable" of symphonies. Some conductors make it sound hopelessly down, licking—savoring—its wounds; others see in it a heroic tragedy. Under Toscanini and Stokowski, for instance, it sounded a thrillingly muscular piece.

Which view is correct? Listener, hear and decide. Because the composer died of virtually self-inflicted cholera (he drank a glass of unboiled water, a *very* risky proposition in Petersburg in 1893) weeks after the premiere, the legend grew that this was a document of suicidal melancholy. Thus, many conductors play it so as to bring out its elements of desperation. (The third movement, for example, is a rather "up" march—but it may be played triumphantly or with overstated, hysterical euphoria, as if it did not believe its own high spirits.) Dirge or glorious fall? It can go either way. (The subtitle, suggested by Chaikofsky's brother and reportedly approved by the composer, means not so much "pathetic" as "having pathos"—which leaves the question wide open.)

A short slow introduction leads off in the depths of the orchestra, the melody assigned to a bassoon. It sounds dire, but when the first movement proper takes off in a relatively fast tempo, that melody is transformed dynamically as an active force in the proceedings. At another tempo change, this time to *Andante* (slow), the lyrical second theme shifts the tone—here is another spot where conductors must deliver a kind of Chaikofsky to us: pining or merely songful? An athletic development spurs us on; after the recapitulation, an elegiacal coda holds us back. We do not yet know where we stand.

The second [slow] movement is an odd item in an odd metre, 5/4. It sounds like a waltz (3/4) with two extra beats—a waltz for two left feet, as it were. Then comes the famous march [third mvt], with a theme known to any man in the street, and an apparently victorious atmosphere. The *Pathétique* would seem to have gone high on power—until we hear the finale [fourth mvt], another slow movement, which is a highly unconventional way to close a symphony. Defeat, now, is inevitable: lugubrious strings, wild tempo fluctuations, a duet of deflated trombone and tuba. But is it the defeat of a vital force or of a loser?

The "Manfred" Symphony, op. 58 1885

Lord Byron's possibly autobiographical character Manfred was something of an emblem for Romantics high on melancholy and quest. He surfaced in a verse play better read than performed and described by Byron as "of a very wild, metaphysical, and inexplicable kind. . . . The scene is in the Alps; the hero is a kind of magician . . . he wanders about invoking [spirits of the earth and air]."

Chaikofsky, too, invokes these spirits plus an authentic Byronic remorse in a combination symphony and tone poem (that is, a traditional four-movement symphony—in b minor, in this case—that carries a programmatic subject). The first movement covers no plot action, but rather presents Manfred generally. The ponderous music heard (in clarinet and bassoon) at the start serves as a motto theme—a Manfred theme, as it were—for the entire work. (It is heard in all four movements.) So this is Manfred: sensitive, self-dramatizing, idealistic, radical. In the second [scherzo] movement, Manfred conjures up the Fairy of the Alps in a waterfall's rainbow, and the music sounds appropriately gurgly and sun-burnished. The trio (middle section) offers what we presume to be the Fairy's song to Manfred (violins accompanied by two harps), after which the motto theme wells up briefly and the waterplay resumes.

The third [slow] movement refers us to the simple life among the mountaineers, a breather in Manfred's endless search for selfhood and a meaning to life. Sure enough, the oboe melody that opens the movement is simplicity itself. But the Byronic hero is, as a rule, alienated, and the motto theme rings out in the trombones with its unappeasable melancholy, set off by a tolling bell. He knows no peace. In the fourth movement he confronts himself and his spirits at an orgy in the underground palace of Arimanes, where Astarte foretells his death. The music suggests a riot more than what we moderns would call on orgy, and the motto signals a change in mood. Astarte's prediction is depicted by horn, strings, and magical harp glissandos (slides up and down the strings). Now the full orchestra sounds the motto theme as Manfred dies to the religious aroma of an organ.

Piano Concerto no. 1 in b flat minor, op. 23 1875

One of the cornerstones of the repertory, this work typifies the Romantic piano concerto—flamboyant emotionalizing, with a heroic test for the soloist's reserves of technique and personal charisma. The opening is famous: the horns anticipate the theme soon to come and the piano crashes in with majestic chords that turn into the accompaniment for the theme, assigned to the violins. Then the piano sounds the theme, resorts to a short, brilliant cadenza (a solo show-off spot), then plays more accompanimental chords as the strings sound the opening theme once again. It is one of the great moments of absolute musical exhilaration, though Classicists fume at its personal "exhibit." Worse yet, it is wasteful, for, having used it to launch his work, the composer discards it—this has all been just so much introduction. Only now comes the first theme, a weirdly jerky passage led off by the piano; this Chaikofsky adapted from a tune sung by beggars in the Ukraine. The lyrical second theme (actually two tunes: a theme group) tenders the necessary contrast, and first and second subjects then confront each other in the development. The recapitulation sorts things out as before, and a stellar cadenza ratifies the soloist's position as the hero of the piece. It's an athletic first movement, even for a Romantic concerto.

The slow [second] movement yields delicacy. The piano is still central, but the overall scoring is lighter. (Note, for instance, the unpretentious opening, with plucked strings supporting a lone flute.) Interestingly, Chaikofsky slips a scherzolike middle section into the otherwise placid slow movement; after a short cadenza, the soloist takes over the main theme from the flute to close the movement as gently as it had opened.

Naturally, the finale [third mvt] returns us to the main business of the virtuoso concerto—lots of tone, power, and momentum. This is what concerto finales are for. A rondo of dance themes, this movement ends in a thrilling apotheosis with all the stops pulled, calling for the most that soloist, orchestra, and conductor can give. Anything less than hair-raising isn't in the ball park. (The classic performance of the piece, to which all veterans refer: Vladimir Horowitz and Arturo Toscanini in an NBC radio broadcast of April 25, 1943. Luckily, RCA Victor preserved it on disc. If you're looking for a recording and don't mind outdated sound, this is the one.)

Violin Concerto in D Major, op. 35 1878

The orchestra provides expectant moments of introduction in anticipation of the first theme, ensuring a real Star Entrance for the soloist. This is a sweet piece, deftly virtuoso if not as dramatic as Chaikofsky can be, though that first theme eventually turns into a rugged polonaise, lending a weight to the first movement as it progresses (as opposed to dropping one on it from the start). But then the slow [second] movement is altogether subdued (Chaikofsky calls it a "canzonetta," little song), its minor-key melody sore with nostalgia. Indeed, the movement is so delicate that the composer doesn't even finish it, but leaps into the finale [third mvt] as if arranging a transfusion of new blood. This finale is the usual dancing rondo, but Chaikofsky handles it with unusual flair even for this flair-crazed era. The media have murdered the word "dazzling"—but it should be revived for this finale, with its shameless virtuoso display. Note the amusing shifts in tempo that lend an almost pictorial air, as if each episode were another snippet of a carnival show overheard and glimpsed from around the corner.

Variations on a Rococo Theme for 'Cello and Orchestra, op. 33 1876

A homage to Mozart's era. The antique-sounding theme (introduced by the 'cello soloist after a few moments of dainty hem-hemming from the orchestra) is Chaikofsky's own, a nice recreation of the eighteenth-century style. Then the variations—seven in all, each one featuring the soloist. Throughout, the composer hews closely to the outline of the original, making it easy to follow the theme through its transformations. It is also intent on recapturing the spirit of Mozart in the spareness of his scoring and the immediacy of the melodic flow. Delightful nostalgia.

Romeo and Juliet 1869; revised 1870

One of the best-known pieces in the repertory, this "fantasy overture" owes its fascination to the combined chemistry of Chaikofsky's musical conciseness and Shakespeare's romantic fire. The composer's sense of music drama was not always acute in the long form of opera, but here he manages to capture the cry, color, and poetry of Shakespeare's play in most effective brevity. There are two central ideas—the ferocity of the Montague-Capulet feud and the innocence of the two lovers. This opposition of war and love is framed by mildly ecclesiastic music suggestive of Friar Laurence, the neutral figure belonging to neither party.

Chaikofsky called this a fantasy overture rather than an overture because he was less concerned with the rigors of form than with abstracting a story in musical images (fantasy means "free in form"). All a "fantasy overture" ends up being, then, is a tone poem in sonata-allegro (i.e., overture) form, with first and second subjects, development, recapitulation. This particular fantasy overture opens with the Friar's churchly music, as much Russian Orthodox as Roman Catholic in sound. (But at least this is an improvement on Chaikofsky's original scoring, which struck his mentor Mily Balakiryef as indicative more of a Haydn quartet than of Mother Church.) The Friar Laurence section acts as introduction; the first theme (or rather theme group) explodes barbarically as the Montagues and Capulets do in the byways of Verona, a street brawl in music. This at length cedes to the love music. Having thus stated his two opposing forces, Chaikofsky faces them off in the development section, builds to a shortened recapitulation, seems about to close with the feud music, and instead reprises the Friar Laurence passage by way of sacred consolation.

Francesca da Rimini, op. 32 1876

Dante met Francesca and her brother-in-law Paolo in the second circle of Hell (reserved for carnal sinners), where as punishment for their adultery they are tossed in an endless, bellowing night by furious winds—the poet was so horrified and moved at hearing Francesca tell her tale that he fainted. Chaikofsky met the pair through Dante's report and turned their saga into the present tone poem. The form is ABA, with a slow introduction, the A depicting the incessant storm that buffets the pair in the underworld and the B (heralded by a clarinet solo) being Francesca's sad narration on the frailty of humankind when aroused by love. The howling winds close the piece when the A returns.

Capriccio Italien, op. 45 1850

Based on popular Italian melodies heard during a stay in Rome, this *Italian Caprice* gets underway rather dolefully but soon picks up in mood and tempo. It's a simple potpourri of tunes; they aren't developed symphonically, merely contrasted and repeated. Thus, the work's charm depends entirely on Chaikofsky's use of instrumentation, for color and "style." The opening trumpet line derives from a real bugle call (the composer's Roman hotel was located next to an army barracks), and the final tune of the set is a tarantella, a dance once thought to be useful in curing victims of the tarantula bite.

Serenade for Strings in C Major, op. 48 1880

Chaikofsky loved this piece. He wrote it simultaneously with the 1812 Overture, which he thought raucous, impersonal, and of no artistic value; the serenade he filled with warmth and intimacy. There are four movements. The first opens in introductory solemnity but soon turns lively. Chaikofsky termed it a "sonatina," which is to say in simplified sonata-allegro form, the second theme rushing in quickly behind the first. The second movement, a salon waltz with

Viennese tang, is the prize of the serenade, always popular with the public; the elegiacal third movement has a wistful appeal. For his finale [fourth mvt], Chaikofsky emphasizes the Slav in him with another slow introduction, this one based on a Russian folk song. Sharp ears may detect a resemblence between the four-square first theme (sounded by the first violins when the tempo picks up) and the introduction to the first movement—which anyway returns in its original form near the end of the finale.

George Balanchine also loved this piece, presumably, as he used it for his ballet, *Serenade,* in 1934.

Marche Slave (Slavic March), op. 31 1876

Chaikofsky dubbed it his "Russian-Serbian March," for its themes are all Russian or Serbian anthems. Brawny and martial, as one might expect, this is the sort of actually rather brutalizing music so much a part of concert and ceremonial life in the days before the glory of war was thoroughly debunked for the corruption it is. Modern audiences are impatient with such pieces, though this one has held on somewhat because of its endearingly high spirits.

1812 Overture, op. 49 1880

Another of the martial pieces so common in the nineteenth century (like Chaikofsky's *Marche Slave* directly above), this "Solemn Overture on the Year 1812" commemorates Russia's successful resistance to Napoleon's invading army. (Thus the use of both French and Russian national anthems, though as it happens the tsarist hymn was not composed until *after* the Napoleonic Wars and properly doesn't belong in an 1812 overture.)

We first hear a slow, solemn passage (adapted from a Russian folk tune). A fraught transition leads to battle music, military rataplans, dramatic hand-to-hand combat among the orchestral choirs, quotation of the "Marseillaise," the French national anthem, and, when logistics permit, the booming of real-life cannon. This is not exclusively a piece of jingoistic airfill, however; reminders of Chaikofsky's great lyrical gift are smuggled in with the uproar, and his use of folk tunes is distinctive and delightful. At length, to signal the Russian victory, the imperial Russian anthem, "God Save the Tsar," wipes out all traces of the "Marseillaise." The composer himself thought this an uninspired piece of jingoism; actually, considering its noisy subject, it's dignified and even charming.

The Ballet Suites:

from Swan Lake, op. 20 1876
from The Sleeping Beauty, op. 66 1889
from The Nutcracker, op. 71 1892

A ballet suite is simply a collection of excerpts from a ballet, arranged so the music may be heard even when a ballet company is not giving the work on some local stage. (Another good reason: ballet conducting and orchestral playing are generally inferior to those of a decent concert ensemble. Today, in the stereo era, the best performances of ballet music are to be heard on records as conducted and played by the great conductors and the top-class orchestras.) However, suites are not a good idea except for the dilletante listener: excerpting robs the ballet—a dramatic form—of its narrative pulse. Furthermore, there is no guarantee that the excerpts are going to be the ones you want to hear.

For these reasons, I warn the reader against so-called *Sleeping Beauty* or *Swan Lake* "suites." First of all, the composer never made these collections of excerpts himself, so one has no guarantee as to what or how much one is hearing—conductors make up these suites pretty much as they choose. Secondly, there is too much wonderful dramatic music in the original works to tolerate the dramatic collapse of the suite treatment, which shreds the story line. Since these suites are primarily heard on records anyway, you might as well spring for a complete recording. I promise you, you won't be sorry.

As to The Nutcracker, let us first clear up one much too prevalent *faux pas.* The ballet is called *The Nutcracker,* period. *The Nutcracker Suite* is the group of excerpts *from* the ballet called *The Nutcracker.* Not to confuse.

Of these three ballets, *The Nutcracker* is the only one for which we have the composer's own arrangement of a suite, op. 71 a. As *The Nutcracker* has less narrative drive than it might, one doesn't lose so much by hearing only excerpts (though, again, this cuts one off from some delightful music). The eight items in the suite don't refer importantly to the *Nutcracker* plot and are also placed out of story order to blend together musically. First comes the "Miniature Overture," called so because it lacks (1) 'cellos and basses and (2) the development section of sonata-allegro: it has the first theme–second theme of the exposition and then simply recapitulates with a tiny coda. Next is a "March" (of children at a Christmas Party), followed by the "Dance of the Sugar Plum Fairy." This is actually the star ballerina's solo (known in ballet circles as her "variation") in the big Pas de Deux at the end of the evening, the duet of the lead male and female dancers. Note the use of celesta, a keyboard instrument sounding like fairy bells, only just invented at the time and unknown in Russia. Chaikofsky is credited with being the first composer to find a use for it in the symphony orchestra. The next five numbers are all *divertissements*—dances having nothing to do with the main action, added to fill out the evening's quota of dance. First is a "Russian Dance" (the famous Trepak), a mysterious "Arab Dance," a perky "Chinese Dance" (performed by mushrooms in Walt Disney's film *Fantasia*), a "Dance of the Flutes," and lastly the "Waltz of the Flowers."

ANTONÍN DVOŘÁK 1841–1904

No convenient umbrella of biographical or aesthetic description covers Antonín Dvořák by way of contextual introduction, comparable to, say, Beethoven's conflict of defiance and transcendence in life and art, or Musorksky's uncouth genius for the expression of the Russian spirit in music. What in particular can one say of Dvořák? His was a successful career, reaching into virtually all forms of music large and small; it suffered failures and showed glories; it remains, in its summits, glorious.

Indeed, Dvořák is now in the process of rediscovery and reassessment as the stereo era puts his work more and more in the limelight. In 1950 or so, only the last three of his nine symphonies were known to the general public; by 1974, there were four different complete sets of the nine, and insiders had added the last three to their two predecessors, numbers five and six, to constitute a "Big Five." (Not only had Dvořák's earlier symphonies lacked for exposure—they didn't even have numbers! Now that the full canon of nine has been revealed, the last five have had to be restationed, Johnnies-come-too-early that they are; but the new positions, held to strict chronological accountability, are clumsy: the former no. 3 is now no. 5, yet the former no. 1 becomes no. 6 and no. 4 turns into no. 8. One still encounters the old system on vintage record jackets.)

Well, how to characterize Dvořák? They call him a folk national, his nation being the Bohemian region of today's Czechoslovakia. Bohemia's musical tradition is a fertile one; in terms both of a creative professional establishment and a loving amateurs' cottage industry, this was a land where music was everywhere available and where nearly everybody assisted in the making of it. (No Czech ever asked another Czech where he or she learned to fiddle: didn't they all have fathers?) Dvořák belongs fervently to that tradition, for his sound is of a highly ethnic impact. Seldom quoting actual Czech melodies, Dvořák seldom appears to be doing anything else, for his use of native dance rhythms is so winning, so appropriate for symphonic development yet so "natural," that one is hard put to tell where symphonic art leaves off and Bohemian life begins. Just as an American composer might borrow the atmosphere of ragtime or jazz without literally utilizing a tune of Scott Joplin's or Duke Ellington's, so did Dvořák track the audio imagery of his native land, in tunes of his own invention but of a generally Bohemian definition. One hears this technique throughout Dvořák's oeuvre, especially in the slow movements and scherzos of his symphonies, when not just sections but a whole entity sings the communication of the folk idyll, of the little village band or the dance medley of the fairgrounds. Moreover, it was specifically as a Czech composer that Dvořák first won international prominence, in his piano duets on native rhythmic types, the Slavonic Dances.

But Dvořák tired of being famous for being Czech. He was, he thought, a composer, not a "Czech composer," and his later symphonies, the Big Five, reveal a growing exploitation of the folk sound less for its charm than for symphonic metamorphosis, for sophistication in the large form, theme against theme or theme growing into theme. A *Western* composer, no mere fiddling Slav, Dvořák even contrived a folk-American symphony—or, at least, thought that he sort of did—in no. 9, "From the New World," replete with suggestions (again, not literal quotations) of Indian and black music. Nor was that all: he flirted with the idea of composing an opera on *Hiawatha*—no doubt it was Longfellow's case-hardened Gitche-Gumee scansion that convinced him not to.

In fine, there is no instant key to Dvořák, no descriptive umbrella. His folk-rhythmic orientation makes him invariably accessible to all and thus, alas, invariably suspect (for snobs and critics): how can anything that catchy be any good? We others, who know what we like, can relish the bluff good nature in him, the rowdy susceptibility and frequent dark nuances and, as we get to know the more impressive works (the cello concerto, the Symphonic Variations, the last five symphonies—especially the powerful no. 7 in d minor), can further grasp the man's suggestive dimensions. As with any gifted artist, the art does not flatter our experience, but enriches it on its own terms; so we invade Dvořák's rhapsodic Bohemia and ignore the critical gamesmanship that would spoil it for us.

Symphony no. 5 (old no. 3) in F Major, op. 76 1875

An odd idea for a symphony—three movements of pliant lyricism topped, suddenly, by a rugged finale. The listener can hardly be blamed for wondering why all the vehemence so late in the work. But there is a reason, if one of greater attraction to the musical analyst than the average listener: tonality. The core of the piece is to be found not in the sweet first movement, nor the haunting second nor the delightful scherzo but in the conflict of minor and Major that besets the fourth. After all, this is a symphony in F Major, and Dvořák asserts his tonality, his harmonic framework, by opposing the work's "home" key (F Major) to the fourth movement's free-spirited first subject (in a minor). Thus the sudden drama: a minor attempts a takeover, but ultimately it is F Major that prevails—that same first subject now blazing brightly in the Major as the work ends.

Structurally, the symphony is more or less conventional. The first movement announces its gentle first theme immediately in the clarinets; its assertive second theme is given out in the full orchestra. The development is rich and agile, and order is maintained when the recapitulation begins with the first theme sounded once more by the clarinets. The tonality of a minor that will figure so largely in the last movement is already importuning the ear in the main theme (in the 'cellos) of the slow [second] movement, which claims A Major in its middle section but returns to the minor after. Then comes an interesting effect: the slightest pause after the slow movement, and the scherzo [third mvt] begins with a brief transitional passage based on the slow movement's main theme (still in the 'cellos). It is as if Dvořák wants us to hear the slow movement turning into the scherzo. The later generates much energy, but the true conflict comes in the finale [fourth mvt] launched by the lower strings with their bid for power in a minor. Not till the very end of the work does F Major finally wrest "its" symphony back.

Symphony no. 6 (old no. 1) in D Major, op. 60 1880

Said the commentator Donald Francis Tovey, regarding the first subject of the symphony, "no man of the world would take this theme so seriously as to make a symphony of it"; but then Dvořák's music does carry a wonderful naiveté about it in both small and large forms, and the symphony that he made of this little tune—for it is subtly present throughout—is, if not worldly, thoroughly adult. Beautifully judged in terms of overall balance, its general effect is of an easeful passage, taking its time to mount to majesty in the finale [fourth mvt].

Many are those who hear Brahmsian echoes (specifically of Brahms' Symphony no. 2, also in D Major) in the work, and this is just, for at the time Dvořák was trying to break out of the Bohemian mould into which contemporaries had put him. Leading the first movement through alternations of power and simplicity, Dvořák moves on to a slow [second] movement of enchanting nocturnelike beauty. The main theme, announced by the violins, undergoes some remarkable transformations such as one expects of a symphonist in need of proving his maturity. Very international. But very local in the scherzo [third mvt]—an example of the Czech specialty called the Furiant. (The name of this strangely shaped dance might be rendered as "swaggerer's step," and bears no etymological relation to the English word, "fury," though the often violent bite of its accent—its count is 1-2-1-2-1-2-1-2-3-1-2-3—suggests a kinship.) The finale balances the first movement with sharp poise, closing in a thrilling *Presto* (very fast) based on the finale's first theme (which is based in turn on the theme that opened the whole work, the naive theme that no "man of the world" could take seriously).

Symphony no. 7 (old no. 2) in d minor, op. 70 1885

Feeling more and more that his typecasting as a Slavic folk stylist was dispossessing his symphonic image of its pan-Western identity, Dvořák composed this work to prove his standing as a musician not of a region but of a tradition. "I will make cause with my roots," he might have said by way of gloss, "back through Schubert and

Haydn"—and one does hear less of Dvořák the Bohemian here than elsewhere. Following Classical lines in layout, the d minor profits from the extended dimensions of Romanticism, both in size and emotional play.

An ominous opening prepares us for the symphony's stormy character, constantly balanced with palliative second subjects and counterstatements. Will the rage win, or the warmth? As in Haydn and Mozart, the two middle movements relax the tension somewhat—at least on the outward level—but an undercurrent of stress is nonetheless never many notes away.

The first movement seems dominated by its main theme, a rumbling d minor menace. Though the soothing B Flat Major second theme follows it remorselessly, it is the menace that one is left with as the movement ends. The distinguished slow [second] movement, however, completes what the B Flat theme started: a statement of the work's hidden sweetness. This is one of the great slow movements of its day, a showpiece of thematic particles stitched into a seamless webbing. The writing for woodwind is particularly intriguing.

The scherzo [third mvt], too, is a gem; note that its main theme is in fact two themes—the real theme in the violins and violas and a countertheme in bassoons and 'cellos. From d minor it slips into D Major for its trio, but returns to d minor (the work's home key) for the repeat of the main theme. Naturally, the finale [fourth mvt] is in d minor, too, tearing right into its main theme so as to leave no ambiguity as to the tenor of *this* piece. But there is ambiguity in the ardent second theme. First articulated by the 'cellos, it is repeated moments later, more grandly and with a whopping timpani accompaniment, as if an eager village band had strayed into the picture. Tragedy or gladness? In the first movement, the minor-key tragedy won out; here, things seem left on a more positive level. Still, it is neither one nor the other for absolute sure. Perhaps that is what gives the work its richness—many claim it is Dvořák's best symphony.

Symphony no. 8 (old no. 4) in G Major, op. 88 1889

This irresistible piece is one of the most nationalistic symphonies going. Every movement seems to communicate folk metaphors—the dancing, the pastoral stillnesses, the age and weight of a people's secular iconography. It is a progressively robust work. It opens with solemnity, in g minor, but quickly reaches for self-affirmation in G Major on the flute, sounding like the sun peeping between clouds. The movement doesn't seem to want to let go, however, and with the slow [second] movement, the work pulls inward. The strings give out an elegiacal motive, answered by bird calls on the flute. But wait: an oboe and flute, then a solo violin takes us into a brighter sound-space, echoed by the full orchestra. The symphony is waking up.

The scherzo [third mvt] ratifies g minor, however, in the form of a lilting waltz—and the G Major trio is downright extrovert. Note a special effect—for his coda (the tail-end of the movement), Dvořák reprises the trio tune, this time not in the waltz time of 3/4 but in the squared-off 2/4. Now we're getting friendly. Sure enough, the finale [fourth mvt] opens with a starchy but gala trumpet fanfare sounding like a summons to some fairgrounds. The fanfare turns into a warm 'cello theme that is treated to a series of variations before it explodes at last in whiplash ferocity. Melodically, this is one of the most satisfying of symphonies. But the work's certain charm lies in its wealth of sheer innocence, so surprised by the sorrowful clarity of its slow movement that it has to outdo itself dancing in the finale.

Symphony no. 9 (old no. 5) in e minor,
"From the New World," op. 95 1893

Nothing less than Dvořák's valedictory to the United States after (actually during—still, the sentiment is one of hail and farewell) his three years as head of the National Conservatory of Music in New York, the "New World" reflects the composer's theory that the profile of American music must be cut along the lines of Indian and black folk melodies. Never quoting from either (notwithstanding an apparent reference to "Swing Low, Sweet Chariot" as the closing theme of the first movement exposition), Dvořák did hope to evoke them, and this he seems to have at least partially done: the persona of the music sounds in spots like nothing else that he wrote, and many writers have insisted on the Indian or black pictorial basis of this or that section—the second movement an evening of slavery and spirituals under the magnolias, the third a party of braves on the hunt.

Maybe so; maybe not. Some few writers claim to hear in the "New

World" the same Bohemian rural revels that so surely inform Dvořák's other works, and they do have a point in that every movement, whatever else one may hear in it, has its moment or two of unmistakably non-American content when Dvořák is simply working within the compass of the generally Western symphony of Haydn, Brahms, et al. For the record, Dvořák did trouble to expose himself to authentic black and Indian music on his American travels, and he did intend to help kick off a native musical style with the "New World."

Like many a symphony of the late 1800s, the "New World" has a motto theme, a tune that makes a distinctive appearance in all four movements—most dramatically, after being hinted at in the introduction, as the first subject of the first movement (played by two horns):

(As so often, it is the first subject of the first movement, this one melody out of many, that figures strategically in the construction of the whole work—this is why it is no exaggeration to speak of the "principal theme" of an entire symphony when referring to the first theme of the first movement, for it provides a generative influence on all that follows. The most obvious example of this first-themeism, as it were, is the familiar buh-buh-buh-*buh* of Beethoven's Fifth: while it is heard in that precise form only in the first movement, its character launches the flight of the whole symphony both musically and dramatically.)

Alert ears will pick up the motto theme illustrated above as it arrives, for it does not change its form each time (as some motto themes do), and tends to show up at big moments in the action, as in the mighty last moments of the work. Frankly, however, one will miss no certain key to the piece if one merely hears what one hears, whatever one hears, for it is one of those warmly human, strikingly active situations in art that communicates instantaneously, and not surprisingly has remained one of the most popular items in the standard repertory since its premiere. Surely nobody does not like it: how can one not?—the vivid first movement, forceful and lyrical by turns (note the perky second subject, introduced on flute and oboe, half southern cakewalk and half Czech tootle)*; the famous *Largo* (very slow) [second mvt] so like a black spiritual that the words for "Goin' Home" were written to be sung to it; the angular, emphatic scherzo [third mvt], with not one but two trio sections, and these as bashful as the scherzo's main theme is impetuous; the defiant finale [fourth mvt], like its three predecessors equalized between the rash and the peaceful and ending in a healthy show of force by all hands until the very last chord, whch fades slowly to nothing.

Piano concerto in g minor, op. 33 1876

Annotator's dish has it that the solo part in Dvořák's piano concerto is unpianistic, physically awkward (especially for the left hand) and crying for revision—and revisions have been forthcoming. However, those pianists who would rather discover Dvořák than appropriate him have found the awkwardness infrequent and the revisions inferior; of late there has been a general return to the composer's original text.

Indeed, the work's flaw lies not in the keyboard writing but in the long first movement, whose domineering first subject (heard in the opening moments in the horns, low strings, and low woodwind) never validates its many would-be developments and recapitulations, forever verging on something but not, somehow, arriving. The slow [second] movement, though, is a gem of lyrical consolation, and the finale [third mvt] follows with a taut sonata-rondo on some highly Bohemian-sounding melodies.

Violin Concerto in a minor, op. 53 1879

Wildly popular in its day, Dvořák's violin concerto has largely, though not entirely, faded from the scene, lacking as it does the robust dynamics and penetratingly rhapsodic thrust of the violin concertos of Brahms and Chaikofsky (both written almost simultaneously with Dvořák's, incidentally). It is a problem piece, said problem being one of formal layout, for, instead of the solid first, sooth-

*Insider's footnote: listen to hear whether or not the conductor slows down here. Most of them do, though Dvořák did not request a change in tempo and the theme loses some of its quirky dash when held back so. Purists like to recall that Arturo Toscanini always took this theme "as marked" (i.e, without slowing down).

ing second, and lightly cathartic third movements of the classical concerto, Dvořák left us a pallid, rather monothematic first movement, an effective (and unusually pictorial—everyone hears something else) second, and a lively third—in other words, not the heavy-to-buoyant of the standard concerto, but a limp-to-buoyant (this is especially apparent when the first movement subsides, without a break, into the second, as if aware that it has not made much of a statement on its own). Not till the third movement rondo does the piece really come alive.

Still, it has its moments, and the soloist does not lack for stellar opportunities. In the rondo [third mvt] he displays his *spiccato* ("marked," i.e., very sharply articulated) technique on a fast-running line while the orchestra attends to the tune, and a bit later (when the rhythm changes), he takes the honors at what sounds like a Bohemian village jam session on a local (originally Ukrainian) dance specialty, the dumka. The episode works so well that the composer brings it back for a short reprise just before the coda.

'Cello Concerto in b minor, op. 104 1895

The last of Dvořák's three concertos (not counting an early one for cello, never orchestrated), this is by far the most successful in terms of making the concerto principle work. Indeed, it is one of the great concertos of its era for its maturity of purpose and individual completeness. Sensitive and even ominous in its minor key, it proceeds from portentous first movement through moving second to still ominous but also lively third, the sense of unity aided by a quotation of the work's opening theme in its final moments.

Beginners, wondering about form, should admire Dvořák's handling of the opening of the concerto, always a tricky moment—for composers, too, have worried about form here especially. With a first and second subject to introduce, and with an orchestra *and* a 'cello soloist with which to introduce them, how is one to satisfy both music and musicians—how find a place for all without sounding loose or long-winded? In his piano and violin concertos, Dvořák brought the soloist in right at the start (which is fine, if virtually unheard of before Beethoven and Mendelssohn), but failed to balance his first and second themes: loose. Other composers got the balance but took too much time about it: long-winded. Here everything works. Dvořák at first holds the soloist back, giving the somber first theme and noble second (on a solo horn, a great moment) to the other instruments and then rounding this off with a Bohemian-sounding closing theme. This, all together, is the *tutti* of the Classical concerto, the orchestral statement of themes. Only now does Dvořák bring in his soloist with the challenge of vivifying his themes so that the movement goes somewhere, so that we follow. In the event, Dvořák exploits development, variation, transformation of themes, until recapitulation brings back the first theme in a sweeping orchestral statement, succeeded by one for the 'cello.

The slow [second] movement pulls us from b minor into G Major in the pastoral clarinet theme that leads off the movement, though a dramatic middle section asserts g minor; the horns take the main theme when it returns. The finale [third mvt] is both dour and glad, sometimes at exactly the same moment. It begins as a march, which builds up to the rondo refrain (sounded by the soloist). Intervening episodes soothe in major keys, and at length Dvořák gives us the refrain switched into the major. At length—but not at last, for he seems too pleased with the movement to end it. It keeps on going, somehow retaining its steam, as when the clarinets surprise us by quoting the opening theme of the first movement.

Slavonic Dances, op. 46; 72 1878; 1886

Not much need be said here, for these ingratiating patterns of Slavic folk rhythms are as easy to follow as to enjoy. They do help fill in Dvořák's dossier as folklorist, never quoting actual folk tunes but rather abstracting their character in melodies of his own invention, and they did (in their orignal form as pieces for piano duet) provide the relatively young and unknown Dvořák with his first taste of fame and financial success.

The dances, mainly Czech but also Ukrainian, Polish, and Serbian, tend to the sophisticated in the second set, written eight years after the first; the pathetic, especially, is more pronounced later than earlier, as if Dvořák were not content anymore with the simple frolic of the dance—as if he would penetrate some emotional abstraction, correlate, dramatize. But whatever the temperament of this or that dance, all are taken whole as earnests of the "national style" in music, surging with the songs of earth, dialect, tradition, festival. Structurally, they are easy to follow, unfolding in an ABA pattern, though both A and B sections are unified by a prevailing rhythm, as if each new melody were the logical consequence of its predecessor. For an invigorating national folk high, the Slavonic Dances make a splendid treat—they are particularly recommended as library builders for children's record shelves. Those who love this type of music and pout for more should address themselves to Leoš Janáček's Lachian Dances and Bedřich Smetana's *The Moldau* (second in his tone poem cycle, *My Native Land*) and the overture to his opera *The Bartered Bride.*

Serenade in E Major for Strings, op. 22 1875

Hearing them, one may think of serenades as being something like small, gentle symphonies with too many movements—sometimes as many as six or seven. These extra movements tend to compromise the clarity of symphonic line—that is, the progression from the conflictive first movement through the slow movement and scherzo to the resolving fourth movement: the oomph. With extra minuets and sonata-allegro movements in the way, it is often hard to tell what a serenade is up to.

No matter. The serenade was not designed to carry the dramatic weight of the symphony—take it as diversion; Haydn and Mozart did. In the spirit of their epoch, Dvořák contrived this event for strings only in five movements—nostalgic opening, minuetty waltz, scherzo, slow movement, and finale (which includes a brief recollection of the opening in its final pages). There is a great deal of counterpoint (two or more independent parts playing at the same time), especially in the finale, in which the various members of the string family seem determined to bluff each other out of the melodic right-of-way. By the time they reach the aforementioned quotation of the first movement, however, they have made up their differences—no! one last confrontation ensues. But nobody wins and everyone ends together.

Symphonic Variations, op. 78
(formerly op. 40) 1877

For some reason this intriguing experiment in "how may I play thee let me count the ways" (twenty-seven, it turns out) has not enjoyed the popularity it surely deserves, for Dvořák's ways with the theme announced at the outset offer a wild ride of melodic, harmonic, and rhythmic modifications. (This is no minor challenge, for the theme itself is an odd one, hard to describe except to say that it manages to sound unassuming and pregnant at the same time.) Ranging wildly in tone, as twenty-seven variations are bound to do if interest be kept keen, the music reaches grand proportions in the last incarnation (a fugue, as so often the case with large-scale variation forms) and then outdoes itself for the usual *re*incarnation, the theme back in its original shape, with trumpets and drums and all shouting it *fortissimo*.

Scherzo Capriccioso, op. 66 1883

Ever since Beethoven invented the scherzo as a replacement for the minuet movements of Haydn and Mozart, it has passed a colorfully various existence, fluttery in one symphony, amusingly clutzy in another, savage, perhaps, in yet another. Having no symphony to belong to, Dvořák's "capricious scherzo" would apparently compensate for its solo status by being all things at once: essentially merry (for scherzo means "joke"), it has its fluttery, clutzy, and even savage moments. Note, for instance, the quasi-ferocious emphasis of the cymbal-crashing first theme (after a short introduction), pumping away like a dance-hall tune run amok, yet note as well the later moment when the harp intrudes with a soothing little cadenza. There is a lot of heart in this caprice.

The "Garland" Tone Poems:
The Water Goblin, op. 107 1896
The Mid-Day Witch, op. 108 1896
The Golden Spinning-Wheel, op. 109 1896
The Wood Dove, op. 110 1896

Karel Jaromír Erben's fairy tales in verse, collected under the title *The Garland*, struck Dvořák as an ideal premise for a tour through the fantasy and freedom of the tone poem. Here was a dare—to narrate Erben's stories through music, meanwhile to dip one's pen deeply into the good-versus-evil, nature-and-magic imagery of the folk-Slavic paint bottle. Music, here, is story—this was the dare. Certain sections of this quartet seem like songs without words set right to Erben's rhymed text; indeed, certain sections are just that, the instruments chanting melodies that correspond exactly to the rise and fall of the *Garland*'s lines, and one may divide the music into "paragraphs" to match the breaks of the originals.

Whether or not one appreciates the Czech-ness of Dvořák's sound here, one may at least enjoy the exactness of his storytelling, and it is recommended that one follow each of these tone poems in reference to the plot synopses that invariably turn up in the concert program or record album notes, thus to "hear" the pictures event by event as Dvořák "sings" them. The tales themselves luxuriate in the gory militancy of storybookland: the water goblin pulls his own half-mortal child to pieces; the mid-day witch reifies a harassed mother's "bogeyman" warnings by showing up and taking over; the golden spinning wheel warbles of how a maid was murdered and her body mutilated by her own stepmother (to the surprise of nobody who was raised on the capers of Grimm stepmothers); and the wood dove coos over the grave of a murderess' victim, driving the former to suicide.

Carnival Overture, op. 92 1891

Carnival is the central panel from a triptych of overtures designed to portray nature, life, and love; eventually they were entitled *In Nature's Realm, A Czech Carnival* (then simply *Carnival*), and *Othello*—love in this case leaning more to jealousy than to romance. But life, in this case, is in highest spirits—not to mention sonata-allegro form: uproarious (first subject) with vendors' cries, revelers, and band music, then more intimately passionate (second subject). In the midst of what promises to be a feverish development section, Dvořák inserts a dreamy interlude—"a pair of straying lovers" was his reading of it—and then closes his carnival, recapitulation, with the first subject in full cry.

EDVARD GRIEG 1843–1907

Despite the endless popularity of his one piano concerto and the incidental music to Henrik Ibsen's play *Peer Gynt,* the Norwegian composer Edvard Grieg has never enjoyed a good press from the critics. "The infinitesimal

Grieg," George Bernard Shaw called him, in response to Grieg's having written an "original part for second piano" to accompany Mozart's piano fantasia in c minor, K. 476. And in his days as reviewer for the magazine *Gil Blas,* Claude Debussy devoted an entire essay to demolishing what he heard as the slick, swooning sweetness of Grieg, whether in songs, piano bits, or large-scale orchestral works.

On the other hand, Grieg's following thinks of him as "the Chopin of the North." The comparison is apt only in that both the Norwegian and the Pole specialized in shortish piano pieces (as opposed to the larger symphonic forms) rooted in the dance rhythms of their respective native lands. Still, as Debussy pointed out, Grieg never synthesized an individualistic "folk" art on the order of the Russian Five (Balakiryef, Rimsky-Korsakof, Musorksky, et al.), and never wrote anything to equal Chopin's haughtily Polish polonaises for piano. "We are left," concludes Debussy, "with a strange and charming taste in our mouths—that of a rose-colored sweet coated in snow."

Piano Concerto in a minor, op. 16 1868

The opening fanfare must be one of the best-known phrases in all symphony. This, however, is not the first subject; *that* follows in the woodwinds after a short flourish at the keyboard. Transitionally, the piano breaks in with a bright, prancey solo reminiscent of Grieg's innumerable short piano pieces, leading to the warm second theme on the 'cellos and woodwind. (Initially, Franz Liszt talked young Grieg into scoring the second theme for trumpet, with results embarrassingly flamboyant even for that flamboyant age; on second thought, Grieg rescored the passage to play as now heard.) With a closing theme based on the opening fanfare, the exposition ends, giving way to a free development section buoyed up more by the basic tunefulness of the themes than by Grieg's ability to develop them. Then the luxurious cadenza (the pianist's big solo spot), and coda.

The rest of the work is easy to follow—a poetic slow [second] movement and a hefty rondo finale [third mvt] adapted from the Norwegian halling (a fast-paced, aggressive dance), opening up in its middle episode into a lovely flute theme that returns triumphantly at the end of the movement. Through it all, one will notice—like it or not—a naiveté so upfront as to risk simplistic inadequacy. One is too aware of "sections" not well integrated, of a piano that would rather play by itself than collaborate with the orchestra. Grieg was a miniaturist, not a symphonist—and yet, it moves. Not because of any

"Norwegian" insights of the nationalist, nor by romantic fluke, but because the innocence of its construction suits the innocence of its melody. This concerto disarms all criticism, even by those who *know* that Grieg could not develop a tune, only compose one. (By the way, listeners whose experience takes in the operetta *Song of Norway* will note some contiguities: Grieg's life and music supplied *Song of Norway* with its plot and score. Two songs, "Legend" and "Hill of Dreams," were drawn from the concerto in particular.)

Incidental Music from Peer Gynt 1876

Technically, Grieg drew up two suites from his score for Henrik Ibsen's play *Peer Gynt,* bearing opus numbers 46 and 55. But as conductors have their own ideas about which of the ten items to play and in which order (*and* whether or not to include the vocal passages for soprano soloist and chorus), let's not try to keep our suites straight but simply concentrate on the music.

Know first of all that the play that inspired this music does not accord with the common view of Ibsen as a Freudian realist; *Peer Gynt* is a lively picaresque about an infuriatingly amoral but attractive adventurer who is as soulless as an onion (Ibsen uses just this simile in his script). Grieg's music accompanies no *Wild Duck* but a farcical and fantastical and poignant exhibit, which explains the variety of the sounds—a moving death scene, for instance, back to back with a piquant Arabian prance.

The best-known items in the suites are an eternal quartet—"Morning," "Ase's Death," "Anitra's Dance," and "In the Hall of the Mountain King." "Morning" needs no extrapolation here, for the melody is instantly familiar. Ase is Peer's mother, a long-suffering woman who breathes her last in Peer's bewildered but unrepentant embrace. Anitra is an Asian vamp, thus the insidious come-hither of piccolo and triangle. The Mountain King captains a band of trolls—not, from the sound of them, a friendly lot.

If you have a choice, expose yourself to the whole of Grieg's score (when buying a recording, check the album to see how many of the pieces you're getting—don't accept fewer than nine), because the less well-known excerpts are as interesting as the familiar ones. Solveig's two songs, for example, offer a haunting picture of the true-loving girl-next-door, too good for the hero but too in love with him to reject him; her "Lullaby," a combination cradle song and dirge, demands to be heard.

Four Norwegian Dances, op. 35 1881

Grieg in a folk-national mood, utilizing—as he rarely did—actual folk material. However "Norwegian" the third movement of Grieg's piano concerto may sound, the melodies are all his; here he occasionally borrows from the public domain. Each of the four dances is laid out in the ABA form so useful in short symphonic movements—a main melodic section, a contrasting middle section, and a repeat of the first section. Neatly orchestrated by someone else (Hans Sitt, otherwise uncelebrated) from Grieg's originals for piano duet (a staple of the home repertory in the late 1800s), this quartet makes no demands on the listener except on those with youngest ears, who may find the invitation to the dance irresistible. (For trivia buffs: Dance no. 2 turned up in the operetta *Song of Norway* as "Freddy and his Fiddle.")

NICOLAI RIMSKY-KORSAKOF 1844–1908

Like his fellow members of the *Moguchaya Kutchka* (Mighty Grouplet) known as the "Russian Five," Rimsky-Korsakof troubled to build an oeuvre along manifestly Russian lines. Conscious of lacking a national musical tradition such as that of France or Germany, the quintet, each in his way, defined the Russian character in their work, borrowing from or invoking folk music, adapting folk tales or history, rooting at the Russian soul. Let the cosmopolitan Chaikofsky write tone poems on *Hamlet, Romeo and Juliet,* or Francesca da Rimini; let him wrestle with the Western symphony of Haydn, Beethoven, Brahms. The mighty Five turned inward to the national core. (Although, to keep the record straight, it should be admitted that the Five's mentor and spokesman Balakiryef helped Chaikofsky plan the composition of both *Hamlet* and *Romeo and Juliet.*)

A more detailed analysis of the aesthetic worked out by the Five may be found in the article on Balakiryef; for now, let it suffice that Rimsky-Korsakof was until recently the best known and most international of the *Kutchka.* Though his Russian sound is as Russian as any, his many operas do not share the forbidding, parochial Slavic solipsism of Borodin's *Prince Igor* or Musorksky's *Boris Godunof.* Indeed, he was celebrated for his gifts as orchestrator, suave with a lilt and brilliance reassuring to Western ears. (Rimsky's textbook on orchestration remains a useful study.) Furthermore, Rimsky eventually rebelled against the gauche amateurism of the Five, renewing his musical training on his own and deploring the ramshackle technique of the other four. A tireless older brother sort to them, all the same, Rimsky has suffered a bad press for completing unfinished works and even polishing the "coarseness" of Musorksky when said coarseness was really more of a barbaric vitality. Even now, when the glories of Musorksky's original *Boris Godunof* have been revealed on stage and disc, most opera houses continue to use Rimsky's more refined version. But to do Rimsky justice, one should know that he was only trying to popularize *Boris Godunof* until its time had come. When his version is at last retired across the board, his ghost will, if ghosts can, smile.

Scheherazade, op. 35 1888

We all know the story: a wicked sultan given to executing his wives on their wedding night is outfoxed by Scheherazade, who fascinates him with her art as storyteller. "Just one more," he tells himself, staying his hand night after night until, a thousand and one nights later, he grants her her life and settles down to marriage with his Eastern Katherine Mansfield.

Now the music. A "symphonic suite," *Scheherazade* is cast in four movements, each with a title allusive to one of the Arabian Nights tales. But the work is not a "symphony with a story" or anything like that. Though the four movements do coexist as the equivalent of a symphonic first movement, scherzo, slow movement, and finale, there are no "stories" here. The composer was adamant on that point. There is no Sultan Theme (though he admitted that a certain theme "seems to suggest" the Sultan), no Sinbad Theme, no Sea Theme, no Festival Theme—none of the highly pictorial concepts that listeners have insisted on finding for themselves. Only one melody was meant connotatively: the sinuous violin solo heard very prominently in all four movements that everyone associates with the tale-spinning Scheherazade. Here, only here, Rimsky agrees with his public. This violin solo does indeed represent his heroine and her seductive narrations; fittingly, it is used at the start of the first, second, and fourth movements, and as a charismatic interlude in the third. (Other themes, by the way, turn up in more than one movement, adding to the sense of overall cohesion.)

What are we to do with a work so imaginal yet so insistent on its lack of images? The very opening of the work, a thunderously menacing theme, is the one that "seems to suggest" the Sultan; it is immediately succeeded by the delicate violin solo, accompanied by the harp, that Rimsky ascribed to Scheherazade. The rest of the first movement, subtitled, "The Sea and Sinbad's Ship," gives in its rocking pageantry the sense of a boat striking through the foam. Scheherazade's slyly fascinating violin theme heralds the second movement, "The Story of the Kalendar Prince." Something like a scherzo in ABA form, this section opens with a typical Rimskyan touch in orchestration: an Oriental melody is passed from instrument to instrument, from the bassoon to the oboe to the strings to the woodwinds to a solo horn. Now comes the B section, a fierce business (don't ask what it signifies; Rimsky says no), then the A section again, in a livelier strain.

The third movement, not unlike a slow movement, offers "The Young Prince and the Young Princess," love music—and the most familiar tune in the piece. Note the return of the main theme of the second movement, speeded up, and a lush interpretation by Scheherazade (the violin again) embellishing her romance.

The fourth movement is a busy one: "Festival in Baghdad; The Ship Goes to Pieces Against the Rock Surmounted by the Bronze Warrior." What Arabian Nights retrospective would be complete without a festival in Baghdad? Toward the end the sea music from the first movement recurs with an unmistakeable air of disaster, and the story is told—but there was no "story," was there? Yet what do we hear at the very end? The solo violin—of the storyteller.

Symphony no. 2, "Antar," op. 9 1868

Though in four movements, this is not a symphony in the strict sense of sonata-allegro end movements, slow movement and scherzo, and key relationships. Rather, it is a tone poem with a hero and heroine, whose characteristic themes (his, especially) provide much of the melodic development in the work. Antar is an Arabian hermit who saves a gazelle from a monstrous bird of prey; the gazelle reveals herself as a fairy queen and grants Antar the three great perquisites of life—vengeance, power, and love.

To follow the work, forget form and let Rimsky's finely turned pictorial gift stoke your imagination. Know only the two significant themes in the piece, heard after a longish slow introduction describing Antar's desert hermitage. First of the two is Antar's theme, a lugubrious but arresting melody deep in the violas; second is that of the fairy queen, an unmissable shimmer on the flute. Both tunes recur throughout the piece, though Antar's is by far the more prominent, serving as a motto theme overall.

The layout is simple: the first movement describes Antar's meeting with the gazelle. The rest are his three rides on the wish-horse: the second movement is Vengeance, the third Power (it sounds like a cute march—shouldn't power be more . . . powerful?), the fourth Love. Antar ends as do all mortals who draw too close to the spirit world, in luxuriating death.

Capriccio Espagnol, op. 34 1887

One of the most extravagantly orchestrated works, this dazzling Spanish Caprice, an Iberian serenade, blends ethnic pastiche and orchestral braggadocio. Just about everyone in the band gets a specialty spot here, for Rimsky revived the old Baroque tradition of *concertante* playing—that is, with constant use of instrumental solos. (The composer emphasized the virtuosi approach by dedicating the score to the players of the premiere performance, listing all sixty-seven of their names on the title page.)

There are five short movements, the last two connected as one. The instrumental solos, whether as melody, accompaniment, or cadenza (the bits that sound like improvised, show-off solos), are too various to mention. Note the little set of theme and five variations in the second movement, on a suitably Spanish-sounding idea, and note as well that the third movement offers virtually the same music as the first but in a different orchestration. The fourth movement, "Scene and Gypsy Song," is the prize of the piece, opening with the "gypsy" theme played as fanfare by horns and trumpets. A solo violin repeats the figure, slips in a fast cadenza, and then comes the Song proper, *highly* Spanish on flute and clarinet and thrown from one part of the orchestra to another. (Trivia buffs will delight to learn that a television musical of the mid-1950s with a score adapted from Rimsky-Korsakof, *The Adventures of Marco Polo,* used this tune for a song called "Xanadu.") The fifth and final movement, a fandango, closes with the music that opened the show.

Suite from The Golden Cock 1907

These extracts from Rimsky's last opera, a wicked satire on idiot monarchy based on a poem by Pushkin, tells of King Dodon, his failed war campaign, his love for the beautiful Queen of Shemakha, and his golden cock, a magical bird who crows peace in good times and alarms in bad. This is dramatic music, set for narration; one cannot follow the events with the help of the suite's vague subtitles, and a proper trot would take too many pages. Frankly, one is advised to make the acquaintance of the complete opera, live or on records, or simply to accept the suite as a comic, horrible, beautiful, grotesque dream.

The Russian Easter Overture, op. 36 1888

The Great Russian Easter in Russian. The composer held the opinion that even music as atmospheric as this could not capture the tang of a true Russian Easter celebration: one had to see it, live, for oneself. But since the Soviets have decreed God counterproductive in the worker's paradise, these ecstatic rites are kept largely off-limits to spectators and we Westerners must make do with this evocative overture, designed to synthesize two religious essences—(1) the grandiose piety of the ritual and (2) the cathartic exhilaration of a pagan spring festival. Using authentic church melodies, Rimsky opens with a slow introduction stating his principal theme in the woodwinds, all on the same notes. The darker instruments take up the tune, but all this soon gives way to a dizzy celebration, popular, basic, enthralled. This is Rimsky upholding the tenets of the "Russian Five": to bring to symphony the folk-spirit of the Russian people.

GABRIEL FAURÉ 1845–1924

Camille Saint-Saëns' pupil and Maurice Ravel's teacher, Fauré occupied the little era between the passionate high Romanticism of Wagner's day and the jazzy neo-Classicism of Stravinsky's, somewhat simultaneously with the impressionism of Claude Debussy. But neither passion nor jazz—nor Debussy's grey and amorphous air-earth-fire-and-water music—stirred Fauré. He resisted the tempo of his time and sought clarity, simplicity, and tuneful formality. All three may be found in the works cited below, which may explain why many people find them "too quiet." Certainly, few composers get as hushy as often as Fauré, but in reply he might have pointed out that volume can be a mask for the insecure. Anyway, when Fauré wanted loud, he wrote it. He composed his opera *Prometheus* for open-air performance by some 400 musicians.

Ballade in f sharp minor for Piano and Orchestra, op. 19 1881

One movement's worth of concerto, moving from slow to moderate to lively in tempo, and from songful sobriety to light refreshment in tone. The piano dominates the opening in a not unChopinesque passage, sparely accompanied by the strings. A solo flute perks this after a bit, and the mood opens up. Throughout, the piano is definitely the main feature, scarcely ever silent and either playing all the tunes or decorating the orchestra line with choice filigree. This is not the dramatic, protagonistic solo writing developed by Paganini and Liszt, however; to close the work Fauré goes in for a silky barcarolle feeling, suggestive of the rocking waves.

Elégie for 'Cello and Orchestra, op. 24 1883

As the term implies, a lamentation, nicely balanced in one short movement. Fauré's gift for self-effacing accompaniments and his generally light touch ideally "place" the 'cello in the orchestral texture (the instrument's low range might otherwise be swamped in orchestral overkill). The solo controls the situation from first to last, imposing its reserve on everyone else. The result is a minute but impeccable little poem.

Dolly, op. 56 1896; orchestrated 1912

A suite composed for piano duet, *Dolly* turned into a ballet in 1912, orchestrated by Henri Rabaud. This is infant music, not for but about them, their worldview, their drives, their personal effects, all chartered in the keen glance of a little girl. First is a charming "Lullaby," in ABA form, slender, petite as Dolly; one wants to tiptoe about. Next comes "Mi-a-ou," not in the least catlike: the title supposedly refers not to a pet but to Dolly's mispronunciation of Raoul, her brother's name. It sounds like children at play. "Dolly's Garden" is Dolly's dream, perfumed with a princess' fine sense of self. "Kitty" waltzes—still not cat sounds; the music belongs to Dolly. A middle section breaks out of the waltz, but the main theme returns at the end. The fifth number is called "Tenderness"; no one will argue with the title, especially not in the light of the piquant oboes and horns of the middle section. How long can little Dolly keep still? Now she must frolic—the finale, "Spanish Dance," presents an extroverted heroine, with drum and tambourine, a hint of the elegant—even luxurious—woman to be.

Masques et Bergamasques, op. 112 1919

Perhaps in reaction to the decadence of late Romanticism, Fauré here recaptures the leaner style of the Classical suite—no programmatic titles, no modern madness of rhythm or harmony, just four movements of crystalline absolute music. We have Overture, Minuet, Gavotte, and Pastorale. The first is lively, an invocation to musical festivity; the Minuet is a proper minuet, something out of Haydn yet not so robust. The Gavotte, too, has an antique ring, a crispness of bobbing perukes (note how in the trio—the B—of the ABA form, Fauré slips the A theme in as an "answer" to the B theme). The closing Pastorale frames a placid look at the rural scene in the composer's characteristic subtle resonance. His less, certainly, is more. (The title, by the way, is untranslatable. Think of it, roughly, as *Masks and Maskers*—the music was originally used in a commedia dell'arte theatre piece.)

Incidental Music to Pelléas et Mélisande, op. 80 1898

Before Debussy made his revolutionary operatic adaptation of Maeterlinck's diaphanous play, Fauré wrote a set of act preludes and accompaniments for a London production starring Mrs. Patrick Campbell as the vividly ambiguous Mélisande. Much of the music in the suite refers to her character. The Prelude prepares generally for the action of tragic enchantment (note the hunting horn at the end—the curtain rises on a forest where the hunter comes upon Mélisande, lost and shivering). The second number, however, "The Spinner," presents Mélisande at her wheel. An oddly turned interlude, a Sicilienne, offers a dance having nothing to do with the play (written for some other occasion, in fact); still, it fits nicely into the suite as sheer music. "Mélisande's Death" captures the sorrow of the play's final scene with Fauré's characteristically affecting simplicity.

VINCENT D'INDY 1851–1931

As a pupil and disciple of César Franck, D'Indy did much to help mobilize a Franck school of symphony, for of other Franckians only Ernest Chausson made much of a splash, and it takes a group to get a movement going. As it was, the little heyday of the Franck Symphony connected the experiments of Franz Liszt in the mid-nineteenth century with the work of Debussy, Ravel, and Dukas (French impressionism) in the early twentieth century, and one still speaks of the Franck movement: Franck, D'Indy, and Chausson.

The credo of the Franck school is cyclicism, which entails two things: (1) a basic motto theme to be varied unceasingly to form numerous subsidiary themes throughout a composition, and (2) the use of prominent themes in more than one movement. Aiming at an overall cohesion, cyclicism is exclusive to no school or period, and may be traced back to Bach. But as a self-conscious Act of Artistic Faith it is associated particularly with the middle and late nineteenth century in general and with Franck and D'Indy in particular. All three of the works analyzed below depend heavily on the cyclic theory—for example, the Symphony on a French Mountain Air has three movements, each built on a variant of the "Air," an adaptation of a folk tune that caught D'Indy's ear on a holiday in southern France.

Symphony no. 2 in B Flat, op. 57 1902

Like any proper Franckian (see the introduction above), D'Indy erects this huge structure on variants of a motto theme—two motto themes, actually. They are heard right at the start of the slow introduction to the first movement, the first in the lower strings and harp, and the second on the flute, almost simultaneously. Not even a trained musician could expect to follow the many transmutations of these two themes on their voyage through the symphony; it is enough to sense their presence and comprehend, intellectually, that D'Indy used them to stretch his work into an almost infinitesimally infrastructured unity—a completeness whose pieces all relate to each other.

It is a grand work, but it does take its time. A lively first movement (after the slow introduction) cedes to an underpowered second [slow] movement. But the third movement—a cross between a slow movement and a scherzo—demands attention for its charming folkish tune given by a solo viola. Not too much has happened so far; it remains for the finale [fourth mvt] to tie it all up with rich polyphonic material (that is, several different strands of melody going on at once) and a climactic restatement of the two motto themes in their original form, one played against the other.

Symphony on a French Mountain Air, op. 25 1886

Not so much a symphony as a concerto, with its three movements and piano soloist, the piece seeks a Romantic unity in a French mountain song, quoted at the very start of the first movement and used as the main themes of all three movements. Expert musicians may thrill to D'Indy's artful adaptation of a simple folk tune into the psychological basis for an entire work; others may enjoy D'Indy's deft sense of instrumental color and bright, transparent sound, so economically disbursed even when the piano is working at full volume.

A concerto's layout, then: fast, "important" first movement, slow second, slight third. As stated before, the "Air" of the title is heard at once, on the English horn. A tender variant of the air sets up a tender slow [second] movement, but a third version, in the third movement, is athletic, played by the woodwinds over a jumpy accompaniment on the piano. Only a touch of calm interferes with the finale's excitement, which mounts to a duel-climax in which piano and orchestra argue over who shall have the last note. It's a draw.

Istar: Symphonic Variations, op. 42 1896

In the Assyrian epic *Izdubar,* Istar is a goddess who undergoes an unusual trial to redeem the life of her dead lover: she must pass through seven doors, paying for her passage at each portal by yielding up some item of jewelry (which, since she's a goddess, is about all she wears). Passing through the seventh door in the height of Assyrian epic chic—bare flesh—she reaches the Waters of Life and with the liquid revives her innamorato.

D'Indy's *Istar* is a theme and variations—with a twist. Instead of announcing his theme and then varying it several times over, growing melodically, rhythmically, and harmonically more complex each time (the usual procedure), D'Indy *starts* with his most obscure variation—no statement of theme—and progressively works his way back through simpler variations until, at the end, he finally sounds the theme itself, naked as Istar is (by then) naked: on flute and piccolo solos thinly backed by violins. Thus the theme, like Istar, gives up its embellishments rather than gains them. One thing D'Indy does build on, though, is the sense of romantic release, for as Istar nears the end of her quest, the tone of the music becomes feverish, soaring at last—just after the flute and piccolo passage—into a rapture of naked delight.

LEOŠ JANÁČEK 1854–1928

Fame came late to Janáček, and when it did it was that isolated Slavic fame that tends not to travel out of Eastern Europe. For a long time he was known only by opera buffs—and dimly at that—for an opera, *Jenůfa,* whose loveliness helped it to cross the ethnic (really, language) barriers. Only lately has interest—in Janáček's five other major operas and his orchestral and chamber music—surged with proper respect. And now that most of his work has been revealed, it turns out that he is one of the geniuses of the modern age, comparable to Stravinsky, Schönberg, Nielsen, and Hindemith in terms of laying an originality upon the massed traditions of Western music.

Like his Czech predecessors Smetana and Dvořák, Janáček was fascinated by the primary cultural colors available to the folklorist. Like theirs, his music always sounds folkish whether he is quoting folk tunes or inventing his own. "The whole life of a man," he once said, "is in the folk music—body, soul, environment, everything. He who grows out of folk music makes a whole man of himself. Folk music binds people together, linking them with other peoples and uniting mankind in a spiritual bond of happiness and blessing."

What sets Janáček apart from the other two Czech composers is his almost obsessive use of the folkish cadence—the rhythm of Czech speech—in music. Especially in his great last period in the 1920s, Janáček bent his musical imagination to the reflection of the folk-cultural karma. The result sounds like no other composer and, sometimes, like the sounds of another world, a sinewy lyricism caught within a fourth dimension of rhythms and repetitions. Taking the "transformation of themes" from the mid-nineteenth century to its natural conclusion, Janáček builds whole works out of one melody that constantly changes its form, a kind of theme and variations in perpetual motion. (Conservatives amongst you will be pleased to know that the 1800s did not so much invent the idea of thematic transformation so much as advertise it; as far back as the Baroque era, Bach exploited the method with gusto, as for example in the Brandenburg Concertos, in which each movement is based on permutations of and corollaries to one principal theme.) The aim, as in the 1800s, is unity. But Janáček's unity is open-ended: he can stop at any point, or he can go on indefinitely.

Janáček is not yet as popular as he will be, so this chapter is a short one. However, I encourage the reader to try the vocal Janáček, who does not show up here. The *Slavonic Mass,* a big work for soloists, chorus, and orchestra, is bound to exhilarate, and the operas are rapidly becoming the sensation of the international repertory. *Jenůfa* is the easiest to like, followed by *Káta Kabanová.* But wonders await in *Příhody Lišky Bystroušky* (The Adventures of the Vixen Sharp-Ears, generally called The Cunning Little Vixen), a comic-tragic satiric fable on the unstoppable continuity of the natural world. Ecologists, especially, when not out picketing a power plant, should enjoy it.

Sinfonietta 1926

Calling it a "little symphony," Janáček is freed of obligations to the form set up by Haydn, Mozart, and Beethoven. He can go his own way—which, throughout his career, Janáček had a habit of doing anyway. There are five movements, and they do as they please, changing tone, tempo, or rhythm with élan. The first movement is all brass and timpani (eleven trumpets!), pushy, sudden. The second movement is less forceful, at times folk-dancey, and the third leans to the lyrical side at first in its stringy pliancy. But the string theme passes to woodwinds and then brass, and the pace quickens and the temperature rises. In the fourth movement, a succession of dances (some of which interfere with each other, rushing in before another has ceased) trips by. Three flutes introduce the fifth movement as violins ripple around them in a characteristic Janáček "riff" (a jazz term for a functional, non-melodic tune used as a kind of placeholder). Other instruments slip in, the atmosphere tenses, and at last—for a touch of eternity—the fanfares from the first movement close the piece, now scored for full orchestra.

Concertino for Piano and Orchestra 1925

Properly, this "little concerto" should not be included in this book, as it calls for only eight instruments: chamber music. But it invites our interest for its chamber-sized version of what a Janáček piano concerto might be like. Anyway, what are rules of exclusion for except to be broken? This is a charming piece, dizzy as a queen and growly as a barnyard. Note how the piano must contend not with instrumental choirs (woodwinds, brasses, strings in groups) as in most concertos, but with solo instruments. Small in shape as well as sound, the work is in four little sections, too short to be called movements. The start-and-stop repetitions of themes, a characteristic of the late Janáček, is very much felt here; be charmed, and consider it a tiny study for your investigation of the bigger works.

Taras Bulba 1918

A tone poem divided, unlike most tone poems, into movements, three of them. Janáček termed the piece a "rhapsody" (denoting a work of nationalistic rhetoric), for it tells of heroism and love amidst a war between Ukrainian Cossacks and Poles. Adapted from Nicolai Gogol, the music follows events leading up to three Cossack deaths, one per movement—first that of Taras' son Andri, then that of Taras' son Ostapof, than that of Taras himself.

The first movement, "The Death of Andri," tells how Taras' son loves a girl of the enemy Poles, starving in siege. The opening slow passage (English horn and violin solos) gently draws on Andri's pining love for his Polish maid, then cedes to more spirited doings in evocation of the coming battle. The love music returns until a tolling bell signals disaster—Andri fights on the Polish side against his own people and falls as a traitor, slain by his father. At last, the English horn and violin keen for Andri.

The second movement, "The Death of Ostapof," turns to Taras' other son. (Note the typical Janáčekian string fragments at the start.) We are on to battle, Cossacks versus Poles. Strings *col legno* (playing with the wood side of the bow) imitate a horse ride, and the opening fragments return. Nervous anticipation. Distracted by sorrow for his dead brother, Ostapof is captured and executed, and as the fragments fly about they suddenly turn into a festive mazurka (a Polish dance) as the Poles celebrate their victory, apparently unaware of the menacing Taras, whose approach is covered by the snarling brass.

The third movement, "The Prophecy and Death of Taras Bulba," tends to the capture and execution of Taras by the Poles, ending in an inspirational promise of future liberty for the Ukraine in a *maestoso* (majestic) passage for brass and strings. As it happened, Janáček composed *Taras Bulba* when the Ukraine was fighting the Soviets for its independence. It lost. Hear this exciting hymn to liberty with ears tuned to the savage ironies of history.

Lachian Dances 1889

Folk dances of Lachia, a region of Janáček's native Moravia, using authentic folk tunes. This was Janáček's first major orchestral work. Those familiar with the complexities of his mature style—the repetition of thematic fragments, the offbeat polyphony (two or more lines of melody at once), the cranky, even outraged folk tune—should grin with delight at the innocence of these six dances, which sound not too unlike the *Slavonic Dances* of Dvořák. That is, they are both suites of dances, simple in structure and harmony, and aiming at a folk-cultural representation in music—Janáček through the use of real folk melodies, Dvořák through very amusing synthetics.

Some of these dances are adaptations of dancelike folk songs, but some are adapted from dances associated with specific rituals of country life. Thus, the first of the six, Starodávný I, relates to courting customs, which is possibly why it both blusters and blushes. The second dance, Požehnaný, is a real charmer, very Slavic in its passing fondness for minor-key tonalities. The roiling Dymák is meant to suggest the blacksmith at his forge. Starodávný II is the first gentle item in the set, the tune given to horns and woodwind, while strings suggest the cutting, angular Janáček of his later years. Then we come to a Čeladenský, lively and, though at times comical, beautifully lyrical when the strings deign to try a moment or two of real song. To close the exhibition, Janáček presents a Pilky, connected with the laying in of firewood for the winter. This pilky is careful at first, but soon tears loose in festive middle section. Then the main tune returns, winding up in a dashing coda.

ERNEST CHAUSSON 1855–1899

Like Vincent d'Indy a disciple of César Franck, Chausson shares with them a dreamy, even idle poetry, sumptuous but precise orchestration, and an energy that is intimate rather than powerful, ascetic rather than importunate. The Franck circle were thought radical in their day and even now not everyone can take them. Franck is "too spiritual," D'Indy "too sluggish." And Chausson? He's the least well known but perhaps the most accessible of the trio. His style is less ostentatiously Franckian than that of D'Indy and Franck himself, especially in the Symphony, cited below. (The Franckians inspired a certain awe in people for their apparent policy of each writing one—which would thenceforth be "the"—symphony. Actually, there was no such policy. D'Indy wrote several symphonies, and Chausson probably would have if he had lived longer. People were misled because the Franckians didn't number their symphonies. In fact, Chausson in particular might have gone on to a great prime if he hadn't died, in a bicycle accident, just when his muse was getting into fettle.)

Symphony in B Flat Major, op. 20 1890

This delightful work lifts the spirituality of the Franckians with Chausson's personal vitality. It is a striking example of how the pupil (Chausson) bends the form of the teacher (Franck) to his own ends; those who admire Franck's well-known Symphony in d minor without loving it may enjoy this same-only-different example of the Franckian symphony.

The format is three movements (slow introduction and strong first movement, slow movement, lively finale), with a motto theme that opens and closes the work and a use of certain themes in more than one movement. The motto theme is stated in the sorrowful introduction. Once the first movement gets going in a faster tempo with a clear-cut first theme (bassoon and horn duet), the work turns agile, even joyful. A neat-sonata-allegro procedure finds the development carefully fragmenting the main themes and the recapitulation remaking them, with the coda piling on a last alteration of the first theme with the fluffy enthusiasm of the harps. The slow [second] movement is intense, rockily forceful, with a middle section defined in the poignant coloration of the English horn. For a finale [third mvt], Chausson leaps into a whirlwind of roiling strings and wind fanfares—but actually this is almost a friendly finale. Sharp ears may detect a subtle transformation of the first movement's main theme into a dancing melody for strings at one point (thematic transformation was an obsession of the Franckians) but no one will miss the triumphant restatement of the motto theme from the symphony's introduction, blared as a brass chorale near the end.

Poème for Violin and Orchestra, op. 25 1896

A sad slow introduction in the orchestra leads into a solo for the violinist, unaccompanied. Here the tone of the whole is established: nostalgic, poetic, pained. The orchestra replies; so far, all is dignified. The soloist is heard again alone, this time in a cadenza showing some spark of technique, and we glide into the *poème* proper, fleeter now, a dream of quasi-ecstatic beauty. As the sole movement continues, the balance of pain and poetry is maintained, with a few climaxes; the structural foundation for the whole is the theme first heard in the solo violin during the introduction.

Much of the music of this era has vanished, especially one-movement concertos on pain and poetry. But this piece has survived, mainly through violinists' admiration of the solo line. Written for a noted virtuoso, Eugène Ysaÿe, the violin part sets off a star nicely—if you don't care for Chausson's poetry, concentrate on the violinist's.

EDWARD ELGAR 1857–1934

Nobilmente (nobly) is a term that one cannot avoid using when discussing Elgar's work. He himself used it often, for his eloquence was gallantry; where other composers might depend on *vivace* (lively) or *maestoso* (grandly), Elgar called for nobility. The question has been raised, though, as to whether his music deserves such treatment. Is it distinguished or merely pompous? The musicologist Edward J. Dent assailed "the chevaleresque rhetoric which badly covers up his essential vulgarity"—and, after all, it was Elgar who wrote the *Pomp and Circumstance* marches.

But it isn't Elgar's fault that his most famous melody is the haughty trio tune (that is, the middle section) of the First *Pomp and Circumstance* march, a memory engraved upon the hearts of high-school graduates and their parents. He left us far more than music to attend commencement ceremonies by. His major orchestral and choral works exhibit qualities that leave all thoughts of marching Pomp behind—rhythmic vitality, exuberance, whimsey, dramatic tension, a real gift for orchestration, and of course the famous *nobilmente,* sometimes forced but more often quite naturally inspired by a penetrating introspection.

Elgar is unshakably English. Photographs of the man show what must appear to American eyes as a tintype of kind: with his rich moustache, his military bearing, his handsome, open features. His oratorios: now, there's England for you, Church of England and cautiously devout. Said one of Elgar's colleagues at the premiere of Elgar's *The Dream of Gerontius* (set to the verses of Cardinal Newman), "It stinks of incense." Perhaps so. Certainly, it is in his non-vocal work that Elgar made his mark.

His fame began with the "Enigma" Variations, a turning point for English music, for Elgar grew up in a country that had lost touch with a venerable musical tradition. Before the Enigma Variations arrived, the national sound consisted of gentlemen amateurs imitating Mendelssohn; it is amazing that Elgar matured in so unstimulating an environment. Where did he get it? There was always the vital British choral tradition, but Elgar had found it within himself. And he stayed himself till the end of his days, the embodiment of the Edwardian style in art, in his confidence and expansiveness. He lived to see the Romantic era that he helped cap turn into a complex of modern eras, but he held true to his type, summing up rather than revising what had preceded him in Western music. He is, at his best, genuinely *nobilmente.*

Symphony no. 1 in A Flat Major, op. 55 1908

The expansive introductory theme in the lower strings supplies a motto for the work; marked *nobilmente e semplice* (noble and simple), it is quintessential Elgar, proud and conservative. One is eager to know what a composer will do with his first symphony—will he stun with experimentation, or with his command of tradition? Will he stun at all? Elgar does stun, traditionally, with a four-movement plan: slow introduction and sonata-allegro first movement, fraught with urgency; scherzo and slow movement, connected by a note held in the strings;

sonata-allegro finale, closing at last with a splended apotheosis of the motto theme played by the full orchestra.

The third [slow] movement is the glory of the piece, its main theme the main theme of the second [scherzo] movement but played much more slowly, and one of its great moments quotes the motto theme, slightly altered, adding to the overall unity of the whole. The slow movement is a touchstone among experts and laymen alike; the conductor Hans Richter likened it to the redemptive beauty of Beethoven's slow movements, and the audience at the world premiere in Manchester brought the concert to a halt after it, *contro bonos mores,* to express their gratitude.

Elgar provides us with a mild program for the work: "a wide experience of human life with a great charity (love) and a *massive* hope in the future." On New Year's Day, 1909, Elgar himself led a performance of the piece in London, inspiring his wife to make a connection between art and the artist's persona: "E. conducted splendidly," she wrote, "& looked *nobilmente* as if he were his music."

Symphony no. 2 in E Flat Major, op. 63 1911

Elgar regarded his second and last symphony as a personal statement—"I have *shewn* myself," he said—though one critic proposed the work as "an epic of the Edwardian age," and detected in its final movement "the motif" of a brilliant sunset. Elgar's own, perhaps? A not entirely apposite epigraph from Shelley was appended to the score:

Rarely, rarely comest thou,
Spirit of Delight!

This is not enough; it provides little hint of the odd conflict of serene and sinister that gives the music its character. In fact, the Spirit of Delight, in the form of a short motto theme (an uprising and backfalling figure heard at the very start in the strings in joyous, almost Richard Straussian, cry) is challenged at the thematic heart of the first movement by a 'cello line uttered over the loathsome pulsing and plucking of the lower strings, a Spirit of Despair.

"I have written the *most extraordinary* passage," wrote Elgar of this moment, "a sort of malign influence wandering thro' the summer night in the garden." Indeed, he had made something of a personal stylistic breakthrough, shattering his (self?-) image as the composer of pomp and circumstance, musician "royal." This repulsive 'cello theme so thrilled Elgar that he reprises it to interfere with the otherwise ingratiating third [scherzo] movement, first in its original scoring and then blared by the full company, assisted by a cheeky tambourine. Light and darkness is the sense of the Second Symphony, though light predominates, particularly in the elegiacal second [slow] movement and the finale [fourth mvt], wherein much *nobilmente* (nobly, Elgar's characteristic marking) disperses the malign influence of the macabre 'cellos.

Violin Concerto in b minor,
op. 61 1910

Outwardly, this work respects the tenets of the classical concerto, but everything in it is just a little different, and one thing is very different. It's a highly personal document; it is wise, amidst all the babbling from critics about Elgar's alleged impersonal emptiness, to consider the piece is the light of the composer's dedication, "Here is enshrined the soul of ______." (A close friend later revealed ______ to be an American woman, Julia H. Worthington.)

One novelty here is the themes themselves: they're all short—stingy, even—as if made for transformation. We hear not first and second themes but first and second theme *groups:* a lot of melody. Another novelty is the last [third] movement. Where one might expect the light rondo finale of the standard concerto, instead we get the longest of the three movements, an almost symphonic conception in sonata-allegro (i.e., first movement) plan, including a quotation from the second [slow] movement. This quotation cues in the work's most famous novelty, a reinvented cadenza. No mere solo spot for the star's virtuoso display, this cadenza is accompanied (the orchestral strings are divided down the line into two groups, and group II plays Elgar's own concoction, the *pizzicato tremolando*—literally "trembling pinch"—by "thrumming" rather than plucking the strings). No confection of thematic fragments either, this cadenza gently reviews all that has preceded, by evocation if not direct quotation—thus satisfying an ideal of overall unity in the concerto that had not been posed before. It is a thrillingly ethereal moment, an unusual and very "right" climax for the voyage from rich first movement through sweet slow movement to richer yet finale.

'Cello Concerto in e minor,
op. 85 1919

Here is a surprise from Elgar the formal conservative of the John Bull marches: a concerto worked out in the symphony's four movements (as opposed to the concerto's three) and, furthermore, a work of remarkable personableness. But then Elgar was never as stodgy as his critics like to say he is. Stodgy? Donald Francis Tovey, a philosopher-king of commentators, called the piece "a fairy-tale." This is an inward-looking entry, lighter than a "big work" yet more spiritual than a "light work." Elgar buffs cherish it; others neglect it. It deserves a chance, however. Hear it as a Briton's manly despair, shy of display yet very personal in expression—especially given the naturally plangent tone of the solo instrument. First movement, scherzo, slow movement, finale: the shape of a symphony, the intimacy of the solo 'cello.

Variations on an Original Theme
(The Enigma Variations), op. 36 1899

What a rousing idea for a theme and variations: Elgar's wife, twelve friends, and the composer himself are depicted in fourteen character sketches—the fourteen variations—derived from a gentle, hesitant theme in g minor! The human subject of each variation is betokened by initials or rubrics (Variation I, for example, is "C.A.E."; Variation X is "Dorabella"),* all identified long ago. But wait—the "enigma" of the title has *not* been identified. This enigma is a secret, alternate theme somewhow connected to the work. "Through and over the whole set," Elgar announced, "another and larger theme 'goes' but is not played." The guesses have been coming ever since. Is it the "pure fool" motive from Wagner's *Parsifal?* "Auld Lang Syne"? "Ta-ra-ra-boom-de-ay"? All have been proposed, but the mystery remains unsolved.

*One of the two sisters in Mozart's opera, *Così Fan Tutte.*

Though these variations are seriously meant as profiles in music, they work as music primarily, as variations on the plaintive violin theme that opens the work. There are almost no programmmatic touches, though Variation VII ("Troyte"—Arthur Troyte Griffith) has been taken as description either of Griffith's reckless disasters as amateur pianist or his friendly but vivid political arguments with Elgar, Griffith being very much the liberal and Elgar being very much not. The composer occupies the fourteenth and final variation ("E.D.U."—Edoo, Alice Elgar's nickname for her husband) with a nice tension, but the prize of the collection is Variation IX ("Nimrod"—August Jaeger, Jaeger meaning "hunter," which Nimrod was, in German), capturing Elgar's best friend in terms of great warmth.

Since we cannot relate to these variations as character portraits—not knowing the characters—it might be best to consider the work as absolute music and simply follow the progress of the theme. As already stated, it opens the work, very minor-key, in the strings.

Var. I: the music sounds more hopeful here, lightened by the timbre of the flute and clarinet, then brought to a thrilling but brief triumphal climax.

Var. II: violins introduce a sinuous, running line.

Var. III: the oboe gives a jittery version of the theme, assisted by other woodwind.

Var. IV: a boisterous passage for full orchestra, then a calmer section.

Var. V: the bassoons recall the theme under a countermelody in the strings. This leads directly into

Var. VI: featuring the violas, giving one of them a solo spot.

Var. VII: a temperamental variation, furious in its downward-driving string runs and pounding timpani.

Var. VIII: a gracious variation, which fades into

Var. IX: a superb slow movement, ceremonial yet meltingly intimate, richly scored for singing strings.

Var. X: fidgety, all muted strings and woodwind.

Var. XI: The basses and bassoons heard between outbursts from the other instruments represent an organist's industrious pedaling.

Var. XII: mainly for 'cellos, and leading directly into

Var. XIII: suggestive of an ocean voyage. The strings billow wave-like, the clarinet whistles salt spray, the timpani tremble hugely.

Var. XIV: a grand finale, with the full orchestra working a somewhat martial atmosphere to gather together the work's loose ends and tie the theme back together, this time in the major mode.

Falstaff, op. 68 1913

This tone poem is a long one (about thirty-five minutes), with full subtitle: "Symphonic study in c minor with two interludes in a minor." And long, in a tone poem, runs the danger of getting too excursive, too scattered and episodic. Elgar found a neat solution to the problem in this musical realization of Shakespeare's less than parfit knight of bawds, beer, and bad companionship to the future King Henry V. Rather than attempt one continuous "symphonic study," Elgar breaks up his narration at two points with his reverielike "interludes." Besides relieving pressure on the forward motion of the music-as-story, the interludes help create the unique savor of the piece.

Unique it certainly is. For Elgar's Falstaff is not precisely the dumpy oaf we tend to think of—this hero claims some romance. He is fat, foolish, and unsatiably appetitive, as before, and we hear him in this form right at the start of the work. But he is capable, in Elgar's hands, of surprising sensitivity; this other Falstaff we hear particularly in the two interludes, dreamy in the solo violin of the first and almost visionary in the second, when a pipes-and-tabor measure precedes a deeply felt theme in the lower strings, used again at the end of the score for Falstaff's death.

Elgar allows four principal divisions for a loose plotline: 1. Falstaff and the Prince, 2. The Boar's Head Inn and the "Gadshill Robbery" (then comes the first interlude, Falstaff's drunken recollection of his youth), 3. a march, battle (and second interlude, queerly nostalgic yet ominously shadowed by coming tragedy), and headlong ride to London for the new King's coronation, and 4. Falstaff's repudiation by King Henry V and death. One clearly hears the King's cool dismissal of his former comrade in orchestral recitative (that is, the instruments seeming to "talk" in solos, with no rhythmic accompaniment), and a fanfare and rude resumption of the coronation march is the final blow. Listen then to the decay of Falstaff in broken phrases. All the significant themes previously heard thrust themselves upon us as if the hero were glimpsing bits of his vainglorious, strangely touching life.

Incidentally, despite the four-part scheme, *Falstaff* is nothing like a symphony. It is a tone poem arranged in a kind of rondoish variation form, for all action proceeds by variation on the central theme, the refrain (as in a rondo) that opens the piece and periodically returns, Falstaff himself "in a green old age."

Serenade for Strings in e minor, op. 20 1892

Not our heroic, prudently experimental Elgar of the later works here but a youthful genteel minstrel of the salons. (Anyway, the serenade is, as a form, technically a forerunner of "salon music" in the first place.) One point of interest is that the third of the three movements quotes material from the first, thus rounding out the piece with typically Elgaresque gesture to Romantic unity.

In the South (Alassio), op. 50 1904

A Virgilian Baedeker, "the thoughts and sensations of one beautiful afternoon" spent ingesting the grandeur of Roman Italy. The pastoral shares with the glorious in this overture, a *canto popolare* (folk song) on the viola following a vigorous ode to the flux of history, as if the picture of marching armies were ceding to the picture of the ruins they leave behind.

Cockaigne (In London Town), op. 40 1901

The weird title denotes London's East End: "Cockneyland." The composer thought this overture proper Cockney—"stout and steaky." But it has the grace of greater London, the expanse from Hampstead Heath to Westminster to Knightsbridge, as well as the energy of the City, the ancient square mile of old Londinium where the Cockneys carry on. A big overture, with first and second subjects, development, and recapitulation, *Cockaigne* is one of Elgar's happiest works. He especially wanted this one to be *popular,* not only fulfilled as art. There is no resisting the jaunty first theme (heard right at the top, quietly, but soon as loud as a pub at lunchbreak)—but notice how well it is brought through from section to section, a very study—if such a thing were possible—in spontaneity.

GUSTAV MAHLER 1860–1911

Depending on one's view, Mahler either expanded the symphony to a brilliantly innovative eloquence of musico-dramatic metaphysics, or inflated the vehicle of Haydn, Mozart, and Beethoven into turgid self-dramatization. Since the Mahler revival of the 1960s, when multiple recordings and performances of his work familiarized the public with the oeuvre as totality, few now hold the latter view. In fact, once one has gone through the nine symphonies, the orchestral song cycle *Das Lied von der Erde* (The Song of the Earth), and the quasi-unfinished Tenth Symphony, one understands why Mahler's conception of symphonic form required the use of huge movements and—sometimes—vocal projection of a poetic text. For this is not just a succession of numbered works, but a series which, in its totality, amounts to an abstraction of the human life cycle—birth, life of innocence, challenge, triumph, and resignation, then death and spiritual transcendance.

"The symphony must be a whole world," Mahler said; anyway, symphonies had been getting bigger through the century that separates Haydn from Mahler. Between them lay the entire Romantic period, a revolutionary era of reorganization, dramatic urgency, and textual or programmatic manipulation. As Mahler started composing, it seemed to be showing those symptoms of decline—decadence and overstatement and distension—that signal a change in epoch. As it happened, the Romantic period never did actually end. Rather, a few years after Mahler died, it went underground for a while, ceding the Western art platform to neo-Classicism, a back-to-Bach-and-Haydn movement sparked as well by satire, jazz, and an overall interest in simple, clear-cut structures, smallness of size, and rejection of Romantic program.

All of this, of course, runs contrary to Mahler. But something went wrong with neo-Classicism. Because after only a few decades, by the mid-1930s, Romanticism was asserting itself again, and since then the aesthetic grid has been ambiguous, episodic, and unmappable. Are we Romantics or Classicists? We seem to be some combination of the two. Mahler's ghost stood by, waiting. And lo, after the Second World War (which may be one of the reasons for the reemergence of Romance, by way of that need for belief in a moral mythology that we call escapism), Mahler underwent a gradual revival.

He had never been forgotten or unheard, of course, but only now was he becoming a vogue. In 1958, after the stereo era had begun, (and stereo is a minimum requirement for Mahler's complex music on records), American record buyers had a choice of two recordings of the Second Symphony, one of the Third, two of the Ninth. As of this writing, there are twelve recordings of the Second in print, seven of the Third, ten of the Ninth. In the 1950s, Mahler had a few champions among conductors—Bruno Walter and Leonard Bernstein, most notably. Now, no conductor's dossier is considered complete without a "Mahler cycle" (*all* of the symphonies docketed on records in personal Interpretations To Be Discussed and Compared).

Mahler had said, "My time will yet come." Now it has; now we can appreciate the visionary, the poet of ferocious and sentimental imagery, the autobiographical symphonist. These were heady qualities even for a Romantic era to take in stride. In his day, Mahler was much more successful as a conductor and administrator (he ran the Vienna State Opera into a golden age). His symphonies were thought . . . well, neurotic. In an article entitled "His Time Has Come" written in 1967, Leonard Bernstein noted Mahler's compulsion to go off the deep end at opposite poles at once: "Can we think of Beethoven as both roughhewn and epicene?" Bernstein asks. "Is Debussy both subtle and blatant? Mozart both refined and raw? Stravinsky both objective and maudlin? Unthinkable. But Mahler, uniquely, is all of these—roughhewn *and* epicene, subtle *and* blatant, refined, raw, objective, maudlin, brash, shy, grandiose, self-annihilating, confident, insecure, adjective, opposite, adjective, opposite." The symphony must be a whole world.

Mahler's symphonies offer a world of mystical speculation on the human condition. Though not all of them are program symphonies, a sense of epic purpose is conveyed all the same through musico-dramatic means. Anyway, half of them make their meaning clear through the use of textual material, sometimes in a small movement and sometimes, as in the Eighth Symphony and *Das Lied von der Erde,* throughout. One can see this enormous symphonic output spanning a three-part arch: symphonies 1 through 4 are the innocent symphonies, longing for simple universals of free-willing life and religious transcendence of death; symphonies 5 through 8 are more personal in scope, the first two on the tragic side, the second two coming out of tragedy towards reaffirmation of the timeless universals; and *Das Lied von der Erde* and the Ninth and (unfinished) Tenth Symphonies conclude the passage with farewells to life and art. Blended in with all this is a kind of textual gloss, an orchestral song cycle of folk lyrics comic and tragic from a collection called *Des Knaben Wunderhorn* (The Boy's Magic Horn). Mahler's settings of these lyrics struck such—for him—archetypal moods that he drew on them in his symphonies, sometimes quoting a line or two but sometimes building whole movements out of them.

With his grotesque marches, his sudden lightning-struck pauses, his constant parodistic references to folk song, Viennese ballroom music, and churchly chorales, his singing soloists and choruses, his apocalyptic climaxes, Mahler gave the nineteenth century what it had been working up to since Beethoven—huge, individualized, conceptual symphonies. His coevals found it all too extreme, but we can deal with it. We may even find that only those with the heightened perspective provided by two world wars and the threat of pushbutton holocaust can appreciate Mahler's musical allegories of belief and dissolution. Who knows? He feels very, very current.

Symphony no. 1 in D Major, "Titan" 1888

Few first symphonies display such exhilarating mastery of form as this one. Fully deserving its nickname (which Mahler borrowed from Jean Paul's novel, *The Titan*), it travels from innocence to heroism in its four movements, broken into two parts, "From the Days of Youth" and "The Human Comedy." This is one of Mahler's shorter symphonies, easy for the neophyte to follow: sonata-allegro first movement, scherzo, slow movement, sonata-allegro finale. (There is also another movement, a charming, simple slow movement between the present first and second movements, but Mahler pulled it out after an early performance. Called the "Bluminé" [Bouquet] movement, it was only recently rediscovered and is seldom performed.)

Originally, Mahler drew up a complex program of explanation. But it is easier to understand the work through the music itself, which tells clearly of youthful pastoral pleasure in the first half, and of defeat and recovery in the second. It is hard to credit the bewilderment and disdain of the symphony's first audiences; what could be easier to comprehend? A dark introduction marked by military fanfares yields to an expressively, *seriously* joyful first movement (note the bird and cuckoo calls), and this is delightfully seconded by the bumptious scherzo [second mvt], a rustic waltz with an odd edge of defiance.

Now comes Part Two. The slow [third] movement is grotesque and bitter; this is the movement that caused the work's first audiences the most trouble, with its macabre first theme—the nursery song "Frère Jacques" in the minor-key—and its parodistic street band plopped in out of nowhere. Not till the finale [fourth mvt] leaps in with its opening thunderclap does one understand the ghoulish, funereal feel of the third movement—that was death, or tragedy; this is the return to life, the victory. As big itself as the first three movements combined, this finale may be considered, along with Bruckner's fourth movements, as the culmination of the development of the dramatic symphony, arching in a great line towards a powerful conclusion to match a powerful first movement.

Symphony no. 2 in c minor, "Resurrection" 1894

An apocalyptic work, as the title suggests. Its great size, number of movements (five), and its use of chorus and soprano and mezzo-soprano soloists may suggest a wildly innovative symphony. But the work is structured along traditional lines. Here is its layout in shorthand:

opening	slow mvt	scherzo	intro	and	finale
1st mvt	2nd mvt	3rd mvt	4th mvt		5th mvt

Taking the short fourth movement as an introduction to the finale, we find the symphony not unlike the regular four-movement symphonies. *Except* it is much longer, it does have voices, and is about something—namely, the rebirth of the spirit, after death, on Judgment Day. This Resurrection is not that of Christ, but the more collective Resurrection that awaits us all.

In order to bring his "picture" home, Mahler uses each of the movements depictively. The long first movement, with its brutal, sudden, tragic opening of trembling violins and violas and bitter 'cello and bass patterns may be heard as if one were contemplating the grave of a dead hero. The music reviews his life and asks (in Mahler's own words) "Why have you lived? Why have you suffered? Is it all some huge, awful joke?" Already, we know, Mahler feels it is not a joke, for an aura of hope and redemption is sensed in one of the movement's principal themes, a major-key motive briefly sounded in the strings.

The second and third movements may be regarded as intermezzos, corollaries to the central scheme launched in the opening and concuded in the finale. The second [slow] movement, in A Flat Major, is positive, pastoral, almost Schubertian in its flowing strings; the third [scherzo] movement is negative, grotesque. Here, too, the strings flow—in dark c minor, while woodwinds squeal and brasses pound. But now we learn why we have lived and suffered. The fourth movement introduces the vocal sections of the work, in a mezzo-soprano solo in D Flat Major, "Urlicht" (Primal Light), words taken from Mahler's favorite folk-song collection, *Des Knaben Wunderhorn* (The Boy's Magic Horn). Ending with, "Dear God will give me a light, will light me to eternal, blessed life!," the song immediately gives way to the fifth movement. Like the first, it opens with a brutal uproar in c minor, this one even more cacaphonous, as if the music of the very spheres themselves were unraveling its line. The last trumpet sounds, inspiring terror and relief. And the dead awaken, marching forth to judgment. The chorus and two women soloists promise release in words partly by Klopstock and partly by Mahler. One cannot miss the sense of release and overturn of former tragedy, especially since Mahler refers back to themes heard in the funereal first movement. But all now is light in E Flat Major. With stupendous festivity, the chorus heralds the Resurrection of mankind: "You will rise again, my heart, in an instant! Your struggle will carry you to God!"

Symphony no. 3 in d minor 1896

This is the longest symphony in the repertory. (There are longer symphonies, but none "in the repertory"—i.e., played with any frequency.) Given Mahler's obsession with themes of life and death, one might expect some apocalyptic behemoth of a work, a kraken waking. Oddly, the symphony is an innocent, friendly, and not very cosmic work. Its essential character was neatly captured by the artist Maurice Sendak—known for his work in whimsically fantastic children's lit—on the cover of the RCA Victor recording of the piece conducted by James Levine. With a child's eye for primary colors, virtues, and trinkets, Sendak presents a moonlit forest filled with costumed animals; in the center, an adolescent angel on a cloud offers a rosy twig to the greyish silhouette of Gustav Mahler, sitting over his score. That, really, is Mahler's Third in essence.

In greater detail, the work is a catalog of simple gifts—to be free, to enjoy the natural outer world and our own inner world of the spirit. Though he eventually published the work without a stated program, the fourth and fifth movements feature a mezzo-soprano soloist and womens' and boys' choirs singing texts from Nietzsche and folk poetry. So there is an overall purpose, a meaning. Choosing from the various movement subtitles that Mahler toyed with, we can erect a kind of trot for the work:

first mvt: "Pan Awakens" and "What the Forest Tells Me"
second mvt: "What the Flowers in the Meadow Tell Me"

third mvt: "What the Animals in the Forest Tell Me"
fourth mvt: "What Man Tells Me"
fifth mvt: "What the Angels Tell Me"
sixth mvt: "What Love Tells Me"

Thus, there is an implied progression, from the larger canvas of the magical green world through communion with its inhabitants into the privacy of the mystical mellow.

The huge first movement is essentially a contest between two "ideas": a dirgelike procession in the minor key and a livelier march in the major; the latter prevails, setting the tone for this work of rapturous self-discovery. The second movement, marked as a minuet, delicately offers the contribution of the flowers; the third, speaking for the animals in the forest, is a folksy scherzo, emphasizing—as Mahler so often did—the natural world as a psychological conception. Toward the end of the movement, Mahler brings in an odd instrument, a valved posthorn (unlike the "natural" posthorn made famous in Mozart's "Posthorn" Serenade, no. 9). This item is so odd that most orchestras have to improvise a substitute for it, such as playing a muted trumpet from an unusual corner of the concert hall. The fourth movement draws us more deeply inside ourselves with a sombre mezzo-soprano solo, the words taken from "The Second Dance-Song" in Nietzsche's *Also Sprach Zarathustra* (Thus Spake Zoroaster): "O humankind! . . . Joy [is] deeper than sorrow!" And, without a break, the joyful fifth movement parades in with its ding-dongs and delights, its mezzo and chorus telling what angels tell, of salvation for all. Again, no break precedes the finale [sixth mvt], an inspired slow movement moving from intimate string song into a glorious *tutti* of major key affirmation. Very few symphonies close with slow movements, and Mahler explains this novelty: "In fast movements . . . everything is motion, change, flow." But a slow movement is the "higher" form of 'quiet being.' "

Symphony no. 4 in G Major 1900

This is generally thought to be the most accessible of Mahler's symphonies, the shortest, the lightest, the most conservative in terms of traditional structuring, the least extreme in dramatic-psychological thrust. Like virtually every Mahler symphony, the Fourth explores the relationship of life and death. But even though the last movement takes the form of a song about the innocent bliss of heaven, one could hear this work without thinking it to be about anything at all.

The first movement (more of a rondo than a true sonata-allegro) opens with sleighbells and odd calls on the flute and clarinet. But the violins quickly step in with a graceful first subject, and the movement soars off into imaginative flights. It is a forthright movement, not in the least tragic—but a touch of the macabre creeps in with the scherzo [second mvt]. Here, a solo violin, deliberately tuned to sound like a cheesy fiddle, suggests the dance of death. An overall pastoral calm informs the music, but that crazed fiddle continually shatters one's piece of mind with its cheerless agility.

The third [slow] movement, however, offers consolation in beautifully long-lined phrases. It is the longest movement, yet it sustains its static transcendance effortlessly. Toward the end, a huge explosion of sound disperses the immobile musical image as wind scatters clouds: the calls of the horn and trumpet sound as if from on high to the faithful. This prepares for the intimate, highly unfinalelike finale, a short, simple song (for soprano soloist) about life in heaven. The words are drawn from *Des Knaben Wunderhorn* (The Boy's Magic Horn), a folk collection, and offer a child's view of the celestial existence, with the emphasis on food and drink, singing and dancing.

Symphony no. 5 in c sharp minor 1902

In three "parts" (five movements, two in the first part and two in the third), the Fifth evolves out of the most dismal horror into a sunny, folksy athleticism. Its first movement is a funeral march, an at times vicious one of shrieking brass and unhinged violins. It opens with a trumpet call, which is developed and then allowed to subside into the first movement's main theme, a moving elegy led by the first violins and 'cellos. The rhythm of the trumpet call harries the elegy, which at last gives way to a strange episode of wildly keening violins fighting a trumpet tune. This section builds to a climax and fades into the rhythm of the trumpet call; the elegy returns in the woodwinds. There follows another episode, launched by muted strings with the melody in the first violins. The trumpet call returns at last as if from a distance, echoed by a lone flute.

The second movement, concluding Part I, is likewise an anguished and stormy business, echoing not only the mood but some of the themes of the first movement as well. A sense of attempted catharsis is felt at times. At one point, 'cellos come forward with a lamentation played against a hushed timpani roll—the 'cellos alone, as if they might change the course of the symphony. But it is too soon yet. The movement picks up energy again, closing at length in a ghostly passage highlighted by unusual string effects. The cellos and basses appear to be ending the movement, but the final note is snatched from them by the timpani.

Part II, a scherzo movement, alters the mood with a series of rustic waltzes with a *concertante* (solo) part for the first horn. This is rich material, for while by itself this waltz-scherzo is ingratiating, within the context of the symphony it becomes an anodyne meant to isolate the emotional fevers of Part I from the relaxation of Part III.

This last part, then, brings us home from tragedy to tranquility. The short but endlessly impressive fourth [slow] movement, *Adagietto* (quite slow), famous for its use in Visconti's film *Death in Venice,* provides a moment of astonishing stationary beauty amidst the ferment of the four other movements, scored as it is entirely for strings with harp accompaniment. With virtually no break, a horn call brings in the big rondo finale [fifth mvt] which caps the proceedings with great good humor. Not just the horn, but a bassoon, an oboe, and a clarinet all suggest possible first subjects. The oboe's second idea sounds right, so the horns lead off with it (actually, all these would-be themes will turn up in the movement). Immediately, the change in the air is patent. For the fun of it, Mahler organizes a fugue, stating the fugue subject in the 'cellos, bringing in the second violins and basses, then the first violins and violas, then expanding outward to the winds and brasses. Themes flutter in and out, including some fragments of the *Adagietto.* At the end, Mahler plays hymnlike brasses against the fugue subject in the woodwinds and strings, which builds to an exhilarating finish.

Symphony no. 6 in a minor 1904

The most out-and-out tragic item of all Mahler's symphonies, no. 6 opens with a forbidding march rhythm that will recur repeatedly throughout the work. Later, a passionate lyrical theme opposes it. These are the two major elements that composers since Beethoven have adopted as the basic dualism of the dramatic symphony—oppression and resistance. Oppression is most fervently expressed in an odd melding of A Major and a minor chords in oboe and trumpet over a nasty tattoo on the timpani; the resistance is sounded by flutes and first violins over gushing violas in F Major—a theme that Mahler reportedly meant as a character portrait of his celebrated wife Alma. It is Mahler's special gift to heighten the tension between the brutal and the ideal with macabre comedy. His sense of irony leads him to end the first movement—after an impressionistically pastoral interlude (pointed by carefully distinguished sets of cowbells) in the development section—on a jubilant note, as if suggesting a triumph to come. Just wait.

The second [scherzo] movement retrieves the tension in a grotesque march like and yet not like that of the first movement. This one glitters shrilly, and its trio (middle section), launched by the oboe, only emphasizes the unsettling, Bosch-like horror of the piece with a disarming imitation of an old-fashioned minuet.

Now it is up to the slow [third] movement to leaven the drama with a more graceful reading of Mahler's mood. We are referred back to the pastoral interlude of the first movement by the use of the cowbells. All action has stopped, and the grotesque seems far more than a movement away. Mahler's profound nostalgia for an ideal rural simplicity inspired several brilliant slow movements; this one is perhaps the best of the lot, unerringly artistic in its abstraction of the national world, the shelter hidden from terror.

But the idyll cannot last, and the ugly march rhythm already established in the first two movemetns as the "motto" of tragedy returns in the finale [fourth mvt]. Too, there are the two famous "hammer-blows" symbolizing strokes of destiny (a third was omitted in revision). Here oppression and resistance fight their last battle. For much of the movement, it appears that resistance will win, and Mahler supplies music of typically mystical transcendence. But oppression wins out at last, and the work ends with that ambiguous but ultimately minor-key blend of A Major and a minor chords over the beating drum. This is fate in its essence, and in this tragic symphony, fate closes the books. An immensely moving work, it has become the most admired of Mahler's symphonies among the inner circle of Mahler buffs, as it was for Viennese composers of the next generation, like Schönberg and Webern.

Symphony no. 7 in e minor,
"The Song of the Night" 1905

Mahler wrote both (relatively) conservative four-movement symphonies for orchestra only and innovative five- and six-movement symphonies calling for vocal soloists and chorus. The Seventh is one of the innovative kind. Though it has no voice parts, its structure is unusual:

1st mvt	"Nightmusic I"	scherzo	"Nightmusic II"	finale
1st mvt	2nd mvt	3rd mvt	4th mvt	5th mvt

The scherzo (Mahler didn't call it one himself, actually) is the shortest of the movements, but the crux of the work's dramatic development, and not only because of its central position. Marked "shadowy" by the composer, it is a ghoulish trip into the arch-Romantic German fantasy world of distortion and parody, perhaps the most effective of all Mahler's spooky scherzos. Balancing the scherzo are the two "nightmusic" movements (whence comes the work's subtitle), each painted in muted colors of the bizarre. And balancing the two Nightmusics are the first and final movements, each glowing with spiritual equanimity and, in the latter, great good humor. Thus, the symphony as a whole offers a progression into terror (through Nightmusic I into the scherzo) and then out of it (through Nightmusic II into the finale). "Nightmusic" by the way, is synonymous in German with "serenade" (as in Mozart's *Eine Kleine Nachtmusik:* A Little Serenade). The first movement, asserting the home key of e minor, is like other Mahler first movements—a broad march (first subject) and a forcefully lyrical violin melody (second subject) in contrast and development after a long, somber slow introduction. The second movement, in c minor, first of the two Mahlerian nocturnes, has a netherworldly, even storybookish quality, as if narrating a heroic romance. In form, it is a rondo, opening with one horn echoing another; this dialogue soon turns into the rondo's main theme:

Here is another march, this one dirgelike to counterstate the triumphal parade in the first movement.

This brings us to the shrill waltz of the d minor scherzo [third mvt], the emotional center of the symphony, containing elements of both the lyrical and the grotesque. The latter makes the bigger impression in Mahler's expressionistic use of bleating woodwind and slithery strings and in his brutal lampoons of the Viennese waltz and the rustic Ländler: the D Major trio (launched by solo oboe) provides a brief surcease. Having lured us into the giddy depths, so to speak, of nightmare, Mahler draws us out again with the mandolin and violin-dominated Nightmusic II [fourth mvt], a much sweeter serenade than Nightmusic I and an almost scientific exercise in nostalgia, as if Mahler's sensibilities are more concerned with self-definition than self-expression. To heighten the color of this *Andante amoroso* (slowly and lovingly), Mahler brings in a guitar and mandolin and amusingly writes a sequence for these two, harp, and strings suggestive of a little nick-of-time tuning up.

The fourth leads us to the fifth [finale] movement, where sentiment and sunniness are enjoyed, not discussed. Here is the completion of our spiritual passage, from an ambiguous opening through freakish trials to the stolid, ultra-Germanic affability known as *Gemütlichkeit.* (Listeners are reminded of both Richard Wagner and Franz Léhar.) A huge rondo, this finale connects back to the first movement at the very end by playing, several times over, its principal theme—a touch of structural cohesiveness also favored by Mahler's contemporary Anton Bruckner.

Symphony no. 8 in E Flat Major, "The Symphony of a Thousand" 1906

Given its subtitle because it calls for combined choruses (boys' choir as well as the usual adult ensemble) and eight vocal soloists as well as a huge orchestra, the Eighth is symphony in structure but a symphonic oratorio in its use of texts, the "Veni, Creator Spiritus" and the final scene of Goethe's huge verse play *Faust.* As much a choral work as a symphony, it doesn't belong in this volume at all but for Mahler's revisionist use of symphonic form as a vehicle for programmatic expression, sometimes vaguely and sometimes so specifically that he used words, as here. But earlier, where he used singers, he used them sparingly, in certain movements. Here is a work so collaborative in its orchestral-formal and vocal-dramatic elements that it is laid out in two "parts" rather than movements. Perhaps it's best not to parse the Eighth as a symphony at all, but simply to hear it with the Latin-German text and an English translation (as invariably supplied in record albums and concert program notes) in front of you.

Incidentally, despite the P. T. Barnumesque hype of the subtitle, the work does not require a thousand performers. But then, what charisma is there in a "Symphony of 200"?

Das Lied von der Erde
(The Song of the Earth) 1908

Though it is more a song-cycle than a symphony, this was to have been Mahler's Ninth Symphony—but superstition cautioned him. Beethoven and Schubert both died after completing their respective Ninths, and Bruckner died with his Ninth unfinished. True, other composers had successfully gone on to the Tenths and beyond—Haydn and Mozart, for instance. But Mahler identified more with Beethoven and Schubert, and theirs was the data that worried him. He thought he saw a way out: give his Ninth Symphony a name—no number—thus leaping the verge unscathed. He could then go on to a "Ninth" (really his Tenth). But fate laughed at Mahler, and he, like his predecessors, died before he could complete a Tenth Symphony.

The Song of the Earth suits this black-comic tale, for it offers a kind of retrospective of life's joy and sadness and ends with a last farewell of morbid beauty, dwindling away to nothing. It comprises six movements—songs, really—and calls for two vocal soloists, a mezzo-soprano and tenor (sometimes a baritone substitutes for the mezzo). The lyrics are translations (into German) from the Chinese, and the orchestra is huge, though only in the first of six songs does Mahler use it consistently full out for power. "The Drinking Song of Earth's Misery" (for the tenor) opens the cycle; like the last of the set it is an extended number, as outgoing in its splendid, beery sorrow—"Dark is life, is death!"—as the last is repressed in resignation. The second number, "Loneliness in Autumn" (mezzo), adds to the melancholy with a ponderous accompanimental line in the violins, but the next three songs lighten the orchestral texture as well as the emotional tone: "Of Youth" (tenor), "Of Beauty" (mezzo), and "The Drunkard in Springtime" (tenor). But then comes the finale, "Farewell" (mezzo), a wintry landscape in music, longingly remembering and slowly fading away. The whole work offers one of the most versatile and affecting sixty minutes in music, comprising the most vital humanity as well as an ascetic renunciation. And of course, it should go without saying that the listener must follow along with text and translation as he listens.

Symphony no. 9 in D Major 1909

Mahler's symphonies either dramatize or abstract his late-Romantic obsession with life, death, and transcendence. The Ninth is his last completed symphony; fittingly, it seems to dwell in death, leaving life and transcendence behind in the earlier work. Those who were close to him claim that he thought of this work as his farewell to art (not to mention life), and throughout the piece are quotations of and variations on a three-note theme known to musicians from Beethoven's use of it in his piano sonata known as "Les Adieux"—the Farewell. This is Mahler's epitaph.

After all his experimentation with the form of the symphony, one is perhaps surprised to find four movements and no voice parts. But these are four rather individualistic movements. In shape alone, the symphony already is unorthodox—two slow movements enclosing two fast ones (both scherzos). The first movement blends two of the composer's most potent sound styles, ecstatic lyricism and the macabre. The movement rises out of quiet fragments, lurches upward as if out of control into a jagged theme for trumpets, and dies away to the sigh of a solo violin. The macabre takes over in the scherzolike second and third movements, laughing mirthlessly at death, perhaps at life as well. The first of the pair resembles the Ländler, the rustic Austrian precursor of the waltz; the second is a rondo, subtitled "Burleske." The one is a dance, the other a storm of defiant cacaphony. Heavy-footed and wailing, the second movement destroys the very principle of the scherzo with its wimpy calamity, and the third movement goes to the other parodistic extreme, so overplaying its sentimentality and bluff energy as to wreck such attitudes in symphony for all who hear it. This is not an easy farewell, nor an easy work. It completely reverses the traditional structure for the dramatic symphony—yet if one were to play the four movements in reverse order, it would make no sense at all.

So far, it has been a spoof of a symphony. The key to its kinetics lies in the fourth movement, a very slow and, at last, resigned piece emphasizing the sweetness of the strings. Rather than pull the work together in conclusion, Mahler cuts the first three movements away—the bitterness, the cackling—and floats his finale statically, as if in tableau. The work is so personal in expression yet so formal that one can only come close to it after hearing the first eight symphonies, for they articulate the joy, the piety, and the tragedy of the life-death cycle in which this is only the closing statement.

Symphony no. 10 in F Sharp Major 1910

Mahler died before he could complete his symphony, leaving the entire five-movement work laid out in what is known as a "short score" (an abbreviated version of a complete manuscript) and the first two movements and a bit of the third in full score. Unlike such unfinished symphonies as Schubert's Eighth and Bruckner's Ninth, then, this is a quasi-finished piece, with all its sections either written or at least indicated. However, details of instrumentation, harmony, and subsidiary lines, and any possible revision that Mahler might have made, are lost to us forever. Since the essential material is there, several musicians have prepared editions of the work, most notably Deryck Cooke. Cooke's "performing version" (as opposed to "completion," which obviously wasn't necessary) is the one invariably heard today. (Cooke prepared two versions. His first, premiered in 1964, was replaced by second thoughts a decade later.)

The first movement, a slow one, is all Mahler's, very slghtly touched up by Cooke. (For years, this first movement was all anyone ever heard of the Tenth.) A symphony almost never opens with a slow movement, but Mahler had long since passed beyond the norm in his structures. The first of two scherzos follows [second mvt], in robust good humor with touches of the grotesque such as Mahler loved; his scherzos always sound as if they're waiting for Godot. This much is Part I.

Part II opens with the short "Purgatorio" [third mvt], a cross between desperation and sweetness, followed by a macabre waltz [fourth mvt], a second scherzo. "Farewell, my lyre," Mahler wrote in his manuscript at this point—but after so much of death and resignation in earlier symphonies, what more can one say on the subject?

The finale [fifth mvt] must redeem it all for us. It is a major movement, a dire ABA form of slow-fast-slow with quotations of themes from earlier movements and a thunderous climax.

This is the summit: his last symphony! We are eager to hear all we can of the composer, yet is this quite the work that "should" follow the ecumenical Eighth, the haunting *Song of the Earth,* the black, mysterious Ninth? Who knows what Mahler would have done with it himself, had he lived to prepare the only authentic performing version there could be?

CLAUDE DEBUSSY 1862–1918

One of the most important figures in the touchy transition from late Romantic (the nineteenth century) into Modern (the twentieth), Debussy more than any of his contemporaries marked the end of symphony as it had been known. Inheriting set forms of orchestral music from the Haydn-Mozart era of the late eighteenth century, the composers of the nineteenth century thought that they could go on endlessly re-evolving an aesthetic within the parameters of symphony, concerto, and the one-movement overture that they themselves turned into the tone poem. But this was not to be, and it was Debussy more than anyone who showed where the new way led.

Somewhat under the influence of the symbolists of avant-garde French literature and the impressionists of avant-garde French painting, Debussy threw music open to their practice—to ambiguity, shadow and color bleeding into each other; all borders, all formal divisions blurred. No more first theme, second theme, development, then orderly recapitulation; no scherzo, slow movement, important finale. The first theme, now, was all there was, endlessly shifting its contours; now all was development; now any movement was equal to any other.

Debussy dispensed with the particularities of the old forms as forms. He never wrote a symphony, a concerto, or an overture, and when he wrote his one completed opera, *Pelléas et Mélisande,* this too proved so unlike opera per se that Debussy's critics refused to call it by that term. With Debussy, orchestral music took its own form anew each time out—a "sketch," an "image," a "prelude." And as he made form ambiguous, so did he treat harmony. Gone, now, was the tonal center—the sense of starting in a particular key and therefore *needing* to end in that key, to assuage the ear—that had ruled music since long before Bach. Debussy's sense of tonality was so free-wheeling—so grey to start with and shifty to continue—that at moments he seemed to be in no key at all. This had never happened before. (It was to happen with great frequency thereafter, to conservatives' discomfort.) Debussy's use of melody, too, was protean, changing its shape and combining with other shapes in ceaseless flux.

Debussy was an innovator of phenomenal foresight, though much of what he accomplished might be seen as a culmination of, not a reaction to, Romanticism. In other words, music had been heading in this direction since Beethoven: for while seeking even greater varieties of unity in music, the Romantics of the 1800s had discovered that artistic revolutions have a habit of never ending, and the ambiguity of form, tonality, and melody was already under investigation by such men as Franz Liszt, César Franck, and Richard Wagner. Though the difference in *sound* is immense, the relationship that connects Liszt and Franck and Wagner to Debussy and all three to the really difficult modernists such as Arnold Schönberg and Alban Berg is not as distended as one might think. Each generation prepared for the next.

For example, Debussy was only following nineteenth-century usage in relating his music to revolutionary aesthetics in literature. Schubert and Schumann together virtually invented the *Lied* (song; used in the sense of art song) through their sensitivity to poetry, and Berlioz based a surprising amount of his output on his reading habits—Shakespeare, Virgil, Scott, Byron. Schubert, Schumann, and Berlioz helped get the Romantic era going; similarly, Debussy forced the issue of modernism in terms that the great symbolist poet Paul Verlaine layed down in his *L'Art Poétique*. "Music before everything else," wrote Verlaine, echoing Ronsard, "and to obtain the effect of music choose the asymmetrical rather than the symmetrical, the odd rather than the even, vaguer and more evanescent, unweighted and unresting."

But how can there be symphonies and concertos without symmetry? How unique and unweighted can those forms become without losing the thematic, harmonic, and rhythmic focus that defines them? Thus Debussy, seconding Verlaine, overthrew the symphonic tradition. His orchestral works cannot be heard as one hears Haydn, Dvořák, Mahler. Whether Classical or Romantic, they all counted on certain priorities of structure that have no place in Debussy. The grey evanescence does not yield our old conflict of the dynamic and the lyric, the patient delineation of a musical syntax. In Debussy, there is no clear-cut beginning, nothing central about the middle sections (except in his piano music), and the end occurs not after a logically worked-up-to climax but wherever the music gives out.

This may suggest an impossibly intellectual listening experience; on the contrary, Debussy is "easier" than his predecessors because one need know nothing of form to enjoy the content. Debussy's use of program is as open as his titles—*The Sea, Festivals, Sirens.* His use of form is whatever you hear. His message is: no message. Color. Shadows. Movement.

La Mer (The Sea) 1905

If you just want to sit back and hear, fine. But if you prefer to listen, asking what is it, what happens there—then you have a task ahead of you. There are no first and second themes, no middle sections, no gradual climaxes here as there are in the average symphony or concerto. Even the tone poems of Richard Strauss will not have prepared you for this vast college, this endless continuity of musical motion. Few annotators have even attempted to analyze it. (It can, of course, be analyzed, but only on a reasonably detailed technical level.) There is both too little and too much to speak of. RCA Victor found a way out of the problem in setting up the liner notes for its Toscanini recording of the piece in the early 1950s: it simpy hired Rachel Carson to write about the ocean, which she did very well.

La Mer has three movements. (Movements? The composer terms them "symphonic sketches," to emphasize their odd form.) The three have titles: "From Dawn to Noon on the Sea," "Play of Waves," and "Dialogue of the Wind and the Sea." All of them sound basically alike, though their mood and tone color will on rehearing assert an inter- as well as an independence. The first sketch portrays the heavy "awakening" of the water as early sunlight glances off its surface. The second is friskier, a congruence of fragmented games. The third is heavy again, suggesting the menace of a storm that never quite breaks. Throughout, the choice of instrumentation is all-important—note the weight of the two harps at the very beginning, for example, or the riot of several independent melodies, woodwinds and strings against horns against brass, at the very end. Let's hear from Carson: "As the surface of the sea itself is the creation and the expression of the unseen depths beneath it, so, underlying his musical recreation of the coming of dawn to the sea and of the wind-driven processions of the waves across the ocean, Debussy has suggested the mysterious and brooding spirit of the deep and hidden waters."

Images for Orchestra:
Gigues (Jigs) 1912
Ibéria 1908
Rondes de Printemps (Spring Round Dance) 1910

These images are, as much in Debussy is, approximate but telling. The first of the three, *Jigs,* is not the jolly prance one might expect.

From the opening—one long note and flute solo followed by a Scotch-jig–like rejoinder from the antique oboe d'amore—then on and away through one mood and another, this is an austere, almost surly piece. *Gigues Tristes* (Sad Jigs), Debussy had originally called it. But they are not precisely sad; rather they are sometimes sad and sometimes provisonally up, or at least jiggy. The oboe d'amore (which had recently been revived by Richard Strauss in his *Symphonia Domestica*) comes in for a plaintive solo toward the end, still on its jiggy Scotch jag, yet somewhow definitively anti-jig.

Ibéria is the most popular of the trio because of its quasi-burlesque Spanish color. It is also the longest, in three sections (with a break between the first and second but not the second and third). First comes "On the Highways and Byways," built largely around one recurring figure (the first tune to be heard once the ethnic rhythm is established). Now bright, now sullen, the trip goes it way amidst a regional savor of castanets, tambourine, and an odd Arabian sound in the woodwinds, representing the Moorish contribution to Spanish music. Next comes "The Perfumes of the Night," a nocturne of high violin tremblings, deep murmurings in the lower strings and harp, darkness and languorous peace. Out of this an eruption of bells and percussion signals daybreak and the third section, "A Holiday Morning." Numerous episodes of canny pictorial scoring tickle each other; no one of them sticks around long enough to identify.

The last of the Images, *Spring Round Dance,* is like *Jigs* in its general plan, a series of dance rhythms somewhat unsettled in tone. In its pictorial idea—its image—*Rondes de Printemps* bears a relationship to Stravinsky's ballet *The Rite of Spring,* though in musical approach Debussy is much less muscular than the Russian, less angular, less folkloristically primitive. But he offers no less of an invitation to the dance.

Nocturnes:
Nuages (Clouds),
Fêtes (Festivals),
Sirènes (Sirens) 1899

Like three poems of the atmospheric but obscure symbolist school that greatly influenced Debussy's musical trajectory (or, like three canvases of an impressionist painter), the three nocturnes "tell" little more than their titles. Whether for composer, poet, or painter, the aim of the new French art *circa* 1900 devolved on the general color of sound (of language; of brush stroke). What are these colors, then? *Clouds* is rosy-grey, pale white, all tinges, muted. *Festivals* is loud and primary, whirling and heterogeneous—note that the title is in the plural, as if several festivals were sparkling simultaneously. *Sirens* is grey again, but a deeper grey—the color of the moon—shaded by a wordless womens' chorus of eight sopranos and eight mezzo-(lower) sopranos.

Is the music just color? No. It is also rhythm—paceless, dreamy progression in *Clouds,* frantic action in *Festivals,* cyclic, timeless undulation in *Sirens.* It is pictures, too, viewed through a mist—the sky, then bursts of light, then the sea. There is little more for the analyst to say here, except to note one sharply pictorial touch in the middle of the middle nocturne, *Festivals,* when the racy procession of rhythms suddenly gives way to a quiet march accompaniment on harps, drums, and strings. Over this, as if from a distance, we hear the fanfare of muted trumpets. Highly symbolic, highly impressionist. And like all things, it passes.

Jeux (**Games**) 1912

A ballet score, but more popular as a concert piece than in its true form as "danced poem." The scenario takes in the flirtation of three tennis players, a boy and two girls. Like any trio, they have some trouble laying out the parameters of their three interlocking relationships; the game is their metaphor, and games their mode. Thus the music folds itself luxuriously around affection, appetite, jealousy. Warm yet always ironic, *Games* manages to touch base with carnal play without losing the timbre of innocence. (Appropos of this, Debussy remarked wryly the built-in intrusive innocence of classical dance: "In a ballet any hint of morality escapes through the feet of the danseuse and ends in a pirouette.")

On a historical level, *Games* exerted a powerful influence on Debussy's contemporaries and successors. Even a novice will catch its distinctly Debussyan ring, but an expert might point out numerous touches of harmonic or rhythmic distinction that quickly passed into the public domain of modern Western music. For instance, note the advanced tonality of the mysterious opening measures—Debussy looking forward to Arnold Schönberg. The music is difficult to follow theme by theme, as it is constantly changing its tune, so to speak—organized on a molecular level and dissolving and resynthesizing ionically. What will catch the ear is Debussy's distinct use of instrumental coloration. With a Stravinsky or a Webern, one notes soloistic effects; with Debussy, one hears combinations of simultaneous "solos."

Prélude à l'Après-Midi d'un Faune (Prelude to [Mallarmé's poem] The Afternoon of a Faun) 1892

Our cosmopolitan modern ears have heard everything. They cannot register the shock with which our great-grandparents greeted this linchpin of modern "decadence"—anti-form, anti-harmony, anti-rhythm—and at that derived from Stéphan Mallarmé's opaquely carnal poem about a dreamy faun. From the perspective of the general public and the critical establishment, Debussy had launched a wicked revolution. To us today, this fey act of musical terrorism is not only easy on the ear but of all Debussy's work easiest to grasp in terms of form.

An ABA structure, like so many symphonic slow movements and scherzos, this languorous item opens in pastoral purity, builds to a vaguely fleshly climax, and ends in purity again: the faun scores only in his dreams. Try to imagine what the audience at the premiere in Paris in 1892, still smarting from the excesses of the operatic Wagner, pianistic and tone-poetic Liszt, and symphonic César Franck (all three revolutionists of one sort or another), made of the naked solo flute that begins the piece. This was not revolution, but world's end! Keeping to the cool colors of the woodwind in his scoring yet using warm-blooded melodies, Debussy plays his piece as if in one unbroken line of fragments, finally reaching a lush, not-quite passionate theme (the B section) that expands and then contracts as the opening music recurs (the second A). Just before the end, the solo flute again sounds its theme (with a solo 'cello), followed by—landmark of art history!—a solo oboe playing the second phrase of the theme, with one note altered to sound like a pre-Gershwin portent of blue American jazz.

Sacred and Profane Dances for Harp and String Orchestra 1904

The *Danse Sacrée,* in d minor, is first, a richly flowing movement for the harp supported sometimes by plucked strings and sometimes by a more melodic line in the violins. The form is a simple ABA. Debussy connects it to the *Danse Profane,* in D Major, with the use of quiet repeated notes in the harp with continue after the waltzlike *Profane Dance* has begun. Here the atmosphere is naturally more unbuttoned, and the soloist enjoys a sumptuous passage in slower time with very little accompaniment, after which the strings reprise the *Profane's* opening theme to the harp's decoration and both finish the piece off, the strings on one plucked note that offers the loudest moment in the whole score.

Marche Ecossaise (Scottish March)
1891; orchestrated 1913

This rarity is included as a curio: written for four-hand piano near the start of Debussy's career and orchestrated at the end. The Debussy of the foggy *Nocturnes* and *Images* is implicit here, not fully formed. Any number of other French composers might have accepted the commission of a Scotsman to work up a march on a traditional Scotch bagpipe tune; still, hints of the later Debussy are not to be missed. There is a Scotch color to the music (as there is to the later *Jigs,* the first of the three *Images*), but only as forced through the radiant Debussyan prism.

FREDERICK DELIUS 1862–1934

All tastes, perhaps, are acquired—but some more so than others in that Delius is like halvah or pralines: too sweet for the average taste. The appreciation is well worth acquiring, however, for under the impressionist murk of melodies luxuriously entwined is a sensitive and original talent. Moreover, though English-born, German-trained, and French-inspired (thus the Debussyist impressionism), Delius was in part American-influenced, for he spent some time as an orange planter in Florida, where he heard the folk music of black America. The Florida visit prompted three of Delius' most intriguing compositions—the *Florida* Suite, an opera on slave life and love called *Koanga,* and *Appalachia* (highly recommended by browsers), which consists of variations on a black folk melody and then a full-throated choral rendering of "Oh Honey, I Am Going Down the River in the Morning."

It might be better for the newcomer to try out *Appalachia* (not cited here because of its choral basis), or *Paris* or *Eventyr* (see below) than to start with the more frequently heard shorter works listed at the end of this chapter. For Delius' short works, deftly colored frescoes though they be, are mood pieces—and the mood, shall we say, is inert. Delius' detractors put his work down as static, opaque, and overly ethereal, lacking in developmental structure. And indeed, Delius' occasional inability to endow his longer works with the organizational impetus that guides the ear reminds us that form is necessary. Art *is* form. (*Life* is content.) Why exposition, development, recapitulation? Here's why: because without form, all music would sound like Delius. His concertos particularly demonstrate the limpness of too loose an organization. On the other hand, melody does matter, and when Delius is "on" his work is rhythmic, engaging, alive, and particularly good at capturing the spirit of a culture, as is *Florida, Paris,* the folk-British *Brigg Fair,* or the Norse *Eventyr,* hectic as a saga.

Violin Concerto 1916

Easily Delius' best concerto, not only because the violin was his own instrument, but because his typical disdain for solid structuring is less pronounced here than elsewhere. We have one movement broken into four sections—moderate, then slow, the moderate again, then a light finale—supported by the propulsion of melodies common to all. The first section brings the soloist forward immediately and keeps him there. A brass fanfare signals the slow section, its main theme (from the soloist) a transformation of the opening theme. A return of the opening music marks the recapitulation for both work and movement, but this is no simple repetition—Delius tacks on a closing section in bouncing $^{12}/_{8}$ metre, with the soloist pulling off a dazzling accompaniment. (This is the equivalent to the third movement of the standard concerto, the dance finale with virtuoso display.) For a coda, the opening music returns a last time, sparsely scored.

Paris, The Song of a Great City 1899

This, Delius' most extended mood piece, is a tone poem worthy of its era, when Richard Strauss led the form into its golden age. There is no specific program, simply an evocation of Paris in general, a mural of colors. Delius calls it a nocturne; it is Paris at night, though the dark, lowering opening exploding into light suggests the stirrings of the city as it awakes and gets into daily gear.

This opening takes some time to gather its energies. Fragments in the wind instruments seem to urge the piece on, but not till the harps and strings set up a sense of light and motion does *Paris* promise some real "music." Even then, the brightness fades briefly—only briefly. *Paris* is in motion now, and Delius pursues a route of sound patterns in varying tempos—playful, festive, ruminative. There is an elegant slow section led off by the strings that grows quite passionate, a dance of castanets, a merry march highlighted by the glockenspiel, a touching violin solo, and a grand finale topped off by a return to the remote fragments of the introduction. Those who have tasted of Paris' precisely misty draft there at the spring must decide if Delius has caught its flavor or not.

Eventyr (Sagas) 1917

The title is Norwegian. Always one of the vaguer tone poets, Delius prefers evocation to narration, so while this music *sounds* pictorial its imagery is abstract, suggestive, purely musical. We hear no true folk tunes. But an air of the North of giants, trolls, berserkers and such pervades, not without the touches of burlesque common to the Norse sagas (which are old enough to constitute perhaps the oldest written body of fiction in post-Roman Europe). As with *Paris,* Delius' other major tone poem, the listener is advised not to trace themes through development, but rather to take in the evocation as it floats, stamps, and jigs by. The highly allusive continuity in fact alludes to nothing: there is no story. Still, one can't resist wondering what is supposed to be happening at one point or another, so indicative is the music—especially at the two startling moments midway along when a male chorus shouts an excited syllable. (For economic reasons, these two cries are somtimes omitted: why hire a whole male chorus just to utter two syllables?)

Typical Delius, *Eventyr* is loosely structured. We open with the 'cellos and basses in disjointed flow, an introduction of impending incidence. Then comes the first real theme, largely in the strings. The tempo picks up, dancing even as the music broods. Now a quiet section, colored by the English horn. The lively brooding returns, climaxing in a tremendous cymbal crash. (The two cries occur just after this point.) Here the action begins to retract, and eventually reaches a restatement of the opening theme in its original string scoring. This, too, climaxes, then fades away on the plucked notes of a solo 'cello.

Florida Suite 1888; revised 1890

Delius is seldom thought of as one of America's folkloric composers, being British (of German extraction). But his spell in Florida as an orange planter fed some southern-American input into his sound style, and natives from Jacksonville to Key West have found the work tastily evocative of the regional twang in its more innocent, pre-Miami land boom days. "Tropical scents for orchestra," Delius termed the suite, which follows twenty-four hours of the plantation life from daybreak through a rich nocturne (night-piece).

The first of the four numbers is "Daybreak—Dance," opening with a dawn haze through which a sinuous oboe tune breaks, setting a tone of oddly vigorous laziness. Sun up in glory, the real business of the day commences: dancing. The second movement, "By the River," introduces an ebb and flow on the violins set off in a middle section by a deeply felt theme accompanied on the harp. Third on the card is "Sunset—Near the Plantation," like the first movement divided into two parts, first nature poetry and then a dance. Delius' sunset is not the blissed-out evanescence of many another nature poet, but virile twilight; the dance yields Delius' typical "American" coloration—one that sounds as Norwegian as Creole. (Indeed, Delius is often compared to Edvard Grieg, the best known of Norwegian composers.) This dance is heftier and more electric than the earlier one, though it subsides as quickly as it exploded, and cedes to a reprise of the opening "sunset" music. Last of the set is "At Night," which opens with the oboe melody from "Daybreak" and proceeds to a limber, haunting depiction of the southern nighttime. Florida—where the alligators play.

Brigg Fair 1917

Subtitled "An English Rhapsody," *Brigg Fair* consists, loosely, of variations and reflections on an English folk song; the rhapsody obtains in two ways: (1) the patriotic (i.e., folkloric) information and (2) the improvisatory nature of the music. Not that the work meanders along, but it does eschew the formal separations, the beginnings and endings, of the classical theme and variations. Variations and *reflections* here. Where Brahms, say, states his theme, erects his variations separately one after the other, then restates the theme for a grand finale, Delius approaches his theme, states it, then dovetails his variations and tangents organically. Brahms' variations are discrete; Delius', homogenized. Thus, the composition does not so much begin as appear to have begun at some point prior to the power of human hearing. Suddenly, flutes, harp, and muted strings are up to something—an introduction, it turns out—and after a bit the theme proper is heard on a solo oboe. It's an English folk song, true enough:

> It was on the fift' of august,
> The weather fine and fair;
> Unto Brigg Fair I did repair:
> For Love I was inclined . . .

(It doesn't rhyme right, but it has an air.)

Six variations pass by quickly, giving way to a placid section reminiscent of the introductory material and featuring an expressive variation of the theme on the violins. Then the fleet variations-molded-on-variations recommence, giving way once more to an introduction-like section followed by another lively set of variations. Now we verge on finale, and soon a final variation tops them all, broad and brilliant, full orchestra. But this, too, passes, and at last the solo oboe intones the theme as it did at the start, dying away, not so much ending as graduating into an unbearable dimension. Reflections on a theme. Conversions, retractions. A rhapsody:

> . . . The green leaves, they shall wither,
> And the branches, they shall die
> If ever I prove false to her,
> To the girl that loves me.

Dance Rhapsody no. 1 1908

"Dance Rhapsody" signifies a quasi-improvisational series of variations and developments on a basic dance melody, heard on the oboe just after the introductory invocations are halted by a loud chord.

From then on, the piece proceeds from mood to mood, as if on endless extensions of the energy of that oboe tune. After an emotional climax, we hear a tender violin solo, a bass oboe, and a grand coda.

Summer Night on the River 1911

One of the shortish mood pieces for which Delius is known—too well known. The uninitiate, happening on these somewhat limp little tone poems, is liable to get restless and close his ears to Delius forever. Too slight, he calls these pieces, too scattered. But this one is the best of its kind; it offers a sensible tuition on the vaporous but evocative world of the impressionist—water, night, stars, natural song. Is this music so limp, after all? Limpid is a better word—that is it texture. Its content is man's appreciation of the green world, its mystery and beauty. Its form is loose, like the river; but like the river it has a current, a direction, a source if not a climax.

Over the Hills and Far Away 1897

Purportedly an "impression of open country"—the moors and hills of Delius' native Yorkshire—this moody tone poem opens with an invocation of the distant prospect by strings and horns, yearning to understand. Shortly, excitement sets in, followed by a rocking, folk-like strain, and then a middle section of sublime calm, the wonder of understanding. This passage rises to a thrilling climax, after which themes already heard recur as the mind draws back in contemplation. Far away is, ultimately, too far. The eye outraces the mind.

The Walk to the Paradise Garden 1906

"Most things in nature," Delius once said, "happen gradually, not abruptly," and many of his short "nature" pieces likewise graduate rather than exalt their thin abstractions of the natural world. This, the best known of the lot, is a case in point. Actually an intermezzo (orchestral interlude) belonging to Delius' opera, *A Village Romeo and Juliet,* the *Walk* starts the opera's two tragic lovers on a tender, reflective journey toward death. It does, indeed, happen gradually, albeit rising to a splendid climax before sinking back into the dreamy netherworld of the opening. Detractors will say, "Nothing occurs in it." Admirers will reply, "Nothing occurs, but much is felt."

Prelude to Irmelin 1892

First flute, then clarinet, then oboe, then violins, all on the same theme, and the music is off, setting the stage for Delius' first opera, *Irmelin* (about a princess of great beauty but cold heart, such as fairy tales delight in and delight to see, at length, ardent with love for Prince Charming). The work is seldom staged, but the prelude is popular in the concert hall for its sinuous, lullaby innocence.

RICHARD STRAUSS 1864–1949

Perhaps the last best seller in music, the most recent composer to exercise that popular touch that familiarizes symphony to millions who never seek out a concert hall, Strauss closed an era. Actually, he not only closed it but survived it by several decades; it was Romanticism, just about to wane when Strauss arrived on the scene (and just reviving when he reached middle age). The Romantics, throughout the 1800s, had been seeking new kinds of musical expression. As the new wave, they experimented with program music, with larger structural forms and a bigger orchestra, with mixed media (voices in symphony), with melancholy, idyllic, or grotesque subject matter (to state their spiritual alienation as men and artists), with ways to remake symphony into a more personal engine of communication.

All these things Strauss inherited; all of them mark his style. Program music was his forte; some of his compositions reached nearly an hour in length and made, his detractors said, an incredible racket; he kept the human voice out of his orchestral works *but* arranged huge orchestrations for songs that in Schubert's day would have been accompanied only by piano or a chamber group; he could set almost anything to music and sometimes did (including his own life—thrice); and, most importantly, carried on the work of Franz Liszt in evolving the flexible new artwork called the symphonic, or tone, poem.

The concerto is the oldest of the big forms, dating back to the little ensembles of the seventeenth century. The symphony came later, with the larger orchestras of the eighteenth century. The tone poem is youngest of all. It is an essentially Romantic conception, in its dramatic basis (the program), its frequent dependence on a textual complement (a poem, say, inscribed in the printed score and mirrored—related, almost—in the music), and its flamboyant personal bent. From the beginning, the concerto and the symphony were devised simply to be music, to sing. The tone poem was devised to be about something, to describe. Inheriting an already developed tone poem from Franz Liszt and several French composers, Strauss took it even farther along, made it richer in characterization, more adaptable in terms of source material, and more plastic in shape. No more the first theme-second theme, development, and recapitulation of traditional symphony: the tone poem tells a tale, and what if one's tale does not call for a "second" theme or a recapitulation?—stories don't recapitulate, after all. Under Strauss, the tone poem found its most elastic form and went into a heyday.

Strauss, too, went into a personal golden age when he discovered the tone poem. He had launched his career in the standard forms—the symphony, the concerto, the sonata. These, as he wrote them, were nothing special. But Strauss knew this, anyway, and wondered what he should do instead. He was a born dramatist; he needed to describe, illustrate, chronicle, comment. His symphony, *Aus Italien* (From Italy, cited below), made a pass at what we might call tone poetics—each of its four movements captured a different aspect of Italian life (and note that it bore a name rather than a number; technically, it was his Symphony no. 2 in G Major). Meanwhile, he wrote an out-and-out tone poem, *Macbeth* (not performed till later), and with a second tone poem, *Don Juan,* stunned listeners with the vitality of symphonic theatre. Seven other tone poems followed, all but one of them equal to the electric eloquence of *Don Juan* (the one dud is the *Alpine Symphony,* though it, too, has its moments). But already, Strauss had moved on to the next stage of musical dramatization, opera, on which he concentrated for the rest of his long life.

The trick in "getting" these Straussian tone poems is to throw out all one's training in Haydn, Beethoven, and so on. Their symphonic movements accord to certain rules of theme-confrontation not useful to the tone poet. They are musicalizing intellectual concepts; he is telling a story. His music adapts to a set action. (This can be taken just so far, however; Strauss himself often lost his temper with those who wanted every theme, every freak of orchestration, explained.) Structurally, the Straussian tone poem does not state, develop, and restate, as does a movement of symphony. Instead, they progress from a beginning through a middle to an end. Thus, Strauss' *Don Quixote* starts with Cervantes' hero losing his grasp on reality and donning his mad armor, continues through several of his adventures, and closes with his death. (An extra depth of narration is provided by two soloists, on the cello and viola, representing Quixote and Sancho Panza respectively.) Or, more loosely, *Also Sprach Zarathustra* (Thus Spake Zarathustra) abstracts the general mood of Nietzsche's book without attempting to make the music "philosophize." Or, most loosely yet, the *Symphonia*

Domestica—a day with the Strauss family—attaches tag themes to Strauss, his wife, and their infant son, but does not offer much in the way of pictorial detail. This is not propaganda; it's music.

One other feature of the Strauss sound needs mentioning, his gift as an orchestrator. No one in music before or after was more adept at drawing allusions out of the various instruments, in creating shapes and colors with them. Even as it presents itself, his music comments on itself—which is why Strauss was so successful in opera. His orchestra offers a psychological subtext running under the action, thus telling a story on several levels at once: what is happening, but *why* it happens. Those who feel up to it should sample Strauss' operas, for they stand among the most intriguing ever composed, not least because the great humanist Hugo von Hofmannsthal wrote the librettos for the best of them. With Hofmannsthal's words and Strauss' music, there is none of the silly, exotic extremism that bedevils much of the opera repertory; poeticized naturalism is their mode. Try *Der Rosenkavalier* (The Cavalier of the Rose) for its radiantly autumnal intimacy, or *Ariadne auf Naxos* for its masterfully grotesque juxtaposition of the two images of eternal woman, the chaste and the earthy. But please do not attempt to hear them without following them, line by line, with an English translation of the libretto (such as is invariably supplied in a record album or sold at performances in the theatre lobby). Listening to opera in a foreign language (German, in this case) without a translation is like going to the movies in a blindfold.

Aus Italien (From Italy), op. 16 1886*

"The work is somewhat new and revolutionary," wrote Strauss after the premiere in Munich, "and the last movement has aroused great opposition . . . I was immensely proud; this is the first work of mine to have met with opposition from the mob, so it must be of some importance." This "symphonic fantasy in G Major" (as opposed to your mere symphony) was revolutionary in its "fantasy" part—that is, its preference for free-form structures and programmatic titles in place of the traditional and purely musical symphonic movements. Strauss, the natural dramatist, did not want to write a Symphony in G Major—the tone poet in him was bursting to come out and *describe*. Thus the work's designation as symphonic fantasy: *Aus Italien* is as much four tone poems (fantasies) as it is a four-movement symphony.

*The Strauss chapter is organized chronologically rather than generically.

As so often with musical "travelogues," the work is to be taken as impressions of places rather than literal depictions—not what you see, but how you feel about seeing it. (The *locus classicus* of this procedure is Beethoven's "Pastoral" Symphony, no. 6, which is not "about" nature but man's relationship to it.) The first movement, "In the Country," has confused listeners; a suggestion of daybreak in the Roman countryside, it feels somehow not important enough for a first movement. Moving from minor to major keys—from a solemn slow introduction to a festive slow main section—it builds in power nicely. The explosion of the bright light of full day toward the end of the movement is exciting, and colored with a sure hand by Strauss the instrumental painter. Still, it feels like a slow movement, not a first movement. It doesn't seem to start anything. The lively second movement, "In Rome's Ruins," on the other hand, is big for a scherzo, and supplies some of the ongoing "push" that "In the Country" lacked. It is not your standard ABA scherzo-and-trio; it is not standard, period. Motives come and go on their own initiative, in a collage of faded imperial glories.

There is no doubting the genre of the slow [third] movement, "On the Beach at Sorrento." This is, no matter what else, a slow movement. It is also the most potent anticipation in *Aus Italien* of the more mature Strauss, both in melody and scoring. No question that this is the movement most attractive to admirers of such prime Strauss material as *Don Juan* and *Der Rosenkavalier.* For the finale [fourth mvt], "Neapolitan Life," Strauss indulges in a little folklorism with a rather off-the-wall use of the folk song "Finiculì, Finiculà." In its day, this movement was considered shockingly undignified, even—such decadence from Strauss—"realistic."

Burleske in d minor for Piano and Orchestra 1886

This is one of the earliest of Strauss' orchestral pieces still alive, as it were—performed—and a Brahmsian influence in terms of structure (classical but expansive), the writing of the solo part (very difficult, calling for a wide stretch of fingers and much reserve of power), and the overall sound is unmistakable. Strauss was not yet totally Strauss, still finding his route by the maps of older masters. This burleske (joke) is equivalent to the sonata-allegro first movement of a piano concerto, with aggressive first theme, lyrical second theme, extended development, recapitulation, cadenza (the soloist's exhibitionist moment), and coda. Why burleske? Why not just "Allegro Vivace in d minor for piano and orchestra"? Possibly because of the unorthodox opening—for four timpani! And then again, why not burleske? The work isn't remotely like a lampoon, but it is fun.

Don Juan, op. 20 1888

The historic importance of this tone poem cannot be overstated. Ever since the reinvention of the opera overture (mainly by Mozart and Beethoven) as a means of dramatic expression, composers had experimented with the idea of a short musical form that would stand by itself as both music and drama. Franz Liszt, with his "symphonic poem," marks a halfway point; with Strauss' *Don Juan,* the first instance of the modern tone poem, the solution was found. Liszt's symphonic poem had a title, atmosphere, and sometimes a narrative illustration or two, but this was only an approach: the structure and sound of the form was still partly rooted in procedures devised for absolute, not dramatic, music. Strauss changed the entire form—with him, everything musical derived from dramatic imperatives. Liszt was laying on, from the outside; Strauss built up, from within.

Intricating its own rather free form on a literary subject (Nikolaus Lenau's long poem, *Don Juan*), this impetuous novelty stunned the musical establishment with its ability to limn an extra-musical subject without losing its impact as sheer music. (It has been called "a one-act 'play' without words.") Some of its effect depends on Strauss' flair for orchestration; some of that flair depends on testing the capacities of the orchestra personnel far beyond precedent. This is tricky music to play, reaching for high and low notes at the ambiguous extremes of players' ranges and demanding breath control of the wind players not called for elsewhere. During rehearsals for the world premiere in Weimar in 1889, the first horn player asked Strauss if Beethoven's Sixth Symphony, the "Pastoral," was really to follow *Don Juan* on the program. It was? "That," replied the exhausted first horn, "remains to be seen."

Lenau's and Strauss' Don Juan is not the frivolous cad sometimes presented (in Mozart's opera *Don Giovanni,* most notably), but a Romantic hero, passionate, poetic, and melancholy, engaged in a search for the womanly ideal. First we hear Juan in his vivacity, then in his prankish good humor, then—prompted by a violin solo—at his most ardent. Soon an autumnal glow spreads through the orchestra, and a tranquil oboe solo paints us an amour. But Juan moves onward, still seeking his one, true Faustian moment of unmitigated beauty. Strauss now presents his hero *as* hero, in a stirring melody for the four horns, bold, affirmative, demanding. These themes vie with each other to narrate the temptations and failures of Juan's life-project, till at last Romantic *Weltschmerz* strikes him and, in a duel, he allows himself to be mortally wounded. Incidentally, you might experience at first-hand the historical development of the tone poem by playing first the Overture to Mozart's *Don Giovanni* (1787) and secondly this alternate version of the same subject. Hearing two master dramatists at work makes not a contest in musical imagery, but a comparison of how Classicism (Mozart) and Romanticism (Strauss) differ in characterizing the eternal figure of the virile libertine—and also, how symphony evolved a flexible form for purposes of narration.

Tod und Verklärung (Death and Transfiguration), op. 24 1889

As so often with Strauss' tone poems, a literary text clues us into the character and action of the music. In this case, the text (by Alexander Ritter) was written *after* the music—inspired by it, in fact; not surprisingly, this is the least specifically evocative of all Strauss' essays in the form. Ritter's poem, which Strauss approved of to the point of having it printed in the score, tells of a man fighting for life on his deathbed. In delirium he reviews his past and finds spiritual release—transfiguration—in death. This is a free enough "guide" for the listener, who may want to read his own picture into Strauss' musical scenario of slow introduction, *Allegro molto agitato* (Lively, very agitated), hopeful woodwind and string solos, renewed agitation, and final redemption in a celestial cascade of melody.

Till Eulenspiegel's Merry Pranks, op. 28 1895

Strauss occasionally got fed up with people asking for detailed guides to his tone poems: what does this tune mean? What is the bassoon saying? The flute sounds so pathetic—is someone ill? Irritably, bored, he would say, "It's just music!" Perhaps we should take *Till* in just that way, as a loose and non-specific two-theme rondo about a legendary prankster of the Middle Ages who is eventually apprehended and hanged for his public nuisances. Each of the two themes characterizes Till as rogue: the first is heard right at the top of the piece in the violins, the second moments later on a solo horn. Thereafter the two intermingle with and bind together various episodes, supporting the overall structure on two levels—physically, by their regular reappearances, and emotionally, by the preciseness with which they suggest the character of Till and the spirit of his adventures.

We open in F Major with the two Till motives. The clarinet uses the first of the two to usher in a bouncy, sly section, obviously the first of the merry pranks. Clarinets also lead into a warm folklike strain that is quickly scattered by rascally laughter. Suddenly, a descending *glissando pizzicato* (a "slide" down plucked strings) on a solo violin heralds a developmental sequence, very attractive, involving both of Till's themes. (The horn theme has turned into a seductive violin motive marked "*liebeglühend,*" glowing with love.) As the piece progresses, Strauss builds tension between these transformations of the two themes and their original forms, finally letting the two confront each other by playing them simultaneously, the first theme on oboes and violins and the second on horns and violas. This is built into a gigantic climax, broken by the unmistakable sounds of Justice (mainly in the brasses) catching up with the public nuisance, Till. He is still laughing up to the very end—but two deep notes in the bassoon and brasses tell of Till's execution, and the clarinet flutters like a soul passing on to heaven. Strauss gives Till the last word in a tiny epilogue back in the opening F Major—Till as eternal irreverance. Eulenspiegel, by the way, means "owlglass," from an old German proverb: "Man recognizes his faults as dimly as the owl looks into the mirror."

Also Sprach Zarathustra
(Thus Spake Zarathustra), op. 30 1896

"Freely after Nietzsche," Strauss explains of this tone poem inspired by the philosopher's searching look at the human condition, one of the more arresting publications of the 1880s. Zarathustra (Zoroaster) leaves his lonely mountain to go among people and lead them into their next and more glorious stages of evolution; his rhapsodic tales, poems, and lectures prompted Strauss' now mystical, now joyful piece in the loosest sense. There is no direct correspondence between music and text, though Strauss did use some of Nietzsche's chapter titles as headings for the different sections of the work. It is a fantasia (free in form), using a few basic themes in variation and repetition for musical, not philosophical, effect.

The introduction, one of the ear-popping splendors of the repertory, is well known to millions through its exposure in the opening sequence of the film *2001: A Space Odyssey* (and through numerous television commercials, quick to exploit voguish cultural phenomena). A more inscrutable side of Zarathustra's teaching follows in "Of the Inhabitants of the Unseen World," though this soon develops into a lyrical passage of restrained beauty for organ and detailed string parts. The livelier "Of the Great Yearning" glides into "Of Joy and Passion" (on a descending harp run) as if in one arching line, for the work unfolds in joined series, dovetailing its several themes and leading one section into another. "The Grave Song," not as sombre as one might think, cedes to the dark, lowering, fuguelike "Of Science," which develops a middle section of frisky pleasure. "The Convalescent" (in the spiritual sense) follows, building to a huge conclusion—or, rather, seeming to. This is only the halfway point, and odd twitterings in the woodwinds eventually turn into a Viennese waltz with violin solo, "The Dance-Song," called vulgar by critics but very much in tune with Nietzsche's dithyrambic human fundamentalism. The tolling of a great bell signals the work's climax, "Song of the Night Wanderer," which closes the piece in a kind of musical metaphysics by opposing two alien keys, C Major in the depths of the orchestra and B Major on high.

Don Quixote, op. 35 1897

This is one of the most sheerly depictive tone poems ever, a brilliant tour de force of dazzling scoring devices and—as analysis reveals—several different things at once: (1) a musical narration based on Cervantes' famous novel, taking its hero from his decision to revive knight errantry through ten of his escapades as the "Knight of the

Rueful Countenance" until self-recognition dwindles the wonderful adventure and he dies; (2) an introduction, theme and ten variations, and finale—or, as Strauss put it, "Fantastic Variations on a Theme of Knightly Character" (each of the variations represents a different episode of the book); and (3) a double concerto for 'cello and viola, the former taking a central position to portray Don Quixote, the latter playing second fiddle as Sancho Panza. If this engaging concatenation of tone poem, variation form, and concerto isn't ingenious, I don't know what is.

The Theme is easy to pick out at first hearing, as it is the very first thing heard, a sprightly yet gallant tune on flutes and oboes. This is Quixote himself, the most empathetically universal stooge in literature, highly romanticized in this long introduction. (Note the short, lovely oboe solo about two minutes into the piece—this is a subsidiary theme, used throughout the piece to symbolize Quixote's obsessive ideal of beauty—Dulcinea, if you like.) After much development of Quixote's theme, meant to depict his investigation into the world of heroic romance, a climax and a sudden ping! (repeated several times) tells us that Quixote's mind has snapped and his reinvention as a lunatic knight is complete. Promptly, Strauss introduces his two soloists: first, the 'cello as Quixote, next the lumbering, plangent Sancho on the viola.

Now, the ten variations on Quixote's theme:

Variation 1: the most famous episode of all, Quixote's battle with the windmills (which he takes to be evil giants).

Variation 2: a classic of musical illustration—Quixote routs a flock of sheep, which Strauss deviously renders, to the life, via shimmering violas and baa-ing brasses.

Variation 3: a dialogue between Quixote and Sancho on the merits of the chivalric life. After each has had his separate say, Quixote's ideal vision is expounded by the full orchestra in the most affecting passage in the work.

Variation 4: Quixote mistakes a band of penitents for varlets, attacks, and is repelled. Another wonderful touch of instrumental dramatization—you will hear the hymn-singing penitents interspersed with Sancho's apprehensive "oh no, not again!" (on clarinet and oboe)—or perhaps these are Quixote's private voices, urging him on: "Smash the varlets!"

Variation 5: as tradition demands, Quixote keeps night-long vigil beside his armor, and has another vision of Dulcinea.

Variation 6: gossipy oboes depict a crude village lass whom Sancho points out as a likely example of the ideal; Quixote refutes this slander.

Variation 7: "Fluttertongued" flutes, harp, and wind machine evoke a ride through the air—all in Quioxote's mind, of course.

Variation 8: A watery mishap. (Conductors must be careful not to drown out a solo violin part here, for this variation is rather heavily scored.)

Variation 9: Two bassoons represent two pompous priests, seen by Quixote as wicked magicians.

Variation 10: A climax in the narration—a friend of Quixote, to cure his folly, challenges him as "The Knight of the White Moon," bests him in combat, and thereby makes Quixote promise to go home.

The finale shows us the death of Quixote, released from madness but from his wondrous dreams as well. What cure was this, and what folly? The variations over, flute and oboe sound the Theme in its original form as at the beginning. The 'cello dims out. It's over.

Ein Heldenleben (**A Hero's Life**),
op. 40 1898

This huge tone poem outrages the critics with its arrogance—the hero of the life, it turns out, is Strauss himself. (Critics have a low tolerance for arrogance . . . in others.) But Strauss' intention was not self-glorification. A year earlier, in *Don Quixote,* he had depicted the ridiculous defeats of an unusual character; here, as a complementary study, he presents the inspiring victories of an ordinary man. In this context, the piece feels less arrogant than enthusiastic.

Episodic in structure, *Ein Heldenleben* is bound together by the hero's theme, the muscular, broadly flowing melody that opens the work and recurs throughout (like the refrain in a rondo). A rather generalized "autobiography" identifies the episodes: first the hero in his essence, then the hero's critics (shrill, yapping woodwinds; another reason for critics to dislike the piece), the hero's love (a solo violin, so prominent in its dialogue with the orchestra that the passage is like something cut out of a concerto), the hero's wartime, the hero's works in peacetime (here Strauss makes it clear who his hero is by quoting liberally from at least eight of his own works; sharp ears might detect the principal theme from *Don Quixote* on the flute and oboe), and the hero's retirement, reminiscences, and transcendent renunciation of earthly matters (more solo violin). It sounds like a full life—but one should remember that Strauss wrote *Ein Heldenleben* fifty-one years before his death, when much lay ahead of him (including, among other things, his three most popular operas, *Salome, Elektra,* and *Der Rosenkavalier*).

Symphonia Domestica (Domestic Symphony), op. 53 1903

Having cast himself as a hero in *Ein Heldenleben* (immediately above), Strauss proposed a tone poem dealing with his other side as husband and father, the hero in his slippers and favorite armchair. Dedicated "to my dear wife and our little boy," this work captures the sounds of the household—relaxation, a lullaby, quarrels, the striking of a clock. In form, it is tone poem merged with the symphony, for its one long movement unfolds in sections as introduction, scherzo, slow movement, and finale, the introduction corresponding to the exposition of a first movement (not the whole movement, just the first statement of themes). The rest of the piece Strauss treats as a huge development, and at the very end he runs a kind of recapitulation. (In other words, this is really like a gigantic sonata-allegro movement—exposition, development, and recapitulation.)

The themes, or theme-groups (since there are so many individual tunes) relate to the three members of the family, brought forward at the start of the work—Papa, friendly ('cellos) and ardent (oboe); Mama, shrewishly unpredictable but loving (flutes, oboes, and violins); and Baby (on the antique oboe d'amore). Lest the listener take the Strauss domicile for a world war, it should be noted that this is a big score designed to make musical rather than autobiographical points. It expands as a symphony expands, for musical emphases. (On the other hand, *some* of that growling and heaving depicts Frau Strauss, a notorious termagant.) It is the musician in Strauss, not the diarist, who builds the piece to a shattering double fugue in the finale: what does a double fugue have to do with domesticity, or anything else? A fugue is a fugue, music pure and, well, not simple.

(A double fugue, by the way, is a fugue with two principal themes. In a one-theme fugue, that theme is repeated and developed in several different horizontal lines, all sounded simultaneously. So a double fugue is more or less like two different possible fugues on the same basic theme going at once. It's quite a feat.)

For those who would like to turn the pages of this family album more or less in order, there is a program; Strauss vacillated between encouraging the listener to hear the work as drama in music and discouraging this approach. In the former mood, he outlined his tale as a kind of "one mad day in the life of" affair. The introduction is simply a set of character sketches, as described above—Papa, Mama, and Baby Strauss. The scherzo, launched by the oboe d'amore, depicts "childish playtime" and "parents' happiness." The movement closes with a lullaby (two clarinets gently accompanied in a cradle barcarolle) and the chimes of the clock striking seven. Now the slow movement, begun by solo oboe and solo flute: nighttime in the Strauss household, rising to a superb *tutti* marked by two harps banging out chords against each other. This is termed the "love scene"; it, too, is ended with the chimes of the clock, this time for seven in the morning. The finale jumps awake for a "merry dispute" (the double fugue).

Some listeners find the *Symphonia Domestica* too large and pushy, also too personal. That's their problem. This is one of Strauss' most brilliant compositions in terms of scoring, structural breadth, and sheer beauty of melody.

"Dance of the Seven Veils" from Salome 1905

Salome, in Strauss' opera (from Oscar Wilde's play), dances so ravishingly that her stepfather Herod offers her anything if she will favor him with a performance. She has just been snubbed by John the Baptist and, obsessed with the desire to kiss his mouth, dances. (She will ask for John's head, get it, kiss it, and be killed at Herod's disgusted command.) The dance affects the comfortable sensuality of the East, incidentally tracing its languorous contours around a phrase associated with Salome's interest in the Baptist's mouth. In modern opera, the music always has an opinion about the characters and their actions.

Suite from Der Rosenkavalier (The Knight of the Rose) 1910

The practice of making suites by clipping bits out of opera scores makes some of us nervous. Much of this music was meant as accompaniment—commentary, really—to a sung play; to leave out the voice parts, to cut and paste, robs the original of its musicodramtic balance. It may sound all right to the uninitiated listener, but the music is not doing what it was designed to do. It's wasteful and disrespectful, like listening to Beethoven's Ninth Symphony while you do the household chores.

As regards *Der Rosenkavalier,* the sunny, lightly psychological romantic comedy set in Maria Theresa's Vienna, this is certainly animated, endearing music. However, without the superb libretto of Hugo von Hofmannsthal, Strauss' score is only half there. There is a wacky plot and sentimental charm going on during—through—the music; without taking it in complete in its context as opera, what do you have? What can I tell you here? It isn't even clear what arrangement of *Rosenkavalier* excerpts makes up a *Rosenkavalier* suite. Strauss himself prepared one, but there are other arrangements made by others, so the contents vary; there is also a Waltz Medley taken from the opera which sometimes gets called "the" *Rosenkavalier* Suite. You may be thinking: if Strauss made up a suite himself, doesn't that make it all right? After all, it's his music. But this is irrelevant to the question of what you can get out of an opera suite with the "opera" translated into an unintelligible code. Anyway, Strauss, one of the sharpest businessmen in the history of music, would have arranged a *Rosenkavalier* can-can and tango medley if his fee had been met.

An Alpine Symphony, op. 64 1915

This is not a symphony but a tone poem, Strauss' last in that form and among his biggest in size. In this one sprawling movement, experts can pick out the equivalent of a "connected" symphony—introduction and "first movement"; scherzo, slow movement, finale and coda. But this is not practical for listening purposes. Think of the piece as a fantasy—a free-form span of countless themes, variations, and repetitions. There is a program: the climb and descent of an Alpine hill in one twenty-four hour period, from deepest night to nightfall. There are twenty-two sections, each running into the next. Since many of them are sharply pictorial, it is relatively easy to follow the progress of the climbing party as it takes in the sights, reaches the full mountain majesty, and returns to earth. Though the scoring is huge and polyphonically complex (that is, sounding two or more themes at once), Strauss deliberately kept the melodies themselves simple and as natural as the scenes they depict. "I wanted to compose, for once," he declared, "as a cow gives milk." (He was also proud of his acute illustrative gift, and once boasted that he could, if he had to, characterize a knife and fork in music.)

Some listeners have found it fulfilling simply to sit back and visualize the events of the climb according to their own lights. Others may want to attend to the twenty-two narrative sections as they unfold. These are, in order: "Night" (dark and static), "Sunrise," "The Ascent," "Entering the Forest" (hunting horns), "Wandering Along with the Brook," "At the Waterfall," "Apparition" (an Alpine sprite materializes in the cascade's rainbow), "On Flowery Meadows," "On the High Pasture" (cowbells and woodwind yodelling), "Getting Lost in Thicket and Undergrowth," "On the Glacier," "Dangerous Moments," "On the Summit" (the emotional climax of the piece—trombones capture the awesome pinnacle of height and space, followed by a frightened, hesitant oboe solo, indicative of the frailty of man in the vastness of nature), "Vision," "Mists Rise," "The Sun Gradually Becomes Obscured," "Elegy," "Calm Before the Storm," "Thunder and Storm, Descent" (perhaps the biggest tempest in all music), "Sunset," "Receding Images," and, as at the opening, "Night."

Le Bourgeois Gentilhomme Suite,
op. 60 1918

Caviar. This is music collected from a production of Molière's comedy, *Le Bourgeois Gentilhomme* (The Parvenu Nobleman), for which Strauss and the translator, Hugo von Hofmannsthal, wrote not just incidental music but also an old-fashioned sort of opera as part of the parvenu protagonist's soirée in the last act. It was a long evening, and a failure, and Strauss pulled off two stunts of salvage—the opera, revised, turned into the brilliant *Ariadne auf Naxos* (performed by itself now), and the best bits of the incidental score turned up in the present suite. There are nine numbers, some quite short and the ninth, within its context, an epic. Throughout, a nostalgic homage to the Baroque era trims Strauss' normally complex canvas, giving an at times chamber (small orchestra) feeling to the whole. The "overture" characterizes the pompous parvenu of the title, announcing the chamber-style scoring at once by opening with strings and piano only. At the end, in a change of mood, the oboe sings a pastoral melody used in the play. Flutes dominate the following "Minuet"; trombone and piano take the lead in the third number, devoted to a fencing lesson. (Turning *gentilhomme* is a more hectic business than the *bourgeois* had thought.) Next comes the "Entrance and Dance of the Tailors," featuring a brilliant (and very tricky) solo for violin in the dance section, a polonaise (Polish dance, always identified by the distinctive ta-ta-*da* of its accompaniment). The fifth number is a minuet adapted from music by one of Molière's coevals, Jean-Baptiste Lully, who himself wrote an incidental score for this same comedy. Another dance follows, this one a courante—very French, but of a Straussian richness in the scoring—and the seventh number, "Cléonte's Entrance," offers another adaptation of a tune by Lully. Next is the prelude to Act II (usually called simply "Intermezzo"), loaded—very lightly, to be sure—with style and deftness. The last and grandest number, "The Dinner" is an example of what used to be called "table music." Starting with a spoof-ceremonial march, it celebrates each new dish with a new musical episode. (It takes an expert to place Strauss' amusing allusions to other works here—to Wagner's *Das Rheingold* in honor of the Rhine salmon, to the evocation of sheep in Strauss' own *Don Quixote* to accompany the leg of lamb, and a combination of Strauss' *Der Rosenkavalier* and Verdi's *Rigoletto,* a snippet of "La Donna è Mobile," when thrushes' tongues are served—the thrush apparently reminding Strauss of the call of an Italian tenor.) To close the scene, Strauss indulges in a deliberate anachronism, the waltz.

The Two Horn Concertos:
No. 1 in E Flat Major, op. 11 1883
No. 2 in E Flat Major 1942

Though composed nearly sixty years apart, these two samples of Strauss' *concertante* (concerto-izing) flair are very much a couple. Besides being in the same key (harmonic structure is more strategic to composition than most listeners realize), both follow the traditional concerto outline of three movements (fast-slow-fast) with a lively first, a mellow second, and a vivacious rondo for the third. Moreover, in both cases the first two movements are not separated by a break. What is different about them is the slightly more advanced harmonic coloration in the later work—only slightly, for while Strauss had developed a flamboyant harmonic palette by the early twentieth century, he eventually simplified his style—Classicized it, as it were. Another distinction may be found in the slow [second] movement of no. 2, wherein Strauss virtually neglects the soloist to meld his horn sound in with that of the orchestra.

One more point. Strauss' father was a famous horn player himself and wildly reactionary in his musical taste. It may be out of respect for papa's low tolerance of the "modern" in music that caused Strauss to write so pure and melodic—so Mozartean—a concerto. But how odd, then, that his second entry in the form should end up in the same simple style—this time out of the autumnal nostalgia of Strauss' last days! Coming along once very early in Strauss' career and a second time very late, the horn concerto as a form entirely avoided the heavy sound style of the radical, middle-period Strauss of *Salome* and *Elektra*.

Oboe Concerto in D Major 1945

A late work, dating from a time when Strauss turned inward, as it were, composing highly neo-Classical pieces of light scoring, simple structure, and Mozartean melody (tunes of a simplistic and "universal" appeal, dependent more on the purity of the melody than on any special rhythmic or harmonic effect). There are three movements, thematically related to each other and connected without a break. The format is traditional: a moderately lively first movement, a pastoral slow movement, and a zippy finale. The soloist is at the fore from the top, lending a elegiacally rustic quality to the whole because of the peculiar natural color of the instrument. Actually, the first movement is much less forceful than is usual with concerto first movements—but then Straussian neo-Classicism calls for transcendence and finesse rather than high drama. The slow [second] movement is lovingly expressed and rather full in tone, the emotional apex of the piece. A cadence for the soloist provides the transition to the finale. Note the coda, a waltz which reminds us that when it comes to a Strauss waltz, the connoisseur celebrates Richard more than Johann. No relation.

Metamorphosen (Metamorphoses) 1945

A work of the most crystalline transcendence, *Metamorphosen* was composed during the worst days of World War II. Hitler's thousand-year Reich had dwindled to its last few days, Europe lay wrecked, and—for some unknown reason—Strauss wrote a serene, highly contemplative study for twenty-three strings (each with its own part) in one long slow movement. Given that Strauss was a natural-born dramatist in music, one asks, "What is it about? Whose metamorphoses? From what into what? Old world into new, perhaps? Decadent culture into death and rebirth?" No one knows. The string lines wind around each other, expand, distend, die. But the quotation of the funeral march [third mvt] from Beethoven's "Eroica" (Symphony no. 3) near the end of the work surely means something.

CARL NIELSEN 1865–1931

The remarkable Dane Carl Nielsen has only recently entered the international repertory after decades of relative obscurity. As the phonograph has done for so many others, it made Nielsen accessible; suddenly it was realized that this composer is not only interesting as a "sound" but important historically for what he did with that fundamental of large-scale composition—ever changing yet basically always what it was—the symphony.

Nielsen is a kind of Beethoven. Making his studies and first personal statements as one era was dying and another being born, Nielsen went through the looking glass and helped organize the new aesthetic simply by composing. Beethoven, of course, arrived as Classicism was ceding to Romanticism; Nielsen saw Romanticism cede to neo-Classicism. But, like Beethoven, he showed the new style mostly by helping to invent it. Highly individualistic (thus his long obscurity), bold, and dramatic, Nielsen often reminds writers of Beethoven, especially in his sharp orientation to the compass points of symphonic structure: Nielsen wanders, but is never lost. (We should mention here Nielsen's "progressive tonality," a system in which the harmonic basis of a symphony is continually transformed and shifted, testing yet "educating" the ear—for example, only his first symphony, in g minor, is described as being "in" a certain key. The others choose new harmonic roots from movement to movement.)

Nielson's are grand symphonies, relatively long and, despite the allusive subtitles, absolute music at its purest. Anyone who has wondered where the modern Beethovens are might investigate this one, for his strengths exert that same admirable power that so invigorates Beethoven. Browsers might start with the Fifth, in either case.

Symphony no. 2, "The Four Temperaments," op. 16 1902

As a very slight programmatic gimmick, each of the four movements depicts one of the classic four human types: a symphony of humours. The first movement, *Allegro collerico,* gives a mostly lively, at times slashing, account of the choleric mentality; lots of *tutti*s here. The second movement, *Allegro comodo e flemmatico,* presents the phlegmatic type in a reserved waltz—this is the scherzo of the symphony with a theme (introduced in the first violins) that changes as the movement develops. (Note, by the way, how the Italian tempo markings for each of the movements includes the applicable "temperament" as well; this is a novelty exclusive to this work.) For a slow [third] movement, we have *Andante malincolico,* the melancholy person, very much so indeed, albeit with great dignity in the middle section, for strings against winds. The finale [fouth mvt] closes the circle with an *Allegro sanguineo* for the confident sort. Another movement big on *tuttis.*

Symphony no. 3, "Sinfonia Espansiva," op. 27 1911

Why "expansive"? Because Nielsen stated his intention to widen the parameters of Danish music with this very work—"I want stronger rhythms, more advanced harmony." It is a kind of Danish "Eroica," doing within its context what Beethoven's Third did in its: expanding the structural and expressive possibility of symphonic form. And like the "Eroica," the "Espansiva" works its revolution even as it utilizes traditional format. The language, paragraphing, and diction are familiar—but the content is new.

A bold symphony, complex and mercurial, always doing something, or doing it over differently—the first movement alone has enough material to outfit a complete symphony. The opening is famous for its spare introductory beats leading up to the dramatic first subject, which leaves its mark on the entire work. The second [slow] movement offers an odd surprise, a wordless soprano and baritone duet which nicely suits the blissful, smoky non-motion of the movement as a whole. A remarkable peacefulness descends in these minutes, and when the two singers enter the picture late in the movement, it comes as no surprise after all—"of course," one thinks. "Every slow movement should have a caroller or two." The scherzo [third mvt] disperses the calm, though Nielsen takes care to "expand" the scherzo's traditional rhythmic devilry with a variety of moods. The marchlike finale [fourth mvt], on the other hand, is vitalized by some *almost* old-fashioned grandeur reminiscent of the Big Tunes favored by Beethoven and Brahms for their finales.

Symphony no. 4, "The Inextinguishable," op. 29 1916

"Music *is* life," said Nielsen, "and, like life, inextinguishable." This is not a program symphony, but one that "theorizes" about the human life-force in musical terms. Thus, the four movements, connected without a break, establish and interpret a basic conflict not resolved until the end. The first movement sets this up neatly with a stormy first-theme group and tender second (launched by the woodwinds), both developed thereafter in intimate opposition. There is no scherzo in the symphony; the second movement acts as a kind of idyllic interlude, lightly scored and somewhat insouciant after the tumult of the first movement. The third [slow] movement returns us to battle, opening with a high-pitched violin line and whacks on the timpani. This is the most potent challenge yet to human/musical indestructability, but—as the fourth movement proves—the life-force wins out in the end.

Symphony no. 5, op. 50 1922

Generally cited as Nielsen's masterpiece, the Fifth marked his first complete break with traditional form. No four movements here—and note, to pick one instance of innovation, the bizarre opening, a wobbling of violas with bassoons puttering around below, as if the work had already begun somewhere else and were coming in on a mysterious transitional passage. This is a piece that takes some getting used to. It is in two large sections, each section containing several separate but connected movements. Themes are shared among them, reworked, and echoed, so that, in a way, it is all one great movement in two episodic parts.

The first part comprises a "first movement" and slow movement. A disquieting anarchy prevails—woodwind squeals! military drumming! modernism!—but never does one lose confidence in Nielsen's sense of totality. The slow movement brings order and calm. Bits of the first movement wander in (the drum, especially), but peace is maintained, even if that nervy drum does break in on the closing clarinet cadenza.

The second part is moodier, more changeable. It starts fast and wild, gets faster, collapses into a slow movement, very much string-oriented, then rears up again in fast tempo for a decisive finale. Throughout, one feels that rhythmic rather than melodic "emotions" have formed the psychology of the work—as if primitive man were telling epic narrative in dance.

Symphony no. 6, "Sinfonia Semplice" 1925

The subtitle is misleading: "simple symphony." Nielsen had planned a light, easygoing work—that sort of simple. But that is not what we hear. Mixed in with idyllic good humor is much parody, grimacing, and sneers. It all starts lightly; four notes on the glockenspiel and a charming first movement presents itself, gentleman quick, not exactly reserved but at least well behaved. But the second movement, dubbed "Humoreske," is frankly mad—giggles, gurgles, and macabre concatenations of noise. If this is simplicity, it is the kind best known to the odd relations who inhabited the boarded-up attic rooms of Victorian England; anyway, it is a form of scherzo, however unusual. The third is the slow movement—Nielsen calls it "proposta seria" (serious proposal), and that it is, compared to what has preceded. After this complex layering of moods, what could more reasonably conclude the work than a fourth movement like a neo-Classical spring, putting all in order with its discipline and method? So Nielsen gives us a theme and variations. The bassoon announces the theme, unaccompanied, a few moments into the movement, and there is a full stop before the nine variations commence. The listener may have some trouble following the progress of the theme as it varies (the transformation is rather involved), but he will certainly recognize the reminders of the screwball second movement in the percussive bleeps and blats of the final variation.

Violin Concerto, op. 33 1911

In form, this is not unlike the traditional three-movement concerto, though the middle slow movement is short enough to be little more than an interval, while there is an unusually long slow introduction to the first movement, virtually a movement in itself. It's a lively piece in all, especially tricky for the soloist but fun for the listener. The introduction, which Nielsen calls "Praeludium" has the air of a Bach prelude at first, with its violin figurations, but soon settles into a pastoral mood, the soloist very much to the fore. At some length, the first movement proper starts with a dignified *tutti* (full orchestra) promptly answered by the soloist. This is a full sonata-allegro movement, complete with cadenza, and if the slow [second] movement makes the tiniest effect, Nielsen closes with a full-fledged rondo finale [third movt] as vivacious as any in the repertory. First prize to the violinist who can hurdle its hazards in one piece.

Clarinet Concerto, op. 57 1928

Five wind players—a flute, oboe, clarinet, bassoon, and horn—formed the Copenhagen Wind Quintet. Out of friendship for them, Nielsen composed a unique piece, his Wind Quintet, op. 43, in which each part mirrors the personality of the original player. For instance, the flutist was a sensitive soul, so the flute part is sensitive; the oboist was friendly, the part likewise; and so on. Then, a brainstorm: Nielsen would write five concertos in the same vein, each one specifically for—and "about"—one of the Quintet. He died after having composed only the flute concerto and the present work, built around the irascible, temperamental character of Aage Oxenfold, the Quintet's clarinettist.

Nielsen's character, while we're sketching, was prone to black mischief, and here he tests Oxenfold's famous lack of patience by bedeviling the clarinet soloist with a snare drum at odd moments of the concerto. It is a one-movement work, through interior sections give us the rough outline of a symphony's four movements: lively first section, slow section, scherzo, and finale. Though Oxenfold's querulousness informs some of the solo part, this is a charming piece, especially when the snare drum is baiting the clarinet and the clarinet is answering back. Note that at the very end the two are still at it, though the snare drum is down to the few peckish taps while the soloist is winding up a genuine melody.

Helios Overture, op. 7 1903

One full day's worth of the Greek sun—its rising out of the silent dark, its passage through the sky, its setting. The triumphant main section of the piece is heralded by blazing fanfares, which return again as the sun starts its descent at the end of the day. *Helios* closes, as it opened, in deep night—the lowest notes of the lower strings.

PAUL DUKAS 1865–1935

Dukas is one of those composers known to most people for only one piece, *The Sorcerer's Apprentice;* unfortunately, he brought this limited popularity upon himself by his very character, whch was both self-critical (and thus sparing of production, for if there were a chance of a project's not turning out superb Dukas would not chance it) and intellectual (and thus not interested in marking his work with any "popular" touch). Expert musicians know him for one item in each of several categories—a highly original piano sonata, a splendid symphony, a ballet called *La Péri* (The Fairy), and an opera of such special flavor that it remains one of the few masterpieces in the form never (as of this writing) to have been recorded, *Ariane et Barbe-Bleue* (Ariane and Bluebeard, a setting of a play by Maurice Maeterlinck very much in the gossamer, ambiguous style of Debussy's opera on a Maeterlinck text, *Pelléas et Mélisande*). Dukas kept active as a teacher (Olivier Messiaen was one of his pupils), but—holding true to his critical code—he destroyed several of his large-scale works just before his death.

Symphony in C Major 1896

Like so many French symphonies, this work is in three movements, omitting the minuet-or-scherzo movement: first movement, slow movement, finale. The first of the three opens snappily, quiets down for a lyrical second theme (in the violins), and closes its exposition with a fanfarelike march in the brasses. The development emphasizes the energy implicit in the themes, so, when the recapitulation has had its say, the overall impression is one of roiling energy cut with a touch of warmth. Note how the coda, though basically restrained, maintains an air of anxiety right up to its last brilliant reprise of the brass fanfares. The slow [second] movement, however, is more intimate, warmly tremulous in its main theme for violins and its transitional horn solo leading the ear from one section to another. In the middle of the movement, Dukas comes slightly forward, building to an expressive climax in a wind chorale. The finale [third mvt] is a virile rondo with a refrain sounded by dark instruments (bassoons, horns, and 'cellos). The intervening episodes offer moments of calm, but the prevailing atmosphere is one of exertion, a kind of lyrical self-defense in festive dress. At the end, Dukas speeds up for a thrilling coda.

The Sorcerer's Apprentice 1897

Those who have seen Walt Disney's *Fantasia* already know the story to which this "scherzo for orchestra" was set, for Mickey Mouse's adventure with the enchanted broom that won't stop heaving water around is exactly the tale that Dukas had in mind. It's an old legend, adapted by Johann Wolfgang von Goethe for a comical poem called "Der Zauberlehrling," which Dukas used as his source.

Goethe's poem is narrated by the apprentice. "For once the old witch-master has gone off," he begins; his tutor's "words and works" he has noted, and tries his hand at charming a broomstick into filling a tub for him. But he can't de-charm his broom, and when he axes it in two, his trouble doubles. At length the sorcerer returns and stills the two brooms. (The Disney version multiplies the horror with not two but an army of goon-brooms who literally flood the premises until the returning magician sweeps all, brooms and water, back to position one.) To know the tale is to follow the music at one's ease.

A mystical introduction prepares for the doings, made impenetrably bizarre by the use of string pluckings and overtones (faint "extra" notes more sensed than heard). The principal theme is gently sounded by a clarinet, echoed by an oboe echoed by a flute—very portentous, yet amusing. The mystical alternates with livelier bits until a whack of the drum silences everybody—here is where the apprentice tries his spell. It seems to be taking: a deep grunt, a couple of stirs, and the broom begins its fetch-and-carry, outlined by three bassoons (the moment is unmissable). Those mystical strings from the introduction signify the spell, the bassoon theme marks the progress of the broom, and soon the music is rolling with fanaticism—the tub is filled, but the crazy broom-thing won't stop! At the height of the noise, a sudden silence and more grunting tell of the axe blow and the renewed vigor of *two* brooms; this sees the work almost to the finish, when alarms signal the master's return. "In the corner, broomstick, broomstick! Back to nothing!" Again, the mystical strings, plus a taste of solo viola—the apprentice whining an apology?

ALYEKSANDR GLAZUNOF 1865–1936

There were two movements in Russian music when Glazunof arrived on the scene. One was the "Moscow" school of Western-minded traditionalists led by Chaikofsky; the other was the innovative nationalistic school presided over by Rimsky-Korsakof. Glazunof studied with Rimsky and is therefore associated with the all-Russians, but his large output (little of which is heard outside of Russia) of Western-styled symphonies, concertos, overtures, string quartets, and such put him in the cosmopolitan camp. It is sad to say, but true, that Glazunof's melodic gift never found an individual style for expression. He is pleasant to hear, but quickly forgotten.

Violin Concerto in a minor, op. 82 1904

Continuing the work of such Romantics as Mendelssohn and Liszt, who helped evolve a more fluid, more soloistic, and more unified concerto out of the Classical model, Glazunof (1) casts his piece in one movement containing the fast-slow-fast outline of the standard three-movement concerto, and (2) carries over his principal themes from one "movement" to the next. The work begins without surprises, as if in a first-movement exposition: the soloist opens the show with the usual first and second themes. But just where one expects a development, the tempo slows down and a "slow movement" ensues. Not till then does one get anything like a development; Glazunof builds a sort of languorous tension up to a cadenza, which leads to a "third movement" rondo, very dancey and full of fine effects for the soloist. Since the whole work is founded on the themes announced at the start, it would be intriguing to follow their evolution through the piece. Unfortunately, Glazunof's themes so lack in distinction that one cannot remember them from one minute to the next.

JEAN SIBELIUS 1865–1957

Sibelius is one of those composers who has benefited from the acclimatizing influence of modern technology—radio concerts, television relays, the LP recording. The who's who in music is an elastic list; names are constantly being added or subtracted. Forty years ago, Sibelius amounted to the short pieces *Finlandia* and *Valse Triste,* the violin concerto, and occasional playings of the Second and Fifth Symphonies. Now, he is abundance, with three symphonies in the regular repertory (nos. 2, 4, and 5) and constant attention to numerous smaller works.

Sibelius is certainly no "difficult" modern, overturning one's expectations of what is beautiful or useful in music. Some of his output is "easier" than the rest, beautiful to the lay ear—and useful to the lazy mind. There are those who can hear *Finlandia* endlessly who will not willingly sit through the forbidding Fourth Symphony a second time. But there are just so many ears to go around, of whatever ambitions, and Sibelius achieved international recognition in the public (as opposed to the critical) sector late in life, long after the year in which he ceased to compose, 1929. As so often in the past, one had to get used to the style, the personal mode; this takes time, repeated hearings. Thus the helpful agency of technological communications in bringing Sibelius home.

It was a far trip. His native country, Finland, is cut off from the Western mainstream by its non-Western language—too difficult for anyone but a Finn to want to speak—and even now a insurgent generation of Finnish composers finds it hard to transmit its talents in foreign climes. Culturally isolated, a solitary, Sibelius dug into his privacy and went his own way musically, resisting—or, more likely, remaining unaware of—the isms of his contemporaries elsewhere in Europe. There is no jazz here, no music hall, no neo-Classical parody, no satiric opera (no opera at all, anyway), no "decadence," no atonalism, no electronic nonsense. A late Romantic, heir to the Wagner generation, Sibelius stayed late-Romantic, never experiencing the dissolution that overtook so many of Wagner's inheritors. They tried to create more Wagner too late, or had to explode Wagner in revoltion, creating anti-Wagner that most people don't want to hear. Sibelius simply created some Sibelius.

Carrying on the nineteenth-century urge toward unity, Sibelius wrote two traditionally structured symphonies and then began to experiment, economizing on the recapitulatory passages that lengthen the Classical-Romantic symphonies. From his Third on, Sibelius' symphonic movements take forms not tried before—leaner, abrupt, not quite finished when the next movement begins. Thus, the Seventh Symphony is written in one long movement. As with Schumann's Fourth Symphony, interior sections (movements) are clearly outlined, but the release of tension in Sibelius's Seventh occurs only at the very end of the work rather than at the ends of separate movements.

Concomitant with Sibelius' groping for unity is his ability to color a work, however long, with one overriding tone, subtle but definable, so that a symphony's four movements exhibit the characteristic "bent" of the whole even in their variety. The classic example of this is the thrillingly dramatic (but to some ears overbearingly gloomy) Fourth Symphony, one of the great realizations of thematic, rhythmic, and harmonic organization in the symphonic form. Those less attracted by compositional processes than by a good time, however, cannot be disappointed here, for, while Sibelius is no anthologist, culling the outback for folk tunes, he does capture a folklike innocence in his melodies. Too, most of his tone-poem subjects derive from Finnish legend, adding to the general air of folk culture that seems to light his music like Arctic sun, for Sibelius' time was one of fierce nationalistic renaissance, when centuries of foreign domination (by Sweden and Russia) gave way to Finnish independence. There is no escaping the feeling that all of Sibelius' music aims to evoke the atmosphere of fjord and forest—is, somehow, telling a Finnish tale. The panorama is felt in sound, not sound pictures, however; this is personal and secret imagery of an entirely musical basis. *Finlandia,* his most popular work, invariably suggests icy Finnish vastnesses to its listeners—but the suggestion is all in the title, which might easily be changed to *Alaska* or *The Creation of the World* with no loss of resonance.

Symphony no. 1 in e minor, op. 39 1899

This is wonderful music, every note, polished with fire and ice and, in Sibelius' fashion, emphasizing neither rhythm nor harmony but melody, a tune burning in the strings over metallic throbbings in the bass instruments. But as intellectuals, we want more than melody; we ask, what does a first symphony tell us of a composer? He *feels,* yes—so do we all—but how much does he *know?*

Received opinion among professional tends to patronize this work. Certainly, Sibelius demonstrates his knowledge of form as it had evolved down to him. How confidently did he evolve it *past* him here? Critics have no quarrel with the first three movements. This first is dramatic, portentous, opening with a lonely call on clarinet over rumbling drums, dying away and then cut off by the emergence of the first movement proper—a siren cry on the violins, a rush of melody, and the brisk pace is set. The second [slow] movement, too, satisfies unqualifiedly, with its back-and-forth of tranquillity and passion. And the scherzo [third mvt] is in Beethoven's forthright vein; its trio tune (middle section) is adapted from the main theme of the slow movement.

The finale [fourth mvt], however, is where "experts" shake their heads. Here is evolution, suddenly, three fourths of the way through. Sibelius knew what he was doing—he labeled the finale "quasi una fantasia" (like a fantasy), meaning free in form and therefore exempt from all rules except its own. In tone, at least, it concludes the work nicely, jumping from static melodic periods to bursts of energy and back again. Moreover, it opens with several versions of the clarinet theme that opened the whole symphony, lending a sense of overall unity. But perhaps we expect even more of a last movement, something to answer questions raised in earlier movements, something finalized, done. Does the finale *finish* the symphony? Listener, decide.

Symphony no. 2 in D Major, op. 43 1901

Sibelius' most popular symphony begins, after some preliminary string thrumming, in the woodwinds, folklike. But a tension soon complicates matters and a first-rate sonata-allegro movement is off and running, though it sometimes pauses as if listening for its own echo. Unlike the grand, extended melodies of the 1880s, these of Sibelius tend to be short, strands to be tied together in repetition and variation. Note the peculiar character of the sound, so suggestive (at least to suggestible ears) of icy Finnish nature spaces, firs neath a midnight sun.

The second [slow] movement climbs out of plucked lower strings into the main theme of the bassoon, a dour, almost Russian-sounding tune fit for Rimsky-Korsakof. Tranquil lyricism is disturbed by roughhewn outcries; much of the movement is snarling, restless drama, and already we expect a powerful last movement to conclude the antagonism of song bedeviled by fury.

Before the finale, however, comes the intercession of the scherzo [third mvt]—talk about restless! It flies headlong until the trio (middle section), heralded by the timpani, appears in the cool idyll of the oboe. This does not last long; the flying throws us onward. But the trio is repeated. Here is the oboe again, backed up by other instruments, spreading its pastoral ease until a gathering swell in the orchestra leads us without a pause into a strangely short-circuited announcement of the rocking first theme of the finale [fourth mvt], which shortly restates itself, now complete and superb. A warm second theme redoubles the sense of achieved calm, though the urgency of the middle movements hovers about, still not expunged. This last movement is a fine example of old-fashioned sonata-allegro, with a clearly marked development section following the exposition just where the 'cellos fiddle variants on the first theme. The entire development amounts to one long crescendo (gradually growing louder) leading up to a tremendous restatement of the first theme (first in its original fragmented form, then in full cry) that ushers in the recapitulation. Here, again, are all the themes heard earlier in the movement, now placed against an undercurrent of anticipation leading up to the last triumphant statement of the first theme, sounding like a cosmic organ, all stops pulled and pedals pounding.

Symphony no. 3 in C Major, op. 52 1907

The first of Sibelius' purely Sibelian (as we call them) symphonies, no. 3 leaves the more traditional nos. 1 and 2 behind in the past as art races on. Now, Sibelius' symphonies grow more compact, less rhetorical but just as dramatic. Thus, no. 3's first movement uses the true sonata-allegro of old, with first theme (the opening), second theme (in the 'cellos), closing theme (on the violins), development, recapitulation, and coda—but how much more fleet this time than in the two earlier symphonies. The folkloric Sibelius of the pastoral dances is only hinted at in the first movement, but he dominates the pleasing second [slow] movement, one of those vaguely pictorial processionals so useful to the symphony when Mendelssohn and Berlioz were around and Romance was in the air. Only one movement remains now, for Sibelius has combined the scherzo and finale into one idea, blending the one's rhythmic force with the other's dramatic power. (Concision!) At first a churning, seemingly timeless whirl, the last movement unexpectedly becomes broad and sonorous on a 'cello tune and works up a grand climax.

Symphony no. 4 in a minor, op. 63 1911

A masterpiece of symphonic organization, eloquent but stark and sullen, not for all tastes. In four movements, it does not accord with the traditional plan of lively end movements surrounding a slow movement and scherzo. Here we get first a slow movement, then a scherzo, another slow movement, and a reasonably lively finale. As so often with Sibelius, each movement relates to the others in terms of atmosphere—one could not imagine any one of these four serving in any other of Sibelius' symphonies.

Even less could one imagine their turning up in another composer's work. For after his first and second symphonies, Sibelius cut himself off from traditional procedures in the structuring of symphonic movement. Not for him, now, the luxury of development sections and recapitulations. His design is tight, sinewy with thematic transformation, stingy with the repetitions that give the ear a chance to assimilate material. The first-time listener is bound to fall behind in a work such as this: it all happens so suddenly. Even the two slow movements seem to outrace one's concentration. But, as with so much of the complex orchestral writing of the twentieth century, a second or third hearing yields perspective; details fall into place, while principal subjects stand out in relief.

The first movement opens low and loud on bassoons, 'cellos, and contrabasses, ceding to a plaintive 'cello solo, the first theme. This builds to a climax, seized by the strings for a rising-falling second theme, and the movement proceeds as so many first movements have before it, into development (odd, muted string figurations derived from the opening bars and embellished with flights of flute and clarinet) and recapitulation (shortened for economy, clarity). The first movement dies away to echoes of the opening, and the second [scherzo] movement picks up on the desolated air in an oboe solo. This is the folksy (though not jolly) Sibelius; for further economy, he ends the movement after the trio (the traditional middle section) without repeating the first section as his predecessors always did.

Everything here is lean—that is the strength of these symphonies of the mature Sibelius—and the third [slow] movement provides not the reflective, lyrical lift of a Mozartean slow movement but a deepening of the work's overall tension. Enervated, almost torn apart, this movement, too, fades away, collapses. The finale [fourth mvt] seeks regeneration, then, more through a kind of musical atonement than through any dramatic triumph. It moves quickly, utilizing some novel touches of scoring, especially in a bizarre passage for rippling, whispering strings, gliding up and down repeatedly, while a glockenspiel sounds a tuneless signal above. The symphony ends, as it began, in a minor: flute and oboe exchange little solos, and the strings close the book.

Symphony no. 5 in E Flat Major,
op. 82 1915; revised 1918

One of the great experiments in the modern symphony: in renovating tradition for new forces of expression. The method codified by Haydn, Mozart, and Beethoven still guides Sibelius in the shape and thrust of this work; but there is novel practice, and novel results. The first movement, for instance, is really two versions of itself, back to back: first a slowish, powerful opening, than a scherzo using the same melodic materials but in a completely different atmosphere. The first half is tense, besieged; it veers and groans. The second half is light, frisky. This is not a first movement simply joined to a second movement—it is *one* movement, for the second [scherzo] half continues the development of themes begun in the first half. It is neither sequel nor transition but continuation. Note the horn theme at the very outset of the first movement, echoed by woodwinds; this is the basis for much that follows. At first, the music may sound less like a movement itself and more like the slow introduction to one, but if this is introduction, it is a long one. The horn is seldom out of hearing, and at one point, when it seems to have reached a climax, the tempo picks up suddenly in a kind of folk-waltz, and the scherzo half of the movement takes over, lifting that horn theme into lively reaches of flute and strings. Soon, the orchestra hits one huge holding pattern of rhythmic tension, faster, louder, pounding the point home.

The second [slow] movement reminds one of a Haydn or Mozart slow movement, with its variations, one after another, on a simple tune. Comes then the odd finale [third mvt]: first theme, second theme, first theme repeated, second theme repeated. The first is a lissome rushing in the strings into which the second unobtrusively wanders. You'll know it when you hear it, for it is one of the most distinctive moments in symphony: a series of slowish but decisive horn signals accompanied by a thrilling countermelody in the woodwinds and 'cellos. Then the first theme slips back in, a little more pregnantly expressed this time, clearly building up to something. Sure enough, the countermelody of the second theme turns up again on flute and clarinet (without, at first, the horn tune), then, as the pace broadens, on the strings as well. The horn call returns, now on the trumpet, and the climax that we have been expecting is reached in the most jarring moment in all of Sibelius: two antagonistic keys going great guns simultaneously. E Flat, the work's home key, wins out in six tutti (full orchestra) chords, thunderous yet austere.

Symphony no. 6 in d minor, op. 104 1923

This serene, even repressed, work has never quite caught on except among Sibelians. The question is, how dramatic must a symphony be—what dynamic melding of melody on rhythm on harmony over the course of several movements is "the minimum"? Conversely, when is a symphony not a symphony?—when it fails to build that arch of climax and release?

But a symphony sets its own objectives; ask yourself, what are its premises? There are four movements—but not the usual four movements. By this time, the last years of his active career, Sibelius had passed the boundary of traditional structuring, past your conventional developments and recapitulations. The first movement opens with an opaque passage for strings, followed by a slightly less diaphanous passage for flutes and oboes. Though the music eventually does pick up somewhat in tone and tempo, it is all rather placid, only dreamily exuberant when it troubles to assert itself—hardly the strong first movement we have come to expect of a symphony. Similary, the slow [second] movement avoids slowness, as if Sibelius had outlawed the "extremes" of symphonic drama, phasing everything down to its moderate essence. The scherzo [third mvt] yields some vitality, but the finale [fourth mvt] keeps a spiritual ceiling on things even as it does open up a little.

A mellow symphony, then. The Sixth does not so much lack drama as resist it, preferring its own interior quasi-drama of themes lapping themes like ruffles on the surface of a stream. No stream can rival the running river—but it knows where it's going, and gets there.

Symphony no. 7 in C Major, op. 105 1924

The drive toward symphonic unity that obsessed so many composers of the 1800s led some of them to attempt one-movement symphonies, though within the one span the definitions of separate movements were easy to spot. There was no real merging of parts, no *organic* unity. All they were doing was attaching the end of one movement to the beginning of the next. A forced cohesion. Arriving at the end of the nineteenth century, Sibelius took up this unfinished business and, in this work especially, finished it. His trick was to dispense with the traditional format of each movement-type (such as the ABA or variation form of the slow movement or the scherzo-and-trio), compressing them structurally. In Sibelius, movements may be so compressed as to sound unfinished. One wants more—and this provides the necessary tension, the ear's eagerness.

Sibelius so revised symphonic form in this piece that at first he thought he'd better call it Fantasia Sinfonica (Symphonic Fantasy), fantasy meaning free in form. But this freedom stretches to fill a symphonic space: one movement, containing several short movements. Analysts disagree as to their number, usually citing either three or five. If there are three movements, the plan is roughly:

slow mvt	scherzo (with slow trio)	slow finale

If five movements:

slow intro	scherzo I	slow mvt	scherzo II	slow finale

The five-movement interpretation states things more clearly, for slow introduction, middle slow movement, and slow finale are a based on the same material (featuring long-lined, epic utterances in the brass instruments). Thus Sibelius compresses: he does not use the traditional recapitulations of the Classical and Romantic symphony in each movement (section), but delays one essential recapitulation till the end of the entire work. Always stirring, moving from heavy to light and back to heavy, it's quite a work.

Violin Concerto in d minor,
op. 47 1903; revised 1905

Sibelius' sole essay in the concerto is irresistible, full of the shimmering lushness and rhythmic ferocity of Sibelius the melodist and nicely developed from section to section by Sibelius the "dramatist." Though close examination reveals novel details of construction in the all-important first movement, more generally the work will not surprise devotees of the traditional concerto from Mozart to Chaikofsky. This is a very moody first movement, caustic as often as rhapsodic, with unexpected cadenzas (the soloist's showy solos) plunked down early as well as late in the movement. An expansive development section forces the melodic elements of the principal themes wide apart, and the somewhat scattered recapitulation does not bring them all together—that sense of release waits for the slow [second] movement, a more positive affair harried by orchestral outbursts but soothed by the soloist's glowing theme. For his finale [third mvt], Sibelius takes to the major key for a dourly prancing rondo. Is it perhaps *too* prancy, considering the gravity of the first movement? Doesn't the first movement pose questions only partly answered in the slow movement and totally ignored in the finale? Maybe not. This is, for all its vigor, an imposing dance; at times, it seems to refer back, in tone, to the testier pages of the first movement. It's a fit finale for a concerto, all right, but its passion bears an Arctic tension under the rhythmic sport.

Four Legends from the Kalevala:

Lemminkäinen and the Maidens of Saari,
op. 22, #1 1895; revised 1897

la, op. 22,
1900
n in Tuonela, op. 22,
95; revised 1897
mminkäinen Journeys Homeward,
op. 22, #4 1896; revised 1900

The Finnish epic, the Kalevala, tells of heroes, maidens, love, death, and wonders, as epics will. These four tone poems—listed above in the preferred order for integral performance—abstract certain episodes of the saga. They do not narrate exactly, but the evocative power of Sibelius' music astonishes even as it draws back from the listener in possessive remoteness. (Like the "Ancient Eight" of Hungarian verse, to which it is related, Finnish epic poetry favors trochaic tetrameter, the scan that Longfellow made notorious in *Hiawatha.*)

The first of the quartet tells of the Kalevala's hero Lemminkäinen and his elopement with the belle of Saari village, one Kyllikki. Soaring with the lad's love, frolicsome for the dancing maidens of Saari, the music eventually comes to favor the former and becomes a valentine of barbaric gallantry.

Second in narrative order is the best known of the quartet, *The Swan of Tuonela.* Lemminkäinen has been dispatched to kill the swan as part of his suit to win fair Kylliki. Tuonela is the equivalent of the underworld in Finnish mythology; the swan floats around it on a black river singing a plangent song. Sibelius hit on a devastatingly simple musical depiction: shimmering strings for atmosphere and a solo English horn (perhaps the most plangent of all instruments) for the swan's concert. At one point the strings usurp the melody, all playing on the same notes. The English horn returns, though the last word of all is had by a solo 'cello.

If the first of this quartet was joyful and the second doleful, *Lemminkäinen in Tuonela* is frightsome, telling of the hero's death by snake bite:

> Lemminkäinen thus did perish,
> Perished thus the fearful suitor,
> In the dark of Death's own river,
> In the depths of Tuonela.

The scoring here is unusually depictive, using the instruments to comment on the tragedy of the hero's death even as they "act" it out.

However, Lemminkäinen's mother manages to bring him back to life with medicines and magic, and he and his sidekick Tiera have quite a time reaching home again, what with getting shipwrecked and lost in a forest and nearly dying of starvation and exposure. These events, in a general way, comprise *Lemminkäinen Journeys Homeward,* built almost entirely of portentous scurrying figures that keep leading up to but do not quite reach a climax until the piece is almost over. Then, a cymbal crash, and we're into a triumphant coda.

Karelia Suite, op. 11 1893

Named for the section of Finland that inspired it (and drawn from music written for a historical pageant), this three-movement suite is rich in folk-quality (but original with Sibelius) tunes. (Sibelius' op. 10, by the way, is the *Karelia* Overture, almost never played.) First comes an Intermezzo, led off by horn calls over tensely muted strings. This quickly develops into quite a parade until the distant air of the opening returns—a hunting party nearing, passing, and moving on. Second is a Ballad, in minuet tempo, featuring some charming instrumental touches—a running 'cello accompaniment shortly after the beginning and an English horn solo over plucked strings toward the end. Last comes a March, full of bounce. The whole business is simple, but cleverly arranged. In our complex world, innocence is achieved, not born.

Incidental Music from Pelléas et Mélisande, op. 46 1905

Maurice Maeterlinck's delicate legendlike play, silk spun of glass, deals with a prince and his gossamer bride, who loves the prince's half-brother. Sibelius wrote music for a production of the play, then extracted several numbers, all wonderfully atmospheric and scored with a light touch for theatre (i.e., small) orchestra. The first piece, "At the Castle Gate," introduces the state of affairs in the kingdom of Allemonde, grave and solid—not the ideal climate for the inertly capricious Mélisande, characterized in the second piece in the fragile simplicity of the English horn. A waltzlike middle section makes a pass at gaiety, but the prevailing somberness chokes it. (A short interval, "At the Seashore," follows "Mélisande," but is often cut.) The third number sets the scene for "A Fountain in the Park": more waltz, more failure to rise above the suffocating dankness of the castle. "The Three Blind Sisters," a song in the play, is scored here for English horn solo followed by a minor-key folkish tune on two clarinets. The air lightens in the woodwindy "Pastorale," a gentle dance that is for many the highlight of the suite—note the continued presence of the English horn. "Mélisande at the Spinning Wheel," self-describing, returns us to the odd mixture of soap opera and faerie that informs Maeterlinck's concept. The seventh piece, an Entr'acte, precedes Act IV with courtly athleticism. More in tune with the drama is "The Death of Mélisande," restrained, then passionate, then restrained again, fading away like the heroine.

En Saga, op. 9 1892; revised 1901

A wildly evocative tone poem devoted to the idea of heroic legend—savagery, magic, romance. There is no specific program. The composer leaves it to the listener to fill in for himself with imagery if he so chooses—taking the mysterious introduction, say, as a camera pan across and down into a troll-infested forest. If you so choose. Mainly, the work fascinates as sheer music. Note how Sibelius creates terrific suspense in that introduction by juxtaposing fragments of themes in the woodwinds with obscure, flightly warnings for *divisi* strings ("divided"—that is, with more than the usual number of separate string parts). At length the music gets louder, faster, more intent, and the movement proper takes off like a ballad of blood and guts strummed on a huge guitar. Don't try to follow the first theme-second theme of sonata-allegro here; the form is individual, though tightly organized. Seldom has a procession of themes felt so spontaneously narrative; each episode works into the next with whiplash inevitability. Eventually a last climactic *tutti* (full orchestra) brings things to a head, and the sounds fade away, closing with one of the principal themes on solo clarinet and another on the 'cellos. Note how the dying melody passes from the 'cellos as a group to a solo 'cello at the very end. Silence in the forest.

Pohjola's Daughter, op. 49 1906

Another of Sibelius' gleanings from Finnish legend, sometimes also called *The Daughter of the North.* A tone poem, it recounts the courtship of a coquettish fairy maid by a vigorous old man who is put through a series of feats to win her—tying an egg into knots, cutting a cake of ice without making any splinters, and such. The sober opening, with its 'cello solo, is typical of Sibelius' ability to conjure up the *sense* of storytelling without actually depicting an event or character. The music soon grows horribly fraught, but cedes to a gentler passage marked by harp and English horn. Next come highly allusive passages (allusive of what, though? We seem to hear the girl's laughter, at any rate), then more dramatic uproar: as legend tells, the old man suffers a grievous wound while pressing his suit. At length the flow of blood is stanched, and philosophical serenity calms the old man's aspiring heart.

Tapiola, op. 112 1925

Tapio is the forest god of Finnish mythology, Tapiola his domain. But if this is a pastorale, it is an uncommonly frenzied one, dominated by the opening striking theme. Episodes suggesting the vast tracts of the northern forests vie with others suggesting the power held static in that mighty wooden army, and so it progresses, from woodwind carols to tumultuous *tutti*s, taking time to suggest timelessness, spacing out its sections to suggest immeasurable expanses. Sibelius is, of course, celebrated for the pictorial allusiveness of his music, but here he has restrained his dramatic spontaneity to achieve the sense of nothing, ever, happening.

Finlandia, op. 26, #7 1899

Not an important but certainly a popular item, this tone poem evokes the natural splendor of Sibelius' native country. A stirring introduction ushers in a lively passage bolstered by drums, cymbals, and triangle, which cedes to an expressive melodic section, hushed with awe of homeland. This is followed by a repeat of the lively passage and a colossal closing.

Valse Triste (Sad Waltz) 1903

The blameless but shallow bit of salon music, part of the incidental score written for a play, *Kuolema* (Death), is, as the title says, a sad waltz. (In the play it is less sad than macabre, for it is danced by a woman in the arms of Death, whom she has mistaken for her late husband.) It is a medley of waltz tunes defty scored for theatre (small) orchestra, capped by three sad chords played by four solo violins.

FERRUCCIO BUSONI 1866–1924

Highly sensual in his sound but deeply intellectual in his approach to composition, Busoni could have been a hero in one of Thomas Mann's tales, the artist torn between the abstracts of his mission on one hand and envy of the simpler, coarse soul of the unobsessed on the other. By blood half German and half Italian, Busoni tried to balance the two, spinning out his Latin song with a Northerner's intellectualism. Busoni was teacher, analyst, conductor, and opera librettist as well as composer, but his times preferred him in a sixth guise as piano virtuoso, as which he was surpassed by no one even in that heyday of virtuosity.

Immersed in the past, responsible to the future, trying to juggle the two into a workable synthesis that would help carry forward the march of art, Busoni was suitable more for legend than popular success. Almost everything he did amounted to a revolution in genre: his piano concerto is in five movements and calls for male chorus, his operas are either "too" short and satirical (*Turandot* and *Arlecchino*) or "too" long and metaphysical (*Doktor Faust*), his piano music too thrilled with Bachian or Lisztian archetypes and too difficult to play. In the 1950s, American television used to program dramas about mad pianists who wrote their colleagues out of the record by composing piano pieces that only they themselves could play—what nonsense! But Busoni actually did this, in his *Fantasia Contrappuntistica* (Contrapuntal Fantasy). He didn't plan it that way; he was just too far ahead of his fellow pianists. His public, too. And we still haven't caught up.

Piano Concerto 1904

Seldom heard because it's such an expensive proposition (a male chorus is needed for the last movement) and also because the piano part is exceedingly difficult without being exhibitionistic, this is one of the great piano concertos ever. Its neglect is an outrage, perpetrated first by Berlin's idiot music critics, who had been gunning for Busoni ever since he introduced a concert series emphasizing new composers (such as Debussy, Sibelius, Nielsen, and Bartók), and continued by timid programmers and disdainful pianists who don't see the point in a concerto that makes them work hard without showing them off.

It's a long work, five movements lasting about an hour. Each movement has been titled generically: the first movement is "Prologue and Introit" (the first complete section of the Mass), the second "Light Piece," the third "Serious Piece," the fourth "Tarantella," the fifth "Song." Thus, instead of the three-movement fast-slow-fast of tradition, Busoni's concerto breaks down into the more expansive:

intro and 1st mvt	scherzo	slow mvt	2nd scherzo	choral finale
1	2	3	4	5

This is structure nobly balanced, for—with the third movement as a root and core—the other movements relate to each other in pairs, sharing themes and moods, the two scherzos as one pair and the outer movements as another.

There is the intellectual-emotional drive of true symphony here, the engine of Beethoven, Brahms, and Mahler, and the purely musical satisfaction—the tunes—is rich. A Brahmsian fiery melancholy endows the first movement, which opens with a full orchestral *tutti* (the statement of themes) at great length before the piano utters a note. The first of the two scherzos [second mvt] is a pungently rhythmic study that sees the piano through the sort of "soloist in conflict with the orchestra" dialogue that sparked so many nineteenth-century concertos—and this dialogue provides the dramatic basis for the slow [third] movement, one of the most beautiful yet assertive such movements to be heard. As a star pianist himself, Busoni knew as well as anyone how to make the instrument sing, and here the concerto principle is electrically activated for confrontation, duel, and treaty. The air is cleared in the second scherzo [fourth mvt] in which both piano and orchestra collaborate on a rather lofty spoof of the frenetic Italian dance, the tarantella. Somehow or other a march insinuates itself into the bumpy texture, a theme from the first scherzo lights in, and a tremendous ka-boom! on the timpani leads to the soloist's cadenza (the concerto's traditional solo "show" spot). Here is where most concertos would end, with this sportive dance. But Busoni has more to tell. Comes now the finale [fifth mvt], with six-part (that is, five lines of "harmony" under the melody) men's chorus singing lines from Oehlenschläger's poem *Aladdin*. This chorus is not just of the movement, it *is* the movement, based on a theme first heard in the first movement (balance!) and offering a thrilling hymn to the eternal life-and-death in the relationship of man and God.

Violin Concerto in D Major 1897

The sound will remind many listeners of Brahms. But since Busoni was a radical (and Brahms a conservative), there is always something odd going on with even the most traditional-sounding passages. In the end, it is all Busoni. It is also all one movement, though a sectional analysis reveals the equivalents of first movement, scherzo, slow movement, and lively finale—like a symphony rather than a concerto. Moreover, these sections are not merely joined at the edges, but are fully integrated into a wholeness by means of the themes, which keep turning up from section to section.

Turandot Suite 1906

A suite is frequently just a collection of excerpts from an opera, ballet, or the incidental music to a play. But in this case the suite came *before* the complete score, by about a decade. *Turandot* is a fantastic fairy tale play by Carlo Gozzi, the eighteenth-century Venetian who revived the grotesque, earthy style of commedia dell'arte (which had fallen into disuse) with a series of extravagant, pantalunatic romances blending every aspect of theatre from tragedy to farce. Eventually, Busoni was to adapt Gozzi's *Turandot* into a shortish opera (some years before Puccini's better-known version of the same source), but first he wrote this cycle of pieces designed to mirror in musical forms the various extremes of Venetian commedia while retaining objectivity: a distillation, in the neo-Classical manner.

The suite does not narrate the tale of the icy virgin princess of China who succumbs to an unknown prince who answers her three riddles. Rather, the suite comments on Gozzi's genre. First is a march, "The Execution [of Turandot's most recent suitor], The City Gates, the Farewell." Then another march for "Truffaldino," a traditional rascal of commedia. Gravely, Busoni introduces "Altoum," the Emperor of China, "Turandot" herself, and "The Harem," to the tune of "Greensleeves." Then comes "Dance and Song," followed by a "Nocturnal Waltz." A "Funeral March and Turkish Finale" concludes, "Turkish" here meaning not literally "of Turkey" but referring to the cymbals-and-triangle oriental orchestration identified as "Turkish" in Mozart's era.

ALBERT ROUSSEL 1869–1937

When Roussel arrived on the scene, French music was just undergoing the revolution of impressionism, that lush, somewhat ambiguous category of sound typified in such a work as Debussy's *La Mer* (The Sea), in which traditional symphonic form is less interesting to the composer than his ineffable evocation of the waves and depths of the ocean. At the same time, a little neo-Classical era brought to Europe—to France especially—a renewed interest in the economical directness of the sounds pursued by Haydn and Mozart, as opposed to Debussy's mysterious inventions and the vastnesses of late Romanticism (as in, for example, Bruckner's and Mahler's huge symphonies). Roussel felt that modern impressionism and old Classicism might be blended. At various times in his career he favored one or the other. But in general we get a feeling in Roussel of Romantic flair combined with Classical order, a willingness to bend music to modern harmonic practices while keeping its structural vitality firm.

Symphony no. 3 in g minor, op. 42 1930

Admirers of the standard four-movement symphony will approve: sonata-allegro first movement, ternary (ABA) slow movement, dancing scherzo, light and mercurial finale. A very Rousselian air of exoticism hangs about the edges of the piece, but most of it carries the sophisticated innocence of ritual neo-Classicism. Notice, for example, the dancing fugue (sophistication) that drops into the middle section of the slow [second] movement on the woodwinds (innocence). For some reason, the work grows lighter in tone as it goes along: the square-cut assertiveness of the first movement and the *Adagio* (very slow) fullness of the second give way to a boulevardier's idea of a scherzo—a waltz, in fact—and a very slender finale in pert Haydnesque style. The concertmaster (the leader of the first violin section, and, by tradition, of the whole orchestra) gets so much solo work in the piece that he will probably be urged to take a bow at the finish.

Symphony no. 4 in A Major, op. 53 1934

The severely neo-Classical Roussel is in evidence here, with a four-movement work to hold the conservative line at a time when oddly shaped (not to mention odd-sounding) symphonies were the rage. Starting off with a slow introduction, Roussel brings in an almost Gershwinesque theme on the English horn that will come to prominence in the second movement; the first movement proper gets going with an *Allegro con brio* (lively with vigor). Then the slow [second] movement, the heart of the symphony, long and rich, pondering its own effusion even as it gushes—that is neo-Classicism for you. The scherzo [third mvt], a gallumphing march, bridges the gap between the recesses of the slow movement and the festive finale [fourth mvt], which begins lightly and soon grows downright impish, with more Gershwinesque touches. This finale is so well constructed that it says all it needs to in what seems like a minute. Precision!—that was the cry of the age.

Sinfonietta for String Orchestra, op. 52 1934

A sinfonietta is a compressed symphony; here, Roussel compresses the instrumentation as well as the size, using only strings. Classicists should not fret: *most* of the forms are scrupulously observed. Instead of our standard layout [first mvt, slow mvt, scherzo, and finale], we get [shortened first mvt, tiny slow mvt, and finale]. It's like a concerto without a soloist. The very short middle movement grows rather intense, and its unexpected leap into the finale (no break between movements) comes as a relief. A graceful piece, highly—as usual with Roussel—rhythmic.

Suites from Bacchus et Ariane 1930

Most composers enjoy setting a ballet score now and then; as Roussel had a natural rhythmic gift, he set more than most. *However.*

What does a composer do with the music if the ballet doesn't become an overnight classic like Leonard Bernstein's *Fancy Free?* Except for the odd revival, the work simply lies on the shelf. Roussel did the smart (also the usual) thing in making two suites of his music for the ballet *Bacchus and Ariane*—but why waste a note? Others extract the best "bits." Roussel extracted the whole thing: Act I became Suite no. 1; Act II, Suite no. 2. The latter is by far more popular.

Don't worry about the story. Ballets being what they are, not much happens. Do notice how spry the music is, supple, sumptuous, comical—it's so good it sounds better without the dancing.

ALYEKSANDR SKRYABIN 1872–1915

Skryabin would have made a good Californian: cults of transcendence and apocalypse were right up his alley. Artistically and intellectually nourished in a Russia increasingly drawn to mysticism and megalomania, he began his career as a pianist-composer of Chopin-like coloration. Later, he took on the blazing, outspoken gaudy of the screwball prophet. Devising a revolutionary harmonic code all his own which was never taken up by any followers (events like Skryabin are produced on a one-shot basis only), he envisioned a messianic role for music. In a few vigorous piano sonatas and works scored for immense orchestras, he stated the case for a "dematerialization" in human life, a soaring beyond the earthly into final mysteries of the spirit.

He was swinging wild. The inscription on the Fifth Piano Sonata reads, "I call you forth to life, hidden influences, sunk in the obscure depths of the Creative Spirit, timid germs of life, I bring you boldness!" His markings for performance left the *lamentoso* and *vivace* of tradition behind: "like a winged caress," "like a shout," "limpid," "threatening," and, to say the least, "strange." For his *Prometheus,* a symphony including piano solo and chorus, he called for a *clavier à lumières,* a piano that "played" colors (projected around the concert hall in clouds and beams of light) instead of notes.

Whether or not one feels ready to follow Skryabin into ecstatic realms, there is much to enjoy in the sweep of his music. Historically, the influence that Skryabin might have exerted was overshadowed by Arnold Schönberg's concurrent revolution, more imposing as compositional technique and without the dizzy metaphysics that tended to embarrass Skryabin's undoubted talent. Schönberg's pieces are the touchstones, Skryabin's only curiosities. But, egad, they don't lack flair.

Symphony no. 4: The Poem of Ecstasy, op. 54 1908

"A Sensual Spectacular!" crows the album cover of a recent recording. "Soaring, surging, shimmering music of naked exaltation!" No doubt Skryabin himself would have seconded the motion, for the erotic was a major component of his mysticism, and the size of the orchestra definitely counts this work among the "spectaculars" of the twentieth century. Cast in one episodic movement, it yearns before it surges, pushing solo instruments to the fore intertwined with sinuous violin lines. Tension sets in with a strong trumpet assertion (one of the main themes in the work), but no, tension drops away, and the luxuriating string sound recurs.

But the trumpet insists, and it takes over. Now the music does tighten up, though it soon relaxes again for more languid caresses. This is the "Poem of Ecstasy," a confrontation of the lazy with the athletic, culminating in a sublimation of the latter when the trumpet theme crashes out in the horns (eight of them, double the usual number), trumpet, organ, bells, and harp while the other instruments wave around them. Skryabin hoped to reclaim humanity from materialism to spirituality with this music, but the piece served more successfully as the accompaniment to a distastefully exquisite ballet arranged so Margot Fonteyn could play an aging artiste reliving her several affairs with younger men amidst a lot of art nouveau drapery.

Symphony no. 5: Prometheus: The Poem of Fire, op. 60 1911

A leading piano part (and a wordless chorus, sometimes replaced by organ) adds to the sumptuousness of this work, one mystical movement scored for large orchestra. Apparently, every theme carried a metaphysical connotation for the composer—the Creative Principle, the Will, and so on—thus making *Prometheus* a wrestling match of flesh and spirit. Moreover, Skryabin composed the piece in his idiosyncratic harmonic system and wrote the piano solo part around his own considerable gifts: in all, a highly personal statement, one that the average listener can hardly hope to receive on the desired level of response. Rather than try to sort through Skryabin's complex program, accept the work as a characteristic outgrowth of late Romanticism, with its cult of personality, its fulsome harmonics, its enthralled sense of mission, its exploded sensationalism. And try to wonder how much more the experience might be worth if today's performances obeyed Skryabin's requisition of a keyboard instrument designed to play (project) colors instead of notes. At least once that anyone knows of, the New York premiere in 1915, such a machine was used—although, rather than cast the colors in the form of light beams and clouds, it simply hurled them flat against a screen. New York was not amused.

Piano Concerto in f sharp minor, op. 20 1897

An early piece, dating from before messianic eroticism obsessed the composer's work; it may strike listeners as a cross between Chopin and Rachmaninof. It has the former's delicacy, the latter's power, and opts for the standard format of the late-Romantic concerto: three movements (fast-slow-fast), a dominating role for the soloist (the piano enters at the start and is seldom silent thereafter), much passion in the first movement, sensuous gentility in the second, exhibition of technique in the third.

RALPH VAUGHAN WILLIAMS 1872–1958

English music, which had been dead for a century, revived with the appearance of Edward Elgar, and where Elgar stopped, Vaughan Williams continued. These were formative years for modern English symphony. Elgar was a cosmopolitan, refining a personal English style out of pan-Western structures and sounds; Vaughan Williams was a nationalist, and brought the resurgent musical spirit home. "Every composer," he wrote, "cannot expect to have a worldwide message, but he may reasonably expect to have a special message for his own people, and many young composers make the mistake of imagining that they can be universal without at first having been local."

A folklorist, Vaughan Williams beat a sociologist's energies into musical poetry, abstracting an atmosphere of authentic Britain within which all his compositions seem to move, even at their most personal. Vaughan Williams, especially in his pastoral mood, is English in its past majesty, its barbaric feudalism, its literature, its folk, its color, its look. Oddly, this is just the sound that composers of Hollywood sound-track accompaniments have tried to imitate when faced with natural panoramas (as in the western film). But their evocation is pygmy next to his. They haven't his ability to suggest breadth and depth in scoring, nor his melodic gift, fluently transforming the local into the universal.

Vaughan Williams *should* be hopelessly parochial, then; too English to travel abroad. But he isn't. Possibly it is his cutting dramatic edge that holds the interest, for in his nine symphonies he, too, experimented with line and shape, with statement, confrontation, and conclusion, as the masters of that form have done since Haydn ratified it 104 times. (107, actually—one is lost and two lack numbers.) Vaughan Williams' Nine (a magic number for a collection—Beethoven, Schubert, Dvořák, Bruckner, and Mahler all died before completing a Tenth) are a varied lot. The First is a choral work with text by Walt Whitman (though in four-movement symphonic form); the Second a loose impression of life in London; the Third a pastorale; the Fourth a slashing, bitter work; the Fifth quasi-Romantic; the Sixth quasi-modernist with experiments in jazz, bitonality (using two keys at once), the grotesque, and the static; the Seventh another choral work (with narrator) and another impression, this of "life" in Antarctica; the Eighth a series of technical stunts; the Ninth something of a retrospective. Any one of them repays investigation (as, by the way, does Vaughan Williams' unstintingly upbeat Falstaff opera, *Sir John in Love,* a trove of melody). But for many the key to Vaughan Williams is turned in his Fantasia on a Theme of Thomas Tallis, a moving descent into English history and tradition.

A London Symphony 1914; revised 1920

This is technically Vaughan Williams' Symphony no. 2 in G Major (he used titles rather than numbers at first; Symphony no. 1, a choral work, is called *A Sea Symphony*). *A London Symphony* remains the most popular of the composer's Nine, though the fun is to be had exclusively through music for its own sake and not through any Baedeker that the title might suggest. As with Beethoven's "Pastoral" (no. 6), the aim is impressionistic, not pictorial—a generalized sense of London rather than an outright tour. (There are a few allusions—Big Ben's chimes in the introduction to the first movement, traffic noises, peddlars' cries and such. But no more than these.)

After a brief introduction, the first movement explodes with vitality, including as its second theme a jovial folkish tune that sounds as American (or Chinese, even) as it does English. The development calms things down somewhat, especially in a sweet episode for strings accompanied by harp; back to the urban bustle for the recapitulation. The composer politely tolerated the suggestion that the slow [second] movement is a picture of Bloomsbury, at the time a genteelly bohemian quarter. But this is gloomy, haunted music: a slow movement, not a place or time. The suggestion of English folk music—a Vaughan Williams specialty—is especially heavy here, and the heartfelt climax of the movement is one of the treasures of English symphony. For recovery, there is the scherzo [third mvt], a bluff dance movement featuring what seems to be an imitation of a harmonica (a street festival?) for a moment of the trio (middle section). A mournfully introspective finale [fourth mvt] turns this into a tragic symphony—the conductor Albert Coates identified the plaintive opening march as that of London's cold, hungry, and unemployed. For an epilogue, Vaughan Williams ends the work as it began, with the spaciousness of the introduction.

Symphony no. 4 in f minor 1935

Some listeners find this abrasive, but it is generally considered Vaughan Williams' symphonic masterpiece for its thrilling consistency of tone amidst a stirring variety of techniques. For a formal unifying device, the composer uses two four-note fragments as generative source material: all the major themes are variants of these two motives. It may sound arbitrary—why *these* four notes?—but what is art without organization?

It is not easy for the first-time listener to pin down these two essential motives, but that doesn't matter, for by the time the work is over you will sense the pervasive unity of the work in the simple resemblance of one theme to another. This is a sharply dramatic venture, very unlike the Vaughan Williams of the Fantasia on "Greensleeves" and other pastoral escapades. The general atmosphere is made manifest at once and retained throughout the stormy first movement. Even the slow [second] movement offers no solace. It is a worried movement, resorting to the briefest of flute solos at its midpoint and only at its end bringing the flute back to expand its little tune in a cadenza. Then the scherzo [third mvt], pushily bumptious, with a slower trio led off by the bassoons and tuba. As with Beethoven's Fifth, this third movement does not officially end, but builds on a crescendo (getting gradually louder) to explode into the finale [fourth mvt], led by a triumphal tune capped with a garish oom-pah tag. The raucous character of the movement only gives way at its end, in an "epilogo fugato" (fugal epilogue), which of course uses as its main themes the two generative motives. (These, by now, should sound like old and not especially likable friends.) In conclusion, Vaughan Williams reprises the opening bars of the first movement, emphasizing the oneness of the work, a musical idea (the whole symphony) in four propositions (movements)—which is, in sum, what the nineteenth century had been leading up to in the symphony all along.

Symphony no. 5 in D Major 1943

This is Vaughan Williams in his ingratiating, pastoral mood, though with a sturdy overlay of drama that eventually comes to dominate the work, asserting itself in the third movement and then expanding eloquently in the fourth only to cede to solemn joy at the very end. The movements each have a formal designation. The first is Preludio, seemingly made of disjunct ideas: a slow, rocking introduction, a faster section with strings constantly in even motion, the introduction again, climaxing and fading away. (Actually, this is standard sonata-allegro form. The "introduction" is the exposition, the faster section the development, and the return of the intro the recapitulation.) The second movement, entitled Scherzo, is just that, a kind of whirling dervish on a cloud ride. The slow [third] movement is called Romanza (romance), which is pretty much what a slow movement is. Here the work grows serious, anticipatory, though the crystalline serenity of Vaughan Williams' rural English sound totally takes over with that expansive, sceptered-isle evocation that composers of Western film soundtracks are always attempting to imitate. This, however, is the genuine article, its technical grasp meeting its emotional reach. It makes a fitting transition, in its hollow final moments, to the finale [fourth mvt], a Passacaglia. This is an old form, tricky to bring off, in which a basic theme is repeated *ad infinitum* while variations play over it. The theme opens the movement in the 'cellos; moments later, the flutes launch a second theme that will return notably at the very end of the work. As the movement goes on, the tension generated by repetitions of the basic theme builds through tempo and rhythm changes, until, climactically, the rocking music of the first movement reappears, followed by the flute tune heard at the start of the finale. In hymnlike peace it closes the work, all strings over a quiet timpani roll in the last bars.

Symphony no. 8 in d minor 1956

This odd item has been called slight and thus dismissed; it is seldom heard. But it isn't slight—it's absurd, deviously and deftly absurd. It should be heard by anyone who loves a good joke or a good symphony. Each movement has a gimmick, or, rather, a *tour de force* of technique. Thus, the first movement is a "variations without theme," the second a spoof of the modern satirist's grotesque scherzo scored only for wind instruments, the third a serious slow movement for strings only, and the finale a toccata calling for the sometimes hysterical assistance of an enlarged percussion section.

In the first movement, a fantasia (free in form), Vaughan Williams does not sound his theme before the variations begin. But you will note a persistent four-note figure (heard at the very start on solo trumpet) dominating the seven variations and their coda, a grand hymnlike passage taken from the string line that launches the third variation. The brief second [scherzo] movement will amuse those familiar with what might be called the *scherzo noir* of Prokofyef and Shostakovitch. After such buffoonery the earnest slow [third] movement is something of a shock, a study in string sonorities featuring solo cadenzas for violin and 'cello. The toccata finale (toccata means "touched"—a piece with a lot of notes) "commandeers," Vaughan Williams explains, "all the available hitting instruments which can make definite notes." It aptly concludes the piece by taking in both the serious and the comic, the former in the dignity of its themes, the latter in the industrious contributions of the percussion battery (five players not counting harp and celesta).

The Lark Ascending 1914;
revised 1920

This is a fifteen-minute romance for violin and orchestra, title courtesy of a poem by George Meredith ("Our valley is his golden cup/And he the wine which overflows/To lift us with him as he goes . . .

Till lost on his aërial rings/In light—and then the fancy sings"). In simple ABA form, the piece compares the lark's flight—the soloist's arabesques over light orchestral accompaniment—to the "love of earth that he instills"—the B section, a sturdy folklike strain. At length, the fancy sings on the violin alone.

Fantasia on a Theme by Thomas Tallis 1909

Tallis was a sixteenth-century composer of church music; Vaughan Williams reinforces the antique imagery of the piece by not only using Tallis' music as a basis for his fantasy, but also setting the work for two string orchestras, separated so that the distinct spaces of sound might suggest the antiphonal (two choirs in alternation) character of sixteenth-century church music.

The theme, once sung to the words "When rising from the bed of death," appears weightily at the start in the lower strings under trembling violins. It is at once repeated by all players at full volume, as luxurious and authentic a national landmark as the English are likely to hear. Now Vaughan Williams exploits the dualism of his orchestra, with statement and response, throwing his development of the theme from one group to the other. A solo viola and then a solo violin heighten the art of texture so basic to this kind of work, seconded by a solo quartet (two violins, viola, and 'cello) as well as the full double orchestra. Throughout, the sense of tradition (Tallis to Vaughan Williams) and the haunting sense of ritual (the churchly color of the scoring) makes this one of the most inspiriting works in the modern repertory.

Fantasia on "Greensleeves" 1934

This piece originated in an orchestral interlude in Vaughan Williams' Falstaff opera, *Sir John in Love*. The use of "Greensleeves" proved so popular that the composer borrowed it for several pieces, the best known being this arrangement for flute, harp, and strings. The simplest of structures gives us the tune itself, a contrasting middle section based on another English song, "Lovely Joan," and "Greensleeves" again.

Overture to the Wasps 1909

From a score of incidental music written for a Cambridge production of Aristophanes' comedy. There is a suite (this piece and four other numbers), but the overture has enjoyed success on its own for its farcical energy (first theme) and folkish beauty (second theme), laid out in traditional sonata-allegro form. At first, we hear the buzzing of you know what (actually, in the play, a "nest" of Athenian jurymen corrupted by pay and power), then an exposition of the two themes, a development, a recapitulation (featuring the second subject, turned into a march, played simultaneously with the first subject), and coda.

SYERGYEY RACHMANINOF 1873–1943

Rachmaninof was the last of the big-time virtuoso composer-performers, a line that goes back at least as far as Mozart. Mozart, of course, turned out to be one of the most eloquent composers, quite aside from his skills as a pianist; Rachmaninof was not comparable as a composer. On the other hand, his gifts as a pianist were extraordinary—you can hear for yourself, as he left numerous recordings of his own and others' music.

Rachmaninof took composition very seriously. Many people think of him as the overstating concocter of lush piano concertos, a self-dramatizer, a pounder and rhapsodizer. Unfair. In temperament, Rachmaninof does appear to resemble the obsessed figures of Romantic hype, with their Sensitivity and gaudy melancholy. He was, in fact, the last of the Romantics in that music underwent a neo-Classical revolution during his lifetime that he, almost alone among Europeans, completely resisted. And by way of obsession, he showed an unnatural interest in the medieval plainsong called the Dies Irae—a set tune used with words promising the Day of Judgment—quoting it often in his work. He even surrendered to Sensitivity to the extent of calling on a hypnotist's assistance to free him from composer's block. (It worked—the extremely popular Second Piano Concerto was the result.)

However, this does not prove the cliché. Rachmaninof's is highly emotional music, but it is neither slapdash nor overstated. Highly traditional in structure, these compositions don't win critics' prizes, but they sure do work as music.

Symphony no. 2 in e minor, op. 27 1907

A longish slow introduction launches this vibrantly plangent work, suggesting the atmosphere of the first movement to come. An English horn solo at last announces the end of the introduction, and the violins sound the sadly sinuous first theme, thereby keeping the promise made by the introduction and establishing an emotional "space" for the work that will seldom be challenged until the final movement.

Few symphonies exploit the minor key so fully as this one. Few symphonies so glory in sorrow—but then this is Rachmaninof—suffering, to him, was a privilege, especially in the context of stormy, doomed defiance. Perhaps the first movement goes on too long about its pitiful condition, but the second [scherzo] movement enlivens the picture. It is not jolly, certainly, but urgently rhythmic (as a scherzo ought to be); its trio (middle section) adds to the sense of motion with rushing figures in the strings. The slow [third] movement presents the Rachmaninof of luscious sighs, Rachmaninof the last—and most—Romantic. But the hyperactive fourth [finale] movement sounds a positive note from the start. A feeling of culmination is aided by a sudden slow section, just before the development, briefly reprising themes from earlier movements, and after wrestling with the dark minor key for a last time, the composer reaffirms the strength and optimism of his finale.

Incidentally, though you may not hear it, this is one of those symphonies with a motto theme, one basic melody that acts as a key to the whole. First heard in the slow introduction, then as the first theme of the first movement, it turns into other themes throughout the symphony, its notes altered but its contour recognizable (at least to the musician). The aim, of course, is unity—relating each movement to a central emotional-melodic premise.

Piano Concerto no. 1 in f sharp minor, op. 1 1891

In Rachmaninof's piano concertos, the piano is not merely the central figure, but the reason for the work. The composer wrote them to display his own astonishing technique and to sublimate his manic-depressive temperament in brooding, theatrical melodrama. This is not the thinking that motivated, say, Mozart's piano concertos, but a more extroverted, almost autobiographical plan. From start to finish, the piano is at the forefront. The overall plan is standard—three movements (fast-slow-fast), the middle slow movement being much shorter than the other two and something of a piano idyll with orchestral murmurs. Note the smashing opening of the first movement, a stern call to battle in clarinets, bassoons, and horns: suddenly the piano races onto the field, fingers flying. The call is repeated, this time with the piano's pounding "assistance." A short cadenza for the soloist, and the plaintive first theme glides in on the violins, to be echoed by the piano. This is very Rachmaninof. The dualism of dynamic fury assuaged by gentle song obtains throughout the work.

Piano Concerto no. 2 in c minor, op. 18 1900

What may be the most popular piano concerto of all time opens with nine introductory chords given by the piano alone in a gradual crescendo (getting louder), until the "home key" of c minor establishes an air of hefty tragedy. Then the orchestra sounds the first theme, dourly expansive, to piano accompaniment. This is developed for a bit, then a clear-cut transitional passage ushers in the rhapsodic second theme (in a major key, for contrast), given by the soloist. This, too, is worked over, and when the development cedes to the recapitulation, the dour first theme has turned into a march with snappy military figures in the piano. The second theme also sounds a little different now, on the solo horn. ("Yes, yes," you say—"but what about the *music*?" Dour, then rhapsodic; both at once; snappily dour, then rhapsodic; as it says above. The drama is embedded in the form and it's built-in antagonism of first and second themes. Listen; you'll hear.)

The second [slow] movement is introverted, at least for Rachmaninof, a nocturne (night-piece), ethereal but repressed. At first the piano accompanies the tune in the clarinet; then the clarinet takes up the accompanimental figure and the piano takes the tune. This is a beautifully judged movement, its sinuous elegance heightened by a violent middle section. The finale [third mvt], lively and dancelike, generally dissipates the heaviness of the first movement, though the home key is still c minor. It's not essential, but not harmful either, to recall that the soulful second theme of this movement once dwelled on the hit parade as "Full Moon and Empty Arms." An industrious climax brings us firmly into the major (with a grand reprise of "Full Moon"), on which happy or at least non-tragic note the work concludes.

Piano Concerto no. 3 in d minor, op. 30 1909

A wildly misleading simplicity rules the opening of this work: slightly accompanied by the orchestra, the piano sounds the first theme, never playing more than one note at a time in each hand. But this is a big, broad, booming piece, and it soon shows its colors, emphasizing an enviable expansiveness of tune. Here we have not Rachmaninof the darkling, wigged-out Romantic, but a serious composer concerned with the problem of form—symmetry, economy, development, conclusion. All the energies of the first movement climax in a monumental cadenza (the soloist's solo showpiece), after which the first theme reasserts its plaintive simplicity. The slow [second] movement extends the rhythmic tensions of the first movement in fiercely yearning self-analysis, and even when a light-fingered middle section gives the pianist a chance to sweeten the atmosphere, one notes that the orchestra's theme (in the woodwinds) is the same sad tune that launched the first movement, now in a slightly altered rhythm. Second movements, in a three-movement concerto, should urge the listener on to resolution, to the final movement; here, Rachmaninof emphasizes this by not ending the second movement at all. Instead, he leads it right into the finale. This is brilliant, vivacious music, as forceful as a big romantic piano concerto can be. Themes from other movements slip in and out of the texture, making for an admirable overall cohesion, and the final pages count as nearly unrivaled in the literature of heroic apotheoses.

Rhapsody on a Theme of Paganini, op. 43 1934

A combination theme-and-variations and one-movement piano concerto, this work draws together one of the founding fathers of the Romantic virtuoso school and the last of that flamboyant line.

Niccolò Paganini, the violinist, and Rachmaninof, the pianist, were both standouts in their respective eras, in terms of personal charisma as well as fabulous technique. Here, the younger man pays tribute to the older in a series of twenty-four variations on a theme found in Paganini's Twenty-four Caprices for Violin Solo, op. 1. It is a double tribute, for besides developing Paganini's tune, Rachmaninof does so in their common frame of reference, the heroic concerto.

The variations generally hew closely to the original melody and are thus easy to follow. But be warned: after a momentary introduction, Rachmaninof sounds not the theme—as we expect—but the first variation. *Then* comes the theme in its pure form (the violins introduce it, naturally), followed by the remaining twenty-three variations. Throughout, the piano is almost never silent. (Paganini would have approved: a star is a star—and in his world, the concerto was the star's show.) The high point of it all for most listeners comes about two thirds of the way through, with the wonderfully songful eighteenth variation, led off by the piano alone, building to a sweeping climax, then dimming back to the solo piano again.

Symphonic Dances, op. 45 1940

This three-part suite is just what the title says it is—dances for orchestra. Rhythm is all-important here. One should feel like dancing. (Rachmaninof hoped to place the music with a choreographer as the basis for a ballet.) The first of the three is a pulsing, assertive piece with an expressively plangent middle section—note the so-Russian use of the mournful woodwind. Next comes a troubled waltz, last a racy Spanish-flavored item opened up at its center by a thoughtful passage featuring some lush violin lines. The Spanish sound returns at the end along with a quotation of the Dies Irae, a medieval church tune promising the Day of Judgment, often used by Rachmaninof. In all the uproar, only a trained musician can spot it.

The Isle of the Dead, op. 29 1907

This insatiably gloomy tone poem was inspired by Arnold Böcklin's painting, *The Isle of the Dead:* dark blue sky, black sea, island of granite dominated by towering trees, and a lone ferry depositing a white figure on the shore. So, then, the music: lapping water, murmurings, a timeless void. Melodies rise up from the general undulation—nothing in particular, a something rather than a clearly articulated theme. Eventually the sound reaches a climax, dies away, and the horns intone the Dies Irae (a medieval tune associated with the Day of Judgment), ushering in a sweeter episode, the melodic center of the piece. The tone turns fraught, forcing some resolution, but what? The Dies Irae is heard again, now on the clarinets echoed by a solo violin, and the opening music returns to close the work. Resolution? None. An endless lamentation for the dead.

GUSTAV HOLST 1874–1934

The terrain of English music lies like fertile land with a mysterious sunken marsh in the middle, for while it shows its vitality in the Baroque era (the seventeenth century) and in the twentieth century, little may be said for it in between: little occurred. A sudden renaissance arrived almost simultaneously with the 1900s and the dignified eruption of Edward Elgar, followed by a next generation of late Romantics: Arnold Bax, Ralph Vaughan Williams, Frederick Delius, and the present subject, Gustav Holst.

Not much need be said here; outside of Britain, Holst's hold on the repertory depends almost exclusively on *The Planets*. Program-note writers make much of Holst's Eastern mysticism and susceptibility to cosmic karma, but his output shows as much interest in Western symphonic tradition as in Oriental and Indian exotica. A short and not well-known work, *Egdon Heath,* has been added below for devotees of literature-in-music.

The Planets, op. 32 1917

A grand idea for a suite: seven numbers, each representing a different planet of the solar system. (Earth isn't included, and Pluto hadn't yet been discovered.) Astrological metaphysics inspired the suite, but only to the extent of supplying Holst with conceptual titles for each piece (e.g., "Saturn, The Bringer of Old Age"). Other than suggesting a context—a musical mood—for each of the seven numbers, the zodiac and its equipment have no bearing on the case. Holst was into astrology, and occasionally cast horoscopes for people—but not in music, please.

The suite opens with "Mars, the Bringer of War," thrilling and ugly in its implacable rhythmic plan, never changing tempo, incapable of evolution, always war. Such intense music tempts a conductor to "play" it big, for sweep or shattering drama—this is a mistake. War is not Mars' passion, but his job. Holst gets his effect in rude, stupid, *unfeeling* power.

Then, what a change in tone: "Venus, the Bringer of Peace." Mars brought out the brass in Holst; here he favors the harp, woodwinds, a solo violin: a lullaby.

"Mercury, the Winged Messenger" might have served as the scherzo of a symphony. Fleet and footsure, it captures a queer caprice by never settling down with any one theme. It darts about from instrument to instrument, preferring the fairy-bell–like celesta, and ends moments after it began.

"Jupiter, the Bringer of Jollity" is the most English of the movements, transplanting the folk festival of Breughel to a Falstaffian greensward. A stirring, more serious transition about one-third of the way in prepares for a solemn carollike middle section that is, for this writer's money, the glory of the whole suite. Holst builds his tune, smack dab in the center of the merrymaking, into a brief but telling ceremonial, a bit of secular devotion taming the pagan revelry. Abruptly, however, the revels reconvene.

"Saturn, the Bringer of Old Age" suggests the ceaseless progression of time. As inexorable in approach as Mars, Saturn, too, uses the effect of a sturdy rhythmic base—the tolling of a cosmic bell. But here the rhythm sometimes varies: age is more giving than war. Gloomy and mystical. Serene. Toward the end it becomes unexpectedly beautiful, freed of its tolling-bell rhythm, expanding its melodic component in the violins.

"Uranus, the Magician" may remind listeners of Paul Dukas' tone poem *The Sorcerer's Apprentice* in its magical-mystery bounce (and because both pieces feature the bassoon). Attend to the invocational four long notes on the brass that open the piece, echoed by tubas and timpani—Uranus' spell, perhaps? Holst uses it as a structural particle, announcing changes of texture with it, especially the macabre middle section, a galumphing march of grotesques—dead souls? These, from the sound of things, are dispersed by the "spell" motive, booming in the brass, resonating in the silence, and plunked out one last time on the harp.

"Neptune, the Mystic" uses a women's chorus, wordless and so unobtrusive as to be more sensed than heard. In fact, the entire movement is more atmosphere than expression, for this quasi-tuneless and -formless cloud-web of a movement aims to close the suite with a suggestion of the void of timelessness beyond our solar system, fading into all space in eternity. A prize of a music critic's ear and tail to the listener who can detect exactly where the music ends and silence begins.

Egdon Heath, op. 47 1927

The Heath, in Thomas Hardy's *The Return of the Native,* is a brooding wasteland symbolic of the blunt dumm of life in Southern England. Holst's tone poem captures brilliantly the grim mood of the novel, especially those pages that relate the Heath's tragic presence to the defiant but doomed heroine, Eustacia Vye. Here is loneliness, barren and brooding, touched by weak upsurges of vitality, as in an attempt at folk song that soon falls victim to the prevailing dinginess. Or here is a thin groaning in the violins, aiming upwards but sinking into despair. Is it the Heath that conquers, or man's own heart of darkness?

ARNOLD SCHÖNBERG 1874–1951

Perhaps the titanic figure in twentieth-century music, Schönberg is sometimes regarded as a tragic hero of modernism, an Oedipus who killed the patriarchy of tradition and took unto corrupt union the motherlode of expanded late-Romantic harmony. The tragedy obtains in that as of Schönberg, the great composer-innovators are no longer figures like Berlioz or Mahler—hard-put to please the public at first yet always approachable—but are now elitists of unapproachable difficulty. Berlioz and Mahler are finally "repertory" composers: of widespread popularity. Schönberg and those who followed his style, however, live a curious double life. On one hand, they are composers of shattering power to their fellow musicians, to historians and critics, and a small segment of the listening community. On the other hand, they are composers whom some ninety percent of the public finds cacaphonous and mad, their music turned upside down or backwards and their aim apparently to blow all symphony apart.

Schönberg started out as the Wagnerian of Wagnerians, immersed in the huge orchestra, the "decadent" (innovatively complex) harmony of *Tristan und Isolde,* the cyclic theme structures by which one basic melody turns into another, which turns into a third, and so on until a huge composition may be built entirely of one central idea. Thus, Schönberg's early works are not "modern" in the present-day Schönbergian sense. *Verklärte Nacht* (Transfigured Night), a string sextet later rescored for string orchestra, reminds one of Wagner's *Tristan,* which the West got under its belt back in the 1800s. Similarly, Schönberg's long tone poem *Pelleas und Melisande* and dramatic song cycle for soloists, chorus, and orchestra, *Gurrelieder,* are largely in the Wagnerian line. But thereafter Schönberg became, remorsefully but compulsively, Schönberg the original and unique. He devised the new sound of the 1900s, twelve-tone music.

Before we tell what, let us ask why? Why devise a new system for composition? Had the old one run out of steam? Obviously, it hadn't, for it is still used today. But Schönberg noticed, as had others, that the lines of Western harmony had steadily been loosening, widening, weaving since about 1800. In Mozart's day the Western ear was precise. It rejected discords. But as the Faustian, Romantic nineteenth century progressed, composers fooled more and more with discords, constantly pushing outward the parameters of what the ear approved. The ear grew imprecise; it had heard too much. By 1900, the ear was no longer a trained organ of perception. It was sophisticated but undiscriminating, and to Schönberg music was therefore a mess. It had lost its sense of beginning and end, its limits. It was like a great, vomit-eating sponge.

So he hit upon a strict method for reorganizing the composition of music. All would be precise again. Fine. But in doing so, he did away with harmony entirely—this is why twelve-tone music sounds so odd. In it, a fixed order of notes is applied over and over, in various pitches and tempos until a piece is over. (Actually, such pieces are never exactly "over." At a certain point, they stop.) Pitch and tempo yield so much variety that a composer never runs out of "music"—one hears virtually no repetition. Yet, in effect the piece is made entirely of one theme. It is like Wagner's cyclicism, but much more arbitrary. And while it sounds crazed to most ears, it is very scientific. (In America, simultaneously with Schönberg, Charles Ives worked out his own solution to the problem of decadent Western harmony, much less scientific but just as arbitrary. Compare, for instance, Schönberg's Variations for Orchestra with Ives' Fourth Symphony.)

The above paragraph offers a simplistic explanation of Schönberg's method. As it is the major revolutionary force in modern music, everyone should be at least conversant with it, so hang on while we delve a little into the technique itself. Schönberg's type of composition is known as twelve-tone, or dodecaphonic (=twelve-tone) music.* The "twelve" in the term

* This is not to be confused with atonal music, another modern revolution. Atonal music is any music without a fixed harmonic "center"—four tone-deaf drunks singing "Sweet Adeline" would be a fine example. Twelve-tone music also has no harmonic center, but it calls for a particular compositional organization: it is a form of atonal music.

derives from the fact that Western music contains only twelve notes. All the high, middle, and low ranges of notes are simply those same twelve in high, middle, or low pitches. (The twelve notes are called the "chromatic scale." You can find them on the piano simply by starting at middle C and moving stepwise upwards from key to key—both black and white—until you get to the next highest C. You have gone from middle C to B and have isolated twelve notes—the only twelve notes there are.)

Now. A twelve-tone composer takes these twelve notes and arranges them in an order—any order he likes. Thus, for example (from Schönberg's Third String Quartet):

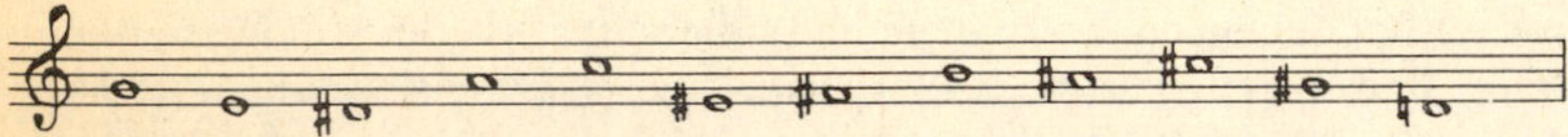

This is called the "row." Out of this basic row, the composer creates a subsidiary row by inverting the distances between the twelve notes—i.e., going up where they went down and vice versa. This is called the "inversion":

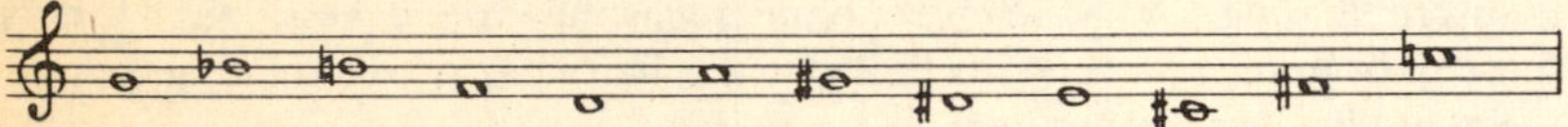

Another subsidiary is arranged by writing down the original row backwards. This is the "retrograde":

One more subsidiary, now, the "retrograde inversion." This is arranged through the same procedure that gave us the inversion (the second row above)—only it is the inversion of the retrograde (the third row):

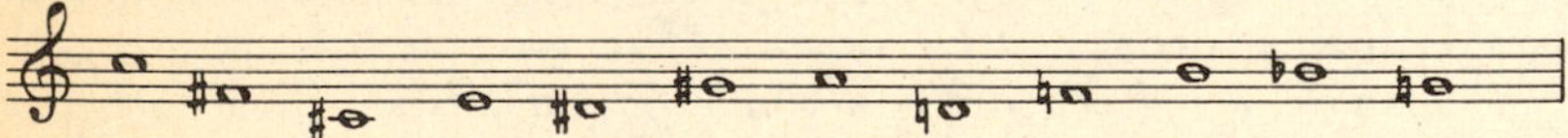

The cynic will say, "All you've got are four arbitrary sets of notes. They're nothing as far as tune quality goes. What can you do with them?" Arbitrary? Yes. Nothing as sheer tune? Yes, sort of. What can you do with them? The works: construct an entire symphony out of them, or a concerto, or an opera, or a string quartet (as Schönberg did, out of the set shown above), or the tiniest song. They are infinitesimally adaptable. In twelve-tone composition, the row and its transformation are repeated, combined, retransformed, and recombined, and sounded in any rhythm at all. It may sound like a limited and overly intellectual approach to the composition of music, but it doesn't sound that way when one hears it. In fact, this may be the most emotional sounding there is. It is difficult mainly because, unlike tonal music (from Bach to Mahler), it does not *repeat* its tunes so that one can get them down. Symphony—symphonic music in general—through roughly 1910, consists of statement, variation, and restatement. Twelve-tone music is entirely variation.

Whether or not one likes the sound, it's there and in these interesting modern times, inescapable. Few major composers don't work in at least some modified form of twelve-tone music nowadays (virtually everyone who uses Schönberg's method adapts it to suit himself), so even the most conservative concertgoers are going to have to face up to twelve-tone sooner or later. Where to start? You might work up to it with Schönberg's *Pelleas und Melisande,* a lush and lovely example of the post-Wagnerian wallowing that twelve-tone music both grew out of and discarded. Then move into twelve-tone itself with Schönberg's piano concerto. Or, better, postpone your introduction to the forbidding Schönberg and first listen to his far more accessible disciple, Alban Berg. Sibelius called Berg "Schönberg's best work."

Verklärte Nacht (Transfigured Night), op. 4 1899; rescored 1917; revised 1943*

Early Schönberg, predating his radicalism that transformed Western music for all time. It was originally a chamber work, a string sextet. But it is more popular in its arrangement for full string orchestra, for which Schönberg simply added in more instruments, amplifying the volume but not otherwise changing the music. The title derives from a poem by Richard Dehmel which inspired the work as Maeterlinck's play *Pelléas et Mélisande* inspired Schönberg's huge tone poem by that name: as an almost line-by-line rendering into music. Dehmel tells of a man and woman walking "through a cold, barren grove." She confesses an infidelity, he forgives her, and in the renewal of their love "the wondrous moonlight" shines down upon them. Following the moods of the poem from darkness into light, the strings shimmer, thrill, harry, caress in music that the most conservative listener, suspicious of the upheaval promised in the word "Schönberg," will not resist. Those who follow along with the full poem as often printed on record jackets or in concert programs

*The Schönberg chapter is organized chronologically rather than generically.

can, of a sort, follow the work as a tone poem, but it is perhaps better to hear it as absolute music, for its own sake. (Dance buffs will offer their own program for the piece, as it is the score used for Anthony Tudor's ballet *Pillar of Fire,* a mainstay of the American Ballet Theatre repertory.)

Pelleas und Melisande, op. 5 1902

This huge tone poem, inspired by Maurice Maeterlinck's gossamer play, offers a unique study in artistic revolution. This is one of the last documents of Romanticism: a huge orchestra, a passionate programmatic narration, a huge and not easily discerned formal structure, and a complex system of Wagnerian leitmotifs—short, plastic themes denoting characters in the drama, pivotal objects, or concepts, all of which are developed for psychological commentary as the story unfolds. It is a stupendous work, containing some of the most gorgeous music of its time, and makes an excellent introduction to the oeuvre of Schönberg, the man who transformed twentieth-century music and, in so doing, organized an elite whose sound has yet to experience the meaning of the word "popular."

In brief, Maeterlinck's play (which Schönberg set to music meticulously, scene by scene) concerns a widowed prince (Golaud) who finds a strange princess (Mélisande) lost in a forest, marries her, and suffers as the neglected third of a love triangle: his halfbrother (Pelléas) loves her, too, and she loves him back. At last, Golaud surprises them together, kills Pelléas and wounds Mélisande fatally. To narrate the tale, Schönberg uses leitmotifs for the three principals, for destiny, for Mélisande's wedding ring, for Golaud's jealousy. These are transformed, mated, broken apart—whatever the action calls for. "I tried to mirror every detail of [the play]," Schönberg wrote, and while his surging orchestra may be too strong for the onion-skin text and transparent faerie of Maeterlinck's original, it certainly yields absorbing drama in sound. Years after *Pelleas,* when Schönberg had passed over into his highly concentrated twelve-tone style, orchestral coloring would become a prime strategy in composition. Smaller ensembles and much solo work would mark the mature Schönberg, and his disciple Anton Webern would take this to such an extreme that he would build whole works on the step-by-step exactness of one or a few notes on one instrument, one or a few on another, and so on. But here, the approach is exactly the opposite: Schönberg uses almost all of his players all the time.

As for form, the work flies by as an hour-length chain of episodes, unified by the constant use of leading themes. However, an ear with a sense of panorama may note the equivalent of a symphony's four movements here: a slow introduction and first movement, a scherzo, a slow movement, and finale.

Five Pieces for Orchestra, op. 16 1908; rescored 1949

It is typical of the modern era, which began to lose interest in the old forms of symphony, concerto, and so on, that Schönberg gives us five *pieces* for orchestra. ("Pieces" are in some ways the form of the 1900s.) At first these were just five shortish movements of music, but at the urging of an annotator Schönberg imposed a touch of program upon them by coming up with subtitles. The first piece, "Premonitions," develops the theme first announced by the 'cellos at the very start, the whole played out over an *ostinato* (steady accompaniment) of great ferocity. Next comes "Yesteryears," a haunting slow movement, properly nostalgic—but remember, the subtitles were composed *after* the music. The third piece, first dubbed "The Changing Chord," was renamed "Summer Morning by a Lake (Colors)." This is mellow music without motion, a study in the shifting colors of the instrumental palette—how to use them as a dynamic in the absence of either melody or rhythm. "Peripeteia" is the fourth piece, and may be translated, roughly, as "Dramatic Climax," to which, not surprisingly, it builds. Last of all, "The Obligatory Recitative," is a puzzler. Recitative is a form of musical expression like speaking—is that what this movement suggests? Not to these ears.

Variations for Orchestra, op. 31 1928

An introduction, theme, nine variations, and finale. This is twelve-tone music (see the article on Schönberg, above), and isn't easy; but one can follow the variations without much trouble because each is distinguished from another in mood, tempo, and instrumental color (though there are no breaks between them). Actually, much of it is quite beautiful, but it takes some getting used to. The introduction is short, ceding to a statement of the theme on 'cellos alone. The first variation is brisk, the second slow with a graceful violin solo, the third brisk again. The fourth variation offers a cockeyed waltz, the fifth a rich adventure in expansive orchestration. Naturally, the sixth follows this with a lighter, quasi-chamber texture, and the seventh redoubles the lightness with the higher-pitched instruments—piccolo, glockenspiel, celesta, and solo violin. Lively now, the eighth variation pushes for the home stretch, and the ninth widens the sound compass with a kaleidoscope of shifting tempos, as if preparing us for the detailed retrospective of the finale. This opens with a reference to the introduction and proceeds to mirror in little the diversity of all that has transpired so far.

An odd footnote, in the "is it coincidence or homage?" department: Luigi Dallapiccola's Variations for Orchestra, also a twelve-tone work, uses a device used here by Schönberg, the four-note theme that, in European notation, spells out BACH. In both works, this theme is introduced in the first pages on trombone. Coincidence? Homage? The two works have the same title and the same "Bach" theme in the same scoring. However one calls it, it's a close one.

Violin Concerto, op. 36 1936

Though its demands on the soloist are such that only the most gifted of virtuosos can get through it, Schönberg's Violin Concerto offers a solo part of no temptation whatsoever to those interested in a splashy star turn. Charisma this work has in plenty; but of exhibitionism, nothing. Gratingly beautiful, moody, incessantly in motion, this masterpiece in the concerto form both plays by the formal rules and breaks them. What are the rules for concerto? A symphonic structure of statement, variation, restatement; a solo role independent of yet collaborative with the orchestra; a sense of soloistic "heroism" and poetry. All these Schönberg accepts, but in so individual a manner as to render them academic, moot points of a passing age.

There is no better way to understand this than to hear the piece itself, especially in conjunction with one of the great violin concertos of the nineteenth century—Brahms', perhaps, or Mendelssohn's or Chaikofsky's. Like theirs, Schönberg's adopts the standard three-movement layout, with a slightly less than fast first movement, a shifty slow movement, and tense finale; unlike theirs, Schönberg's makes its points not in the contrast of soloist and orchestra, but in their balance. When the soloist in the Brahms reaches his cadenza near the end of the first movement, we receive it from within the context of having heard the soloist "master" the work's flow of melody as the central expounder or developer of material. The cadenza, then, is like a celebration of the soloistic role. But a comparable moment in the first movement of Schönberg's concerto does not affect us comparably; there, when the violin suddenly takes off on its own, unaccompanied, we feel cut off from the work as an entity, alienated from—not attracted to—sound.

Piano Concerto, op. 42 1942

A landmark in the evolution of the solo concerto, the work has made many converts to the advanced idiom of "modern" music. (Some call it modern; actually, it's almost forty years old.) This music travels some distance, taking the ear with it—and note that its one movement contains sections corresponding to the traditional four movements of a symphony: a slow first movement, a biting scherzo, a slow movement, and a march finale. Schönberg even supplies us with a loose, emotional subtext for these four sections: "Life was so easy (first section) but suddenly hate exploded around us (second section). The situation became grave (third section) but life goes on (fourth section)."

It is interesting to hear what became of the virtuoso piano concerto of the 1800s under Schönberg's complex twelve-tone method of composition. (For an explanation of twelve-tone procedure, see the introduction above.) The concerto principle still operates—the statement and counterstatement of soloist and orchestra, their mingled roles of leader and accompanist, the entrances and exits, the cadenzas, the breadth and width of the texture of sound. Yet the overall effect, amidst Schönberg's sometimes expressionistic autograph, is unique to the concerto form—quixotic, given to short melodies piled on top of each other rather than the long melodic periods that we're used to. You may not "understand" the work as you feel you do in Mozart or Beethoven. But you may easily grow to like it.

CHARLES IVES 1874–1954

Charles Ives' career is unique in music. In brief: he wrote pieces so advanced in conception and so difficult to execute that almost none of them was performed in its time. Rather than pander his gifts to prevailing tastes, Ives earned a living as an insurance man. He gave up composing halfway through his life, and in his last decades began to be discovered. After his death, recordings and concerts of his work proliferated. He became a regular feature of the repertory—popular—and his experiments in musical time and space, in modern harmony and rhythm, were hailed as preceding those of the Europeans who had been credited with inventing them. He is now generally regarded as America's greatest composer.

Ives was really radical, a terror to the "ladybirds" and "Rollos" (his code words for unambitious concertgoers) who couldn't believe their ears. "You goddarn sissy-eared mollycoddle," he told a hissing conservative after a performance of Carl Ruggles' *Men and Mountains,* "when you hear strong masculine music like this, stand up and use your ears like a man!"

At least Ruggles' music was, occasionally, played. Orchestras had trouble just getting through Ives in one piece, for he thought nothing of composing what appeared to be several different pieces in one, all contrary as to rhythm, harmony, and melody. "I worked out combinations of tones and rhythms very carefully by kind of prescriptions," he wrote, "in the way a chemical compound which makes explosions would be made . . . And I did what I wanted to, quite sure that the thing would never be played, and perhaps *could* never be played." Radical. In his gargantuan Fourth Symphony, a sixth trumpet plays exactly one note—once—in the entire work. In 1920, a rare public attempt was made on an Ives piece, "Decoration Day" (a movement of his *Holidays Symphony*) by the National Symphony Orchestra in Carnegie Hall. "At the end of each section," he reported, "one little violinist in the back row was the only one playing, all the others having dropped by the wayside. I doubt if there was a single measure that was more than half played."

Like his pseudo-Italian score marking, "*con blasto,*" Ives was his own strange device, a new idea in every direction. His subject matter was odd—New England holidays and locales, Protestant ecstasy, out-of-key marching bands on parade, barn dances. His sense of melody was, frankly, way off-the-wall. His use of the "collage" effect (antagonistic musical streams running into each other) came fifty years before its vogue. His habit of quoting extensively from hymn tunes, patriotic songs, and folk material did not even carry the "quaint" respectability of the folkish touches in, say, Dvořák. It was just crazy.

No, it wasn't. Ives was abstracting his time and place in music, northeastern rural America at the turn of the century. The hymn tunes and Reveille and "Turkey in the Straw," the events and locations, the religious introspection, the unprecedented synthesis of *shapes* in music—all this was by way of interpreting the American cosmos in musical terms. Ives is great not because he beat Stravinsky and Schönberg to the far side of avant-garde, but because, in a music world so dominated by European styles that no one had any idea what a genuine American voice might sound like, Ives found that voice.

No wonder his coevals rejected him. They were not prepared to deal with an American montage, much less one so individualized as this. When Ives grew quiet, it was to score unanswered questions or the New England winter; when he grew lively, he turned into a town band, or two or three of them at once; when he grew loud, weak men hissed, like the mollycoddle after Ruggles' *Men and Mountains*. Ruggles, Ives' colleague, was hard to take, but his sound amounted to an ambiguous continental epic: Ives delved into little things of life in a specific way. He drafted one's intellect.

And, of course, he didn't take his music seriously "enough," with his *con blasto* and "Camptown Races" and "Columbia, the Gem of the Ocean" coming at you together—not even in the same key!—and the "wrong" final chord of the Second Symphony. Yet, what a richness of expression lies behind the fun. This is why Ives is great. As Americans, we can hear ourselves coming alive in his panorama, in his hymn tunes and folk ditties. A painter paints what he sees; Ives wrote what he heard. He left us a repertory of piano-accompanied songs the truth and beauty of which no American has so much as rivaled, plus chamber music, piano and organ solos, and orchestral works, some of which are traditional in conception, some of which show a transition from tradition to revolution, and some of which tear the roof off the old folks' home. With Ives, you'd best stay young. We leave the last word to the comparably iconoclastic Arnold Schönberg, who jotted down this poem in his late exile in Los Angeles. It takes one to know one:

> There is a great Man living in this country—a composer.
> He has solved the problem how to preserve one's self and to learn.
> He responds to negligence by contempt.
> He is not forced to accept praise or blame.
> His name is Ives.

Symphony no. 1 in d minor 1898

Those who have heard tell of Ives' great American eccentricities will be surprised when this symphony begins, for—as his graduation exercise under study with Horatio Parker at Yale—it is a reasonably traditional work, academic homage to Brahms and Dvořák. No slow introduction—the first movement takes off pronto with a first theme, and from there on follows standard sonata-allegro procedure. It's amazing how middle-European the soon-to-be proto-American Ives could sound, but everyone must start somewhere. Most kingpin explorers of brave new worlds wiped their eyes open with respectful tours of dead cities—Beethoven's First Symphony, culled from Haydn; Schönberg's *Gurrelieder* (Songs of Gurre), a symphonic song cycle in debt to Wagner; Stravinsky's First Symphony, a homage to his teacher Rimsky-Korsakof.

As a full-blown Romantic symphony, Ives' First is engaging if twice-told, all the more engaging for those who have heard the wildly advanced work of the mature Ives. After the balance of lyricism and storm in the first movement, the second [slow] movement isolates a sense of lamenting nostalgia, opening up beautifully at its climax. At moments, one hears something of the true Ives to come, but the scherzo [third mvt] could be the work of anyone, with its youthfully pedantic canonic entries (one voice after another entering separately, as in "Row, Row, Row Your Boat") and waltz trio (the middle section). A grand finale of sonata-allegro dash and romance concludes with a Chaikofskyan coda.

Symphony no. 2 1902

No way around it: Ives was unexpected. But the Second symphony is an ideal introduction for the less ambitious listener, who may want something between conventional and crackpot. Both are present here—Ives is moving into radical from traditional—and this allows one to hear Ives' peculiar style as it was just before it, as it were, over-became. Here we are halfway to Ives. (Though halfway was too far already for Ives' generation, who postponed this work's premiere for almost fifty years by simply refusing to perform it.)

Ives tended to treat the symphony as a consciousness-raising event for the ears. Be prepared for a barrel of quotations of all sorts—Beethoven, Brahms, Wagner, "America, the Beautiful," "Turkey in the Straw," "Camptown Races," and hymn tunes—all tossed high in an air of the mind as an impressionist (such as Debussy) might set the sea or fireworks to music: to show you what his senses "show" him. These are not pictorial symphonies, but abstract adventures of sound as caught by a fellow American writing when

Beethoven, Brahms, "Camptown Races," and hymns were the jumble in his ear.

There are five movements, though the first might be thought of as a long slow introduction to the second, as it is short and runs into the second without a break. Flowing strings and a savor of Bach dominate the opening, and even if he does hear the horns dally with "Columbia, the Gem of the Ocean," the newcomer may be forgiven for wondering what is so radical about the piece. Without warning, the pace picks up and the full orchestra steps in for the second movement with a correction in tone: the Bach-like strings have yielded to woodwinds under a more local influence. True, a European feeling is still (partly) in the air—Brahms is especially thick in this movement. But if this is a regular sonata-allegro movement, it is peppered with fleeting but unerring allusions to the midcult American soundscape.

The third [slow] movement, in ABA form, suggests choir and organ music, exerting considerable power after a placid beginning and closing just after a short but telling reference to "America, the Beautiful." The fourth movement is a second slow movement, but a little one, and might also be taken as an introduction to the succeeding movement. Certainly it has a masterfully invocational air (plus another taste of "Columbia, the Gem of the Ocean"), and seems to fade right into the zippy finale [fifth mvt], a grabbag of pop tunes. (For a second theme we get "Old Black Joe" on horn with a farmer's fiddle decorating it overhead.) Not having graduated past conventional symphonic structure yet, Ives gives us a full recapitulation, so those who didn't believe that they heard "Old Black Joe" in a symphony can hear it for themselves a second time, now embellished in the woodwind. The quotations of American song come so fast in this movement that no commentator hopes to get them all. Use your ears, and don't be offended by the closing quotation of reveille and the rude *blat!* of the final chord. The insult is aimed at academics.

Symphony no. 3,
"The Camp Meeting" 1904

Having written a basically conventional symphony as his First and one of convention-turning-into-innovation as his Second, Ives exploded, rose high, and fell jubilantly to earth in his Third as the Ives we celebrate, a happy-go-cranky, earnest nonconformist synthesizing the sounds, colors, and moods of his age. (Oddly, the manipulation of quotations of popular tunes for comic effect, so typical of Ives, is completely absent in this strongly spiritual work.)

The Third earned its subtitle through Ives' generative use of gospel hymns, not merely quoted but used as main themes throughout the work's three movements; these three movements are laid out in an unlikely pattern: slow-fast-slow. A stirring sense of middle-class religion is felt from the start. The first movement (subtitled "Old Folks Gatherin' "), more grand than slow, is built on a reserved—a Protestant—piety. The brisker second movement ("Children's Day") reportedly represents "the games which little children played while their elders listened to the Lord's word." A marching energy endows these hymn tunes (including "There Is a Fountain Filled with Blood" at the very start of the movement) with a highly symphonic feeling of linear motion; in the end, this renders the hymns all the more affecting. The third movement ("Communion") is the most cerebral of the three, an early exception to the old rule that symphonies don't end with slow movements (cf. Chaikofsky's Sixth and Mahler's Ninth, respectively shortly before and just after Ives' Third). Stately and deeply felt unto its closing chimes (distant church bells), it is a perfect conclusion to this quite pietistic symphony, for after the righteous optimism of the first movement and the militant air of community in the second, the third brings us closer to the oneness of man's relationship to God—what Quakers call the "inner light." An interesting alternate view of Ives the true believer, to balance Ives the madcap satirist.

Symphony no. 4 1916

The only one of Ives' symphonies that really must be termed difficult—both to perform and, if one is squeamish, to hear. The Fourth stands as a culmination of Ives' technique and aesthetic, a huge reorganization of the numerous experiments he had made in form, melody, harmony, quotation of popular and church music, instrumentation, programmatic subtext, collage effect: music as idea and altogether stupendous.

It was one of his last works (like Rossini and Sibelius, he ceased composing halfway through his life), and one of the very few he got to hear performed, at least in part: the New York Philharmonic attempted the first two movements of the Fourth in 1927, creating a sensation of public outrage, a failure *fou*. But now that the times have caught up with Ives—Leopold Stokowski led the work's first complete performance in Carnegie Hall in 1965, fifty years late—we prize this piece as one of the great events in American music. It is not a relic, nor a point of historical transition, nor an educational study. It is a superb symphony.

"The aesthetic program," wrote Ives' confidant, Henry Bellaman, "is that of the searching questions of What? and Why? which the spirit of man asks of life. This is particularly the sense of the prelude [first mvt]. The three succeeding movements are the diverse answers in which existence replies." "Diverse" is the word; at times you will hear enough material for several different symphonies—and I mean *different,* each coming from some distinctive space of mood and tempo—all going on at once. Seldom in this work does the full orchestra appear to act as a body; it is constantly breaking up into mutually antagonistic units, which is why it is so difficult to perform. (When Stokowski conducted the world premiere, he enlisted the aid of several associate conductors to keep all the players together.) This arbitrary layered effect—music on music on music—is, like Ives' constant allusions to hymns and songs, no stunt. It is an abstraction of the sound environment of Ives' America, and means to suggest pictures to the listener, such as the passing of an amateurishly off-key marching band, or the dismal flair of a cocktail pianist at a soirée heard through a hubbub.

The first movement is truly a prelude, a short lead-in to the rest of the work and the launching pad for the symphony's central proposition: the "what? and why? which the spirit of man asks of life." There are two semi-orchestras, the main group (including piano and a vocal choir) and a body of strings with harp. This second group enters early on and, independent of everything else in the movement, calmly shreds the hymn tune "Bethany." The focus of the movement is another hymn, "Watchman, Tell Us of the Night," brought to the surface by the chorus after a strong opening of almost baleful beauty.

The second movement, first of the answers to Ives' questions, is a kind of scherzo. Ives called it "not a scherzo . . . but rather a comedy—in which an exciting, easy, and worldly progress through life is contrasted with the trials of Pilgrims in their journey through the swamps and rough country." Numerous allusions to traditional tunes (from "Turkey in the Straw" to Reveille) and more of the divided orchestration score this passage of life, and with a harder edge than ever before in Ives' music (though his sense of humor—and zest for ragtime—survives intact). Note a quintessentially Ivesian episode in which a kitschy violinist and an improvisatory pianist share a non-duet, oblivious of the noise around them. And pity the violas—their parts call for them to end the movement after everyone else, as if they had fallen behind.

The third is a slow movement, refreshingly orderly after the maniacally haphazard second movement, for this answer to the what? and why? is planned as "an expression of the reaction to life into formalism and ritualism." To emphasize the isms, the system of it all, Ives lays out the movement as a great double fugue (the most systematized form in music), and draws his themes from the hymns, "From Greenland's Icy Mountains" and "All Hail the Power": method and belief.

The fourth movement offers grand finale—an "apotheosis," says Ives, of the first three movements. The questions were put in the first movement, answered in the second and third; now Ives remixes the dialogue. For if the comedy of the second movement showed us the chaos of life, and the double fugue of the third movement presented the human need for order, the finale reposes the questions and rephrases the answers: perhaps the very capacity to ask the questions is all the answer there is. Once again, the orchestra is subdivided; a special percussion group opens the movement by itself, drumming a rhythm which it stubbornly continues to drum through to the end. As in the prelude, a hymn provides a conceptual base for the movement—"Nearer, My God, to Thee"—intoned wordlessly by the chorus. The connection between finale and prelude is highly detailed (though not easy to hear), giving the symphony a cyclic feeling of voyage and regeneration. From its remote beginning, the finale grows in volume, then dies down and away.

Holidays Symphony 1913

The title of this four-movement work is really *New England Holidays*—Ives decided not to use the word symphony "because I was getting somewhat tired of hearing the lily boys say, 'This is a symphony?—Mercy?—where is the first theme of 12 measures in C Major?—Where are the next 48 measures of development leading nicely into the second theme in G?' " And it is true that a symphony is not just any four (or three, or whatever) movements thrown together; one expects a certain constituency of parts, organization, unity. On the other hand, the symphony had changed its form remarkably in the hundred years separating Haydn and Ives, and the "lily boys" were having very little say in what comprises a symphony. Don't look, then, for a scherzo or slow movement—or, as Ives warns, a first and second theme-combination. Leave the agonies of classification to the academics.

In any case, there is a unity of program here: each of the four movements recalls an American holiday from each of the four seasons, the whole "based on something of the memory that a man has of his boyhood holidays." The man being Ives, these are New England holidays, celebrated in small-town, late-nineteenth-century Connecticut. With love and humor, nostalgic but satirical as well, the composer gives us an aural panorama of such occasions—the military bands and amateur fiddlers, the community wingdings, patriotism and tradition, even the weather—and, of course, those Ivesian allusions to church and pop music, from "The Girl I Left Behind Me" and "Yankee Doodle" to "Turkey in the Straw" (which turns up out of kilter in the barn-dance episode of the first movement).

The first movement, "Washington's Birthday," opens with a bleak evocation of the New England winter, testing Calvinist righteousness with the more superb righteousness of Mother Nature. The orchestra—strings, especially—mirrors this dour relationship, snow on snow, until a fanfare breaks in and a young people's dance gets going with two-step and fare-thee-well (note that joyous informality of the so-called jew's harp, synchronous with the off-rhythm "Turkey in the Straw" on the flute). At the end, a sentimental Last Dance is succeeded by a ghostly allusion to "Good Night, Ladies."

"Decoration Day" [second mvt] reflects what was once a spiritually significant memorial with hymn-singing, a marching band (which explodes into life just after Taps), and a last moment of surprised introspection. Then we hear the more outgoing "Fourth of July" [third mvt], whose understated opening Ives explains as a boy's gloating anticipation on the night before. But day dawns soon. "Cannons on the green," Ives cites as his elements, "Village Band on Main Street, fire crackers . . . Churchbells, lost finger, fifes, clam-chowder, a prize-fight, drum-corps, burnt shins, parades (in and out of step) . . . and the day ends with the sky-rocket over the Church-steeple, just after the annual explosion sets the Town Hall on fire." Thus, Ives' famous collage effect, which preceded that of the "moderns" of the 1960s by about fifty years, and which breaks all rules of "sane" composition for pictorial effect. Although, Ives observes, if "this is pure program music—it is also pure abstract music."

"Fourth of July" is very brief; "Thanksgiving and/or Forefathers' Day" [fourth mvt] is very long and calls for chorus (to sing "God! Beneath Thy Guiding Hand"), and some listeners find it too elaborate in the context of the first three movements. It also dates from an earlier period than the other three. But there is no rule that demands proportion of symphonic movements, no rule on when different movements have to be written, and no rule (not since Beethoven's Ninth) forbidding the use of chorus in a symphonic finale. Ask yourself, does this solemn, Protestant, and patriotic movement cap the first three successfully or doesn't it? That is the only issue.

Three Places in New England 1914

Also called the First Orchestral Set (there is a Second as well, much less popular at the present writing). This was one of the few of Ives' compositions that he heard performed, and he was appreciative of the difficulties he posed for players used to Mendelssohn and Brahms. "Just like a town meeting—every man for himself," he said of one of the early American performances in 1930. "Wonderful how it all came out!" Probably because of this early exposure, the *Three Places* remains one of Ives' most popular works, and has even caught on in Europe. First of the three locales is "Boston Common," specifically at the "St. Gaudens" (Augustus St. Gaudens' bas-relief of Colonel Robert Gould Shaw and the Fifty-Fourth Regiment, black troops who fought in the Civil War). The music of this movement uses "Old Black Joe" and two Civil War songs, "Battle Cry of Freedom" and "Marching Through Georgia." It moves quietly, as if conjuring up the memorial out of a haze, eventually framing the silhouette of a march to a distant, and irregular, drum.

The second place, "Putnam's Camp, Redding, Connecticut," offers a jaunty memorial to the Revolutionary War in the form of a boy's fantasies as he surveys the battle site years later during a Fourth of July picnic. Unlike the first movement, with its single-minded military tread, "Putnam's Camp" is episodic, ever changing its shape to suit Ives' imagistic panorama, including a famous moment when two bands playing at different speeds pass each other in mad duet. The set closes at "The Housatonic [River] at Stockbridge," inspired by a poem by Robert Underwood Johnson—"Contented river! in thy dreamy realm . . . "—and by a visit to the spot itself. "We walked in the meadows along the river," says Ives, "and heard the distant singing from the church across the river. The mists had not entirely left the river and the colors, the running water, the banks and trees were something that one would always remember." This brief movement is like a prelude, a piece limited in size and devoted to the working out of one central idea in an unchanging accompanimental texture. Out of the swirls of mist, Ives builds to a substantial climax, an explosion that leaves that mist of strings hovering in the air. After a moment, they evaporate.

Central Park in the Dark 1906

Times and spaces change; when this piece was published in the early 1950s, Ives added the words "Some Forty Years Ago" to the title, so as to distinguish *his* park from the present one. His park is not dangerous, God knows, but it is weird. Pale string lines laze around in slow spirals in continuous motion (throughout the piece, completely unrelated to everything else that happens) while the rest of the orchestra offers echoes of popular music from different sources, most notably a carousel's mechanical ragtime. These intrusions collide, scream, and suddenly cut off. In the silence following, we hear the torpid strings still winding out their slow circles of sound. Times and spaces: a study.

The Unanswered Question 1906

"A cosmic landscape," Ives called it. Like *Central Park in the Dark* (immediately above), with which he paired it, *The Unanswered Question* is an exercise in the relationship of different sets of musical images, played together. The elements are: very, very hushed strings; a psychotic, repetitive trumpet; and woodwinds in reply to the trumpet. These are symbols. Ives says the strings represent "The Silences of the Druids Who Know, See, and Hear Nothing." The trumpet asks "The Perennial Question of Existence." The woodwinds search for "The Invisible Answer." What happens? The Druids (strings) hover. The trumpet restates the Question. The woodwinds worry the answer, hunt for it, and fail to find it.

MAURICE RAVEL 1875–1937

Ravel was so French that his personal style might be taken as a key to French style in general: clarity, simplicity, formality, eccentricity. He was, mainly, a miniaturist—suites of short numbers, one-act operas, the famous *Bolero* built entirely on one tune endlessly repeated. He was also a first-rate technician, loving musical puzzles—how, for example, to hold the ear's attention in that selfsame *Bolero* through all those repetitions? He was a parodist of forms and ethnic modes (especially Spanish); anachronistic perspectives were a specialty, the reviewing of an old sound style through the modernist's lens. Ravel is highly polished, never spontaneous. A critic complained of the artificial impeccability of one of Ravel's pieces. "Has it not occurred to him," the composer asked, "that I may be artificial by nature?"

It is a swank style, the more so because of a creeping sense of humor in the most serious pieces and also because of one of the most celebrated gifts for orchestration in the history of symphony. Ravel's talent for "coloring" a score by his sensitivity for his instrumentation was so acute that he ended up orchestrating much of the music that he originally composed for solo piano—and it is his scoring of Musorksky's piano suite, *Pictures at an Exhibition,* that is so frequently played today. His study of the potentialities of instrumental sound never ceased: ten years before his death, working on a violin-and-piano sonata, he telegrammed to a violinist friend, "Come at once with your violin and the Twenty-Four Caprices of Paganini." He ranks with Berlioz, Rimsky-Korsakof, Bartók, and Richard Strauss for deftness and brilliance of orchestration.

Do not let anyone tell you that Ravel was a dilletante (some might try because of his relatively small output and that cliché about his "artificiality"). He was a craftsman; that takes study and labor. True, he was careless about the blending of old styles with new, but so what? That was his prerogative. His parodistic works are not meant as education or commentary—they comprise his personal eclecticism. One does not enter *Le Tombeau de Couperin* (The Tomb of Couperin, an antique suite by Ravel) as if entering a classroom. Nor does one properly hold his *Daphnis and Chloé* responsible for authentic revivals of primitive Greek modes. It's listener's choice to hear what he pleases to hear, and composer's choice to write on the same rule.

Piano Concerto in G Major 1931

An apparent homage to George Gershwin has made the work an instant favorite among many listeners who do not care much about symphonic music. Opening with a lithe, antique-sounding first theme, the concerto soon turns to the unmistakable air of American jazz, which dominates the movement, especially in a dreamlike sequence during the development section. That Ravel is a subtler artist in this style does not in the least take away from the *Rhapsody in Blue* and other Gershwin compositions; if anything, Ravel's prudently articulated "jazz" makes Gershwin's more athletic autograph all the more potent. The second [slow] movement is exquisitely Ravellian—refined, nostalgic, simple—launched by a lengthy passage for the soloist. (Note the breadth of the theme; most symphonic themes are short and elastic; this one, like those of Schubert, seems never to end at all.) If the first movement recalled Gershwin, the second recalls Mozart, the "father" of the piano concerto—father especially of the blissfully lyrical middle slow movement. (The critic Martin Cooper hears in this movement the guiding genius of Fauré, Ravel's teacher and a master of melodic clarity, of tunes so ample that they are their own development.) The brief third movement combines Gershwin and Mozart, jazz and lyricism, in a racy rondo.

Piano Concerto in D Major for the Left Hand 1931

A weird opening—one contrabassoon creeping like the kraken through the deep of the lower strings—warns us that we are in for a dramatic work. The soloist's forceful entry seconds the motion. This is an extremely difficult solo part—writing for one hand does not "halve" the pianist's obligations, but rather doubles them, charging one hand with the work of two, encompassing the entire keyboard. (This is no idle exercise—the pianist Paul Wittgenstein commissioned the piece because he had lost his right arm in World War I.)

This yearning, troubled work is in one movement, and does not contain the equivalents of slow movement and finale (as some one-movement concertos do). It is one long movement: exposition, development (plus new episodes), and recapitulation. The development features a harsh march rhythm over which the piano soloist dances rather heavily, followed by a kind of primitive wail on the tenor saxophone. Other instruments pick up the theme as the march continues. Some perspective sets in with the recapitulation—the work feels more grand now than fantastical, and an expansive cadenza for the soloist (reworking familiar material) leads to a short coda. It's a rich piece, as textured in its moods as a silent film; try hearing it a second time immediately after the first. Then, its tricky construction will fall into place nicely.

Mother Goose Suite 1912

Originally composed for piano duet and then expanded, orchestrated, and staged as a ballet, *Mother Goose* collates Sleeping Beauty, Beauty and the Beast, and other denizens of Storybookland into one continuous movement of separate episodes. Throughout, the scope is sophisticated simplicity, children's tales and childlike tunes laid out by a master of mood and shape. First is "Sleeping Beauty's Pavane," a tiny little business for flute, finished off by ethereal muted violins. "Tom Thumb" follows, featuring the oboe. Tom is lost in a wood and has been leaving a trail of bread crumbs—but these are eaten by birds, who may startle the listener by turning up, cheeping lustily, for a few moments. "Laideronette [Little Ugly], Empress of the Pagodas" presides not over Eastern temples but over "pagodes" and "pagodines," little animals who play music through nutshells. All the same, the savor of the East is unmissable: a child's musical picture of China, perhaps. The fourth piece of the set is "The Conversation of Beauty and the Beast," a lazy waltz ceding to the enchanted dignity of "The Fairy Garden."

Valses Nobles et Sentimentales
1910; orchestrated 1912

Like several other of Ravel's better-known works, these "noble and sentimental waltzes" started out as a piano suite and were later orchestrated. In this case, the orchestral version was made to accompany a ballet called *Adélaïde; or, The Language of Flowers*. Its ornately tender scenario has not survived, but the music certainly has, both in its solo-piano and the present version. There are seven waltzes plus an epilogue, each striking a different mood. The first is discordant, the second delicate, and so it goes, up to a seventh waltz of such outgoing energy that an epilogue is needed to play us out, as it were—and, incidentally, to sum up the whole event with a few references to foregoing material.

Le Tombeau de Couperin
(The Tomb of Couperin) 1917; orchestrated 1919

Originally a six-movement piano suite, this work throws open the "tomb" of not only composer François Couperin, but that of eighteenth-century French music in general. In its piano form especially it revived the popular harpsichord dance suite of that time, and though the melodies are all original with Ravel, stylistically he has recreated the sound, as well as the forms, of Couperin's era. It is, in other words, a neo-Classical tribute, like so many other works of the 1910s and '20s—Stravinsky's *Pulcinella,* for instance, a reworking of tunes composed by the eighteenth-century Pergolesi.

There are four numbers: Prélude, Forlane, Menuet, and Rigaudon. The first is of course an opening invocation, but the other three are all dances—the Forlane a slightly jumpy Italian form, the Menuet that versatile measure that proved so useful to the symphony of the Haydn-Mozart period, and the Rigaudon a sample of the piquant folk art of Provence. (The composer did not orchestrate two other movements from the original piano score, a fugue and a highly pianistic toccata.) What Ravel has done with these four pieces in the orchestral setting is, typically, a *tour de force* of instrumental finesse; his "effects" are always embedded within the texture of mood, never thrown in for mere dazzle. Note how the trumpet outlines the essential resilience of the main section of the Rigaudon, balanced, in the slower middle section, by the perky woodwinds.

Rhapsodie Espagnole
(Spanish Rhapsody) 1907

A suite of four movements, extravagantly Spanish and a showpiece for an ambitious (and huge) orchestra. Unlike some works evoking

Spain in color and rhythm, Ravel's is not written with an outsider's ears; no less an authority than Manuel de Falla claimed that it "surprises one by its [genuinely] Spanish character. . . . This 'Hispanization' is . . . achieved . . . through the free use of the modal rhythms and melodies and ornamental figures of our 'popular' music, none of which has altered in any way the natural style of the composer."

Why should it? Ravel's natural style draws on just the abandon and mystery associated with the Spanish sound, revealed with comparable elegance and energy in his *Alborada del Gracioso* and *Bolero* (both cited below). The four movements here comprise a prelude, two dances, and a lively finale. "Prelude to the Night" opens the work with a theme of four descending notes that is repeated, with a few interruptions, throughout (and that returns twice more later on). Its ethereally sinister tone derives from Ravel's scoring: widely spaced, high in the violins and low in the violas, both groups muted. Having defined his atmosphere, Ravel goes on to the two dances, the lively Malagueña and a brooding Habañera. Last and longest is "Feria" (Fiesta), an opulent holiday complete with castanets and nervy riot. A lazy middle section allows for a siesta and some more of the *concertante* (solo instrumental) writing for which the score is famous. The riot returns for the closing.

Daphnis and Chloé Suites 1911

Like such other famous ballets as Stravinsky's *The Firebird, The Rite of Spring, Petrushka,* and *Pulcinella,* Debussy's *Jeux,* Respighi's Rossini-derived *La Boutique Fantasque* (The Madcap Boutique), and De Falla's *The Three-Cornered Hat,* this work was composed for Dyagilef's Ballets Russes, the first generative force in dance to integrate all artistic elements into a conceptual whole. This is not mere music, then, but revolutionary ethno-artistic agitation—a Greek love story plotted in modernistically pagan terms and scored to blend the Classical majesty of Louis XVI's court painters with a superannuated pre-Raphaelite innocence. (Or so Ravel claimed.)

This anachronistic perspective was a Ravel specialty, though many listeners find the sounds comfortingly "Greek," diaphanously suitable for the nymphs and shepherds of the story in their Pan-haunted forest. There are two suites, both of which call for optional chorus. Suite no. 1 consists of a luminous "Nocturne," and "Interlude," and a "Warriors' Dance"—for pirates intrude into the sacred grove bent on rape. They are discouraged (by Pan), and Suite no. 2 is concerned mainly with celebration. First, "Sunrise," a famous example of Ravel's mastery of orchestration in solo bits and *tutti* (full orchestra) effects. (Those who would compare French and German styles in art might play Ravel's *Daphnis* sunrise back to back with the cosmic first minute of Richard Strauss' *Also Sprach Zarathustra,* also devoted to a sunrise.) Next, "Pantomime" exploits the woodwind choirs for yet more brilliant shimmer, and "General Dance" concludes the work with one of the most ambitious expressions of savage debauch ever committed to music paper.

Alborada del Gracioso
(The Clown's Morning Song) 1905; orchestrated 1918

Originally a piano piece (from the suite called *Miroirs,* Mirrors), the Alborada is one of Ravel's several splurges in Spanish folklore. (The Alborada, sung at dawn, is the "opposite" of a serenade, night music.) String thrummings suggest the alborada's indispensable adjunct, the guitar. Fragments of themes dart from oboe to English horn to clarinet, followed by the real business of the day, dance rhythms. Except for a subdued episode highlighted by a mournful bassoon solo, the brief work continues to elaborate the moody drive of the dance.

Bolero 1928

Bolero was written for Ida Rubinstein's ballet company. It is, by Ravel's own admission, "orchestral tissue without music." The piece is unique: one great crescendo (gradual intensity of volume) on one simple repeated melody lasting nearly twenty minutes. Some hate its monotony; some are hypnotized. Certainly there is a problem of repetitiousness in both rhythm and tune—but it was because the problem challenged the composer that he wrote *Bolero* in the first place. It is a study in obsession, take it or leave it. Two military drums tap out the rhythm and a solo flute introduces the Arabic-Spanish sounding theme (Ravel's own, however) that we will hear so much of. The tune passes to other woodwinds—a solo clarinet, a solo bassoon. Throughout, the pace is firm and slow. (Ravel once reproached Toscanini for taking it too fast, but the conductor replied that Ravel's requested tempo was too draggy; you are liable to hear some diverseness of speed between performances faithful to Ravel and others, revisionist like Toscanini.) Only one major effect (besides the kaleidoscopic instrumentation) dispels the unyielding single-mindedness of the work, a sudden change of harmony at the end, exhilarating after so much regularity.

La Valse (The Waltz) 1920

A murky turbulence in the lower instruments opens this medley of waltzes, part homage to and part burlesque of the Viennese tradition of Johann Strauss, Jr. (The work was originally entitled *Wien,* Vienna.) First proposed and only later used as a ballet, *La Valse* cries out for choreography, as one sentimental, athletic, or sinister melody follows another. It is a fantastic charade, glittering with the savage self-righteousness of imperial gaiety and ending in sheer panic. As always with Ravel, use of instruments provides a precision of coloration (oboe and trumpet solos, especially). But the main effect is that of the insatiable increments and distortions of the waltz rhythm, rising up out of cloudy tremblings for sport, relaxation, and, eventually, horror.

REINHOLT GLIER 1875–1956

Originally of Belgian family, Glier brings up the rear in the Russian wing of the Western repertory, seldom mentioned and seldom heard. He seems not to have run afoul of Soviet authorities. Indeed, he made his peace with "Socialist realism" by incorporating folk melodies of the Russian outback in his in any case highly old-fashioned music: plenty of melody, lush scoring, and conservative harmony. Glier is the composer of one of music's odder items, a two-movement concerto for coloratura soprano, which Joan Sutherland has recorded.

Symphony no. 3 in b minor, "Ilya Mouromyetz," op. 42 1911

In this electronuclear age, a popular and semi-popular symphony may be defined as those that adapt, respectively, well and moderately well, to disc. That lets *Ilya Mouromyetz* out. It's so long that even with lengthy cuts it barely squeezes onto one record, and while record-buyers will tolerate two-record symphonies in Mahler and Bruckner (plus Beethoven's Ninth and the odd exception such as Shostakovitch's Seventh), they are most likely to ignore something this big and unfamiliar.

However, the work repays investigation. It's a program symphony, with a complex legend to recount. Ilya is a *bogatir* (pronounced bog-a-*tir*), a folk hero of Herculean strength. The reader may taste of the uncompromising extremism of Ilya's story in learning that this hero is introduced to us having spent the first thirty years of his life sitting motionless—that's just the *beginning* of the tale! It seems that Ilya breaks his coma to become a *bogatir* on the advice of two wandering gods and befriends an already established hero who passes on to Ilya his folk-heroic wisdoms when about to die. That's the first movement.

In the second movement, Ilya conquers a ferocious brigand named Nightingale (Solovyey, in Russian) for his ability to sing sweetly. Alternatively, he can bellow, and of course does both here. The third movement pictures the feast of Vladimir, the local prince; Ilya drags in Nightingale, forces him to display his vocal technique, and beheads him.

Another villain turns up in the fourth movement, Batiga the Wicked, whose breath is so foul that it fells Christians. Ilya and his cohort slay Batiga and his pagan host. But a second battle with men whose corpses arise undead and double—so that every one slain becomes two—climaxes Ilya's career. He and his crew are magically turned to stone.

Who can resist a tale with that much bravado? Glier is at pains to reconstruct the events pictorially, with much use of the darker instruments (the trombone especially) to suggest the murky wonders constantly afoot. A slow introduction to the first movement sounds a number of themes basic to the entire work, and as excitement mounts and the strings describe a long and rapid descent, the first movement proper takes off in lively tempo. Already, one can hear fragments of the slow introduction turning into full-out themes even as these themes are changing their shape to dramatize Ilya's story. It is not clear how the athletic first movement fits in with the gloss—certainly nothing suggests anyone's having sat motionless for thirty years (which the highly pictorial Richard Strauss would certainly have found some way to do). Still, the atmosphere of adventure is richly laid.

The second movement, telling of the meeting with Nightingale, is the slow movement. Much of it is devoted to his birdsong (flutes and other woodwind), underlined by a flowing melody in the violins. At the end, the twitterings grow intense as trombones, bassoons, and double basses bellow. A complete change of tone welcomes us to the scherzo [third mvt], detailing Nightingale's concert at Vladimir's feast. The main section sounds Russian and hearty, the trio (middle section) grisly—Nightingale's chirps and bellows. The frenetic finale [fourth mvt] concentrates on Ilya's valor, tapering down to a close of muted strings and deep bass notes when Ilya undergoes his unexplained ossification.

MANUEL DE FALLA 1876–1946

A passionately nationalistic composer, de Falla made himself an expert in the cosmopolitan traditions of Spanish music, with its Moorish, Jewish, Gypsy, and Middle-Eastern influences changing the face of its art no less than its history. He was a fanatic on the subject and bent his creative impulses to a *pro patria* program, working exclusively in native forms and on native subjects. When the Royal Academy of Fine Arts in Madrid announced a competition for a national opera, it was de Falla who won it, with the luridly naturalistic *La Vida Breve* (Life Is Short). Then, one day in 1907, he went to Paris for a week's diversion . . . and stayed seven years.

De Falla was not the first foreign composer to undergo a stylistic revision in what was then still the capital of the Western music world; in contact with such composers as Debussy and Ravel he widened his aesthetic parameters, building on his Spanish foundation with the airier sophistication of French music—impressionism and neo-Classicism. He remained, to the end, Spanish. But he shows a French overlay that at once lightens and deepens his sense of Spanish self.

Nights in the Gardens of Spain 1915

A piano concerto. Or, more exactly, "Symphonic Impressions for Piano and Orchestra" (as de Falla called it), for the piano takes a major but not perhaps sufficiently leading role in the *concerto* sense.

Certainly, the soloist is prominent, and adds a lush savor to these three almost violently suave nocturnes. The first movement, "At the Generalife" (one of the buildings of the Alhambra in Grenada), begins with a raw, simple tune in the violas which, expanded, provides the bulk of the material. The second movement, "Distant Dance," is not the slow movement one might expect, but a lighter rendering of the mystery that informed the first movement. The piano plays a major part here, also providing the sudden transposition into the lively third movement, "In the Gardens of the Mountains of Cordoba," which follows without a break. As sharply colored as the first movement, this finale shares with it an edge of brutality. The night is not always tender.

Three Dances from The Three-Cornered Hat 1919

The dance version of Pedro de Alarcón's short novel, *The Three-Cornered Hat,* was written for Dyagilyef's Ballets Russes. It retells the old comic trope of a pompous official's attempted seduction of a young husband's alluring wife (foiled, of course). The three excerpts extracted from the score are "The Neighbors' Dance," a svelte piece of moonlit merrymaking, "The Miller's Dance"—the miller being the husband in the case and his dance a stamping, rhythmic business heralded by cadenzas for French and English horn solos; and the "Final Dance," a celebration sparked by a perky repeated figure and closed with a sizzle of castanets. Ever the nationalist, de Falla identifies the three dances by their native genres—respectively, Seguidillas, Farruca, and Jota.

Ritual Fire Dance from El Amor Brujo (The Demon Lover) 1915

El Amor Brujo is a ballet with songs about a gypsy girl who must exorcise the ghostly memory of her former faithless lover in order to claim a love life with a new young man. This excerpt, popular out of the ballet context as a solo item, is the exorcism itself. (The full title is *Ritual Fire Dance To Drive Off Evil Spirits.*) Opening with an ominous trill in the lower strings joined by a heavy rhythmic tread, the piece then turns to a wailing oboe melody (in the ballet, the heroine sings wordlessly over this; her part may be omitted if the dance is played alone), more trills, and a now mysterious-now furious second theme. Then all of this is repeated and capped by *fortissimo* (very loud) chords.

CARL RUGGLES 1876–1971

Ruggles is a textbook case of an American perennial, the crackpot genius—a composer of such vast line and thrust that he remains over-huge for many listeners fifty years after his half-dozen or so works were written. In his own time he (with Charles Ives) marked the first breakaway in American music from imitation of European models. Simultaneously, George Gershwin, John Alden Carpenter, and Aaron Copland were sifting through jazz to establish an urban, quasi-popular energy in symphony, but Ruggles and Ives dwelled in the opposite extreme, abstracting an aural experience for the countryside. (Copland was later to join them there.) Ives investigated small-town, middle-class New England life; Ruggles framed a continental epic. He is comparable to Walt Whitman in his mythopoetics, his attempt to encompass the spirit of an insurgent people in his art.

This is wildly rhapsodic, densely concentrated music—Ruggles' longest item lasts less than twenty minutes. Don't be put off by Ruggles' reputation as a nonconformist (thoroughly merited, by the way), for what was considered hissably dissonant in the 1920s and '30s is not so menacing today, and if you can forget about listening for first and second themes and instead grasp Ruggles' compositions as totalities, you may well be thrilled. *Sun-Treader,* especially, is highly recommended.

Sun-Treader 1931

This short but sprawling masterpiece was once thought "impossible" to play or hear; premiered in Paris in 1932, it wasn't performed in America until 1966, when Ruggles got to audition his piece for the first time—at the age of eighty-nine. (Luckily, an excellent recording by Michael Tilson Thomas and the Boston Symphony on Deutsche Grammophon label fills the gap for us between *Sun-Treader*'s infrequent appearances.) The title is borrowed from Browning's apostrophe to the dead Shelley in *Pauline:* "Sun-Treader, life and light be thine forever!" Rather than an elegy, however, Ruggles' tone poem is a heroic, even fabulous adventure spun off the inspiring grandeur of the epithet "Sun-Treader." Don't identify the meaning; don't explain. *Feel* it. For it is built more on "feelings" than on themes and development. The central sound image of the piece is heard right at the start: rising, flying brass over pounding timpani. This is used three times in all; in between its appearances, lyrical passages vie with intense, fighting passages, as if panning back on the picture of a continental expanse harried and celebrated by an aggressive humanity trying to come to terms with nature and history.

Men and Mountains 1924; revised 1936

Ruggles' few compositions are short but immense. Here, he shows his mythic credentials straight off in the source of his title, a line from William Blake: "Great things are done when men and mountains meet." A kind of non-technological counterpart to Hart Crane's poem, *The Bridge* (of the same era), *Men and Mountains* hymns the freewheeling openness of permanently youthful America, staging its ambitious self-dramatization from ocean to ocean across some natural, ancient truth that it can accept only in terms of conqueror and vanquished. The work is in three movements. First, "Men" (subtitled "a rhapsodic Proclamation for Horn and Orchestra") proposes the flesh-and-blood half of the mythopsychological meeting. A surprisingly tender slow movement follows in "Lilacs," a rest cure slipped between the thundering men and their rocky, geological alter-egos, emphasizing string textures. "Marching Mountains" returns us to the war/love affair of natural and asserted forces, beaten out with the aid of on-and-off throbbing drums. An elegiacal middle section refers back to the mood of "Lilacs," after which more great things are done and the epic partnership is affirmed on the timpani at the close.

ERNÖ DOHNÁNYI 1877–1960

As composer, pianist, conductor, and teacher, Dohnányi (formerly called Ernst von Dohnányi) is better known in his native Hungary than elsewhere. There, his Brahmsian lyricism once overshadowed the more adventurous sound of Béla Bartók and Zoltán Kodály, two radically folk-oriented Hungarian composers. But now Bartók and Kodály are national classics, while Dohnányi has faded away except for the piece cited below, a favorite for its witty instrumentation.

Variations on a Nursery Tune, op. 25 1913

The highly dramatic introduction sounds as if it were anticipating the last trumpet rather than a set of variations for piano and orchestra on "Twinkle, Twinkle, Little Star"—or, as the Europeans generally call it, "Ah, vous dirai-je, Maman." But at length the sense of impending apocalypse dies away, and the piano soloist enters with the theme. For the first six variations, the music hews closely to the original tune; then it branches out. Variation no. 7 is a sumptuous Viennese waltz, no. 8 a dour march, no. 9 a grotesque minor-key scherzo (its bassoon opening and skippy pacing may remind some of Dukas' *The Sorcerer's Apprentice*). Variation no. 10 is a grand one, reminiscent of Rachmaninof. It builds to a cymbal crash and a triumphant restatement of the theme, whereupon the wind instruments continue with the theme in chorale style, while the piano and harp comment rather urbanely between phrases. A fugal finale leads to the coda, in which the theme is heard one last time, a little ruined by a sleepy bassoon.

OTTORINO RESPIGHI 1879–1936

A talented composer whose individual voice is of that recondite, even academic kind that speaks mainly to other musicians, Respighi might have faded away but for the three tone poems of Roman sights and senses, cited below. And these three are, of course, widely popular more for their "sonic spectacular" aspect than for their atmospheric beauties. (When stereo came in the late 1950s, devotees of hi-fi celebrated the charisma of their equipment with playings of Respighi's three Roman carnivals.) Yet there is no little imagination at work here.

Fountains of Rome 1916

Four (connected) sections, each depicting a different fountain at a different time of day. First, "The Valle Giulia Fountain at Dawn" etches a pastoral landscape—a suburban fountain. A burst of horns and bells calls us to "The Triton Fountain at Morning," a flip and playful passage. More exuberant yet more grandiose is "The Trevi

Fountain at Noon"—don't expect to hear Respighi allude to the tourists who hang around the Trevi tossing in coins and making wishes. No, this is the emotional climax of the piece, thrilled with its horn, trumpet, and trombone calls, and as it quiets down it imperceptibly drifts into the delicate undulations of "The Villa Medici Fountain at Sunset." A suggestion of bird cries on clarinet and flute lead to a hushed, nightfalling final page.

Pines of Rome 1924

As the festive opening attests, Respighi's is as much the modern Rome of the *dolce vita* as the classical Rome of the S.P.Q.R. While its predecessor, *Fountains of Rome,* gave us depictions of four fountains, *Pines* yields views of Roman pine trees in four sections, dovetailed at the edges (as in Fountains) to form one four-part tone poem. The first pines to be heard from are those of the Villa Borghese, against which we note the avid games of schoolchildren, not excluding a rude noise on the trumpet (presumably some child's offpitch toy instrument). Suddenly, the mood changes. Dark, even dank mutterings in the lower voices of the orchestra transport us to pines overlooking catacombs. A distant trumpet against slow-moving strings paints a beautiful scenic picture; then, for drama, a hymnlike chant rises up from the depths of the old caverns. The chant sounds remarkably like Hollywood's American Indian soundtrack music, but no matter—this is a gravely impressive evocation, easily the great moment in Respighi's three Roman tone poems. The mood changes again; now we stand on the Janiculum Hill in the moonlight. A brief cadenza on the piano opens this episode, superceded by a clarinet, then strings, then the full orchestra. After a while, the limpid sounds die away, the clarinet sings again, and a nightingale marks the moment for us, carolling straight from life on a phonograph or (nowadays) tape recording. We move on to the fourth section, this one on the pines along the Appian Way. Here is classical Rome in its blasted glory, heard in the tramping of a ghost army. Shadowy plaints on the English horn. Military signals in the brass. The tramping builds, and suddenly the shadows fall away and the abstract army comes back to life in its old splendor, "mounting in triumph to the Capitol," as the composer notes in the score.

Roman Festivals 1928

Disturbed by the heavy textual bias of the early twentieth-century tone poem, Respighi sought in his three Roman tone poems to release music from its reliance on extramusical program (as in, say, Richard Strauss' *Till Eulenspiegel's Merry Pranks*). So, we get vague pictures but no real story line here. As in the more popular *Pines of Rome* and *Fountains of Rome,* the format is four connected sections, each one separate in mood and melody (no tunes from one section turn up in another). The four festivals silhouetted herein are the Circenses (from the days of the Empire), a Christian-era Jubilee, and the more modern October Festival and Epiphany Eve. Circenses is a riot of calls to the arena, the mob's outcry, and the hymn of doomed martyrs. The pious Jubilee gets excited as pilgrims reach the summit of Monte Mario and view the holy city; the orchestra reflects their ecstasy with a festive procession that eventually dies out on a horn call and the tolling of deep bells. The October holiday is joy from start to finish, culminating in a prankish serenade. La Befana—the night before Epiphany—offers a folkish Rome of the dancing populace, including a cheap waltz and the traditional saltarello, the whole exploding in a collage of antagonistic rhythms, as if several different parties were going off at once.

ERNEST BLOCH 1880–1959

Though there have been many famous and relatively famous composers of Jewish descent over the years, few of them have tried to develop a "Jewish school" in symphony the way such nationalist composers as Musorksky, Vaughan Williams, or Janáček abstracted folk sounds and images in music for their respective cultures, Russian, English, and Moravian. Ernest Bloch is an exception. His formative influences are many, joining Bach with the odd harmonics of the East, and these with the harmonic revolution launched by Debussy. Worked in among the three is a deliberate attempt to capture something Jewish in music. What, exactly, would this be? Bloch tells us: "the freshness and naiveté of the patriarchs; the violence of the Books of the prophets; the savage love of justice; the despair of Ecclesiastes; the sorrow and immensity of Job; the sensuality of the Song of Songs. . . . It is this that I endeavor to hear in myself and transcribe into music: the sacred emotion of the race that slumbers in our souls."

On the other hand, if Musorksky, Vaughan Williams, or Janáček are invariably heard seeking some essence in their backgrounds, Bloch—Swiss-born but an American resident from about 1915 on—is pan-Western in his outlook, as intrigued by medieval and Renaissance sounds as by Jewish. He thought nothing of adapting an American Indian theme for his Violin Concerto; Indian emotion, too, struck him as sacred and potentially symphonic. Still, it is the Jewish emotion that gives us Bloch at his height, robed in talmudic grandeur and fury. In the end, it is Solomon and the Books that inspired Bloch's most personal splendor.

Israel Symphony 1916

Three (not four) movements, a choral (with soloists) finale, and a programmatic scheme saluting two ancient Jewish holidays make this an unusual symphony. But three-movement symphonies were becoming a regular event in the 1900s, choral finales are as veteran as Beethoven's Ninth, and programmatic symphonies were no novelty after the imagistic 1800s of Berlioz, Liszt, and Richard Strauss.

The two religious celebrations break the work into two parts. Part One, devoted to Yom Kippur, a serious "Day of Atonement" on which the devout settle an annual account with God, comprises a short, slow first movement and a faster second movement. The form is rhapsodic—that is, free in form, built on contrasts of the heroic and the lyrical. Part Two, the choral finale, tackles the more joyful Succoth, "Feast of Booths," a harvest rite (the text is a French translation of traditional Jewish prayers to God, sometimes performed in English in America). Bloch put his all into this work—the "sacred emotion of the race," as he put it—and unifies his tripartite picture by running his three movements into each other and retaining themes from the first movement in the last. From the meditative through the chilling to the sacramental, the work grows in power with a simple beauty that must be called "popular" in this period of sometimes alienative or intellectual symphonic composition.

Violin Concerto 1938

Surely the opening page constitutes the only instance of a Jewish violin concerto taking off with an American Indian first subject. But then this is not one of Bloch's more ethnic works, and his sound here is less given to his characteristic talmudic passion than to a more general passion of balladeering heroism. The Indian theme is apparently a genuine Indian melody; it contributes to the distinctive atmosphere of the first movement, one of those long now lyric-now assertive first movements whose style was laid down in the nineteenth century. That was the heyday of the virtuoso celebrity—and we need a virtuoso here, not only to dazzle with his technique but to dominate emotionally in the rugged and singing "halves" of the first movement, the short but widely gauged second [slow] movement, and the diversely rhythmic finale [third mvt]. Note that the Indian savor touches all three movements, always making its strongest utterance in the opening sections. Note as well that Bloch reuses themes from the first movement in the second and third. The final reappearance of the first movement's first subject (the Indian theme) at the very end of the finale gives a nice feeling of resolution.

Schelomo, Hebrew Rhapsody for 'Cello and Orechestra 1916

The 'cello solo is the voice of Solomon (Schelomo), king, moralist, and poet—"I have seen all the works that are done under the sun; and, behold, all is vanity and vexation of the spirit." Solomon opens the work in an introductory cadenza and dominates the succeeding sounds of luxury, barbarism, and brooding meditation. Bloch's most popular work, it is also his most candidly Jewish, as colorful as the soundtrack score for a Biblical epic—a one-movement concerto of free-form meandering (thus the designation as "rhapsody") that makes a splendid counterpart to Ecclesiastes. "All goeth unto one place; all are of the dust, and all turn to dust again."

BÉLA BARTÓK 1881–1945

Bartók amazes. That folklorist, that eclectic, that experimentalist, that radical with the heart of a conservative, that barbarian. He is one of the most respected composers of the twentieth century, although unlike his colleagues Debussy, Schönberg, Stravinsky, and Ives he created no new style, form, or procedure. Hungarian, he collaborated with his compatriot Zoltán Kodály to collect and publish Hungarian folk music, which till then had been largely confused (outside Hungary) with gypsy shtick. Having thus educated Western ears to the true nature of Hungarian music, the two foremost Hungarian musicians could then synthesize this nature in their symphonic composition. This synthesis is not mere quotation. Those who have heard George Gershwin's *Rhapsody in Blue* or *An American in Paris* will understand how the folklorist operates. The method is to write one's own music in the native idiom, thus refreshing the ear with new images on the basic icon. It is an adventure in self-ratification, a quest for communal identity.

We're very used to folklorists in symphony. From Haydn to Mahler, the great symphonists of the Classic and Romantic eras regularly programmed folkish touches in their works—dance movements, quotations of authentic material, recreations of folk style, and so on. But with Bartók the practice feels more exotic. For one thing, Hungarian music sounds odd to the rest of us; for another, it is Bartók's pleasure to emphasize the peculiarity of Hungarian culture with savage, slashing rhythms and brutal orchestration. Like Stravinsky in *The Rite of Spring* and *The Firebird,* Bartók used primitivism as a means to a heightened *national* expression: what you are is what you were.

Besides the barbaric Bartók, there is the Bartók of what is known as the "night music"—a delicately evocative impressionism comprising musical twitterings and murmurs suggestive of night in a forest or out on the plains. This sound is especially useful to Bartók in his slow movements. Actually, there are many distinct Bartókian idioms, better encountered on the spot in concert hall or on record than in verbal description. *Hear* the man; start anywhere. (Those who like a sense of artistic evolution might want to work their way chronologically through Bartók's six string quartets, which sum up the epiphanies of his career in little.)

Concerto for Orchestra 1944

In the old *concerto grosso* of the late seventeenth century and early eighteenth, a small group of solo instruments played against a larger group. The soloists comprised the *concertino,* the main orchestral body the *ripieno* ("full group"). Later, in the early eighteenth century, came the solo concerto, in which a single virtuoso played against the orchestra. The concerto for orchestra is an outgrowth of the twentieth century; it combines the two early forms. Thus: the use of ensemble soloists (the *concertino*) remains, but this ensemble is not fixed—any instruments or group of instruments may suddenly break free of the mass sound and take the lead. One moment there may be a single soloist, then three woodwinds, say, then no soloist at all.

Bartók's Concerto for Orchestra is the best known of this genre, perhaps his most popular work. Besides offering a tempting showcase to first-rate orchestras, letting their personnel cut loose on their own for a change, it has the charm of emotional progression as it moves from the nervous tension of the first movement to a pleasant enjoyment of its own vigor in the last. It is in five movements, breaking down into slow introduction and first movement, scherzo, slow movement, "interrupted intermezzo," and finale. As often with Bartók, the middle slow movement commands the center of a symmetrical line, for as we move along, the speed of the movements decreases to the center, then picks up again *from* the center:

fast	medium	slow	medium	fast
1st mvt	2nd mvt	3rd mvt	4th mvt	5th mvt

A spell of anticipation is laid down in the slow introduction to the first movement, and when the movement proper (subtitled "Introduction") gets underway, it is in a rush of thematic fragments, no clear tune appearing until the tempo pulls back for a plaint on the oboe, soon passed to other instruments. This movement gives us the barbaric Bartók, raging, pounding, and gliding through a spectrum of instrumental colors. He relaxes in the second movement, the first of the work's two scherzos, subtitled "Game of Pairs." The game, of course, relies on pairs of instruments—two bassoons open the movement, two oboes follow, then two clarinets, two flutes, and so on. (Two harps score the game's highest points with wild glissando effects—i.e., sliding up and down the strings.) The third [slow] movement, "Elegy," is not the lyrical slow movement of Mozart or Bruckner, but a taut episode, an anchor for the work; in its big middle section it reprises a theme heard earlier, in the introduction to the first movement. The fourth movement, "Interrupted Intermezzo," is the second scherzo, a buffoonish piece despite its tender, folklike main theme. At the direct center of the movement, the interruption occurs, made by a clarinet playing what sounds like a Spanish paso doble (two step):

Operetta buffs recognize it as Prince Danilo's famous "Maxim's" song from *The Merry Widow*. But Bartók's son tells us that his father meant to spoof the second half of the monotonous theme in the first movement of Shostakovitch's Seventh Symphony (the "Leningrad"), a theme associated with the march of the Nazi war machine—a theme that Bartók, among others, found unbearably vulgar. The interrupted theme does come back (in the strings) after all this noisy meddling, but the spell has been broken and it dies away in a huff. The fifth movement, "Finale," cuts up with a whirlwind of perpetual motion.

Piano Concerto no. 2 1931

Like many of Bartók's major works, the Second Piano Concerto looks for a symmetry in the three-movement structure. In place of the concerto's traditional fast-slow-fast layout, however, Bartók drops a scherzo into the exact center of the work, breaking the slow movement into corresponding halves. Likewise, the first and third movements balance each other, sharing the same motor-driven fury and even a few themes. Thus, we have a work whose first half mirrors its second:

violent "1st mvt"	slow mvt begun— scherzo—slow mvt finished	violent rondo
1st mvt	2nd mvt	3rd mvt

The second movement is the most interesting of the three, with its veiled strings suspended in slow motion, its almost improvisatory piano part and pointillistic orchestral commentary—this quintessential Bartókian elegy is typical of his "night music" style, so-called for its expressionistic adaptation of the nocturne. The middle section—the scherzo—is a toccata of pounding piano that (at the work's midpoint) relates back and forward to the two end movements.

Piano Concerto no. 3 1945

Bartók's last completed work (he died before he could finish the last page), the Third Piano Concerto is also one of his most popular pieces. It is thought that he *planned* it to be popular: demoralized by penury and neglect in his American exile, Bartók apparently set out to compose something that *had* to be liked, something less difficult than he might have written. In any case, the concerto is out of Bartók's topmost drawer—at least the first two thirds of it—and a fascinating study in how to impress the ear with a folk-native sound without taking a full-fledged folklorist's holiday. In each of the three movements, the "sense" of Hungary is unmissable. Yet like many ethnic specialists, Bartók does not quote any folk material; he simply writes his own.

Bartók's native savor is pervasive. It lifts the lively first movement with the imagist's eyes, sighted on the folk fiddle, the dance at the tavern, the plains and forests. The prize of the work is the second [slow] movement, an ABA structure of meticulous beauty. The A section presents a tender dialogue between a gauze of string sound and a chorale played by the soloist. The B gives way to Bartók's mystical, shrilling "night music" idiom, made of fragmentary tremblings and twitterings. When the A returns, decorated by the pianist's Bach-like solo, remnants of the B shimmer around it. There is no break between the second and third movements: a gong sounds and the vivacious finale is off and away. It is generally admitted that this last movement does not equal the first two in terms of melodic interest, but its insistent rhythmic vitality does what the rondo finales have traditionally done for the concerto: winds it up with the stamping energy of the dance and some virtuoso brilliance from the soloist.

Violin Concerto no. 2 1938

Until very recently this was known simply as Bartók's Violin Concerto, without a number. But the performance in 1958 of a two-movement violin concerto (presumably unfinished) plus its continued presence on the fringes of Bartók's oeuvre has necessitated a "no. 1" and "no. 2." Still, the present work remains "the" Bartók Violin Concerto, being far superior to the older work. As so often with this composer, the format is symmetrical: the traditional three movements of the concerto structure are planned so that the first and third balance each other, sharing principal themes as if they were two possible movements on the same material.

The opening reminds one of the opening of Mendelssohn's violin concerto in its dramatic spareness—a bit of strumming introduction in the strings and the soloist leaps in with the first theme. The approach is still direct and sudden even a century after Mendelssohn first tried it. For the rest of the first-movement exposition, Bartók is largely at his ease, spinning out a second theme as relaxedly lyrical as the first, but the tempo quickens for the development, and the lengthy cadenza that caps the movement yields some brilliant virtuoso acrobatics.

The second [slow] movement is a theme and six variations, the theme opening the movement, played by the soloist. After a brief answer from the strings, the soloist leads off with the first variation, an embellished version of the theme so filled out with extra notes that one is reminded of the "thin person inside the fat person" mentioned by encouraging dieticians. The soloist retains the lead in the second and third variations. But as of the fourth variation the texture as well as the theme fills out in the full orchestra. By the sixth variation, however, the soloist again holds forth over minimal accompaniment (plucked strings in steady rhythm), and the soloist closes the movement with a restatement of the original theme.

The third [finale] movement is like a roughhewn dance version of the first, retailoring its themes for the faster, more keenly virtuosic tradition of the concerto finale. But since Bartók intends this movement to balance with the first, he casts it not in rondo form, but as a "first movement" sonata-allegro. Thus, it is less a concerto finale than a concerto first movement played as a finale. It's moody music, featuring both the "barbaric" as well as the lyrical Bartók.

Viola Concerto 1945

This work was left in sketches at Bartók's death, drafted in cryptic shorthand on disordered papers that included bits of other works and presented corrections of first thoughts literally on top of the originals. It looked like a 3-D comic book viewed without the magic glasses. Bartók's ally, Tibor Serly, arranged the sketches in order, deciphered them, and filled them out: finished the work. How much of it is true Bartók and how much Serly we don't know; we're grateful to have it at all, for it makes a rich farewell to art, ofttimes bitter and satiric, and everything that a man who felt betrayed by poverty and faint praise might lay down as last words.

A noteworthy beginning: the viola announces the first theme *solo,* sparsely accompanied. Soon the music develops tension and volume, while the soloist stays at the forefront virtually throughout, as often decorating themes as stating them. This is a sonata-allegro movement, with development and recapitulation following the opening exposition. The recapitulation ends with a sense of loss—but it does not end, after all, for the soloist's cadenza cedes to a bassoon solo, and this cedes to the second [slow] movement. This is an ABA form of beautiful, nearly motionless meditation. The tiny B section is a flight of sighs and groans, after which the tranquil first section returns (punctuated by B's sighs) only to fall headlong into the third movement, an exciting rondo finale in Bartók's vein of dancing barbarism. This movement is not much respected by analysts, but some listeners find its drive appealing—and, of course, much of its success depends on the gifts of the solo violist. Since Mozart's day, stellar chemistry has been crucial to the concerto as form, art, and entertainment.

Divertimento for String Orchestra 1939

Antiquing has been one of the prime activities of the twentieth century. Here Bartók resurrects the divertimento of Haydn and Mozart, a form related to the symphony but—like the serenade—lighter in tone. Bartók is no slavish archeologist, but a synthesizer, and his divertimento blends the usage of the eighteenth century with his own very modern emotional outlook, his Hungarian melodic palette, and his particular sense of formal symmetry. Thus, while his all-string orchestra frequently makes use of the *concertante* of the old days (in which a solo or group of soloists plays against the main orchestral body), we have a dour middle movement sandwiched between two lively ones, plus a measure of Bartókian satire in the finale.

The first of the three movements is instant reminiscence—melody (in the violins), pure Bartók; texture of sound, very *concerto grosso*. A lively sonata-allegro movement, it closes with a placid coda after much variety of tempo. The second [slow] movement is rather non-divertimento in its funereal pace and shell-shocked rage (note year of composition); the whole thing plays as a stifled shriek. But the finale [third mvt] picks us up again, with a frolicsome rondo filled with cute instrumental effects—including a "gypsy fiddle" cadenza for solo violin and, toward the end, a burlesque polka.

Music for Strings, Percussion, and Celesta 1936

Lest one think of the above as dismally limited personnel in terms of sound variety, remember that percussion takes in not only various drums but piano, harp, xylophone and—by the way—celesta. (The title should properly have stood as Music for Strings and Percussion.) Clearly, Bartók has limited his resources as the poet uses the "limitations" of rhyme and metre: to concentrate the means of expression.

There are four movements, not corresponding to the traditional four movements of a symphony (e.g., the first movement is not symphonically substantial, and there is no scherzo). The first movement is a slow, very tightly controlled fugue; its energy derives not from speed but from its own accumulation of mass as one melodic line coils around another. A musical version of a snake pit. After a loud climax, the whole thing unwinds itself—one critic compared it to the opening and closing of a fan.

The second movement is lively, a succession of dance tunes and developments of them. With its vitality and variety, it might well have provided the first movement of a symphony—and note how Bartók exploits the battery (percussion section) and divides his strings for a Baroque-like statement-counterstatement rivalry-collaboration.

The third [slow] movement is essential Bartók, an example of his "night music" style, made up of odd shimmers, an expressionistic nocturne. Now the study in instrumental coloration has reached high gear, and Bartók gets sounds out of his players that you may never have associated with these particular instruments. As in the first movement, a point of culmination is reached, and the movement works its way back to its beginning, a hollow xylophone solo.

The finale [fourth mvt] is a dancy rondo of superb mettle, bewildered at its climax by the reappearance of the fugue theme from the first movement. Rallying, the dance reasserts itself and suddenly ends.

Suite from The Miraculous Mandarin 1919

There are several ways to make a ballet suite. The oldest, most useful with ballets having separate numbers, is to extract the "best" (or most popular) and string them out in some order conducive to happy listening. But more modern ballets do not usually have separate numbers—where to start the extraction, where to end? Does one cut chunks from the ongoing texture? Bartók's solution here is to play the first two thirds or so of the full score (having omitted one section), then close with a "concert ending." Thus, as drama, the suite concludes before the story does. But as music the suite satisfies, and gives us a chance to hear the music when no ballet company is offering the work complete on stage.

The mandarin of the title is the third customer (after an old man and a shy young man) of a prostitute working with three thugs. They strip him of his valuables and try to kill him, but he has become so obsessed with the woman that he will not die. They smother him, stab him, hang him—in vain. His eyes are fixed on the girl; he must have her; he lives. Only when she sympathetically embraces him does the mandarin, his dream fulfilled, succumb.

For this lurid plot, Bartók fashioned an eerie, demented score, expressive of the sensuality, ruthlessness, and passion of the plot. One needs to see it staged, see how the music works with the story—but it is such interesting music that a vague understanding of the action will keep one absorbed. Note the sometime Oriental character of the piece, in the Mandarin's honor.

Dance Suite 1923

One of Bartók's most arresting studies in the folk-Hungarian (and even a little Arabian) sound. There are five movements of dance tunes plus a retrospective finale, all six parts linked into one sectional movement by the use of a refrain—a unifying theme whose reappearances tie it all together. The refrain is not heard at first. The opening movement takes off on a bassoon theme and some heavy-footed development of it before the refrain shows up, hesitantly, on the violins. Suddenly, we are plunged into the second dance, Bartók at his most barbaric; this time the refrain is given to the clarinet. This brings us to the third movement, the first gladsome dance in the set, one of the most frankly Hungarian passages in all music. The refrain sounds final now—Bartók gives us a "false finish" (don't clap!) and we move on into the pseudo-Arabian fourth movement, thinly langourous. This movement ends with a brief allusion to the refrain, leading on to a dour, almost non-melodic fifth movement, a study in rhythm. It is over in moments, and acts as something like a prelude to the grandiose finale, wherein Bartók treats us to developments of themes heard earlier. A last, delicate restatement of the refrain precedes a propulsive coda.

HEITOR VILLA-LOBOS 1881–1959

A Brazilian of great folkloric flair, Villa-Lobos deserves to be better known than he is in North America (especially because the Brazilian musical idiom shows its bloodlines with that of the United States in the cakewalk and "creole" jazz). He was incredibly prolific, and enjoyed a slight vogue in America during Franklin D. Roosevelt's Good Neighbor Policy in the 1930s. But since the 1950s his sharply characterized music has fallen by the wayside. Sad loss. Villa-Lobos was never afraid of being "too" tuneful, and often scared critics with his very likeability. Those with a hankering for good, South American guitar music might sample his Concerto for Guitar.

The Bachianas Brasileiras

These are nine suites written from the 1920s to the 1940s, scored variously for groups from flute and bassoon duet to large orchestra and designed to fold the imaginative fancies of a Brazilian tone poet into the batter of Bach's formal procedures. The overall title for the series might translate as "Brazilian Bacheries"; admirers of Bach's structural clarity might be delighted to learn what a modern composer with a sharp pictorial eye and sense of humor can do with the old suite. Antique and novel at once, the Bachianas Brasileiras even add Brazilian subtitles of specific local description to the generic Prelude and Gigue (jig) of Bach's era (as in nos. 2, 4, and 7, examined below). Special note must be made of the fourth movement of no. 2, subtitled "The Little Train of the Caipira"—a charming recreation of a steam-driven railroad hop in the interior—and of no. 5, for soprano and eight 'cellos (and therefore out of our compass here), a bizarrely beautiful composition found highly effective in initiating the doubter into the mysteries of "classical music."

Bachianas Brasileiras no. 2 1930

A four-movement suite for orchestra—Prelude, Aria, Dance, and Toccata—devoted to the more popular side of the Brazilian character. The prelude, for instance, is also entitled "Song of the Capadocio" (boulevardier), and does not fail to sing it, complete with bluesy ornamentation. The Toccata doubles as "The Little Train of the Caipira," a tour de force in which the essential quality of the toccata (touched, meaning one touches, or plays, a great many short, fast notes) is used to portray the progress of a little Brazilian train from one station to another. At his most definitively Brazilian here, Villa-Lobos has a field day with a number of odd local instruments.

Bachianas Brasileiras no. 4 1930–1953

Four movements for orchestra whose generic titles—Prelude, Chorale, Aria, and Dance—belie the fragrant Brazilian mystique of the subtitles—Introdução, Canto do Sertão (Song of the Jungle), Cantiga, Mindinho. Oh, this is Brazilian music all right, for if the strings-only prelude shows a strong affiliation to Bach, the other three urge a colorfully local impression upon the listener, not least in the infinitely repeating xylophone note in the Song of the Jungle or the modernistic fiesta of the final Dance.

Bachianas Brasileiras no. 7 1942

Like its brother Bachianas, no. 7 is very upfront with its formal affinities to Father Bach and no less ingenuously Brazilian. What a lot of conga hides behind the cool Classical layout!—Prelude, Gigue, Toccata, Fugue. But then these are all tours of one sort or another through the Brazilian culture ethos as much as they are Suites for Orchestra.

Guitar Concerto 1951

Those who have not heard the guitar utilized as a solo instrument may be surprised at its resources, though naturally Villa-Lobos has kept his orchestral forces small so as not to drown out the soloist. There are the traditional three movements, fast-slow-fast. After a few bars of rhythmic beat, the soloist enters, playing against the orchestra's thematic fragments with runs and scales. After a bit, the guitar sounds a genuine theme, a lyrical line repeated sequentially at falling pitches; then various instruments trade off a tune while the guitar pounds out repeated chords. The structural scale is small, the mood intimately ceremonial, with no clear-cut sense of exposition, development, and recapitulation: more runs and scales, more chords, and the first movement has, suddenly, finished. The slow [second] movement shows off the woodwinds in solos almost as much as the guitar, but it does enjoy a healthy cadenza at the close, according to the player's whim and powers of invention. (This is a rare instance of the cadenza not being written out by a twentieth-century composer; instead, Villa-Lobos recommends four progressions of tempo.) The finale [third mvt] is a jagged business, with excitingly wide-flung solos for the guitar. Again, the woodwinds are favored among the orchestra players for their complementary timbre and volume.

ZOLTÁN KODÁLY 1882–1967

A Hungarian deeply into folk music, Kodály is often compared with his compatriot Béla Bartók simply in order to throw the former's conservatism and the latter's modernistic adaptability into relief. (The "control" for the comparison is that both worked toward abstracting the sound of sung and spoken Hungarian in their melodies and rhythms.) Note the years of Kodály's lifetime: these were fraught times for the concertgoing public, never sure from minute to minute what new Faustian wonder might be thrust upon them. No doubt much of the public prefered the melodically more assimilable Kodály to his colleague—but why choose? Each has something to tell us.

Dances of Galánta 1933

A one-movement suite of folk melodies traced by folklorists to Galánta, a Hungarian market town once important as a way station on the journey from Vienna to Budapest when the one was the haughty cosmopolis of the Austro-Hungarian empire and the other a twin-cities affair (Buda and Pest) amounting to a provincial capital. The form of these dances is easy to follow—a rondo with a slow introduction. There is a principal theme, the main "dance," as it were, dusky with gypsy allure. This theme is suggested in the introduction: one by one, instruments toy with it until a solo clarinet cadenza ends the introduction and begins the flow of dance tunes. You will hear this theme again as a refrain between the other melodies, most amusingly near the end when a climactic torrent of gypsy fiddles suddenly cuts off for cadenzas from flute, oboe, and the clarinet again, leading into a wild gypsy coda.

Dances of Marosszék 1930

A medley of folk melodies native to Marosszék, a region of Hungary. This is in form a rondo, which means that one main theme leads off and keeps recurring between hearings of subsidiary themes. Here the main theme is a ponderous gypsy plaint, scored with an eye on the local color. Of greater interest, however, is an unusual subsidiary episode made up of a series of solos sounding like bird-calls on oboe, then flute, then piccolo, violin, and contrabass. The finale, as one might hope, is fiddler's choice, a zippy whirlwind of gypsy feet.

Variations on a Hungarian Folk Song, "The Peacock" 1939

Introduction, theme, sixteen variations, and finale, all devolved on an old Hungarian song, "Peacock Has Gone Flying." The variations are relatively easy to follow, especially given the year of composition, when a set of variations might whirl by in such scattered complexity that one could not hope to trace the original tune in its variant guises. In the introduction, lower strings hint at the theme (i.e., the "Peacock" song), followed by a lush development in the full orchestra, but not till a solo oboe is heard, briefly, does Kodály state the theme itself. Then we're off, with each variation separated from the next by a full stop so the listener may catch his breath and compute the altitude of the Peacock's ever-diverging flight. The early variations stick close to the theme, but later ones take on a flair of their own, such as the eleventh variation, a plangent duet for English horn and clarinet, joined by other woodwinds and strings for a rich medley of intertwining lines; or the twelfth variation, an *Adagio* (very slow) for the upper strings with ruminations on horn and harp; or the thirteenth variation, a funeral march. Thereafter, the theme reasserts itself, until the sprightly finale restates it in more or less pure form.

Háry János Suite 1926

Kodály's most popular work is a collection of excerpts from his musical play about a tale-teller who would be called János Háry outside of

Hungary (Hungarians always put the surname first). To allay our suspicions that old János' memories of having visited the Imperial court at Vienna (where he saw the Empress feeding the livestock, including a two-headed eagle) and defeating Napoleon pretty much singlehanded might be somewhat imaginary, Kodály appeals to a Hungarian superstition: any announcement greeted by a listener's accidental sneeze must be true. The suite opens with the sneeze—hear it a-borning, rising, and detonating—and then goes into "Prelude: The Fairy Tale Begins," a romancer's preparation—but whose, Háry's or Kodály's? Next is the perky "Viennese Musical Clock," one of of the items that János spies on his tour of the royal palace at Schönbrünn. A solo violin ushers in the austere "Song," used several times in the play; note the use of the cimbalom, a kind of armchair piano played like a xylophone, ultra-Hungarian. A buffoonish march depicts "The Battle and Defeat of Napoleon": Háry may take this episode seriously, but Kodály doesn't. At the end we get a mock cortège for the fallen with saxophone solo. The delightfully more-Hungarian-than-thou "Intermezzo," cimbalom to the fore, covers a scene change; it's what used to be known as "curtain music." Last is "The Entrance of the Empreror and His Court," receiving the heroic János with full honors. Marie-Louise, the princess of Austria-Hungary, János recalls, was crazy mad for him. But he returned to his village belle, Örzse.

IGOR STRAVINSKY 1882–1971

Launching his career as a Romantic Russian nationalist and a pupil (for one year) of Nicolai Rimsky-Korsakof, continuing it in Paris as the composer of huge ballet scores—the suave fairy tale *The Firebird,* the fantastic/grotesque *Petrushka,* the brutal *Rite of Spring*—then turning to the smaller orchestra and transparent architecture of neo-Classicism, and closing his career as an adept of difficult modern techniques, Stravinsky always surprised the ear. No matter what "period" he was in, he never sounded like anyone else working with the same materials. All efforts to pigeonhole him are overthrown. In the musical pantheon, where extravagant individualism is a minimum requirement, Stravinsky stands out.

He left examples of virtually every genre of musical composition (including ragtime), yet everything he touched sounds new. Take opera, for instance. Stravinsky's one evening-length operatic entry (there are several one-acts), *The Rake's Progress,* does not remotely satisfy the traditional conditions for music drama: a comic-tragic plot suggested by Hogarth's famous series of engravings, a Mozartean sound slyly adapted for modern harmony, unheard-of comings and goings in both action and music, satire and sadness—a masterpiece. But one of a kind.

One may traipse through Stravinsky's output and virtually never find any form that hasn't been reinvented in some way. Below are cited examples of the symphony, the concerto, the tone poem, complete ballets and ballet suites; to each one Stravinsky applied a loving fondness for melody, a dry wit, an amazing structural sense, and a wildly perverse sense of rhythm. It is in this area, perhaps, that he made his greatest contribution to twentieth-century music. Rhythm in symphony had grown a little stale by 1900. Claude Debussy, another revolutionary, reinvented rhythm by clouding the traditional rhythmic stresses; Stravinsky exploded them. For example, compare a typical rhythm of Western music:

1-2-3-4 1-2-3-4 1-2-3-4

to what Stravinsky did with it in a famous moment of *The Rite of Spring:*

1-2-3-4 1-2-3-4 1-2-3-4 1-2-3-4 1-2-3-4 1-2-3-4

Stravinsky, in a way, was a one-man rite of spring for twentieth-century music.

There really is no way to detail the diversities of Stravinsky's style in his long career in this limited space. Let your ears take you through them by chance. Certainly the Stravinskyan autograph is distinctive and immediately recognizable (not least when slavishly imitated, as in Hollywood sound-track scores). Some people find it on the arid side, more commentative than simply expressive, but the "feeling" in Stravinsky is not as upfront as that in Schubert or Chaikofsky. Stravinsky's is more layered, ambiguous, complex.

Don't limit yourself to the symphonic works listed below. Try *L'Histoire du Soldat* (The Story of a Soldier), a work for chamber (small) orchestra and speakers in which an allegory about temptation and the spirit is juxtaposed with nervous musical parodies. Or try the monumental *Oedipus Rex,* a shortish opera based on Sophocles and sung in Latin (a narrator keeps one up on the action) by soloists and chorus who never move, an operatic frieze. Or *Ragtime,* a study in American jazz for eleven instruments, one of the earliest experiments in America's elite syncopations that were to dominate the musical scene in the 1920s. You may find, if you tour the Stravinskyan landscape, that you have heard twentieth-century music—its first principles, trends, and novelties—in little.

Fireworks, op. 4 1908*

This little tone poem was written so early in Stravinsky's career that he was still using the traditional opus numbers (which he soon

*The Stravinsky chapter is organized chronologically rather than generically.

dropped). But *Fireworks* is anything but traditional. In its icy whirling patterns of sound-color it marked a stylistic breakthrough for a composer till then associated with a quietly Westernized Russian nationalism as the pupil of Rimsky-Korsakof. But here he showed himself radical, pan-Western, and non-folkloric. Though he never did break entirely with the platonic ideal of a Russian art (for he never wished to), he became, from here on, an uncompromisingly individualistic and unclassifiable composer.

Free in form, *Fireworks* starts hectic, slows down for a mysterious middle section remarkably reminiscent of the mystical opening bars of Paul Dukas' *The Sorceror's Apprentice,* then speeds up again—two views of the phenomenon once known as pyrotechnics, the bursting upward rush, and the dreamy detonations.

The Firebird Suites 1916; 1919; 1945

The Firebird was the first of Stravinsky's trend-setting scores for Dyagilyef's Ballets Russes, composed in 1910 and premiered that year with choreography of Michel Fokine. However, the three suites of excerpts extracted from the complete hour-long score date from later years.

The first of the three is distinguished by its fidelity to the lush orchestration of the original; the second, by its smaller scoring; the third by its larger share of musical numbers. Each of the three offers a different selection of *Firebird* highlights, and while Stravinsky buffs have their separate preferences, it is the second that is usually heard—if only because it calls for fewer instrumentalists than the first and is "conveniently" shorter than the third.

Actually, the best way to hear the music is in its complete form (one record's worth of music, by the way), for it is all worth hearing. It is a fairy tale of innocence versus evil, the former represented by Prince Ivan and the latter by the magician Kashchey the Deathless and his army of ghouls. Intervening for Ivan is the Firebird, and providing romantic interest is a group of princesses under Kashchey's spell. Given that one isn't hearing the full score, he will probably be getting the 1919 suite, which tells the story in little. An Introduction sets the tone with deep, growly opening measures, woodwind twitterings, and magical string effects. This runs into "The Firebird" herself, followed by "The Firebird's Dance," suggesting her precisely mercurial presence. After a full stop comes the lyrical heart of the suite, "The Princesses' Round-Dance," a haunting moment. But this is succeeded by "The Hellish Dance of King Kashchey," an orgy of barbaric dynamics (note, however, that a lovely violin melody soars above the grotesquerie at one point). Kashchey vanquished, we hear a "Lullaby," oddly but effectively led by the bassoon, and the "Finale" completes the cycle of fairyland beauty, built on one theme (solo horn, at first) repeated over and over to a tremendous climax.

Petrushka 1911

One of the great ballet scores in terms of dramatic momentum as well as musical richness, this astonishing work was once thought too sophisticated for most ears, though much of it is as simple as folk music. Written for Dyagilyef's Ballets Russes, it triumphed on its Parisian premiere—but the players of the Vienna Philharmonic, rehearsing the first production outside of France, thought the music "dirty." Even the supportive Dyagilyef had mixed feelings: "You end your ballet," he told the young composer, "on a question!"

The whole ballet poses a question: how unreal is fantasy, after all? The action centers on the public and "private" lives of three carnival puppets: a shy clown (Petrushka=Little Peter), a pretty ballerina whom Petrushka loves, and a brutal blackamoor who at length smashes Petrushka onstage in front of an audience. The crowd is horrified at such lifelike spontaneity from mannequins, but the string-master picks up the "dead" Petrushka and shows them all—see? just a dummy. But later, the fairgrounds deserted, the master sees the ghost of the puppet mocking him overhead. Is Petrushka "real"? That is the musical question on which Stravinsky ends his score. "Well," he once said anent Dyagilyef's complaint, "at least he understood that much."

The music, though a thrilling listening experience in itself, thrives when it is heard as accompaniment to the ballet as intended. Stravinsky's music, Michel Fokine's choreography, and Alexandre Benois' decor were all meant to collaborate equally in posing the basic question: is the art real? To hear without "seeing" is to drop out of the debate entirely, for the atmosphere of the fantastic, of the grotesque, of tragedy disguised in comedy, depends as much upon stage dressing and kinetics as upon Stravinsky's score. (Those who have access to tours of the American Ballet Theatre can see their excellent production, a careful replica of the original.)

The orchestration is especially allusive—Martin Cooper has likened it to a giant accordion in its buzzing folkish energy and to a Fauvist painting in its use of layers. A piano of almost concerto-level brilliance adds to the cutting tone, the sense of riot always on the edge, and perhaps the most Fauvist effect of all is found in the famous *Petrushka* fanfares, the discordant screams that abstract the work's basic question, the dualism of fantasy-reality. (The oddly abrasive sound of these fanfares is achieved through use of bitonality, writing in two keys at once.)

But at least Stravinsky did write the action into his music. One can follow the narrative with an inner eye as one hears—the shrill Petersburg crowd, the little diversions of the carnival (an organ grinder, a dancer who plays the triangle as she prances), the drum-roll announcing the puppet master, the dance of his three star attractions, Petrushka's pathetic courtship of the ballerina behind the scenes, the ballerina's flirtation with the blackamoor, the crowd again, dancing and reveling, the scuffle between Petrushka and the moor, the latter's murder of the former, and at last the ambiguous ending.

Le Sacre du Printemps (The Rite of Spring) 1912

"Pictures of Pagan Russia," the subtitle declares—the tribal fertility gala of primeval humankind, never secure about the seasonal cycle from any one year to the next. *The Rite of Spring* is a ballet, and there is no *Rite of Spring* suite—this is the whole thing. Its premiere in Paris in 1913 prompted one of most famous riots in musical history. Even the sophisticated were not ready for this first example in the new genre of primitivistic art. Everything—the music, Vaslaf Nizhinsky's choreography, and Nicholas Roerich's designs—aimed at presenting the elemental in man, the unconscious all-truths. What one sees is a pagan festival, a succession of dances, athletic games, the teaching and benediction of seers and ages, and a ritual human sacrifice. What one hears, away from the ballet stage, is such action impressed into sound with all the savage rhythmic impetus and mystical ectasy that the situation requires.

As in Stravinsky's earlier Ballets Russes scores, *The Firebird* and

Petrushka, the orchestration of the melodies provides a distinct coloration. *The Firebird* is styled for fairy tale, *Petrushka* for grotesquerie—*The Rite of Spring* for atavism. It is not all brutal by any means; some of it is almost ethereally quaint, solitary, rapt. The very first notes, for example, are sounded by a solo bassoon suggesting the first stirrings of life. There is a great deal of solo work from the woodwind throughout, in fact, their cool concoctions almost refreshing amidst the vicious inexorability of the brasses and the orgasmic whooping of the percussion.

Savagery, even when synthesized for art, was not what Paris had in mind in 1913. Today, we admire Stravinsky's ability to suggest prehistoric simplicity through a complex musical anthropology of ugly rhythm and ferocious instrumental color. But the opening-night public resisted with a demonstration. Carl Van Vechten, who was there, called it "war over art." Someone behind him rose to his feet in the uproar and, galvanized either by Stravinsky's music, Nizhinsky's choreography, or the occasion, "began to beat rhythmically on the top of my head with his fists. My emotion was so great that I did not feel the blows for some time." Hear it for yourself now, keeping in mind the essential evocation of the springtime sacrament of a prehistoric people. But attend to what the composer once said in this matter: "The idea came from the music, and not the music from the idea. I have written a work that architectonic, not anecdotal."

Song of the Nightingale 1917

It is usual for composers to arrange concert suites of excerpts from their ballet scores, but this suite is excerpted from an opera, *Solovyey* (The Nightingale), known in the West by its French title, *Le Rossignol,* because it was premiered, in French, in Paris. The plot of the opera tells of a miraculous nightingale who entrances the Emperor of China and his court until a mechanical bird usurps its place, whereupon it departs, only to return to sing for Death in return for his sparing the ailing Emperor's life. The music is drawn from sections of the opera's second and third acts, and since the excerpts combine as one movement, the suite is, in effect, a tone poem.

The Chinese-flavored score is reasonably pictorial. First we hear the Emperor's court dizzily preparing for the Nightingale's court debut. The music grows ceremonial for the "Chinese March" of the emperor and his dignitaries, though it includes a few pompously "wrong" notes. A lengthy flute cadenza introduces the Song itself, sinuous and more distinctive than beautiful. A bit more ceremonial busy music brings us to the performance of the mechanical nightingale, a cold, fluid oboe over throbbing harp. The trumpet solo that follows derives from the song of a fisherman (heard in all three short acts of the opera), but of course here his moralistic poetry is missing its words:

> Death, with the voice of the birds themselves,
> Conquers the celestial soul.

Right enough, we hear music depicting the emperor on what will surely be his deathbed. The mechanical bird tries his cold song, to no avail. But here is the flute: the real nightingale has returned. Its song sends Death away, the Emperor recovers, and the trumpet closes the work with a reprise of the fisherman's song:

> Listen! The voices of birds
> Speak for the celestial soul.

Pulcinella Suite 1922

Here's a textbook case of neo-Classicism for those who wonder about the term. The suite is a shortened version of a ballet whose action derives from the commedia dell'arte tradition and whose melodies belong not to Stravinsky but to Giovanni Battista Pergolesi, a well-known composer of the early eighteenth century. Arranging these antique melodies according to his whim, Stravinsky reconstructs the past within a modern musical context. It is ancient art revitalized by a fresh viewpoint. In other terms, Stravinsky is not like the retoucher who preserves a faded painting, but the synthesist who paints his own version of old mastery. This is neo-Classicism—the modern "reverting" to the old, using its discrete forms (i.e., Renaissance comedy and Baroque music) in a chamber scoring (i.e., for smallish orchestra, about thirty-five players). *Pulcinella* is a ballet comprising twenty numbers and calling for three vocal soloists. For the suite, Stravinsky dropped the singers and arranged eleven of the numbers into eight movements, from Sinfonia (symphony, here meaning overture) to Finale. The scoring is both a homage to and a satire of the orchestra of Pergolesi's day, for while Stravinsky calls for a *concertino* string group constantly playing off the rest of the instruments (as in the old *concerto grosso*), he also has his players pulling stunts now known to Pergolesi's contemporaries. The second number, called Serenata, features some eerie string effects, and the seventh number, *Vivo* (lively) presents some of the dirtiest trombone playing east of New Orleans.

Divertimento from Le Baiser de la Fée (The Fairy's Kiss) 1928

"Divertimento" (amusement) is simply an older term meaning "suite," and in fact this is a suite drawn from a ballet. This Fairy is one of the colder sorts; her kiss brings death. However, the suite as here assembled (*"Sinfonia"* [Overture], "Swiss Dances," "Scherzo," and *"Pas de Deux"*) makes no attempt to mirror the ballet's story. Its interest is not narrative but technical: all the themes are Chaikofsky's. Picking from the older composer's piano and vocal music and generally avoiding the better-known melodies, Stravinsky made free use of the originals, with a quaint result—the music sounds like both Chaikofsky and Stravinsky at once. Impossible, you say: you're right. Two such different styles—Chaikofsky so lyrical, so conservatively "ballet"; Stravinsky so acerb and intellectual. Both opinions underrate these two giants. The experiment shows how modern Chaikofsky was, and how melodic Stravinsky. Here they are, together again for the first time, two highly Russian composers exercising their roots.

Apollo (Apollo Musagète)
1928; revised 1947

For string orchestra. George Balanchine's choreography gives us Apollo and three muses, Calliope, Polyhymnia, and Terpsichore, dancing separately and together; Stravinsky claims the work as an exercise in the working out of various poetic metres in music. The sound style is ice-clear Stravinsky—bold, angular, charming in spite of itself. "The Birth of Apollo" opens the ballet by way of prelude with slow introduction, a lively middle section, and a repeat of the slow. Then a violin cadenza ushers in Apollo's solo dance, followed by a dance for Apollo and the Muses that starts out—but does not finish—as a waltz. Each of the muses now takes her solo. Calliope's is yearning (with a grand bit for solo 'cello), Polyhymnia's ditsy, Tersichore's expansive. Apollo has another solo, then dances with Terpsichore. A lengthy final dance brings the quartet together again, and the traditional ballet "apotheosis" refers back to the slow music of the introduction.

About the two titles: that in parenthesis was the work's original name; after the revision Stravinsky took to calling the piece simply *Apollo.*

Capriccio for Piano and Orchestra
1929; revised 1949

This piece was written for the same reason that so many piano concertos of Mozart's day were written—as something to play for guest appearances. Fittingly, then, the piece respects Mozart's format: three movements, fast-slow-fast (although the three are connected without a break). A schizophrenic introduction launches the work with opposing energies of coarse and gentle, but once the first movement gets going, charm is the informing mode. As a coda, the introduction returns. Then comes the slow [second] movement, then the pert finale [third mvt], which gives the piece its title (it is marked *Allegro capriccioso* = lively and capricious). Classical concerto tradition called for the soloist to test his weight in the first movement, his song in the second, and his verve in the third. So it is here.

Violin Concerto in D Major 1931

A motto theme, heard in all four movements, binds the work together, though the theme tends to obscure itself in development when it shows up. It is the first thing one hears, one long spread chord played by the violin soloist with the 'cellos and basses, plus three shorter chords. (Thus, the motto "theme" is really more of a motto sound, the peculiar sound of those chords.)

The first movement, subtitled Toccata, is lively, *brillante,* emphasizing its first theme and closing with a bizarre figure for the soloist endlessly repeated while the orchestra sees to the tunes. (A toccata is a piece with "a lot of notes," as it were, and keeps everyone busy plunking them out.) The two middle movements are titled Aria I and Aria II ("aria" referring to their form, ABA, sometimes called song, or aria, form). These two movements taste lavishly of J.S. Bach, especially the second of the pair, a stately business with Baroque embellishments. (The motto theme is heard three times here, slightly disguised, at the very top of the movement—the A; just before the middle section—the B; and again at the return of the main—A—section.) The fourth movement is a typical concerto finale in that the soloist gets to show off his virtuosity; it is also typical in form—a rondo, and very staccato—the players are constantly plucking, hammering, biting. The motto theme is embedded in the main refrain of the rondo, but so transformed as to be untraceable. Stravinsky is so devious.

Symphony in C 1940

An unexpectedly traditional format gives us first movement, slow movement, scherzo, and finale. There is even a short slow introduction to the first movement, after which the winsome, precisely churned-up first movement chugs pleasantly along in that typically Stravinskyan imprint of Classical (Haydn-Mozart) sounds in natty modern dress. "What can one say about a score that is so unmysterious and so easy to hear?" the composer himself has asked—the second [slow] movement, for instance, so like the Mozartean slow movement in its songful melody lightly accompanied, contrasting middle section, and recapitulation. The second and third [scherzo] movements run together, without a break (coarse lower strings announce the transition). The finale [fourth mvt] begins with a murky slow introduction on the bassoons (repeated later in the movement) but soon turns lively. Ironically, the coda (tail-end) of the movement loses all energy in a sequence of quiet woodwind chords, another angle on Stravinsky's ceaseless experiments in sound as space.

Danses Concertantes 1942

The title means "Orchestral Dances in Concertante Style," *concertante* meaning "a soloistic use of the instruments." Though the work has been adopted by ballet companies and bears descriptive titles drawn from the dance world, it was written for its own sake, as a concert piece. There are five continuous movements. The first, "March—Introduction," invokes a sense of occasion, meanwhile warning of the peculiar quality of these "concerto dances": constant coming and going of instrumental solos. The second movement, *"Pas d'Action"* (Narrative Dance—classical ballet terms tend to the French), confronts angularity with tenderness. Third is *"Thème Varié"* (Varied Theme), a wistful theme and four lengthy variations. The fourth movement, *"Pas de Deux"* (Dance for Two), is heralded by woodwind and string flourishes, and begins rather unpretentiously for a Big Moment (the *pas de deux* is usually the gala event of any ballet). Twice, the rhythm is interrupted by the flute for a flowery cadenza; other instruments, too, put in their oars at various times—*concerto* dances, remember. For a closing, Stravinsky brings back the opening music for a "March—Conclusion."

Scènes de Ballet 1944

Billy Rose attempted to outdo the by-then-late Florenz Ziegfeld by buying the sumptuous Ziegfeld Theatre, mounting in it a symptuous revue devoted to all aspects of the arts, decorating the lobby sumptuously with the work of Salvador Dali, and throwing a sumptuous champagne-drenched opening night bash for the revue, which he called *Seven Lively Arts*. This show would have everything—jazz from Benny Goodman, choice comedy from Bert Lahr and Beatrice Lillie, a Broadway chorus line, a Cole Porter score—and Alicia Markova and Anton Dolin in a ballet choreographed by George Balanchine and composed by Igor Stravinsky, this same *Scènes de Ballet*, slightly cut to fit an overly sumptuous evening. It was a good idea for a show but it fizzled, mainly because much of the material wasn't very good. (Porter's score, except for "Ev'ry Time We Say Goodbye," was almost awful; long before the New York premiere, Lillie dubbed the evening *Seven Deadly Arts.*)

Scènes de Ballet has survived. It has no plot or theme whatever—pure music, pure dance. After a brief Introduction, the corps (the ballet "chorus") takes over in an oddly metred dance scored for odd wind solos. A touch of "busy music" on two clarinets and piano leads into the ballerina's solo, lightly edgy. At its end, this brings the work to its first full stop. Now the tempo slows for "Pantomime," featuring some cutely meticulous string writing. "Pas de Deux," very slow, is launched by a solo trumpet quickly joined by solo horn. There is a prankish interlude in faster tempo, but then the dance retrieves its grandeur again on trumpet and horn. With no warning, we plunge into another "Pantomime" leading into the male dancer's solo, another tiny "Pantomime," another dance for the corps (featuring the clarinets), and a grave "Apotheosis" based on the music of the introduction.

Throughout, Stravinsky emphasizes solo work, "coloring" the music kaleidoscope-style. It's delightful and tricky to follow and Rose was impressed: you hire class, you get class. Still, he wanted to tone down the scoring for the Broadway public—the scoring of Stravinsky, perhaps the most perceptive painter in the instrumental palette. After the opening night of the Philadelphia tryout, Rose wired Stravinsky: "YOUR MUSIC GREAT SUCCESS STOP COULD BE SENSATIONAL IF YOU WOULD AUTHORIZE ROBERT RUSSELL BENNETT RETOUCH ORCHESTRATION STOP BENNETT ORCHESTRATES EVEN COLE PORTER." Stravinsky wired back: "SATISFIED WITH SUCCESS."

Symphony in Three Movements 1945

This remarkable work is worth fifty hearings and days of study. In its twenty-two minutes it contains musical, pictorial, and emotional references to World War II as certainly as *The Waste Land* abstracted a mythopoeia for the post–World War I era. Stravinsky claimed that the composition of the work felt programmatic to him (the program relevant to the war) but that the piece as composed is not programmatic—and then cited instances of pictorial reference, a few of which are cited below. "The symphony was written under the pressure of world events . . . without participation of what I think of as my will, they excited my musical imagination."

So: the first movement "deals with" (is suggested by? retreats from?) "scorched earth tactics in China." The piano is prominent. The second [slow] movement, in ABA form with a brusquely genteel main theme introduced by the violins, is just music: "Composers combine notes. That is all." The third movement (which follows without a break) evokes an array of "goose-steping soldiers," slides into a tense fugue announced by piano and harp—the "stasis and turning point"—and rises to a triumph, that "of the Allies." The final outlandish chord—"rather too commercial," Stravinsky observes—caps the Allied overturn of Nazi barbarism.

There are too many details of scoring, construction, and so on to list here. But veteran listeners may catch allusions to the "cat" (clarinet) theme of Prokofyef's *Peter and the Wolf* in the first movement and the first number from Act II of Rossini's *The Barber of Seville* in the main theme of the second movement. Don't worry about form—hear *feeling* instead. Stravinsky protects himself, but personal projection comes through all the same.

Ebony Concerto 1945

Stravinsky was always receptive to popular music as sources for regeneration in symphony, and this commission from jazzman Woody Herman for a concerto for clarinet and jazz band is not as unlikely as it might sound. The layout is traditional, anyway, in the fast-slow-fast of the old "Italian" concerto—though the clarinet never takes over the work as a protagonistic soloist. Perhaps this is more of a concerto for (jazz) orchestra.

The first movement sets up a jiving tone in a typical Stravinskyan rhythmic plan, nervous and pushy. The use of the drums suggests an African hunting dance, the freely jamming piano a hot southern night down by the tracks. The slow [second] movement is altogether blue; moments of it bear a striking affinity with passages from Leonard Bernstein's musical *On the Town,* written a year earlier. The third movement opens with a tiny slow introduction (used later in the movement), then flips into a *Con moto* (with motion). A few repeated chords of a not entirely jazzy harmonics close the piece.

Orpheus 1948

Another Balanchine ballet, this one on the perennial subject of the musician in art, love, and death. This was Balanchine's second major staging of the tale, as he and The American Ballet (not to be confused with the present American Ballet Theatre) had taken on the dancing obligations for the Metropolitan Opera in the mid-1930s, culminating in a daring and disliked production of Gluck's *Orfeo ed Euridice* in 1936, directed by Balanchine and designed by Pavel Tchelitchev. Observed Lincoln Kirstein, the American Ballet chief, "It was by way of a reckless manifesto."

The present work, created for Ballet Society (the precursor of the New York City Ballet), is anything but reckless: poised, conservatively articulate, classical. It is superb music. Opening with Orpheus mourning the death of Euridice, Stravinsky offers descending notes on the harp under string chords. Then comes the first dance, a lively business led by a *scherzando* (joking) solo violin. The Angel of Death then has a solo and conducts Orpheus to hell, to trembling violins over a trombone, then a trumpet. Isamu Noguchi designed *Orpheus*' premiere, and one of his best ideas seems to have been a transparent curtain that fell every so often to signal a change of scene while Stravinsky sounds a brief "interlude." One such is now heard, and the curtain rises again on a "Dance of the Furies," agitated but not frightening, a stylized version of hell. Indeed, its frisky strings and noncommittal trumpet solos are almost friendly, until a new turn in the sound begins to suggest a certain frenzy. Now comes what must always be a great moment in Orpheus adaptations, his address and soothing of hell's anger. In opera, the poet sings; here, of course, he dances, to a firm rhythm of plucked strings and harp. Another "interlude": the doomed stretch out their arms to Orpheus and beg to hear more; he obliges. Hell, too, is moved. The furies bind Orpheus' eyes (viola solo, then trumpets) and produce Euridice—on their trip earthward, he must not look at her. A slow, woodwindy pas de deux for the two lovers, all the more intriguing because Orpheus cannot see. But he must see, and looks, and Euridice falls dead. A desolate "interval." The bacchantes rush in and tear Orpheus to pieces, as legend tells. But as with the Dance of the Furies, this is stylized rage, though it does eventually grow vindictive in its banging string chords. In an apotheosis, Apollo takes Orpheus to heaven to the accompaniment of the descending harp line that opened the work. A catch-22 of neo-Classical art—which this Orpheus certainly is—is that theatre is theatre and the audience will bring its own romanticism to the most austere rituals. Try to remain unmoved by the final page; I dare you.

Agon 1957

This ballet score caught Stravinsky both going and coming, right on the verge of a stylistic evolution. In his seventies by then, he began composition in 1953 in his neo-Classical autograph familiar to admirers of his earlier scores. But other work interrupted *Agon,* and when he returned to it in 1956, Stravinsky had graduated himself from neo-Classicism into a more advanced harmonic usage. Could the ear stand a work that began in one style and ended in another? (This had also happened to Stravinsky years before, while working on his short opera *The Nightingale.* He had composed the first of its three brief acts in a simple, folk-Russian style. Four years later, returning to the piece after a hiatus, he had become a full-fledged neo-Classicist, and the shift in signature from Act I to Act II is amusing to hear.)

Stravinsky's solution in *Agon* was to revise, so slightly, the earlier portion of the work so the gap in style would not jar. Still, one does hear it—and as if to reassure the listener that the composer remembers who he was, he finishes off the work with a reprise of its less sophisticated opening music.

Agon is a Balanchine ballet, created for the New York City Ballet; the title, a Greek word signifying the contest of two main characters in a theatrical work, is meaningless here—translate it as *"Ballet."* The structure is a little weird: fifteen short movements broken into four groups. A nervous opening for trumpets and horns sets up the work's unusual stop-and-start atmosphere; the second dance then asserts regularity in its rhythmic violin figure. Note the constant use of solo effects; Stravinsky uses a big orchestra here, but not necessarily all at once, choosing some instruments for this dance, others for that. So the dances come and go, changing mood and timbre (sound "color") at each new section. The modern feeling sets in early on, but it doesn't prove disturbing; indeed, these dances prove charming even in the *Angst* of modernism. At last, as a lagniappe, Stravinsky tosses us a restatement of his opening fanfare, sounding brightly juvenile after so much advanced harmony. Perhaps the title does have a meaning after all. The work *is* a contest: between one composer's two styles.

Movements for Piano and Orchestra 1959

In his youth, Stravinsky led the avant garde. But after *The Rite of Spring* and *Les Noces* and the *Symphony of Psalms* he had been too busy evolving his personal style to worry about staying "contemporary," and by the late 1940s radical critics in Europe—where one is up-to-the-minute or *kitsch* (sentimentalistic pop art)—had written him off. Suddenly, in the 1950s, Stravinsky got rhythm, as it were, all over again. This is one of his most advanced pieces, respectably avant garde for its time and one of his least enjoyable works.

Movements, warns the title, in the austere modern style of Schönberg's, Berg's, or Webern's "pieces for orchestra." There are five short movements, each identified as to tempo by the merest metronome marking, no *Allegro* or *Andante.* (Maelzel's metronome is the little tick-tock machine used to determine tempos as a clock tells time, once a fixture on middle-class pianos). All traditional rituals of melody, harmony, and rhythm are overthrown for Schönberg's twelve-tone system (see the Schönberg article for details), and there is not much for the commentator to say short of an unreadably complex analysis. Listen, as in the somewhat similar work of Anton Webern, to the meticulous use of instrumental coloration, especially in regard to the piano's balance with the rest of the smallish orchestra.

ANTON WEBERN 1883–1945

There are three star "moderns" in the firmament, "modern" here meaning difficult, associated with twelve-tone music. (Twelve-tone procedure, devised by Arnold Schönberg, is discussed in the article on Schönberg.) The leader of the trio is Schönberg, the most popular is Alban Berg, and the most difficult—intellectual, "dry," unapproachable—is Webern.

Analysts disagree as to whether Webern is a kind of last Romantic, working out of the shredded traditions of the nineteenth century, or a kind of first modern, taking the style of the arguably Romantic Schönberg and Berg and reducing it to its non-Romantic elements. One thing is sure: however odd Webern's music may sound when you first hear it, a slight familiarity with it will uncover its beauties, and even the most conservative ear will have to admit that "something is there."

The present volume is not the place to extrapolate Webern's highly concentrated, even atomized compositional practices. His works are *very* short; his whole life's work amounts to some four hours of music in all, including symphonic movements lasting less than a minute. This is not a stunt. Webern's music is, each time out, a precise study in technique; one should hear as if looking through a microscope.

With that kind of effort demanded of the listener, Webern's music never earned even the half-hearted popularity of Schönberg's and Berg's. Not only the general public but also the avant-garde establishment neglected him; here is one radical who has never known real vogue. Yet somehow, almost mysteriously, he has been promoted to twentieth-century classic. His highly charged exactness and kaleidoscopic studies in instrumental coloring eventually influenced young composers to an amazing degree. Practising musicians, at least, have no trouble absorbing Webern's soundscape, and he may be said to have passed on the open "secrets" of his style to a host of younger composers from Olivier Messiaen and Pierre Boulez to Karlheinz Stockhausen. He might have left a larger body of work, but for a freak accident that took his life just after World War II; he was shot, apparently in some misunderstanding, by a soldier of the American occupation forces. Incidentally, one may see his name written as Anton von Webern—the family, of noble lineage, used the particle; Webern himself seems to have dropped it in his youth.

Six Pieces for Orchestra, op. 6 1910

Six extremely little pieces, showcasing Webern's characteristically concentrated approach. Here, every note counts—seriously: as color (by virtue of the sound quality of the instrument playing it), as space (by virtue of its range, high or low, in relation to the notes preceding or following it), and as time (obviously, since there is so little time in the work). The first piece is slow enough for one to catch the shifting colors, spaces, and times as the notes slip by. The second piece is harsh and jerky; the third intensely tiny, the fourth a snarling funeral march featuring the percussion instruments, which open and close it. The fifth piece, also slow, opens with a superb effect in the lower strings, trembling in their deepest registers like the grumbles of ghosts. They also close the piece, this time—for balance—from on high. The sixth and last piece supplies a slow fade away to nothing.

Five Pieces for Orchestra, op. 10 1913

Less than five minutes long, this is possibly the most precisely worked out item in the symphonic repertory. The scoring calls exclusively for solo instruments: four woodwind players, three brass players, several percussionists, and four solo string players—and each of them plays what amounts to a soloist's part. It sounds like some dozen concertos going on at once without an orchestral body to hold anyone together. But Webern has stripped away all accompaniment, and the listening experience should deepen one's awareness of the color and texture of instrumental music. The mood of the five pieces goes from calm to lively to slow to flowing to lively again. However, such terms are always relative even when Webern uses them himself. To help focus the mind, he also produced vague titles for each of the pieces: "Prototype," "Transformation," "Return," "Memory," and "Soul."

Symphony, op. 21 1928

Webern uses the word "symphony" here in its oldest sense, meaning "orchestral work." Certainly this is not what most people think of as a symphony: it is well under ten minutes long and consists of two movements, both of them more concerned with technical procedures than developing a dramatic line. The first movement is a canon—one theme sounded by different sources entering at successive intervals (e.g., a group performance of "Row, Row, Row Your Boat"). However, here Webern varies the theme at each entrance, so you won't be able to follow it. Don't listen for anything; just hear. The second movement is a theme-and-variations. The theme is sounded by the clarinet, followed by seven variations and a coda. The variations are too obliquely derived for anyone to hope to follow them. Instead, notice Webern's use of instrumental color, an important feature of his style.

Concerto, op. 24 1934

Technically out of the compass of this book for its small forces, the work bears as full title, "Concerto for Flute, Oboe, Clarinet, Horn, Trumpet, Trombone, Violin, Viola, and Piano." Nine parts: chamber music. But Webern's style is so nuclear, so precisely reduced, that this chamber piece stands as a virtual abbreviation of an orchestral work. Moreover, it presents the listener with a rare opportunity to "hear" serialism in operation, for the shape of the all-basic tone row here is such that one can clearly follow its repetitions and permutations as it moves from instrument to instrument and pitch to pitch.

There are three short movements. The first, *Etwas lebhaft* (rather lively), opens with overlapping three-note phrases in oboe, flute, trumpet, clarinet, and piano that all vaguely resemble each other. As the movement continues, one may notice other such correlations, as if the twelve-tone system of primal row and endless restatements were opening itself up for an aural cross-section. The same row of course informs the material of the second movement, *Sehr langsam* (very slow)—though now the melodic outline is less abrasive. The third movement, *Sehr rasch* (very quick) closes with recollections of the opening three-note phrases.

ALBAN BERG 1885–1935

Along with Anton Webern, Berg is the most famous of those who adopted the complex twelve-tone system of composition devised by Arnold Schönberg. But Berg is by far the most popular of twelve-tone composers—including Schönberg. For Berg shows a smashing heart of poetry and tragedy, while Schönberg and Webern sound too "intellectual"—too dry—to most ears. (For a brief description of twelve-tone, or dodecaphonic music, see the introduction to the Schönberg chapter.) Berg, too, can be difficult, but usually not after the first time. Exposure and familiarity can make us contemptuous of simple music, but it feeds our interest in the complex.

Berg was not prolific, but what he did produce was invariably masterwork. His Violin Concerto, for example, for all its atomic constructions telescoped into endlessly expanded transformations and reflections, is music of great sensitivity. One may parse it for technique for days, but ultimately it is a profoundly emotional hearing experience. Similarly, we admire and discuss the progression of technique of Berg's first opera, *Wozzeck,* to his second, *Lulu;* still, it is the dramas themselves, dramas in music, that thrill us.

A good place to start with Berg is to hear not his orchestral or operatic works but a chamber piece, the Lyric Suite for string quartet. (Berg also arranged three movements of this piece for orchestra, cited below.) This is a very intimate introduction; you might then try the Violin Concerto, much bigger but no less intimate, inspired by the ugly, early death of a beautiful young actress.

Violin Concerto 1935

A classic of the repertory, very "modern," very weird, very moving. It is dedicated "to the memory of an angel," this being Manon Gropius, a lovely eighteen-year-old actress who was stricken with infantile paralysis and died after a year of torment. Berg and his wife were close friends of Manon's parents Alma Mahler and Walter Gropius, and Berg was badly shaken. This concerto has been taken as an exorcism of his horror. It is in two parts, with two (connected) movements in each part; the standard interpretation reads the first part as a portrait of Manon Gropius and the second part as an abstraction of her death as tragedy and transcendence.

The concerto is a twelve-tone work, very freely utilizing the style of composition developed by Arnold Schönberg (outlined in the introduction to the Schönberg chapter). Besides the basic "tone row" of the twelve notes to be used as the fundamental theme-material of the work, Berg employs a Carinthian folk tune and a Bach chorale, "Es Ist Genug!" (It Is Enough). The average listener probably won't notice how or when they are used, and it doesn't matter anyway. It is enough to follow the overall emotional development of the work from the expression of character in Part I to the expression of action in Part II. Don't listen for first or second themes—there are none here. Instead, concentrate on the way Berg "speaks" through the soloist, playing his poetry against the rougher textures of the orchestra. The work opens and closes in darkness—plaintive, dreamy, calm. Part I: the first movement suggests Manon's sensitivity and the second, her vivacity. Then Part II: catastrophe erupts in the third movement, then subsides for a lamentation and, of a kind, recovery in the fourth movement. Then darkness again, as at first.

Chamber Concerto 1925

Limited resources: violin and piano soloists and thirteen wind instruments. There are three (connected) movements, each scored a little differently—piano and winds in the first movement, violin and winds in the second [slow] movement, and both soloists with the winds in the finale. This is Berg just before he adopted (more exactly, adapted—and very freely) Arnold Schönberg's twelve-tone method of composition, and the sound is advanced but not horribly difficult. Indeed, its whimsy should appeal. The first movement, in fact, is a "Thema scherzoso con variazioni" (Scherzo theme and variations), though it will be easier to sit back and enjoy the scherzo quality than to pick out the specific theme and its transformations. The slow movement offers the violinist a main chance to display his emotional palette and technique, and the pianist joins him for the finale, a rondo based not on a recurring melody, but a recurring *rhythm.* Very tricky.

Three Movements from the Lyric Suite 1928

The *Lyric Suite* is a six-movement string quartet. From it, Berg extracted the second, third, and fourth movements and arranged them for full string orchestra, with minor adjustments. In this form, the music has become one of his most popular works; its lyrical appeal—its emotional songfulness—disarms those dubious of "modern" music (by which they mean "modern"-sounding, which hardly applies to a work written in 1928 anyway). The first of these three movements is an *Andante amoroso* (slow, lovingly) of immediate attraction; the second a weird intermission featuring unusual bowing and plucking procedures and highly divided strings (that is, with more than the usual number of separate groupings); and the third is a properly climactic summing up of importunate resonance, closing in morbid calm.

Three Pieces for Orchestra, op. 6 1915

One striking new symphonic form developed in the twentieth century is the orchestral suite of very short movements with no title other than the number of parts, as here. Of course, the idea of an original suite is not new, but the word "suite" implies a series of some kind, and was almost always organized around some theme, as with, say, Gustav Holst's *The Planets.* Berg's three pieces here are Prelude, Round Dance, and March. The Prelude begins in mystery, eventually yielding a principal theme, a yearning line in the first violins. This is developed briefly, and the movement subsides into the mysterious non-melodic buzz of its opening. The Round Dance is clumsy and friendly, and should remind Mahler buffs of his peasant-dance scherzo movements. Longest of the three, the brutal March uses a simplistic sonata-allegro to work up to a succession of ferocious climaxes. In one of them, the boiling orchestra suddenly drops away, ceding the sound space to the timpani, whose blows dwindle from fff (*molto fortissimo*=very, very loud) to pp (*pianissimo*=very quiet).

EDGAR VARÈSE 1885–1965

Of Varèse, the *New College Encyclopedia of Music* says, "His compositions, which owe nothing to tradition, include several works for large or unusual orchestras." This is putting it mildly. Said Varèse himself, "I do not write experimental music. My experimenting is done before I make the music. Afterwards, it is the listener who must experiment."

Lionized as a pioneer who never ceased seeking his west, Varèse spent his long career (headquartered in the United States despite his French birth and training) in search of a new "space" for music, a science of sonority. Each of his works seems to suggest one possibility in his search, but he moved ever on, eventually reaching out to electronic music—as an idea—before the means to compose it were refined.

Don't be afraid of Varèse, but be prepared for a surprising amount of percussion work. (The electronic music of Varèse, as all other electronic music, is not dealt with in this book.) Much of Varèse's music was avant garde too long ago to be thought radical today. If you have a choice, try *Arcana* (cited below), and consider Varèse's statement: "An artist is never *ahead* of his time, but most people are *behind* their own time."

Arcana 1927; revised 1960

Once considered incoherent and decadent, *Arcana* now seems intelligible and, with its 120-person orchestra, invigorating. The key to it is one basic figure that supplies the melody for the entire sixteen-minute piece. It is a kind of theme-and-variations, the theme being the heavy-footed tune heard at the very start, and the variations running far afield of it in tone and style (you will hear allusions to the patriotic march, the cabaret concert, jazz, Stravinsky, and so on). The orchestra is not only huge but diverse, including hecklephone, two sarrusophones, four triangles, two coconuts (an instrument, not the fruit), and güiros (a Cuban gourd scratched with sticks). The title, by the way, is the plural of *arcanum,* a mystic wisdom open only to initiates. Friends, hear—and be you now initiates, too.

Intégrales 1925

A shrill clarinet opens the work with a more-or-less one-note fanfare. Other instruments take up the pattern, accompanied by popping, marching, pushing percussion. This is one entailment on Varèse's search for new structural identities for sound—"music made of sound set free." Other identities, which follow the opening section, include obsessively whistling piccolos, long-held notes, repeated notes, and references to the opening clarinet fanfare, including a quasi-oriental oboe solo. Is the sound set free? The listener decides.

Ionisation 1931

One of Varèse's smaller works, this calls for thirteen players and thirty-seven instruments—all percussion. They bang, they gong, they ting, they shake, they glitter—and of all thirty-seven only the piano, celesta, and chimes can actually play notes (as opposed to the tuneless noise of, say, the castanets, sleigh bells, maracas, and other leprechauns of the percussion glen). Amusingly, Varèse does not use his three tune-carriers for tunes. He wants to work entirely in rhythm, plus make some secondary distinction in the "colors" of different instruments.

Hyperprism 1924

The focus of this four-minute piece is the contrast of wind (woodwinds and brasses) and percussion instruments. As usual with Varèse, there are many of the latter, including sleigh bells, gongs, drums, and siren. The percussion instruments open the work—no tunes—followed by the winds—"tunes" of a sort, more like fanfares. Soon the two groups are heard together, but never in collaboration until the last moment.

BOHUSLAV MARTINŮ 1890–1959

Martinů offers the exception to the rule that Czech composers deal lavishly in syntheses of the native sound style. Smetana, Dvořák, and Janáček all, in various ways, are national composers. Martinů is international. Drawn at first to France (in the 1920s and '30s) and then to the United States (from 1941 on) when the Nazi crunch threatened to squash him, Martinů changed his style constantly, absorbing new forms and devices as he moved west. He is never too "modern" for the conservative and always ingenuously delightful, though he rose admirably to tragedy when necessary (as in the *Memorial to Lidice,* cited below).

Unfortunately, though he was *almost* popular in his lifetime, often played and well spoken-of if never a concert headliner, since his death his reputation has dimmed except among musicologists. Even his best works retain the most tenuous hold on the repertory in his two adopted countries, though he is a regular event in the musical life of Czechoslovakia.

Symphony no. 6: Fantaisies Symphoniques 1953

Originally, Martinů was going to call it the "New Fantastic Symphony"—then changed his mind to avoid association with Berlioz. Now termed "symphonic fantasies," the work remains fantastic not in the Berliozian sense of wild and hallucinatory but in its use of fantasy (free) form (as opposed to the more defined sonata or ABA forms of more conventional symphonic movements).

There are three movements. The first, opened and closed by a strangely ethereal slow passage, is lively, featuring one theme that in melody and harmony has to be one of the most American-sounding moments in all symphony. (Martinů's compatriot Dvořák also managed to sound both American and Czech in his "New World" Symphony, written, like Martinů's Sixth, as a result of time spent in America.) The second [scherzo] movement achieves some furious rhythmic—not to mention dramatic—expansion; the third and last is the slow movement, deflating the energy built up in the first two movements with an austere sorrow. Typical fantasy, the music is moody, interestingly episodic—note the almost perky clarinet solo in the middle of the movement, another "American" effect from this most cosmopolitan of composers.

Piano Concerto no. 3 1948

Written for Rudolph Firkusny, this work demands the most of its soloist in terms of technique and endurance. The format is conventional, commencing with a stormily lyrical first movement that counters the piano line with Czech-folkish strains in the violins and woodwinds. The slow [second] movement opens passionately and never settles into the gracile poise of the Mozartean slow movement—this is assertive music, faster than "slow" and in its racy emotional climate virtually a continuation of the first movement. The dominating thematic figure is an odd trainlike motion (usually in the strings) which plays against the piano, sometimes as accompaniment and sometimes as challenge. The jerky finale [third mvt] is notably folklike, as if the cosmopolitan Martinů were reminding us that "Czech born is Czech forever." An interesting effect of this piece is that its three movements seem almost to run at the same speed, as if they were three allegros back to back.

Violin Concerto no. 2 1943

Martinů is in eclipse at present, but back in the 1940s and '50s this was one of his most popular works, savored for its wonderful lyricism. (It was written for Misha Elman.) The composer was living in the United States then, yet he reverted to an almost primitive folk style for this work, as if attempting to recreate the musical atmosphere of his native Czechoslovakia. A violinist himself, he spun out a most grateful solo part—this is a real virtuoso's showpiece, touching all bases from fiddle fun to fierce artistry. The first movement is ardent rather than lively, the second [slow] movement tenderly intimate, the finale [third mvt] a roughhewn dance movement culminating in an absurdly tricky cadenza that cuts off seconds before the orchestra shuts the work closed.

Memorial to Lidice 1943

World War II called up a new genre in symphony, anti-Nazi music. Symphonies, tone poems, and even a few concertos were written to inspire and focus morale, many of them prompted by specific incidents of Nazi brutality. This is one of those, a threnody for the Czech village of Lidice, totally wiped out by the Germans in retaliation for the Resistance assassination of "Hangman" Heydrich, Gauleiter of Bohemia-Moravia. (Three thousand hostages in Prague and Brno were also slaughtered.) The word "Lidice" quickly came to symbolize the worst penalty of war, the incidental terrorizing of non-combatants.

At the time, a few people thought that music had no place in the war effort, that its poetry could only disguise the horror, not unmask it. But now, decades later, the music stands on its own as a tone poem not of current event but of tragedy belonging to no one time. A discordant opening gives us Martinů's "fix" on the twin images of oppression and resistance; they are heard both in conflict and in a strange harmony, almost a symbiosis. Hymnlike in the strings, the music resists terror, crying survival, surging to a brave finish when the horns quote the opening four notes of Beethoven's Fifth—the so-called "Victory" theme of the Allied Powers.

JACQUES IBERT 1890–1962

Ibert just hangs onto the repertory in the two works cited here; all the rest of his considerable output is seldom heard even in his native France. As *Escales* is a "pops" item and *Divertissement* a lampoon, Ibert is generally thought of as a lightweight—but his career was launched by the Paris premiere of his tone poem *La Ballade de la Geôle de Reading: The Ballad of Reading Gaol,* after Oscar Wilde's brutal verses.

Escales (Ports of Call) 1922

This is one of those rare works that manage to be both offbeat and mainstream at the same time—offbeat to highbrow symphony buffs, who disdain it as a cheesy travel poster of a piece, yet mainstream to many casual listeners who encounter it happily on records, radio, and at Kostelanetz-like "Promenade" concerts. It is pleasant music, if hardly compelling. There are three movements, one each for Italy, North Africa, and Spain.

"Rome-Palermo," the first port-of-call, opens with simple aplomb on a flute solo that announces, straight on, "Adventure!" Lush strings-and-harp passages suggest sumptuous seas, other sections suggest hustly port towns—seedy and prankish episodes—until the strings and harp seem to put the ear out to sea again. The brief second movement and port is Nefta, in Tunisia, where a prominent oboe solo sets the tone for elegant tropical sensuality. Last of the trio is "Valencia," with the now-torrid–now-languid effects common to the Spanish soundscape. At first on the easygoing side, the movement builds to a fiery conclusion.

Divertissement 1930

This is very funny music, orginally written to accompany a production of Labiche's popular comedy, *The Italian Straw Hat.* First, an

Introduction warns the ears about what is to come with odd instrumentation and a few amusingly stupid tunes. But lo, a succeeding Cortège promises sobriety—for maybe twelve seconds. Suddenly, the tempo picks up; various instruments try out tiny solos in a festive march. Listen carefully for a minuscule quotation of the Wedding March from Mendelssohn's *A Midsummer Night's Dream* at two different points. Nothing really gets settled in this movement—everything started is abruptly dropped; at the end, we get a reprise of the opening slow march. Next is a Nocturne, which also starts out sober and, perversely, continues so, despite a brief but overwrought piano cadenza at the very end. A Waltz now has its joke in that a portentous introduction leads up to a maddeningly insignificant woodwind tune. At least the strings know what a waltz is for, and they oblige with a gooey Johann Straussian air. The movement then completely falls apart with a zesty spoof of palm-court-type salon music. A Parade is next, nearing and passing cutely. For his Finale, Ibert pulls off a gallop made up of one part circus music, one part ballet chase scene, and one part gall. A delight.

SYERGYEY PROKOFYEF 1891–1953

One of the great originals of the twentieth century, Prokofyef managed to sound different from everyone else despite his working in the forms that everyone else was using—piano sonatas, string quartets, symphonies, concertos, operas, ballets. He could be experimental or traditional. What set him apart was his sound style as a whole: his biting, angular, abrasive melodies, his delight in the grotesque, his tumultuous rhythmic drive, his ability to blend quaintness and satire with the most beautifully tuneful passages.

The composer himself, on the occasion of his fiftieth birthday in 1941, outlined the "five lines of development" that guided his composition:

1. Classical—i.e., traditional
2. Innovatory—new harmonic idioms and mediums
3. Toccata—rapid, rhythmically precise motion
4. Lyrical
5. Scherzo—comic

These are not in chronological order, but spontaneous; almost any of Prokofyef's works shows all five in some proportion. Obviously, such expressive sophistication is not to all tastes. Some listeners resent the intrusion of the bizarre upon the beautiful. Others are baffled by the sly complexity of tone hidden in the ostensive simplicity of design. Unfortunately, among those who didn't "get" Prokofyef's style were the policy-makers of the Central Committee of the Communist Party in Prokofyef's homeland, Russia. Thinking a bloody revolutionary period not conducive to the composition of music—even music so wildly cynical and desperate as his—the young virtuoso pianist and composer left Russia for the West (mainly Paris) in 1918. However, his work remained more popular back in Russia than in the free world, and eventually homesickness plus a desire to create in his native cultural habitat sent him East again in 1933.

Music, like everything else in the Soviet Union, is hostage to state tyranny, specifically in that Soviet composers are expected to write music that is invariably simple and heroic, preferably using programmatic messages of political propaganda. This is the notorious "Socialist realism." Though spared the purge of 1937 through the personal intervention of Stalin, Prokofyef was brought to account for his individuality in 1948, when *Pravda* published the Central Committee's detailed condemnation of just about every front-rank composer then living in Russia. Shostakovitch, likewise assaulted, apologized, promised to do better, and hoped the times would change. Prokofyef, however, nonchalantly insulted the Committee at his *viva voce* hearing, turning his back on them when his indictment was read out. Ironically, he had once defended the Soviet system to his non-Communist friends in the West, and even composed his Second Violin Concerto, in 1935, heavily on the lyric side as if to affirm his willingness to meet Socialist realism at least partway.

Because of this political context, we listen to Shostakovitch always wondering how much of his music represents his personal wishes and how much a slavey's command. But Prokofyef composed mostly at liberty. Even after he returned to the Soviet Union, he was not so harassed by policy as some of his colleagues. He is an acquired taste. The Central Committee never acquired it, but we can, especially if we prepare ourselves for the at-times grim melding of lyricism and satire. Consider making your acquaintance with the *Scythian Suite,* a stupendous explosion of barbaric glitter, or the Third Piano Concerto, a unique combination of lively innocence and frolicsome nostalgia, one of Prokofyef's less tart entries. Classicists, who admire economy of presentation above all, should investigate the First Symphony, dubbed "Classical" for its wry homage to the simpler symphony of the Haydn era.

Symphony no. 1 in D Major, "Classical," op. 25 1917

What could be simpler than this old-fashioned symphony, using the format developed, experimented with, and at last ratified by Haydn?

The cut of melody and harmony is that of Prokofyef, *enfant terrible.* But the overall shape and function of the four movements accord with the old conventions. Critics thrill to the historical importance of the work, one of the formative examples of the neo-Classical revival. As it happens, though, Prokofyef imposed the old fashion upon himself as a discipline—he wanted to test his grasp of basics. If he succeeded, *then* he could go off on his own tangents.

This is not a strict copy of Haydn and company, but a modernist's retrospective of their style. In sound—in the personality of the themes and their instrumentation—the piece is of course pure Prokofyef. The lively first movement immediately establishes the neo-Classical soundscape: witty, parodistic, shrewdly quaint. We open at the gallop, though by the second subject (shrilly elegant violins leaping over wide spaces), things have calmed down somewhat. After a slow [second] movement of piquant songfulness we pass over into hardcore satire in the third movement, a gavotte rather than the expected minuet. Violins and woodwind combine to spell out the tinny Prokofyef autograph, seconded by a trilling flute-and-oboe collaboration in the trio section over a "drone bass" (in imitation of a bagpipe) in the lower strings. (Prokofyef liked this gavotte so much he later used it in his ballet *Romeo and Juliet.*) The finale [fourth mvt] winds it all up with insistent but not overbearing vitality. Note a typical touch in the woodwindy second theme: a batch of rapid repeated notes.

Symphony no. 5 in B Flat Major, op. 100 1944

This is an energetic work, featuring a dynamic slow movement and perhaps the great satiric scherzo of modern times. As if to make up for the animation of these two middle movements, the first movement is slower than most, broadly gesturing at some heroic ideal with certain sardonic misgivings. The pride of the movement is its coda, a thrilling expansion tacked on just when one expects the music to fade out.

It wouldn't be Prokofyef without burlesque, and the scherzo [second mvt] supplies the expected high jinks with an icy, whiplash gaiety. The trio (middle section), both preceded and followed by a shrill woodwindy bit, offers an emotional contrast to the main part of the scherzo, though the sense of power that it unleashes is very central to the work in general. When the scherzo proper returns, it is in the process of development rather than the exact repetition demanded by tradition, and near the end it delights in a series of lightninglike downward-driving runs in the strings. Follows then the slow [third] movement, akin to the first movement in its idealism and an effective bridge from scherzo to finale [fourth mvt], which after all must resolve the work's question of mood and color. This the finale at first does with a slow introduction recalling the first movement's first subject. When the finale assumes its own rather dashing tempo, it becomes clear that Prokofyef has simply transferred the "information" of earlier movements into that of the finale. A great deal of the melodic material here actually does derive from the first movement, most notably a perverse theme that repeatedly emphasizes a "wrong" note. This the composer uses at the very end for harmonic tension: that wrong note turns out to be the wrongest possible for the home key, B Flat. By hammering on it again and again, Prokofyef can all the better confirm the release of harmonic tension when he finally trades the "wrong" note in for the right one.

Symphony no. 6 in e flat minor, op. 111 1946

Ennervated loneliness marks the opening of the first movement, aided by the minor key and reticent scoring. Then, a change: a brisk march, redoubling the air of alienation. But now another change: the first theme returns in fast tempo accompanied by whacks on cymbal and woodblock. This is the development section, rephrasing the loneliness of the opening in livelier but more crushing terms. This is vitality, but maleficent vitality: evil. The fury recedes, and the recapitulation reaffirms the non-affirmation of the opening.

A tragic symphony? It began so, and so it continues, in a slow [second] movement of strained lyricism. This is an expansive elegy that constantly tries to reassure itself but constantly loses its dignity in wails of anguish. Note, for example, the beautiful line for 'cellos early on—but note as well the savage figure for timpani, piano, and several bass instruments later on, heralded by "clockwork" plonks on woodblock and plucked strings. With such manic effects built into his slow movement, Prokofyef needs no scherzo. So we move right on to the finale [third mvt], which begins with misleadingly benign zip, punctuated by a stamping figure like the heel-and-toe of a village dance. Still, the atmosphere is something less than delighted. More and more we sense the isolation of the first two movements as it might be stated in an atmosphere of false gaiety. At length, tragedy reasserts its hold in a restatement of the first movement's opening theme in two blistering climaxes.

Symphony no. 7, op. 131 1952

Originally conceived as a "children's symphony," the Seventh has been dismissed as lightweight, some analysts suggesting that Party pressure may have forced Prokofyef to make it more "popular" (i.e., simple) than he wanted to. Whatever the reason, it is a simple symphony, regular in structure, old-fashioned in appeal, and highly melodic. It opens sparely, in gloomy c sharp minor, the first subject in the violins. Other instruments roll and rumble as the theme is developed, and soon a lyrical second subject is disclosed by the lower instruments. The violins take up the tune, bringing to it a rhapsodic expansion familiar to lovers of Prokofyef's ballet scores *Romeo and Juliet* and *Cinderella*. There is a rather off-the-wall closing theme involving woodwinds and bells, a development and full recapitulation. The movement dies away to fragments of the first subject and, at the end, a "wrong-note" major-key chord on the piano.

Keeping to the simple but unwilling to suppress his native satire, Prokofyef provides a silly waltz for the second [scherzo] movement, with a brief restrained trio led by violins and solo oboe, a repeat of the trio, and an amusingly bombastic coda. The third [slow] movement is short and witty; some listeners are put off by its failure to rise above its own sense of humor, but it does have some affecting moments.

The finale [fourth mvt] in D Flat Major is more successful, a raging hoopla of prancy solos and assorted buffoonery. To lift the heart, Prokofyef quotes the big lyrical tune from the first movement toward the close, and follows this with the strange theme that originally succeeded it. The symphony seems to have ended—no . . . the vivacious opening tempo returns for a lightning finish.

Piano Concerto no. 2 in g minor, op. 16 1913

This barbaric item opens as if in a dream, but rips into an athletic extroversion soon enough, featuring the biggest cadenza (the soloist's show-off spot) imaginable. The second [scherzo] movement is famous with annotaters for its multitude of tuneless notes on the piano (what melody there is is mainly provided by the orchestra). The third movement, termed an "intermezzo" (interval), once shocked the sensitive for its rude, tramping opening. Actually, this is an at-times charming movement that acts as a restrained second scherzo. Those who hope for a slow movement somewhere along the way haven't anticipated Prokofyef the *enfant terrible*. No slow movement. The finale [fourth mvt] brings the work home in cascades of thrill-seeking, soloistic heroism, *very* concerto.

Piano Concerto no. 3 in C Major, op. 26 1921

One of the most popular piano concertos of the twentieth century, this is also one of the most difficult in terms of challenge to the soloist's endurance. Though the first movement opens slowly, with a sweet melody on the clarinets, the tempo soon picks up, the soloist leaps in with the first subject, and an *Allegro* (lively) of more or less non-stop action proceeds. Buffoonish touches in the scoring (such as the castanets that accompany the second subject) keep the ambience comic. But there is no denying the affecting power of the slow [second] movement, a theme and five variations. The theme launches the movement, played by the orchestra; the pianist takes the first variation, leading the orchestra through a tempestuous tempo change for the second variation (note the trumpet helpfully outlining the theme). The third variation is also fast, the theme losing much of its original shape. But the slower, reflective fourth variation, ranging yet farther from the original *melody,* recaptures its intimate *character*. The vigorous fifth variation leads into a restatement of the theme in its basic form, embellished by rapid-fire figures on the keyboard. The finale [third mvt] honors the jolly rondo of tradition, varying in tone and tempo. At the end, a thrilling wash of sound finds the orchestra torn between assisting the pianist and obliterating him. It takes a strong player to achieve even a draw.

Piano Concerto no. 5 in G Major, op. 55 1932

This is a wild one. Five short movements—lively, moderate, explosive, slow, and lively again—seemed so little like a concerto (as organic form) to the composer that at first he thought of calling it "Music for Piano and Orchestra." It isn't played often (mainly because the solo part is so difficult), but its terse assertiveness provides an unusual experience. Outgoing in its first two movements, the work goes a little mad in its central section, a toccata (literally "touched"—because it uses a great many notes in a small space of time). Then comes a slow [fourth] movement, somewhat less than tender; the finale [fifth mvt] is most outgoing of all.

Violin Concerto no. 1 in D major, op. 19 1917

Piquant is the word for this piece, dreamily bizarre rather than turbulent or sardonic (two moods common to the composer). No, here he is neither huge nor satiric, but poised and almost reticent, though he certainly puts the soloist through a virtuoso's paces. The violinist almost never gets a rest; he opens the work with a sinuous first theme as if in reverie (Prokofyef marks it *sognando*=dreaming). For contrast, the second theme (marked *narrante*=storytelling) has a bite which carries into the development section until a shortened recapitulation simply restates the first theme (on flute, at first) while the solo violin and the harp decorate it with sheerest filigree.

Rather than the slow movement of tradition, the second movement offers a scherzo like a fairy on a rampage, bitty but menacing. The soloist sets the tone for the finale [third mvt] with a dancing tune, but later a more lyrical mood takes over. By the end of the work, we are not surprised to hear the first theme of the first movement (in the solo and first violins) vie for prominence with the dance tune. After this tidy bid for overall unity, the third movement ends in an almost note-for-note replica of the ending of the first movement.

Violin Concerto no. 2 in g minor, op. 63 1935

The soloist, unaccompanied, opens the work with a somber first theme that dominates the first movement through exposition, development, and recapitulation. Similarly, the second [slow] movement is dominated by its main theme; this is the glory of the concerto, Mozartean in its brilliance of song. In performance, it almost always ends in that nervous, clammy, thrilled silence of an audience that wishes it could throw poise to the winds and clap its hands off in appreciation. The tension, however, is swallowed up in the finale [third mvt], a rhythmic rather than melodic movement veering from uncouth waltz to stamping aggressiveness.

Sinfonia Concertante for 'cello and orchestra, op. 125 1952

A reworking of a viola concerto dating from 1938, the present "concertoish symphony" is one of Prokofyef's last major compositions. It's a big work, with expansions of development and variations not always found in the concerto form. The first movement deals largely with decorations of the opening theme, a vigorous hut-two-three-four. It is the central second movement, a combination of slow movement and scherzo, that contains complex structural procedures. This long movement, longer than many concertos, acts almost as if it would be a whole work in itself—episodic, sharply angular at one point and sentimental at another. There is a cadenza for the soloist relatively early on; later, he plays a tricky accompanimental figure under two clarinets while the tambourine throws a little party for itself. After such drollery even a taut theme-and-variations finale [third mvt] has its hands full bringing the work to climax and resolution.

Suites from Romeo and Juliet 1935

Prokofyef's *Romeo and Juliet* must be the most popular evening-length ballet score after the big three of Chaikofsky (*Swan Lake, The Sleeping Beauty, The Nutcracker*). He put his best into it, and the result is so dramatic that the music actually does as well in concert as it does in the theatre. However, the excerpts drawn for the suites are not arranged in story order, so one's listening is liable to get a little nerve-wracking. Ideally, one might invest in a recording of the complete score.

There are two suites, both made while the composer was waiting for his finished score to reach the stage. (Several Russian theatres agreed to mount it and then reneged; it finally received its premiere in Brno, Czechoslovakia, in 1938.) Suite no. 1 opens with "Folk Dance," a jumpy number for a street scene. A perky "Scene" (in ballet parlance, a movement covering some plot action) leads on to a "Madrigal," a slow section drawn from the Capulet ballroom scene where Romeo and Juliet meet. The following "Minuet" describes the pompous arrival of the guests for the ball, whereupon the alternately prancy and shrilling "Masks" depicts three uninvited arrivals—Romeo, Mercutio, and Benvolio, from the Montague side of the famous feud, in capes and dominoes. "Romeo and Juliet" accompanies the balcony scene, mirroring Shakespeare's poetry with muted beauty from the orchestra, notably a chaste flute solo. This remarkable instrumental evocation of stealthy sensuality is dispelled by the last number, "The Death of Tybalt," tackling the Tybalt-Mercutio duel, the Tybalt-Romeo duel, and Tybalt's funeral procession, with Tybalt's mother keening over the corpse.

The second suite opens with a brilliant expression of "The Montagues and the Capulets" in the full dress of their feud: a brief introduction of snarling brasses suddenly cuts away to an eerie shimmer of violins; then a heavy, regular rhythm sets in as the proud Veronese nobles show their mettle. (In the ballet, this music describes the Capulets at their ball, not the Montagues as well.) In a middle section, a solo flute transforms the main theme into something light and slender; then it returns in its original haughty heft. The second number, "Juliet as a Young Girl," is capricious, innocent, tender. "Friar Laurence" sounds properly thoughtful; "Dance of the Five Couples" is a lively smidgeon of a street scene heightened by a passing festival. Perhaps the most beautiful single item in the score is "Romeo and Juliet Before Parting," a slow movement of great depth with a weirdly touching finish. A short interval, "Dance of the Maids with the Lilies," brings us to "Romeo at Juliet's Tomb," from the final scene of the ballet. Note how Prokofyef brings Juliet's cortège in as if from the distance: we hear the music from Romeo's point of view, waiting in the tomb. Thus the level of shuddering sorrow overlaid upon the funeral music.

Cinderella Suites 1941

There are three suites from the complete score, arranged in 1946. But one generally hears either the whole ballet or excerpts chosen by a conductor without regard to what suite it belongs to. Since the music is dramatically keyed to the story as few ballet scores are, its's important that—if one must hear excerpts—they be played in story order so one may enjoy Prokofyef's quite distinctive view of the fairy tale according to the logic of his form.

This Cinderella is the familiar waif of the cinders with weak father, nasty stepmother, mean stepsisters, fairy godmother, Prince Charming, midnight flight, and telltale slipper. But the plot is thickened with characterful touches, all of which affect the musical projections of the tale. The two sisters, for instance, Khudishka (Scrawny) and Kubishka (Dumpy), are grotesque foils to the central love plot. The scene in which the fairy godmother sends Cinderella to the ball, the ball itself, and the prince's globe-trotting search for the nameless beauty of the slipper are played out in the elaborate "variations" (solo dances) with which ballets drop all pretense of dramatic continuity and just stand there and dance. The godmother's warning about leaving the ball at midnight is strongly portrayed: roiling strings over a twelve-note theme in the brasses. There is even, for the fun of it, a quotation of the famous March from Prokofyef's opera *The Love For Three Oranges* in the ball scene. I urge the listener to pass up the "highlights" discs and spring for a complete recording. An excellent Russian performance conducted by Gyennady Rozhdyestvyensky, available on the Angel-Melodiya label, fills two records and includes an excellent number-by-number analysis of the score.

Lieutenant Kijé Suite, op. 60 1934

These five numbers are excerpts from Prokofyef's 1933 soundtrack score for a movie spoof of the tsarist bureaucracy. It's a blithe burlesque. The plot premise of the film derives from the rule that the tsar is infallible: when he mistakes the phrase *"Porootchiki zhe"* (The lieutenants, however . . .) for *"Porootchik Kijé"* (Lieutenant Kijé), that fortuitous lieutenant must therefore be invented. First of the five pieces is "The Birth of Kijé," suggesting the military community with an opening and closing cornet fanfare and some march spoofs led by "fife and drum." "Romance" is a doleful song (also arranged for baritone solo, but seldom performed with a singer), "The Wedding of Kijé" a boozy party held by the cornet, "and "Troika" a lurching ride on a three-horse sleigh (this, too, offers a baritone in an alternate version, singing, "A woman's heart is like an inn: the whole world fits therein"). "Troika" opens with a stately announcement of its theme—then the ride begins, the theme on saxophone, bassoon, and 'cellos while a sense of motion is conveyed by fleetly pounding strings, harp, piano, drum, triangle, and sleigh bells. Last comes "The Burial of Kijé"—for even an abstracted mortal must die. True, his death calls for a certain kind of elegy; Prokofyef gives us nostalgia mingled with comedy by recalling tunes from earlier parts of the suite, and closes with a touch of the opening cornet fanfare by way of taps. Under this, the lowest instrument (the contrabass) sounds its highest note, as if a cry in the distance.

Suite from The Love for Three Oranges, op. 33 bis 1924

Prokofyef's opera of 1919 is based on a play of the same name by the flamboyant Venetian Carlo Gozzi. Bent on reviving the moribund spirit of *commedia dell'arte,* Gozzi told—comic-romantically—of a fairy-tale prince under a ban of enchantment who finds three princesses inside three oranges, eventually finding his happy ending with one of them. Gozzi's Punch-and-Judy style suited Prokofyef to the note, and the result is a wacky, wonderful partnership of romance and grotesquerie. To construct this suite of excerpts from the opera, the composer either left out the vocal lines or replaced them with instruments. First comes "The Crackpots," drawn from the opera's prologue, when various special-interest groups of theatre buffs (the Crackpots, Empty-Heads, and Lovers of Tragedy, Comedy, and Romance) lobby for the entertainment they prefer. Ultimately, of course, all get what they want, for true *commedia* is something of a grabbag. The second number is an "Infernal Scene," devoted to a game of cards, good magician versus evil witch. Next comes the famous "March," depicting the loony pomposity of the fairy-tale court, followed by a "Scherzo," hurry music connected with the Prince's search for his three oranges. Fifth, "The Prince and the Princess," is love music, pure and simple—well, not so pure, given Prokofyef's taste for spoof. Last comes the exit music of the villains of the piece, "Flight."

Scythian Suite (Ala and Lolly), op. 20 1915

Four numbers drawn from an ambitious ballet projected (for Dyagilyef's Ballets Russes) but never completed, this suite stands with Stravinsky's *The Rite of Spring* as examples of the primitivistic movement in ballet. It calls for huge orchestra, delighting in barbaric splendor and arrogance, and tells of the Scythians, an ancient nomadic people of the steppes of southern Russia, sun-worshippers. Ala is the daughter of the sun, Lolly a Scythian hero. The subtitle listed above was to have been the name of the ballet.

Some ballet it would have been, too, some extravaganza of savage poetry, to judge from the music. First comes "The Adoration of Vyelyes and Ala," Vyelyes being the Sun and the ceremony inspiring much weight, color, and movement from the orchestra. Most devout of all, perhaps, are the three flutes with pastoral echo effects in a subdued middle section. Then come the bad guys: "The Enemy God and Dance of the Evil Ones." The plot takes a twist in "Night," as the Enemy God threatens Ala under cover of darkness. Ending with a run on a solo harp and a quietly dissonant chord in the strings, "Night" anticipates a resolution in "Lolly's Departure and the Procession of the Sun": battle music (including what sounds like the cries of great birds) depicts Lolly's fight to save Ala. Ultimately, what saves her is the sunrise—the power of light, which disperses evil. The music changes at this point to capture the growing brilliance of the sun show, building to a tremendous climax by repeating the same figures over and over with greater volume each time.

Peter and the Wolf, op. 67 1936

Like Benjamin Britten's *The Young Person's Guide to the Orchestra*, *Peter and the Wolf* is music with a purpose: to isolate the characteristic timbres of different instruments so as to familiarize the uninitiated. There is a story—told by a narrator—and each person or animal in the action is identified with a specific instrument. The bird is heard on the flute; the duck on the oboe (a Russian duck, very doleful); the cat, elegant and spry, on the clarinet; the grandfather on the bassoon; the dread wolf on three horns; the hunters (as rifle shots) on the drums; and Peter in a boyishly heroic march on the strings. Ideal (in fact, intended by the composer) for kids.

ARTHUR HONEGGER 1892–1955

"I attach great importance to the architecture of music . . . my great model is Johann Sebastian Bach." So Honegger defined his position as one of the leading influences of the neo-Classical revival in the 1920s. A member—at least nominally—of the group of French composers known as The Six, Honegger was much less attracted than the other five were to a blending of simplicity and clarity with the racy sound of popular music. (For more on the aesthetics of The Six, see the introductory article to Francis Poulenc.) Swiss, anyway, not French, and of a training and termperament that looked back to the great German rather than French masters, Honegger was the first of The Six to dissociate himself from the satire and whimsy for which they were famous in their youth.

He often felt as if he were writing in a vacuum. "The most important attribute of a composer," he observed, "is that he be dead." Honegger has never enjoyed a wild popular success for his back-to-Bach economy of presentation and his dry, "intellectual" sound, not even posthumously. Detractors might say that his melody sounds as if it were reporting on itself, turning itself in for disciplinary action lest it prove too ardent, too moving. Yet, within his chosen parameters, Honegger has resonance. Newcomers might try *Pacific 231,* an evocation of railway locomotion dating from the machine craze in art in the 1920s, a lively artifact.

Symphony no. 2 (for String Orchestra and Trumpet) 1941

(Actually the trumpet part, called for only in the final movement, is marked *ad lib,* meaning it's conductor's choice whether to use it or, if preferred, an oboe or clarinet. Honegger simply wants to emphasize a hymnlike violin line which might otherwise get lost in the sound of the other strings. The "foreign" timbre of the brass or wood instrument, playing along with the violins, ensures that the hymn tune will stand out.)

This somewhat depressed work is laid out in three movements, Honegger's usual plan for a symphony. Although he denied having any program in mind, the world status at the time of composition in late 1941—France fallen, Hitler's war machine plowing through Russia, England standing alone for freedom—must surely have inspired the unnerving antagonism of depression (the obsessive solo viola figure in the opening) and violence that dominates the first movement. The slow [second] movement is the heart of the work. The composer thought it "gloomy" and "a little desperate" and predicted that conductors would try to cheer it up by taking its *Adagio mesto* (sad and very slow) faster than they ought. The finale [third mvt], however, remixes the elements of despair and fury expressed earlier in a quick tempo that grows rhythmically more adventurous with the use of accents on off-beats. At last the trumpet (or oboe or clarinet) chimes in with the hymn tune—a ray of hope?

Symphony no. 3, "Liturgical" 1946

Honegger's characteristic three movements give a rounded shape to his symphonies rather than the square cut of the more usual four; he tends to center attention on the middle slow movement. The subtitle, "Liturgical," denotes the mottos assigned to each of the movements: the first, a turbulence, is marked "Dies Irae" (Day of Wrath—Judgment Day); the second, stricken but hopeful, is "De profundis clamavi" (Out of the depths I cried), a thrilling recovery from disaster that sings of the heroism of sheer survival; the third, "Dona nobis pacem" (Give us peace), begins with a caustic march, builds to bitter defiance, and culminates in the sweet bendiction of peace.

Pastorale d'Été (Summer Pastorale) 1920

The epigraph to the score, "J'ai embrassé l'aube d'été" (I have embraced the dawn of spring), a snippet of Rimbaud's *Les Illuminations,* sums up the blithe, bird-thou-never-wert spirit of this tone poem. As tranquilly upfront and glowing as dawn in the Swiss mountains, where Honegger wrote the piece while on vacation, the music utilizes two themes—first, the opening horn melody; second, the livelier tune introduced a little later on clarinet—in the ABA form of a symphonic slow movement. A is the first theme, B the second, and the repeat of the A, after a bit of development to a soaring climax, features the two themes played simultaneously.

Pacific 231 1923

The 231 was a locomotive built for weight and speed. Ubiquitous in the 1920s, when Western art adressed itself to machine power for both mythopoetic and satiric purposes, this tone poem does not so much follow the course of a train trip as suggest its impact on the senses. As it happens, listeners insist on taking the piece in strictly graphic terms, hearing the coughing and sputtering of the engine (at the very start, in strings playing on the bridge of the instrument, which produces a dull, brittle tone, followed by "flutter-tonguing" flutes, horns, and trumpets), the warm-up and take-off (tuneless pushing in the lower instruments), the hurtling voyage on iron, and at last the ponderous arrival. Honegger ridiculed this approach, insisting in his turn on the integrity of his non-evocative music as a study in rhythmic dynamics.

In vain. *Pacific 231* really does sound like a train trip, and that's the way it goes. (Those who agree with Honegger and find his abstract concept lacking in the pictorial tizzy of train flight might check out Heitor Villa-Lobos' *Bachianas Brasileiras* no. 2, which contains a more ingenuous and folksy picture of the iron ride called "The Little Train of the Caipira.")

Rugby 1928

This is not to be taken as program music, Honegger said, merely as a suggestion of the burly, competitive aggression of a rugby game. A "platonic" tone poem, then. Honegger called this type of composition "mouvement symphonique" (symphonic movement), to distinguish it from the pictorial tone poem of the Richard Strauss type. As one might expect, this is jerky, explosive music, and one may be forgiven for letting visions of scrimmages, and cheering fans dance in one's head. Honegger's defenders may cry, "Look, he could have named it *Perpetual Motion* or something equally abstract just as appropriately." But he didn't.

DARIUS MILHAUD 1892–1974

In some ways the naughtiest of all in an era of engagingly infantile pranksterism in French music, Milhaud eventually grew to be his country's senior mid-twentieth-century musician. He was prolific (his opus numbers, not listed here because they are so infrequently used, reached into the 400s) and versatile. His sources included Harlem jazz, South American rhumba, regional and folk music, Jewish canticle, medieval plainsong, Baroque gallantry. No one was more cosmopolitan.

Yet no one was more French. Thrown up in the neo-Classical revival of the 1920s, where action (and outraged reaction) centered in Paris, Milhaud headed the group then known as the *Nouveaux Jeunes* (New Youth), or The Six. One of the aims of these six earnestly incorrigible composers was to blend the forms of serious music with the flamboyant sound of pop—music hall, cabaret, operetta. Working on this bias, Milhaud won early fame for two linchpins in the evolution of modern music, the ballets *La Création du Monde* (The Creation of the World) and *Le Boeuf sur le Toit* (The Ox on the Roof), the first composed in the idiom of black jazz, the second in the invigorating brouhaha of Brazilian dances.

So unorthodox, so revolutionary were The Six in what they planned to do for music (*to* music, said their critics) that one might chart their complex aesthetics as a series of "Down withs": Down with four-movement symphonies! Down with the virtuoso violin and piano concertos! Down with chamber music scored for the same old strings and woodwinds! and so on. They wanted to widen the parameters of serious music, renew its—to them—moribund life force. Oddly, the very openness of their enthusiasms proved limiting after a while. They began to need a renewal of their own—which they could only find in the four-movement symphony, the concerto, the string quartet, and so on. And when the smoke cleared, the Six had broken up to go their separate ways, and Milhaud had embarked on a tour through musical forms both traditional and innovative.

Perhaps his dexterity kept him from being better known; this is the age of the specialist, and Milhaud did it all, all too well. His distinctive palette of styles is such that one may hear him and still not feel that one has figured him out; dip in anywhere and sample him at whim. You're only young once.

Suite Provençale 1936

Evoking Milhaud's native Provence, the suite draws on tunes composed by André Campra, a musician of the Baroque era and a fellow native. Eight numbers, some quite short, capture in orchestration as well as melody the atmosphere of Mediterranean Provence of the bizarre landscapes, the riotous colors, the shrill sun: a place that Cézanne might have painted. (And indeed, Cézanne, too, was Provençal.)

Each number is identified by its tempo marking. *Animé* (animated) ushers us in with a town-band sort of parade. *Très modéré* (Very moderate) follows, sounding like a piece broken off of a story; it concludes with a tiny *Vif* (fast). Third in line is a prankish *Modéré* . . . and so it goes, pictures of Provence. Note the especially Provençal flavor of the last number, *Vif* again, with off-the-wall piccolos and stupid "Provençal drum" to suggest the ethnic fife-and-drum dance once known as the *tambourin*.

La Création du Monde (The Creation of the World) 1923

Milhaud's rigorous investigation of the techniques of black jazz (including on-the-spot research in nightclubs in London and Harlem) led to this remarkable melding of the innocent, the bittersweet, the savage, and the ramshackle. It is popular as a concert piece, but it's a ballet score, the intent being to dramatize the African's primitive world-creation mythology—the fierce gods, the stirrings of first life, the elemental spring.

Western art in the 1910s and '20s manifested great interest in primitive culture, in abstracting the fundamentals of the human imagination in advanced musical forms. This led to such events as Stravinsky's *The Rite of Spring,* Prokofyef's *Scythian Suite,* Ravel's *Daphnis and Chloé,* John Alden Carpenter's *Skyscrapers* (all designed for the ballet stage) and this jazzy piece of Milhaud's. Some of the works cited above reach back to barbaric life; one lunges forward into the urban machine civilization. But all were agreed on one point—the importance of jazz as a musical expression of mankind in its essence. Thus, here, the prominence of the piano singing its decadent backroom jive, the emphasis on drums and cymbals, the intrusive saxophone, the soloistic use of the strings (two violins, one 'cello, one bass). Try to hear Milhaud's score as its first public did, viewing Fernand Léger's anthropogenic jungle decor of clouds and colors, parrots, baboons, tribesmen. Or place it, for fun, in some ghetto *boîte* in the 1920s. It works either way.

Le Boeuf sur le Toit (The Ox on the Roof) 1919

Overnight, this little ballet score got so chic that a nightclub named itself in its honor. Its musical source is Brazilian dance music, its action concerns the absurd, slapsticky non-events occurring in an American bar during Prohibition, "*le régime sec*" (the dry regime), as the French dubbed it. The ballet's scenario was worked out by Jean Cocteau, in keeping with Milhaud's plan to merge the popular in music with classical form and training. "Here," explained Cocteau, "I avoid subject and symbol. Nothing happens, or what does happen is so crude, so ridiculous, that it is as though nothing happens . . . . It is an American farce, written by a Parisian who has never been in America."

Cocteau hadn't; Milhaud had just returned from Brazil, where he was bowled over by the vitality of the samba, rhumba, and conga. Melodies run riot here, and to tie it all together Milhaud uses a simple rondo form (that is, with a principal theme, a refrain, recurring between contrasting episodes). The refrain is heard immediately, and will be easy to place thereafter. Note another characteristic of the period, polytonality (writing in two or more keys at once). Absolutely delightful, just the sort of transfusion that the neo-Classical revival of the time was hoping to make into the tired blood of post-Romantic symphony. For regional coloration, Milhaud calls for a weird South American percussion instrument, the guitebaro, but recommends a substitute, if necessary: sandpaper, "comme en ont les jazz."

WALTER PISTON 1894–1976

Piston makes a difficult study for the commentator. His music is not what conservatives call modern; in fact he is embarrassingly enjoyable. But he has written that he does not favor analysis of his compositions by way of advance preparation: "Indeed, I could wish that my music be first heard without the distraction of preliminary explanation." He has resisted program music in general—the tone poem, the dramatic overture, the scenic or pictorial symphony, and so on. For the stage, he has written only the ballet *The Incredible Flutist.* To Piston, symphony is not narrative or depiction but musical form: symphonies and concertos, with no titles or other extramusical decoration. They are not about anything. You sit and listen.

More difficult yet is the lack of obvious stylistic devices in Piston's work; is he jazz, folkish Americana, urban tension, radical epic, old-fashioned, ultra-modern? None of the above; he is Piston. Always. Highly individual. His lack of a stylistic tag sets him apart rather than fades him, and his distinctive sound is unmistakable. He just doesn't parse easily for the layman. Furthermore, he never seems to write on an off-day: any one piece stands up to the same high levels as all the others. This handicaps his chapter—which works to single out, since all are first-rate?

In any case, Piston's position as a great composer is secure and most likely will ripen with time; the quality of his work is just too high to be neglected long. (Certainly, his academic texts, *Harmony, Counterpoint,* and *Orchestration,* have become the standard works in those subjects, and on a global scale—*Harmony,* for instance, has been translated into Chinese, Japanese, and Korean.) For us, it is a matter of getting used to the Piston sound and form and getting away from the Romantic conception of music as self-dramatization. Said Piston, in regard to his Sixth Symphony (and one may extend the statement to define Piston's view of music in general), "The symphony was composed with no intent other than to make music to be played and listened to."

Symphony no. 2 1943

Piston's characteristic signature is not one ever thought of as folklorically American, but certain themes here bear the stamp of the popular American voice—a touch of ragtime in the first movement, a hint of black blues in the second. The work opens somewhat darkly, but as the line expands it brightens, and the second subject of the perfect sonata-allegro first movement is a woodwindy tune with a raggy, toe-tapping air. The development section builds to a climax almost shocking in the movement's relaxed context, but the reappearance of the raggy theme reminds one of the generally assertive personality of American music.

On the other hand, the slow [second] movement is beautifully lyrical. It is built entirely of two themes (heard at the start, one on bassoon and the other on clarinet) and simply states and restates these two in one unbroken line until a climax blows all development away and affirms the two themes one final time. The short finale [third mvt] is a lively affair, throwing the aggressiveness of the style (Piston's? America's?) into relief. The drive of the rhythm is irresistible.

Symphony no. 6 1955

A classic four-movement symphony; strong first movement, scherzo, rich slow movement, bright finale. The energetic opening of the first movement is balanced by a sinuous second subject in the woodwind, but this is a more poetic than dramatic movement overall, and eventually fades away. A fleet scherzo [second mvt] succeeds it, so shy as to be almost dainty about its percussion. Retaining the intimacy, a solo 'cello leauches the slow [third] movement, and another solo, this on the flute, presents a second theme. It is as if, after the understated first movement and tiny, deft scherzo, Piston were writing a symphony in little. And true enough, the arch of this movement through to its climax and back to the 'cello strain of its inception never quite breaks out of its self-imposed parameters. But the finale [fourth mvt], one of Piston's typical studies in rhythmic motion, upsets the formula with its brash and strident energy.

Symphony no. 7 1960

Three, not four movements, in the sleek modern style. A first movement that veers between dour and hectic sets up a tension of expectation in the listener, although by the coda (the tail-end of the movement) a subdued last word from the horns prepares for the wholly different world of the slow [second] movement, a pastoral haven lauched by solo oboe. Like so many slow movements of modern symphonies, this is the central anchor of the symphony, balancing two fast outer movements with one long arching line expanded out of one focal theme as opposed to the more episodic structures preferred in the 1800s. Thus, the entire movement seems to complement the opening oboe theme, which at last returns on English horn, set off by a wan farewell on the flute. The finale [third mvt] is a typical Piston finale, rambunctiously punctilious—*precisely* pushy—yet still pleasantly melodic. Reaching back to the energy of the first movement, it pulls the "show" together across the span of the slow movement, a real vaudeville finish.

Concerto for Orchestra 1933

Béla Bartók wrote the best-known but by no means the only concerto for orchestra, a form that uses all (or most of) the players, not just one, as its soloists. Piston's is a brief work, its three movements totaling under fifteen minutes. He refers us to the Baroque era, when the concerto was king of symphonic forms, invoking ancient sounds, structures, and rhythms in the first movement, meanwhile turning a kaleidoscope of instrumental coloration. Bustling in and out of the texture are solos, pairings, groups—a note, a phrase, a tiny song. In the second movement—where one would expect the slow third of the concerto's traditional fast-slow-fast layout—Piston gives us a lively, at times jazzy dance. But the finale [third mvt] starts very slowly, down in the tuba, where the theme of a theme-and-variations is announced. The brasses offer their version of the theme, the woodwinds correct them, very gently, and the strings put in their variation, picking up the tempo and the overall mood.

Suite from The Incredible Flutist
1938

Piston's only foray into stage music, *The Incredible Flutist* is a ballet of idyllic frivolity about the visit of a circus to a small town, the flutist being a snake charmer who is also highly successful with women. The suite, arranged in 1940, uses about half the full 1938 score in eleven numbers played without a break. Starting with a highly anticipatory introduction suggesting "Siesta Hour in the Marketplace," the music brings the square alive with vendors and customers. Comes then a tango danced by the four daughters of a merchant, lazy in its main strain, sultry in its brief middle section, and most satisfying when the strings take the first strain on its repeat. The circus steps into town with all the commotion beloved of such events (including two barks of a dog at the end). Now the Flutist has his solo on his instrument of choice, after which a tangy minuet and (after a piano cadenza) a convivial "Spanish Waltz" take stage. Then mystery: veiled strings as "Eight O'Clock Strikes." The Flutist and one of the merchant's daughters perform a "Siciliano" (a gentle rocking dance, like a pastoral lullaby). For a finale, Piston presents us with a polka which builds from lithe and little into stamping aggression.

PAUL HINDEMITH 1895–1963

Hindemith is a musician's musician, impetuously technical. One seems to hear him acknowledging a challenge in each work, like a sportsman—how to meld the sounds of the brass with those of the strings for contrast in rhythm and melody? How to reclaim the old virtuoso concerto for picky modern ears? How to compose large-scale orchestral works without writing the same old symphonies? Hindemith's music is like a study of something, an intellectual's concert series.

And indeed, there are those who find Hindemith too dry, too thoughtful, all "method"—like the "back-to-Bach" movement associated with neo-Classicism in the 1920s but with Germany especially and Hindemith in particular. Or like the type of composition known as *Gebrauchsmusik* ("useful music"), referring to pieces written for a practical purpose, such as amateur performance or to widen the repertory of the less glamorous instruments (a sonata, say, for bassoon or English horn). Incredibly prolific, Hindemith appears in chronicle as the very opposite of the Romantic composer, who *feels* his way through creation. Hindemith systematizes.

But let us rather praise Hindemith's discipline than hold it against him. Music is not invariably the self-dramatizing poetry of the extremist. And if anyone wants to complain of Hindemith's intellect, his "now I do this type of thing" and "here I do that," let him first hear the wonderful, quite spontaneous-sounding *Symphonic Metamorphosis of Themes by Carl Maria von Weber.*

Hindemith lacks charisma, whether as viola soloist, conductor, academician, or creator. Even his staunch defiance of Nazism, when his homeland went mad, lacked the popular resonance of certain other dissenters, for Hindemith was anti-political, not a crusader. He even wrote an opera, *Mathis der Maler* (Mathis the Painter; see below), to argue in favor of the artist's isolation in society. Thomas Mann—now there was a dissenter for epic. Hindemith is your behind-the-scenes character, too easily overlooked or, when seen, too distant to like. He is accessible—but *you* must come forward.

Symphony in E Flat 1940

An interesting document for those who wonder whatever became of the symphony. The same four movements of old still work: sturdy sonata-allegro first movement, slow movement, scherzo and trio, sturdy finale. Restively glorious, as if it would like to sound triumphant but the times (note year of composition) forbid it, the symphony opens with a fanfarelike first subject in the brass, echoed by full orchestra. This first theme pretty much controls the first movement, as the only slightly less aggressive second theme (introduced in the strings and immediately imitated by the woodwinds) is merely a variant of it. The second [slow] movement redoubles the atmosphere of the first less restively, allowing for solo lines in a kind of air space. But the scherzo [third mvt] reins the work in, relaxing only for the pastoral trio, begun by solo oboe. When the main scherzo theme returns, it now serves as a transition to the finale [fourth mvt], which follows it after the briefest pause. Now Hindemith must make something of the quasi-military tension he has stored up; this he does with the aid of an intermezzo, a "betweenness" launched spang in the middle of the movement by the woodwinds, twice bolstered by an odd effect on the cymbal—struck, Hindemith directs, while a knitting needle is held to it. When the movement continues as before, we feel reasonably "finished" by it, especially since an apparent ending does not end after all but pulls back for some cadenzalike commentary from the woodwind. Then comes coda, furious, grand, conclusive.

Symphony, Mathis der Maler (Mathis the Painter) 1934

In the grim 1930s, with communism glowering in Russia and fascism in Italy and Germany actively threatening their free neighbors, Hindemith wondered about the artist's relationship with society. Shall he turn his back, be ideal and private? Or shall he use art moralistically, politically? Untimately, Hindemith solved the problem in an odd compromise. Rather than politicize—but rather than do nothing as well—he wrote an opera, *Mathis der Maler,* picturing the great painter Mathis Grünewald in relation to his society, that of the Peasants' Rebellion of 1524–25. That rebellion, the last (and most bloody) of a series of peasant uprisings that had begun in the fourteenth century, was of course fired by the lure of freedom, at the time a relatively new idea. Freedom, too, was on Hindemith's mind, and he collected his self-doubts and ambivalences in the character of Mathis—the *Painter,* the title seems to insist: the painter, you actors in history, you tyrants, politicians, landowners, and peasants who threaten art with real life. Ultimately, Mathis' raised consciousness is lowered again by the behavior of the peasants, whom he discovers to be just as oppressive in power as the authorities had been, and he quits all sides but that of art. Art for art's sake is his understanding, because art's sake is, within the humanistic scope, noble, ethical, generous work.

Nazi opposition to Hindemith's aesthetics postponed the premiere of the opera, so meanwhile Hindemith extracted three scenes from it (deleting the voice parts) to make a three-movement symphony. (Actually, it's as much a suite as a symphony.) The movements bear titles taken from the three panels of the real-life Grünewald's famous triptych painted for the Altar of St. Anthony's Church at Isenheim in Alsace. The first movement, "Angelic Concert," is the prelude to the opera, a confrontation of religious tunes and a more outgoing, earthy lyricism. Thus Hindemith collates the two possible existences—the obscure spirituality of the ivory tower and life out in the human world of history. The lean second movement, "Entombment," acts as a transition to the raptly sculpted recesses of the finale [third mvt], "The Temptation of Saint Anthony." This is adapted from a dream sequence in the opera, wherein Mathis sees himself as Anthony plagued by demons (as in Grünewald's famous panel). Though the fierce music is by no means as gruesome as the goings-on in Grünewald's painting, the final pages, given to an ancient hymn tune, wonderfully reflect Hindemith's hero's sense of mission and commitment—as maker of art, not war.

Symphony, Die Harmonie der Welt (The Harmony of the World) 1951

"World" here means "universe"—the music of the spheres. As with Hindemith's *Mathis der Maler* Symphony, this is a three-movement work drawn from an opera bearing the same name. *Mathis der Maler* turned on the function of the artist in society; *Die Harmonie der Welt* similarly deals with Johannes Kepler, the great German astronomer of the late Renaissance who among other things determined that the natural mathematics of music might provide a physics for the universe.

The present symphony, then, is a metaphysical work, one better "received" than analyzed except on a rigorously technical level, not for us here assembled. The movements, entitled "Musica Instrumentalis" (Machine Music), "Musica Humana" (Human Music), and

"Musica Mundana" (World Music), might be heard as a progressively inspired and inspiring collation of abstract images, taking the spirit ever more deeply into the mystical geometry of world-order.

Violin Concerto 1939

The soloist is on top of things from the start, introducing all the principal themes one after another to answering celebration from the orchestra. This is a lyrical work, a kind of homage to the rhapsodic virtuoso concertos of the 1800s. We contemporaries all too often suffer acerbic "commentary" in our contemporary concertos along with melodic benison; ours is a satiric age. But here Hindemith plans his dramatic contrast less harshly than his coevals did. Indeed, this is almost a Romantic work for all of Hindemith's neo-Classical preciseness. Note the relaxed beauty of the slow [second] movement, introduced by a pastoral woodwind passage, and the perky gaiety of the rondo finale [third mvt]. Overall the sound is Hindemith's, the format that of the nineteenth century. Does that make this work old-fashioned? Hindemith writes, we should "minimize the word *new* in the term 'new art' and emphasize the word *art*."

Der Schwanendreher (The Swan-Turner) 1935

A concerto for viola, Hindemith's own instrument (he played the premiere with the Concertgebouw Orchestra under Willem Mengelberg in Amsterdam in 1935). The work is scored for chamber (small) orchestra, with violins and violas omitted so as not to overshadow the solo part. The composer himself supplies the "medieval" program: "A fiddler happens upon a merry company and performs his repertory collected in foreign parts: songs serious and cheerful, and finally a dance. A right good musician, he develops and decorates the melodies, preluding and improvising as fancy dictates and ability permits."

This is an inspired premise for a viola concerto; Hindemith builds his work on folk tunes such as any "right good musician" might develop and decorate. The first movement is based on "Zwischen Berg und Tiefem Tal" (Between Hill and Deep Dale), the second [slow mvt] on "Nun Laube, Lindlein, Laube" (Now Flower, Linden, Flower), with a prankish middle section on "Der Gutzgauch auf dem

Zaune Sass" (The Cuckoo sat on the Fence). The finale [third mvt] is the most pleasing, that promised dance in the form of a theme and variations. It is here that the composer explains his title, for the theme is "Seid Ihr nicht der Schwanendreher?" (Aren't You the Swan-Turner?)—the turner being the spit-boy at medieval feasts.

Concert Music for Strings and Brass 1930

Though Hindemith was quite capable of writing a traditional symphony (as with the Symphony in E Flat, cited above), he joined with his contemporaries in questioning the validity of the four-movement format as the primary engine of orchestral drama. A hundred years before Hindemith, a composer naturally reached for the symphony as form; by the 1900s, one did not necessarily work in the sometimes too insistently major enterprise of the symphony, wherein every less than superb passage is a slap in Beethoven's face. So, Hindemith "invents" his own genre: "concert music," nice and vague.

This is a study in scoring: brass choir (four horns, four trumpets, three trombones, and a bass tuba) against the strings. Two movements. The first is in two sections, a lively, almost bouncy one followed by a shortish slow passage. The second is in ABA form: fast and insistent, then a brief slow center, followed by the fast again (the shape of a traditional scherzo movement in a symphony). Enjoy the contrast that Hindemith draws between the burnished gravity of the brasses and the more flexibly emotional strings. Notice the contrasting colors, motions, spaces. And be one up on your neighbor: note, as he might not, the short but fetching touch of Gershwinesque jazz in the violins in the second movement at the end of the slow middle section, repeated by the strings at the very end of the piece.

Symphonic Metamorphosis of Themes by Carl Maria von Weber 1943

One of Hindemith's most popular works, this is a delightful caravan of transformations on melodies originally used by Weber in pieces for piano duet over a century ago. In four sections, it opens in brilliant bustle, but the second piece offers exotica (much percussion and chinoiserie) in an old Chinese tune borrowed for Weber's incidental music for a production of Friedrich Schiller's *Turandot.* (Schiller's play, based on an earlier work by the flamboyant Venetian Carlo Gozzi, has also seen service in operatic campaigns under Puccini and Busoni.) The first number was a mere arrangement of Weber, but now Hindemith gives true metamorphosis in a set of eight variations on the Chinese theme. The third piece provides a lyrical interlude, a kind of heavy-footed lullaby, and for finale Hindemith tries out a march. Throughout, the melodies that launch each of the four sections are old ones—but the way they are used (scored, harmonized, elaborated, and varied) is new: Hindemith's way.

ROGER SESSIONS 1896–

Some artists are born modern; Sessions grew into it, and for a long time was cited as the foremost "difficult" American composer. It sounds like a backhanded compliment, but in fact among musicians and the fancier European critics a lack of "modernism" is considered puerile in a composer. By 1945, a composer who expected to be Taken Seriously had to work in at least some adaptation of the twelve-tone technique developed by Arnold Schönberg.

Now, it happens that many composers have worked and continue to work in much less advanced sound systems. In America, Walter Piston and Alan Hovhaness both resisted the twelve-tone idiom without sounding old hat in the least. But it is true that there is a certain pressure on composers to abandon the standard Western harmonic system—and of course their personal tastes may lead them into twelve-tone or atonalism anyway. (Atonalism means composing without using the standard harmonic system; twelve-tone is a form of atonalism utilizing a specific procedure.) There is a kind of principle in vogue that every country shall have at least one resident twelve-tone genius. Italy had Luigi Dallapiccola. Germany had Bernd Alois Zimmermann and still has Hans Werner Henze. England has Humphrey Searle.

And the United States has Sessions. (It also has Elliott Carter, but he came along later, after Sessions had filled the gap.) Not that Sessions turned Modern for unholy reasons, nor was he drafted against his will. But it has worked out that Sessions is the, as it were, grand old American atonalist—the man who, for European critics, distinguished American music. Obviously, his temperament and training were such that the Schönbergian idiom suited him. He reached out to it, did not start with it. But now it is his, and history has been served: we, too, have our certified modernist of long standing. Those wondering where to start should consider the violin concerto, a relatively early work perched between traditional and avant garde and a fund of sweet bequests.

Symphony no. 3 1957

Like Walter Piston—but unlike most other contemporary American composers—Sessions does not favor pre-performance analysis of his music for listeners. However, like Piston, he is willing to sketch outlines of the movements provided one understand that these are more like reports of what the work has turned out to be rather than Statements of Purpose. And it's true that with such absolute music as this, there is little to do short of an extensive trot in technical language. Much, much music is of this absolute kind—Mozart's symphonies, for example. The best way to hear them is simply to hear them.

Still, some general observations always help. Overall, the work's four movements correspond roughly to the first movement-scherzo-slow movement-finale of the traditional symphony. The first is industriously reflective, ending on a down note. The second is *very* scherzo, in the old ABA form, though the return of the A section is not a simple repetition, but a variation. The trio (the B) is easy to distinguish: stormy violins and trombones answered by placid woodwinds and horns, and so on, back and forth. The third [slow] movement is, for much of its length, gentle and yearning, but draws up nervously at one point and never quite regains its poise, though its opening music is repeated at the end. A touch of jazz—the great American signature—sparks the opening of the finale [fourth mvt], a sharply rhythmic conclusion to the whole.

Rhapsody for Orchestra 1970

The rhapsody, as form, is a lyric and/or heroic work of improvisational character—a brave fantasy, so to speak. The violent opening of Sessions' rhapsody leaves no doubt of its heroic aggressiveness, but the lyrical asserts itself as well, notably in a middle section led by the violins, after which the atmosphere of the opening returns. But this is not all: Sessions closes with a contemplative epilogue of recitative ("spoken" music) for trombone, then 'cello, then viola, then violin. In the last moments, the insistent opening returns, pow!

Violin Concerto 1935

The format is that of a symphony—four movements, a lyrical, shortish first movement, a scherzo, an interrupted slow movement, and a lively finale. But the soloist stands very much to the fore; few works put him through the soloistic wringer more than this one, and it's a safe bet that the difficulty of the solo part is the main reason that Sessions' concerto is not heard more often. (Not that violinists can't play it—the general level of technique among world-class—i.e., international star—violinists is very high. But why trouble to master a work that isn't popular in the first place? is the prevailing attitude.)

Sessions' structure is interesting in that the normally all-important first movement and the slow [third] movement are both overshadowed by the scherzo [second] movement and the puckish finale [fourth mvt]. Hardly have we gotten used to the graceful, endless line of the first movement than the soloist takes a brief cadenza, a tiny recapitulation ensues in the orchestra, and the movement falls dead in the contrabass section. Similarly, the slow movement is even briefer, and is suddenly cut off by the soloist's solo flight in a new, giddy tempo—and we're off and running with the last movement.

Note, by the way, a a canny innovation: Sessions omits the entire violin section from his scoring to set off the sound of the soloist's unique fiddle.

The Black Maskers Suite 1923

Early Sessions, a suite drawn from his incidental music for a production of Andryeyef's odd allegorical play *The Black Maskers* at Smith College. In four movements—Dance, Scene, Dirge, and Finale—Sessions gives us a miniature of Andryeyef's tale of a masquerade, held in a castle symbolic of the human soul, that gets out of hand, destroying the castle and the truth-questing man who lives there. The Dance is uncurbed, absurd, agonized, and villainous—masks confront the truth-seeker. The Scene accompanies the masquerade in ABA form, the B a duet of bass flute and viola. The Dirge tolls for the dead truth-seeker (and for thee, friends). The Finale depicts the collapse of the castle in a mood promising redemption; this is the outstanding number in the suite, and always surprises concertgoers who "never thought I could like modern music."

VIRGIL THOMSON 1896–

Like Charles Ives, Carl Ruggles, and George Gershwin, Virgil Thomson is American Unique. Nobody else—ever—sounds like him, though he (like his three colleagues) often sounds like something else—hymn tunes, folk songs, piano solos, dance types. Resolutely uninfluenced by the many several isms of his time, Thomson hewed close to what might be called the greater American sound, melding an informal folklore on an acute and concise sense of form.

Thomson is tidy, pointed, fleet. Music he wrote in the 1920s is not unlike that he wrote in recent years, for his style evolved early on and suited him perfectly. He is best known for two absurdist operas with librettos by Gertrude Stein, *Four Saints in Three Acts* and *The Mother of Us All* (whose heroine is Susan B. Anthony, one of the pioneers of the women's movement). He is also one of the rare composers (such as Berlioz and Debussy) to sustain an important column of music criticism for an extended stint, in this case for the New York *Herald Tribune* from 1940 to 1954. Thomson's oeuvre includes a wide variety of works, including some eight movie soundtrack scores, in which Thomson so excelled that the whole genre of movie music was upgraded in the nation's artistic consciousness.

Symphony on a Hymn Tune
1928; revised 1944

The hymn, which provides principal material in all four movements, is known by different names in various regions (and by various Protestant denominations) of America. It is first heard in its pure form early on in the strings after a bit of anticipatory introduction that culminates in a somewhat less than reverent trombone solo. From then on, this melody is never more than a page or two away, as it varies and vies with other folk- or hymnlike figures. These also carry over from movement to movement, so that the entire work is an exercise in righteous Christian economy, a deal a horsetrader might admire: a whole symphony made out of three or four tunes in the public domain!

The first movement, besides arranging these themes in no particular order, closes with an unspeakably beery cadenza for trombone, piccolo, 'cello, and violin solos. The second is the slow movement, with a flavor of Bach (and ending, for some reason, with the suggestion of a distant railway train), the third virtually a scherzo, and the fourth a gala reprise of more or less the entire first and third movements. Throughout, the characteristic innocence of Thomson's sound is challenged by the wilful discords and shocks of an *enfant terrible*—very '20s, very Paris, which is where Thomson happened to be at the time of composition.

'Cello Concerto 1950

These three movements have titles. First is "Rider on the Plains," a traditional concerto first movement in sonata form with a western gait. The second [slow] movement offers "Variations on a Southern Hymn," the hymn tune ("Tribulation") phrased on the 'cello, then taken up by a ghoulish string-and-woodwind choir as the variations commence. There are ten in all, plus a plaintive cadenza for the soloist. The rondo finale [third mvt], "Children's Games," uses the xylophone and another hymn, "Yes, Jesus Loves Me," to keep things lively.

Three Pictures for Orchestra:

The Seine at Night 1947
Wheat Field at Noon 1949
Sea Piece with Birds 1952

Though its locale is Paris, *The Seine at Night* did not draw from Thomson anything like a Debussyan nocturne. There is a strong hint of impressionist curves and coloration, true—but the sturdy, unambiguous (and sometimes simplistically discordant) harmony identifies Thomson the eternal American folklorist. (For a taste of true impressionism, try hearing Debussy's *La Mer*—The Sea—just after hearing Thomson's version of the Seine.) A dramatic score, this, thrilled with the continuity of life as seen in the flowing power of an ancient city's lifeblood.

Wheat Field at Noon finds Thomson on more familiar ground, though this is not the Thomson of the brassy hymn tunes and marches. It's almost a secret score, withholding more than it tells—and, in that deviousness, all the more telling. A complex technique is at work here, but Thomson himself says, "The value of the procedure lies . . . not in its ingenuity but in whatever suggestive power it may be found to have." Three *pictures* for orchestra.

Sea Piece With Birds, last and shortest of the trio, is, in the composer's words, "an attempt to portray the undertow of the sea, the surface tension of the waves, and the flight of birds as they sail back and forth above the sea." Like the waters themselves, the music is fickle to shape, constantly rephrasing itself, black, and heaving. At the end, trumpets imitate the cries of birds.

Suite from The River 1937

The River was a documentary film put out by the Department of Agriculture to dramatize the ill effects of anti-ecological exploitation, in this case that of the Mississippi River. Here, Thomson rescues four movements' worth of his incidental score for the movie, which is seldom seen today even in revival houses. This is a vigorous, prancy business, not at all the plangent pomposity one might expect of a government commercial—but then, as directed by Pare Lorentz, *The River* was an artistic achievement that transcended its own pragmatism.

The first of the four movements is "The Old South," a loose potpourri of Americana from the hymn tune to the banjo dance, arranged in no special order. "Industrial Expansion in the Mississippi Valley" opens coolly on a solo flute, but then the trumpet seriously intones "A Hot Time in the Old Town Tonight," which Thomson builds into a jaunty scherzo, closing with a trombone solo line marked "free and corny." The third movement, "Soil Erosion and Floods," begins austerely on wind and brass solos but develops into an impassioned chorale with nasty timpani thumping out each beat. The "Finale" (no other title) perks things up with a quotation of "The Bear Went over the Mountain" and closes on a reprise of the hymn tune heard in the first movement.

Suite from The Plough That Broke the Plains 1936

Like the *River* Suite, this is a selection of numbers from a film score written for a documentary. Also like it, it went far to improve the writing of soundtrack music, at the time largely a hogwash of emotionalism and imitations of Romantic symphony. Thomson, with his elegant sense of style and his folkloric Americana, proved a tonic. A text of excerpts from the movie's narration precedes each section in the score, but the atmospheric music works well on its own. After a short "Prelude," we move into a "Pastorale" (subtitled "Grass") and thence to "Cattle," in which guitar, banjo, and washtub and the quotation of a few cowboy songs give the suite some down-home legitimacy. Next comes "Blues" (subtitled "Speculation"); for this corrupt side of capitalism, Thomson gives us a musical "corruption": jazz, complete with saxophones and an acrid odor. The brief "Drought" follows mainly to provide a bridge to "Devastation," the last and longest number, a retrospective in mood and color.

Two Suites from Louisiana Story 1948

In the 1930s and '40s, Thomson wrote several movie scores, throwing into relief the banal overkill of the Hollywood hack with a lithe sense of tone and a deft folkish touch. *Louisiana Story,* Robert Flaherty's "semi-documentary" about the coming of industrialization to the bayou country, derived its narrative shape in the point of view of a fourteen-year-old Acadian, or Cajun, boy. (The Cajuns are longtime Louisiana natives of French origin.) The boy's innocence dovetails nicely with that of Thomson's music, which uses a few Cajun melodies for authenticity.

The *Louisiana Story* score turned out so well that Thomson extracted two separate suites from it. The first, called simply *Louisiana Story,* is in three movements: Pastorale, focusing on the bayou water roads in a sweet barcarolle threatened by the intrusion of an oil prospector's amphibious marsh buggy; Chorale, a blend of folk tune and hymn depicting the boy's frolic with a pet raccoon; and a Passacaglia, accompanying an egg raid on an alligator's nest (thus the somewhat reptilian crawl of the movement) and closing in a Fugue as the boy struggles to capture one of the beasts.

The second suite is *Acadian Songs and Dances.* Its seven sections, self-describing, are "Sadness," "Papa's Time," "A Narrative," "The Alligator and the 'Coon," "Super-sadness," "Walking Song," and "The Squeeze Box."

GEORGE GERSHWIN 1898–1937

This Gershwin thing isn't just a style anymore, it's a historical movement, and justly so. For in his mélange output of pop tunes, piano ripples, musical comedy and movie musical scores, orchestral compositions, and his one full-length opera, Gershwin made an important point for American art—that this commercial marketplace representing democratic taste combines the vernacular with genius in its self-expressive forms. Like his colleagues Irving Berlin and Jerome Kern, Gershwin borrowed from ragtime and jazz. Using popular music as his base, he created a personal style that adapted well to the forms of concert music.

Significantly, a line from one of the first songs Gershwin composed (to his brother Ira's lyrics) runs "The real American folk song is a rag," and cites it as a "rhythmic tonic for the chronic blues." Ragtime and blues, American sounds. But the real American folk song is the work of individuals, not a folk. Such songs as "The Man I Love," "Fascinating Rhythm," "How Long Has This Been Going On?," and "Oh, So Nice" played tricks with melody, harmony, and rhythm that pop music had never been "bright" enough to play before. By the time Gershwin composed the opera *Porgy and Bess,* a wildly eloquent picture of the black subculture in a Charleston backwater, Gershwin had proved that the American pop tune is as capable of expressive expansion as the finest European "art song."

Similarly, Gershwin proved that serious music needn't be exclusive to serious listeners. But any attempt to distinguish Gershwin's orchestral music from everyone else's on the populist angle is naive and snobbish. Gershwin's more ambitious compositions certainly get their kick from the popular idiom, no question. However, his sense of structure and development, while immature, are not all that inferior to that of the average conservatory graduate. Gershwin was a primitive of sorts, but he was also a genius: he *created* a sound. Other composers have used the harmonic and melodic identities of American pop with greater dexterity than Gershwin—Darius Milhaud, Ernst Křenek, and Aaron Copland, for instance. But they borrowed the noises, adapted them; Gershwin *was* that noise. It was that natural with him. "Blue" is not a practice with Gershwin: it's what he sounds like, pure. That's the genius of it. And as for primitivism, *Porgy and Bess* is still unrivaled after nearly half a century among all American operas for richness of expression and dramatic power.

Concerto in F 1925

Those who wonder where this remarkable but quite innocent piece stands in lists might think of it in terms of Grieg's piano concerto. Grieg, like Gershwin, was basically a miniaturist, used to working in small forms—songs and short piano pieces. (Gershwin made the transition to the large form, opera, in *Porgy and Bess,* ten years after the concerto.) The challenge of true symphony, to such an artist, is profound. A big work is not a succession of joined little works, not a medley. A big work is an organism of little parts interacting in *extensions* of themselves—in statement, variation, and restatement. In this, Gershwin, like Grieg, proves himself game but definitely overparted. He doesn't stretch far enough: we can hear the seams where the parts are joined. These are less three movements than three medleys.

Still, this concerto (like Grieg's) works. It *shouldn't* hold together—any musician can prove on paper that it doesn't—but somehow it does when you hear it. Its rude freshness, its urchin's energy, its happy neglect of technique—its novelty—make it not a failed classical concerto but a classical concerto successfully de-classified. It's its own master.

Anyway, it does accord with the classical three-movement layout, fast-slow-fast. The brash first movement is tied together by a Charleston rhythm (that is, with an off-beat accent like that in the song "Charleston": 12345678). After a noisy opening, it dissolves into a lyrical theme introduced on the piano; smooth song then vies with nervous intermediary figures throughout a lengthy development run more by simple restatement than genuine variation (which is what development is). Then, instead of a full recapitulation, Gershwin simply restates, *grandioso,* his principal lyrical theme. The second [slow] movement depends upon the blues rather heavily at first, then picks up for a dancey middle section featuring real "Gershwin" piano—an agile left hand and a rippling, quicksilver right. For the finale [third mvt], we get a drivingly rhythmic showpiece that reworks themes from the first two movements and closes with a most *grandioso* yet reprise of the big tune from the first movement.

Rhapsody in Blue 1924

Historically, this is the most important of Gershwin's orchestral compositions, as it marked the emergence of his populist's talent in the concert hall, and on a historic occasion. Understand the mood of the times: "jazz," in the 1920s, was used imprecisely to cover virtually all American pop music, excluding old-fashioned waltzes and other such sententiae. The "jazz band" was simply any group playing pop tunes, usually for dance purposes, with clarinet, saxophone, trumpet, bass fiddle, and others improvising their way along.

Now, jazz was already being mooted as this great American invention, our Contribution. To help solemnize the coming out, the self-styled "King of Jazz," Paul Whiteman, hired New York's Aeolian Hall for an "Experiment in Modern Music"—namely, an orchestral concert not of symphonies, overtures, or tone poems, but of contemporary American pop music. The program, on February 12, 1924, revealed such entries as Zez Confrey's piano spots (including his "Kitten on the Keys"), orchestral arrangements of such pop tunes as "Alexander's Ragtime Band" and "Limehouse Blues," a "before and after" showing how "jazz treatment" reinvents a song . . . and the *Rhapsody in Blue.*

Until Gershwin came onstage in the penultimate slot to play the piano part in his one-movement "jazz concerto," the afternoon had not gone well. Now, it exploded. This, finally, was weird dynamite, a piano concerto built entirely on the character and apprehension of pop music. The work is part of the culture now; you can't imagine what a shock it was in 1924. Here was no "jazz treatment" of a song, no "Kitten on the Keys," but a legitimate—a Serious—composition in the common idiom, written by a most uncommon but certainly not highbrow talent. In fact, Gershwin was at that point so unpolished that he wasn't able to orchestrate the piece; Ferdé Grofé, later the composer of the *Grand Canyon Suite,* handled the scoring. (Originally, Grofé arranged the piece for Whiteman's smallish ensemble, but its continued popularity with orchestras bigger, so to speak, than a jazz box prompted an expanded orchestration. This is the one heard today.)

Listeners' astonishment at the *Rhapsody's* premiere started with the opening measure, a sleazy clarinet trill sliding up to the bluesy melody that sets the tone for the whole piece. The *Rhapsody* proceeds entirely on its own (i.e., non-traditional) devices, now tranquil, now agitated; themes are repeated, counterstated, varied, but on a free-wheeling American plan having little reference to great Western tradition. Generally, the air is that of a scherzo—a joke—but there is an emotional core to it all, and at length a highly sentimental episode takes stage, one of the most familiar tunes in all symphony. This yields to a piano solo of hushed, rivet-gun ratatat—a tiny toccata, actually—that is quickly melded onto themes heard earlier. A brilliant recapitulation and finale wraps it all up with a last crashing affirmation of the clarinet theme that began it all. Taut, incisive, expertly defined in what it is that had not been before, the *Rhapsody* (in, yes, Blue—though for the record it starts and ends in B Flat Major) is not fun to analyse because its constituent parts dovetail so neatly. It must be heard, not talked about.

Second Rhapsody for Orchestra with Piano 1931

Note the "for Orchestra with Piano" rather than "For Piano and Orchestra." This is less a concerto than an orchestral work with a featured piano part (though the piano leads off as a solo). Originally written for the movie musical *Delicious* to underscore sequences set in Manhattan, the *Second Rhapsody* reveals the basis for Gershwin's sound coloration: urban jive. Much of his music has the character of "city music," as if composed in homage to the energy of the uprearing American machine of neon, els, bars, and subway holes. A city boy himself, Gershwin hymns the democratic hubbub of town, not the gentle epic of country. So it is here; if much of this neglected work sounds like a rehash of the one-time-only technique that created the *Rhapsody in Blue,* Gershwin buffs should at least try it once.

Variations on "I Got Rhythm" 1934

"I Got Rhythm" is one of the songs most closely associated with Ethel Merman, who introduced it to the public in the musical *Girl Crazy* in 1930. No one should have trouble following the irreverant peregrinations of the tune through Gershwin's highly rhythmic study hall, and devotees of the *Rhapsody in Blue* will be glad to learn that the *Variations* are a *concertante* work, scored for piano soloist and orchestra. (The Gershwin autograph is, let's face it, jazz-rag piano.) Surely everyone knows the melody of "I Got Rhythm" by heart. Those who don't should pay attention to its first full statement, after a "jazzy" introduction, by the piano alone. Then the fun begins.

An American in Paris 1928

"My purpose here is to portray the impressions of an American visitor in Paris, as he strolls about the city and listens to various street noises and absorbs the French atmosphere . . . I've not endeavored to represent any definite scenes in this music." So Gershwin tells us not to think too clinically in terms of narrative: *impressions* at most. But at the premiere, Gershwin and the composer-critic Deems Taylor together concocted a detailed program after all. What does this prove? That music is always music in the first place, pure music, and that you can turn music into description after the fact if you use enough words.

Anyway, the opening of *An American in Paris* does have the air of a brisk street tour. Are those taxi horns? A quiet passage (English horn prominently featured) deters the American briefly, and as he walks on the jaunty character of the opening turns even more so. It swaggers. Now a solo violin is heard; in their notes, Gershwin and Taylor supposed this to be a prostitute making her pitch. This is quickly over, however, and a kind of upbeat blues (the tune on a solo trumpet) changes the character of the piece—homesickness, say Gershwin and Taylor. This informal nostalgia is very humanly portrayed, at least to the American ear, for the sounds are so energetic, so new world; Gershwin has jumped back into his favorite setting, the American city. Paris is forgotten. The back-home feeling not only does not disperse—it is redoubled by a jazzy dance passage led by two trumpets. According to Gershwin and Taylor, the American has met another American. They celebrate, and now the "homesick" theme retruns in triumph. They stroll—the walking music of the opening returns, Gershwin in Paris. And for a coda, the "homesick" theme.

ROY HARRIS 1898–1979

Now somewhat withdrawn from prominence with the late emergence of Charles Ives, the incremental celebrity of Aaron Copland, and the variety of Leonard Bernstein, Roy Harris was, back in the 1930s, a white hope of American symphony. He was prolific, enticingly but simply dramatic in sound, never radical in harmony or rhythm. Best of all, he was committed to the symphony as a form (many of his colleagues were not). The public watched for Harris' continuity, and he was cited as one of the most effortlessly American of composers.

Douglas Moore noted Harris' western origin (Oklahoma) with relish and called him "a sort of musical Walt Whitman." But after the first wave of enthusiasm began to ebb, as waves will, Copland spoke for the musical community in noting Harris' "insecure critical faculty" as a detriment in his composition. Faulty craftmanship was sabotaging his natural gifts. Yet, said Copland, "Plenty of Americans have learned how to compose properly, and it has done us little good. Here is a man who, perhaps, may not be said to compose properly but who will do us lots of good."

Harris has immediacy, a blessing and a curse combined. The bounty obtains in his ease of communication; his impact is sensual as well as cerebral. But the drawback obtains in the suspicion of posterity, lips pursed like a Calvinist's on Saturday night. But who knows? Harris may yet have it both ways. If nothing else, he did contribute importantly to the early growth of an American style in the big form, the symphony.

Symphony no. 1, "Symphony 1933" 1933

Harris' international triumph was to be won with his Third Symphony, five years after this one. But already the stirrings of an original talent were hard to miss. Almost everyone agreed that the work's certain qualities lay in the direct emotional address of its melody and the vigor of its rhythm. Both are in evidence right from the top of the first movement, planned for a kind of eager dignity, as befits a youthful work that is going to turn out to be an important one. By the time the strings glide in with a nervously innocent, lyrical second theme, one's attention is held, focused, and a sort-of quotation (on timpani) of the famous buh-buh-buh-*bum* of Beethoven's Fifth does not distract but rather draws one closer in.

The second [slow] movement, which dominates the work by force of mood, opens hesitantly and soon settles into a lamentation with flights of self-consolation from the woodwinds. Its curious combination of the barren and the self-sufficient is absolute music at its purest (that is, music for music's sake), but many listeners insist on hearing in it a picture of the central American plains and their plain people.

The finale [third mvt] refers back to the first movement in the tone (and drum-beating) of its opening. But this is the athletic third of the piece, taut and flying forward. Its energy is not unbeatable—a strange passage for plucked strings and woodwinds stops all momentum for a bit. But the tempo picks up again, and only in the final pages does Harris pull back, fist clenched in restrained fury.

Symphony no. 3 1938

With this work, Harris rose to the front rank; it remains a touchstone in the tradition of the American symphony, no less exhilarating now than when it was hailed as, literally, the Great American Symphony. A one-movement work of five continuously flowing and thematically related but distinct sections, it plots its dramatic trajectory not so much on the conflict of themes stated, developed, then restated (as in, say, Beethoven), but rather on the antagonism of the various sections, each to the other. Harris' drama here is horizontal, extended backwards and forwards, and it makes the work sound "bigger" than its actually rather economical twenty minutes. No wonder it won such praise on its premiere in 1939, by the Boston Symphony under Serge Koussevitsky (a great friend to modern American music). But "Let's not kid ourselves," says Harris. "My Third Symphony happened to come along when it was needed." Harris underrates himself. It is not only a case of the right work at the right time, for the Third remains popular and admired today, music to pleasure the soul long after it has ceased to fill a cultural gap.

As to the music itself: Again, there are five sections, played in one unbroken line. Harris has outlined these sections for us as "Tragic" [first sect], all on the strings, dark and sombre; then "Lyric" [second sect], ushered in by a slow descending line on the flute and adding woodwinds and horns to the strings. The pace has quickened, the theme-flow grown more assertive. An English horn, then oboe, pull us into the third section, "Pastoral," the pace even livelier and the tone friendlier, lighter. As the moments pass, however, tension sets in; the brass instruments challenge each other, and soon we arrive at the forceful fourth section, "Fugue," heralded by pounding drum and dominated by the brass (with string commentary). Eventually, the strings take up the motion, the brass and drum the commentary, and as the drum bangs out a steady rhythm, we pass through the fifth section, "Dramatic-Tragic," to a dark finale.

Symphony no. 7 1954

This is a highly concentrated work, a one-movement and—almost—a one-theme symphony, as the melodic material largely comprises variations on a single theme. Everything seems to proceed out from the thin, aching violin line heard at the outset, which will return with formidable effect at the very end of the piece. The heavy, clomping accompaniment in the lower instruments is repeated over and over while the violin line shifts harmony, rhythm, and melody: this is a passacaglia, a variation form in which a set accompaniment recurs indefinitely under the changing tunes. The passacaglia occupies the first half of the symphony, the second half being dancier though no less heavy. Incidentally, that first half offers possibly the best chance in all symphony for one to *hear* a passacaglia unfolding, for Harris has divided the fixed accompaniment (deep and brooding) from the ever-changing melody (high in the violins) so no one can miss the distinction between the (unvaried) bass line and the variation line.

FRANCIS POULENC 1899–1963

The Russians have a Five—the "Mighty Grouplet" of Balakiryef, Rimsky-Korsakof, Musorksky, Borodin, and Cui, associated with nationalistic, anti-Western theories of composition. The French have a Six—Poulenc, Milhaud, Honegger, Auric, Durey, and Tailleferre—and their much more loosely conceived movement sprang from a rejection of their predecessors in French music—the religious passion of the César Franck school on one hand, and the too-too refinement of Claude Debussy and impressionism of the other. The Six called themselves *Les Nouveaux Jeunes* (New Youth), but everyone else called them Les Six. Hating the muddled extremism of late Romanticism, they forced French music to reconsider its ancient options of economy and clarity, the hallmarks of Classicism. But neo-Classicists are not mere reactionaries, and this new youth recaptured tradition with innovation—American jazz, Parisian music hall ditties, Latin American rhythms, impertinent satire. Like many things, these were right for a certain time and place but not right anywhere after; following their heyday in the 1920s, the Six pretty much disbanded as a movement and went their separate ways.

Poulenc's particular case amuses, for a lightness of touch so infected his style that his serious often sounds racy, flip, comical—even, in the most high-toned forms, popular. Perhaps in only one well-known work, his opera *Dialogues of the Carmelites,* does he undertake to move the listener with a profound beauty; everywhere else, Poulenc remains a part-time harlequin. Celebrated by singers for his captivating song cycles, he collates the precision of the trained musician with the gaiety of the pop primitive: he is wry and exquisite, garish and elegant, saucy and pensive, sonorous and small-scaled, a modern version of Classicism as arranged by Pierrot. The great masters of seventeenth- and eighteenth-century French music, Lully and Rameau, would die all over again after hearing Franck or his disciple D'Indy. But they might relish Poulenc.

Concert Champêtre (Rustic Concerto) for Harpsichord and Orchestra 1928

Absolutely delightful. The harpsichord is a lot trendier now than it was in 1928, but it guaranteed this neo-Classical affidavit the witness of authenticity—early keyboard concertos were written for harpsichord, the piano not having been invented yet. And Poulenc gets very Classical here. Admirers of Mozart's piano concertos will have to get used to Poulenc's gutsy rhythmic surprises and discordant diversions, but otherwise this concerto relates back to its "purer" days before the Romantics of the 1800s made it an ecstatic emotional-philosophical star turn. Three movements, fast-slow-fast, with a slow, (mock?) solemn introduction and some unexpected slow passages cut into the first movement. Unlike Mozart's piano, Poulenc's harpsichord enters the proceedings early on, but those who know the beauty of a Mozartean slow [second]movement will see what Poulenc's Classicism is driving at in this tenderly melodic second movement. A raucous finale rounds off the event.

As to the title, this offers no program for the music; Poulenc wrote the work for Wanda Landowska, who lived in a (rustic) region native also to Diderot and Rousseau. "This," Poulenc wrote, "explains the refined [pastoral] character of some of my melodic material."

Concerto in d minor for Two Pianos and Orchestra 1932

We have every reason to expect a confirmed neo-Classicist like Poulenc to give us the concerto layout favored in Haydn and Mozart's day: lively first movement; slow, lyrical second; livelier yet third. But the neo in neo-Classicism calls for renovations on—and well as revival of—tradition, and Poulenc gives us two schizophrenic outer movements, each containing dreamy, anti-lively interludes amidst the hoopla of castanets, café fanfares, and vaudeville "traveling music." Even the middle movement, which starts out with a gently childlike tune such as Mozart might have envied, gets rather het up for a slow movement, with highly romantic surges on the strings and a feverishly nostalgic climax before the childlike theme returns at the close.

Incidentally, the insolently popular air of the two outer movements, which frequently threaten to turn into something less like a concerto and more like a musical comedy potpourri, is no slip of Poulenc's pen. The lowdown "popular" amounted to a fetish among Poulenc and his colleagues in their group called "The Six." With it, they hoped to reinvigorate French symphony with a vitality to counteract the to-their-ears effete luxuriousness of late-Romantic decadence.

Concerto in g minor for Organ, Strings, and Timpani 1938

A lot of organ here; the soloist is almost never at rest, a natural hazard of the reduced orchestra (strings and kettledrums but no woodwinds or brass, or other percussion). Moreover, the concerto is not in the usual three movements (fast-slow-fast), but in one large movement broken up into seven sections alternating fast and slow tempos after a slow introduction of—for Poulenc—unusual stateliness. An air of uneasiness pervades each ensuing section, whether jolly or lyrical; perhaps it is the strange air of the awesome organ, always an odd character in the company of other instruments. Not till the unusual final section, a gradual fading away dominated by viola and 'cello solos, does the piece sound content with itself. An odd, not unpopular, item.

Sinfonietta 1947

As the word implies, a little symphony. But what type of little? It's not short—in fact, it's as long as any of Haydn's symphonies, for example. It gives full measure in symphonic "shape"—four movements: traditional sonata-allegro first, scherzo, slow movement, and finale. But Poulenc thought it too light, too pleasant, too complacently daffy to earn its degree as a rightful symphony. "I was dressing," he said, "too young for my age." And yet that very quality of imposed youthfulness proves—here, at least—an utter delight. Neo-Classical Poulenc has recreated the spirit of the old transparently structured symphony of dancing Haydn and lyrical Mozart in the days before Beethoven completed their experiments in turning the symphony into an engine of organic musical drama. Students of form will find this a convenient exercise for the tracing of first and second themes, development, and recapitulation in the first movement, or of ABA neatness in the scherzo [second mvt]. Lay buffs in search of an exuberant listening high will enjoy it, non-intellectually, no less.

Suite Française (French Suite) 1935

Six short items for chamber orchestra, each adapted from a collection of dances by the sixteenth-century composer, Claude Gervaise. The melodies, harmony, and tempos belong to Gervaise, but the choice of instrumentation is Poulenc's, giving a netherworldly air to an otherwise strictly Renaissance situation. (This is another tenet of the neo-Classicism that so attracted Poulenc—a ready quotation of the music of the past.) Renaissance and Baroque buffs take note—they're playing your song.

KURT WEILL 1900–1950

Famous forever as Bertolt Brecht's collaborator on *The Threepenny Opera*, Weill maintained two separate and consecutive careers. The first he spent as *enfant terrible* of the neo-Classical scene in Germany in the 1920s, melding academic procedure with the new sounds of jazz. After the Nazis chased him out of Europe, he launched a second career as an innovator in American musical comedy; listeners will place him as the composer of "September Song," "My Ship," and "Speak Low" (from *Knickerbocker Holiday*, *Lady in the Dark*, and *One Touch of Venus*, respectively).

But the coarse-grained sardonicism of "The Ballad of Mack the Knife" (the "Moritat" from *The Threepenny Opera*) brings us closer to the "serious" Weill of studies with Ferruccio Busoni followed by composition in the traditional forms of quartet, sonata, concerto, and symphony. Weill's sound in these forms borrows the acid commentary of expressionism, and he found the perfect commentative complement in Bertolt Brecht, with whom he wrote not only *The Threepenny Opera* but a vicious Marxist opera called *Rise and Fall of Mahagonny City*, both in the "death is a cabaret" climate of post–World War I Berlin. This Brechtian Weill, experts will tell you, is the great Weill, especially when heard through recordings of his songs made by his wife, Lotte Lenya. (The experts are right: Lenya's hard-bitten voice,

Brecht's brilliant lyrics, and Weill's distinctive atmosphere combine in one of the most striking situations of sheer style available to the ear.)

Lately, Weill has undergone a period of reassessment and popularity. If it continues, the Second Symphony (below) will surely become a repertory item, for its mordant rhetoric—a bored grimace painted into an almost Bach-like clarity of structure—is one of the most original sounds in modern music.

Symphony no. 1 1921

One kaleidoscopic movement twisting from mood to mood, restless even in calm and bitter when lively, Weill's first symphony ends up being more poignant and moving than it thinks it is. Its brusque epiphanies are also telling, however. Remember the time and place—a ruined Germany just after the world war it so blithely inaugurated. Whether deliberately or not, Weill cannot help but capture in certain basic harmonic and melodic colorings the human condition, *loco* Central Europe, *anno* a shaky armistice.

On a background that shifts and reforms in ceaseless schizophrenia, Weill pits rage and despair against more constructive emotions, gradually bringing the latter forward to victory. An almost chamber-like scoring (that is, with solo instruments to the fore) gives an intimate character to it all, and toward the end two hopeful-sounding violins in duet presage an unmistakeably jubilant and then exhortative (lower strings) conclusion.

A footnote. Weill prefaced his manuscript with an epigraph drawn from Johannes Becher's avant-garde play, *Workers, Peasants, and Soldiers: A People's Awakening to God*. Becher was a pacifist and socialist, so dedicated to Marxism that he made himself a mechanical mouth for Party causes—even unto revising *Workers* to purge it of its anti-dialectical "errors," such as the mention of God. Apparently, Weill's symphony is meant as an abstraction of Becher's play on some level, though—as so often with program music—one may enjoy the work without attending to the program in the least.

Symphony no. 2 1938

Three movements, not four—fast-slow-fast, like a concerto. A brief slow introduction breaks into the first phrases of a funeral march (trumpet solo), then erupts in a turbulent *Allegro molto* (very lively) movement. It's distinctive music, biting yet pleasing—but that is

Weill, the sardonic grim one with the unstoppable melodic gift. This first movement is even in traditional sonata-allegro form, though the recapitulation is complicated by a wonderfully calm moment, woodwinds over pulsing strings, just before the turbulence returns to close the movement.

The slow [second] movement offers another funeral march, lightened by a flute duet *cum* 'cello trio developing the principal theme. This is followed by an unexpectedly lyric trombone and then a beautiful violin passage before the tortured whirlwind atmosphere of the first movement returns to the business of a funeral march, grief. This is tragic music; those who say that Weill cannot feel—and those there are—ought to hear this movement.

Having set up something Weill concludes the work with a finale [third movement] matched with the first movement, just as turbulent, though not so fast, a rabid series of dance tunes. A rondo, it presses within its recurring themes a grotesque woodwind march episode and ends with a bouncy tarantellalike coda. So—a tiny funeral prelude, a raucous first movement, a funereal slow movement, and a rousing but unfriendly dance finale. That's what it is. No stories, no program. Symphony in three movements.

Kleine Dreigroschenmusik (Little Threepenny Music=Suite from The Threepenny Opera) 1929

A year after its premiere, Weill made a suite of seven numbers from his and Bertolt Brecht's masterpiece, *The Threepenny Opera*, a savage indictment of corporate and freelance crime in the context of the London underworld. (As source for his libretto, Brecht helped himself to John Gay's famous ballad opera of 1728, *The Beggar's Opera*, thus the London setting. Generally, Brecht preferred to set his anti-capitalist musicals and operas in Chicago.)

The Threepenny Opera (*Die Dreigroschenoper* in German) is scored for a tinny, tiny band. This suite calls for a few more instruments, though it remains relatively chamber-sized (fourteen pieces and percussion), and holds to the acerbic, twenties-jazz "decadence" of the original. The first item, an overture in ABA form with weird Baroque clang, is non-vocal; all the other excerpts were originally songs, and naturally lose most of their meaning without singers. But

Weill's music is so intriguing that one recommends this suite as a listening, if not an intellectual, experience. And now that you've let the suite introduce you to the music, listen to the original work in its full verbal glory. (A good recording to get is the original cast of the 1976 Lincoln Center production, in English, on the Columbia label.)

AARON COPLAND 1900–

The most limited list of significant American composers would include Copland—not because he is so popular, so prolific, or for his contribution to the evolution of American forms in symphony, but because he as much as anyone has defined the native sound in serious music.

Copland surfaced after Charles Ives and Carl Ruggles had already initiated our historic breakaway from the European influence in symphony, from the imitations of Wagner and Mendelssohn, the labored attempts to found an American school on academic copies of everything that had already been done. But Ives and Ruggles were radicals, almost never performed. The next generation, Copland's, changed all this. Among their several remarkable apprehensions was this one: American *popular* music (ragtime, jazz, blues, musical comedy) has vitality. Why not borrow that vitality for symphony? Such thinking produced such works as George Gershwin's *Rhapsody in Blue*, Darius Milhaud's *La Création du Monde* (French music but in a Harlem-derived idiom), and two works by the young Copland, his *Music for the Theatre* and his Piano Concerto. This was the 1920s, and the savor of jazz was prized. "An easy way to be American in musical terms," Copland pronounced it; given the times, it was the only way.

Other ways were quickly found, and Copland has since employed several different personal styles, including a more-or-less non-derivative "public" voice not easily described (it is generally referred to as Copland's "austere" style); a rivetingly authentic folklike voice (which has given us a few classics of the American repertory—*Appalachian Spring*, for example); and, since 1950, a highly modernist sound that some people find unfriendly. In all these styles—jazz, "austere," folkish, and mid-century modern—Copland has shown an extraordinary talent for presiding over the continual reinvention of a national art. Personally, I would rank him with Ives, Ruggles, and no one else as the great producers of American symphony in the twentieth century.

Dance Symphony 1930

At first, Copland gave his symphonies names instead of numbers. Later, he went back and called the *Organ Symphony* his First (taking out the organ part) and the *Short Symphony* his Second; this *Dance Symphony*, however, remains unnumbered. It is built of excerpts culled from an early ballet, *Grohg* (inspired by a viewing of F.W. Murnau's silent film version of *Dracula*, *Nosferatu*), whence its title: these are dances. They are arranged as a slow introduction and three movements, fast-slow-fast, played without a break. After the pale vacua of the introduction, the lively first movement is colorful relief with its dizzy xylophone and piano figures. A brief, slow bridge dominated by sinuous string lines leads to the middle [slow] movement, a slow waltz (in *Grohg*, this music accompanied the "Dance of the Young Girl Who Moves as if in a Dream"). This works up to a splendid climax with wild runs up and down the harp keyboard; moments later the third movement follows. This devilish finale, a carnival of off-kilter rhythms, will undo any but the most alert orchestra. Near the end, Copland allows for the two-time intrusion of an odd little episode of wheedling violins over groaning, oom-pahpahs in the lower strings.

Short Symphony (Symphony no. 2) 1933

Well, it is short. Like many symphonies of its era, it is in three rather than four movements, a practice which related to the French influence on neo-Classicism. (Three-movement symphonies were a neo-Classical favorite and an old French tradition as well.) The first movement is rather sonata-allegro, with a schizophrenic first theme (heard right at the start) and a highly assertive second theme (an upward rush of strings), development, and shortened recapitulation. Without an interval, the second [slow] movement slips in with an antiquely modern (i.e., neo-Classical) sound, and there is also no interval before the dashing finale [third mvt], which amusingly quotes from the two earlier movements while making its own points.

Symphony no. 3 1946

A stylistic breakaway from the popular ethnic idiom of *El Salón México*, the *Lincoln Portrait*, and *Appalachian Spring*, Copland's Third is in four movements. The first opens with a precise introduction of major themes: a simple string tune, a simple viola and oboe tune, and a stronger third tune on the brass instruments (which will figure importantly in the third movement). The second [scherzo] movement is based on a square-cut subject first heard on violas and a solo horn; as one expects of a scherzo, this movement opens up the work rhythmically, while the succeeding third [slow] movement deepens it lyrically. Beginning with a recognizable transformation of the brass theme from the first movement (now heard high up in still, hushed violins), this movement seems to stop dead, then takes wing again on a flute solo which inspires a whole series of kaleidoscopic impressions until the former brass theme returns on solo violin and piccolo, a striking moment of "recognition." A vital and even somewhat old-fashioned finale [fourth mvt] concludes the symphony, enclosed by a bold fanfare.

Suite from Appalachian Spring 1944

Appalachian Spring is a Martha Graham ballet devoted to the joys and shyness of a young couple living in the wilderness of pioneer Pennsylvania. (Graham borrowed the title from one of Hart Crane's poems. The standard German translation of the ballet's title, *Frühling in Pennsylvanien*—Spring in Pennsylvania—seems more apt, since the Appalachian Mountains only just reach the southern border of the state.) The ballet was scored for a chamber orchestra of thirteen instruments (to fit the small hall in the Library of Congress, where the work was first staged), and there is a suite of excerpts using that small scoring. But the *Appalachian Spring* suite as commonly heard is that made by Copland for full orchestra.

This is superb music, as classic an entry in American musical annals as Graham's choreography is in those of American dance. No less limber in its fuller orchestration than in its chamber scoring, the music glows with that spark of authenticity, the uniqueness of the universal. I envy anyone who gets to discover this music, who experiences the precise warmth of the Introduction and readies himself for the rest. Having set the tone, Copland speeds up the tempo and moves into balletic action: the pioneer community, the young couple, their neighbors, the doings. Then comes a tender passage—a pas de deux (duet dance) for the couple. The tempo picks up again and the music turns public (note the piano) for some dances in a folkish vein. The dances grow wilder, providing a solo for the bride. Then a transition leads us into a quotidian picture of the couple's new life together. This is cast as a theme and variations, the theme being that of an old Shaker hymn, "Simple Gifts," first sounded, so simply, on a solo clarinet:

> 'Tis the gift to be simple,
> 'Tis the gift to be free,
> 'Tis the gift to come down
> Where we ought to be . . .

The variations grow progressively more flamboyant in scoring while staying faithful to the outline of the theme, and a final variation of roughhewn grandeur brings us to a finale as chaste as sunlight streaming down through green leaves.

Suite from Billy the Kid 1939

This is a likely subject for an American ballet, with choreography by Eugene Loring for Ballet Caravan (but usually identified with American Ballet Theatre) set off by Copland's quotation of several cowboy tunes. His suite retains most of the score, starting with an open, spacious sound suggestive of the wide prairie. It quickly picks up a little movement without altering tempo, then starts the action off in a frontier town (piccolo chirps "Great Granddad"). The melodies are all so western in cut that only an expert can tell folklore from mythopoeia—though no one will miss "Git Along, Little Dogies" on oboe and trumpet. In the ballet, we see Billy's outlaw life inaugurated in a tragic accident, and the quiet passage opened by woodwind solos accompanies a nocturnal card game under the stars (a variant of "Oh, Bury Me Not on the Lone Prairie" on the violins). This is succeeded by a posse hunt for Billy, his capture, escape, a dalliance with his girl, and death.

Music for the Theatre 1925

This early work shows off the jazzy Copland of the '20s. The "theatre" of the title refers to the "theatre orchestra"—the smallish band regularly employed, of old, in the pits of the nation's average-sized playhouses. So, for a pop group: a pop sound. This is a suite in five movements. The first, "Prologue," gives off an aggressive trumpet fanfare and then quiets moodily down for an oboe solo. Second is

"Dance"—*very* jazz, with driving off-rhythms. An "Interlude" presents the blues, "Burleske" a sneaky scherzo, and "Epilogue" drowses soothingly (note the opening fanfares now assigned to a less provocative solo clarinet).

Quiet City 1939; revised 1940

This short piece was originally part of Copland's incidental score to Irwin Shaw's play *Quiet City*, tried out for two performances by the Group Theatre and then withdrawn. The music has survived: Copland rescored this atmospheric urban impression for English horn, trumpet, and strings. It is slow, slower, slowest, then just slow again, delicate-wiry and remote. Late town, quiet people. The sense of a great, crowded space is set up in the antithesis of placid string velvet against the two nervous solo instruments. Later, the work turns more lyrical, drawing all sounds together. At the end, the whole thing seems to be slipping away from the ear down a side street.

El Sálon México (Mexican Dance Hall)
1936

One of the nicer bequests of the Rooseveltian Good Neighbor Policy (which promoted an interest in Latin American culture), this salute to Mexican music both literally quotes from and impressionistically suggests the native sound. The composer calls his form a "modified potpourri"—a string of tunes stated, slightly developed, combined, restated. One of Copland's most endearing entries, it starts slow but quickly sharpens its rhythmic angles and picks up steam, abetted by an enlarged percussion section (including the Mexican gourd). Then all motion halts for a lyrical passage launched by a solo clarinet. Soon enough the pace has picked up again, always mindful of the ins and outs of the wayward Latin dance pulse. A pounding finale caps the study in song and dance south of the border.

Danzón Cubano 1942

The *danzón*, says Copland, "is not the familiar hectic, flashy, and rhythmically complicated type of Cuban dance. It is more elegant and curt and is very precise as dance music goes." So is it here. In an almost lyrical strain, the *danzón* sways and struts but never gets a real fling going: Dionysus in a conservative mood. There are two main sections, each with its own unshared themes. The division between the two is marked by a piano and contrabass duet.

A Lincoln Portrait 1942

A special piece with a text to be spoken by a narrator. (Actors with a populist or Biblical profile are preferred: Melvyn Douglas, Henry Fonda, Gregory Peck, and Charlton Heston have all recorded it; perhaps more to the point, so have Adlai Stevenson and Carl Sandburg.) The words are drawn from Lincoln's letters and speeches, and wind around Copland's musical abstraction of Lincoln as man, historical figure, and mythic avatar. The introduction suggests immense stature and troubled times, then turns gentle, then sturdy. Now a change in mood, with perky variants of "Camptown Races": American folk. This section is urged on to a brilliant, whirlwind climax, giving way to a hymnlike tune, at which point the narration begins (the music continues as underscoring). The text closes with the final words of the Gettysburg Address.

WILLIAM WALTON 1902–

English music was conservative when Walton first made his mark in the early 1920s; Walton, then, was radical. His style has vastly mellowed since, and as one of Britain's senior composers he is today thought of as the grand captain of the old guard. But a thorough investigation of his oeuvre reveals an autograph that shifts around in tiny eras of its own, defying classification. He is easy on the ear, but not innocuous—and his early "entertainment" *Façade* (a suite of short parodistic musical pieces accompanying Edith Sitwell's absurd poetry) remains a landmark of twentieth-century innovation (see below).

Walton's versatility, which led him to compose at least one example in each of many genres from opera and oratorio to chamber music, brought him at last to the cinema, where he devised the soundtrack scores to Laurence Olivier's films of *Richard III*, *Hamlet*, and *Henry V*. Excerpts from these have been recorded on one disc (now available on the Seraphim label), and are recommended to all.

Viola Concerto 1929; revised 1961

There are not many concertos for the viola, which has always been overshadowed by the more glamorous violin and the heftier 'cello. We are lucky that this one is so good. Highly dramatic under a light overlay of pathetic and morbid sentimentality, it respects the three-movement tradition of the concerto form but sets aside the ancient fast-slow-fast format for a slowish-fast-fast genre all its own.

The first movement starts sweet and grows sour; the second movement is a kind of scherzo, resolutely mercurial. This is the soloist's showpiece, where he dances. The bassoon launches the finale [third mvt], quickly answered by the soloist, and a genteel collaboration is respected thereafter. At the very end comes a passage critics love to cite, wherein Walton has the strings play the bassoon figure while the soloist transcendently reprises the theme with which he opened the work.

Variations on a Theme by Hindemith 1963

The theme is taken from Hindemith's 'cello concerto, and is heard (mainly on flute and oboe) right at the start. Nine very free variations follow, a long and busy finale (a culmination of the variation "effects" already heard), and a coda. This is one of Walton's liveliest pieces, treating Hindemith's theme to a kaleidoscope of textures and melodies; the average listener should expect to lose track of the original theme early on. No matter: the point is to relish the music, not hunt down its transformational clues.

Façade Suites 1922

This is true delight. *Façade* is a ground-zero of neo-Classical textual clarity. It consists of preposterous poems by Edith Sitwell (e.g., "In a room of the palace/Black Mrs. Behemoth/Gave way to wrath/And the wildest malice . . .") read in a rhythm set down to collide with a succession of self-contained musical spoofs. The aim was to establish a genre of the abstract in poetry to complement that of painting and sculpture. The result is unique and droll. Walton's musical Baedeker includes a fox trot, tango, tarantella, hornpipe, polka, rustic yodel—

The neo-Classical, parodistic outrageous avant-garde Works. Because Sitwell's verses are hard to catch without an eye glued to the text, many people prefer to hear Walton's lampoons without the recitation (a ballet version, too, has replaced the words with another abstract art, the dance). As suite (there are two), *Façade* is nothing but music and makes for elegant listening. However, the ambitious, who take their art in historical perspective, will want to investigate the original version for orchestra and reader(s). Some juicy voices have attempted Walton's tricky rhythms on disc—Vera Zorina, Hermione Gingold, Fenella Fielding and Michael Flanders, Peggy Ashcroft and Paul Scofield, and even Sitwell herself.

Portsmouth Point Overture 1925

Inspired by a Rowlandson print of the Portsmouth waterfront in full cry, as English as Bass ale, this is a merry business. It's very much of its time, showing a slight Stravinskyan influence in its multiple rhythms and dissonant, brittle humor. Yet it has the air of timeless English folk music, robustly atmospheric in its evocation of freight-hauling, sailors on leave, and merrymaking among the locals.

Scapino Overture 1940

A "comedy overture" Walton calls it, having modeled it on the commedia dell'arte rascal Scapino, that not-always-faithful servant and purse-crazed prankster. Written to commemorate the Chicago Orchestra's fiftieth anniversary, *Scapino* is an overture without a work to precede; it would serve nicely as a curtain raiser to Molière or Congreve. It's all for farce, but it has romance, too—as witness the trembling 'cello solo in the development, accompanied by violins and violas imitating guitars.

ARAM KHATCHATURYAN 1903–1978

As a Soviet composer, a Georgian of Armenian family, Khatchaturyan followed the nationalist school set up by Glinka and The Five (Rimsky-Korsakof, Musorksky, et al.). The aim was to fashion a Russian (as opposed to Western-influenced) musical tradition. Thus, Armenian folk tunes and rhythms flood

Khatchaturyan's compositions, and, while he is not above working in the symphony and concerto of Western derivation, he is definitely most successful in his strictly nationalist ballet and theatre scores—*Gayane*, *Spartacus*, *Masquerade*—where he is more concerned with melody and folk color than with the archlike structures of Western symphony. In fact, he came late to musical methodology of any kind, having enrolled in a music school in Moscow at age nineteen, not even being able to read music. The critic Gerald Abraham likened him to "an eager, intelligent child who has just been given the run of a toyshop."

Piano Concerto 1936

This work is old-fashioned for the 1930s, but not for the dictates of the Party's Central Committee, which demanded "Socialist realism" in Soviet music (i.e., simple tunes, simple structure, optimistic character: "democratic" procedure, or else). Khatchaturyan upholds the bravura (heroic soloist) bent of the Lisztian piano concerto with a turbulent first movement, lyrical slow movement, and hectic third movement. The first is so big it takes up half the piece, peaking in a discordant cadenza (the soloist's "improvisatory" exhibition) like a small movement in itself; a dazzling upward run crashes into the re-entry of the orchestra for a short loud-louder-loudest coda. The slow [second] movement soothes, not entirely, the turbulence, with a violin theme of Armenian atmosphere. Folkish touches bring out the best in this composer, always, and this movement is the prize of the piece. After a contrasting middle section, the folklike theme returns ecstatically in the strings to a hammering piano accompaniment, fading out in a tender coda. Then the finale [third mvt]: a pushy whirlwind that balances the splintery passions of the first movement with passions of its own.

Violin Concerto 1940

A classical concerto, in a format that Mendelssohn and Brahms would have found unaltered from what they were used to. The first movement, for instance: a vigorous first theme, lyrical second theme, big development and cadenza, recapitulation of the first two themes, topped off by a big coda. Not much personality here, except for the admirably Armenian-styled tune that occupies the "second half" of the first theme (really a first theme group). The slow [second] movement fares better, opening with an odd, unsettled introduction that finally settles into a waltzlike accompaniment for the soloist's entry. As so often in violin concertos, this central movement is dominated by the soloist's rhapsodic embellishments of the principal theme. Crazed fanfares seize the ear for the finale [third mvt], a rondo with a heavy folk overlay. Note how the racy but gently dancelike quality of the first theme is balanced by some furiously dramatic episodes.

Gayane Ballet Suites 1942

(The title is frequently, but wrongly, transliterated as *Gayne*; the right pronunciation is *Ga*-ya-nuh.) It's easy to talk down to this music, for it is barbarically simple and all melody—so easily humiliated, some will say, by comparison with the wildly detailed rhythms of Stravinsky's ballet scores. But what's awful about simplicity? This is iresistible music, Khatchaturyan's masterpiece.

The folk in this case is Armenian and the ballet's setting is a collective farm. Officially, there are two *Gayane* suites, but the choice of which extracts to play from the evening-length score is really up to the conductor—certain numbers, anyway, are more popular than others. One that you can count on hearing is the "Sabre Dance," a viciously insistent item with a taunting, languorous saxophone melody at its center. The other numbers are all worth hearing; if you're considering investing in a recording—the only way to get a solid sampling of the music short of attending a performance of the ballet itself—your best bet is the two-record set on RCA Victor conducted by Loris Tjeknavorian. This is the most complete performance available and the most exciting. Moreoever, the liner notes provide a detailed, number-by-number analysis.

LUIGI DALLAPICCOLA 1904–1975

For reasons unknown, it is the custom in music to let public interest in a composer lapse for a few years after he dies. While in painting or sculpture the loss of an artist *excites* interest and raises prices on his pieces, in music we tend to bury a composer's vogue with his body, at least for a while. Dallapiccola now suffers that desuetude, having died in 1975, though he was one of the three or four most distinguished European composers of the post–World War II period. He was a modern—useless word; aren't we all? But even in the forefront of the avant garde, Dallapiccola held himself answerable to the heritage of Italian song; within the sometimes cacaphonous context of the twelve-tone system (for more details, please see the article on Arnold Schönberg), one heard Dallapiccola singing. His modernism was variable, ranging from the sort of thing that conservatives tend to walk out on to the tuneful simplicity of his renovation of Giuseppe Tartini's ancient violin music in the two *Tartiniana*s (below).

Unfortunately, Dallapiccola's best works do not suit the parameters of this book, and can only be mentioned here. One is his one-act opera, *Il Prigioniero* (The Prisoner), an excruciating study of hallucination and idealism in the mind of one of totalitarianism's victims. Another is a choral work, *Canti di Prigionia* (Songs of Prison), texts drawn from three eloquent prisoners of the past—Mary Stuart, Boethius, and Savonarola.

Variations for Orchestra 1954

These aren't exactly the theme and variations one is used to in, say, Brahms (the "Haydn" Variations) or Elgar (the "Enigma" Variations). Dallapiccola was writing twelve-tone music by this time, and his "theme" as such is therefore the non-thematic tone row of twelve-tone composition, that arrangement of notes in a certain order that is repeated endlessly throughout the work in transpositions, reversals, and other variations. Thus, you will not hear a theme brought through a passage of developments; rather, listen to the developments for their own sake as studies in contrasting moods and colors. There are eleven variations in one continuous flow, opening with a trombone's brooding intonation of a famous trope of musical allusion—the four letters B, A, C, and H are spelled out in musical notation (Europeans write our B^b as B and our B as H). This "Bach" theme dominates the first variation, ceding to the violently noisy second variation. And so it goes, each variation contrasting with its predecessor. The third variation is scored in chamber (small orchestra) style, every line heard clearly; the fourth is a pastorale; the fifth untamed and modern; the sixth emphasizes a melody; the seventh plays one group of instruments against another in concerto style; the eighth is a study in rhythm, the ninth in instrumental color, the tenth serious and secret, the eleventh a finale and the closest Dallapiccola—or twelve-tone music in general—can come to a restatement of his "theme."

Two Pieces 1947

Generally known as "Two Pieces for Orchestra" in the U.S., this is twelve-tone music used very freely (for an explanation of the twelve-tone idiom, please see the article on Arnold Schönberg). Dallapiccola typically deals in absolute forms here, autotelic situations rather than pictorial images or "suggestions." The first of the pair is a Sarabande (an old, slow Spanish dance with a gracefully provocative pulse) and the second is a Fanfare and Fugue.

The Sarabande, hushed throughout, begins in the strings with dreamy languor, stressing the orchestra as an ensemble of first-desk (soloist level) players. Such markings in the score as "flexible," "like a breath of air," "like a shadow," "as if speaking," and "with romance" are needed to cast this veiled spell. After the briefest pause, a drum roll lauches the short Fanfare, succeeded by the Fugue (hammering violins lead off). Though this is unquestionably advanced music, it makes for fine listening, and need not deter even the least experienced ears: pure music.

The Two Tartinianas for Violin and Orchestra 1951; 1956

"Tartiniana" might be translated as "Essences of Tartini." Giuseppe Tartini was an eighteenth-century violinist, composer, and developer of playing technique. Taking Tartini's melodies and adapting them for the more advanced compositional textures of today, Dallapiccola points out that the difference between original Tartini and Dallapiccola-ized Tartini lies in the simplicity of eighteenth-century counterpoint (the combining of two or more "lines" of sound into a viable whole). Counterpoint, in those days, was subservient to the main melodic line. Once the tune was set, the other lines—the "counterpoint"—were carefully fit to it. In Dallapiccola's day, however, counterpoint knew no such strictures, and his experiment is to drop Tartini's self-assured melodies into the more perilous contrapuntal environment of modern music. The sense of the antique remains, of course—but in a fresh and vital context, for Dallapiccola is the admirer of tradition who hated traditionalism. He understands and renews.

There are two Tartinianas, both (to close with the spirit of Tartini) calling for violin soloist (but no other violins). The orchestras are smallish, the scale of the movements attentive to old rules of balance and "good taste." The *First Tartiniana* unfolds in four movements, slow-fast-slow-fast. The *Second Tartiniana*, in five movements, is perhaps the more interesting of the pair. Opening with a slowly rocking Pastorale, it switches to a hearty Bourrée (a French dance), slips in a brief Intermezzo (the violin soloist doesn't play in this), then goes into another festive dance sparked by harp and celesta accompaniments. The fifth movement gives full value as finale with a theme and variations. Here's the square-cut theme, announced straightaway by the soloist, immediately worked over in five variations, and at last repeated twice in its original form with orchestral embellishment.

DMITRI SHOSTAKOVITCH 1906–1975

Shostakovitch's death robbed the international stock of composers of one of its few remaining giants. Of his generation, only Benjamin Britten and Aaron Copland stood the odious but inevitable comparison—and the former was known more for opera than symphony and the latter has never blown the mind with a "big one," the bold, vital, profound piece that reshapes our mythology with modern imagery. Shostakovitch had the big ones to his credit (if in some cases size alone proved unequal to mythopoeia), and worked in a variety of forms, from short piano pieces to operas and huge programmatic symphonies.

His Western reputation, now in disuse, ran a gauntlet of times and mores. At first, in the late 1920s, he was a promising *enfant terrible,* not above (indeed happily right down into and grinning, take it or leave it) the parody and burlesque of neo-Classicism. In the mid-1930s, opinion shifted; then, Shostakovitch was the victim of repression, an artist trapped in the totalitarianism of Stalin's Russia. As of the German assault on Russia in 1941, when the Soviets became our allies, Shostakovitch underwent further mutation, this time as a symbol of Russian valor, teaching history a musical lesson in defiance and patriotism even as the Russians themselves taught it in steel and flesh to the Nazis. Came then the cold war; passions cooled. Now Shostakovitch was a composer like any other—a master, certainly, but one whose work might be praised or blamed in critical and popular circles without reference to political flux. Now that he is dead, he is under the ban of qualified neglect usually accorded recently deceased composers (for reasons that no one has explained as well as Edmund Burke: "I must see the Things, I must see the men"). Probably somewhere around 1990, his music will be granted a revival—perhaps championed by a prominent conductor—with much critical reevaluation, a biography or two, and a lush recording of all fifteen symphonies, complete in one album.

Two points in the above paragraph deserve fuller expression, that of Shostakovitch's neo-Classical (as opposed to Romantic) style and his vile treatment by the Soviet censors for his lack of "Socialist realism"—i.e., Socialist propaganda. Shostakovitch's individuality infuriated the policy-makers of the Central Committee, who insisted on simple tunes, simple harmony, and simple tales on the good fortune of life in the Soviet idyll. Shostakovitch's discordant satire, his experiments with harmony and structure, and lackadaisical attitude toward Socialist realism brought him censure in 1936. Citing Shostakovitch's opera *The Lady Macbeth of Mtsensk District* and his ballet *Clear Stream, Pravda* damned the composer for his "modernist formalism"—in other words, for his expression of himself in his art on his own terms: for his freedom. So was launched a state ban that was not resolved until Shostakovitch humiliatingly subtitled his Fifth Symphony "a Soviet artist's practical, creative reply to just criticism" in 1937.

Among Shostakovitch's stylistic peculiarities that so irritated Soviet honchos was his sardonic sense of humor, often allowed to subvert the most heroic symphonies by taking over the scherzo movements with a slapstick black comedy. This is one aspect of his highly developed neo-Classical urge, the "modernist formalism" of parody, allusion, and discrete structuring, perhaps the most easily heard of all Shostakovitch's signature "sounds." Shostakovitch is very much a Classicist, yet he is very much a romantic, too; if some of his symphonies show the dry angularity of his Classical approach—small, controlled, carefully shaped so one may hear the shape as it passes—some others show the self-dramatizing outreach of the romantic—large, emotional, instinctual. Compare, for example, his spare Ninth Symphony, with its facetious salute to Haydn, to the Eighth, with its expansive, despairing tragic line. Both wartime symphonies, the second and third of a "war trilogy," they emphasize two different angles of the composer's style. While the romantic in him tends to overstate or fall into an occasional banality, the Classicist has the unfortunate habit of alienating some listeners with rigorous restraints. He sounds, to them, unspontaneous—"intellectual"—and they cry for Mozart instead. They want to *feel.* But Shostakovitch is not less spontaneous than Mozart, if more intellectual; the Russian wants as much as the Austrian from melody, but he wants more from his audience in the way of mental responses to his asked questions.

By the end of his career, Shostakovitch enjoyed as close a relationship with his countrymen, artist to audience, as he could have hoped for. More or less exempt from party censure (by virtue of his high international standing) provided he didn't make too false a move, he knew as few contemporary composers do the excitement of being truly important in the culture. A latest work by Shostakovitch would sell out the biggest Russian halls with thousands turned away at each performance. We in America haven't this electric atmosphere for art; we prefer film and rock to symphony. To comprehend Shostakovitch and what he represents, in music, in Russia, one must realize how much his fellow citizens counted on the consolation of his imagery. He made them feel.

Symphony no. 1 in F, op. 10   1925

Listeners who have grown fat on the classic symphonies from Haydn to Chaikofsky in this key or that, major or minor, must ready themselves for the harmonic constructions of the modern era, an ambitious regimen that embraces neither the major or the minor but both: this symphony is in F—period! (More recent symphonies tend not to be in any key at all.) Even experts are not always sure how to gauge the harmonic plan of Shostakovitch's big works, and record-bin browsers may notice that some recordings of this piece announce it as a symphony in F Major, others as a symphony in f minor.

We, however, are less concerned with the intricacies of composition than with the overall effect. We want to know, generally, what is going on; and we are hard put to say in simple terms. The basic form is familiar—four movements: first movement, scherzo, slow movement, finale—but a certain moodiness keeps each from making its familiar effect. True, the two strong end movements sound basic, conceptual, important. But elusive suggestions of ulterior conceptions, of other bases, flit in and out. Then, too, the scherzo [second mvt] in ABA form, offsets its skittery A and ghostly B with a strange, angry coda; and the reflective slow [third] movement leavens its lyricism with trumpet calls. The simpler epoch of Schubert's pure-song slow movements and Chaikofsky's emotional directness has ceded to a more finely nuanced era.

Symphony no. 5 in d minor, op. 47   1937

One of Shostakovitch's best (certainly most popular) works, the Fifth is big, forthright, sentimental, and brave. Historically something of a linchpin, it dates from a time when many composers, from Russia to the U.S., had begun to move away from the brittle, parodistic "intellectualism" of the neo-Classical revival and into the more feeling arena of Romanticism. For Shostakovitch, the Fifth marked not only a Romantic liberation from parody but also a liberation from official Party censure for earlier, allegedly anti-Soviet (i.e., complex and original) composition.

"A Soviet artist's practical, creative reply to just criticism," Shostakovitch called this symphony; we'll never know whether he really meant it or was simply yielding, as any slave must, to his master's plan. It is at least true that the Fifth shows a new directness in Shostakovitch's once complex sound structures, though if anything he is even more original than before. The newcomer to Shostakovitch may eat his cake and have it, too: he may sample the grotesque and desperate world of modern art aided by a simplicity of form and candor of communication.

Sonata-allegro first movement, scherzo, slow movement, finale—all here, very formal. Given extra foundation by an important slow [third] movement with no brasses but unusually intense string textures, the work proceeds from a martial, somewhat spare first movement through a satiric scherzo [second mvt]—a touch of the old prankish Shostakovitch here, sounding like a cotillion of overweight fairies—and the moving recesses of the slow movement, which fill with a tautness of importunate clarinets under the string melody, on to the boisterous completion of the heroic finale [fourth mvt]. The Party was pleased; here, it declared, was a "positive" symphony. Alyexyey Tolstoy dubbed it the "Symphony of Socialism" and prepared a gloss on the movements: the first is "the masses working underground" and "gigantic factory machinery and its victory over nature"; the scherzo is "the athletic life of the happy inhabitants of the [Soviet] Union"; the slow movement "represents the synthesis of Soviet culture, science and art. As for the finale, it is the image of the gratitude and enthusiam of the masses."

Well, a romantic, melodic Shostakovitch surprises his detractors, political and otherwise. Yet the eccentric who burst upon the scene with raving contemporaneity in his First Symphony is with us still. Note the trio (middle) section of the scherzo, when a solo violin with a penchant for Viennese glissandos (sliding from one note to another) spoofs the folksy *Schmerz* of Gustav Mahler.

Symphony no. 6 in b minor, op. 54 1939

Laid out in three rather than four movements, no. 6 combines the work of a first and second movement in its lengthy first, a powerful but somewhat defeated stretch of sound that shows little relation to the two lively movements that follow, a sort of scherzo [second mvt] and a sort of rondo finale. Shostakovitch buffs cite the wonderful instrumental variety; non-believers admit the tense attraction of the first movement and even esteem its wishful interlude for solo flute, but find the second and third movements too shallow to resolve the tension.

Symphony no. 7 in C, "Leningrad," op. 60 1941

Well received at its first American hearing (under Arturo Toscanini in 1942) in gratitude for the amazing Russian resistance to Hitler's army—and in particular admiration for the resolute citizens of besieged Leningrad—no. 7 was planned to abstract a national ideal of heroism. The composer used the siege of Leningrad as his model. The first movement, he said, is conflict; the last, victory.

Musically, this first movement tenders one of the great programmatic depictions in all symphony: the approach of the enemy. This comes midway in the movement, after a traditional exposition of first, second, and closing themes, the last a misleadingly calm moment of piccolo and violin solos. Then it comes—a snare drum beating out a military tattoo very quietly, as if from the far distance. This is the German army nearing Leningrad. A new theme is heard over the drum, a march, first on the strings *col legno* ("with the wood," i.e., playing with the wooden rather than the hair side of the bow, an almost "noteless" sound), then on the flute, then on other instruments, again and again, relentlessly, the drum never ceasing, the accompaniment varying but the theme itself not varied, again and yet again—twelve times in all (some conductors cut one of the repetitions). At last the battle is engaged and all hell—what war is—breaks loose. A lengthy recapitulation follows then as an elegiacal postmortem, but the fist of Russian defiance is clearly still upraised even as the last moments are given to the Nazi snare drum and march theme.

The other three movements of this giant symphony complete the picture of national resolve: the scherzo [second mvt], no joke here but a hollow, moving threnody with a raucous trio section; the heavy slow [third] movement, its middle section harrowed by threats of coming action; and the finale [fourth mvt] of conclusive victory.

That war is over now, and our former allies have become an ugly enemy. Though this does not alter the exhilaration of the symphony as music, it has unfortunately put a damper on the work's present status in America. It was not often heard here until détente made it acceptable again to remember Leningrad and what happened there. For those who might like to hear, Shostakovitch tells.

Symphony no. 8 in c minor,
op. 65 1943

Second of Shostakovitch's symphonic "war trilogy," no. 8 is the tragic opus, lacking the glorious defiance of the Seventh and the cheeky recovery of the Ninth. It is a brutalized protest, battered by its own themes and instrumentation to an exhausted close. Five, not four, movements comprise the structure, with a large first movement planned to combine the properties of first and slow movements in one. A humorless scherzo comes next, and the third movement is a kind of secondary scherzo, a ruthless march dominated by its *ostinato* (—obstinate thing, the rhythmic figure repeated throughout the movement). No breaks separate the third from the fourth and fifth movements, and they appear to offer three different views of the hoplessness of war—a stinging, a repressed, and at last a resigned anguish.

Symphony no. 9 in E Flat Major,
op. 70 1945

No doubt the end of World War II called for a festive symphony—but surely not one this puckish? At least, so it was thought at the time. The Ninth has had to live with critical condescension, if popular amusement, ever since.

Ninth symphonies carry a certain responsibility about them, as if, because Beethoven made it his biggest work, all his followers (and virtually anyone who writes symphonies is such) must tread Master's path. Look at the record—most post-Beethoven symphonists who reach a Ninth did tend to (try to) outdo themselves. Schubert's Ninth is not only his masterpiece in the form but one of the great symphonies ever, and surely Anton Bruckner felt himself to be making a Beethoven-Schubert connection when he sensed that his Ninth was to be the culmination of his life's work. So overwhelming is this "Ninth" aura that Gustav Mahler feared that fate would strike him down once he completed *his* Ninth, so he craftily gave his would-be Ninth a title instead of a number (*Das Lied Von der Erde*—The Song of the Earth) and went on to write a Tenth which he dubbed the Ninth. (It's not nice to fool Mother Nature: fate struck him down anyway while he was composing a Tenth.)

So no wonder some writers patronize this cute little piece, so outrageously concise—especially when compared to the huge symphonies that Shostakovitch was writing as a rule by then. Those writers are fools. This Ninth is a delight, from the clear-cut first and second themes of the sonata-allegro first movement through slow movement, scherzo and extra slow movement to the impishly dazzling rondo of the finale. Yes, the work has five rather than four movements, but the fourth—a dialogue between heavy brass and bassoon—functions as a longish introduction to the finale, and the loving burlesque of the "simple" symphony of Papa Haydn really does recreate the symphony of less grandiose days. There are too many charms to list here, but please note the absurd second theme of the first movement, a march tune scored in the style of Harpo Marx.

Symphony no. 10 in e minor,
op. 93 1953

Possibly Shostakovitch's masterpiece in the symphony, the Tenth displays none of the banalities or overinflated conclusions that some listeners feel mar some of the others, even the better ones. This one is sharply judged throughout and rich as life. It is an elusive masterpiece, for while its general effect is tragic, only the long first movement bears a consistently tragic tone, hollow in its clarinet, flute, and closing piccolo solos.

Technically, there is no slow movement for lyrical communication; of the four movements, the two middle ones function virtually as two scherzos. The brief second movement is a brutal riot with a military feel to it, the third an importunate waltz in c minor that appears to change its mood after a refreshing horn call. At first, the weirdly plaintive English horn seems to urge the woodwinds to resist the horn call—but suddenly the strings and percussion leap into action. The movement is still in c very minor, but at least it's showing some vitality. At length, however, the energy fails, and a solo violin sounds the movement's main theme against the horn call. Shostakovitch ends the movement with ambiguity, though, as if suggesting that tragedy may be overthrown: he gives the strings a harmonically inappropriate chord in a minor to sustain while flute and piccolo play repetitions of the movement's opening theme in its original c minor. The tonal imbalance is precisely anticipatory and uncommitted. Obviously, the finale must decide things—which is just what a finale is for.

At the start, the tragedy seems to carry through in the finale [fourth mvt], too. It opens with a very long slow introduction, led, so emptily, by solo woodwinds in turn "improvising" on a theme. But eventually the mood does change, and the movement becomes a whirlwind of angry, joyous, and bewildered fragments racing each other in circles. There is one interlude, in which music from the introduction returns. But a solo bassoon knocks this aside and the whirlwind blows on to a non-tragic (but perhaps not victorious) conclusion in E Major.

What makes it a masterpiece? Simply stated, it works. Not only does it lack obvious flaws, it evidences the old saw about "the sum being more than the parts"—which is exactly how the best symphonies *do* work. Taken alone, any of these four movements is admirable though odd; taken together, they play off each other so well that oddity cedes to completeness of individual vision: movement 1 is continued—differently—by movement 2, which is contrasted to movement 3, which is both improved upon and corrected by the introduction to movement 4, which then changes attitude and refers back to certain parts of all three preceding movements, closing in a wild ride of unfocused energy. Perhaps its ambiguity is what makes it—ironically—so finished a work. In great music, the listener puts out as much effort as the composer.

Symphony no. 11 in g minor,
"The Year 1905," op. 103 1957

The aborted workers' revolution in Petersburg in 1905 is often called the dress rehearsal for 1917, but it was really more like a disastrous bare-stage runthrough of muffed cues, messy technical production, and ill-focused direction. Here is Shostakovitch's musical recreation of the event, four movements subtitled "The Palace Square," "January 9," "Eternal Memory," and "Alarm." No question, the composer caught the sudden stillnesses and explosions of history, but somehow this lengthy work never strikes off the needed spark despite a unified presentation (no breaks between movements) in which principal themes (including a few old revolution songs) are repeated or interrelated throughout.

For instance, the opening moments brilliantly suggest the icy void of the square before the Tsar's Winter Palace: harp and thinly harmonized strings spread over a wide range create an empty, itchy expectancy by their very lack of itchiness, while drums and trumpets put trouble in the air. Then comes a carmagnole ("Listen!," composed by prisoners) on the flutes, completing the picture: empty square, ready army, a band of workers approaching to demonstrate for some civil liberties. This much is superb, but unfortunately Shostakovitch plays with these same materials with little development for the entire movement, thus sagging the tension.

January 9 (January 22 by Western calendars) of 1905 was "Bloody Sunday," when Father Gapon led a peaceable multitude into a massacre by the guards of the Winter Palace, and the second movement, the core of the symphony, describes the encounter. Where before all was frozen, here it is furious action, eventually dissolving into the slow [third] movement, a requiem for the fallen. The fourth movement—its first theme built on another of 1905's revolutionary airs, "Tremble, You Tyrants!"—takes a while to work out its pledge of future revolutionary triumph.

As already mentioned, Shostakovitch uses a few themes repeatedly (sometimes in mutation, sometimes as simple restatements) to bind his four movements around a central plan—a great idea. But the movements themselves are too distended, too static; what should have been a sweeping statement of introduction, conflict, lamentation, and finale instead comes off as an overbearing binge of slogans.

Still, the work displays to the fullest the composer's characterful orchestration, and some listeners find it an inspiriting adventure in the contrast of energy and immobility.

Symphony no. 14, op. 135 1969

Technically, this work does not belong in this book, for it is more a vocal event than a symphony, a song cycle for soprano, bass, and chamber (small) orchestra of strings and percussion on eleven texts by Federico García Lorca, Guillaume Apollinaire, Wilhelm Karlovich Küchelbecker, and Rainer Maria Rilke—on the subject of death. Then why is it here? Because it is one of Shostakovitch's finest endeavors, an exacting collaboration of words and music—every line, every melody pointed to dramatic disclosure. As such, it sneaks in here by way of recommendation to the reader in search of edification off the purely instrumental track.

Symphony no. 15 in A, op. 141 1971

What is one to make of this work, half innocent pantalunacy and half questing introspection? What was Shostakovitch trying to say?—for although the symphony has no stated program, few listeners agree that it's "nothing but music." Somewhere in these four movements—lively spoof (or is it?), sombre slow movement, tasty scherzo, and haunting finale—lies, surely, a message. So allusive is the piece that commentators have driven themselves to solve its puzzle like whodunit buffs tracking a butler. Some have called it autobiographical, a four ages of man: the silly season of infancy, sober maturity, second childhood, and at last a measured farewell ending with a reminder of the silly infancy of the first movement, as if in cyclic evolution. No one, however, has been able to explain the quotation of prominent themes from three operas, Rossini's *William Tell* and Wagner's *Tristan und Isolde* and *Der Ring des Nibelungen*. The two Wagner quotations (the "fate" motive from the *Ring* at the very start of the fourth movement and the first three notes of the *Tristan* prelude in the first violins a tiny bit later) must elude the beginner. But it is impossible to miss the famous gallop from the *William Tell* Overture as it cuts a merry swath through the first movement.

Concerto no. 1 for Piano in c minor, op. 35 1933

Nominally, this is Shostakovitch's first piano concerto, but the scoring is so peculiar that one wants to amend the title as if in warning—Concerto for Piano and Orchestra of Strings Only Plus One Crazed Trumpet. There are four movements, though the third is little more than an introduction to the finale, thus keeping to the classic three-movement concerto. The first movement is slightly martial, politely dizzy; the second, by contrast, presents a pensive triologue among the three "roles" in this play: piano, strings, and trumpet. The third movement consists of two piano meanderings separated by a handsome string theme. Before one has absorbed that, comes the fourth movement, a rondo, downright dizzy this time, with many rapidly repeated notes and a touch of hee-haw in the strings. The trumpet really comes out here, leading one episode on a spoof of Italian folk song, and the piano enjoys a good old-fashioned cadenza based, for reasons unknown, on Beethoven's "Rage over a Lost Penny."

Concerto no. 1 for violin in a minor, op. 99 1955

The work was written for David Oistrakh. Each of its four movements has a characterological subtitle. The first is "Nocturne"(night piece, a transparent evocation of moonlit moods), the second is "Scherzo," the third "Passacaglia" (a slow dance in which the bass line is repeated *ad infinitum* while the melody changes), the finale a rondo dubbed "Burlesca" (burlesque). We moderns can take four-movement (as opposed to the traditional three) concertos in our stride, but we may congratulate Shostakovitch for not having omitted the hoary cadenza, for he has made of this former ritual of virtuoso display an integral part of the proceedings, placing it between the third and fourth movements. There it acts as a lengthy exorcism, drawing us out of the heavy slow movement (the "Passacaglia") into the barbaric zest of the rondo. The cadenza is thus used for structural unification; at the same time, we get the virtuoso display all the same.

'Cello Concerto in E Flat Major, op. 107 1959

A deservedly popular work (written for Mstislav Rostropovich), diverse and intriguing from the sneaky first theme of the first movement (in the solo part, right at the start) to the same sneaky theme that rounds off the finale. Laid out in four movements with only one break (between the first and second), the concerto really accords with the ancient three-movement shape, for the third movement is nothing more than a protracted cadenza based on second-movement material. Beginners used to the Classical concerto of Mozart's era—sonata-allegro first movement, slow second, and rondo finale—will find one such here, made vivid by the brooding, plangent bulk of the 'cello in contrast to Shostakovitch's bright scoring, come woodwind, come horn (the latter notably in the first movement recapitulation, when it sounds the second theme while the soloist strums a virulent accompaniment).

OLIVIER MESSIAEN 1908–

In a magazine interview, when his seventieth birthday was celebrated in his native France with a month-long retrospective of his work, Messiaen called music "a language that can reach the secret parts of existence. It's an abstract language which addresses the subconscious more than the conscious." What are his great themes? "Human love, faith, and divine love . . . nature, especially the song of birds."

Birds are a major inspiration to Messiaen; his attempts to recreate and even analyze their music in his compositions form his most identifying feature. "For me," says Messiaen, "birds are the greatest of artists." He has traveled the world noting their cries, he taking down their dictation on music paper, his wife (the pianist Yvonne Loriod) capturing the sound on tape. But Messiaen's soundscape extends far beyond this expression of the natural world. Like such other twentieth-century composers as Ives, Schönberg, Webern, Carter, and Hovhaness, Messiaen has made such a study of music's constituent parts that his music often sounds as if he had extracted one or two elements from the whole to concentrate on them to the detriment of the others. Schönberg's mature style suggests that melody were the only force active in the music. In Webern, instrumental color seems predominant; in Hovhaness, rhythm. With Messiaen, rhythm seems separated from melody, as his percussion and woodwind sections seem independent of his strings and brasses and his indispensable solo lines for piano and Ondes Martenot (a kind of electrified piano).

For some, Messiaen points the way to the music of the future; his disjointed yet secretly single-minded soundscape feels contemporary and progressive without sinking into the grotesquerie and negativism that marks so much modern art. His works are intellectually conceived, yet they have a direct and quite sensual appeal.

Turangalîla Symphony 1948

This is a huge work—ten movements, a tremendous orchestra with prominent solos for piano and Ondes Martenot, four key themes that recur throughout the work, and a virtually untranslatable Sanskrit word for a title. Messiaen has called the piece a "song of love" and a "hymn of joy," and it is meant to explore this joyful love on a cosmic level.

Such a gigantic business cannot be charted in detail here; let us travel loosely. The first movement, termed "Introduction," presents in a collage of riot two of the key themes, a threatening one for trombones and a gentle one for clarinets. Then the piano takes a full cadenza, unaccompanied, and the movement proceeds in a passage remarkably reminiscent of Charles Ives, made up of unharmonious rhythmic and melodic sections playing against each other.

The second movement, "Love Song I," is a hectic rondo, its refrain comprising two themes, one for trumpet and a weirdly undulating motive for Ondes Martenot and strings. Note the bizarre cry of the Ondes at the close of the movement—it sounds almost like a human scream.

The third movement, "Turangalîla I," is if possible even odder than its predecessors, suggesting a tropical jungle in upheaval. By this time the listener is aware that Messiaen's movements do not correspond to the old opening, slow movement, scherzo, and finale—but then the classical symphony had been edged out of practice some years before *Turangalîla,* anyway. There is no set form in the symphony nowadays; thus, *Turangalîla*'s fourth movement, "Love Song II," may be parsed, approximately, as a mixture of scherzos. Again, the connection with Ives is very strong, and the Ondes contributes more of its humanoid cry.

The fifth movement, "Joy of the Stars' Blood," is more unified, a lively dance movement. Messiaen has identified the movement as an expression of the metamorphic ecstasy of the union of true lovers; thematically, it is based on the key trombone theme, and much of it is pleasantly repetitive, building up to a brief piano cadenza and a tremendous reaffirmation of the trombone theme by all the brasses.

The sixth movement, "Garden of Love's Sleep," is a complete changeover, a slow movement, hypnotically static in its single phrase on the Ondes repeated over and over with piano and woodwind decoration suggestive of the sounds of the natural world (especially Messiaen's famous bird calls). If the symphony as a whole may be viewed as an odyssey of joyful love, this is its rest period. The Ondes theme is the third of Messiaen's four key themes; as a "love theme" it is the most important of the four.

The piano opens the seventh movement, "Turangalîla II," an at times menacing situation depending heavily on exotic percussion. Here Messiaen deals with the fourth of his key themes, a progression of chords rather than a melody. The composer has likened the movement, as image, to the climactic torture scene in Poe's "The Pit and the Pendulum."

For the long eighth movement, "Development of Love," Messiaen sets out to develop all that has been heard so far, using all four key themes and the illustrative colors of the piano and Ondes to bring this retrospective on love to a climax. As the development section of a sonata movement forces the issues raised in the exposition, so does this movement act upon the first seven movements of the work.

The remaining two movements finish the piece off. "Turangalîla III" [ninth mvt] reclaims the sometimes tuneless rhythmic bases of the work, and the finale [tenth mvt—the only tenth mvt, I might add, in this entire book] presents a joyously repetitive brass fanfare and restates the all-basic "love theme" from the sixth movement in a grand *tutti* led by the Ondes.

Oiseaux Exotiques (Exotic Birds) 1956

By the composer's count, some forty different birds are represented here in their natural calls, a new one launched just about every other moment. The scoring is truly exotic, mixing a Debussyan impressionism with more modern sounds, and—as often in Messiaen—keeping the piano in the forefront. Because of the little spaces of silence that separate the various rhythmic sections, the work feels very episodic, a suite of bird calls rather than a unified movement.

ELLIOTT CARTER 1908–

Intellectually austere (very little vocal music), Carter is regarded in Europe as America's leading composer, and the reluctance of programmers to keep his music before the public is an outrage. "No," say those responsible. "He is too modern; the public does not want to hear him." But how can the public develop the taste without regular exposure? Modern music is difficult for many people, but not once one gets used to it. Anything new is strange.

For economic reasons, Carter's chamber music is kept more current in live performances (fewer musicians to hire) than his orchestral work. But the major compositions have been recorded, so, till the time comes, we can buy ourselves little museums of the Carter repertory and attend private concerts on our stereo systems.

The Carter façade of Renaissance polymath, rugged individual, and cultural synthesist is the real Carter, and behind the cliché stands a vital talent. He has made an individual contribution to the science of expression—his "metrical modulation," a technique for changing the rhythmic pulse of music (say, from fast to moderate, or moderate to slow) in even gradations while the music is playing.

More interesting to the average listener is the singular happenstance of success that Carter enjoys. Each "major piece," as it appears, actually turns out to be major (this is not always the case with his colleagues). Also helpful is Carter's precision as an annotator (in program notes and record sleeves) of his own music, especially since the practice of composers glossing their work has been an American habit since the 1930s.

Symphony no. 1 1942

This lovely work, from early in Carter's career, precedes the more advanced idiom for which he is best known. This music has a folkloric rural sound, designed, says Carter, to "suggest the characteristic beauties of Cape Cod, where it was written, and something of the extraordinary cultural background of New England, which this landscape brings to mind." There are three movements (no scherzo). The first movement, *Moderately, wistfully,* opens quietly, with the yearning, dreamy quality of woodwinds phrased against dancing strings.

Many will be reminded of Copland's *Appalachian Spring* (which postdates the present work by two years). The movement is in ceaseless motion. Suddenly, in its last moments, it pauses for a clarinet cadenza and a closing chord. The second [slow] movement, *Andante serioso* (slowly and seriously), carries through the mood of the first movement in a dignified vein, perhaps in allusion to the transcendentalist rocks of the New England intellectual landscape. The finale [third mvt], a rondo, takes off in a lithe burst in the violins. Note the certain change of pace every so often—this is a signature of Carter's style. At length, a touch of woodwindy jazz brings down the curtain.

Variations for Orchestra 1955

Like many contemporary composers, Carter is more concerned with variation than restatement. His music is eternally in mutation, so meticulously that one cannot follow the transformation of his themes: they are already undergoing transformation virtually as soon as they are sounded. So, here we have a theme-and-variations without the guidelines you would expect of Mozart or Brahms. Carter's Variations do not *clearly* start or stop varying, nor do they allow for distinct numbers identified by particular rhythm, harmony, melody, or instrumentation. These Variations vary too fluidly, too completely, for the ear to follow.

And yet, part of Carter's plan is to "neutralize" (Carter's word) the energy of the variation form by "confronting" variations of the theme with the theme itself. It is a kind of chaos patrolled by order. Perhaps it's best for the listener not to attempt to isolate the theme and its variations, but to approach the piece as a sensual experience—which all music is, at root, anyway. But do notice, after all the plays on texture and rhythm have been made, how the trombones storm into apparent cacaphony with a nasty statement of the first half of the theme. Then, a chord which seems to promise the end of the work instead gives way to hushed strings which finish the theme off and, suddenly, stop. An intriguing close.

Concerto for Orchestra 1969

The piece was inspired by a poem called *Vents* (Winds) by a Frenchman curiously named St. John Perse, which deals in transformation, as music does also. There are four movements (not separated by breaks, however), each emphasizing different facets of orchestral sound. The lively (windtorn?) first movement mostly features the 'cellos, with leading parts for percussion instruments. The second movement puts the higher strings and woodwinds forward. The third loses altitude, choosing the lower-sounding instruments and a tenuous sense of motion. The fourth movement picks up the tempo and exploits such relatively bright instruments as the oboe, trumpet, and viola, getting progressively faster as the work nears its close. (Graduated fluctuations of tempo are a Carter specialty, so much so that his phrase for the technique, "metrical modulation," has entered the lexicon of modern music.)

Double Concerto for Harpsichord, Piano, and Two Chamber Orchestras
1961

An arresting symmetry binds this work: its two halves mirror each other, so that the continuous but discrete sections comprise two alternate routes into a center (the slow movement), starting either at the beginning or the end, thus:

introduction	harpsichord cadenza	scherzo	slow mvt	fast mvt	piano cadenza	coda
sounds gradually gathering		featuring piano		featuring harpsichord		sounds gradually diminishing

A double concerto is, of course, a concerto with two soloists—here, harpsichord and piano. But Carter has doubled his orchestra as well—halved it, actually, so that each of the two soloists plays with his own little band. Obviously, this is a work conceived to showcase spatial concepts in music: circles and straight lines of sound, shapes, patterns, relationships. Says Carter, "There was a desire to get down to the physical origins of musical sound and to take off from there."

SAMUEL BARBER 1910–1981

One of the better-known American composers, Barber has established his reputation for a strong sense of form, a natural melodic gift, and a sharp flair for "color"—the ability to create a mood through the attitude, so to speak, of the instrumentation. He is, simply, listenable. Though he grew up during a period of radical music (the time of Henry Cowell, George Gershwin, George Antheil, and Aaron Copland), Barber never reached what the layman thinks of as "modern" music, the weirdly discordant and apparently unstructured music that isn't so listenable.

Maybe listenable is too glib a word. In a time when most composers seem to have lost touch with the bulk of their audience, Barber can be liked as well as admired. In fact, his best-known work, a vocal item, is unique for its exceptionable appeal to novices and experts both. This is *Knoxville "Summer of 1915,"* a fifteen-minute monologue for soprano and orchestra set to the words of James Agee. Startingly unpretentious considering the strong response it engenders, it touches the listening American with that profound identification of the present in the past that so often is mistaken for nostalgia. If you have not heard this remarkable work, by all means hie yourself to the store and latch on to a recording of it. (There have been three—two by Eleanor Steber and one by Leontyne Price; Steber's first effort, available on the Odyssey label, is the best of the three.)

Symphony no. 1, op. 9 1936

A compact plan. Barber retains the old four-movement layout of the Classical symphony, but has shortened his movements and connected them in one four-part work. Moreover, Barber redoubles his economy by using the two principal themes of the "first movement" as the main themes of the other "movements." Thus, the stentorian first theme that launches the work turns into the skittish theme of the succeeding scherzo section, and the lyrical second theme that followed the first becomes the basis, when the scherzo has dwindled dizzily away, for a "slow movement" [third section]. Meanwhile, Barber has been building the tension, and by the middle of the slow section the symphony is raging. This gives way to the finale, a graceful but weighty slow dance measure (based on the first theme—note, however, that other versions of the principal themes appear, including an intrusive trumpet solo on the scherzo melody). A compelling study in "less is more."

Piano Concerto, op. 38 1962

Here's a thrilling piece, one that will surely catch on as a repertory item. It is traditional in structure, observing the fast-slow-fast layout of old, yet the intense contributions of the soloist and the relationship of themes from one movement to another mark this as a Romantic work. It opens with the piano alone, an introductory cadenza announcing the principal themes of the movement. The orchestra and soloist collaborate on a full exposition: taut, luscious first theme and lyrical second theme (oboe solo). The development leads up to another cadenza, and with a mighty cymbal crash the recapitulation finishes off the first movement. The second [slow] movement is of an eerie beauty. The third movement is a dynamic rondo made breathless by its odd metre (5/8, an out-of-whack beat). The overall impression is one of anxious, relentless energy.

Violin Concerto, op. 14 1940

The soloist delivers the lyrical first subject right at the start, while a touch of old blue jazz perks the rhythmic second subject when it first turns up on solo clarinet. Out of these two ideas Barber plans a warm movement, very lyrical. The slow [second] movement emphasizes the warmth, as expected, though its middle section is tense, and the tension is retained when the main theme of the movement returns. Thus, the slow movement acts as a transition from the lyrical first movement to the excited finale [third mvt], *Presto in moto perpetuo* (very fast in perpetual motion).

Capricorn Concerto for Flute, Oboe, Trumpet, and Orchestra, op. 21 1944

Named for Barber's house in Mt. Kisco, New York, op. 21 is a delightful throwback to the Baroque era. It is a *concerto grosso,* in which the three soloists (the *concertino*) are pitted against a string orchestra (the *ripieno*). Barber's choice of soloists is especially apt for the retrospective in that the Baroque concerto favored solos from the woodwind (flute and oboe here) and brass (the trumpet), not only the string instruments and almost never the keyboard (harpsichord, in those days) that we moderns expect to hear in a concerto. In fact, it is the soloistic use of woods and brasses that helps define the shrill and tinny sound of the Baroque.

Three movements. The first varies in tempo: introduction (in the strings), lively, then a slow passage for the three soloists, the lively music again (the *ritornello,* or refrain), a trumpet solo in slow time, and a last taste of the *ritornello* by way of coda. The second movement is not the traditional slow movement, but a scherzo *and* slow movement combined in ABA form. The A is a ditsy scherzo and the B the slow "movement." The energetic finale [third mvt] takes off on a fanfare and winds it all up nicely, soloists to the fore.

Adagio for Strings, op. 11 1938

This is the slow movement of Barber's string quartet no. 1 (1936), rescored for a full string orchestra. One can see why it's so popular on its own: its rather ancient grace suggests a tragedy resisted, transcended by some greater inner resource. Like something by Bach, it does not set first subject against second subject but simply works out the implications of the severe opening music, intensifying the "space" of sound to a great climax, then fading back into shadow.

Second Essay for Orchestra,
op. 17 1942

There are poems, fantasies, études (studies), scherzos (jokes), and just plain "pieces" for orchestra—why not essays as well? Barber's Second Essay makes a splendid showpiece for orchestra (many woodwind solos) besides being sharply etched drama that swells to great excitement on strictly musical—i.e., non-programmatic—means. The sinuous main theme is heard immediately on a solo flute and repeated by a bass clarinet. Now other woodwinds pass in over the thumping of a drum and the awakening of the strings. A surge of expectancy is in the air, yet all is still being worked out from the opening flute theme. Even the middle section, a fugue launched by a clarinet and taken up by one instrument after another, is derived from that opening theme. Thus, the piece is like a great line extended from one point—from the solo flute to a grand *tutti* climax, then on to a hymnlike coda.

Overture to The School for Scandal,
op. 5 1931

Richard Brinsley Sheridan's *The School for Scandal* is one of the finest of English comedies, a text on human nature besides being a superb farce. At its edges, tongues flap fondly with ceaseless dish; in its core, timeless truths of just dessert stalk the hypocrite, the rakehell with the good heart, the aged husband, and the young bride. Frankly, one hears neither Sheridan's spirit nor his sensitivity in Barber's overture. The spirit is supposed to be heard (after an introductory fanfare) in the first subject (gossipy violins chewing a rumor), the sensitivity in the plangent second theme (solo oboe). But the chattering violins do not render the malice of Sheridan's scandal-mongers and the lyrical theme, too, is short on style. It's flat, too solemnly pathetic. This is not real Sheridan, then; you may enjoy it as sheer music.

WILLIAM SCHUMAN 1910–

Schuman is one of those composers who take a little getting us to and then, suddenly, sound like an old friend. He is of the third generation of American composers (Samuel Barber, Alan Hovhaness, Elliott Carter et al.), landed after Ives and Ruggles had already made their bequests and after the second group of Copland, Gershwin, and such has begun to amass a prestigious American oeuvre. Schuman's style is not as easily identified as that of any of these others; his brash, imaginative autograph is his own but it doesn't adapt to labels—jazzman, folklorist, crackpot visionary, whatever. Take him on his terms, without historical "preparation" or detailed secondary readings.

Symphony no. 3 1941

At first glance it is unconventionally structured: two parts, each containing two connected movements. It would appear to be a four-movement symphony—but these are not the traditional symphonic movements. Part I is a Passacaglia and Fugue, Part II is a Chorale and Toccata. Forget slow movement, scherzo, and the like. The passacaglia is a variation form in which a set theme is repeated continuously under the variations; that theme is introduced on the violas. After providing the material energy for the entire passacaglia movement, it fades into the fugue, launched by four horns. Note the separate entrances of variations on and counterstatements to the fugue theme all playing against each other —this is the essence of the fugue form. The chorale that opens Part II is more lyrical, a neat complement to the more rhythmic and showy tendencies of the concluding toccata.

A Song of Orpheus 1961

The "song" that inspired this "fantasy for 'cello and orchestra" is from Shakespeare's *Henry VIII:*

> Orpheus with his lute made trees,
> And the mountain tops that freeze,
> Bow themselves, when he did sing . . .

The 'cello soloist opens the piece alone, playing a musical setting of the words that Schuman composed for a production of the play in the 1940s. Bit by bit the orchestra steals in under; as soloists or as a group, the other instruments enter into dialogue with the 'cello. The composer explains that "all the music grows out of the melodic line of the song which is stated at the very beginning of the composition." A fantasy is, in form, free-willing, taking whatever shape it wants; thus, Schuman gives the song its head and lets it wander, closing as he began with the 'cello quietly reasserting its post as songmaster.

New England Triptych 1956

"Three Pieces for Orchestra After William Billings." Billings was an eighteenth-century American composer who, says Schuman, embodies "the spirit of sinewy ruggedness, deep religiosity, and patriotic fervor that we associate with the Revolutionary period." Though Schuman's elaborations of Billings' melodies came years before any talk of Bicentennial, this is that sort of endeavor, fine antiquarian browsing. The first piece, "Be Glad Then, America," opens with a stirring introduction, then slides into fragments of a patriotic anthem; Schuman does not just play it, but takes it apart for examination. The second piece is "When Jesus Wept," a reasonable facsimile of Billings' original, and the finale, "Chester," evokes patriotism with a rousing march: "Our troops advance with martial noise. . . . And gen'rals yield to beardless boys."

In Praise of Shahn 1969

Subtitled a "Canticle for Orchestra," this piece rages and keens in memory of the artist Ben Shahn. It was Schuman's intention to abstract in music two qualities of Shahn's character, "unabashed optimism" and "a searching poignancy"; neither is apparent in the dynamic opening section. An earnest string sound pulls one closer and now, only, does the canticle (a Biblical song) begin to make its effect, still compressed into a string line. It is one of Schuman's finest inspirations, and continues for quite some time. Restless figures on the brass and woodwinds scatter it, however, and the mood changes to one of fury and horror which carries through to the end.

ALAN HOVHANESS 1911–

A key to the art of Hovhaness may be turned in digesting his statement concerning one of his works: "My Symphony no. 4 probably has spiritual influences of the composers Yegmalion, Gomidas Vartabed, and Händel." The absurd billing of the well-known Westerner with the two completely mysterious Easterners—as if all three enjoyed a comparable vogue—is typical Hovhaness: naive, solipsistic, eclectic, and involved with "spiritual influences" of all sorts.

Hovhaness is not a primitive (a natural talent, unrefined by technical training), though he at times sounds it. On the contrary, he has built on his education with exhaustive research into the musical styles of the East (he himself is half-Armenian). Moreover, he is one of the most industrious of composers, not remotely a dabbler. But his intention, frequently, is to intricate a kind of primitivism through a mystical, hallucinatory, cultist sound—an acid rock of symphony. Many buffs of serious music cannot relate to Hovhaness; a lot of people who don't regularly encounter Beethoven or Mahler find Hovhaness just the thing. His is one of the most distinctive signatures in the book of composers; if you're intrigued, try *Mysterious Mountain* (immediately below), or sample *"And God Created Great Whales"*, for humpback whale solo (on tape) and orchestra. Californians in particular find that one grand karma.

Symphony no. 2, "Mysterious Mountain," op. 132 1955

A work of impenetrable transcendence. The mountain of the title is mysterious not only in the composer's ambiguously evocative sounds, but in its lack of programmatic identity: what mountain where? Hovhaness does not tell. "Mountains are symbols," he states, "of man's attempt to know God. . . . To some, the Mysterious Mountain may be the phantom peak, unmeasured, thought to be higher than

Everest, as seen from great distances by fliers from Tibet. To some it may be the solitary mountain, the tower of strength over a countryside—Fujiyama, Ararat, Monadnock, Shasta, or Grand Teton." Everyone hears something different here—but everyone hears *something*. This is provocative music, one of the few symphonic compositions of recent years likely to become a popular favorite. There are three movements, two lyrical and introspective spaces surrounding a double fugue. Majestic in its immobile contemplation, the first movement casts a wonderful spell, amplified by the second movement with its churchly chorale of strings. Midway through the second movement, a second theme breaks in in fast tempo—now the fugue is really rolling—and what might be termed the "mountain" theme dominates the texture to splendid effect. The third movement returns us to earth in a solemn chant of muted brasses under a dancing violin line. This gives way to the music of the first movement, even more compelling on its second hearing, hovering weightlessly, an enigma in the form of a hymn.

Symphony no. 4, op. 165 1957

The characteristic Hovhanessian Oriental mystery opens the first movement, which the composer calls "a hymn and fugue." Timeless, spaceless sounds interspersed with brass chorales; then the fugue, energetic and mellifluously Baroque. The marimba, an African xylophone, launches the second movement, a chain of dances. Here especially Hovhaness exploits his penchant for the Eastern timbre (tone color). A real xylophone replaces the marimba, succeeded by timpani, glockenspiel, vibraphone, harp: a percussionist suite. The third movement offers another hymn and fugue, rising to a grand ceremony of sound in brass, chimes, and gong.

Symphony no. 7, "Nanga Parvat," op. 178 1959

Nanga Parvat ("Without Trees") is one of the world's more remote mountains, snowbound in Kashmir. For this salute to its forbidding majesty, Hovhaness composed a symphony for wind instruments (that is, woods and brasses) and percussion in his habitual three movements. The first, *Con ferocità* (ferociously), uses incessant drum rhythms to suggest the barbaric power of the Himalayas. The second movement, "March," depicts (in the composer's words) "wild improvised marches in raucous woodwinds and false brass unisons," with Hovhaness' typical use of repetitive melody in unvarying accompanimental textures. The third movement, "Sunset," closes the short work with a solemn native pageant. An odd echo of Christian worship peeks through the otherwise Eastern gauze; at the end, Hovhaness likens his high woodwind tone clusters (groups of adjacent notes played together) to "shafts of light through craggy peaks."

Symphony no. 15, "Silver Pilgrimage," op. 199 1963

Like many of Hovhaness' symphonies, "Silver Pilgrimage" uses hazy sound-pictures in accordance with a very loose program. The tonal atmosphere and spiritual inspiration are Eastern—Indian, to be exact (*Silver Pilgrimage* is a novel by one M. Anantanarayan)—and, like Hovhaness' many Eastern-flavored symphonies, this one deals in hypnotic repetitions as a magician deals in spells. If you don't like it, get out of the magic.

The first movement, "Mount Ravana," features a ceaseless buzz of quietly chattering violins and lowering or frantic comments from other instruments. "Marava Princess" [second mvt] is not dissimilar in technique, though here the melody is more directly articulated, and toward the end the movement turns engagingly rhythmic. "River of Meditation" [third mvt] opens as a pageant of bells and drums, but eventually becomes an endless flute solo on a very free schedule. (Note, again, the almost toneless string chatter, a special component of the work.) For a finale, the fourth movement, "Heroic Gates of Peace," suggests the uplifted truth of geoemotional harmony. An ecumenical message somewhat comparable to that of the finale of Beethoven's Ninth Symphony, this movement uses long melodic lines, triumphal drumming, swirling strings, and a hint of Renaissance church music to hymn the millennium. But where Beethoven unleashes an exciting volume of sound, Hovhaness keeps to a motionless instrumental texture and static melody.

Fra Angelico, op. 220 1967

An autobiographical work, perhaps, for Fra Angelico, like Hovhaness, was a Western artist who turned East for inspiration (or so the composer tells us). The three violins heard at the start are meant to suggest "celestial music" with their upward swooping—one of the more bizarre invocations in contemporary symphony. The next episode is dominated by 'cellos moving against a suspended backdrop of strings; this is followed by yet more religious initiation. The sense lies in the overall effect, not in any piece of it: thus the murmurs, the repetitions, the lack of sturdy rhythmic energy. Hovhaness says, "Come into the dream." The murmurs grow louder as each instrument contributes to a gentle cacaphony—each playing at his own speed—that suddenly turns into a riot of trombone slides and shrilling horns. It's like a fanfare gone mad. Having reached a deeper level of ecstasy (one hopes), we witness a glorious adoration, which at length wafts off into a yet higher realm modeled on the opening "celestial" swooping of the violins.

BENJAMIN BRITTEN 1913–1976

The best known of modern English composers, Britten was universally hailed in his homeland for his regeneration of the almost-dead spirit of English opera. Starting in 1945 with *Peter Grimes,* a brutally insular piece on the alienation of an inarticulate iconoclast in an East Anglian fishing village, and continuing with *Albert Herring* (1947), *Billy Budd* (1951), and *The Turn of the Screw* (1954) among others, Britten paraded an astonishing versatility of genre as if to rewrite the native opera singlehandedly. His great gift, undoubtedly, was for music theatre.

That gift informed also his orchestral output. The "drama" of symphony does not fail in Britten: one senses the arch of line as his pieces unfold, the thrusting toward a resolution. Britten loves his variations. Two of the five works cited here are theme-and-variation types, and one entire opera, the aforementioned *Turn of the Screw* (after Henry James' story), works out its sixteen scenes as an introduction and theme followed by fifteen variations, one to a scene! The composer's interest in the voice limited his non-vocal output, and those who want to hear more of him without resorting to an outright tour of opera should address themselves to the *War Requiem,* a mass for the dead using Wilfred Owen's poetry as well as the set Latin text, or to the *Spring Symphony,* an engaging choral work that travels from winter to summer via lyrics from Anonymous to Auden.

Sinfonia da Requiem, op. 20 1940

A symphony that acts like a mass. Though there is no chorus, no churchly text, still the atmosphere of grief and transcendence is deeply felt. The first movement, subtitled "Lacrymosa," opens with a pounding beat out of which a thought rises in the 'cellos; this builds into the single main theme, eternally soaring upward yet falling back down, more in grief than transcendence. With no break the riotous second movement, "Dies Irae" (Day of Judgment), charges onto the scene, at first in tiny dots and dashes but soon with awesome power. An odd middle section, a march, adds to the tension with its treading accompaniment and alto saxophone solo. Again, no break takes us to the transcendent finale [third mvt], "Requiem Aeternam." Although the listener may not be aware of it on first or second hearings, all three movements share common thematic material. (For instance, the gentle melody played by three flutes at the very start of the third movement is the same tune that is played repeatedly against the saxophone solo in the second movement.) Thus, Britten expresses three different moods—keening, fury, and elegy—while making one unified statement.

Simple Symphony (for strings), op. 4 1934

Britten called this Classical four-movement work "simple" not only because its structure and scoring (for strings only) are transparent but also because he culled all the themes from pieces composed in his adolescence. "Boisterous Bourrée" [first mvt] is a sonata-allegro movement: forthright minor-key first theme, innocent major-key second theme, simple development played out in one gradual crescendo and reversed recapitulation (second theme first, first theme last in a quiet coda). "Playful pizzicato" [second mvt] is a scherzo in which the strings are plucked (*pizzicato*), not bowed, throughout. The slow [third] movement, "Sentimental Saraband," is the emotional center of the work, heavy and haunting with an ancient charm. The "Frolicsome Finale" [fourth mvt] brings us home with Haydnesque vitality.

Variations on a Theme of Frank Bridge, op. 10 1937

Frank Bridge was Britten's major composition teacher from boyhood on, and this homage takes the form of nine variations and a fugue for string orchestra, the theme taken from Bridge's *Three Idylls for String Quartet.* It turned out to be Britten's first big success, a standout in its genre. For while many variation works tend to tie their separate variations together in unified presentation—a progression of variations—Britten deliberately changes his mood at each successive variation, giving the whole the disjunct effect of a suite. Hear how sectional the work is. First, the assertive, restless introduction, fading into the theme as stated by solo quartet (two violins, viola, and 'cello—Bridge's original scoring), then by full string orchestra. Next comes the first variation, an *Adagio* (very slow) of deep chords in the lower strings with flighty comments in the violins. Then the second variation, a march; then the third, a gracious, waltzlike tune; and so on—each new variation an entirely new idea in form and tone. The sixth variation tenders a spoof on the Viennese waltz, with some odd scoring effects; the seventh is a bit of "perpetual motion." The last variation, a fugue, is the biggest, leading up to a restatement of the original theme.

The Young Person's Guide to the Orchestra (Variations and Fugue on a Theme of Purcell), op. 34 1945

This is two pieces in one. First, it is, as the title tells, an introduction to the instruments of the orchestra: music with a purpose. Second, as music for its own sake, it is a set of variations and fugue based on a hefty tune left by the Baroque composer Henry Purcell. To insure the tyro's comprehension, a narrator calls off the instruments as they are introduced one by one.

Obviously, this is an ideal chance to isolate in one's mind the various timbres of the playing families—also an ideal introduction to the art of the variation form, for Britten keeps the Purcell original very much in the ear even as he plays around with it. A caveat on recordings: a few of the many LP versions of the piece simply play the music—*Variations and Fugue on a Theme of Henry Purcell*—without the *Young Person's Guide.* Check the cover credits. (Narrators tend to hail from the world of show business: you may be sure that they will have arranged for prominent billing.) If there's a narrator, there is also the *Guide.*

Four Sea Interludes and Passacaglia from Peter Grimes, op. 33 a and b 1945

Britten's opera *Peter Grimes* tells of a brutish nonconforming fisherman and his failure to relate to his fellow citizens in an English seacoast village. These five pieces (sometimes the four sea interludes are heard without the passacaglia) are all preludes and interludes designed to reflect the stage action, setting tone before the rise of the curtain or developing the events of a previous scene while the curtain is down and the set being changed. Thus, they lose much of their meaning when heard outside the operatic context. But as music they are so evocative of the sea—tide flow, sunplay, storm—that they belong alongside Debussy's *La Mer* (The Sea) as the standard abstraction of the ocean in orchestral music.

I think we really have to forget about the dramatic, *Peter Grimes* function of these pieces and treat them as the strictly musical entries that their concert title makes of them: four "sea" interludes and a passacaglia. The first of the sea pieces, "Dawn," depicts the calm dignity of the seashore's morning: flutes and violins on high suggesting seagull cries; harp, clarinets, and violas reaching forth like the sea's arms; low brass growling with power and possession. "Sunday Morning," second and brightest of the sea pictures, offers solemn church bells in horns, festive flights in the woodwinds, and, for contrast, a songlike passage for lower strings. Next is "Moonlight," trimly depicted as if in shafts breaking through a glowering overcast. Lonely, haunted, hopeful music. "Storm," self-describing, completes the quartet.

The passacaglia, plucked up from the tragic center of the opera, bears no reference to the sea. It is a mood piece devoted to the despairing of Grimes. Note the passacaglia form: a fixed bass line (heard at the very start in the lower strings) is repeated throughout, unchanged, while other figures shift freely over it. The first melody is heard on a plaintive solo viola, and at length the viola finishes the piece off in a "concert ending" (i.e., specially composed for performance out of the opera house).

LEONARD BERNSTEIN 1918–

Bernstein the conductor, author, lecturer, proponent of radical chic, and philosopher-king of the midcult bohemia sometimes threatens to eclipse Bernstein the composer, especially in recent years when his talk sounds more distinguished than his music. The American Wunderkind of the 1940s, a Candide out on the wonderful town, Bernstein became the first American conductor of international celebrity as well as the only composer since George Gershwin to attempt a rapprochement between the popular native sound and the penetration of serious music.

There was some tradition for him to draw on, but much development to his credit as well. Like Kurt Weill, he would consummate the evolution of our musical theatre. Like Gershwin, he understood what made music popular better than people did. Like Charles Ives, Carl Ruggles, and Aaron Copland, he would seek an American order in the march of symphonic forms and make them over to suit the culture. As of *circa* 1950, Bernstein was to head, direct, and carry the standard for the next generation of American composers. Some thirty years after, we ask: did it happen?

It did not. Bernstein's best ballet score of several remains *Fancy Free,* back in 1944; his best of three symphonies is his first, the "Jeremiah," from 1942; his work for the musical theatre does not so much decline after *West Side Story* in 1957 as thud into the abyss. Bernstein may still catch his second wind and all this will change; till then we must salute his talent, at its freshest, in its youth—the friendly innocence of his urban cacaphony in *Fancy Free* and the musical it inspired, *On the Town,* athletic, boozy, rudely healthy; the tautly elicited trauma of *The Age of Anxiety,* suggested by W.H. Auden's emblematic poem; the hieratic passion of the "Jeremiah" Symphony. Those willing to dilute their symphonic draught with a little under-the-counter pop infusion should invest in recordings of Bernstein's musicals, particularly *On the Town* and *Candide* (*not* the trivialized 1973 revival, but the original 1956 production, infinitely preferable).

Symphony no. 1, "Jeremiah" 1942

Says Bernstein, "As for programmatic meanings, the intention . . . is not one of literalness but of emotional quality." This is not a symphony about Jeremiah but one to reflect his heavy relationship with an errant people. The first movement, "Prophecy," reads an impassioned lecture to the corrupt citizenry of Jerusalem, fulminating, pleading (most eloquently in the woodwinds). But the pleas of Jeremiah need the overstatement of drums and brass; the movement soars to an angry peak and, as if anticipating failure, fades away. There has been no Great Awakening. This Old Testament Solzhenitsyn, like his modern counterpart, does not get through to his audience. But the wages of weakness and decadence is destruction. This Bernstein covers in a vicious scherzo [second mvt], "Profanation." It starts lightly, but nervously, and grows into a din of attack and rapine. The third and last movement, "Lamentation," calls for a mezzo-soprano soloist to intone Jeremiah's keening elegy (in Hebrew, from the Book of Lamentations). The entire movement is given over to the lament, a moving and sensual relief after the fury and violence of the preceding movements. "How doth the city sit solitary, that was full of people! how is she become as a widow! . . . Turn Thou us unto Thee, O Lord, and we shall be turned; renew our days as of old."

Symphony no. 2, "The Age of Anxiety"
1949

With its important piano soloist, this is as much a concerto as a symphony; moreover, it is a program symphony, for Bernstein based it on W.H. Auden's *The Age of Anxiety: A Baroque Eclogue,* writing six movements to correspond to the six parts of Auden's poem. In truth, the piano is not featured strongly enough to rate the work a full-fledged concerto, perhaps because the soloist is meant to speak for a detached or alienated sensibility. (In its original version, since revised, the piano dropped out of the last movement entirely except for one chord of bashful involvement.) Other instruments get chances to speak for themselves while collaborating on an existential worldview, but it is the piano that one notices.

Now, the program. "The Prologue" introduces, in a kind of imporvisation, four lonely people in a Manhattan bar. "The Seven Ages," a discussion among the four, offers a strange set of variations: each variation departs from the variation that preceded it rather than from one basic theme. "The Seven Stages," finds the four, deeper into drink and discussion, trying to resolve, not deepen, their problems of spiritual pain.

That much is Part One. Part Two begins with "The Dirge," aptly named, as the four—three men and a woman—sit in a cab, suspended motionless in music, as it were, on their way to the woman's apartment. A lively passage for the piano and other percussion instruments (drums, harp, glockenspiel, celesta, and xylophone) depicts "The Masque": the sad, late-night party at the woman's apartment. Despite the outgoing flavor of this jazzy music, the party more or less dissolves. Bernstein shows this musically by having the orchestra cut out suddenly while the piano keeps on playing. Then a trumpet solo glides in, signaling "The Epilogue," an inspiring attempt to find some individual value in the morass, some belief in self. The pianist assists with his personal affirmation in the form of a cadenza (his solo "spot") near the end.

Symphony no. 3, "Kaddish" 1963

The modern symphony depends on the programmatic use of sung or spoken text to a degree unheard of in the nineteenth century and early twentieth. Thus, Bernstein's Third Symphony is really less a symphony than a happening for narrator, soprano, chorus, and orchestra. The Kaddish is a Jewish prayer for the dead, highly emotional in character—but Bernstein has written that the prayer itself is as much a celebration of God as a giver of life as it is a requiem for those he taketh away; this bimodal purpose informs all three movements of the symphony, "Invocation" and the first Kaddish (for chorus); "Din-Torah" (Judgment by Law) and the second Kaddish (for soprano); and "Scherzo," the third Kaddish (for boy's choir) and finale. Though the music is not easy to follow, the text will keep the listener tuned into the composer's ideas and images.

Serenade for Violin Solo, Strings, and Percussion (after Plato's Symposium) 1954

Five sections of violin concerto, in one movement, inspired by the Platonic dialogue on love and lovers; each of the five reflects Bernstein's reading of the succession of speakers at a banquet. The soloist begins, alone, for Phaedrus; Pausanias throws in his thoughts after the various string groups have entered in turn, ushering in an *allegro* (lively) movement. Sections for Aristophanes (lighter) and Erixymachus (very fast) lead up to a beautiful slow passage, mirroring Agathon's salute to the love life in the understated beauty of the soloist's song. Then Socrates enters the picture, interrupted by an almost jazzily boisterous Alcibiades. After the soloist's cadenza, the tranquil mood of the opening closes the work.

On the Town Suite 1944

Three dances lifted from a high-spirited musical comedy about three sailors on twenty-four-hour leave in New York. (Betty Comden and Adolph Green wrote the libretto, Jerome Robbins laid out the extensive choreography, and Bernstein, of course, composed the music.) The first of the dances, "The Great Lover," captures the rhythmic hustle of the metropolis, pacing the streets in quest of romance, getting elbowed and shoved, eternally pesky. Second is an *andante* (medium slow), "Lonely Town: Pas de Deux," originally staged as a male-female dance duet to express in movement what one of the sailors has just expressed in song: being alone in a city full of people. To muted accompaniment, a trumpet intones a theme from the song. Soon a fuller orchestra takes up a development of the theme, climaxing grandly, then withdrawing to the air of the opening, the trumpet tune now on the English horn. Biggest of the trio is "Times Square: 1944," avid honky-tonk based largely on the musical's theme song, "New York, New York (It's a helluva town)."

Overture to Candide 1956

What could more appropriately prepare a public for this engagingly satiric "comic operetta" than a dazzling rondo overture in E Flat Major, with cutting main subject, tender subsidiary subject, alarms and episodes, and a Rossinian crescendo for a coda? Based on Voltaire's picaresque spoof of Leibnizian optimism, *Candide* occasionally lost control of its satiric component and appeared to believe in its own sentimentality (a revision in 1973 repaired this fuzziness of tone). But the overture never relaxes its ironic bite. A short fanfare calls in the first theme group of flying woodwinds, a ridiculously self-important can-can, and thunderous war music (accompanying the destruction of Westphalia in the show). Then comes the sweet subsidiary theme, from Candide's duet with his loved one, Cunegonde, "Oh, Happy We," with a charming countermelody playing above it. The fanfare and first theme return, followed by the subsidiary theme, at first under an odd little turn in the woodwinds—as if to hold the attractive melody at a distance, "sabotage" it with a joke—and then *fortissimo* (very loud), with its countermelody. It fades. Full stop. Then: a slow crescendo such as Rossini made famous, wherein the orchestra plays the same figure over and over again while continually growing louder. (The tune of this coda is sliced out of Cunegonde's aria, "Glitter and Be Gay.") Fanfare and both main themes giddily trade off last words before the final chord.

HANS WERNER HENZE 1926–

Henze is the compleat modern, with his insistent experimentation with traditional forms, his prolificacy, his striking gifts for the stage (which have yielded at least three absolutely first-rate operas), his *Angst*-filled war with critics who find him too conservative and audiences who find him too advanced, his blending of Schönberg's twelve-tone compositional procedure with Italianate lyricism, plus—Henze the performer—his public appearances as conductor and pianist and—Henze the man—his leftist totalitarian politics.

In Europe, Henze is ubiquitous; in America, he is rarely heard, and at that only because concerts must program a living composer every so often or be laughed out of the annals. Americans have to seek Henze out on disc (Deutsche Grammophon, the leading German record company, makes a point of recording Henze's important work, though these issues tend to go out of print quickly; move fast, if you're interested). Since Henze is one of the few really acute opera composers, why not take a chance on one of his operas? The ideal starting point is *Der Junge Lord* (The Young Lord), a black comedy full of burlesques and surprises.

Symphony no. 3 1949

Anyone who fears that the modernists just can't cut it in the symphony should hear this one. It is, of course, progressive in its harmony; no one can call Henze a throwback. But he is interested in the symphony as form, and knows that nothing will come of nothing—tradition holds the back of his mind as he writes. A musician who examined the score would place various procedures as ancient and familiar, but what you *hear* is a sharply dramatic work sounding like nothing heard before (despite overtones of Stravinsky). There are three movements, each with a title. The first, "Apollo's Invocation," opens and closes in wild magic, setting off a graceful dance measure. The second movement, "Dithyramb," is, as the title suggests, not exactly a slow movement, though it functions as a lyrical interval between the two outer movements (and relates to them in its use of the wild outbursts they also share). The finale, "Oath Poetry," is the wildest of the three, though not consistently, a Dionysiac counter to the Apollonian opening.

Symphony no. 6 (for two chamber orchestras)
1968

The aim here is constant contrast in that there are two orchestras, each playing sometimes with and sometimes against the other. Moreover, the contrast of concerto is also applied here in that there is a ceaseless picking out of solo instruments for fleeting solo work. (In other words, there is really a concerto for orchestra for two separate orchestras.) There are three more or less interchangeable movements, played continuously without a break, and a great deal of what can only be termed weird noise. The concept of contrast is especially exploited in the middle movement, wherein nine different musical atmospheres are presented, each one promptly answered by an opposing atmosphere—loud versus soft, say, or placidity versus rage. This procedure Henze adapted from a poem by a Cuban revolutionary, Miguel Barnet ("Where it says a great white ship/It should say cloud/Where it says grey/It should say a land distant and forgotten. . ."). Henze operates the European office of radical chic.

Violin Concerto no. 1 1947

Early Henze, his first entry in the twelve-tone idiom of Arnold Schönberg. It is "modern," in the conservative's derogatory sense, but there is charm in a violin concerto even in such advanced surroundings, something to focus on amidst all the alleged cacaphony: a soloist's star turn. No question that this is a stellar number for the soloist, and it remains one of Henze's more appealing works for orchestra. There are four movements: an almost traditionally shaped first movement, a tiny marchlike scherzo, a slow movement, and a raucous finale.

Ode to the West Wind 1953

A 'cello concerto, inspired by Shelley's poem ("O wild West Wind, thou breath of Autumn's being,/Thou, from whose unseen presence the leaves dead/Are driven like ghosts from an enchanter fleeing. . ."). Henze's structure is made to mirror Shelley's; since the poem comprises five sonnet stanzas, the concerto is in five movements, with the first and second and then the fourth and fifth joined at the edges to make, really, three movements. Moreover, each of the five musical sections corresponds in tone with Shelley's stanzas. Henze describes his sections as Introduction and Sonata [i.e., sonata-allegro movement], Variations, and Funeral Music and Apotheosis. Or, in terms of poetry: Invocation and Statement, Developments, and Tragedy and Higher Statement. Or, in terms of the listening experience: Introduction and First Movement, Slow Movement, and Finale. The 'cello soloist is never permitted to "show off" in concerto style; he is, rather, used to focus attention on the intimate poetry of the original, less a virtuoso than a bashful bard. "O Wind, If winter comes, can Spring be far behind?"

GLOSSARY

absolute music: music for its own sake, with no subject matter—as opposed to program music, which characterizes a person, dramatizes an event, or tells a story.

aria: ("air") song. Aria, or song, form, is ABA—a main section, a contrasting section, and a repeat of the main section.

arioso: ("songlike") a kind of singing or playing halfway between recitative and song.

atonalism: the practice of writing music without traditional Western harmony. To the average ear, it is more than mere dissonance, rather a continuously intelligible sound.

ballad opera: an eighteenth-century English forerunner of modern musical comedy, in which a play was performed with songs dropped blithely into the plot, usually with original lyrics set to popular tunes.

barcarolle: "boat" music, imitating the rock of the waves.

basso ostinato: ("steady bass") a lower line repeated throughout a composition while the upper parts change.

battery: the percussion section of the orchestra.

bravura: ("heroic") referring to an especially virtuosic passage.

buffo: "comic."

cadenza: ("cadence") originally an improvised and later (after 1800) usually written-out embellishment for solo voice or instrument. It is a "cadence" in that it began as a kind of valedictory decoration just before the end of a movement or piece, though it later turned up at any point in a composition.

canon: a composition in which one part is imitated by one or more parts so that their successive entries overlap (as in the popular singing of "Row, Row, Row Your Boat").

cantabile: "singing."

cantata: a vocal piece—as opposed to a sonata, an instrumental piece. The cantata is usually a work for soloists and chorus in several sections.

carmagnole: a song associated with a political revolution.

cembalo: (see clavicembalo).

chamber music: music composed to be performed by small forces—a string quartet, for example.

chorale: a hymnlike passage scored for one family of instruments.

clavicembalo: the harpsichord; also called cembalo.

closing theme: in sonata-allegro form, the last theme in the exposition.

coda: ("tail") the final "bit" used to finish off a movement.

concertante: using prominent instrumental solos.

concertino: (see concerto grosso).

concerto grosso: a concerto in which a group of soloists (the *concertino*) plays in *balanced* contrast to the rest of the orchestra (the *ripieno*).

continuo: short for *basso continuo* ("fixed bass"), meaning the back-up instrument(s) in seventeenth- and eighteenth-century orchestral music that played continually along with the strings to provide a solid harmonic and rhythmic foundation—usually harpsichord, sometimes with bassoon and/or 'cello.

counterpoint: the combination of two or more independent parts in harmonic collaboration.

counterstatement: a contrasting rejoinder to a symphonic theme.

crescendo: a gradual intensifying of volume.

cyclic unity: a practice popular from the mid-1800s on, in which one basic theme, by constant transformation, supplied the material for all the main themes in a given work.

decrescendo: a gradual lessening of volume.

development: in sonata-allegro movements, the middle section, in which themes from the exposition are varied, transformed, played around with: developed.

dodecaphony: (see twelve-tone)

double concerto: a concerto for two soloists.

electronic music: music either wholly or partly using electronic noises played on tape.

"end" movements: the first and last movements in a work.

entr'acte: a piece of music played between the acts of an opera or play, invariably after the interval just before the rise of the curtain.

étude: "study."

exposition: in sonata-allegro (or any other) movements, the first main section, in which the movement's principal themes are introduced.

finale: the final movement or section of a work.

fluttertonguing: a method of playing on wind instruments in which the tongue is rolled, yielding a "fluttery" buzz; introduced by Richard Strauss (on the flutes) in his tone poem *Don Quixote.*

fugato: "in the style of a fugue."

fugue: a composition in which several independent melodic lines—all repetitions or variations of a basic line—are combined into a harmonious texture. The basic line—the "subject"—opens the fugue alone. At intervals, other lines—the "answer," the "countersubject," and such—join the basic line until there are three or four continuous lines playing at once.

Gebrauchsmusik: ("useful music") a German term dating from the 1920s meaning music written for practical purposes, such as for amateur use or as "make music," so to speak, for players of instruments that lack a rich literature (a bassoon sonata, for instance).

glissando: ("sliding") a quick swish from one note to another, taking in all the notes in between.

home key: speaking harmonically, the fundamental key of a composition, to which it is traditionally bound to return at the end of a movement or at the end of a whole work.

impressionism: a style of music, inspired by the symbolist movement in French poetry, in which the sounds obliquely evoke subject matter—program music, as it were, through a mist. Debussy, Dukas, and Delius are the composers most associated with impressionism.

legato: smooth and connected—as opposed to staccato ("detached").

leitmotif: ("leading theme") a musical theme associated with a person, thing, or idea.

libretto: the words to a work of music theatre.

lyricism: songfulness.

measure: the most basic unit of a musical score—a molecule of music (also called a "bar").

medley: a sequence of themes or songs, not developed symphonically but simply strung together into a movement, one after the other.

monothematic: having one theme only.

motto theme: a theme that symbolizes the dramatic core of a work, usually the first theme heard. It is then repeated in later movements, and is sometimes transformed into other themes by means of variation.

nocturne: ("night piece") a composition suggestive of the night—misty, dark, mysterious, perhaps tinged with melancholy.

"occasional" music: music composed to accompany a specific event.
oratorio: a work of music theatre composed on a sacred theme and meant to be sung in concert rather than staged.
ostinato: ("steady thing") a rhythmic figure that is repeated while the music above it changes.
overture: ("opening") a piece played, before the curtain rises, to introduce an opera, ballet, or play.
pas de deux: "dance for two."
Passacaglia: most frequently, a variation form in which a theme is repeated in the bass while other melodies play in sequence above it.
polyphony: music combining several different (and equally important) lines of melody at once—as opposed to homophony, which is based on one line of melody with non-intrusive accompaniment.
potpourri: ("stew") a succession of tunes—synonymous with medley.
prelude: (1) a short piece in one movement based on one essential melodic or rhythmic idea; (2) an introductory movement.
recapitulation: in sonata-allegro form, the last third of a movement, in which the themes stated in the exposition and varied in the development are restated *more or less* in their original form.
recitative: a cross between singing and speaking; in symphony, usually an instrumental solo, without accompaniment, that sounds as if the player were reciting or declaiming through his instrument rather than "singing" through it.
repertory item: a piece encountered with some frequency in the concert hall.
rhapsody: 1. ecstatic music; 2. a work of nationalistic or epic subject matter.
riff: a jazz term referring to a melodic fragment, usually used as a transition from one phrase to another.
ripieno: (see *concerto grosso*).
ritornello: in composition using solo instruments or voices, a recurring orchestral interlude.
romance: (1) song; (2) a loose term for a songlike piece.
rondo: ("round") a form in which a main theme, the refrain, recurs between one major subsidiary theme and several episodes.
siciliano: a gentle, rocking piece.
sinfonia: the old Italian work for "symphony," used *circa* 1600 to mean an overture or prelude or ritornello played by an orchestra.
sonata-allegro: a form of symphonic movement consisting of exposition, development, and recapitulation. In the exposition, principal themes are stated, in the development they (or subsidiary themes) are varied, and in the recapitulation the exposition is repeated. Also called sonata form.
staccato: "disconnected"—as opposed to legato, "connected."

subject: in symphonic movements, a major theme. One usually speaks of subjects in sonata-allegro movements, in which the two main themes are called the first and second subject.

suite: a composition comprising several movements. These may be independent movements of absolute music (as in Bach's Suites for Orchestra), movements relating to each other as parts of a whole (as in Holst's *The Planets*), or excerpts from an opera or ballet score (as in Chaikofsky's *Nutcracker Suite*).

tarantella: a quick, jumpy dance of Italian folk origin.

timbre: the "color" of a sound.

toccata: ("touched piece") (1) a piece played rapidly with a lot of short notes—with, in other words, a lot of finger work; (2) in Baroque music, a brass fanfare.

tone cluster: a group of adjacent notes played together.

trill: an ornament consisting of the rapid alternation of two adjacent notes.

trio: the middle section of a scherzo, minuet, or dance movement. This section was customarily composed for three instrumental solos—i.e., a trio. After the custom broke down, the section kept its name.

tutti: a passage for full orchestra.

twelve-tone technique: a method of composition developed by Arnold Schönberg. It rejects traditional Western harmony for a complex organizational system of its own. For an explanation, please see the introduction to the Schönberg chapter.

virtuoso: an accomplished musician.

INDEX

All works are listed alphabetically by composer; certain works are also listed alphabetically by title as a cross-reference to anticipate possible confusion of title or composer.